HEART OF DARKNESS

AN AUTHORITATIVE TEXT
BACKGROUNDS AND SOURCES
CRITICISM

THIRD EDITION

A NORTON CRITICAL EDITION

Joseph Conrad
HEART OF DARKNESS

AN AUTHORITATIVE TEXT
BACKGROUNDS AND SOURCES
CRITICISM

THIRD EDITION

Edited by

ROBERT KIMBROUGH

PROFESSOR EMERITUS OF ENGLISH
UNIVERSITY OF WISCONSIN

W · W · NORTON & COMPANY · *New York* · *London*

Copyright © 1988, 1971, 1963 by W. W. Norton & Company, Inc.

Library of Congress Cataloging in Publication Data

ISBN 0-393-95552-4

W. W. Norton & Company, Inc., 500 Fifth Avenue, New York, N.Y. 10110
www.wwnorton.com

W. W. Norton & Company Ltd., Castle House, 75/76 Wells Street,
London W1T 3QT

5 • 6 • 7 • 8 • 9 • 0

Contents

Introduction

In the fall of 1889, Joseph Conrad simultaneously began his first piece of fiction, *Almayer's Folly*, and his search for a way to get command of a riverboat on the Congo. The first act was impulsive and casual; the second, long-planned and calculatingly carried out. The first seemed mere whim; the second, the natural extension of a boyhood dream and present vocation as a seaman. But the actual significance of these two acts proved to be just the reverse of their appearance, for his Congo adventure so broke Conrad's health that he was delayed in resuming a life aboard ship, while his period of convalescence was occupied with increasingly satisfying creative writing. Although Conrad returned to sea twice before *Almayer* was finished in 1894, his new career as a writer took a decisive turn when he sat down to start *An Outcast of the Islands* even before *Almayer* had been accepted for publication. These two works were published in 1895 *(Almayer)* and 1896 *(Outcast)*, and, in spite of losing time on two abortive projects, Conrad completed *The Nigger of the "Narcissus"* and a volume of five short stories, *Tales of Unrest*, in 1897. During 1898, he wrote and published *Youth*, the first of his Marlow tales, and in the fall began the second, *Heart of Darkness*. Published in the spring of 1899, *Heart of Darkness* rounded out a crucial decade in Conrad's life.

For half of those ten years, Conrad worked in obscurity, sharing only with his aunt news of his progress in writing. With the publication of *Almayer*, however, fame and publicity came quickly, and by the time of *Heart of Darkness* Conrad was an established literary figure on intimate terms with John Galsworthy, Stephen Crane, H. G. Wells, Ford Madox Ford, and Henry James—just to mention fellow novelists. This rapid transition from a life of isolation to one of fellowship, from seaman to landsman, from captain to writer—indeed, from bachelor to family man— is part of the romance of Conrad's biography. What is immediately important is that by the fall of 1898 Conrad was so securely established as a master of his new craft and so settled in his new way of life that he was ready to experiment artistically with very private material. *Heart of Darkness*, while putting to rest one phase of Conrad's life, marks the beginning of another.

Conrad's earlier narratives are primarily objective, descriptive, and thematically clear; *Heart of Darkness* tends to be interior, suggestively analytic, and highly psychological. In short it introduces a new mode into Conrad's fiction: the symbolic. Ian Watt believes that *Heart of*

Darkness is not only the first but also the only symbolic work by Conrad.
To work successfully within such a mode, a writer must know well the
craft of writing—how to manipulate words and events in the most
suggestive ways—and be willing to look into the self, the ultimate source
of all symbols. By 1898, Conrad was ready to try. At a later point, he
may have been in doubt about his success: "What I distinctly admit is
the fault of having made Kurtz too symbolic or rather symbolic at all.
But the story being mainly a vehicle for conveying a batch of personal
impressions I gave rein to my mental laziness and took the line of least
resistance" (letter, December 2, 1902). This Norton Critical Edition of
Heart of Darkness is designed to allow the reader to evaluate Conrad's
seemingly casual remark.

The Text

   Heart of Darkness first appeared in 1899 as "The Heart of Darkness"
in *Blackwood's Magazine* in three parts (February, March, and April),
after which it was revised for inclusion by Blackwood in 1902 in a separate volume, *Youth: A Narrative; and Two Other Stories* (the third being
The End of the Tether). All subsequent publications of *Heart of Darkness*, whether reprints or newly set editions, stem from this version of
the story, rather than from the one in manuscript or the one in *Blackwood's*. The next significant appearance was in 1917—the story had been
reprinted in America in serial form and in three *Youth* volumes—when
Conrad wrote an "Author's Note" for a reprint by Dent in London of
the *Youth* volume of 1902. Then, in 1920, Doubleday brought out the
first collected works of Conrad in a limited American edition, called the
"Sun-Dial." At the same time, William Heinemann in London was
preparing a limited English edition of the collected works, which appeared
in 1921. The first general collected editions were brought out simultaneously in 1923 in New York by Doubleday and in London by Dent.
Because Conrad kept publishing, further collected editions were needed
after his death in 1924, but an editor of *Heart of Darkness* cannot consider them authoritative because Conrad had no chance to correct, revise,
or even approve them.
   Conrad's literary executor, Richard Curle, reported that although much
of Conrad's work is "extant in at least six different states—the manuscript, the corrected typescript, the serial form, the American book form,
the English book form, and the collected edition book form," it was "the
last alone that Conrad considered his final text" (Richard Curle, *The
Last Twelve Years of Joseph Conrad*, Garden City, NY, 1928). Although
we know from letters that Conrad took great interest in the 1923 Doubleday and Dent collected editions, Bruce Harkness in *Heart of Darkness and the Critics* (San Francisco, 1960) has shown (and the present
editor has verified) that the *Youth* volumes in these two collections are
printed from the same plates that were made in America for the 1920
"Sun-Dial" *Youth* volume, a work that is most unreliable both because

there is no evidence that Conrad had a chance to oversee the publication and because it is filled with error. Hence, one must move back to the 1921 Heinemann *Youth* volume as a possible copy-text for *Heart of Darkness*.

The Heinemann *Collected Works* is not a reprint, but a separate edition, the type of which was distributed after 780 sets had been printed. Conrad kept abreast of the production and worked closely with the editors on various of the volumes. Departures from the *Heart of Darkness* of 1902 are few, but do present a clarity of phrase and a consistency of syntax found in no other state of the story. The 1921 edition has been used, then, as the copy-text for the present edition.

Because there are, however, four significant forms of the text behind Conrad's "final" one—the nearly complete manuscript, the partial typescript, the *Blackwood's Magazine* version of 1899, and the Blackwood *Youth* volume of 1902—the present edition carries in its footnotes a selection of variant readings that permits the reader to follow Conrad as he worked toward establishing the final meaning and art of his text. The manuscript is a "clean" one; it moves steadily forward, having no long insertions, taking no false tacks, showing few second thoughts, and containing almost no revisions longer than a sentence. Because it is the most explicit of the extant versions, many passages that were later suppressed help one understand the meaning of the final text of *Heart of Darkness*. The magazine version is less explicit, omitting words, phrases, and one whole scene, but it has only one totally rewritten passage and only one other fully revised. The 1902 version differs from the magazine mainly in matters of style, in smoothness of phrase and syntax, but Conrad did tone down noticeably two descriptions of the native woman who appears toward the end of the story. Although no major changes appear in the 1921 edition, it is the most polished and consistent in style of all previous editions and reprints.

Nevertheless, the present text contains fifteen substantive and some two thousand accidental departures from 1921. Substantive changes are usually taken to refer to matters of wording, and accidentals, to matters of punctuation and capitalization. As the two words imply, a substantive variant is felt to be one that consciously changes meaning, while an accidental variant is felt to be indifferent with regard to meaning. But such a separation is artificial, for the way a sentence is pointed can change its implied meaning just as forcefully as can a change in its wording. The pointing of Marlow's sentences provides a case in point.

Twenty-five years ago, when I undertook the first Norton Critical Edition of *Heart of Darkness*, I was absolutely enchanted by Conrad's manuscript: its uninhibited flow, its simple directness. My instinct was to edit the manuscript for printing, but I was dissuaded because orthodox textual bibliography conservatively said: do not rush to change what the author did not change in the last text approved by that author. Thus my first (and second) edition represents the most reliable text of *Heart of Darkness* published since the authoritative 1921 version.

Today, orthodoxy has changed: while the "final" text still claims authority, the manuscript and the copy provided to a publisher's copy editor also have been granted a special kind of authority. Specifically, if a clear rationale of punctuation (and capitalization) within the manuscript and typescript of a work has been ignored by the publishing-house editor who prepared copy for the printer, then the editor of a critical edition of that work is justified in reclaiming the author's intentions through the reestablishment of the original rationale of punctuation. In the present case, Conrad's punctuation of the manuscript and typescript of *Heart of Darkness* is light; Blackwood's (both in *Blackwood's Magazine* and in *Youth*) is heavy—lots of colons and semicolons and exclamation points and question marks and restrictive commas.

For the complete story and for further justification for the adjustment of house-introduced accidentals, see the excellent work of Marion Michael and Wilkes Berry, "The Typescript of 'The Heart of Darkness,'" *Conradiana* 12 (1980): 147–55. But, in short, Conrad's practice was to have his wife, Jessie, type his manuscripts; he would then correct and change the typescript before sending it to the publisher; and when possible he always wanted to read proof before final printing. Once under contract for *Heart of Darkness* (as the subsection "Writing the Story" in Backgrounds and Sources, below, indicates) Conrad wrote feeling the pressure of deadlines, but Jessie fell sick after typing fifty-seven pages (and four lines) of manuscript, which came to thirty-five pages of typescript. Conrad corrected and changed these pages but sent the rest of the manuscript, pages 58–90, directly to David Meldrum, Blackwood's London literary agent. Meldrum had this balance of the manuscript typed and returned to Conrad, but sent the first thirty-five typed pages on to Edinburgh. Conrad corrected the typed version of manuscript pages 58–90, marked where he thought the first installment could end, and sent the lot to Edinburgh. Most of the manuscript lying behind the thirty-five pages typed by Jessie is lost; on the other hand, we have no further typed copy or corrected proofs for any part of the rest of the manuscript, which survives almost without interruption or loss. But a rationale of punctuation can be established by studying the hand changes in the typescript and by collating the places where the surviving manuscript and the typescript coincide and by studying the original punctuation in the rest of the manucript.

By reinstating the simple, direct flow of the manuscript, I have reestablished the speaking voice of Marlow that was originally heard on the *Nellie*. In so doing, I have also returned to him fifteen original words or phrases that never made it into print and whose absence was never later corrected by Conrad. None of the following emendations is purely "editorial"; each is fully substantiated by the manuscript (and in some few cases, the typescript). In the following list, after the page and line number, the new reading is given, followed by the 1921 printed version:

11.1:   on, *for* in
15.43:   appears, *for* appeared

17.20:   drooped, *for* dropped
18.22:   excavations hanging, *for* excavations, or hanging
19.15:   of, *for* or
21.32:   later on, *for* later
21.39   Caravans. *(omitted by first printer, and thereafter)*
25.6:   Triumphant, *for* Because triumphant
26.35:   later on, *for* later
33.26:   had, *for* has
39.9:   shore, *for* short
50.30:   found time for it., *for* found time for!
58.35:   shadow of the forest, *for* shadows of the forests
71.22:   the faith, *for* faith
75.13:   black, *for* back

Thus, this text, based upon a full study of all extant states of the story, from original draft through collected edition, is the most authoritative one printed since Conrad's death and is the only one to publish extensive portions of Conrad's manuscript.

In the following annotation, readings from the manuscript are identified as *Ms*; from the typescript, as *Ts*; from the magazine, as *Maga*; and from the first book form, as *1902*. Note †, on page 7, is an example of a reading in the *Maga* version that differs from 1902 and 1921 (the extant *Ms* does not begin until page 9 of the present text). Note *, page 9, is an example of a phrase in the *Ms* that was eliminated in the typescript of the *Maga* version. And note †, page 22, is an example of a reading that Conrad crossed out before the manuscript was typed. Not all variants have been included, only those that the editor feels lead toward a fuller, richer understanding of Conrad's art, either technically or thematically. *My remarks in these bibliographical footnotes are all in italics.*

The remaining annotations have been restricted to the definition of obscure words and phrases not readily found in a good dictionary and the identification of proper nouns. No notes try to identify people and places that had a "real" existence outside the story. Conrad's letter to Richard Curle (below, p. 232) makes it quite clear that he believed that such annotation did him a disservice; still, the reader curious to match the details of biography to the details of fiction has only to study "Conrad in the Congo" in the Backgrounds and Sources section. Nor have I given hints toward a "reading" of the story, either through direct statement or by suggesting analogues or by cross-referencing background material. All the help a reader may need to develop an individual interpretation can be found in the Backgrounds and Sources and Criticism sections, which follow the text.

Backgrounds and Sources

The Backgrounds and Sources selections have been divided into four subsections. "The Congo" gives, after a modern historical sketch, contradictory views and opinions of Belgian activity in the Congo contemporary with Conrad's own visit and concludes with a history of modern Zaire. The record of Conrad's "personal impressions" in letters, journals, and essays has been assembled in the second subsection, "Conrad in the Congo." Then, the actual, matter-of-fact way in which Conrad went about translating his deeply personal experiences into art is revealed in the third subsection, "Writing the Story." The last subsection, "Conrad on Life and Art," is a collection of philosophical and aesthetic ideas from Conrad's essays. Each subsection is interesting in its own right; however, each is intended primarily as a critical tool to be used in gaining a richer appreciation of *Heart of Darkness*. The first subsection sets the story within its historical context, but also provides the reader with the kind of information needed to appreciate Conrad's irony. The second subsection offers all that Conrad ever biographically recorded concerning his Congo experience, the artistic projection of which is *Heart of Darkness*. The third subsection reminds us that, autobiographical though it may be, the story was to Conrad a significant but objective work of art; indeed, his concern for cash may come as a shock to the romantically inclined. And the fourth subsection is not a medley of random Conradian opinions, but a carefully chosen group of statements that shed light on the themes and the artistic methods of *Heart of Darkness*.

In "The Congo" subsection, the most important addition to this third edition is the work of the distinguished historian John Hope Franklin on the fascinating life of George Washington Williams, who was in the Congo at the same time as Conrad. They followed the same itinerary and visited the same places; in fact, each stayed overnight with the missionary George Grenfell at Bolobo. In early August, they may well have been at Stanley Pool at the same time, Conrad having just arrived overland from Matadi and about to start out for Stanley Falls, Williams having just returned from Stanley Falls and Grenfell's mission and about to cross the river into the French Congo and then into other African states. Williams's experience in the Congo is particularly revealing because he went there as a complete devotee of King Leopold but was immediately appalled by what he saw; when he arrived in Stanley Falls, at the center of the "heart of darkness," he composed a full, public letter to Leopold—which, of course, the public and the king ignored. I am most grateful to Professor Franklin for allowing me to include the results of his scholarship. Franklin's editing of Williams's three reports on conditions in the Congo retains the original printing-house layout and typographical errors. With his permission, I have modified that layout and corrected those errors.

Also in "The Congo" subsection are two new maps, the Congo in 1890 and Zaire in 1987, and a new essay on the history of the Congo from the death of Leopold to the present rule of President Mobutu. This essay was researched and written by my assistant, Lynne Rice, who was particularly helpful in the fresh collation of all the states of *Heart of Darkness*.

"Conrad in the Congo" opens with a brief but complete biographical sketch of Conrad by Muriel Bradbrook and closes with comments from Albert Guerard on Conrad's transmission of the experience of life into the experience of art. All of the other pieces are from Conrad. Fortunately, Frederick Karl had completed the first two volumes of his *Collected Letters of Joseph Conrad* before this edition went to press, enabling me to edit and to reprint here, with his kind permission, the authoritative version of Conrad's correspondence, some of which was not previously available to the public before Karl's monumental undertaking (which is planned to run to eight volumes). Since the second edition of this work, Zdzislaw Najder has reedited Conrad's journals from the 1890 Congo experience and has kindly allowed me to reprint his introductions and his editions of "The Congo Diary" and the "Up-river Book." Both of these works, to me, are fascinating because they show us how vastly different from Marlow's were the external facts of Conrad's overland journey from Matadi to Kinshasa and his river journey up the Congo from Kinshasa to Stanley Falls. (In this regard, one might arrange to view the "The Congo" segment of the television series *River Journeys*, which shows how much and how little has changed since Conrad's day.)[1]

The titles and notes (except where labeled) are mine. The map of the Congo in 1890 contains the major geographical references within the story proper and within the various essays and accounts that follow. My editorial omissions are indicated by three asterisks: * * *

Criticism

The three most important events in *Heart of Darkness* criticism since the second edition of this book are the public remarks of Chinua Achebe on Conrad's racism, the film *Apocalypse Now*, and the publication of Ian Watt's *Conrad in the Nineteenth Century*. Each proved so engaging and provocative in its own right that each stimulated further critical responses and each serves as a starting point for the grouping of the new essays in this section. In order to make room for them, I have had to drop all but two of the excellent essays that I included in the first and second editions. Retained are Robert F. Haugh, who reviews the main approaches taken to *Heart of Darkness* from publication through 1954, and Albert J. Guerard, whose book *Conrad the Novelist* remains, for me, the finest and most important of all Conrad criticism.

Achebe, best known for his now-classic novel, *Things Fall Apart*, not only allowed me to use his remarks but revised them specially for this edition. Wilson Harris, although from Guyana, defended Conrad, as a

---

1. "The Congo," written by, directed by, and featuring Michael Wood, coproduced by RKO Pictures and BBC-TV, was presented over PBS by WETA, Washington ,D.C.. and is available from RKO Pictures, Inc., New York City, or Churchill Films, Los Angeles.

fellow novelist, from Achebe's attack. Frances B. Singh, writing from India, also attacks Conrad's colonialism, but C. Ponnuthurai Sarvan, writing from the University of Zambia, defends Conrad.

Francis Ford Coppola's film *Apocalypse Now* was controversial from the beginning, even before release, and has remained a campus favorite in the United States. Syndicated movie reviewer Mike Wilmington loved it; journalist Robert LaBrasca did not. William M. Hagen, both a Conrad scholar and a student of film, traces the narrative development of the film from behind the camera and with reference to Conrad's story. E. N. Dorall, writ·· · from the University of Malaya, presents a balanced appreciation ot both works of art.

The last seven essays are more typical literary criticism. Each can be read on its own, but together they provide a variety of ideas on "Impressionism and Symbolism in *Heart of Darkness*," the title I have given to my selections from Ian Watt, who proved devilishly hard to edit; his remarks on *Heart of Darkness* run over a hundred pages and the entire book is relevant to Conrad's story. I am grateful to Professor Watt for trusting me with his words, but he may not be grateful to me for including Robert Baker's seething review of his book. Bruce Johnson's reaction to Watt is not so vitriolic and is a bit more constructive. Garrett Stewart finds both Conrad and Marlow lacking in moral strength, but Juliet McLauchlan, the keeper of Conrad's flame in England, defends both Conrad and Marlow against both Watt and Stewart. And I was drawn to Michael Levenson's essay not only because it is very good but also because his approach, like mine, is through the writing of the text.

I first heard Ian Watt on Conrad's impressionism and symbolism in *Heart of Darkness* when we were on the same panel at the First International Conrad Conference in 1974 in Canterbury, Kent, where I had been invited to speak on the text from the point of view of an editor. Because I had twice edited the work, read all of the criticism on it, and taught the story numerous times, I had a lot to say—but not on editing. After Watt was through, I began by stating my title—"Phallic Futility and Folly in *Heart of Darkness*." Two women walked out of the room. Because lunchtime was announced, I never finished my paper, and I never got around to preparing it for inclusion among the conference papers before Norman Sherry's deadline. Some years later, John Batchelor, then a fellow conference participant, now an Oxford don, asked me to edit *Youth* (1902) as part of his Conrad collection within The World's Classics. I agreed, mainly because I wanted to return to my essay. But I should have remembered that exit by those women, for Oxford University Press found the language in my approach to the story too shockingly sexual for their readers and they asked to cut the most offending passages. It looked as if I would never be able to get my long-hatched but still hidden ideas before an audience larger than one. Then Norton asked for a third edition, and I said to myself, What the hell, modesty be damned.

The selections have been arranged chronologically, and most of the items have been included in their entirety. In no case should the editing be taken as a judgment on the quality of the omitted material. Finally, I have renumbered footnotes where necessary, eliminated page references to the text, adjusted all quotations of the story to conform to the present text, omitted specific notation of material elsewhere in this collection of criticism, and added some cross-references to material outside the collection.

A Guide to Bibliography

The last section of the book is vastly different from the bibliographies in each of the first two Norton Critical Editions of *Heart of Darkness*. Not only have Conrad studies proliferated, but also access to those studies has been eased because of the availability of annual printed bibliographies on Conrad and because of the availability of the MLA Bibliography through on-line computers in almost every library. Therefore, the present bibliography is no longer annotated, and just enough material is included to get someone oriented within and started on Conrad scholarship and criticism.

Acknowledgments

My aim in every respect has been reliability and completeness, but I could not have hoped to accomplish this end had I not received help from many quarters: from the secretaries of the Department of English of the University of Wisconsin, who did much of the typing; from the staff of the Wisconsin Memorial Library, who tracked down and obtained through interlibrary loan all editions and important reprints of the story; from the Newberry Library and the Vassar College Library, which allowed me to use their 1921 Heinemann editions; from the Yale University Library, which granted permission to use and to publish excerpts from Conrad's manuscript; from the Henry W. and Albert A. Berg Collection (New York Public Library: Astor, Lenox, and Tilden Foundations), which allowed me to study and to quote the thirty-five-page typescript; and from the Conrad estate, which allowed this work to appear yet another time.

The Text of
HEART OF DARKNESS

THE WORKS OF JOSEPH CONRAD

YOUTH

A NARRATIVE

AND TWO OTHER STORIES

. . . But the Dwarf answered : " No ; something human is dearer to me than the wealth of all the world."—GRIMM'S TALES

LONDON: WILLIAM HEINEMANN

Author's Note

The three stories in this volume[1] lay no claim to unity of artistic purpose. The only bond between them is that of the time in which they were written. They belong to the period immediately following the publication of *The Nigger of the "Narcissus,"* and preceding the first conception of *Nostromo,* two books which, it seems to me, stand apart and by themselves in the body of my work. It is also the period during which I contributed to *Maga;*[2] a period dominated by *Lord Jim* and associated in my grateful memory with the late Mr. William Blackwood's encouraging and helpful kindness.

Youth was not my first contribution to *Maga.* It was the second. But that story marks the first appearance in the world of the man Marlow, with whom my relations have grown very intimate in the course of years. The origins of that gentleman (nobody as far as I know had ever hinted that he was anything but that)—his origins have been the subject of some literary speculation of, I am glad to say, a friendly nature.

One would think that I am the proper person to throw a light on the matter; but in truth I find that it isn't so easy. It is pleasant to remember that nobody had charged him with fraudulent purposes or looked down on him as a charlatan; but apart from that he was supposed to be all sorts of things: a clever screen, a mere device, a 'personator,' a familiar spirit, a whispering 'daemon.' I myself have been suspected of a meditated plan for his capture.

That is not so. I made no plans. The man Marlow and I came together in the casual manner of those health-resort acquaintances which sometimes ripen into friendships. This one has ripened. For all his assertiveness in matters of opinion he is not an intrusive person. He haunts my hours of solitude, when, in silence, we lay our heads together in great comfort and harmony; but as we part at the end of a tale I am never sure that it may not be for the last time. Yet I don't think that either of us would care much to survive the other. In his case, at any rate, his occupation would be gone and he would suffer from that extinction, because I suspect him of some vanity. I don't mean vanity in the Solomonian

1. *Youth: A Narrative; and Two Other Stories* [*Heart of Darkness* and *The End of the Tether*], first published in 1902. *Heart of Darkness* was originally published in 1899. Conrad's introduction to *Youth* was first published in 1917. The copytext for this edition is Heinemann 1921.

2. Familiar abbreviation for *Blackwood's Magazine.*

sense.[3] Of all my people he's the one that has never been a vexation to my spirit. A most discreet, understanding man. . . .

Even before appearing in book-form *Youth* was very well received. It lies on me to confess at last, and this is as good a place for it as another, that I have been all my life—all my two lives—the spoiled adopted child of Great Britain and even of the Empire; for it was Australia that gave me my first command. I break out into this declaration not because of a lurking tendency to megalomania, but, on the contrary, as a man who has no very notable illusions about himself. I follow the instincts of vainglory and humility natural to all mankind. For it can hardly be denied that it is not their own deserts that men are most proud of, but rather of their prodigious luck of their marvellous fortune: of that in their lives for which thanks and sacrifices must be offered on the altars of the inscrutable gods.

Heart of Darkness also received a certain amount of notice from the first; and of its origins this much may be said: it is well known that curious men go prying into all sorts of places (where they have no business) and come out of them with all kinds of spoil. This story, and one other, not in this volume,[4] are all the spoil I brought out from the centre of Africa, where, really, I had no sort of business. More ambitious in its scope and longer in the telling, *Heart of Darkness* is quite as authentic in fundamentals as *Youth*. It is, obviously, written in another mood. I won't characterize the mood precisely, but anybody can see that it is anything but the mood of wistful regret, of reminiscent tenderness.

One more remark may be added. *Youth* is a feat of memory. It is a record of experience; but that experience, in its facts, in its inwardness and in its outward colouring, begins and ends in myself. *Heart of Darkness* is experience too; but it is experience pushed a little (and only very little) beyond the actual facts of the case for the perfectly legitimate, I believe, purpose of bringing it home to the minds and bosoms of the readers. There it was no longer a matter of sincere colouring. It was like another art altogether. That sombre theme had to be given a sinister resonance, a tonality of its own, a continued vibration that, I hoped, would hang in the air and dwell on the ear after the last note had been struck.

After saying so much there remains the last tale of the book, still untouched. *The End of the Tether* is a story of sea-life in a rather special way; and the most intimate thing I can say of it is this: that having lived that life fully, amongst its men, its thoughts and sensations, I have found it possible, without the slightest misgiving, in all sincerity of heart and peace of conscience, to conceive the existence of Captain Whalley's personality and to relate the manner of his end. This statement acquires some force from the circumstance that the pages of that story—a fair half of the book—are also the product of experience. That experience belongs (like *Youth's*) to the time before I ever thought of putting pen to paper.

3. See Ecclesiastes 1.14. 　　　　　4. *An Outpost of Progress.*

As to its 'reality,' that is for the readers to determine. One had to pick up one's facts here and there. More skill would have made them more real and the whole composition more interesting. But here we are approaching the veiled region of artistic values which it would be improper and indeed dangerous for me to enter. I have looked over the proofs, have corrected a misprint or two, have changed a word or two—and that's all. It is not very likely that I shall ever read *The End of the Tether* again. No more need be said. It accords best with my feelings to part from Captain Whalley in affectionate silence.

1917   J.C.

Heart of Darkness

I

The *Nellie*, a cruising yawl, swung to her anchor without a flutter of the sails and was at rest. The flood had made, the wind was nearly calm, and being bound down the river the only thing for it † was to come to and wait for the turn of the tide.

The Sea-reach of the Thames stretched before us like the beginning of an interminable waterway. In the offing the sea and the sky were welded together without a joint and in the luminous space the tanned sails of the barges drifting up with the tide seemed to stand still in red clusters of canvas, sharply peaked with gleams of varnished sprits. A haze rested on the low shores that ran out to sea in vanishing flatness. The air was dark above Gravesend,[1] and farther back still seemed condensed into a mournful gloom brooding motionless over the biggest, and the greatest, town on earth.

The Director of Companies was our Captain and our host. We four affectionately watched his back as he stood in the bows looking to seaward. On the whole river there was nothing that looked half so nautical. He resembled a pilot which to a seaman is trustworthiness personified. It was difficult to realise his work was not out there in the luminous estuary, but behind him, within the brooding gloom.

Between us there was as I have already said somewhere, the bond of the sea. Besides holding our hearts together through long periods of separation it had the effect of making us tolerant of each other's yarns—and even convictions. The Lawyer—the best of old fellows—had, because of his many years and many virtues, the only cushion on deck and was lying on the only rug. The Accountant had brought out already a box of dominoes and was toying architecturally with the bones. Marlow sat cross-legged right aft, leaning against the mizzen-mast. He had sunken cheeks, a yellow complexion, a straight back, an ascetic aspect, and with his arms dropped, the palms of hands outwards, resembled an idol. The Director satisfied the anchor had good hold made his way aft and sat down amongst us. We exchanged a few words lazily. Afterwards there was silence on board the yacht. For some reason or other we did not begin that game of dominoes. We felt meditative and fit for nothing but

† *Maga:* us
1. Gravesend is the last major town in the Thames estuary, twenty-six miles east of London, on the south shore (in Kent) where Essex forms the north shore.

placid staring. The day was ending in a serenity of still and exquisite brilliance. The water shone pacifically, the sky without a speck was a benign immensity of unstained light, the very mist on the Essex marshes was like a gauzy and radiant fabric hung from the wooded rises inland and draping the low shores in diaphanous folds. Only the gloom to the west brooding over the upper reaches became more sombre every minute as if angered by the approach of the sun.

And at last in its curved and imperceptible fall the sun sank low, and from glowing white changed to a dull red without rays and without heat, as if about to go out suddenly, stricken to death by the touch of that gloom brooding over a crowd of men.

Forthwith a change came over the waters, and the serenity became less brilliant but more profound. The old river in its broad reach rested unruffled at the decline of day after ages of good service done to the race that peopled its banks, spread out in the tranquil dignity of a waterway leading to the uttermost ends of the earth. We looked at the venerable stream not in the vivid flush of a short day that comes and departs for ever but in the august light of abiding memories. And indeed nothing is easier for a man who has, as the phrase goes, "followed the sea" with reverence and affection, than to evoke the great spirit of the past upon the lower reaches of the Thames. The tidal current runs to and fro in its unceasing service crowded with memories of men and ships it has borne to the rest of home or to the battles of the sea. It had known and served all the men of whom the nation is proud, from Sir Francis Drake to Sir John Franklin,[2] knights all, titled and untitled—the great knights-errant of the sea. It had borne all the ships whose names are like jewels flashing in the night of time, from the *Golden Hind* returning with her round flanks full of treasure, to be visited by the Queen's Highness and thus pass out of the gigantic tale, to the *Erebus* and *Terror*, bound on other conquests—and that never returned. It had known the ships and the men. They had sailed from Deptford, from Greenwich, from Erith— the adventurers and the settlers; kings' ships and the ships of men on 'Change; Captains, Admirals, the dark "interlopers" of the Eastern trade, and the commissioned "Generals" of East India fleets.[3] Hunters for gold or pursuers of fame they all had gone out on that stream, bearing the sword, and often the torch, messengers of the might within the land, bearers of a spark from the sacred fire. What greatness had not floated on the ebb of that river into the mystery of an unknown earth? . . . The dreams of men, the seed of commonwealths, the germs of empires.

The sun set; the dusk fell on the stream and lights began to appear along the shore. The Chapman lighthouse, a three-legged thing erect on a mud-flat, shone strongly. Lights of ships moved in the fairway—a

---

2. Sir Francis Drake sailed the *Golden Hind* in the service of Elizabeth I; Sir John Franklin (1786–1847) in 1845 led an exploring party in the *Erebus* and *Terror* in search of the Northwest Passage, but by the winter of 1848–49 all hands were dead. See below, p. 144.

3. Deptford, Greenwich, and Erith are three ports between London and Gravesend; the 'Change is the "Wall Street" of London; and "interploprers" were ships that trespassed on the rights of the trade monopolies such as the East India Company with its large transports engaged in regular general trade.

great stir of lights going up and going down. And farther west on the upper reaches the place of the monstrous town was still marked ominously on the sky, a brooding gloom in sunshine, a lurid glare under the stars.

"And this also," said Marlow suddenly, "has been one of the dark places of the earth."

He was the only man of us who still "followed the sea." The worst that could be said of him was that he did not represent his class. He was a seaman, but he was a wanderer too, while most seamen lead, if one may so express it, a sedentary life. Their minds are of the stay-at-home order, and their home is always with them—the ship—and so is their country—the sea. One ship is very much like another and the sea is always the same. In the immutability of their surroundings the foreign shores, the foreign faces, the changing immensity of life glide past, veiled not by a sense of mystery but by a slightly disdainful ignorance, for there is nothing mysterious to a seaman unless it be the sea itself which is the mistress of his existence and as inscrutable as Destiny. For the rest, after his hours of work, a casual stroll or a casual spree on shore suffices to unfold for him the secret of a whole continent, and generally he finds the secret not worth knowing. The yarns of seamen have a † direct simplicity, the whole meaning of which lies within the shell of a cracked nut. But Marlow was not typical (if his propensity to spin yarns be excepted) and to him the meaning of an episode was not inside like a kernel but outside,* enveloping the tale which brought it out only as a glow brings out a haze, in the likeness of one of these misty halos that, sometimes, are made visible by the spectral illumination of moonshine.

His remark did not seem at all surprising. It was just like Marlow. It was accepted in silence. No one took the trouble to grunt even, and presently he said very slow:

"I was thinking of very old times, when the Romans first came here, nineteen ‡ hundred years ago—the other day. . . . Light came out of this river since—you say Knights? Yes, but it is like a running blaze on a plain, like a flash of lightning in the clouds. We live in the flicker—may it last as long as the old earth keeps rolling! But darkness was here yesterday. Imagine the feelings of a commander of a fine—what d'ye call 'em—trireme [4] in the Mediterranean, ordered suddenly to the north; run overland across the Gauls in a hurry; put in charge of one of these craft the legionaries—a wonderful lot of handy men they must have been too—used to build, apparently by the hundred, in a month or two, if we may believe what we read. Imagine him here—the very end of the world, a sea the colour of lead, a sky the colour of smoke, a kind of ship about as rigid as a concertina—and going up this river with stores, or orders, or what you like. Sandbanks, marshes, forests, savages, precious

---

† Ms begins here, but reads an effective for a direct
* Ms: outside in the unseen
‡ Ms and Ts: eighteen
4. A "trireme" was a galley with three ranks of oars, one above another; "Falernian wine," below,

was a famous ancient wine from Campania and should not be confused with Neapolitan Falerno; and "Ravenna," below, now inland, was the chief Roman naval base in northern Italy on the upper Adriatic.

little to eat fit for a civilised man, nothing but Thames water to drink.
No Falernian wine here, no going ashore. Here and there a military
camp lost in a wilderness like a needle in a bundle of hay—cold, fog,
tempests, disease, exile, and death—death skulking in the air, in the
water, in the bush. They must have been dying like flies here. Oh yes—
he did it. Did it very well too, no doubt, and without thinking much
about it either, except afterwards to brag of what he had gone through
in his time, perhaps. They were men enough to face the darkness. And
perhaps he was cheered by keeping his eye on a chance of promotion to
the fleet at Ravenna, by and by, if he had good friends in Rome and
survived the awful climate. Or think of a decent young citizen in a
toga—perhaps too much dice, you know—coming out here in the train
of some prefect, or tax-gatherer, or trader even—to mend his fortunes.
Land in a swamp, march through the woods, and in some inland post
feel the savagery. The utter savagery had closed round him—all that
mysterious life of the wilderness that stirs † in the forest, in the jungles,
in the hearts of wild men. There's no initiation either into such mysteries. He has to live in the midst of the incomprehensible which is also
detestable. And it has a fascination too, that goes to work upon him.
The fascination of the abomination—you know. Imagine the growing
regrets, the longing to escape, the powerless disgust, the surrender—the
hate."

He paused.

"Mind," he began again, lifting one arm from the elbow, the palm of
the hand outwards, so that with his legs folded before him he had the
pose of a Buddha preaching in European clothes and without a lotus-
flower—"Mind, none of us would feel exactly like this. What saves us
is efficiency—the devotion to efficiency. But these chaps were not much
account really. They were no colonists, their administration was merely
a squeeze, and nothing more, I suspect. They were conquerors, and for
that you want only brute force—nothing to boast of, when you have it,
since your strength is just an accident arising from the weakness of others. They grabbed what they could get for the sake of what was to be
got. * It was just robbery with violence, aggravated murder on a great
scale, and men going at it blind—as is very proper for those who tackle
a darkness. The conquest of the earth, which mostly means the taking it
away from those who have a different complexion or slightly flatter noses
than ourselves, is not a pretty thing when you look into it too much.
What redeems it is the idea only. An idea at the back of it, not a sentimental ‡ pretence but an idea; and an unselfish belief in the idea—
something you can set up, and bow down before, and offer a sacrifice
to. . . ."

---

† Ms p. 14, *is missing*. P. 15 *begins thirteen lines
below:* not much account
* Ms: got. That's all. The best of them is they didn't
get up pretty fictions about it. Was there, I wonder, an association on a philanthropic basis to
develop Britain, with some third rate king for a pres-

ident and solemn old senators discoursing about it
approvingly and philosophers with uncombed
beards praising it, and men in market places crying
it up. Not much! And that's what I like! No! No!
It was just, *etc.*
‡ Ms: mouthing

He broke off. Flames glided on the river, small green flames, red flames, white flames, pursuing, overtaking, joining, crossing each other—then separating slowly or hastily. The traffic of the great city went on in the deepening night upon the sleepless river.† We looked on, waiting patiently—there was nothing else to do till the end of the flood; but it was only after a long silence, when he said in a hesitating voice, "I suppose you fellows remember I did once turn fresh-water sailor for a bit," that we knew* we were fated, before the ebb began to run, to hear about one of Marlow's inconclusive experiences.

"I don't want to bother you much with what happened to me personally," he began, showing‡ in this remark the weakness of many tellers of tales who seem so often unaware of what their audience would best like to hear; "yet to understand the effect of it on me you ought to know how I got out there, what I saw, how I went up that river to the place where I first met the poor chap. It was the farthest point of navigation and the culminating point of my experience. It seemed somehow to throw a kind of light on everything about me—and into my thoughts. It was sombre enough too—and pitiful—not extraordinary in any way—not very clear either. No. Not very clear. And yet it seemed to throw a kind of light.

"I had then, as you remember, just returned to London after a lot of Indian Ocean, Pacific, China Seas—a regular dose of the East—six years or so, and I was loafing about, hindering you fellows in your work and invading your homes, just as though I had got a heavenly mission to civilise you. It was very fine for a time, but after a bit I did get tired of resting. Then I began to look for a ship—I should think the hardest work on earth. But the ships wouldn't even look at me. And I got tired of that game too.

"Now when I was a little chap I had a passion for maps. I would look for hours at South America, or Africa, or Australia and lose myself in all the glories of exploration. At that time there were many blank spaces on the earth and when I saw one that looked particularly inviting on a map (but they all look that) I would put my finger on it and say: When I grow up I will go there. The North Pole was one of these places I remember. Well, I haven't been there yet and shall not try now. The glamour's off. Other places were scattered about the Equator and in every sort of latitude all over the two hemispheres. I have been in some of them and . . . well, we won't talk about that. But there was one yet—the biggest—the most blank, so to speak—that I had a hankering after.

"True, by this time it was not a blank space any more. It had got filled

---

†Ms: river. A big steamer came down all a long blaze of lights like a town viewed from the sea bound to the uttermost ends of the earth and timed to the day, to the very hour with nothing unknown in her path[,] no mystery on her way, nothing but a few coaling stations. She went fullspeed, noisily, an angry commotion of the waters followed her spreading from bank to bank—passed, vanished all at once—timed from port to port, to the very hour.

And the earth suddenly seemed shrunk to the size of a pea spinning in the heart of an immense darkness full of sparks born, scattered, glowing, going out beyond the ken of men. We looked on, etc.
*Ms p. 17 ends; pp. 18–29 missing.
‡Ts p. 10: showing himself in this remark curiously like most tellers of tale who seem always so strangely unawares, etc.

since my boyhood with rivers and lakes and names. It had ceased to be a blank space of delightful mystery—a white patch for a boy to dream gloriously over. It had become a place of darkness. But there was in it one river especially, a mighty big river that you could see on the map, resembling an immense snake uncoiled, with its head in the sea, its body at rest curving afar over a vast country and its tail lost in the depths of the land. And as I looked at the map of it in a shop-window it fascinated me as a snake would a bird—a silly little bird. Then I remembered there was a big concern, a Company for trade on that river. Dash it all, I thought to myself, they can't trade without using some kind of craft on that lot of fresh water—steamboats! Why shouldn't I try to get charge of one. I went on along Fleet Street,[5] but could not shake off the idea. The snake had charmed me.

"You understand it was a Continental concern, that Trading Society; but I have a lot of relations living on the Continent, because it's cheap and not so nasty as it looks—they say.

"I am sorry to own I began to worry them. This was already a fresh departure for me. I was not used to get things that way, you know. I always went my own road and on my own legs where I had a mind to go. I wouldn't have believed it of myself, but then—you see—I felt somehow I must get there by hook or by crook. So I worried them. The men said, 'My dear fellow,' and did nothing. Then—would you believe it—I tried the women. I, Charlie Marlow, set the women to work—to get a job! Heavens! Well, you see, the notion drove me. I had an aunt, a dear enthusiastic soul. She wrote: 'It will be delightful. I am ready to do anything, anything for you. It is a glorious idea. I know the wife of a very high personage in the Administration and also a man who has lots of influence with,' etc. etc. She was determined to make no end of fuss to get me appointed skipper of a river steamboat, if such was my fancy.[†]

"I got my appointment—of course; and I got it very quick. It appears the Company had received news that one of their Captains had been killed in a scuffle with the natives. This was my chance and it made me the more anxious to go. It was only months and months afterwards, when I made the attempt to recover what was left of the body, that I heard the original quarrel arose from a misunderstanding about some hens. Yes, two black hens. Fresleven—that was the fellow's name, a Dane—thought himself wronged somehow in the bargain, so he went ashore and started to hammer the chief of the village with a stick. Oh, it didn't surprise me in the least to hear this and at the same time to be told that Fresleven was the gentlest, quietest creature that ever walked on two legs. No doubt he was, but he had been a couple of years already out there engaged in the noble cause, you know, and he probably felt the need at last of asserting his self-respect in some way. Therefore he whacked the old nigger mercilessly while a big crowd of his people watched

5. A central business street in London.
† Ts, canceled: I'm curious how women are out of touch with the reality of facts. Yes. They are out of it, they are out of it. Yet I really believe they can carry through anything in the world—up to a certain point.

him, thunderstruck, till some man—I was told the chief's son—in desperation at hearing the old chap yell, made a tentative jab with a spear at the white man—and of course it went quite easy between the shoulder-blades. Then the whole population cleared into the forest expecting all kinds of calamities to happen, while, on the other hand, the steamer Fresleven commanded left also in a bad panic, in charge of the engineer, I believe. Afterwards nobody seemed to trouble much about Fresleven's remains till I got out and stepped into his shoes. I couldn't let it rest, though, but when an opportunity offered at last to meet my predecessor, the grass growing through his ribs was tall enough to hide his bones. They were all there. The supernatural being had not been touched after he fell. And the village was deserted, the huts gaped black, rotting, all askew within the fallen enclosures. A calamity had come to it, sure enough. The people had vanished. Mad terror had scattered them, men, women, and children, through the bush and they had never returned. What became of the hens I don't know either. I should think the cause of progress got them, anyhow. However, through this glorious affair I got my appointment before I had fairly begun to hope for it.

"I flew around like mad to get ready and before forty-eight hours I was crossing the Channel to show myself to my employers and sign the contract. In a very few hours I arrived in a city that always makes me think of a whited sepulchre. † Prejudice no doubt. I had no difficulty in finding the Company's offices. It was the biggest thing in the town and everybody I met was full of it. They were going to run an oversea empire and make no end of coin by trade.

"A narrow and deserted street in deep shadow, high houses, innumerable windows with venetian blinds, a dead silence, grass sprouting between the stones, imposing carriage archways right and left, immense double doors standing ponderously ajar. I slipped through one of these cracks, went up a swept and ungarnished staircase, as arid as a desert, and opened the first door I came to. * Two women, one fat and the other slim, sat on straw-bottomed chairs knitting black wool. The slim one got up and walked straight at me—still knitting with downcast eyes—and only just as I began to think of getting out of her way, as you would for a somnambulist, stood still, and looked up. Her dress was as plain as an umbrella cover, and she turned round without a word and preceded me into a waiting-room. I gave my name, and looked about. Deal table in the middle, plain chairs all round the walls, on one end a large shining map marked with all the colours of a rainbow. There was a vast amount of red—good to see at any time because one knows that some real work is done in there—a deuce of a lot of blue, a little green, smears of orange, and, on the East Coast, a purple patch, to show where the jolly pioneers of progress drink the jolly lager-beer. However, I wasn't going into any of these. I was going into the yellow. Dead in the centre. And the river was there—fascinating—deadly—like a snake. Ough. A door opened, a white-haired secretarial head, but wearing a compassionate expression, appeared, and a skinny forefinger beckoned me into the sanctuary. Its light was dim and a heavy writing-desk squatted in the middle. From behind that structure came out an impression of pale plumpness in a frock-coat. The great man himself. He was five feet six, I should judge, and had his grip on the handle-end of ever so many millions. He shook hands, I fancy, murmured vaguely, was satisfied with my French. *Bon voyage.*

"In about forty-five seconds I found myself again in the waiting-room with the compassionate secretary who full of desolation and sympathy made me sign some document. I believe I undertook amongst other things not to disclose any trade secrets. Well, I am not going to.

"I began to feel slightly uneasy. You know I am not used to such ceremonies and there was something ominous in the atmosphere. It was just as though I had been let into some conspiracy—I don't know— something not quite right, and I was glad to get out. In the outer room the two women knitted black wool feverishly. People were arriving and the younger one was walking back and forth introducing them. The old one sat on her chair. Her flat cloth slippers were propped up on a foot-warmer and a cat reposed on her lap. She wore a starched white affair on her head, had a wart on one cheek, and silver-rimmed spectacles hung on the tip of her nose. She glanced at me above the glasses. The swift and indifferent placidity of that look troubled me. Two youths with foolish and cheery countenances were being piloted over and she threw at them the same quick glance of unconcerned wisdom. She seemed to know all about them and about me too. An eerie feeling came over me. She seemed uncanny and fateful. Often far away there I thought of these two, guarding the door of Darkness, knitting black wool as for a warm pall, one introducing, introducing continuously to the unknown, the other scrutinising the cheery and foolish faces with unconcerned old eyes. 'Ave! Old knitter of black wool. *Morituri te salutant.*'[6] Not many of those she looked at ever saw her again—not half—by a long way.

"There was yet a visit to the Doctor. 'A simple formality,' assured me the secretary with an air of taking an immense part in all my sorrows. Accordingly a young chap wearing his hat over the left eyebrow, some clerk I suppose—there must have been clerks in the business, though the house was as still as a house in a city of the dead—came from some-where upstairs, and led me forth. He † was shabby and careless, with ink-stains on the sleeves of his jacket, and his cravat was large and bil-lowy under a chin shaped like the toe of an old boot. It was a little too early for the Doctor, so I proposed a drink and thereupon he developed a vein of joviality. As we sat over our vermuths he glorified the Com-pany's business and by and by I expressed casually my surprise at him

6. "Hail! . . . Those who are about to die salute   † Ms p. 30 *begins here.*
you."

not going out there. He became very cool and collected all at once. 'I am not such a fool as I look, quoth Plato to his disciples,' he said sententiously, emptied his glass with great resolution, and we rose.

"The old doctor felt my pulse, evidently thinking of something else the while. 'Good! Good for there,' he mumbled, and then with a certain eagerness asked me whether I would let him measure my head. Rather surprised, I said Yes, when he produced a thing like callipers and got the dimensions back and front and every way, taking notes carefully. He was an unshaven little man in a thread-bare coat like a gaberdine with his feet in slippers, and I thought him a harmless fool. 'I always ask leave, in the interests of science, to measure the crania of those going out there,' he said. 'And when they come back too?' I asked. 'Oh, I never see them,' he remarked, 'and, moreover the changes take place inside, you know.' He smiled as if at some quiet joke. 'So you are going out there. Famous. Interesting too.' He gave me a searching glance and made another note. 'Ever any madness in your family?' he asked in a matter-of-fact tone. I felt very annoyed. 'Is that question in the interests of science too?' 'It would be,' he said without taking notice of my irritation, 'interesting for science to watch the mental changes of individuals on the spot, but . . .' 'Are you an alienist?'[7] I interrupted. 'Every doctor should be—a little,' answered that original imperturbably. 'I have a little theory which you Messieurs who go out there must help me to prove. This is my share in the advantages my country shall reap from the possession of such a magnificent dependency. The mere wealth I leave to others. Pardon my questions, but you are the first Englishman coming under my observation. . . .' I hastened to assure him I was not in the least typical. 'If I were,' said I, 'I wouldn't be talking like this with you.' 'What you say is rather profound and probably erroneous,' he said with a laugh. 'Avoid irritation more than exposure to the sun. Adieu. How do you English say, eh? Good-bye. Ah! Good-bye. Adieu. In the tropics one must before everything keep calm.' . . . He lifted a warning forefinger. . . . 'Du calme, du calme. Adieu.'

"One thing more remained to do—say good-bye to my excellent aunt. I found her triumphant. I had a cup of tea—the last decent cup of tea for many days—and in a room that most soothingly looked just as you would expect a lady's drawing-room to look, we had a long quiet chat by the fireside. In the course of these confidences it became quite plain to me I had been represented to the wife of the high dignitary and goodness knows to how many more people besides as an exceptional and gifted creature—a piece of good fortune for the Company—a man you don't get hold of every day. Good Heavens! And I was going to take charge of a two-penny-half-penny river-steamboat with a penny whistle attached! It appears however I was also one of the Workers, with a capital—you know. Something like an emissary of light, something like a lower sort of apostle. There had been a lot of such rot let loose in print

7. In Conrad's day, a kind of psychiatrist.

and talk just about that time, and the excellent woman living right in the rush of all that humbug got carried off her feet. She talked about 'weaning those ignorant millions from their horrid ways,' till, upon my word, she made me quite uncomfortable. I ventured to hint that the Company was run for profit.

" 'You forget, dear Charlie, that the labourer is worthy of his hire,' she said brightly. It's queer how out of touch with truth women are! They live in a world of their own and there had never been anything like it and never can be. It is too beautiful altogether, and if they were to set it up it would go to pieces before the first sunset. Some confounded fact, we men have been living contentedly with ever since the day of creation, would start up and knock the whole thing over.

"After this I got embraced, told to wear flannel, be sure to write often and so on—and I left. In the street—I don't know why—a queer feeling came to me that I was an impostor. Odd thing, that I, who used to clear out for any part of the world at twenty-four hours' notice with less thought than most men give to the crossing of a street, had a moment—I won't say of hesitation, but of startled pause before this commonplace affair. † The best way I can explain it to you is by saying that for a second or two I felt as though instead of going to the centre of a continent I were about to set off for the centre of the earth.

"I left in a French steamer and * she called in every blamed port they have out there, for as far as I could see the sole purpose of landing soldiers and custom-house officers. I watched the coast. Watching a coast as it slips by the ship is like thinking about an enigma. There it is before you—smiling, frowning, inviting, grand, mean, insipid, or savage, and always mute with an air of whispering—Come and find out. This one was almost featureless, as if still in the making, with an aspect of monotonous grimness. The edge of a colossal jungle so dark green as to be almost black, fringed with white surf, ran straight, like a ruled line, far far away along a blue sea whose glitter was blurred by a creeping mist. The sun was fierce, the land seemed to glisten and drip with steam. Here and there greyish, whitish specks showed up, clustered inside the white surf, with a flag flying above them perhaps—settlements, some centuries old, and still no bigger than pin-heads on the untouched expanse of their background. We pounded along, stopped, landed soldiers, went on, landed custom-house clerks to levy toll in what looked like a God-forsaken wilderness with a tin shed and a flag-pole lost in it, landed more soldiers—to take care of the custom-house clerks—presumably. Some I heard got drowned in the surf, but whether they did or not nobody seemed particularly to care. They were just flung out there, and on we went. Every day the coast looked the same, as though we had not moved, but we passed various places—trading places—with names like Gran' Bassam, Little Popo, names that seemed to belong to some sordid farce acted in front of a sinister back-cloth. † The idleness of a passenger, my isolation amongst all these men with whom I had no point of contact, the oily and languid sea, the uniform sombreness of the coast, seemed to keep me away from the truth of things within the toil of a mournful and senseless delusion. The voice of the surf heard now and then was a positive pleasure, like the speech of a brother. It was something natural, that had its reason, that had a meaning. Now and then a boat from the shore gave one a momentary contact with reality. It was paddled by black fellows. You could see from afar the white of their eyeballs glistening. They shouted, sang; their bodies streamed with perspiration; they had faces like grotesque masks—these chaps; but they had bone, muscle, a wild vitality, an intense energy of movement that was as natural and true as the surf along their coast. They wanted no excuse for being there. They were a great comfort to look at. For a time I would feel I belonged still to a world of straightforward facts; but the feeling would not last long. Something would turn up to scare it away. Once, I remember, we came upon a man-of-war anchored off the coast. There wasn't even a shed there and she was shelling the bush. It appears the French had one of their * wars going on thereabouts. Her ensign drooped limp like a rag, the muzzles of the long six-inch ‡ guns stuck out all over the low hull, the greasy, slimy swell swung her up lazily and let her down, swaying her thin masts. In the empty immensity of earth, sky, and water, there she was, incomprehensible, firing into a continent. Pop, would go one of the six-inch guns; a small flame would dart and vanish, a little white smoke would disappear, a tiny projectile would give a feeble screech— and nothing happened. Nothing could happen. There was a touch of insanity in the proceeding, a sense of lugubrious drollery in the sight; and it was not dissipated by somebody on board assuring me earnestly there was a camp of natives—he called them, enemies—hidden out of sight somewhere.

"We gave her her letters (I heard the men in that lonely ship were dying of fever at the rate of three a day) and went on. We called at some more places with farcical names where the merry dance of death and trade goes on in a still and earthy atmosphere as of an overheated cata-comb; all along the formless coast bordered by dangerous surf, as if Nature herself had tried to ward off intruders; in and out of rivers, streams of death in life, whose banks were rotting into mud, whose waters, thick-ened into slime, invaded the contorted mangroves that seemed to writhe at us in the extremity of an impotent despair. Nowhere did we stop long enough to get a particularised impression, but the general sense of vague and oppressive wonder grew upon me. It was like a weary pilgrimage amongst hints for nightmares.

† Ms: back-cloth. Of all my life this passage is the part the most unreal.
* Ms: their heroic wars
‡ Ms: ten-inch; Ts and Maga: eight-inch; 1902: six-inch

"It was upward of thirty days before I saw the mouth of the big river. †
We anchored off the seat of the government. But my work would not
begin till some two hundred miles farther on. So as soon as I could I
made a start for a place thirty miles higher up.

"I had my passage on a little sea-going steamer. Her captain was a
Swede and knowing me for a seaman invited me on the bridge. He was
a young man, lean, fair, and morose, with lanky hair and a shuffling
gait. As we left the miserable little wharf he tossed his head contemp-
tuously at the shore. 'Been living there?' he asked. I said, 'Yes.' 'Fine lot
these government chaps—are they not?' he went on speaking English
with great precision and considerable bitterness. 'It is funny what some
people will do for a few francs a month. I wonder what becomes of that
kind when it goes up country?' I said to him I expected to see that soon.
'So-o-o!' he exclaimed. He shuffled athwart keeping one eye ahead vig-
ilantly. 'Don't be too sure,' he continued. 'The other day I took up a
man who hanged himself on the road. He was a Swede too.' 'Hanged
himself! Why, in God's name!' I cried. He kept on looking out watch-
fully. 'Who knows! The sun too much for him, or the country perhaps.' *

"At last we opened a reach. A rocky cliff appeared, mounds of turned-
up earth by the shore, houses on a hill, others with iron roofs amongst
a waste of excavations hanging to the declivity. A continuous noise of
the rapids above hovered over this scene of inhabited devastation. A lot
of people, mostly black and naked, moved about like ants. A jetty pro-

† Ms: river where my work was waiting for me. We
went up some twenty miles and anchored off the
seat of the government. I had heard enough in
Europe about its advanced state of civilization: the
papers, nay the very paper vendors in the sepulchral city were boasting about the steam tramway
and the hotel—especially the hotel. I beheld that
wonder. It was like a symbol at the gate. It stood
alone, a grey high cube of iron with two tiers of
galleries outside towering above one of those ruin-
ous-looking foreshores you come upon at home in
out-of-the-way places where refuse is thrown out.
To make the resemblance complete it wanted only
a drooping post bearing a board with the legend:
rubbish shot here, and the symbol would have had
the clearness of the naked truth. Not that a man
could not be found even there, just as a precious
stone is sometimes found in a dustbin.
    I had one dinner in the hotel and found out the
tramway ran only twice a day, at mealtimes. It
brought I believe the whole government with the
exception of the governor general down from the
hill to be fed by contract. They filled the dining
room, uniforms and civil clothes[,] sallow faces,
purposeless expressions. I was astonished at their
number. An air of weary bewilderment at finding
themselves where they were sat upon all the faces,
and in their demeanour they pretended to take
themselves seriously just as the greasy and dingy
place that was like one of those infamous eating
shops you find near the slums of cities, where
everything is suspicious, the linen, the crockery,

the food[,] the owner[,] the patrons, pretended to
be a sign of progress; as the enormous baobab on
the barren top of the hill amongst the government
buildings[,] soldier's huts, wooden shanties, cor-
rugated iron hovels, soared, spread out a maze of
denuded boughs as though it had been a shade
giving tree, as ghastly as a skeleton that posturing
in showy attitudes would pretend to be a man.
    I was glad to think my work only began two
hundred miles away from there. I could not be too
far away from that comedy of light at the door of
darkness. As soon as I could I left for a place thirty
miles higher up. From there I would have to walk
on the caravan road some hundred and seventy
miles more to the starting point of inland navigation.
    I had my passage, etc.
* Ms: perhaps.
    The little steamer had no speed to speak of and
I was rather impatient to see the first establishment, the shore station of my company. We had
left the coast belt of forest and barren, stony hills
came to view right and left of the stream, border-
ing flat strips of reedy coarse grass. [Canceled: As
we rounded a point I heard far ahead a powerful
and muffled detonation as of a big gun. After a
time there was another. It reminded me of the ship
shelling the continent. "What's that?" I asked.
"Railway station," answered the Swede curtly,
preparing to make a crossing to the south bank.]
    At last we opened a reach, etc.

jected into the river. A blinding sunlight drowned all this at times in a
sudden recrudescence of glare. 'There's your Company's station,' said
the Swede pointing to three wooden barrack-like structures on the rocky
slope. 'I will send your things up. Four boxes did you say? So. Farewell.'

"I came upon a boiler wallowing in the grass, then found a path leading up the hill. It turned aside for the boulders and also for an undersized railway truck lying there on its back with its wheels in the air. One
was off. The thing looked as dead as the carcass of some animal. I came
upon more pieces of decaying machinery, a stack of rusty rails. To the
left a clump of trees made a shady spot where dark things seemed to stir
feebly. I blinked, the path was steep. A horn tooted to the right and I
saw the black people run. A heavy and dull detonation shook the ground,
a puff of smoke came out of the cliff, and that was all. No change appeared
on the face of the rock. They were building a railway. The cliff was not
in the way of anything, but this objectless blasting was all the work going
on.

"A slight clinking behind me made me turn my head. Six black men
advanced in a file toiling up the path. They walked erect and slow,
balancing small baskets full of earth on their heads, and the clink kept
time with their footsteps. Black rags were wound round their loins and
the short ends behind waggled to and fro like tails. I could see every rib,
the joints of their limbs were like knots in a rope, each had an iron collar
on his neck and all were connected together with a chain whose bights
swung between them, rhythmically clinking. Another report from the
cliff made me think suddenly of that ship of war I had seen firing into a
continent. It was the same kind of ominous voice; but these men could
by no stretch of imagination be called enemies. They were called criminals and the outraged law like the bursting shells had come to them, an
insoluble mystery from the sea. All their meagre breasts panted together,
the violently dilated nostrils quivered, the eyes stared stonily uphill. They
passed me within six inches, without a glance, with that complete,
deathlike indifference of unhappy savages. Behind this raw matter one
of the reclaimed, the product of the new forces at work, strolled despon-
dently carrying a rifle by its middle. He had a uniform jacket with one
button off and seeing a white man on the path hoisted his weapon to his
shoulder with alacrity. This was simple prudence, white men being so
much alike at a distance that he could not tell who I might be. He was
speedily reassured and with a large, white, rascally grin, and a glance at
his charge, seemed to take me into partnership in his exalted trust. After
all, I also was a part of the great cause of these high and just proceedings.

"Instead of going up I turned and descended to the left. My idea was
to let that chain-gang get out of sight before I climbed the hill. You
know I am not particularly tender; I've had to strike and to fend off. I've
had to resist and to attack sometimes—that's only one way of resisting—
without counting the exact cost—according to the demands of such sort
of life as I had blundered into. I've seen the devil of violence, and the
devil of greed, and the devil of hot desire; but by all the stars these were

strong, lusty, red-eyed devils that swayed and drove men—men, I tell you. But as I stood on this hillside I foresaw that in the blinding sunshine of that land I would become acquainted with a flabby, pretending, weak-eyed devil of a rapacious and pitiless folly. How insidious he could be too I was only to find out several months later and a thousand miles farther. For a moment I stood appalled, as though by a warning. Finally I descended the hill, obliquely, towards the trees I had seen.

"I avoided a vast, artificial hole somebody had been digging on the slope, the purpose of which I found it impossible to divine. It wasn't a quarry or a sandpit, anyhow. It was just a hole. It might have been connected with the philanthropic desire of giving the criminals something to do. I don't know. Then I nearly fell into a very narrow ravine, almost no more than a scar in the hillside. I discovered that a lot of important drainage-pipes for the settlement had been tumbled in there. There wasn't one that was not broken. It was a wanton smash-up. At last I got under the trees. My purpose was to stroll into the shade for a moment, but no sooner within than it seemed to me I had stepped into the gloomy circle of some Inferno. The rapids were near and an uninterrupted, uniform, headlong rushing noise filled the mournful stillness of the grove where not a breath stirred, not a leaf moved, with a mysterious sound, as though the tearing pace of the launched earth had suddenly become audible.

"Black shapes crouched, lay, sat between the trees, leaning against the trunks, clinging to the earth, half coming out, half effaced within the dim light, in all the attitudes of pain, abandonment, and despair. Another mine[8] on the cliff went off followed by a slight shudder of the soil under my feet. The work was going on. The work! And this was the place where some of the helpers had withdrawn to die.

"They were dying slowly—it was very clear. They were not enemies, they were not criminals, they were nothing earthly now, nothing but black shadows of disease and starvation lying confusedly in the greenish gloom. Brought from all the recesses of the coast in all the legality† of time contracts, lost in uncongenial surroundings,* fed on unfamiliar food, they sickened, became inefficient, and were then allowed to crawl away and rest. These moribund shapes were free as air—and nearly as thin. I began to distinguish the gleam of the eyes under the trees. Then glancing down I saw a face near my hand. The black bones reclined at full length with one shoulder against the tree, and slowly the eyelids rose and the sunken eyes looked up at me, enormous and vacant, a kind of blind, white flicker in the depths of the orbs which died out slowly. The man seemed young—almost a boy—but you know with them it's hard to tell. I found nothing else to do but to offer him one of my good Swede's ship's biscuits I had in my pocket. The fingers closed slowly on it and held—there was no other movement and no other glance. He had tied a bit of white worsted round his neck—Why? Where did he get it.

8. British for a high-explosive change.   * Ms: strangeness
† Ms: pomp

Was it a badge—an ornament—a charm—a propitiatory act? Was there any idea at all connected with it. It looked startling round his black neck this bit of white thread from beyond the seas.

"Near the same tree two more bundles of acute angles sat with their legs drawn up. One, with his chin propped on his knees, stared at nothing in an intolerable and appalling manner. His brother phantom rested its forehead as if overcome with a great weariness; and all about others were scattered in every pose of contorted collapse, as in some picture of a massacre or a pestilence. While I stood horror-struck one of these creatures rose to his hands and knees and went off on all-fours towards the river to drink. He lapped out of his hand, then sat up in the sunlight crossing his shins in front of him, and after a time let his woolly head fall on his breastbone.

"I didn't want any more loitering in the shade and I made haste towards the station. When near the buildings I met a white man in such an unexpected elegance of get-up that in the first moment I took him for a sort of vision. I saw a high, starched collar, white cuffs, a light alpaca jacket, snowy trousers, a clean † necktie, and varnished boots. No hat. Hair parted, brushed, oiled, under a green-lined parasol held in a big white hand. He was amazing and had a pen-holder behind his ear.

"I shook hands with this miracle and I learned he was the Company's chief accountant and that all the book-keeping was done at this station. He had come out for a moment, he said, 'to get a breath of fresh air.' The expression sounded wonderfully odd with its suggestion of sedentary desk-life. I wouldn't have mentioned the fellow to you at all only it was from his lips that I first heard the name of the man who is so indissolubly connected with the memories of that time. Moreover I respected the fellow. Yes. I respected his collars, his vast cuffs, his brushed hair. His appearance was certainly that of a hairdresser's dummy, but in the great demoralisation of the land he kept up his appearance. That's backbone. His starched collars and got-up shirt-fronts were achievements of character. He had been out nearly three years and, later on, I could not help asking him how he managed to sport such linen. He had just the faintest blush and said modestly, 'I've been teaching one of the native women about the station. It was difficult. She had a distaste for the work.' Thus this man had verily accomplished something. And he was devoted to his books, which were in apple-pie order.

"Everything else in the Station was in a muddle—heads, things, buildings. Caravans. Strings of dusty niggers with splay feet arrived and departed; a stream of manufactured goods, rubbishy cottons, beads, and brass-wire set into the depths of darkness and in return came a precious trickle of ivory.

"I had to wait in the station for ten days—an eternity. I lived in a hut * in the yard, but to be out of the chaos I would sometimes get into the accountant's office. It was built of horizontal planks and so badly put

† Ms: clear silk; *Maga* and 1902: clear   * Ms: tent

together that as he bent over his high desk he was barred from neck to heels with narrow strips of sunlight. There was no need to open the big shutter to see. It was hot there too; big flies buzzed fiendishly and did not sting but stabbed. I sat generally on the floor, while of faultless appearance (and even slightly scented) perching on a high stool he wrote, he wrote. Sometimes he stood up for exercise. When a truckle-bed with a sick man (some invalided agent from up-country) was put in there, he exhibited a gentle annoyance. 'The groans of this sick person,' he said, 'distract my attention. And without that it is extremely difficult to guard against clerical errors in this climate.'

"One day he remarked without lifting his head, 'In the interior you will no doubt meet Mr. Kurtz.'* On my asking who Mr. Kurtz was he said he was a first-class agent, and seeing my disappointment at this information he added slowly, laying down his pen, 'He is a very remarkable person.' Further questions elicited from him that Mr. Kurtz was at present in charge of a trading-post, a very important one, in the true ivory-country, at 'the very bottom of there. Sends in as much ivory as all the others put together. . . .' He began to write again. The sick man was too ill to groan. The flies buzzed in a great peace.

"Suddenly there was a growing murmur of voices and a great tramping of feet. A caravan had come in. A violent babble of uncouth sounds burst out on the other side of the planks. All the carriers were speaking together, and in the midst of the uproar the lamentable voice of the chief agent was heard 'giving it up' tearfully for the twentieth time that day. . . . He rose slowly. 'What a frightful row,' he said. He crossed the room gently to look at the sick man and returning said to me, 'He does not hear.' 'What! Dead?' I asked, startled. 'No. Not yet,' he answered, with great composure. Then alluding with a toss of the head to the tumult in the station-yard, 'When one has got to make correct entries one comes to hate those savages—hate them to the death.' He remained thoughtful for a moment. 'When you see Mr. Kurtz,' he went on, 'tell him from me that everything here'—he glanced at the desk—'is very satisfactory. I don't like to write to him—with those messengers of ours you never know who may get hold of your letter—at that Central Station.' He stared at me for a moment with his mild, bulging eyes. 'Oh, he will go far, very far,' he began again. 'He will be a somebody in the Administration before long. They, above—the Council in Europe, you know—mean him to be.'

"He turned to his work. The noise outside had ceased, and presently in going out I stopped at the door. In the steady buzz of flies the home-ward-bound agent was lying flushed and insensible; the other bent over his books was making correct entries of perfectly correct transactions; and fifty feet below the doorstep I could see the still tree-tops of the grove of death.

* Ms: canceled: Klein (and the next three times; thereafter, Kurtz).

"Next day I left that station at last, with a caravan of sixty men, for a two-hundred-mile tramp.

"No use telling you much about that. Paths, paths, everywhere; a stamped-in network of paths spreading over the empty land, through long grass, through burnt grass, through thickets, down and up chilly ravines, up and down stony hills ablaze with heat; and a solitude, a solitude, nobody, not a hut. The population had cleared out a long time ago. Well if a lot of mysterious niggers armed with all kinds of fearful weapons suddenly took to travelling on the road between Deal and Gravesend catching the yokels right and left to carry heavy loads for them, I fancy every farm and cottage thereabouts would get empty very soon. Only here the dwellings were gone too. Still I passed through several abandoned villages. There's something pathetically childish in the ruins of grass walls. Day after day with the stamp and shuffle of sixty pair of bare feet behind me, each pair under a 60-lb. load. Camp, cook, sleep, strike camp, march. Now and then a carrier dead in harness, at rest in the long grass near the path, with an empty water-gourd and his long staff lying by his side. A great silence around and above. Perhaps on some quiet night the tremor of far-off drums, sinking, swelling, a tremor vast, faint; a sound weird, appealing, suggestive, and † wild—and perhaps with as profound a meaning as the sound of bells in a Christian country. Once a white man in an unbuttoned uniform, camping on the path with an armed escort of lank Zanzibaris,[9] very hospitable and festive—not to say drunk. Was looking after the upkeep of the road, he declared. Can't say I saw any road or any upkeep, unless the body of a middle-aged negro, with a bullet-hole in the forehead upon which I absolutely stumbled three miles farther on may be considered as a permanent improvement. I had a white companion too, not a bad chap, but rather too fleshy and with the exasperating habit of fainting on the hot hillsides miles away from the least bit of shade and water. Annoying, you know, to hold your own coat like a parasol over a man's head while he is coming to. I couldn't help asking him once what he meant by coming there at all. 'To make money, of course. What do you think?' he said scornfully. Then he got fever and had to be carried in a hammock slung under a pole. As he weighed sixteen stone[1] I had no end of rows with the carriers. They jibbed, ran away, sneaked off with their loads in the night—quite a mutiny. So, one evening I made a speech in English with gestures, not one of which was lost to the sixty pairs of eyes before me, and the next morning I started the hammock off in front all right. An hour afterwards I came upon the whole concern wrecked in a bush—man, hammock, groans, blankets, horrors. The heavy pole had skinned his poor nose. He was very anxious for me to kill somebody, but there wasn't the shadow of a carrier near. I remembered the old doctor—

---

† Ts, p. 35, *ends here and refers to Ms, p. 58, fourth line.*
9. The natives of Zanzibar were used as mercen-aries throughout Africa.
1. 224 pounds.

'It would be interesting for science to watch the mental changes of individuals on the spot.' I felt I was becoming scientifically interesting. However, all that is to no purpose. On the fifteenth day, I came in sight of the big river again and hobbled into the Central Station. It was on a back water surrounded by scrub and forest, with a pretty border of smelly mud on one side and on the three others enclosed by a crazy fence of rushes. A neglected gap was all the gate it had, and the first glance at the place was enough to let you see the flabby devil was running that show. White men with long staves in their hands appeared languidly from amongst the buildings strolling up to take a look at me and then retired out of sight somewhere. One of them, a stout, excitable chap with black moustaches informed me with great volubility and many digressions, as soon as I told him who I was, that my steamer was at the bottom of the river. I was thunderstruck. What, how, why? Oh it was 'all right.' The 'Manager himself' was there. 'All quite correct.' Everybody had behaved splendidly! splendidly! 'You must,' he said in agitation, 'go and see the General Manager at once. He is waiting.'

"I did not see the real significance of that wreck at once. I fancy I see it now—but I am not sure—not at all. Certainly the affair was too stupid—when I think of it—to be altogether natural. Still. . . . But at the moment it presented itself simply as a confounded nuisance. The steamer was sunk. They had started two days before in a sudden hurry up the river with the Manager on board, in charge of some volunteer skipper, and before they had been out three hours they tore the bottom out of her on stones and she sank near the south bank. I asked myself what I was to do there—now my boat was lost. As a matter of fact I had plenty to do in fishing my command out of the river. I had to set about it the very next day. That and the repairs when I brought the pieces to the station took some months.

"My first interview with the Manager was curious. He did not ask me to sit down after my twenty-mile walk that morning. He was commonplace in complexion, in feature, in manners, and in voice. He was of middle size and of ordinary build. His eyes of the usual blue were perhaps remarkably cold and he certainly could make his glance fall on one as trenchant and heavy as an axe. But even at these times the rest of his person seemed to disclaim the intention. Otherwise there was only an indefinable, faint expression of his lips, something stealthy—a smile—not a smile—I remember it, but I can't explain.† It was unconscious, this smile was, though just after he had said something it got intensified for an instant. It came at the end of his speeches like a seal applied on the words to make the meaning of the commonest phrase appear absolutely inscrutable. He was a common trader, from his youth up employed in these parts—nothing more. He was obeyed, yet he inspired neither love nor fear, nor even respect. He inspired uneasiness—that was it. Uneasiness. Not a definite mistrust—just uneasiness—nothing more.

---

† Ms: explain. It could be seen from a distance as he walked about the station grounds, a silent perambulating, glancing figure—with the air of being very much alone. It was unconscious, etc.

You have no idea how effective such a . . . a . . . faculty can be. He had no genius for organising, for initiative, or for order even. That was evident in such things as the deplorable state of the station. He had no learning, and no intelligence. His position had come to him—why? Perhaps because he was never ill. He had served three terms of three years out there. Triumphant health in the general rout of constitutions is a kind of power in itself. When he went home on leave he rioted on a large scale—pompously. Jack ashore—with a difference in externals only. This, one could gather from his casual talk. He originated nothing, he could keep the routine going—that's all. But he was great. He was great by this little thing that it was impossible to tell what could control such a man. He never gave that secret away. Perhaps there was nothing within him. Such a suspicion made one pause—for out there there were no external checks. Once when various tropical diseases had laid low almost every 'agent' in the station he was heard to say, 'Men who come out here should have no entrails.' He sealed the utterance with that smile of his as though it had been a door opening into a darkness he had in his keeping. You fancied you had seen things—but the seal was on. When annoyed at meal-times by the constant quarrels of the white men about precedence he ordered an immense round table to be made for which a special house had to be built. This was the station's mess-room. Where he sat was the first place—the rest were nowhere. One felt this to be his unalterable conviction. He was neither civil nor uncivil. He was quiet. He allowed his 'boy'—an overfed young negro from the coast—to treat the white men, under his very eyes, with provoking insolence.

"He began to speak as soon as he saw me. I had been very long on the road. He could not wait. Had to start without me. The up-river stations had to be relieved. There had been so many delays already that he did not know who was dead and who was alive and how they got on—and so on, and so on. He paid no attention to my explanations and, playing with a stick of sealing-wax, repeated several times that the situation was 'very grave, very grave.' There were rumours that a very important station was in jeopardy and its chief, Mr. Kurtz, was ill. Hoped it was not true. Mr. Kurtz was. . . . I felt weary and irritable. Hang Kurtz, I thought. I interrupted him by saying I had heard of Mr. Kurtz on the coast, 'Ah! So they talk of him down there,' he murmured to himself. Then he began again assuring me Mr. Kurtz was the best agent he had, an exceptional man, of the greatest importance to the Company; therefore I could understand his anxiety. He was, he said, 'very, very uneasy.' Certainly he fidgeted on his chair a good deal, exclaimed, 'Ah! Mr. Kurtz,' broke the stick of sealing-wax and seemed dumbfounded by the accident. Next thing he wanted to know 'how long it would take to'. . . . I interrupted him again. Being hungry, you know, and kept on my feet too, I was getting savage. 'How can I tell,' I said. 'I haven't even seen the wreck yet. Some months, no doubt.' All this talk seemed to me so futile. 'Some months,' he said. 'Well. Let us say three months before we can make a start. Yes. That ought to do the affair.' I flung out of his hut (he lived all alone in a clay hut with a sort of verandah) muttering to myself my opinion of him. He was a chattering idiot. Afterwards I took it back when it was borne in upon me startlingly with what extreme nicety he had estimated the time requisite for the 'affair.'

"I went to work the next day, turning, so to speak, my back on that station. In that way only it seemed to me I could keep my hold on the redeeming facts of life. Still, one must look about sometimes; and then I saw this station, these men strolling aimlessly about in the sunshine of the yard. I asked myself sometimes what it all meant. They wandered here and there with their absurd long staves in their hands like a lot of faithless pilgrims bewitched inside a rotten fence. The word 'ivory' rang in the air, was whispered, was sighed. You would think they were pray-ing to it. A taint of imbecile rapacity blew through it all like a whiff from some corpse. By Jove! I've never seen anything so unreal in my life. And outside, the silent wilderness surrounding this cleared speck on the earth stuck me as something great and invincible, like evil or truth, waiting patiently for the passing away of this fantastic invasion.

"Oh, those months! Well, never mind. Various things happened. One evening a grass shed full of calico, cotton prints, beads, and I don't know what else, burst into a blaze so suddenly that you would have thought the earth had opened to let an avenging fire consume all that trash. I was smoking my pipe quietly by my dismantled steamer and saw them all cutting capers in the light with their arms lifted high when the stout man with moustaches came tearing down to the river, a tin pail in his hand, assured me that everybody was 'behaving splendidly, splendidly,' dipped about a quart of water, and tore back again. I noticed there was a hole in the bottom of his pail.

"I strolled up. There was no hurry. You see the thing had gone off like a box of matches. It had been hopeless from the very first. The flame had leaped high, driven everybody back, lighted up everything—and collapsed. The shed was already a heap of embers glowing fiercely. A nigger was being beaten near by. They said he had caused the fire in some way; be that as it may, he was screeching most horribly. I saw him later on for several days sitting in a bit of shade looking very sick and trying to recover himself. Afterwards he arose and went out—and the wilderness without a sound took him into its bosom again. As I approached the glow from the dark I found myself at the back of two men, talking. I heard the name of Kurtz pronounced, then the words, 'take advantage of this unfortunate accident.' One of the men was the Manager. I wished him a good evening. 'Did you ever see anything like it—eh? it is incred-ible,' he said, and walked off. The other man remained. He was a first-class agent, young, gentlemanly, a bit reserved, with a forked little beard and a hooked nose. He was stand-offish with the other agents and they on their side said he was the Manager's spy upon them. As to me, I had hardly ever spoken to him before. We got into talk and by and by we strolled away from the hissing ruins. Then he asked me to his room, which was in the main building of the station. He struck a match and I perceived that this young aristocrat had not only a silver-mounted dressing-case but also a whole candle all to himself. Just at that time the Manager was the only man supposed to have any right to candles. Native mats covered the clay walls; a collection of spears, assegais,[2] shields, knives, was hung up in trophies. The business entrusted to this fellow was the making of bricks—so I had been informed; but there wasn't a fragment of a brick anywhere in the station, and he had been there more than a year—waiting. It seems he could not make bricks without something, I don't know what—straw maybe. Anyway it could not be found there, and as it was not likely to be sent from Europe it did not appear clear to me what he was waiting for. An act of special creation perhaps. However, they were all waiting—all the sixteen or twenty pilgrims of them—for something; and upon my word it did not seem an uncongenial occupation, from the way they took it, though the only thing that ever came to them was disease—as far as I could see. They beguiled the time by backbiting and intriguing against each other in a foolish kind of way. There was an air of plotting about that station, but nothing came of it, of course. It was as unreal as everything else—as the philanthropic pretence of the whole concern, as their talk, as their government, as their show of work. The only real feeling was a desire to get appointed to a trading-post where ivory was to be had, so that they could earn percentages. They intrigued and slandered and hated each other only on that account—but as to effectually lifting a little finger—oh no. By Heavens! There is something after all in the world allowing one man to steal a horse while another must not look at a halter. Steal a horse straight out. Very well. He has done it. Perhaps he can ride. But there is a way of looking at a halter that would provoke the most charitable of saints into a kick.

"I had no idea why he wanted to be sociable, but as we chatted in there it suddenly occurred to me the fellow was trying to get at something—in fact, pumping me. He alluded constantly to Europe, to the people I was supposed to know there—putting leading questions as to my acquaintances in the sepulchral city, and so on. His little eyes glittered like mica discs—with curiosity—though he tried to keep up a bit of superciliousness. At first I was astonished, but very soon I became awfully curious to see what he would find out from me. I couldn't possibly imagine what I had in me to make it worth his while.[†] It was very pretty to see how he baffled himself, for in truth my body was full only of chills and my head had nothing in it but that wretched steamboat business. It was evident he took me for a perfectly shameless prevaricator. At last he got angry and to conceal a movement of furious annoyance he yawned. I rose. Then I noticed a small sketch in oils, on a panel, representing a woman draped and blindfolded carrying a lighted torch. The background was sombre—almost black. The movement of

2. Slender throwing spears.
† *Ms and Maga*: while. His allusions were Chinese to me. It was, *etc.*

the woman was stately, and the effect of the torchlight on the face was
sinister.

"It arrested me and he stood by civilly holding an empty half-pint
champagne bottle (medical comforts) with the candle stuck in it. To my
question he said Mr. Kurtz had painted this—in this very station more
than a year ago—while waiting for means to go to his trading-post. 'Tell
me, pray,' said I, 'who is this Mr. Kurtz?'

" 'The chief of the Inner Station,' he answered in a short tone, looking away. 'Much obliged,' I said laughing. 'And you are the brickmaker
of the Central Station. Every one knows that.' He was silent for a while.
'He is a prodigy,' he said at last. 'He is an emissary of pity, and science,
and progress, and devil knows what else. We want,' he began to declaim
suddenly, 'for the guidance of the cause entrusted to us by Europe, so
to speak, higher intelligence, wide sympathies, a singleness of purpose.'
'Who says that?' I asked. 'Lots of them,' he replied. 'Some even write
that; and so *he* comes here, a special being, as you ought to know.' 'Why
ought I to know?' I interrupted really surprised. He paid no attention.
'Yes. To-day he is chief of the best station, next year he will be Assistant-
Manager, two years more and . . . but I dare say you know what he will
be in two years' time. You are of the new gang—the gang of virtue. The
same people who sent him specially also recommended you. Oh, don't
say no. I've my own eyes to trust.' Light dawned upon me. My dear
aunt's influential acquaintances were producing an unexpected effect
upon that young man. I nearly burst into a laugh. 'Do you read the
Company's confidential correspondence?' I asked. He hadn't a word to
say. It was great fun. 'When Mr. Kurtz,' I continued severely, 'is General Manager, you won't have the opportunity.'

"He blew the candle out suddenly and we went outside. The moon
had risen. Black figures strolled about listlessly, pouring water on the
glow, whence proceeded a sound of hissing; steam ascended in the
moonlight; the beaten nigger groaned somewhere. 'What a row the brute
makes!' said the indefatigable man with the moustaches appearing near
us. 'Serve him right. Transgression—punishment—bang! Pitiless, pitiless. That's the only way. This will prevent all conflagrations for the
future. I was just telling the Manager. . . .' He noticed my companion
and became crestfallen all at once. 'Not in bed yet,' he said with a kind
of servile † heartiness; 'it's so natural. Ha! Danger—agitation.' he vanished. I went on to the river-side, and the other followed me. I heard a
scathing murmur at my ear, 'Heaps of muffs—go to.' The pilgrims could
be seen in knots gesticulating, discussing. Several had still their staves
in their hands. I verily believe they took these sticks to bed with them.
Beyond the fence the forest stood up spectrally in the moonlight and
through the dim stir, through the faint sounds of that lamentable courtyard, the silence of the land went home to one's very heart—its mystery,
its greatness, the amazing reality of its concealed life. The hurt nigger

† *Ms and Maga:* obsequious

moaned feebly somewhere near by and then fetched a deep sigh that made me mend my pace away from there. I felt a hand introducing itself under my arm. 'My dear sir,' said the fellow, 'I don't want to be mis-understood and especially by you who will see Mr. Kurtz long before I can have that pleasure. I wouldn't like him to get a false idea of my disposition. . . .'

"I let him run on, this papier-mâché Mephistopheles, and it seemed to me that if I tried I could poke my forefinger through him and would find nothing inside but a little loose dirt, maybe. He, don't you see, had been planning to be Assistant-Manager by and by under the present man, and I could see that the coming of that Kurtz had upset them both not a little. He talked precipitately and I did not try to stop him. I had my shoulders against the wreck of my steamer hauled up on the slope like a carcass of some big river animal. The smell of mud, of primeval mud by Jove, was in my nostrils, the high stillness of primeval forest was before my eyes; there were shiny patches on the black creek. The moon had spread over everything a thin layer of silver—over the rank grass, over the mud, upon the wall of matted vegetation standing higher than the wall of a temple, over the great river I could see through a sombre gap glittering, glittering as it flowed broadly by without a murmur. All this was great, expectant, mute, while the man jabbered about himself. I wondered whether the stillness on the face of the immensity looking at us two were meant as an appeal or as a menace. What were we who had strayed in here? Could we handle that dumb thing, or would it handle us? I felt how big, how confoundedly big, was that thing that couldn't talk and perhaps was deaf as well. What was in there? I could see a little ivory coming out from there and I had heard Mr. Kurtz was in there. I had heard enough about it too—God knows! Yet somehow it didn't bring any image with it—no more than if I had been told an angel or a fiend was in there. I believed it in the same way one of you might believe there are inhabitants in the planet Mars. I knew once a Scotch sailmaker who was certain, dead sure, there were people in Mars. If you asked him for some idea how they looked and behaved he would get shy and mutter something about 'walking on all-fours.' If you as much as smiled he would—though a man of sixty—offer to fight you. I would not have gone so far as to fight for Kurtz, but I went for him near enough to a lie. You know I hate, detest, and can't bear a lie, not because I am straighter than the rest of us, but simply because it appals me. There is a taint of death, a flavour of mortality in lies—which is exactly what I hate and detest in the world—what I want to forget. It makes me miserable and sick like biting something rotten would do. Temperament, I suppose. Well, I went near enough to it by letting the young fool there believe anything he liked to imagine as to my influence in Europe. I became in an instant as much of a pretence as the rest of the bewitched pilgrims. This simply because I had a notion it somehow would be of help to that Kurtz whom at the time I did not see—you understand. He was just a word for me. I did not see the man in the name any more than you do.

Do you see him? Do you see the story? Do you see anything? It seems to me I am trying to tell you a dream—making a vain attempt, because no relation of a dream can convey the dream-sensation, that commingling of absurdity, surprise, and bewilderment in a tremor of struggling revolt, that notion of being captured by the incredible which is the very essence of dreams. . . ."

He was silent for a while.

". . . No, it is impossible; it is impossible to convey the life-sensation of any given epoch of one's existence—that which makes its truth, its meaning—its subtle and penetrating essence. It is impossible. We live, as we dream—alone. . . ."

He paused again as if reflecting, then added:

"Of course in this you fellows see more than I could then. You see me, whom you know. . . ."

It had become so pitch dark that we listeners could hardly see one another. For a long time already he, sitting apart, had been no more to us than a voice. There was not a word from anybody. The others might have been asleep, but I was awake. I listened, I listened on the watch for the sentence, for the word that would give me the clue to the faint uneasiness inspired by this narrative that seemed to shape itself without human lips in the heavy night-air of the river.

". . . Yes—I let him run on," Marlow began again, "and think what he pleased about the powers that were behind me. I did! And there was nothing behind me! There was nothing but that wretched old mangled steamboat I was leaning against while he talked fluently about 'the necessity for every man to get on.' 'And when one comes out here, you conceive, it is not to gaze at the moon.' Mr. Kurtz was a 'universal genius,' but even a genius would find it easier to work with 'adequate tools—intelligent men.' He did not make bricks—why, there was a physical impossibility in the way—as I was well aware; and if he did secretarial work for the Manager, it was because 'no sensible man rejects wantonly the confidence of his superiors.' Did I see it? I saw it. What more did I want? What I really wanted was rivets, by Heaven! Rivets. To get on with the work—to stop the hole. Rivets I wanted. There were cases of them down at the coast—cases—piled up—burst—split! You kicked a loose rivet at every second step in that station yard on the hillside. Rivets had rolled into the grove of death. You could fill your pockets with rivets for the trouble of stooping down—and there wasn't one rivet to be found where it was wanted. We had plates that would do but nothing to fasten them with. And every week the messenger, a lone negro, letter-bag on shoulder and staff in hand, left our station for the coast. And several times a week a coast caravan came in with trade goods—ghastly glazed calico that made you shudder only to look at it, glass beads value about a penny a quart, confounded spotted cotton handkerchiefs. And no rivets. Three carriers could have brought all that was wanted to set that steamboat afloat.

"He was becoming confidential now, but I fancy my unresponsive

attitude must have exasperated him at last, for he judged it necessary to
inform me he feared neither God nor devil, let alone any mere man. I
said I could see that very well, but what I wanted was a certain quantity
of rivets—and rivets were what really Mr. Kurtz wanted—if he had only
known it. Now letters went to the coast every week. . . . 'My dear sir,'
he cried, 'I write from dictation.' I demanded rivets. There was a way—
for an intelligent man. He changed his manner; became very cold and
suddenly began to talk about a hippopotamus; wondered whether sleeping on board the steamer (I stuck to my salvage night and day) I wasn't
disturbed. There was an old hippo that had the bad habit of getting out
on the bank and roaming at night over the station grounds. The pilgrims
used to turn out in a body and empty every rifle they could lay hands on
at him. Some even had sat up o' nights for him. All this energy was
wasted though. 'That animal has a charmed life,' he said, 'but you can
say this only of brutes in this country. No man—you apprehend me?—
no man here bears a charmed life.' He stood there for a moment in the
moonlight with his delicate hooked nose set a little askew and his mica
eyes glittering without a wink, then with a curt Good-night, he strode
off. I could see he was disturbed and considerably puzzled, which made
me feel more hopeful than I had been for days. It was a great comfort to
turn from that chap to my influential friend, the battered, twisted, ruined
tin-pot steamboat. I clambered on board. She rang under my feet like
an empty Huntley & Palmer biscuit-tin kicked along a gutter; she was
nothing so solid in make, and rather less pretty in shape, but I had
expended enough hard work on her to make me love her. No influential
friend would have served me better. She had given me a chance to come
out a bit—to find out what I could do. No. I don't like work. I had
rather laze about and think of all the fine things that can be done. I
don't like work—no man does—but I like what is in the work—the chance
to find yourself. Your own reality—for yourself—not for others—what
no other man can ever know. They can only see the mere show, and
never can tell what it really means.

"I was not surprised to see somebody sitting aft on the deck with his
legs dangling over the mud. You see I rather chummed with the few
mechanics there were in that station, whom the other pilgrims naturally
despised—on account of their imperfect manners, I suppose. This was
the foreman—a boiler-maker by trade—a good worker. He was a lank
bony yellow-faced man with big intense eyes. His aspect was worried
and his head was as bald as the palm of my hand; but his hair in falling
seemed to have stuck to his chin and had prospered in the new locality,
for his beard hung down to his waist. He was a widower with six young
children (he had left them in charge of a sister of his to come out there),
and the passion of his life was pigeon-flying. He was an enthusiast and
a connoisseur. He would rave about pigeons. After work hours he used
sometimes to come over from his hut for a talk about his children and
his pigeons; at work when he had to crawl in the mud under the bottom
of the steamboat he would tie up that beard of his in a kind of white

serviette[3] he brought for the purpose. It had loops to go over his ears. In the evening he could be seen squatted on the bank rinsing that wrapper in the creek with great care, then spreading it solemnly on a bush to dry.

"I slapped him on the back and shouted 'We shall have rivets!'" He scrambled to his feet exclaming 'No! Rivets!' as though he couldn't believe his ears. Then in a low voice, 'You . . . eh?' I don't know why we behaved like lunatics. I put my finger to the side of my nose and nodded mysteriously. 'Good for you!' he cried, snapped his fingers above his head, lifting one foot. I tried a jig. We capered on the iron deck. A frightful clatter came out of that hulk and the virgin forest of the other bank of the creek sent it back in a thundering roll upon the sleeping station. It must have made some of the pilgrims sit up in their hovels. A dark figure obscured the lighted doorway of the Manager's hut, vanished, then a second or so after the doorway itself vanished too. We stopped and the silence driven away by the stamping of our feet flowed back again from the recesses of the land. The great wall of vegetation, an exuberant and entangled mass of trunks, branches, leaves, boughs, festoons motionless in the moonlight, was like a rioting invasion of soundless life, a rolling wave of plants piled up, crested, ready to topple over the creek to sweep every little man of us out of his little existence. And it moved not. A deadened burst of mighty splashes and snorts reached us from afar as though an ichthyosaurus[4] had been taking a bath of glitter in the great river. 'After all,' said the boiler-maker in a reasonable tone, 'why shouldn't we get the rivets?' Why not, indeed! I did not know of any reason why we shouldn't. 'They'll come in three weeks,' I said confidently.

"But they didn't. Instead of rivets there came an invasion, an infliction, a visitation. It came in sections during the next three weeks, each section headed by a donkey carrying a white man in new clothes and tan shoes bowing from that elevation right and left to the impressed pilgrims. A quarrelsome band of footsore sulky niggers trod on the heels of the donkey; a lot of tents, camp-stools, tin boxes, white cases, brown bales would be shot down in the courtyard and the air of mystery would deepen a little over the muddle of the station. Five such instalments came, with their absurd air of disorderly flight with the loot of innumerable outfit shops and provision stores that, one would think, they were lugging, after a raid, into the wilderness for equitable division. It was an inextricable mess of things decent in themselves but that human folly made look like the spoils of thieving.

"This devoted band called itself the Eldorado Exploring Expedition and I believe they were sworn to secrecy. Their talk however was the talk of sordid buccaneers. It was reckless without hardihood, greedy without audacity, and cruel without courage. There was not an atom of foresight or of serious intention in the whole batch of them, and they did not seem aware these things are wanted for the work of the world. To tear

3. French form for table napkin.   4. A huge prehistoric kind of crocodile.

treasure out of the bowels of the land was their desire, with no more moral purpose at the back of it than there is in burglars breaking into a safe. Who paid the expenses of the noble enterprise I don't know; but the uncle of our Manager was leader of that lot.

"In exterior he resembled a butcher in a poor neighbourhood and his eyes had a look of sleepy cunning. He carried his fat paunch with ostentation on his short legs and during the time his gang infested the station spoke to no one but his nephew. You could see these two roaming about all day long with their heads close together in an everlasting confab.

"I had given up worrying myself about the rivets. One's capacity for that kind of folly is more limited than you would suppose. I said Hang!— and let things slide. I had plenty of time for meditation and now and then I would give some thought to Kurtz. I wasn't very interested in him. No. Still, I was curious to see whether this man who had come out equipped with moral ideas of some sort would climb to the top after all and how he would set about his work when there."

II

"One evening as I was lying flat on the deck of my steamboat I heard voices approaching—and there were the nephew and the uncle strolling along the bank. I laid my head on my arm again and had nearly lost myself in a doze when somebody said—in my ear as it were—'I am as harmless as a little child, but I don't like to be dictated to. Am I the Manager—or am I not? I was ordered to send him there. It's incredible.' . . . I became aware that the two were standing on the shore alongside the forepart of the steamboat just below my head. I did not move. It did not occur to me to move. I was sleepy. 'It *is* unpleasant,' grunted the uncle. 'He had asked the Administration to be sent there,' said the other, 'with the idea of showing what he could do; and I was instructed accordingly. Look at the influence that man must have. It is not frightful?' They both agreed it was frightful, then made several bizarre remarks: 'Make rain and fine weather—one man—the Council—by the nose'— bits of absurd sentences that got the better of my drowsiness, so that I had pretty near the whole of my wits about me when the uncle said, 'The climate may do away with this difficulty for you. Is he alone there?' 'Yes,' answered the Manager; 'he sent his assistant down the river with a note to me in these terms: "Clear this poor devil out of the country and don't bother sending more of that sort. I had rather be alone than have the kind of men you can dispose of with me." It was more than a year ago. Can you imagine such impudence?' 'Anything since then?' asked the other hoarsely. 'Ivory,' jerked † the nephew; 'lots of it—prime sort— lots—most annoying, from him.' 'And with that?' questioned the heavy rumble. 'Invoice,' was the reply fired * out, so to speak. Then silence. They had been talking about Kurtz.

† Ms: jerked out   * Ms: spat

"I was broad awake by this time but, lying perfectly at ease, remained
still, having no inducement to change my position. 'How did that ivory
come all this way?' growled the elder man who seemed very vexed. The
other explained that it had come with a fleet of canoes in charge of an
English half-caste clerk Kurtz had with him; that Kurtz had apparently
intended to return himself, the station being by that time bare of goods
and stores, but after coming three hundred miles had suddenly decided
to go back, which he started to do alone in a small dugout with four
paddlers, leaving the half-caste to continue down the river with the ivory.
The two fellows there seemed astounded at anybody attempting such a
thing. They were at a loss for an adequate motive. As for me, I seemed
to see Kurtz for the first time. It was a distinct glimpse: the dugout, four
paddling savages, and the lone white man turning his back suddenly on
the headquarters, on relief, on thoughts of home perhaps, setting his
face towards the depths of the wilderness, towards his empty and desolate
station. I did not know the motive. Perhaps he was just simply a fine
fellow who stuck to his work for its own sake. His name, you understand,
had not been pronounced once. He was: 'that man.' The half-caste who
as far as I could see had conducted a difficult trip with great prudence
and pluck was invariably alluded to as: 'that scoundrel.' The 'scoundrel'
had reported that the 'man' had been very ill—had recovered imperfectly. . . . The two below me moved away then, a few paces, and strolled
back and forth at some little distance. I heard: 'Military post—doctor—
two hundred miles—quite alone now—unavoidable delays—nine
months—no news—strange rumours.' They approached again just as the
Manager was saying, 'No one, as far as I know, unless a species of wandering trader—a pestilential fellow snapping ivory from the natives.' Who
was it they were talking about now? I gathered in snatches that this was
some man supposed to be in Kurtz's district, and of whom the Manager
did not approve. 'We will not be free from unfair competition till one of
these fellows is hanged for an example,' he said. 'Certainly,' grunted the
other; 'get him hanged! Why not? Anything—anything can be done in
this country. That's what I say; nobody, here, you understand *here*, can
endanger your position. And why? You stand the climate—you outlast
them all. The danger is in Europe, but there before I left I took care to.
. . .' They moved off and whispered, then their voices rose again. 'The
extraordinary series of delays is not my fault. I did my possible.'† The
fat man sighed, 'Very sad.' 'And the pestiferous absurdity of his talk,'
continued the other; 'he bothered me enough when he was here. "Each
station should be like a beacon on the road towards better things, a
centre for trade of course but also for humanising, improving, instructing." Conceive you—that ass! And he wants to be Manager! No, it's.
. . .' Here he got choked by excessive indignation, and I lifted my head
the least bit. I was surprised to see how near they were—right under me.
I could have spat upon their hats. They were looking on the ground

† Ms *canceled after* possible: Can I help him being alone?

absorbed in thought. † The Manager was switching his leg with a slender twig; his sagacious relative lifted his head. 'You have been well since you came out this time?' he asked. The other gave a start. 'Who? I? Oh! Like a charm—like a charm. But the rest—oh, my goodness! All sick. They die so quick, too, that I haven't the time to send them out of the country—it's incredible!' 'H'm. Just so,' grunted the uncle. 'Ah! my boy, trust to this—I say trust to this.' I saw him extend his short flipper of an arm for a gesture that took in the forest, the creek, the mud, the river— seemed to beckon with a dishonouring flourish before the sunlit face of the land a treacherous appeal to the lurking death, to the hidden evil, to the profound darkness of its heart. It was so startling that I leaped to my feet and looked back at the edge of the forest, as though I had expected an answer of some sort to that black display of confidence.* You know the foolish notions that come to one sometimes. The high stillness confronted these two figures with its ominous patience, waiting for the passing away of a fantastic invasion.

"They swore aloud together—out of sheer fright, I believe—then, pretending not to know anything of my existence, turned back to the station. The sun was low; and leaning forward side by side, they seemed to be tugging painfully uphill their two ridiculous shadows of unequal length, that trailed behind them slowly over the tall grass without bending a single blade.

"In a few days the Eldorado Expedition went into the patient wilderness, that closed upon it as the sea closes over a diver. Long afterwards the news came that all the donkeys were dead. I know nothing as to the fate of the less valuable animals. They no doubt, like the rest of us, found what they deserved. I did not inquire. I was then rather excited at the prospect of meeting Kurtz very soon. When I say very soon I mean it comparatively. It was just two months from the day we left the creek when we came to the bank below Kurtz's station.

"Going up that river was like travelling back to the earliest beginnings of the world, when vegetation rioted on the earth and the big trees were kings. An empty stream, a great silence, an impenetrable forest. The air was warm, thick, heavy, sluggish. There was no joy in the brilliance of sunshine. The long stretches of the waterway ran on, deserted, into the gloom of overshadowed distances. On silvery sandbanks hippos and alligators sunned themselves side by side. The broadening waters flowed through a mob of wooded islands. You lost your way on that river as you would in a desert and butted all day long against shoals trying to find the channel till you thought yourself bewitched and cut off for ever from everything you had known once—somewhere—far away—in another existence perhaps. There were moments when one's past came back to one, as it will sometimes when you have not a moment to spare to

† Ms canceled twice: in their atrocious thoughts.
* Ms: confidence. But there was nothing, there could be nothing. The thick voice was swallowed up, the confident gesture was lost in the high stillness that fronted these two mean and atrocious figures with its ominous air [of] patient waiting, etc. [Canceled: a comparison of the voice and gesture to bursting shells and blasted rocks.]

yourself; but it came in the shape of an unrestful and noisy dream remembered with wonder amongst the overwhelming realities of this strange world of plants and water and silence. And this stillness of life did not in the least resemble a peace. It was the stillness of an implacable force brooding over an inscrutable intention. It looked at you with a vengeful aspect. I got used to it afterwards. I did not see it any more. I had no time. I had to keep guessing at the channel; I had to discern, mostly by inspiration, the signs of hidden banks; I watched for sunken stones; I was learning to clap my teeth smartly before my heart flew out when I shaved by a fluke some infernal sly old snag that would have ripped the life † out of the tin-pot steamboat and drowned all the pilgrims; I had to keep a look-out for the signs of dead wood we could cut up in the night for next day's steaming. When you have to attend to things of that sort, to the mere incidents of the surface, the reality—the reality I tell you—fades. The inner truth is hidden—luckily, luckily. But I felt it all the same; I felt often its mysterious stillness watching me at my monkey tricks, just as it watches you fellows performing on your respective tight-ropes for—what is it? half a crown a tumble. . . ."

"Try to be civil, Marlow," growled a voice, and I knew there was at least one listener awake besides myself.

"I beg your pardon. I forgot the heartache which makes up the rest of the price. And indeed what does the price matter if the trick be well done? You do your tricks very well. And I didn't do badly either since I managed not to sink that steamboat on my first trip. It's a wonder to me yet. Imagine a blindfolded man set to drive a van over a bad road. I sweated and shivered over that business considerably, I can tell you. After all, for a seaman, to scrape the bottom of the thing that's supposed to float all the time under his care is the unpardonable sin. No one may know of it, but you never forget the thump—eh? A blow on the very heart. You remember it, you dream of it, you wake up at night and think of it—years after—and go hot and cold all over. I don't pretend to say that steamboat floated all the time. More than once she had to wade for a bit, with twenty cannibals splashing around and pushing. We had enlisted some of these chaps on the way for a crew. Fine fellows—cannibals—in their place. They were men one could work with, and I am grateful to them. And, after all, they did not eat each other before my face: they had brought along a provision of hippo-meat which went rotten and made the mystery of the wilderness stink in my nostrils. Phoo! I can sniff it now. I had the Manager on board and three or four pilgrims with their staves—all complete. Sometimes we came upon a station close by the bank clinging to the skirts of the unknown, and the white men rushing out of a tumble-down hovel with great gestures of joy and surprise and welcome seemed very strange, had the appearance of being held there captive by a spell. The word 'ivory' would ring in the air for a while—and on we went again into the silence, along empty reaches,

† Ms: bowels

round the still bends, between the high walls of our winding way,†
reverberating in hollow claps the ponderous beat of the stern-wheel.
Trees, trees, millions of trees, massive, immense, running up high, and
at their foot, hugging the bank against the stream, crept the little begrimed
steamboat like a sluggish beetle crawling on the floor of a lofty portico.
It made you feel very small, very lost, and yet it was not altogether
depressing, that feeling. After all, if you were small, the grimy beetle
crawled on—which was just what you wanted it to do. Where the pilgrims imagined it crawled to I don't know. To some place where they
expected to get something, I bet! For me it crawled towards Kurtz—
exclusively; but when the steam-pipes started leaking we crawled very
slow. The reaches opened before us and closed behind, as if the forest
had stepped leisurely across the water to bar the way for our return. We
penetrated deeper and deeper into the heart of darkness. It was very quiet
there. At night sometimes the roll of drums behind the curtain of trees
would run up the river and remain sustained faintly, as if hovering in
the air high over our heads till the first break of day. Whether it meant
war, peace, or prayer we could not tell. The dawns were heralded by the
descent of a chill stillness. The woodcutters slept, their fires burned low,
the snapping of a twig would make you start. We were wanderers on a
prehistoric earth, on an earth that wore the aspect of an unknown planet.
We could have fancied ourselves the first of men taking possession of an
accursed inheritance, to be subdued at the cost of profound anguish and
of excessive toil. But suddenly as we struggled round a bend there would
be a glimpse of rush walls, of peaked grass-roofs, a burst of yells, a whirl
of black limbs, a mass of hands clapping, of feet stamping, of bodies
swaying, of eyes rolling under the droop of heavy and motionless foliage.
The steamer toiled along slowly on the edge of a black and incomprehensible frenzy. The prehistoric man was cursing us, praying to us, welcoming us—who could tell? We were cut off from the comprehension
of our surroundings; * we glided past like phantoms, wondering and secretly
appalled, as sane men would be before an enthusiastic outbreak in a
madhouse. We could not understand because we were too far and could
not remember because we were travelling in the night of first ages, of
those ages that are gone, leaving hardly a sign—and no memories.
    "The earth seemed unearthly. We are accustomed to look upon the
shackled form of a conquered monster, but there—there you could look
at a thing monstrous and free. It was unearthly and the men were. . . .
No they were not inhuman. Well, you know that was the worst of it—
this suspicion of their not being inhuman. It would come slowly to one.
They howled and leaped and spun and made horrid faces,‡ but what

† Ms: way higher than the corridor of a temple, as
still, as sonorous, reverberating, etc.
* Ms: surroundings. It could only be obtained by
conquest—or by surrender, but we passed on
indifferent, surprising, less than phantoms, wondering and secretly etc.
‡ Ms: faces. You know how it is when we hear the

band of a regiment. A martial noise—and you
pacific father, mild guardian of a domestic heart-
stone [sic] suddenly find yourself thinking of carnage. The joy of killing—hey? Or did you never,
when listening to another kind of music, did you
never dream yourself capable of becoming a saint—
if—if. Aha! Another noise, another appeal, another

thrilled you was just the thought of their humanity—like yours—the thought of your remote kinship with this wild and passionate uproar. Ugly. Yes, it was ugly enough, but if you were man enough you would admit to yourself that there was in you just the faintest trace of a response to the terrible frankness of that noise, a dim suspicion of there being a meaning in it which you—you so remote from the night of first ages—could comprehend. And why not? The mind of man is capable of any-thing—because everything is in it, all the past as well as all the future. What was there after all? Joy, fear, sorrow, devotion, valour, rage—who can tell?—but truth—truth stripped of its cloak of time. Let the fool gape and shudder—the man knows and can look on without a wink. But he must at least be as much of a man as these on the shore. He must meet that truth with his own true stuff—with his own inborn strength. Prin-ciples? Principles won't do. Acquisitions, clothes, pretty rags—rags that would fly off at the first good shake. No. You want a deliberate belief. An appeal to me in this fiendish row—is there? Very well. I hear, I admit, but I have a voice too, and for good or evil mine is the speech that cannot be silenced. Of course, a fool, what with sheer fright and fine sentiments, is always safe. Who's that grunting? You wonder I didn't go ashore for a howl and a dance? Well, no—I didn't. Fine sentiments, you say? Fine sentiments be hanged! I had no time. I had to mess about with white-lead and strips of woollen blanket helping to put bandages on those leaky steam-pipes—I tell you. I had to watch the steering and circumvent those snags and get the tin-pot along by hook or by crook. There was surface-truth enough in these things to save a wiser man. And between whiles I had to look after the savage who was fireman. He was an improved specimen; he could fire up a vertical boiler.[5] He was there below me and, upon my word, to look at him was as edifying as seeing a dog in a parody of breeches and a feather hat walking on his hind legs. A few months of training had done for that really fine chap. He squinted at the steam-gauge and at the water-gauge with an evident effort of intrepidity—and he had filed teeth too, the poor devil, and the wool of his pate shaved into queer patterns, and three ornamental scars on each of his cheeks. He ought to have been clapping his hands and

---

response. All true. All there—in you. Not for you tho' the joy of killing—or the felicity of being a saint. Too many things in the way, business, houses, omnibuses, police[,] the man next door. You don't know my respectable friends how much you owe to the man next door. He is a great fact. There[']s very few places on earth where you haven't a man next door to you or something of him, the merest trace, his footprint—that's enough. You heard the yells and saw the dance and there was the man next door to call you names if you felt an impulse to yell and dance yourself. Another kindly appeal too, and, by Jove, if you did not watch yourself, if you had no weak spot in you where you could take refuge, you would perceive a responsive stir. Why not! Especially if you had a brain. There's all the past as well as all the future in a man's mind. And no kind neighbor to hang you promptly. The discretion of the wilderness, the night, the darkness of the land that would hide everything. Principles? Principles—acquisitions, clothes, rags, rags that fall off if you gave yourself a good shake. There was the naked truth—dancing, howling, praying, cursing. Rage. Fear. Joy. Who can tell. It was an appeal. Who's that grunting? You don't think I went ashore to dance too. Not I. I had to mess about with white lead and strips of blanket bandaging those leaky steam pipes—I tell you. And I had to watch the steering, and I had to look after the savage who was fireman. He was being improved—he was improved. He could fire up a vertical boiler, etc.

5. Boiler of relatively simple construction, easily fired, and requiring little space.

stamping his feet on the bank, instead of which he was hard at work, a thrall to strange witchcraft, full of improving knowledge. He was useful because he had been instructed; and what he knew was this—that should the water in that transparent thing disappear the evil spirit inside the boiler would get angry through the greatness of his thirst and take a terrible vengeance. So he sweated and fired up and watched the glass fearfully (with an impromptu charm, made of rags, tied to his arm and a piece of polished bone as big as a watch stuck flatways through his lower lip) while the wooded banks slipped past us slowly, the shore noise was left behind, the interminable miles of silence—and we crept on, towards Kurtz. But the snags were thick, the water was treacherous and shallow, the boiler seemed indeed to have a sulky devil in it, and thus neither that fireman nor I had any time to peer into our creepy thoughts.

"Some fifty miles below the Inner Station we came upon a hut of reeds, an inclined and melancholy pole with the unrecognisable tatters of what had been a flag of some sort flying from it and a neatly stacked wood-pile. This was unexpected. We came to the bank and on the stack of firewood found a flat piece of board with some faded pencil-writing on it. When deciphered it said: 'Wood for you. Hurry up. Approach cautiously.' There was a signature, but it was illegible—not Kurtz—a much longer word. 'Hurry up!' Where? Up the river? 'Approach cautiously.' We had not done so. But the warning could not have been meant for the place where it could be only found after approach. Something was wrong above. But what—and how much? That was the question. We commented adversely upon the imbecility of that telegraphic style. The bush around said nothing and would not let us look very far, either. A torn curtain of red twill hung in the doorway of the hut and flapped sadly in our faces. The dwelling was dismantled, but we could see a white man had lived there not very long ago. There remained a rude table—a plank on two posts; a heap of rubbish reposed in a dark corner, and by the door I picked up a book. It had lost its covers, and the pages had been thumbed into a state of extremely dirty softness, but the back had been lovingly stitched afresh with white cotton thread, which looked clean yet. It was an extraordinary find. Its title was *An Inquiry into some Points of Seamanship* by a man Towser, Towson— some such name—Master in His Majesty's Navy. The matter looked dreary reading enough with illustrative diagrams and repulsive tables of figures and the copy was sixty years old. I handled this amazing antiquity with the greatest possible tenderness lest it should dissolve in my hands. Within, Towson or Towser was inquiring earnestly into the breaking strain of ships' chains and tackle, and other such matters. Not a very enthralling book, but at the first glance you could see there a singleness of intention, an honest concern for the right way of going to work which made these humble pages thought out so many years ago luminous with another than a professional light. The simple old sailor with his talk of chains and purchases made me forget the jungle and the pilgrims in a delicious sensation of having come upon something unmistakably real.

Such a book being there was wonderful enough, but still more astounding were the notes penciled in the margin, and plainly referring to the text. I couldn't believe my eyes! They were in cipher! Yes, it looked like cipher. Fancy a man lugging with him a book of that description into this nowhere and studying it—and making notes—in cipher at that! It was an extravagant mystery.

"I had been dimly aware for some time of a worrying noise and when I lifted my eyes I saw the wood-pile was gone and the Manager aided by all the pilgrims was shouting at me from the river-side. I slipped the book into my pocket. I assure you to leave off reading was like tearing myself away from the shelter of an old and solid friendship.

"I started the lame engine ahead. 'It must be this miserable trader— this intruder,' exclaimed the Manager looking back malevolently at the place we had left. 'He must be English,' I said. 'It will not save him from getting into trouble if he is not careful,' muttered the Manager darkly. I observed with assumed innocence that no man was safe from trouble in this world.

"The current was more rapid now, the steamer seemed at her last gasp, the stern-wheel flopped languidly, and I caught myself listening on tiptoe for the next beat of the float,[6] for in sober truth I expected the wretched thing to give up every moment. It was like watching the last flickers of a life. But still we crawled. Sometimes I would pick out a tree a little way ahead to measure our progress towards Kurtz by, but I lost it invariably before we got abreast. To keep the eyes so long on one thing was too much for human patience. The Manager displayed a beautiful resignation. I fretted and fumed and took to arguing with myself whether or no I would talk openly with Kurtz, but before I could come to any conclusion it occurred to me that my speech or my silence, indeed any action of mine, would be a mere futility. What did it matter what any one knew or ignored? What did it matter who was Manager? One gets sometimes such a flash of insight. The essentials of this affair † lay deep under the surface, beyond my reach and beyond my power of meddling.

"Towards the evening of the second day we judged ourselves about eight miles from Kurtz's station. I wanted to push on, but the Manager looked grave and told me the navigation up there was so dangerous that it would be advisable, the sun being very low already, to wait where we were till next morning. Moreover, he pointed out that if the warning to approach cautiously were to be followed we must approach in daylight— not at dusk or in the dark. This was sensible enough. Eight miles meant nearly three hours' steaming for us and I could also see suspicious ripples at the upper end of the reach. Nevertheless, I was annoyed beyond expression at the delay, and most unreasonably too, since one night more could not matter much after so many months. As we had plenty of wood and caution was the word, I brought up in the middle of the stream. The reach was narrow, straight, with high sides like a railway

6. Each blade on the paddle-wheel.
† Ms: affair, its meaning and its lesson, lay deep, *etc.*

cutting. The dusk came gliding into it long before the sun had set. The current ran smooth and swift, but a dumb immobility sat on the banks. The living trees, lashed together by the creepers and every living bush of the undergrowth, might have been changed into stone, even to the slenderest twig, to the lightest leaf. It was not sleep—it seemed unnatural, like a state of trance. Not the faintest sound of any kind could be heard. You looked on amazed and began to suspect yourself of being deaf—then the night came suddenly and struck you blind as well. About three in the morning some large fish leaped and the loud splash made me jump as though a gun had been fired. When the sun rose there was a white fog, very warm and clammy, and more blinding than the night. It did not shift or drive, it was just there standing all round you like something solid. At eight or nine perhaps, it lifted, as a shutter lifts. We had a glimpse of the towering multitude of trees, of the immense matted jungle, with the blazing little ball of the sun hanging over it—all perfectly still—and then the white shutter came down again smoothly as if sliding in greased grooves. I ordered the chain which we had begun to heave in to be paid out again. Before it stopped running with a muffled rattle, a cry, a very loud cry as of infinite desolation, soared slowly in the opaque air. It ceased. A complaining clamour, modulated in savage discords, filled our ears. The sheer unexpectedness of it made my hair stir under my cap. I don't know how it struck the others; to me it seemed as though the mist itself had screamed, so suddenly and apparently from all sides at once did this tumultuous and mournful uproar arise. It culminated in a hurried outbreak of almost intolerably excessive shrieking which stopped short, leaving us stiffened in a variety of silly attitudes and obstinately listening to the nearly as appalling and excessive silence. 'Good God! What is the meaning. . . .' stammered at my elbow one of the pilgrims, a little fat man with sandy hair and red whiskers, who wore side-spring boots, and pink pyjamas tucked into his socks. Two others remained open-mouthed a whole minute, then dashed into the little cabin, to rush out incontinently and stand darting scared glances, with Winchesters at 'ready' in their hands. What we could see was just the steamer we were on, her outlines blurred as though she had been on the point of dissolving and a misty strip of water perhaps two feet broad around her—and that was all. The rest of the world was nowhere as far as our eyes and ears were concerned. Just nowhere. Gone, disappeared, swept off without leaving a whisper or a shadow behind.

"I went forward and ordered the chain to be hauled in short, so as to be ready to trip the anchor and move the steamboat at once if necessary. 'Will they attack?' whispered an awed voice. 'We will all be butchered in this fog,' murmured † another. The faces twitched with the strain, the hands trembled, slightly, the eyes forgot to wink. It was very curious to see the contrast of expressions of the white men and of the black fellows of our crew, who were as much strangers to that part of the river as we,

† Ms: mumbled

though their homes were only eight hundred miles away. The whites, of course greatly discomposed, had besides a curious look of being painfully shocked by such an outrageous row. The others had an alert, naturally interested expression, but their faces were essentially quiet, even those of the one or two who grinned as they hauled at the chain. Several exchanged short grunting phrases which seemed to settle the matter to their satisfaction. Their head-man, a young broad-chested black, severely draped in dark-blue fringed cloths, with fierce nostrils and his hair all done up artfully in oily ringlets, stood near me. 'Aha!' I said, just for good fellowship's sake. 'Catch 'im,' he snapped with a bloodshot widening of his eyes and a flash of sharp teeth—'catch 'im. Give 'im to us.' 'To you, eh?' I asked; 'what would you do with them?' 'Eat 'im!' he said curtly, and leaning his elbow on the rail looked out into the fog in a dignified and profoundly pensive attitude. I would no doubt have been properly horrified had it not occurred to me that he and his chaps must be very hungry, that they must have been growing increasingly hungry for at least this month past. They had been engaged for six months (I don't think a single one of them had any clear idea of time as we at the end of countless ages have. They still belonged to the beginnings of time—had no inherited experience to teach them, as it were) and of course, as long as there was a piece of paper written over in accordance with some farcical law or other made down the river, it didn't enter anybody's head to trouble how they would live. Certainly they had brought with them some rotten hippo-meat which couldn't have lasted very long anyway, even if the pilgrims hadn't, in the midst of a shocking hullabaloo, thrown a considerable quantity of it overboard. It looked like a high-handed proceeding, but it was really a case of legitimate self-defence. You can't breathe dead hippo waking, sleeping, and eating and at the same time keep your precarious grip on existence. Besides that, they had given them every week three pieces of brass wire each about nine inches long, and the theory was they were to buy their provisions with that currency in river-side villages. You can see how *that* worked. There were either no villages, or the people were hostile, or the director, who like the rest of us fed out of tins with an occasional old he-goat thrown in, didn't want to stop the steamer for some more or less recondite reason. So, unless they swallowed the wire itself or made loops of it to snare the fishes with, I don't see what good their extravagant salary could be to them. I must say it was paid with a regularity worthy of a large and honourable trading company. For the rest, the only thing to eat—though it didn't look eatable in the least—I saw in their possession was a few lumps of some stuff like half-cooked dough of a dirty lavender colour, they kept wrapped in leaves and now and then swallowed a piece of, but so small that it seemed done more for the look of the thing than for any serious purpose of sustenance. Why in the name of all the gnawing devils of hunger they didn't go for us—they were thirty to five—and have a good tuck-in for once amazes me now when I think of it. They were big powerful men with not much capacity to weigh the consequences, with courage, with strength, even yet, though their skins were no longer glossy and their muscles no longer hard. And I saw that something restraining, one of those human secrets that baffle probability, had come into play there. I looked at them with a swift quickening of interest—not because it occurred to me I might be eaten by them before very long, though I own to you that just then I perceived—in a new light, as it were—how unwholesome the pilgrims looked, and I hoped, yes I positively hoped, that my aspect was not so—what shall I say?—so—unappetising: a touch of fantastic vanity which fitted well with the dream-sensation that pervaded all my days at that time. Perhaps I had a little fever too. One can't live with one's finger everlastingly on one's pulse. I had often 'a little fever,' or a little touch of other things—the playful paw-strokes of the wilderness, the preliminary trifling before the more serious onslaught which came in due course. Yes—I looked at them as you would on any human being with a curiosity of their impulses, motives, capacities, weaknesses, when brought to the test of an inexorable physical necessity. Restraint! What possible restraint? Was it superstition, disgust, patience, fear—or some kind of primitive honour? No fear can stand up to hunger, no patience can wear it out, disgust simply does not exist where hunger is, and as to superstition, beliefs, and what you may call principles, they are less than chaff in a breeze. Don't you know the devilry of lingering starvation, its exasperating torment, its black thoughts, its sombre and brooding ferocity? Well, I do. It takes a man all his inborn strength to fight hunger properly. It's really easier to face bereavement, dishonour, and the perdition of one's soul—than this kind of prolonged hunger. Sad, but true. And these chaps too had no earthly reason for any kind of scruple. Restraint! I would just as soon have expected restraint from a hyena prowling amongst the corpses of a battlefield. But there was the fact facing me—the fact, dazzling, to be seen, like the foam on the depths of the sea, like a ripple on an unfathomable enigma, a mystery greater—when I thought of it—than the curious, inexplicable note of desperate grief in this savage clamour that had swept by us on the river-bank behind the blind whiteness of the fog.

"Two pilgrims were quarrelling in hurried whispers as to which bank. 'Left.' 'No, no, how can you? Right, right, of course.' 'It is very serious,' said the Manager's voice behind me; 'I would be desolated if anything should happen to Mr. Kurtz before we came up.' I looked at him and had not the slightest doubt he was sincere. He was just the kind of man who would wish to preserve appearances. That was his restraint. But when he muttered something about going on at once I did not even take the trouble to answer him. I knew, and he knew, that it was impossible. Were we to let go our hold of the bottom, we would be absolutely in the air—in space. We wouldn't be able to tell where we were going to—whether up or down stream or across—till we fetched against one bank or the other—and then we wouldn't know at first which it was. Of course I made no move. I had no mind for a smash-up. You couldn't imagine a more deadly place for a shipwreck. Whether drowned at once or not, we were sure to perish speedily in one way or another. 'I authorise you to take all the risks,' he said after a short silence. 'I refuse to take any,' I said shortly, which was just the answer he expected, though its tone might have surprised him. 'Well, I must defer to your judgment. You are Captain,' he said with marked civility. I turned my shoulder to him in sign of my appreciation and looked into the fog. How long would it last? It was the most hopeless look-out. The approach to this Kurtz grubbing for ivory in the wretched bush was beset by as many dangers as though he had been an enchanted princess sleeping in a fabulous castle. 'Will they attack, do you think?' asked the Manager in a confidential tone.

"I did not think they would attack, for several obvious reasons. The thick fog was one. If they left the bank in their canoes they would get lost in it as we would be if we attempted to move. Still I had also judged the jungle of both banks quite impenetrable—and yet eyes were in it, eyes that had seen us. The river-side bushes were certainly very thick, but the undergrowth behind was evidently penetrable. However, during the short lift I had seen no canoes anywhere in the reach—certainly not abreast of the steamer. But what made the idea of attack inconceivable to me was the nature of the noise—of the cries we had heard. They had not the fierce character boding of immediate hostile intention. Unexpected, wild, and violent as they had been they had given me an irresistible impression of sorrow. The glimpse of the steamboat had for some reason filled those savages with unrestrained grief. The danger if any, I expounded, was from our proximity to a great human passion let loose. Even extreme grief may ultimately vent itself in violence—but more generally takes the form of apathy. . . .

"You should have seen the pilgrims stare! They had no heart to grin or even to revile me, but I believe they thought me gone mad—with fright maybe. I delivered a regular lecture. My dear boys, it was no good bothering. Keep a look-out? Well, you may guess I watched the fog for the signs of lifting as a cat watches a mouse, but for anything else our eyes were of no more use to us than if we had been buried miles deep in a heap of cotton-wool. It felt like it too—choking, warm, stifling. Besides, all I said, though it sounded extravagant, was absolutely true to fact. What we afterwards alluded to as an attack was really an attempt at repulse. The action was very far from being aggressive; it was not even defensive in the usual sense; it was undertaken under the stress of desperation and in its essence was purely protective.

"It developed itself, I should say, two hours after the fog lifted, and its commencement was at a spot, roughly speaking, about a mile and a half below Kurtz's station. We had just floundered and flopped round a bend when I saw an islet, a mere grassy hummock of bright green in the middle of the stream. It was the only thing of the kind, but as we opened the reach more I perceived it was the head of a long sandbank or rather of a chain of shallow patches stretching down the middle of the river. They were discoloured, just awash, and the whole lot was seen just under

the water exactly as a man's backbone is seen running down the middle
of his back under the skin. Now, as far as I did see, I could go to the
right or to the left of this. I didn't know either channel, of course. The
banks looked pretty well alike, the depth appeared the same, but as I had
been informed the station was on the west side I naturally headed for
the western passage. †

"No sooner had we fairly entered it than I became aware it was much
narrower than I had supposed. To the left of us there was the long uninterrupted shoal and to the right a high steep bank heavily overgrown
with bushes. Above the bush the trees stood in serried ranks. The twigs
overhung the current thickly, and from distance to distance a large limb
of some tree projected rigidly over the stream. It was then well on in the
afternoon, the face of the forest was gloomy, and a broad strip of shadow
had already fallen on the water. In this shadow we steamed up, very
slowly as you may imagine. I sheered her well inshore, the water being
deepest near the bank as the sounding-pole informed me.

"One of my hungry and forbearing friends was sounding in the bows
just below me. This steamboat was exactly like a decked scow. On the
deck there were two little teak-wood houses with doors and windows.
The boiler was in the fore-end and the machinery right astern. Over the
whole there was a light roof supported on stanchions. The funnel projected through that roof and in front of the funnel a small cabin built of
light planks served for a pilot-house. It contained a couch, two camp-
stools, a loaded Martini-Henry[7] leaning in one corner, a tiny table, and
the steering-wheel. It had a wide door in front and a broad shutter at
each side. All these were always thrown open, of course. I spent my days
perched up there on the extreme fore-end of that roof, before the door.
At night I slept, or tried to, on the couch. An athletic black belonging
to some coast tribe and educated by my poor predecessor was the helmsman. He sported a pair of brass earrings, wore a blue cloth wrapper
from the waist to the ankles, and thought all the world of himself. He
was the most unstable kind of fool I had ever seen. He steered with no
end of a swagger while you were by, but if he lost sight of you he became
instantly the prey of an abject funk and would let that cripple of a steamboat get the upper hand of him in a minute.

"I was looking down at the sounding-pole and feeling much annoyed
to see at each try a little more of it stick out of that river when I saw my
poleman give up the business suddenly and stretch himself flat on the
deck without even taking the trouble to haul his pole in. He kept hold
on it though, and it trailed in the water. At the same time the fireman,
whom I could also see below me, sat down abruptly before his furnace
and ducked his head. I was amazed. Then I had to look at the river
mighty quick because there was a snag in the fairway. Sticks, little sticks,
were flying about, thick; they were whizzing before my nose, dropping
below me, striking behind me against my pilot-house. All this time the

---

† Ms canceled: east and eastern
7. A breech-action military rifle that takes a cartridge with an especially large power charge.

river, the shore, the woods were very quiet—perfectly quiet. I could only hear the heavy splashing thump of the stern-wheel and the patter of these things. We cleared the snag clumsily. Arrows, by Jove! We were being shot at! I stepped in quickly to close the shutter on the land-side. That fool-helmsman his hands on the spokes was lifting his knees high, stamping his feet, champing his mouth, like a reined-in horse. Confound him! And we were staggering within ten feet of the bank. I had to lean right out to swing the heavy † shutter and I saw a face amongst the leaves on the level with my own looking at me very fierce and steady, and then suddenly, as though a veil had been removed from my eyes, I made out deep in the tangled gloom, naked breasts, arms, legs, glaring eyes—the bush was swarming with human limbs in movement, glistening, of bronze colour. The twigs shook, swayed, and rustled, the arrows flew out of them, and then the shutter came to. 'Steer her straight,' I said to the helmsman. He held his head rigid, face forward, but his eyes rolled, he kept on lifting and setting down his feet gently, his mouth foamed a little. 'Keep quiet!' I said in a fury. I might just as well have ordered a tree not to sway in the wind. I darted out. Below me there was a great scuffle of feet on the iron deck; confused exclamations; a voice screamed, 'Can you turn back?' I caught sight of a V-shaped ripple on the water ahead. What? Another snag! A fusillade burst out under my feet. The pilgrims had opened with their Winchesters and were simply squirting lead into that bush. A deuce of a lot of smoke came up and drove slowly forward. I swore at it. Now I couldn't see the ripple or the snag either. I stood in the doorway, peering, and the arrows came in swarms. They might have been poisoned, but they looked as though they wouldn't kill a cat. The bush began to howl. Our wood-cutters raised a warlike whoop; the report of a rifle just at my back deafened me. I glanced over my shoulder and the pilot-house was yet full of noise and smoke when I made a dash at the wheel. The fool-nigger had dropped everything to throw the shutter open and let off that Martini-Henry. He stood before the wide opening, glaring, and I yelled at him to come back, while I straightened the sudden twist out of that steamboat. There was no room to turn even if I had wanted to, the snag was somewhere very near ahead in that confounded smoke, there was no time to lose, so I just crowded her into the bank, right into the bank where I knew the water was deep.

"We tore slowly along the overhanging bushes in a whirl of broken twigs and flying leaves. The fusillade below stopped short as I had foreseen it would when the squirts got empty. I threw my head back to a glinting whiz that traversed the pilot-house in at one shutter-hole and out at the other. Looking past that mad helmsman who was shaking the empty rifle and yelling at the shore, I saw vague forms of men running bent double, leaping, gliding, distinct, incomplete, evanescent. Something big appeared in the air before the shutter, the rifle went overboard,

† Ms: beastly heavy

and the man stepped back swiftly, looked at me over his shoulder in an extraordinary, profound, familiar manner, and fell upon my feet. The side of his head hit the wheel twice and the end of what appeared a long cane clattered round and knocked over a little camp-stool. It looked as though after wrenching that thing from somebody ashore he had lost his balance in the effort. The thin smoke had blown away, we were clear of the snag, and looking ahead I could see that in another hundred yards or so I would be free to sheer off away from the bank, but my feet felt so very warm and wet that I had to look down. The man had rolled on his back and stared straight up at me; both his hands clutched that cane. It was the shaft of a spear that, either thrown or lunged through the opening, had caught him in the side just below the ribs; the blade has gone in out of sight after making a frightful gash; my shoes were full; a pool of blood lay very still gleaming dark-red under the wheel; his eyes shone with an amazing lustre. The fusillade burst out again. He looked at me anxiously, gripping the spear like something precious, with an air of being afraid I would try to take it away from him. I had to make an effort to free my eyes from his gaze and attend to the steering. With one hand I felt above my head for the line of the steam whistle and jerked out screech after screech hurriedly. The tumult of angry and warlike yells was checked instantly and then from the depths of the woods went out such a tremulous and prolonged wail of mournful fear and utter despair as may be imagined to follow the flight of the last hope from the earth. There was a great commotion in the bush; the shower of arrows stopped; a few dropping shots rang out sharply—then silence, in which the languid beat of the stern-wheel came plainly to my ears. I put the helm hard a-starboard at the moment when the pilgrim in pink pyjamas, very hot and agitated, appeared in the doorway. 'The Manager sends me. . . . 'e began in an official tone and stopped short. 'Good God!' he said glaring at the wounded man.

"We two whites stood over him and his lustrous and inquiring glance enveloped us both. I declare it looked as though he would presently put to us some question in an understandable language, but he died without uttering a sound, without moving a limb, without twitching a muscle. Only in the very last moment as though in response to some sign we could not see, to some whisper we could not hear, he frowned heavily, and that frown gave to his black death-mask an inconceivably sombre, brooding, and menacing expression. The lustre of inquiring glance faded swiftly into vacant glassiness. 'Can you steer?' I asked the agent eagerly. He looked very dubious, but I made a grab at his arm and he understood at once I meant him to steer whether or no. To tell you the truth, I was morbidly anxious to change my shoes and socks. 'He is dead,' murmured the fellow immensely impressed. 'No doubt about it,' said I tugging like mad at the shoe-laces. 'And by the way, I suppose Mr. Kurtz is dead as well by this time.'

"For the moment that was the dominant thought. There was a sense of extreme disappointment as though I had found out I had been striving after something altogether without a substance. I couldn't have been more disgusted if I had travelled all this way for the sole purpose of talking with Mr. Kurtz. Talking with . . . I flung one shoe overboard and became aware that that was exactly what I had been looking forward to—a talk with Kurtz. I made the strange discovery that I had never imagined him as doing, you know, but as discoursing. I didn't say to myself, 'Now I will never see him,' or 'Now I will never shake him by the hand,' but, 'Now I will never hear him.' The man presented himself as a voice. Not of course that I did not connect him with some sort of action. Hadn't I been told in all the tones of jealousy and admiration that he had collected, bartered, swindled, or stolen more ivory than all the other agents together. That was not the point. The point was in his being a gifted creature and that of all his gifts the one that stood out pre-eminently, that carried with it a sense of real presence, was his ability to talk, his words—the gift of expression, the bewildering, the illuminating, the most exalted and the most contemptible, the pulsating stream of light or the deceitful flow from the heart of an impenetrable darkness.

"The other shoe went flying unto the devil-god of that river. I thought, By Jove! it's all over. We are too late; he has vanished—the gift has vanished by means of some spear, arrow, or club. I will never hear that chap speak after all—and my sorrow had a startling extravagance of emotion, even such as I had noticed in the howling sorrow of these savages in the bush. I couldn't have felt more of lonely desolation somehow had I been robbed of a belief or had missed my destiny in life. . . . Why do you sigh in this beastly way, somebody? Absurd? Well, absurd. Good Lord! mustn't a man ever. . . . Here, give me some tobacco." . . .

There was a pause of profound stillness, then a match flared, and Marlow's lean face appeared worn, hollow, with downward folds and dropped eyelids with an aspect of concentrated attention; and as he took vigorous draws at his pipe it seemed to retreat and advance out of the night in the regular flicker of the tiny flame. The match went out.

"Absurd!" he cried. "This is the worst of trying to tell. . . . Here you all are each moored with two good addresses like a hulk with two anchors, a butcher round one corner, a policeman round another, excellent appetites, and temperature normal—hear you—normal from year's end to year's end. And you say, Absurd! Absurd be—exploded! Absurd! My dear boys, what can you expect from a man who out of sheer nervousness had just flung overboard a pair of new shoes? Now I think of it, it is amazing I did not shed tears. I am, upon the whole, proud of my fortitude. I was cut to the quick at the idea of having lost the inestimable privilege of listening to the gifted Kurtz. Of course I was wrong. The privilege was waiting for me. Oh yes, I heard more than enough. And I was right, too. A voice. He was very little more than a voice. And I heard—him—it—this voice—other voices—all of them were so little more than voices—and the memory of that time itself lingers around me, impalpable, like a dying vibration of one immense jabber, silly, atrocious, sordid, savage, or simply mean without any kind of sense. Voices, voices—even the girl herself—now. . . ."

He was silent for a long time.

"I laid the ghost of his gifts at last with a lie," he began suddenly. "Girl! What? Did I mention a girl? Oh, she is out of it—completely. They—the women I mean—are out of it—should be out of it. We must help them to stay in that beautiful world of their own lest ours gets worse.† Oh, she had to be out of it. You should have heard the disinterred body of Mr. Kurtz saying, 'My Intended.' You would have perceived directly then how completely she was out of it. And the lofty frontal bone of Mr. Kurtz! They say the hair goes on growing sometimes, but this—ah—specimen was impressively bald. The wilderness had patted him on the head, and behold, it was like a ball—an ivory ball; it had caressed him and—lo!—he had withered; it had taken him, loved him, embraced him, got into his veins, consumed his flesh, and sealed his soul to its own by the inconceivable ceremonies of some devilish initiation. He was its spoiled and pampered favourite. Ivory! I should think so. Heaps of it, stacks of it. The old mud shanty was bursting with it. You would think there was not a single tusk left either above or below the ground in the whole country. 'Mostly fossil,' the Manager had remarked disparagingly. It was no more fossil than I am, but they call it fossil when it is dug up. It appears these niggers do bury the tusks sometimes—but evidently they couldn't bury this parcel deep enough to save the gifted Mr. Kurtz from his fate. We filled the steamboat with it and had to pile a lot on the deck. Thus he could see and enjoy as long as he could see because the appreciation of this favour had remained with him to the last. You should have heard him say, 'My ivory.' Oh yes, I heard him. 'My Intended, my ivory, my station, my river, my . . .' everything belonged to him. It made me hold my breath in expectation of hearing the wilderness burst into a prodigious peal of laughter that would shake the fixed stars in their places. Everything belonged to him—but that was a trifle. The thing was to know what he belonged to, how many powers of darkness claimed him for their own. That was the reflection that made you creepy all over. It was impossible—it was not good for one either— trying to imagine. He had taken a high seat amongst the devils of the land—I mean literally. You can't understand? How could you—with solid pavement under your feet, surrounded by kind neighbours ready to cheer you or to fall on you, stepping delicately between the butcher and the policeman, in the holy terror of scandal and gallows and lunatic asylums—how can you imagine what particular region of the first ages a man's untrammelled feet may take him into by the way of solitude— utter solitude without a policeman—by the way of silence—utter silence, where no warning voice of a kind neighbour can be heard whispering of

---

† Ms: worse. That's a monster-truth with many maws to whom we've got to throw every year—or every day—no matter—no sacrifice is too great— a ransom of pretty, shining lies—not very new perhaps—but spotless, aureoled, tender. Oh, she, *etc.*

public opinion. These little things make all the great difference. When they are gone you must fall back upon your own innate strength, upon your own capacity for faithfulness. Of course you may be too much of a fool to go wrong—too dull even to know you are being assaulted by the powers of darkness. I take it no fool ever made a bargain for his soul with the devil. The fool is too much of a fool or the devil too much of a devil—I don't know which. Or you may be such a thunderingly exalted creature as to be altogether deaf and blind to anything but heavenly sights and sounds. Then the earth for you is only a standing place—and whether to be like this is your loss or your gain I won't pretend to say. But most of us are neither one nor the other. The earth for us is a place to live in, where we must put up with sights, with sounds, with smells too, by Jove!—breathe dead hippo so to speak and not be contaminated.† And there, don't you see, your strength comes in, the faith in your ability for the digging of unostentatious holes to bury the stuff in— your power of devotion not to yourself but to an obscure, back-breaking business. And that's difficult enough. Mind, I am not trying to excuse or even explain—I am trying to account to myself for—for—Mr. Kurtz— for the shade of Mr. Kurtz. This initiated wraith* from the back of Nowhere honoured me with its amazing confidence before it vanished altogether. This was because it could speak English to me. The original Kurtz had been educated partly in England and—as he was good enough to say himself—his sympathies were in the right place. His mother was half-English, his father was half-French. All Europe contributed to the making of Kurtz, and by and by I learned that most appropriately the International Society for the Suppression of Savage Customs had entrusted him with the making of a report for its future guidance. And he had written it too. I've seen it. I've read it. It was eloquent, vibrating with eloquence, but too high-strung I think. Seventeen pages of close writing. He had found time for it. But this must have been before his—let us say—nerves went wrong and caused him to preside at certain midnight dances ending with unspeakable rites, which—as far as I reluctantly gathered from what I heard at various times—were offered up to him— do you understand—to Mr. Kurtz himself. But it was a beautiful piece of writing. The opening paragraph however, in the light of later information, strikes me now as ominous. He began with the argument that we whites, from the point of development we had arrived at, 'must necessarily appear to them [savages] in the nature of supernatural beings— we approach them with the might as of a deity,' and so on, and so on. 'By the simple exercise of our will we can exert a power for good practically unbounded,' etc. etc. From that point he soared and took me with him. The peroration was magnificent, though difficult to remember, you know. It gave me the notion of an exotic Immensity ruled by an august Benevolence. It made me tingle with enthusiasm. This was the unbounded power of eloquence—of words—of burning noble words.

† Ms canceled after contaminated: To say there's no dead hippo won't do. And there, etc.   * Ms canceled: ghost

There were no practical hints to interrupt the magic current of phrases, unless a kind of note at the foot of the last page, scrawled evidently much later in an unsteady hand, may be regarded as the exposition of a method. It was very simple and at the end of that moving appeal to every altruistic sentiment it blazed at you luminous and terrifying like a flash of light- ning in a serene sky: 'Exterminate all the brutes!' † The curious part was that he had apparently forgotten all about that valuable postscriptum because later on when he in a sense came to himself, he repeatedly entreated me to take good care of 'my pamphlet' (he called it) as it was sure to have in the future a good influence upon his career. * I had full information about all these things, and besides, as it turned out I was to have the care of his memory. I've done enough for it to give me the indisputable right to lay it, if I choose, for an everlasting rest in the dust- bin of progress, amongst all the sweepings and, figuratively speaking, all the dead cats of civilisation. But then, you see, I can't choose. He won't be forgotten. Whatever he was he was not common. He had the power to charm or frighten rudimentary souls into an aggravated witch-dance in his honour, he could also fill the small souls of the pilgrims with bitter misgivings—he had one devoted friend at least, ‡ and he had con- quered one soul in the world that was neither rudimentary nor tainted with self-seeking. No, I can't forget him, though I am not prepared to affirm the fellow was exactly worth the life we lost in getting to him. I missed my late helmsman awfully—I missed him even while his body was still lying in the pilot-house. Perhaps you will think it passing strange this regret for a savage who was no more account than a grain of sand in a black Sahara. Well, don't you see, he had done something, he had steered; for months I had him at my back—a help—an instrument. It was a kind of partnership. He steered for me—I had to look after him, I worried about his deficiencies, and thus a subtle bond had been created of which I only became aware when it was suddenly broken. And the intimate profundity of that look he gave me when he received his hurt remains to this day in my memory—like a claim of distant kinship affirmed in a supreme moment.

"Poor fool! If he had only left that shutter alone. He had no restraint, no restraint—just like Kurtz—a tree swayed by the wind. As soon as I had put on a dry pair of slippers I dragged him out, after first jerking the spear out of his side, which operation I confess I performed with my eyes shut tight. His heels leaped together over the little door-step; his shoul- ders were pressed to my breast; I hugged him from behind desperately. Oh! he was heavy, heavy; heavier than any man on earth, I should imagine. Then without more ado I tipped him overboard. The current snatched him as though he had been a wisp of grass and I saw the body roll over twice before I lost sight of it for ever. All the pilgrims and the Manager were then congregated on the awning-deck about the pilot- house chattering at each other like a flock of excited magpies, and there

---

† *Ms canceled:* Kill every single brute of them.   his future, his career.
* *Ms:* upon 'my career.' His Intended, his ivory,   ‡ one devoted friend at least, *not in Ms*

was a scandalised murmur at my heartless promptitude. What they wanted
to keep that body hanging about for I can't guess. Embalm it, maybe.
But I had also heard another and a very ominous murmur on the deck
below. My friends the wood-cutters were likewise scandalised, and with
a better show of reason—though I admit that the reason itself was quite
inadmissible. Oh, quite! I had made up my mind that if my late helmsman was to be eaten, the fishes alone should have him. He had been a
very second-rate helmsman while alive, but now he was dead he might
have become a first-class temptation and possibly cause some startling
trouble. Besides, I was anxious to take the wheel, the man in pink pyjamas showing himself a hopeless duffer at the business.

"This I did directly the simple funeral was over. We were going half-
speed, keeping right in the middle of the stream, and I listened to the
talk about me. They had given up Kurtz, they had given up the station;
Kurtz was dead and the station had been burnt—and so on, and so on.
The red-haired pilgrim was beside himself with the thought that at least
this poor Kurtz had been properly revenged. 'Say! We must have made
a glorious slaughter of them in the bush. Eh? What do you think? Say?'
He positively danced, the bloodthirsty little gingery beggar.[8] And he had
nearly fainted when he saw the wounded man! I could not help saying,
'You made a glorious lot of smoke, anyhow.' I had seen from the way
the tops of the bushes rustled and flew that almost all the shots had gone
too high. You can't hit anything unless you take aim and fire from the
shoulder, but these chaps fired from the hip with their eyes shut. The
retreat, I maintained—and I was right—was caused by the screeching of
the steam-whistle. Upon this they forgot Kurtz, and began to howl at
me with indignant protests.

"The Manager stood by the wheel murmuring confidentially about
the necessity of getting well away down the river before dark at all events,
when I saw in the distance a clearing on the river-side and the outlines
of some sort of building. 'What's this?' I asked. He clapped his hands in
wonder. 'The station!' he cried. I edged in at once, still going half-speed.

"Through my glasses I saw the slope of a hill interspersed with rare
trees and perfectly free from undergrowth. A long decaying building on
the summit was half buried in the high grass; the large holes in the
peaked roof gaped black from afar; the jungle and the woods made a
background. There was no enclosure or fence of any kind, but there had
been one apparently, for near the house half a dozen slim posts remained
in a row, roughly trimmed, and with their upper ends ornamented with
round carved balls. The rails or whatever there had been between had
disappeared. Of course the forest surrounded all that. The river-bank
was clear and on the water side I saw a white man under a hat like a
cart-wheel beckoning persistently with his whole arm. Examining the
edge of the forest above and below, I was almost certain I could see
movements—human forms gliding here and there. I steamed past pru-

8. British slang for "red-headed rascal."

dently, then stopped the engines and let her drift down. The man
on the shore began to shout, urging us to land. 'We have been attacked,' screamed the Manager. 'I know—I know. It's all right,' yelled back
the other, as cheerful as you please. 'Come along. It's all right. I am
glad.'

"His aspect reminded me of something I had seen—something funny
I had seen somewhere. As I manoeuvred to get alongside I was asking
myself, 'What does this fellow look like?' Suddenly I got it. He looked
like a harlequin. His clothes had been made of some stuff that was brown
holland probably, but it was covered with patches all over, with bright
patches, blue, red, and yellow—patches on the back, patches on the
front, patches on elbows, on knees, coloured binding round his jacket,
scarlet edging at the bottom of his trousers, and the sunshine made him
look extremely gay and wonderfully neat withal because you could see
how beautifully all this patching had been done. A beardless boyish face,
very fair, no features to speak of, nose peeling, little blue eyes, smiles
and frowns chasing each other over that open countenance like sunshine
and shadow on a wind-swept plain. 'Look out, Captain!' he cried; 'there's
a snag lodged in here last night.' What! Another snag? I confess I swore
shamefully. I had nearly holed my cripple, to finish off that charming
trip. The harlequin on the bank turned his little pug-nose up to me.
'You English?' he asked all smiles. 'Are you?' I shouted from the wheel.
The smiles vanished and he shook his head as if sorry for my disappointment. Then he brightened up. 'Never mind!' he cried encouragingly.
'Are we in time?' I asked. 'He is up there,' he replied with a toss of the
head up the hill and becoming gloomy all of a sudden. His face was like
the autumn sky, overcast one moment and bright the next.

"When the Manager, escorted by the pilgrims, all of them armed to
the teeth, had gone to the house, this chap came on board. 'I say, I don't
like this. These natives are in the bush,' I said. He assured me earnestly
it was all right. 'They are simple people,' he added; 'well, I am glad you
came. It took me all my time to keep them off.' 'But you said it was all
right,' I cried. 'Oh, they meant no harm,' he said and as I stared he
corrected himself, 'Not exactly.' Then vivaciously, 'My faith, your pilot-
house wants a clean-up!' In the next breath he advised me to keep enough
steam on the boiler to blow the whistle in case of any trouble. 'One good
screech will do more for you than all your rifles. They are simple people,' he repeated. He rattled away at such a rate he quite overwhelmed
me. He seemed to be trying to make up for lots of silence and actually
hinted, laughing, that such was the case. 'Don't you talk with Mr. Kurtz?'
I said. 'You don't talk with that man—you listen to him,' he exclaimed
with severe exaltation. 'But now. . . .' He waved his arm and in the
twinkling of an eye was in the uttermost depths of despondency. In a
moment he came up again with a jump, possessed himself of both my
hands, shook them continuously while he gabbled: 'Brother sailor . . .
honour . . . pleasure . . . delight . . . introduce myself . . . Russian
. . . son of an Arch-Priest . . . Government of Tambov . . . What!

Tobacco! English tobacco; the excellent English tobacco! Now, that's
brotherly. Smoke! Where's a sailor that does not smoke.'

"The pipe soothed him and gradually I made out he had run away
from school, had gone to sea in a Russian ship; ran away again; served
some time in English ships; was now reconciled with the Arch-Priest.
He made a point of that. 'But when one is young one must see things,
gather experience, ideas, enlarge the mind.' 'Here!' I interrupted. 'You
can never tell! Here I met Mr. Kurtz,' he said, youthfully solemn and
reproachful. I held my tongue after that. It appears he had persuaded a
Dutch trading-house on the coast to fit him out with stores and goods
and had started for the interior with a light heart and no more idea of
what would happen to him than a baby. He had been wandering about
that river for nearly two years alone, cut off from everybody and everything. 'I am not so young as I look. I am twenty-five,' he said. 'At first
old Van Shuyten would tell me to go to the devil,' he narrated with keen
enjoyment; 'but I stuck to him, and talked and talked till at last he got
afraid I would talk the hind-leg off his favourite dog, so he gave me some
cheap things and a few guns and told me he hoped he would never see
my face again. Good old Dutchman, Van Shuyten. I sent him one
small lot of ivory a year ago so that he can't call me a little thief when I
get back. I hope he got it. And for the rest, I don't care. I had some
wood stacked for you. That was my old house. Did you see?'

"I gave him Towson's book. He made as though he would kiss me,
but restrained himself. 'The only book I had left and I thought I had lost
it,' he said, looking at it ecstatically. 'So many accidents happen to a
man going about alone, you know. Canoes get upset sometimes—and
sometimes you've got to clear out so quick when the people get angry.'
He thumbed the pages. 'You made notes in Russian?' I asked. He nodded. 'I thought they were written in cipher,' I said. He laughed, then
became serious. 'I had lots of trouble to keep these people off,' he said.
'Did they want to kill you?' I asked. 'Oh no!' he cried, and checked
himself. 'Why did they attack us?' I pursued. He hesitated, then said
shamefacedly, 'They don't want him to go.' 'Don't they?' I said curiously. He nodded a nod full of mystery and wisdom. 'I tell you,' he
cried, 'this man has enlarged my mind.' He opened his arms wide, staring at me with his little blue eyes that were perfectly round."

III

"I looked at him, lost in astonishment. There he was before me in
motley as though he had absconded from a troupe of mimes, enthusiastic, fabulous. His very existence was improbable, inexplicable, and altogether bewildering. He was an insoluble problem. It was inconceivable
how he had existed, how he had succeeded in getting so far, how he had
managed to remain—why he did not instantly disappear. 'I went a little
farther,' he said, 'then still a little farther—till I had gone so far that I
don't know how I'll ever get back. Never mind. Plenty time! I can man-

age. You take Kurtz away quick—quick—I tell you.' The glamour of youth enveloped his parti-coloured rags, his destitution, his loneliness, the essential desolation of his futile wanderings. For months—for years— his life hadn't been worth a day's purchase—and there he was gallantly, thoughtlessly alive, to all appearance indestructible solely by the virtue of his few years and of his unreflecting audacity. I was seduced into something like admiration—like envy. Glamour urged him on, glamour kept him unscathed. He surely wanted nothing from the wilderness but space to breathe in and to push on through. His need was to exist and to move onwards at the greatest possible risk and with a maximum of privation. If the absolutely pure, uncalculating, unpractical spirit of adventure had ever ruled a human being, it ruled this be-patched youth. I almost envied him the possession of this modest and clear flame. It seemed to have consumed all thought of self so completely that even while he was talking to you, you forgot that it was he—the man before your eyes—who had gone through these things. I did not envy him his devotion to Kurtz, though. He had not meditated over it. It came to him and he accepted it with a sort of eager fatalism. I must say that to me it appeared about the most dangerous thing in every way he had come upon so far.

"They had come together unavoidably, like two ships becalmed near each other, and lay rubbing sides at last. I suppose Kurtz wanted an audience because on a certain occasion, when encamped in the forest, they had talked all night, or more probably Kurtz had talked. 'We talked of everything,' he said quite transported at the recollection. 'I forgot there was such a thing as sleep. The night did not seem to last an hour Everything! Everything! . . . Of love too.' 'Ah, he talked to you of love! I said much amused. 'It isn't what you think,' he cried almost passionately. 'It was in general. He made me see things—things.'

"He threw his arms up. We were on deck at the time, and the head-man of my wood-cutters lounging near by turned upon him his heavy and glittering eyes. I looked around, and I don't know why, but I assure you that never, never before did this land, this river, this jungle, the very arch of this blazing sky appear to me so hopeless and so dark, so impenetrable to human thought, so pitiless to human weakness. 'And ever since you have been with him, of course?' I said.

"On the contrary. It appears their intercourse had been very much broken by various causes. He had, as he informed me proudly, managed to nurse Kurtz through two illnesses (he alluded to it as you would to some risky feat) but as a rule Kurtz wandered alone far in the depths of the forest. 'Very often coming to this station, I had to wait days and days before he would turn up,' he said. 'Ah! it was worth waiting for—sometimes.' 'What was he doing? exploring or what?' I asked. Oh! Yes. Of course he had discovered lots of villages, a lake too—he did not know exactly in what direction; it was dangerous to inquire too much—but mostly his expeditions had been for ivory. 'But he had no goods to trade with by that time,' I objected. 'There's a good lot of cartridges left even

yet,' he answered, looking away. 'To speak plainly, he raided the country,' I said. He nodded. 'Not alone, surely!' He muttered something
about the villages round that lake. 'Kurtz got the tribe to follow him, did
he?' I suggested. He fidgeted a little. 'They adored him,' he said. The
tone of these words was so extraordinary that I looked at him searchingly.
It was curious to see his mingled eagerness and reluctance to speak of
Kurtz. The man filled his life, occupied his thoughts, swayed his emotions. 'What can you expect!' he burst out; 'he came to them with thunder and lightning, you know—and they had never seen anything like
it—and very terrible. He could be very terrible. You can't judge Mr.
Kurtz as you would an ordinary man. No, no, no! Now—just to give
you an idea—I don't mind telling you, he wanted to shoot me too one
day—but I don't judge him.' 'Shoot you!' I cried. 'What for?' 'Well, I
had a small lot of ivory the chief of that village near my house gave me.
You see I used to shoot game for them. Well, he wanted it and wouldn't
hear reason. He declared he would shoot me unless I gave him the ivory
and then cleared out of the country because he could do so, and had a
fancy for it, and there was nothing on earth to prevent him killing whom
he jolly well pleased. And it was true too. I gave him the ivory. What
did I care! But I didn't clear out. No, no. I couldn't leave him. I had to
be careful, of course, till we got friendly again for a time. He had his
second illness then. Afterwards I had to keep out of the way, but I didn't
mind. He was living for the most part in those villages on the lake.
When he came down to the river, sometimes he would take to me and
sometimes it was better for me to be careful. This man suffered too
much. He hated all this and somehow he couldn't get away. When I
had a chance I begged him to try and leave while there was time; I
offered to go back with him. And he would say yes—and then he would
remain—go off on another ivory hunt—disappear for weeks—forget
himself amongst these people—forget himself—you know.' 'Why! he's
mad,' I said. He protested indignantly. Mr. Kurtz couldn't be mad. If I
had heard him talk only two days ago I wouldn't dare hint at such a
thing. . . . I had taken up my binoculars while we talked and was looking at the shore, sweeping the limit of the forest at each side and at the
back of the house. The consciousness of there being people in that bush,
so silent, so quiet—as silent and quiet as the ruined house on the hill—
made me uneasy. There was no sign on the face of nature of this amazing tale † that was not so much told as suggested to me in desolate exclamations, completed by shrugs, in interrupted phrases, in hints ending
in deep sighs. The woods were unmoved like a mask—heavy like the
closed door of a prison—they looked with their air of hidden knowledge,
of patient expectation, of unapproachable silence. The Russian was
explaining to me that it was only lately that Mr. Kurtz had come down
to the river, bringing along with him all the fighting men of that lake
tribe. He had been absent for several months—getting himself adored, I

† *Ms and Maga:* tale of cruelty and greed that was, *etc.*

suppose—and had come down unexpectedly, with the intention to all appearance of making a raid either across the river or down stream. Evidently the appetite for more ivory had got the better of the—what shall I say—less material aspirations. However, he had got much worse suddenly. 'I heard he was lying helpless, and so I came up—took my chance,' said the Russian. 'Oh, he is bad, very bad.' I directed my glass to the house. There were no signs of life, but there were the ruined roof, the long mud wall peeping above the grass, with three little square window-holes no two of the same size, all this brought within reach of my hand, as it were. And then I made a brusque movement and one of the remaining posts of that vanished fence leaped up in the field of my glass. You remember I told you I had been struck at the distance by certain attempts at ornamentation, rather remarkable in the ruinous aspect of the place. Now I had suddenly a nearer view and its first result was to make me throw my head back as if before a blow. Then I went carefully from post to post with my glass, and I saw my mistake. These round knobs were not ornamental but symbolic; † they were expressive and puzzling, striking and disturbing—food for thought and also for vultures if there had been any looking down from the sky; but at all events for such ants as were industrious enough to ascend the pole. They would have been even more impressive, those heads on the stakes, if their faces had not been turned to the house. Only one, the first I had made out, was facing my way. I was not so shocked as you may think. The start back I had given was really nothing but a movement of surprise. I had expected to see a knob of wood there, you know. I returned deliberately to the first I had seen—and there it was black, dried, sunken, with closed eyelids—a head that seemed to sleep at the top of that pole, and with the shrunken dry lips showing a narrow white line of the teeth, was smiling too, smiling continuously at some endless and jocose dream of that eternal slumber.

"I am not disclosing any trade secrets. In fact the Manager said afterwards that Mr. Kurtz's methods had ruined the district. I have no opinion on that point, but I want you clearly to understand that there was nothing exactly profitable in these heads being there. They only showed that Mr. Kurtz lacked restraint in the gratification of his various lusts, that there was something wanting in him—some small matter which when the pressing need arose could not be found under his magnificent eloquence. Whether he knew of this deficiency himself I can't say. I think the knowledge came to him at last—only at the very last. * But the wilderness had found him out early, and had taken on him a terrible vengeance for the fantastic invasion. ‡ I think it had whispered to him things about himself which he did not know, things of which he had no conception till he took counsel with this great solitude—and the whisper had proved irresistibly fascinating. It echoed loudly within him because

---

† *Ms and Maga*: symbolic of some cruel and forbidden knowledge. They were, *etc*.
* *Ms*: last. If so, then justice was done. But, *etc*.

‡ *Ms and Maga*: invasion. It had tempted him with all the sinister suggestions of its loneliness. I think, *etc*.

he was hollow at the core. . . . I put down the glass, and the head that
had appeared near enough to be spoken to seemed at once to have leaped
away from me into inaccessible distance.

"The admirer of Mr. Kurtz was a bit crestfallen. In a hurried, indistinct voice he began to assure me he had not dared to take these—say,
symbols—down. He was not afraid of the natives; they would not stir till
Mr. Kurtz gave the word. His ascendancy was extraordinary. The camps
of these people surrounded the place and the chiefs came every day to
see him. They would crawl. . . . 'I don't want to know anything of the
ceremonies used when approaching Mr. Kurtz,' I shouted. Curious, this
feeling that came over me that such details would be more intolerable
than those heads drying on the stakes under Mr. Kurtz's windows. After
all, that was only a savage sight while I seemed at one bound to have
been transported into some lightless region of subtle horrors, where pure,
uncomplicated savagery was a positive relief, being something that had
a right to exist—obviously—in the sunshine. The young man looked at
me with surprise. I suppose it did not occur to him that Mr. Kurtz was
no idol of mine. He forgot I hadn't heard any of these splendid mono-
logues on, what was it? on love, justice, conduct of life—or what not. If
it had come to crawling before Mr. Kurtz, he crawled as much as the
veriest savage of them all.† I had no idea of the conditions, he said:
these heads were the heads of rebels. I shocked him excessively by laughing. Rebels! What would be the next definition I was to hear. There had
been enemies, criminals, workers—and these were—rebels. Those
rebellious heads looked very subdued to me on their sticks. 'You don't
know how such a life tries a man like Kurtz,' cried Kurtz's last disciple.
'Well, and you?' I said. 'I! I! I am a simple man. I have no great thoughts.
I want nothing from anybody. How can you compare me to . . . ?' His
feelings were too much for speech and suddenly he broke down. 'I don't
understand,' he groaned. 'I've been doing my best to keep him alive and
that's enough. I had no hand in all this. I have no abilities. There hasn't
been a drop of medicine or a mouthful of invalid food for months here.
He was shamefully abandoned. A man like this, with such ideas.
Shamefully! Shamefully! I—I—haven't slept for the last ten nights. . . .'

"His voice lost itself in the calm of the evening. The long shadow of
the forest had slipped downhill while we talked, had gone far beyond the
ruined hovel, beyond the symbolic row of stakes. All this was in the
gloom while we down there were yet in the sunshine, and the stretch of
the river abreast of the clearing glittered in a still and dazzling splendour
with a murky and over-shadowed bend above and below. Not a living
soul was seen on the shore. The bushes did not rustle.

"Suddenly round the corner of the house a group of men appeared,
as though they had come up from the ground. They waded waist-deep
in the grass in a compact body bearing an improvised stretcher in their
midst. Instantly in the emptiness of the landscape a cry arose whose

† Ms: all. And his was a sturdy allegiance, soaring bravely above the facts which it could see with a
bewilderment and a sorrow akin to despair. I had, etc.

shrillness pierced the still air like a sharp arrow flying straight to the very
heart of the land. And as if by enchantment streams of human beings—
of naked human beings—with spears in their hands, with bows, with
shields, with wild glances and savage movements, were poured into the
clearing by the dark-faced and pensive forest. The bushes shook, the
grass swayed for a time, and then everything stood still in attentive
immobility.

" 'Now, if he does not say the right thing to them we are all done for,'
said the Russian at my elbow. The knot of men with the stretcher had
stopped too, half-way to the steamer, as if petrified. I saw the man on
the stretcher sit up, lank and with an uplifted arm, above the shoulders
of the bearers. 'Let us hope that the man who can talk so well of love in
general will find some particular reason to spare us this time,' I said. I
resented bitterly the absurd danger of our situation, as if to be at the
mercy of that atrocious phantom † had been a dishonouring necessity. I
could not hear a sound, but through my glasses I saw the thin arm
extended commandingly, the lower jaw moving, the eyes of that apparition shining darkly far in its bony head that nodded with grotesque jerks.
Kurtz—Kurtz—that means 'short' in German—don't it? Well, the name
was as true as everything else in his life—and death. He looked at least
seven feet long. His covering had fallen off and his body emerged from
it pitiful and appalling as from a winding-sheet. I could see the cage of
his ribs all astir, the bones of his arm waving. It was as though an animated image of death carved out of old ivory had been shaking its hand
with menaces at a motionless crowd of men made of dark and glittering
bronze. I saw him open his * mouth wide—it gave him a weirdly vora-
cious aspect as though he had wanted to swallow all the air, all the earth,
all the men before him. A deep voice reached me faintly. He must have
been shouting. He fell back suddenly. The stretcher shook as the bearers
staggered forward again, and almost at the same time I noticed that the
crowd of savages was vanishing without any perceptible movement of
retreat, as if the forest that had ejected these beings so suddenly had
drawn them in again as the breath is drawn in a long aspiration.

"Some of the pilgrims behind the stretcher carried his arms—two shot-
guns, a heavy rifle, and a light revolver-carbine—the thunderbolts of
that pitiful Jupiter. The Manager bent over him murmuring as he walked
beside his head. They laid him down in one of the little cabins—just a
room for a bed-place and a camp-stool or two, you know. We had brought
his belated correspondence, and a lot of torn envelopes and open letters
littered his bed. His hand roamed feebly amongst these papers. I was
struck by the fire of his eyes and the composed languor of his expression.
It was not so much the exhaustion of disease. He did not seem in pain.
This shadow looked satiated and calm as though for the moment it had
had its fill of all the emotions.

"He rustled one of the letters, and looking straight in my face said, 'I

† Ms: phantom who ruled this land had been, *etc.*   * Ms: it open its

am glad.' Somebody had been writing to him about me. These special recommendations were turning up again. The volume of tone he emitted without effort, almost without the trouble of moving his lips, amazed me. A voice! a voice! It was grave, profound, vibrating, while the man did not seem capable of a whisper. However, he had enough strength in him—factitious no doubt—to very nearly make an end of us, as you shall hear directly.

"The Manager appeared silently in the doorway; I stepped out at once and he drew the curtain after me. The Russian, eyed curiously by the pilgrims, was staring at the shore. I followed the direction of his glance.

"Dark human shapes could be made out in the distance, flitting indistinctly against the gloomy border of the forest, and near the river two bronze figures leaning on tall spears stood in the sunlight under fantastic head-dresses of spotted skins, warlike and still in statuesque repose. And from right to left along the lighted shore moved a wild and gorgeous apparition of a woman.

"She walked with measured steps, draped in striped and fringed cloths, treading the earth proudly with a slight jingle and flash of barbarous ornaments. She carried her head high, her hair was done in the shape of a helmet, she had brass leggings to the knees, brass wire gauntlets to the elbow, a crimson spot on her tawny cheek, innumerable necklaces of glass beads on her neck, bizarre things, charms, gifts of witch-men, that hung about her, glittered and trembled at every step. She must have had the value of several elephant tusks upon her. She was savage and superb, wild-eyed and magnificent; there was something ominous and stately in her deliberate progress. And in the hush that had fallen suddenly upon the whole sorrowful land, the immense wilderness, the colossal body of the fecund and mysterious life seemed to look at her, pensive, as though it had been looking at the image of its own tenebrous and passionate soul. †

"She came abreast of the steamer, stood still, and faced us. Her long shadow fell to the water's edge. Her face had a tragic and fierce aspect of wild sorrow and of dumb pain mingled with the fear of some struggling, half-shaped resolve. She stood looking at us without a stir and like the wilderness itself, with an air of brooding* over an inscrutable purpose. A whole minute passed and then she made a step forward. There was a low jingle, a glint of yellow metal, a sway of fringed draperies, and she stopped ‡ as if her heart had failed her. The young fellow by my side growled. The pilgrims murmured at my back. She looked at us all as if her life had depended upon the unswerving steadiness of her glance. Suddenly she opened her bared arms and threw them up rigid above her head as though in an uncontrollable desire to touch the sky, and at the

† Ms and Maga: soul. And we men looked at her— at any rate I looked at her.
* Ms: implacable brooding
‡ Ms and Maga: and she stopped. Had her heart failed her, or had her eyes veiled with that mournfulness that lies over all the wild things of the earth seen the hopelessness of longing that will find out sometimes even a savage soul in the loneliness [Maga: lonely darkness] of its being? Who can tell. Perhaps she did not know herself. The young fellow, etc.

same time the swift shadows darted out on the earth, swept around on
the river, gathering the steamer in a shadowy embrace.† A formidable
silence hung over the scene.

"She turned away slowly, walked on following the bank and passed
into the bushes to the left. Once only her eyes gleamed back at us in the
dusk of the thickets before she disappeared.

" 'If she had offered to come aboard I really think I would have tried
to shoot her,' said the man of patches nervously. 'I had been risking my
life every day for the last fortnight to keep her out of the house. She got
in one day and kicked up a row about those miserable rags I picked up
in the storeroom to mend my clothes with. I wasn't decent. At least it
must have been that, for she talked like a fury to Kurtz for an hour
pointing at me now and then. I don't understand the dialect of this tribe.
Luckily for me, I fancy Kurtz felt too ill that day to care, or there would
have been mischief. I don't understand. . . . No—it's too much for me.
Ah, well, it's all over now.'

"At this moment I heard Kurtz's deep voice behind the curtain: 'Save
me—save the ivory, you mean. Don't tell me! Save *me!* Why, I've had
to save you. You are interrupting my plans now. Sick. Sick. Not so sick
as you would like to believe. Never mind. I'll carry my ideas out yet—I
will return. I'll show you what can be done. You with your little ped-
dling notions—you are interfering with me. I will return. I. . . .'

"The Manager came out. He did me the honour to take me under
the arm and lead me aside. 'He is very low, very low,' he said. He
considered it necessary to sigh, but neglected to be consistently sorrowful. 'We have done all we could for him—haven't we. But there is no
disguising the fact, Mr. Kurtz has done more harm than good to the
Company. He did not see the time was not ripe for vigorous action.
Cautiously. Cautiously. That's my principle. We must be cautious yet.
The district is closed to us for a time. Deplorable. Upon the whole, the
trade will suffer. I don't deny there is a remarkable quantity of ivory—
mostly fossil. We must save it, at all events—but look how precarious
the position is—and why? Because the method is unsound.' 'Do you,'
said I looking at the shore, 'call it "unsound method"?' 'Without doubt,'
he exclaimed hotly. 'Don't you?' . . . 'No method at all,' I murmured
after a while. 'Exactly,' he exulted. 'I anticipated this. Shows a complete
want of judgment. It is my duty to point it out in the proper quarter.'
'Oh,' said I, 'that fellow—what's his name—the brickmaker will make a
readable report for you.' He appeared confounded for a moment. It seemed
to me I had never breathed an atmosphere so vile, and I turned mentally
to Kurtz for relief—positively for relief. 'Nevertheless, I think Mr. Kurtz
is a remarkable man,' I said with emphasis. He started, dropped on me
a cold heavy glance, said very quietly, 'He *was*,' and turned his back on

† Ms: embrace. Her sudden gesture was as startling
as a cry but not a sound was heard. The formidable silence of the scene completed the memorable
impression. *Maga:* embrace. Her sudden gesture

seemed to demand a cry, but the unbroken silence
that hung over the scene was more formidable than
any sound could be. *1902:* embrace. A formidable
silence hung over the scene.

me. My hour of favour was over; I found myself lumped along with
Kurtz as a partisan of methods for which the time was not ripe. I was
unsound. Ah, but it was something to have at least a choice of nightmares.

"I had turned to the wilderness really, not to Mr. Kurtz who, I was
ready to admit, was as good as buried. And for a moment it seemed to
me as if I also were buried in a vast grave full of unspeakable secrets. I
felt an intolerable weight oppressing my breast, the smell of the damp
earth, the unseen presence of victorious corruption, the darkness of an
impenetrable night. . . . The Russian tapped me on the shoulder. I
heard him mumbling and stammering something about 'brother seaman—couldn't conceal—knowledge of matters that would affect Mr.
Kurtz's reputation.' I waited. For him evidently Mr. Kurtz was not in
his grave; I suspect that for him Mr. Kurtz was one of the immortals.
'Well,' said I at last, 'speak out. As it happens, I am Mr. Kurtz's friend—
in a way.'

"He stated with a good deal of formality that had we not been 'of the
same profession' he would have kept the matter to himself without regard
to consequences. He suspected 'there was an active ill-will towards him
on the part of these white men that. . . .' 'You are right,' I said, remembering a certain conversation I had overhead. 'The Manager thinks you
ought to be hanged.' He showed a concern at this intelligence which
amused me at first. 'I had better get out of the way quietly,' he said
earnestly. 'I can do no more for Kurtz now and they would soon find
some excuse. What's to stop them. There's a military post three hundred
miles from here.' 'Well, upon my word,' said I, 'perhaps you had better
go if you have any friends amongst the savages near by.' 'Plenty,' he
said. 'They are simple people—and I want nothing, you know.' He stood
biting his lip, then: 'I don't want any harm to happen to these whites
here, but of course I was thinking of Mr. Kurtz's reputation—but you
are a brother seaman and. . . .' 'All right,' said I after a time. 'Mr.
Kurtz's reputation is safe with me.' I did not know how truly I spoke.

"He informed me, lowering his voice, that it was Kurtz who had ordered
the attack to be made on the steamer. 'He hated sometimes the idea of
being taken away—and then again. . . . But I don't understand these
matters. I am a simple man. He thought it would scare you away—that
you would give it up, thinking him dead. I could not stop him. Oh I
had an awful time of it this last month.' 'Very well,' I said. 'He is all
right now.' 'Ye-e-es,' he muttered not very convinced apparently. 'Thanks,'
said I, 'I shall keep my eyes open.' 'But quiet—eh?' he urged anxiously.
'It would be awful for his reputation if anybody here. . . .' I promised a
complete discretion with great gravity. 'I have a canoe and three black
fellows † waiting not very far. I am off. Could you give me a few Martini-
Henry cartridges?' I could and did with proper secrecy. He helped himself with a wink at me to a handful of my tobacco. 'Between sailors—

† *Ms:* three fellows

you know—good English tobacco.' At the door of the pilot-house he turned round—'I say, haven't you a pair of shoes you could spare?' He raised one leg. 'Look.' The soles were tied with knotted strings sandal-wise under his bare feet. I rooted out an old pair at which he looked with admiration before tucking it under his left arm. One of his pockets (bright red) was bulging with cartridges, from the other (dark blue) peeped 'Towson's Inquiry,' etc. etc. He seemed to think himself excellently well equipped for a renewed encounter with the wilderness. 'Ah! I'll never, never meet such a man again. You ought to have heard him recite poetry—his own too it was, he told me. Poetry!' He rolled his eyes at the recollection of these delights. 'Oh, he enlarged my mind!' 'Good-bye,' said I. He shook hands and vanished in the night. Sometimes I ask myself whether I had ever really seen him—whether it was possible to meet such a phenomenon! . . .

"When I woke up shortly after midnight his warning came to my mind with its hint of danger that seemed in the starred darkness real enough to make me get up for the purpose of having a look round. On the hill a big fire burned, illuminating fitfully a crooked corner of the station-house. One of the agents with a picket of a few of our blacks armed for the purpose was keeping guard over the ivory, but deep within the forest red gleams that wavered, that seemed to sink and rise from the ground amongst confused columnar shapes of intense blackness, showed the exact position of the camp where Mr. Kurtz's adorers were keeping their uneasy vigil. The monotonous beating of a big drum filled the air with muffled shocks and a lingering vibration. A steady droning sound of many men chanting each to himself some weird incantation came out from the black flat wall of the woods as the humming of bees comes out of a hive, and had a strange narcotic effect upon my half-awake senses. I believe I dozed off leaning over the rail till an abrupt burst of yells, an overwhelming outbreak of a pent-up and mysterious frenzy, woke me up in a bewildered wonder. It was cut short all at once and the low droning went on with an effect of audible and soothing silence. I glanced casually into the little cabin. A light was burning within, but Mr. Kurtz was not there.

"I think I would have raised an outcry if I had believed my eyes. But I didn't believe them at first—the thing seemed so impossible. The fact is, I was completely unnerved by a sheer blank fright, pure abstract ter-ror, unconnected with any distinct shape of physical danger. What made this emotion so overpowering was—how shall I define it—the moral shock I received, as if something altogether monstrous, intolerable to thought and odious to the soul had been thrust upon me unexpectedly. This lasted of course the merest fraction of a second and then the usual sense of commonplace deadly danger, the possibility of a sudden onslaught and massacre, or something of the kind, which I saw impending was positively welcome and composing. It pacified me, in fact, so much that I did not raise an alarm.

"There was an agent buttoned up inside an ulster and sleeping on a chair on deck within three feet of me. The yells had not awakened him; he snored very slightly. I left him to his slumbers and leaped ashore. I did not betray Mr. Kurtz—it was ordered I should never betray him—it was written I should be loyal to the nightmare of my choice. I was anxious to deal with this shadow by myself alone—and to this day I don't know why I was so jealous of sharing with any one the peculiar blackness † of that experience.

"As soon as I got on the bank I saw a trail—a broad trail through the grass. I remember the exultation with which I said to myself, 'He can't walk—he is crawling on all-fours—I've got him.' The grass was wet with dew. I strode rapidly with clenched fists. I fancy I had some vague notion of falling upon him and giving him a drubbing. I don't know. I had some imbecile thoughts. The knitting old woman with the cat obtruded herself upon my memory as a most improper person to be sitting at the other end of such an affair. I saw a row of pilgrims squirting lead in the air out of Winchesters held to the hip. I thought I would never get back to the steamer and imagined myself living alone and unarmed in the woods to an advanced age. Such silly things—you know. And I remember I confounded the beat of the drum with the beating of my heart and was pleased at its calm regularity.

"I kept to the track though—then stopped to listen. The night was very clear, a dark blue space sparkling with dew and starlight in which black things stood very still. I thought I could see a kind of motion ahead of me. I was strangely cocksure of everything that night. I actually left the track and ran in a wide semicircle (I verily believe chuckling to myself) so as to get in front of that stir, of that motion I had seen—if indeed I had seen anything. I was circumventing Kurtz as though it had been a boyish game.

"I came upon him and if he had not heard me coming, I would have fallen over him too, but he got up in time. He rose, unsteady, long, pale, indistinct like a vapour exhaled by the earth, and swayed slightly, misty and silent before me while at my back the fires loomed between the trees, and the murmur of many voices issued from the forest. I had cut him off cleverly, but when actually confronting him I seemed to come to my senses; I saw the danger in its right proportion. It was by no means over yet. Suppose he began to shout. Though he could hardly stand there was still plenty of vigour in his voice. 'Go away—hide yourself,' he said in that profound tone. It was very awful. I glanced back. We were within thirty yards from * the nearest fire. A black figure stood up, strode on long black legs, waving long black arms across the glow. It had horns—antelope horns, I think—on its head. Some sorcerer, some witch-man, no doubt; it looked fiend-like enough. 'Do you know what you are doing?' I whispered. 'Perfectly,' he answered raising his voice for that single word; it sounded to me far off and yet loud like a hail through a speaking-trumpet. If he makes a row we are lost, I thought to myself.

† Ms and Maga: dismal blackness　　　　　　　　* Ms: of; Maga and 1902: from

This clearly was not a case for fisticuffs, even apart from the very natural aversion I had to beat that Shadow—this wandering and tormented thing. †
'You will be lost,' I said—'utterly lost.' One gets sometimes such a flash of inspiration, you know. I did say the right thing, though indeed he could not have been more irretrievably lost than he was at this very moment when the foundations of our intimacy were being laid—to endure—to endure—even to the end—even beyond.

" 'I had immense plans,' he muttered irresolutely. 'Yes,' said I, 'but if you try to shout I'll smash your head with. . . .' There was not a stick or a stone near. 'I will throttle you for good,' I corrected myself. 'I was on the threshold of great things,' he pleaded in a voice of longing with a wistfulness of tone that made my blood run cold. 'And now for this stupid scoundrel. . . .' 'Your success in Europe is assured in any case,' I affirmed steadily. I did not want to have the throttling of him, you understand—and indeed it would have been very little use for any practical purpose. I tried to break the spell, the heavy mute spell of the wilderness that seemed to draw him to its pitiless breast by the awakening of forgotten and brutal instincts, by the memory of gratified and monstrous passions. This alone, I was convinced, had driven him out to the edge of the forest, to the bush, towards the gleam of fires, the throb of drums, the drone of weird incantations; this alone had beguiled his unlawful soul beyond the bounds of permitted aspirations. And, don't you see, the terror of the position was not in being knocked on the head—though I had a very lively sense of that danger too—but in this, that I had to deal with a being to whom I could not appeal in the name of anything high or low. I had even like the niggers to invoke him—himself—his own exalted and incredible degradation. There was nothing either above or below him—and I knew it. He had kicked himself loose of the earth. * Confound the man! he had kicked the very earth to pieces. He was alone—and I before him did not know whether I stood on the ground or floated in the air. I've been telling you what we said—repeating the phrases we pronounced—but what's the good. They were common everyday words—the familiar vague sounds exchanged on every waking day of life. But what of that? They had behind them, to my mind, the terrific suggestiveness of words heard in dreams, of phrases spoken in nightmares. Soul! If anybody had ever struggled with a soul I am the man. And I wasn't arguing with a lunatic ‡ either. Believe me or not, his intelligence was perfectly clear—concentrated, it is true, upon himself with horrible intensity, yet clear, and therein was my only chance—barring, of course, the killing him there and then, which wasn't so good on account of unavoidable noise. But his soul was mad. Being alone in the wilderness, it had looked within itself and, by Heavens I tell you, it had gone mad. I had—for my sins, I suppose—to go through the ordeal of looking into it myself. No eloquence could have been so

† Ms and Maga: thing that seemed released from one grave only to sink forever into another. 'You will, etc.

* Ms canceled: of every restraint.
‡ Ms and Maga: mad man

withering to one's belief in mankind † as his final burst of sincerity. He struggled with himself too. I saw it—I heard it. I saw the inconceivable mystery of a soul that knew no restraint, no faith, and no fear, yet struggling blindly with itself. I kept my head pretty well, but when I had him at last stretched on the couch, I wiped my forehead while my legs shook under me as though I had carried half a ton on my back down that hill. And yet I had only supported him, his bony arm clasped round my neck—and he was not much heavier than a child.

"When next day we left at noon, the crowd, of whose presence behind the curtain of trees I had been acutely conscious all the time, flowed out of the woods again, filled the clearing, covered the slope with a mass of naked, breathing, quivering, bronze bodies. I steamed up a bit, then swung down-stream, and two thousand eyes followed the evolutions of the splashing, thumping, fierce river-demon beating the water with its terrible tail and breathing black smoke into the air. In front of the first rank along the river three men plastered with bright red earth from head to foot strutted to and fro restlessly. When we came abreast again they faced the river, stamped their feet, nodded their horned heads, swayed their scarlet bodies; they shook towards the fierce river-demon a bunch of black feathers, a mangy skin with a pendent tail—something that looked like a dried gourd; they shouted periodically together strings of amazing words that resembled no sounds of human language; and the deep murmurs of the crowd, interrupted suddenly, were like the responses of some satanic litany.

"We had carried Kurtz into the pilot-house. There was more air there. Lying on the couch he stared through the open shutter. There was an eddy in the mass of human bodies and the woman with helmeted head and tawny cheeks rushed out to the very brink of the stream. She put out her hands, shouted something, and all that wild mob took up the shout in a roaring chorus of articulated, rapid, breathless utterance.

" 'Do you understand this?' I asked.

"He kept on looking out past me with fiery, longing eyes, with a mingled expression of wistfulness and hate. He made no answer, but I saw a smile, a smile of indefinable meaning, appear on his colourless lips that a moment after twitched convulsively. 'Do I not?' * he said slowly, gasping, as if the words had been torn out of him by a supernatural power.

"I pulled the string of the whistle, and I did this because I saw the pilgrims on deck getting out their rifles with an air of anticipating a jolly lark. At the sudden screech there was a movement of abject terror through that wedged mass of bodies. 'Don't! don't you frighten them away,' cried some one on deck disconsolately. I pulled the string time after time. They broke and ran, they leaped, they crouched, they swerved, they dodged the flying terror of the sound. The three red chaps had fallen flat, face down on the shore as though they had been shot dead. Only

---

† to one's belief in mankind, *added* 1902.   * *Ms and Maga:* 'I will return.'

the barbarous and superb woman did not so much as flinch and stretched tragically her bare arms after us over the sombre and glittering river.

"And then that imbecile crowd down on the deck started their little fun and I could see nothing more for smoke.

"The brown current ran swiftly out of the heart of darkness bearing us down towards the sea with twice the speed of our upward progress. And Kurtz's life was running swiftly too, ebbing, ebbing out of his heart into the sea of inexorable time. The Manager was very placid, he had no vital anxieties now, he took us both in with a comprehensive and satisfied glance: the 'affair' had come off as well as could be wished. I saw the time approaching when I would be left alone of the party of 'unsound method.' The pilgrims looked upon me with disfavour. I was, so to speak, numbered with the dead. It is strange how I accepted this unforeseen partnership, this choice of nightmares forced upon me in the tenebrous land invaded by these mean and greedy phantoms.

"Kurtz discoursed. A voice! a voice! It rang deep to the very last. It survived his strength to hide in the magnificent folds of eloquence the barren darkness of his heart. Oh, he struggled, he struggled. The wastes of his weary brain were haunted by shadowy images now—images of wealth and fame revolving obsequiously around his unextinguishable gift of noble and lofty expression. My Intended,† my station, my career, my ideas—these were the subjects for the occasional utterances of elevated sentiments. The shade of the original Kurtz frequented the bedside of the hollow sham whose fate it was to be buried presently in the mould of primeval earth. But both the diabolic love and the unearthly hate of the mysteries it had penetrated fought for the possession of that soul satiated with primitive emotions, avid of lying fame, of sham distinction, of all the appearances of success and power.

"Sometimes he was contemptibly childish. He desired to have kings meet him at railway stations on his return from some ghastly Nowhere, where he intended to accomplish great things. 'You show them you have in you something that is really profitable, and then there will be no limits to the recognition of your ability,' he would say. 'Of course you must take care of the motives—right motives—always.' The long reaches that were like one and the same reach, monotonous bends that were exactly alike, slipped past the steamer with their multitude of secular[9] trees looking patiently after this grimy fragment of another world, the forerunner of change, of conquest, of trade, of massacres, of blessings. I looked ahead—piloting. 'Close the shutter,' said Kurtz suddenly one day; 'I can't bear to look at this.' I did so. There was a silence. 'Oh, but I will wring your heart yet!' * he cried at the invisible wilderness.

"We broke down—as I had expected—and had to lie up for repairs at the head of an island. This delay was the first thing that shook Kurtz's

---

† Ms: My Intended, my ivory, my station, my career, my ideas.

9. A French form (like *serried* on p. 45 and *ser-* viette on p. 32, above), *secular* means simply "aged" or "ancient."

* Ms: 'Oh! but I will make you serve my ends.'

confidence. One morning he gave me a packet of papers and a photo-graph—the lot tied together with a shoe-string. 'Keep this for me,' he said. 'This noxious fool' (meaning the Manager) 'is capable of prying into my boxes when I am not looking.' In the afternoon I saw him. He was lying on his back with closed eyes, and I withdrew quietly, but I heard him mutter, 'Live rightly, die, die.† . . .' I listened. There was nothing more. Was he rehearsing some speech in his sleep, or was it a fragment of a phrase from some newspaper article. He had been writing for the papers and meant to do so again, 'for the furthering of my ideas. It's a duty.'

"His was an impenetrable darkness. I looked at him as you peer down at a man who is lying at the bottom of a precipice where the sun never shines. But I had not much time to give him because I was helping the engine-driver to take to pieces the leaky cylinders, to straighten a bent connecting-rod, and in other such matters. I lived in an infernal mess of rust, filings, nuts, bolts, spanners, hammers, ratchet-drills—things I abominate because I don't get on with them. I tended the little forge we fortunately had aboard; I toiled wearily in a wretched scrap-heap—unless I had the shakes too bad to stand.

"One evening coming in with a candle I was startled to hear him say a little tremulously,* 'I am lying here in the dark waiting for death.' The light was within a foot of his eyes. I forced myself to murmur, 'Oh, nonsense!' and stood over him as if transfixed.

"Anything approaching the change that came over his features I have never seen before and hope never to see again. Oh, I wasn't touched. I was fascinated. It was as though a veil had been rent.‡ I saw on that ivory face the expression of sombre pride, of ruthless power, of craven terror—of an intense and hopeless despair. Did he live his life again in every detail of desire, temptation, and surrender during that supreme moment of complete knowledge? He cried in a whisper at some image, at some vision—he cried out twice, a cry that was no more than a breath:

" 'The horror! The horror!'

"I blew the candle out and left the cabin. The pilgrims were dining in the mess-room and I took my place opposite the Manager, who lifted his eyes to give me a questioning glance which I successfully ignored. He leaned back, serene, with that peculiar smile of his sealing the unex-pressed depths of his meanness. A continuous shower of small flies streamed upon the lamp, upon the cloth, upon our hands and faces. Suddenly the Manager's boy put his insolent black head in the doorway and said in a tone of scathing contempt:

---

† Ms: die nobly

* Ms and Maga: querulously

‡ Ms and Maga: rent. I saw on that ivory visage the expression of strange pride, of mental power, of avarice, of blood-thristiness, of cunning, of excessive terror, of intense and hopeless despair. Did he live his life through in every detail of desire[,] temptation[,] and surrender during that short and supreme moment? [Ms only continues:] He cried at some image, at some vision, he cried with a cry that was no more than a breath—

"Oh! the horror!"

I blew the candle out and left the cabin. Never before in his life had he been such a master of his magnificent gift as in his last speech on earth. [Canceled: The eloquence of it.]

The pilgrims, etc.

" 'Mistah Kurtz—he dead.'

"All the pilgrims rushed out to see. I remained and went on with my dinner. I believe I was considered brutally callous. However, I did not eat much. There was a lamp in there—light—don't you know—and outside it was so beastly, beastly dark. I went no more near the remarkable man who had pronounced † judgment upon the adventures of his soul on this earth. The voice was gone. What else had been there? But I am of course aware that next day the pilgrims buried something in a muddy hole. *

"And then they very nearly buried me.

"However, as you see, I did not go to join Kurtz there and then. I did not. I remained to dream the nightmare out to the end and to show my loyalty to Kurtz once more. Destiny. My destiny! Droll thing life is—that mysterious arrangement of merciless logic for a futile purpose. The most you can hope from it is some knowledge of yourself—that comes too late—a crop of unextinguishable regrets. I have wrestled with death. It is the most unexciting contest you can imagine. It takes place in an impalpable greyness with nothing underfoot, with nothing around, without spectators, without clamour, without glory, without the great desire of victory, without the great fear of defeat, in a sickly atmosphere of tepid scepticism, without much belief in your own right, and still less in that of your adversary. If such is the form of ultimate wisdom then life is a greater riddle than some of us think it to be. I was within a hair's-breadth of the last opportunity for pronouncement, and I found with humiliation that probably I would have nothing to say. This is the reason why I affirm that Kurtz was a remarkable man. He had something to say. He said it. Since I had peeped over the edge myself, I understand better the meaning of his stare that could not see the flame of the candle but was wide enough to embrace the whole universe, piercing enough to penetrate all the hearts that beat in the darkness. He had summed up—he had judged. 'The horror!' He was a remarkable man. After all, this was the expression of some sort of belief; it had candour, it had conviction, it had a vibrating note of revolt in its whisper, it had the appalling face of a glimpsed truth—the strange commingling of desire and hate. And it is not my own extremity I remember best—a vision of greyness without form filled with physical pain and a careless contempt for the evanescence of all things—even of this pain itself. No. It is his extremity that I seem to have lived through. True, he had made that last stride, he had stepped over the edge, while I had been permitted to draw back my hesitating foot. And perhaps in this is the whole difference; perhaps all the wisdom, and all truth, and all sincerity, are just compressed into that inappreciable moment of time in which we step over the threshold of the invisible. Perhaps. I like to think my summing-up would not have

† Ms and Maga: had so unhesitatingly pronounced.
* Ms p. 207 ends here followed by a new page now numbered p. 75, which picks up the story thirty-two words later: the end and to show my loyalty to Kurtz once more. The Ms concludes with pages numbered 75 through 99.

been a word of careless contempt. Better his cry—much better. It was
an affirmation, a moral victory paid for by innumerable defeats, by
abominable terrors, by abominable satisfactions. But it was a victory.
That is why I have remained loyal to Kurtz to the last, and even beyond,
when a long time after I heard once more not his own voice but the
echo of his magnificent eloquence thrown to me from a soul as translucently pure as a cliff of crystal.

"No, they did not bury me, though there is a period of time which I
remember mistily, with a shuddering wonder, like a passage through
some inconceivable world that had no hope in it and no desire. I found
myself back in the sepulchral city resenting the sight of people hurrying
through the streets to filch a little money from each other, to devour
their infamous cookery, to gulp their unwholesome beer, to dream their
insignificant and silly dreams. They trespassed upon my thoughts. They
were intruders whose knowledge of life was to me an irritating pretence
because I felt so sure they could not possibly know the things I knew.
Their bearing, which was simply the bearing of commonplace individuals going about their business in the assurance of perfect safety, was
offensive to me like the outrageous flauntings of folly in the face of a
danger it is unable to comprehend. I had no particular desire to enlighten
them, but I had some difficulty in restraining myself from laughing in
their faces so full of stupid importance. I daresay I was not very well at
that time. I tottered about the streets—there were various affairs to settle—grinning bitterly at perfectly respectable persons. I admit my behaviour was inexcusable, but then my temperature was seldom normal in
these days. My dear aunt's endeavours to 'nurse up my strength' seemed
altogether beside the mark. It was not my strength that wanted nursing,
it was my imagination that wanted soothing. I kept the bundle of papers
given me by Kurtz not knowing exactly what to do with it. His mother
had died lately, watched over, as I was told, by his Intended. A clean-
shaved man with an official manner and wearing gold-rimmed spectacles called on me one day and made inquiries, at first circuitous, afterwards suavely pressing, about what he was pleased to denominate certain
'documents.' I was not surprised because I had had two rows with the
Manager on the subject out there. I had refused to give up the smallest
scrap out of that package and I took the same attitude with the spectacled
man. He became darkly menacing at last and with much heat argued
that the Company had the right to every bit of information about its
'territories.' And, said he, 'Mr. Kurtz's knowledge of unexplored regions
must have been necessarily extensive and peculiar—owing to his great
abilities and to the deplorable circumstances in which he had been placed;
therefore. . . .' I assured him Mr. Kurtz's knowledge however extensive
did not bear upon the problems of commerce or administration. He
invoked then the name of science. 'It would be an incalculable loss if,'
etc. etc. I offered him the report on the 'Suppression of Savage Customs'
with the postscriptum torn off. He took it up eagerly but ended by sniff-
ing at it with an air of contempt. 'This is not what we had a right to

expect,' he remarked. 'Expect nothing else,' I said. 'There are only private letters.' He withdrew upon some threat of legal proceedings and I saw him no more, but another fellow calling himself Kurtz's cousin appeared two days later and was anxious to hear all the details about his dear relative's last moments. Incidentally he gave me to understand that Kurtz had been essentially a great musician. 'There was the making of an immense success,' said the man who was an organist, I believe, with lank grey hair flowing over a greasy coat-collar. I had no reason to doubt his statement, and to this day I am unable to say what was Kurtz's profession, whether he ever had any—which was the greatest of his talents. I had taken him for a painter who wrote for the papers, or else for a journalist who could paint—but even the cousin (who took snuff during the interview) could not tell me what he had been—exactly. He was a universal genius—on that point I agreed with the old chap who thereupon blew his nose noisily into a large cotton handkerchief and withdrew in senile agitation bearing off some family letters and memoranda without importance. Ultimately a journalist anxious to know something of the fate of his 'dear colleague' turned up. This visitor informed me Kurtz's proper sphere ought to have been politics 'on the popular side.' He had furry straight eyebrows, bristly hair cropped short, an eyeglass on a broad ribbon, and, becoming expansive, confessed his opinion that Kurtz really couldn't write a bit—'but Heavens! how that man could talk! He electrified large meetings. He had the faith—don't you see—he had the faith. He could get himself to believe anything—anything. He would have been a splendid leader of an extreme party.' 'What party?' I asked. 'Any party,' answered the other. 'He was an—an—extremist.' Did I not think so? I assented. Did I know, he asked, with a sudden flash of curiosity, 'what it was that had induced him to go out there?' 'Yes,' said I and forthwith handed him the famous Report for publication if he thought fit. He glanced through it hurriedly, mumbling all the time, judged 'it would do,' and took himself off with this plunder.

"Thus I was left at last with a slim packet of letters and the girl's portrait. She struck me as beautiful—I mean she had a beautiful expression. I know that the sunlight can be made to lie too, yet † one felt that no manipulation of light and pose could have conveyed the delicate shade of truthfulness upon those features.* She seemed ready to listen without mental reservation, without suspicion, without a thought for herself. I concluded I would go and give her back her portrait and those letters myself. Curiosity. Yes. And also some other feeling perhaps. All that had been Kurtz's had passed out of my hands: his soul, his body, his station, his plans, his ivory, his career. There remained only his memory and his Intended—and I wanted to give that up too to the past, in a way—to surrender personally all that remained of him with me to that oblivion which is the last word of our common fate. I don't defend myself. I had no clear perception of what it was I really wanted. Perhaps

† *Ms and Maga:* yet that face on paper seemed to be a reflection of truth itself. One felt, *etc.*

* *Ms and Maga:* features. She looked out trustfully. She seemed ready, *etc.*

it was an impulse of unconscious loyalty or the fulfilment of one of those ironic necessities that lurk in the facts of human existence. I don't know. I can't tell. But I went.

"I thought his memory was like the other memories of the dead that accumulate in every man's life—a vague impress on the brain of shadows that had fallen on it in their swift and final passage, but before the high and ponderous door, between the tall houses of a street as still and decorous as a well-kept alley in a cemetery,† I had a vision of him on the stretcher opening his mouth voraciously as if to devour all the earth with all its mankind. He lived then before me, he lived as much as he had ever lived—a shadow insatiable of splendid appearances, of frightful realities, a shadow darker than the shadow of the night, and draped nobly in the folds of a gorgeous eloquence. The vision seemed to enter the house with me—the stretcher, the phantom-bearers, the wild crowd of obedient worshippers, the gloom of the forests, the glitter of the reach between the murky bends, the beat of the drum regular and muffled like the beating of a heart, the heart of a conquering darkness. It was a moment of triumph for the wilderness, an invading and vengeful rush which it seemed to me I would have to keep back alone for the salvation of another soul. And the memory of what I had heard him say afar there, with the horned shapes stirring at my back in the glow of fires within the patient woods, those broken phrases came back to me, were heard again in their ominous and terrifying simplicity. * I remembered his abject pleading, his abject threats, the colossal scale of his vile desires, the meanness, the torment, the tempestuous anguish of his soul. And later on I seemed to see his collected languid manner when he said one day 'This lot of ivory now is really mine. The Company did not pay for it. I collected it myself at a very great ‡ personal risk. I am afraid they will try to claim it as theirs though. H'm. It is a difficult case. What do you think I ought to do— resist? Eh? I want no more than justice.' . . . He wanted no more than justice—no more than justice! I rang the bell before a mahogany door on the first floor and while I waited he seemed to stare at me out of the glassy panel—stare with that wide and immense stare embracing, condemning, loathing all the universe. I seemed to hear the whispered cry, 'The horror! The horror!' **

"The dusk was falling. I had to wait in a lofty drawing-room with three long windows from floor to ceiling that were like three luminous and bedraped columns. The bent gilt legs and backs of the furniture shone in indistinct curves. The tall marble fireplace had a cold and monumental whiteness. A grand piano stood massively in a corner with dark gleams on the flat surfaces like a sombre and polished sarcophagus. A high door opened—closed. I rose.

"She came forward all in black with a pale head, floating towards me

† Ms and Maga: well-kept sepulchre
* Ms and Maga: simplicity: 'I have lived— supremely! [Maga only: What do you want here?] I have been dead—and damned.' 'Let me go—I want more of it.' More of what? More blood, more heads on stakes, more adoration, rapine, and murder. I remembered, etc.
‡ Ms and Maga: at my
** Ms: cry, 'Oh! the horror!'

in the dusk. She was in mourning. It was more than a year since his
death, more than a year since the news came; she seemed as though she
would remember and mourn for ever. She took both my hands in hers
and murmured, 'I had heard you were coming.' I noticed she was not
very young—I mean not girlish. She had a mature capacity for fidelity,
for belief, for suffering. The room seemed to have grown darker as if all
the sad light of the cloudy evening had taken refuge on her forehead.
This fair hair, this pale visage, this pure brow,† seemed surrounded by
an ashy halo from which the dark eyes looked out at me. Their glance
was guileless, profound, confident, and trustful. She carried her sorrowful head as though she were proud of that sorrow, as though she would
say, I—I alone know how to mourn for him as he deserves. But while
we were still shaking hands such a look of awful desolation came upon
her face that I perceived she was one of those creatures that are not the
playthings of Time. For her he had died only yesterday. And by Jove,
the impression was so powerful that for me too he seemed to have died
only yesterday—nay, this very minute. I saw her and him in the same
instant of time—his death and her sorrow—I saw her sorrow in the very
moment of his death.* Do you understand? I saw them together—I heard
them together. She had said with a deep catch of the breath, 'I have
survived'—while my strained ears seemed to hear distinctly, mingled
with her tone of despairing regret, the summing-up whisper of his eternal condemnation.‡ I asked myself what I was doing there, with a sensation of panic in my heart as though I had blundered into a place of
cruel and absurd mysteries not fit for a human being to behold.** She
motioned me to a chair. We sat down. I laid the packet gently on the
little table and she put her hand over it. . . . 'You knew him well,' she
murmured after a moment of mourning silence.

" 'Intimacy grows quickly out there,' I said. 'I knew him as well as it
is possible for one man to know another.'

" 'And you admired him!' she said. 'It was impossible to know him
and not to admire him. Was it?'

" 'He was a remarkable man,' I said unsteadily. Then before the
appealing fixity of her gaze that seemed to watch for more words on my
lips I went on, 'It was impossible not to. . . .'

" 'Love him,' she finished eagerly, silencing me into an appalled
dumbness. 'How true! how true! But when you think that no one knew
him so well as I! I had all his noble confidence. I knew him best.'

" 'You knew him best,' I repeated. And perhaps she did. But with
every word spoken the room was growing darker and only her forehead
smooth and white remained illumined by the unextinguishable light of
belief and love.

" 'You were his friend,' she went on. 'His friend,' she repeated a little
louder. 'You must have been if he had given you this and sent you to

† Ms: pure brow, this candid brow, seemed, etc.
* Ms: death. It was too terrible.
‡ Ms: condemnation. I tell you it was terrible. I
asked, etc.
** Ms and Maga: behold. I wanted to get out. She
motioned, etc.

me! I feel I can speak to you—and oh, I must speak. I want you—you who have heard his last words—to know I have been worthy of him. . . . It is not pride. . . . Yes! I am proud to know I understood him better than any one on earth—he told me so himself. And since his mother died I have had no one—no one—to—to. . . .'

"I listened. The darkness deepened. I was not even sure whether he had given me the right bundle. I rather suspect he wanted me to take care of another batch of his papers which after his death I saw the Manager examining under the lamp. † And the girl talked, easing her pain in the certitude of my sympathy she talked, as thirsty men drank. I had heard that her engagement with Kurtz had been disapproved by her people. He wasn't rich enough or something. And indeed I don't know whether he had not been a pauper all his life. He had given me some reason to infer that it was his impatience of comparative poverty that drove him out there.

" '. . . Who was not his friend who had heard him speak once?' she was saying. 'He drew men towards him by what was best in them.' She looked at me with intensity. 'It is the gift of the great,' she went on and the sound of her low voice seemed to have the accompaniment of all the other sounds full of mystery, desolation, and sorrow I had ever heard— the ripple of the river, the soughing of the trees swayed by the wind, the murmurs of the crowds,* the faint ring of incomprehensible words cried from afar, the whisper of a voice speaking from beyond the threshold of an eternal darkness. 'But you have heard him. You know!' she cried.

" 'Yes, I know,' I said with something like despair in my heart, but bowing my head before the faith that was in her, before that great and saving illusion that shone with an unearthly glow in the darkness, in the triumphant darkness from which I could not have defended her—from which I could not even defend myself.

" 'What a loss to me—to us,' she corrected herself with beautiful generosity. Then added in a murmur, 'To the world.' By the last gleams of twilight I could see the glitter of her eyes full of tears—of tears that would not fall.

" 'I have been very happy—very fortunate—very proud,' she went on. 'Too fortunate. Too happy for a little while. And now I am unhappy for—for life.'

"She stood up. Her fair hair seemed to catch all the remaining light in a glimmer of gold. I rose too.

" 'And of all this,' she went on mournfully, 'of all his promise and of all his greatness, of his generous mind, of his noble heart nothing remains—nothing but a memory. You and I. . . .'

" 'We shall ‡ always remember him,' I said hastily.

" 'No!' she cried. 'It is impossible that all this should be lost—that

---

† Ms and Maga: lamp. But in the box I brought to his bedside there were several packages [Maga only: pretty well alike, all] tied with shoe-strings and probably he had made a mistake. And the girl, etc.

* Ms, Maga and 1902: the wild crowds; 1917: the crowds

‡ Ms: I will

such a life should be sacrificed to leave nothing—but sorrow. You know what vast plans he had. I knew of them too—I could not perhaps understand—but others knew of them. Something must remain. His words at least have not died.'

" 'His words will remain,' I said.

" 'And his example,' she whispered to herself. 'Men looked up to him—his goodness shone in every act. His example. . . .'

" 'True,' I said, 'his example too. Yes, his example. I forgot that.'

" 'But I do not. I cannot—I cannot believe—not yet. I cannot believe that I shall never see him again, that nobody will see him again, never, never, never!'

"She put out her arms, as if after a retreating figure, stretching them black and with clasped pale hands across the fading and narrow sheen of the window. Never see him! I saw him clearly enough then. I shall see this eloquent phantom as long as I live and I shall see her too, a tragic and familiar Shade resembling in this gesture another one, tragic also and bedecked with powerless charms, stretching bare brown arms over the glitter of the infernal stream, the stream of darkness. † She said suddenly very low, 'He died as he lived.'

" 'His end,' said I with dull anger stirring me, 'was in every way worthy of his life.'

" 'And I was not with him,' she murmured. My anger subsided before a feeling of infinite pity.

" 'Everything that could be done . . .' I mumbled.

" 'Ah, but I believed in him more than any one on earth—more than his own mother, more than—himself. He needed me. Me! I would have treasured every sigh, every word, every sign, every glance.'

"I felt like a chill grip on my chest. 'Don't,' I said in a muffled voice.

" 'Forgive me. I—I—have mourned so long in silence—in silence. . . . You were with him to the last? I think of his loneliness. Nobody near to understand him as I would have understood. Perhaps no one to hear. . . .'

" 'To the very end,' I said shakily. 'I heard his very last words. . . .' I stopped in a fright.

" 'Repeat them,' she murmured in a heart-broken tone. 'I want—I want—something—something—to—to live with.'

"I was on the point of crying at her, 'Don't you hear them.' The dusk was repeating them in a persistent whisper all around us, in a whisper that seemed to swell menacingly like the first whisper of a rising wind. 'The horror! The horror!' *

" 'His last word—to live with,' she insisted. 'Don't you understand I loved him—I loved him—I loved him.'

"I pulled myself together and spoke slowly.

" 'The last word he pronounced was—your name.'

"I heard a light sigh and then my heart stood still, stopped dead short

† Ms: the infernal stream that flows from the heart of darkness.
* Ms: wind. 'Oh! the horror!'

by an exulting and terrible cry, by the cry of inconceivable triumph and of unspeakable pain. 'I knew it—I was sure!' † . . . She knew. She was sure. I heard her weeping; she had hidden her face in her hands. It seemed to me that the house would collapse before I could escape, that the heavens would fall upon my head. But nothing happened. The heavens do not fall for such a trifle. Would they have fallen, I wonder, if I had rendered Kurtz that justice which was his due? Hadn't he said he wanted only justice? But I couldn't. I could not tell her. It would have been too dark—too dark altogether. . . ."

Marlow ceased and sat apart, indistinct and silent, in the pose of a meditating Buddha. Nobody moved for a time. "We have lost the first of the ebb," said the Director suddenly. I raised my head. The offing was barred by a black bank of clouds, and the tranquil waterway leading to the uttermost ends of the earth flowed sombre under an overcast sky— seemed to lead into the heart of an immense darkness.

---

† Ms: I was sure!' She knew! She was sure! It seemed to me the house would collapse, the heavens would fall upon my head. But nothing happened. The heavens do not fall for such a trifle. Would they have fallen, I wonder, if I had rendered Kurtz justice. Hadn't he said he wanted only justice? But I couldn't. I could not tell her. It would have been too dark—too dark altogether."

Marlow ceased [for canceled: he was silent. Then the following compounded predicate is added above the line] and sat in the pose of a meditating Voudha. Nobody moved for a time. "We have lost the first of the ebb," said the Director suddenly. I looked around. The offing was barred by a black bank of clouds and the tranquil waterway that leads [jor canceled: leading] to the uttermost ends of the earth flowing sombre under an overcast sky seemed to lead into the heart of an immense blackness.

Maga: like 1902 and Heinemann, except I looked around for I raised my head.

For a discussion of the ending, see Ford Madox Ford, below, p. 212.

BACKGROUNDS
AND SOURCES

A Map of the
CONGO FREE STATE
1890

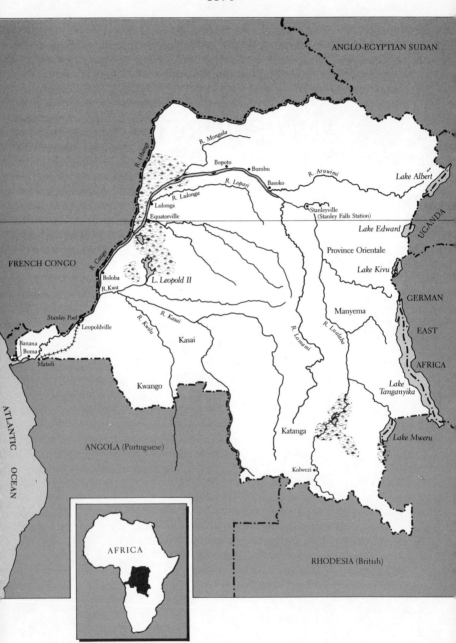

The Congo

The mission which the agents of the State have to accomplish on the Congo is a noble one. They have to continue the development of civilisation in the centre of Equatorial Africa, receiving their inspiration directly from Berlin and Brussels. Placed face to face with primitive barbarism, grappling with sanguinary customs that date back thousands of years, they are obliged to reduce these gradually. They must accustom the population to general laws, of which the most needful and the most salutary is assuredly that of work.

—KING LEOPOLD II, OF BELGIUM, 1898

Carlyle says that 'to subdue mutiny, discord, widespread despair by manfulness, justice, mercy, and wisdom, to let light on chaos, and make it instead a green flowery world, is beyond all other greatness, work for a God!' Who can doubt that God chose the King for His instrument to redeem this vast slave park. * * * King Leopold found the Congo * * * cursed by cannibalism, savagery, and despair; and he has been trying with a patience, which I can never sufficiently admire, to relieve it of its horrors, rescue it from its oppressors, and save it from perdition.

—H. M. STANLEY, 1898

The kodak has been a sore calamity to us. The most powerful enemy that has confronted us, indeed. In the early years we had no trouble in getting the press to 'expose' the tales of the mutilations as slanders, lies, inventions of busy-body American missionaries and exasperated foreigners who had found the 'open door' of the Berlin-Congo charter closed against them when they innocently went out there to trade. * * * Yes, all things went harmoniously and pleasantly in those good days, and I was looked up to as the benefactor of a down-trodden and friendless people. Then all of a sudden came the crash!

—MARK TWAIN, "King Leopold's Soliloquy," 1905

MAURICE N. HENNESSY

[The Congo Free State: A Brief History, 1876 to 1908] †

Stanley was the most remarkable explorer of them all. A Welshman by birth, he was endowed with the fiery Celtic imagination of his ances-

† From *Congo*, by Maurice N. Hennessy (London: Pall Mall Press, 1961) 13–27. Reprinted by permission.

tores. In his early years he went to America, became an American citizen and worked for the *New York Herald*. Although Stanley is best known for his African journeys, he could easily have claimed fame in another field, for he was a great journalist. He had travelled most of the known world for his newspaper and proved himself to be one of the truly remarkable reporters of his time. When, between the years 1856 and 1871, Livingstone disappeared into the African bush, the *New York Herald* sent Stanley to the Congo to find him. After searching for 236 days he succeeded. He found something else also—an entirely new career and one which was to change not only his own life by the whole course of African history.

So clamorous was the exploration and colonisation vogue that it was quite evident that trouble was just around the corner. The Portuguese (the original pioneers), the British, the Dutch and the French were particular rivals, and to such an extent that there was serious danger of open war.

Sitting back in Europe watching the whole performance was a man who was monarch of a nation itself less than fifty years old. He was Leopold II of Belgium. He was a man of inordinate ambition, and centred his designs on Africa and particularly on the Congo. Possibly he saw that, due to its geographical position, its narrow approach to the sea, and the particular mystery of its interior, the Congo basin had escaped much of the depredation of the slave trade. Probably he also realised that he stood less likelihood of opposition if he set his heart on this particular area.

In 1876 Leopold called a conference in Brussels to examine the African situation and, as he expressed it, 'to open to civilisation the only part of our globe where Christianity has not penetrated and to pierce the darkness which envelops the entire population'. Here * * * we find the exalted language that was in reverse proportion to the nobility of the real intent. As a result of this conference, an International African Association was formed; very quickly it became, to all practical purposes, the personal organisation of Leopold. The success of this move encouraged the wily king to conceive another idea. He formed the International Association of the Congo.

* * *

While Leopold was looking to his own interests, the rivalry for Africa became more intense. The saner participants realised that the prize was too great to be lost by the risk of war, and consequently, in 1884, a conference was called in Berlin by Bismarck. Its purpose was to attempt to iron out the differences between the nations with territorial ambitions in Africa and at the same time to draw up a set of rules for would-be exploiters which would prevent open conflict. Up to this point the general pattern had been for each country's exploration parties to push inland from the coast until they met each other. They were then faced with the alternatives of making a gentleman's agreement or fighting it out there and then. The latter did not appeal very much in the bush, especially as all concerned were fully occupied fighting climatic conditions and the dread diseases of the tropics. On the other hand, many of the gentleman's agreements were of short duration and were by no means the kind of pacts that were likely to stand the test of time or form a firm basis for future peace. The conference at Berlin laid down certain rules, heard and decided on the claims of such nations as France and Portugal, and at the same time produced the most high-sounding resolutions, couched, according to pattern, in language as hypocritical as it was inapt. The main safeguard against an all-out clash was a unanimously approved resolution by the signatory nations that each nation should notify the others of its plans for colonisation, and at the same time outline the territories within which it proposed to operate.

* * *

The granting of concessions to various companies was a natural sequel to the kind of rule Leopold established and to his lust for wealth. In all cases, he ensured that a large part of any profits went to himself, but in order to foster this end, an abundance of labour was a primary requirement. Consequently, quite early on a system of work as a tax medium was initiated. Each chief was authorised to collect taxes; he did so by demanding that individuals should work for a specific period of time for a minimum payment. This, of course, was another name for slavery. The so-called taxpayers were treated like prisoners; their work was carried out under the supervision of armed sentries, and, as can be easily imagined, the system lent itself to all kinds of tyranny, brutality and subsequent reprisals by the natives. In one concession alone one hundred and forty-two Africans were killed. The spirit of bitterness and hatred generated in the people was quite terrifying, but little could be done about it as there was not enough control in the area to prevent the various agents from misusing their power.

* * *

Leopold retained control of the Congo Free State until [his death in] 1908. In a statement addressed to Monsieur Beernaert, Belgian Minister of Finance, on August 5th, 1889, he made known his intention of willing the state to the Belgians. He wrote: 'I have therefore made, as Sovereign of the Independent State of the Congo, the Will that I send you. I ask you to communicate it to the Legislative Chamber at the moment which shall appear to you the most opportune.' He used the words 'most opportune' with a reason; he was about to ask for a loan of one hundred and fifty million francs and was really offering the Congo as a *quid pro quo*. The money was granted—a fact which proved that whatever else may be said, the monarch had the confidence of the Belgian people in the early days of the state just as he had of his colleagues at Berlin.

SIR HARRY JOHNSTON

[George Grenfell: A Missionary in the Congo] †

In December 1885, when the missionaries of all denominations had scarcely ceased acclaiming heartily the creation of the "Congo Free State"[1] as an alternative to the extension of Portuguese influence (the Baptists being amongst the warmest friends of King Leopold's enterprise), Grenfell wrote a note at Stanley Pool complaining that the State was already beginning to infringe the provisions of the Act of Berlin by claiming all the land as State property and refusing sites to a missionary society as well as to the Dutch Trading House.

In 1890 he writes in his diary: "Bula Matadi has become disliked amongst the people of the Upper Congo, and is called Ipanga Ngunda, which means 'Destroys the country.' In May 1890 Grenfell first complains of the action of the Congo State officials in regard to ivory, which had been made a Government monopoly, in practice, if not in theory. The representative of the State at Bumba on the northern Congo was said to fire on all canoes carrying ivory westwards, whilst he also prevented canoes going eastwards from Bopoto to purchase ivory. "The State officers having a commission on the ivory they get, they are keen about securing all they can."

On June 17, 1890 Grenfell's diary records the first hint being given as to the possibility of *Concessionnaire* companies coming into existence on the Congo. He had received the information from an American, Colonel Williams, who went up the Congo as far as the Stanley Falls, and told Grenfell on his return that an American agent at Brussels (Mr. Sanford) had been discussing with the King in 1888 the idea of creating such companies to deal with the development of the State.

JOHN HOPE FRANKLIN

Stalking George Washington Williams *

It was almost forty years ago that I had the experience, but I remember it as distinctly as if it were yesterday. In the spring of 1945 I was just beginning to work on a book that was to be called *From Slavery to Free-*

† From *George Grenfell and the Congo* (2 vols.), 1. 445–47. New York. Copyright 1910 by D. Appleton & Co. Reprinted by permission of the publisher.

Johnston (1858–1927) was a distinguished anthropologist and prolific writer on Africa.

1. It is not clear how the official title of "L'Etat Indépendant du Congo" came to be rendered "Congo Free State," this translation not being strictly correct. Stanley—the wish being father to the thought—seems to have originated the common English name, "Congo Free State." The native name is "Bula Matadi," the nickname originally given to Stanley *[Johnston's note]*.

* From *George Washington Williams: A Biography* (Chicago: The U of Chicago P, 1985) xv–xvii. Reprinted by permission.

dom: A History of Negro Americans. A good way to being, I thought, was to read the shelves in the library of North Carolina College at Durham, where I was teaching, to see what, if anything, had been written on the subject, aside from Carter G. Woodson's *The Negro in Our History*, published in 1922. To my astonishment, my eyes fell on a two-volume work, *A History of the Negro Race in America from 1619 to 1880; Negroes as Slaves, as Soldiers, and as Citizens*, by George Washington Williams. I discovered that the work had been published in 1882 by a reputable publisher, G. P. Putnam's Sons, was about one thousand pages long, and, beginning with African civilization, covered virtually every aspect of the Afro-American experience in the New World. I saw that it was carefully researched—with plenty of footnotes—logically organized, and well written. Upon examining the card catalogue I learned that Williams was the author of still another work, *A History of Negro Troops in the War of the Rebellion*, published in 1887 by Harper and Brothers.

Among the many things I later learned was that Williams was destined for a life of adventure and excitement almost from the time of his birth in 1849 in Bedford Springs, Pennsylvania. With virtually no education, he ran away from home in 1864—at fourteen years of age—and joined the Union Army. After the Civil War, during which he saw action in various battles, he went to Mexico and fought with the forces that overthrew Maximilian. Returning to the United States, he enlisted in the Tenth Cavalry, one of the four all-Negro units of the regular United States Army, from which he received a medical discharge in 1868.

Williams received a first-rate education at the Newton Theological Institution; semiliterate as an entrant, he became a polished writer and speaker within five years. At the age of twenty-five, following his graduation and marriage, he was installed as pastor of the Twelfth Baptist church in Boston. The following year, he went with his wife and young son (born in Boston earlier that year) to Washington, where he edited *The Commoner*. Soon afterward he settled in Cincinnati, pursuing a varied career as pastor; columnist for the Cincinnati *Commercial*; lawyer, after studying with President William Howard Taft's father; first black member of the state legislature; and historian of his race.

In 1890 Williams went to study conditions in the Belgian Congo under the patronage of the railroad magnate, Collis P. Huntington. After an extensive tour of the country, he wrote an *Open Letter* to King Leopold II, assailing him for his inhuman policies in the Congo. Although he had written a report to President Benjamin Harrison, at the president's request, there was little reaction in the United States to his attacks on King Leopold. Williams then went to England with his English "fiancée" (he was separated from his wife), intending to write a lengthy work on Africa. Illness overtook him, however, and he died in Blackpool at forty-one years of age.

Williams had a wide acquaintance among important personages in various parts of the world. He had at least one lengthy interview in Brus-

sels with King Leopold II. He knew Sir William Mackinnon, a British
shipping magnate, and George Grenfell, the British missionary. In the
United States he met and talked with Presidents Rutherford B. Hayes,
Grover Cleveland, and Benjamin Harrison. Senator George F. Hoar of
Massachusetts was one of his staunchest supporters. In Ohio he counted
Governor Charles Foster, Senator John Sherman, Judge Alphonso Taft,
Murat Halstead (editor of the Cincinnati *Commercial*), and Senator
Charles Fleischmann among his friends. He also had contact with such
literary figures as Henry Wadsworth Longfellow, George Bancroft, and
George Washington Cable.

He knew Frederick Douglass; Congressman John Mercer Langston;
T. Thomas Fortune, editor of the New York *Freeman*; Richard T. Gree-
ner, an early black graduate of Harvard; Robert Terrell, the first black
judge in the District of Columbia; and such leading black Bostonians as
Judge George L. Ruffin, the civic leader James M. Trotter, and Lewis
Hayden, abolitionist and legislator. It would be my good fortune to find,
from time to time, correspondence between Williams and his many
acquaintances that would greatly assist me in putting together the missing pieces of the Williams story.

GEORGE WASHINGTON WILLIAMS

A Report upon the Congo-State and Country to the President of the Republic of the United States of America †

St. Paul de Loanda,
Province of Angola, (S. W. Africa).
October 14th 1890.

To the President of the Republic of the United States of America:

I have the honor to submit herewith a Report upon the conditions of
the State of Congo, and the country and people over which it claims
jurisdiction.

During my interview with you at the Executive Mansion, Washington, D.C., Monday morning December 23d 1889, I promised to prepare for you a Memorandum of the International Law and sentimental
reasons why the Government of the Republic of the United States should
ratify the General Act of the Conference of Berlin, (1884–1885) recognizing *L'Etat Indépendant du Congo*, and assuming certain obligations
in regard to it, especially as to neutrality.

In an interview with the Honorable JOHN SHERMAN, Chairman of the

† From John Hope Franklin, *George Washington Williams: A Biography* (Chicago: U of Chicago P, 1985)
1985) 264–79. Reprinted by permission.

Senate Committee on Foreign Relations, I learned that he entertained the same views as yourself, in regard to the danger of annulling the traditions of a century, of violating the Monroe Doctrine, and of approaching the stormy circle of European politics. The Senator seemed pleased that I was going to furnish a Memorandum on "l'Acte Général de la Conférence de Berlin," and promised to suspend action on the act until I had completed my investigations. Two days later I sailed for Europe, on my way to the Congo, (Southwest-Africa).

Upon my return to Brussels, early in January, I found the atmosphere about the Palace rather cool. Officials, who formerly greeted me cordially, now avoided me, and wrapped themselves in an impenetrable reserve. It had become known that I was going to visit the Congo, and every possible influence was exerted to turn me aside from my mission. An officer of the King's Household was dispatched to me for the purpose of persuading me not to visit the Congo. He dwelt upon the deadly character of the climate during the rainy seasons, the perils and hardships of travelling by caravans, and the heavy expenses of the voyage, which would cost, he said, £400 (Dollar 2,000). I simply replied, that I was going.—After this the King sent for me, and received me very cordially. I did not care to lead up to a conversation on the Congo, and consequently I strove to turn the conversation to other topics. But I soon saw that there was but one thing about which His Majesty cared to converse, and I made up my mind to allow him to do all the talking, as far as was possible. He said that STANLEY had told him the Congo would not be worth a shilling without a railway; that it was difficult to travel in the country, and more difficult to obtain wholesome food for white men; that he hoped I would postpone my visit to the Congo for at least five years; and that all necessary information would be furnished me in *Brussels*. In reply I told His Majesty that I was going to the Congo *now*, and would start within a few days. "Then you cannot go on the State-Steamers, and must rely upon the Mission-Steamers," responded His Majesty in an impatient tone of voice. I made no reply, but simply turned the conversation to the Anti-Slavery Conference of the Powers. At a convenient moment I took my leave of His Majesty and quitted the Palace. A young nobleman of Belgium with whom I had been on terms of good fellowship, and who knew all the political gossip of the Court, told me that Mr. HENRY S. SANFORD, an American citizen, who has resided in Belgium for twenty-five or thirty years, suspected one of two things in connection with my mission to the Congo, viz: that I came as the representative of an American company to open up trade and commerce in the Congo, or that I was the agent of his enemies in America who wished to prove the falsity of his statements in reference to the fertility of the country and the volume of trade.

I crossed the Channel to England on the night of the 21st day of January 1890, and arrived in London the following morning. I purchased my African travellers-outfit at the Army and Navy Store, and on the 28th of January I left for Liverpool, from which port I sailed for the

Congo on the 30th of January, in the British and African Steam Navigation Co's steamer "Gaboon." I wrote you a brief letter from Liverpool, intimating the opposition my mission met with in Brussels.

The voyage from Liverpool to the capital of the State of Congo, (Boma) occupied fifty three days; but I was afforded abundant time and opportunity of visiting all the important ports on the West Coast of the African Continent.

Permit me, at this point, to make a statement personal to myself, but not irrelevant to this Report. I was among the very first of public men in America to espouse the cause of *l'Association Internationale du Congo*. I wrote a series of articles on African geography, during the winter of 1883–1884, in which I combated Portugal's claim to the Congo. In April 1884, I presented an argument before the Senate Committee on Foreign Relations, urging the passage of a resolution recognizing the flag of *l'Association Internationale du Congo*, as the flag of a friendly Government. The resolution passed on the 10th of April, and on the 22nd the Secretary of State, the Honorable FREDERICK J. FRELINGHUYSEN, sent an order instructing the officers of the army and navy of the Republic to salute the flag of *l'Association Internationale du Congo* as the flag of a friendly Government.

Shortly after this I went to Belgium to place before the King certain plans for the perfection of the labor-system in the Congo; and they met the approbation both of the King and HENRY M. STANLEY. On the 21st of August 1889, I published an elaborate historical paper on the Congo; and a few weeks later, at the reunion of the *Anti-Slavery Leaders* at Boston, I offered a resolution, requesting the President of the Republic of the United States to accept the invitation of the King of the Belgians to be represented in an Anti-Slavery-Conference of the Powers of Europe, to unify action upon the land and sea looking towards the abatement of the slave-trade, around and upon the African Continent. Within a few days a representative was appointed, and I sailed for Europe to do whatever I could to promote the success of this notable Conference. I remained at Brussels two months.

Thus much to prove how deeply I have been interested in the success of the Congo State, the overthrow of the African Slave-Power, and the spread of civilization. I have never entertained any other than friendly feelings towards the King of the Belgians and his African State; and my report deals only with those matters *which have come under my personal observation*, or the truth of which has been established by the testimony of competent and veracious witnesses.

The establishment of a State in the Valley of the Congo is due to His Majesty Leopold II, King of the Belgians. On the 13th and 14th days of September 1876, he convened at his Palace at Brussels, a company of distinguished African travellers who represented Germany, Austria-Hungary, France, England, Italy, Russia and Belgium. The object of this Conference was to devise the best means of opening the Congo-country to commerce and civilization. On the 20th and 21st days of

June 1877, another meeting was held at Brussels, when the Conference took definite shape, and *l'Association Internationale du Congo* was formed under the Presidency of the King of the Belgians. He employed HENRY M. STANLEY as his Chief-Agent to proceed to the Congo and secure the country as His Majesty's personal possession. MR. STANLEY was supposed to have made treaties with more than four hundred native Kings and Chiefs, by which they surrendered their rights to the soil. And yet many of these people declare that they never made a treaty with STANLEY, or any other white man; that their lands have been taken from them by force, and that they suffer the greatest wrongs at the hands of the Belgians. I have never met a chief or tribe or native, man, woman or child, from Banana, the mouth of the Congo River, to Stanley-Falls at its headwaters, who expressed any other sentiment towards the Congo State than that of hatred, deeply rooted in an abiding sense of injury, injustice and oppression. In Russia, Creta and Ireland the constituted authorities have some support from among the people; but in the Congo State there is not one solitary native who would put out his hand to aid the Congo State Government.

Although the majority of the treaties alleged to have been made by MR. STANLEY, were only witnessed by his servantboy "Dualla," they were accepted as genuine in Europe and America. Having possessed itself of a vast tract of land in the Congo, *l'Association Internationale du Congo*, of which the King of the Belgians was President and treasurer, now sought to obtain recognition in Europe. Failing to secure the countenance of a single Power, the *Association* appealed to the Republic of the United States of America. Its representative was the Hon. HENRY S. SANFORD, a citizen of the United States, who had resided in Belgium for twenty-five or thirty years. Mr. SANFORD had been many years in the diplomatic service, and was well qualified for this delicate mission. He was fortunate to find at Washington a President who was the son of a Baptist clergyman, whose fame chiefly arose from his extreme anti-slavery sentiments and work for the slave in ante-bellum days. Moreover, the Secretary of State was the son of one of the earliest and most eminent of the Presidents of the American Colonization Society. Mr. SANFORD's course was plain; he appealed to American sentiment and commercial interest; and the manner in which the flag of the *Association* was recognized, I have already described.

Germany and France now saw that it was the moment to call for a Conference of European Powers, engaged in the unseemly scramble for commerce upon the African Continent. But, after several private conferences between Germany and France, it was decided to invite the Republic of the United States of America on account of its supposed relations to Liberia; and at length the programme was so extended as to include all the Great-Powers and the Scandinavian States. The Republic of the United States received an invitation to join the Congo Conference at Berlin on the 10th of October, 1884, presented by Baron VON ALVEN-SLEBEN, Envoy Extraordinary and Minister Plenipotentiary of His Majesty the Emperor of Germany. The invitation declared that "the Governments of Germany and France are of opinion, that it would be well to form an agreement on the following principles:

1st. Freedom of commerce in the basin and the mouths of the Congo;

2nd. Application to the Congo and the Niger of the principles adopted by the Vienna Congres, with a view to sanctioning free navigation on several international rivers, which principles were afterwards applied to the Danube;

3rd. Definition of the formalities to be observed, in order that new occupations on the coast of Africa may be considered effective.

On the 17th of October Mr. FRELINGHUYSEN, Secretary of State, addressed a reply to Baron VON ALVENSLEBEN's note of invitation, and said:

"The Government of the United States views in this announcement and invitation an expression of the wish of the German Government to recognize the importance of the unimpeded traffic of the Congo Valley and the West Coast of Africa, and to secure its free enjoyment to all countries. This Government, entertaining the same views, to which it has given effect by its recognition of the flag of the *International Association of the Congo*, will have pleasure in accepting the invitation of His Imperial Majesty's Government, and will instruct the representative of the United States at Berlin to take part in the proposed Conference, on the understanding (so far as this Government is concerned) that the business to be brought before the Conference is to be limited to the three heads mentioned in your note, dealing solely with the commercial interests of the Congo region and of Western Africa, and that while taking cognizance of such establishment of limits to international territorial claims in that region as may be brought before it as matters of fact, the Conference is itself not to assume to decide such questions. The object of the Conference being simply discussion and accord, the Government of the United States, in taking part therein, reserves the right to decline to accept the conclusions of the Conference."

This then was a clear statement of the views and attitude of the Government of the Republic of the United States in regard to the proposed Conference of Berlin upon Congo and West African affairs. The Secretary of State never altered his views or positions from first to last; and he never permitted his Government to become a party to a scheme of seizing and dividing the Congo-country among certain European Powers, one of the foulest crimes of modern diplomatic history! One plenipotentiary told me that when he went to a certain European Statesman, and asked that his Government be given more territory, this Chairman of the Committee on "Distribution" exclaimed: "I have given away all the territory that is on the map!" This was not in reference to the Congo-State alone, for there is the French Congo and the Portuguese Congo as well; and the amount of territory passed upon at Berlin was 2,400,000 square miles.

The Conference met at Berlin on the 15th of November 1884, and under the Presidency of Prince BISMARCK, continued in session, excepting a few adjournments, until the 26th February 1885; and after signing the General Act, the august Conference adjourned.

L'Etat Indépendent du Congo was created and became the successor of *l'Association Internationale du Congo*. The King of the Belgians was now requested, or rather became the natural chief of the new State, as he had been of the *Association*; but there was a constitutional obstacle in the way of his Majesty assuming the legal headship of this African State. Article LXII (62) of the Belgian Constitution provides,—"The King cannot be at the same time chief of another State, without the consent of the two Chambers. Neither of the two Chambers can discuss this subject unless two-thirds at last of the members composing it be present, and the resolutions can only be passed providing it is supported by two-thirds of the votes." I translate and insert here the record of the proceeding by which LEOPOLD II became the Sovereign of the Congo State. "The Belgian Legislative Chamber, by a resolution, adopted in the Chamber of Representatives the 28th of April 1885, and in the Senate April 30th 1885, authorized His Majesty LEOPOLD II, King of the Belgians, to become the Chief of another State, in conformity with article 62 of the Belgian Constitution." The resolution is as follows: "His Majesty LEOPOLD II, King of the Belgians, is authorized to become the Chief of the State founded in Africa by *l'Association Internationale du Congo*. The union between Belgium and the new State shall remain exclusively personal."

On the 1st of August 1885, His Majesty notified the Powers that the possessions of *l'Association Internationale du Congo* would in the future constitute *l'Etat Indépendant du Congo*; that he had assumed, in accord with the *Association*, the title of "Soverain de l'État Indépendant du Congo;" that the relation between Belgium and this State was exclusively personal, and that it was to remain perpetually neutral.

On the 30th of October 1885, His Majesty, as Sovereign of the Congo State, issued a Decree creating three Departments for his new State Government, and naming three chiefs, 1st *Département of Foreign Affairs, including Justice,* with three Bureaux: *a.* Foreign Affairs, *b.* Postal and Maritime, *c.* Judicial affairs; 2nd *Département of Finance; a.* General taxes, *b.* Land Department, *c.* Pay and Auditor's Department; 3rd *Département of Interior: a.* Administration, *b.* Roads and communications, *c.* Army and Navy.

The three heads of departments constituted a council, under the Presidency of the Sovereign, who is the absolute Ruler. His councelors may recommend but can never share his authority. He makes all the laws under the title of "Decrees," and from his decisions there is no appeal. His Government is denominated as local, the European portion of the Congo-State.

In the Congo there is a Governor-General, in charge of the State, who issues such laws as he feels are necessary under the title of "*ordonances,*" but except they are reïssued as a "Decree" by the Sovereign within six months, they are *null and void*. There are an Inspector-General, Secretary-General, Procurer-General, Finance-General, Judges and Commissaires of Districts. There are postmasters, transport-officers and clerks of various kinds.

A small portion of the country, claimed by the *Independant State of Congo*, is divided into Military Districts; the rest is *dominated* by natives whose lawful possession it is. There are eleven Military Districts, viz: 1. Banana, 2. Boma, 3. Matadi, 4. Manyanga, 5. Lukunga, 6. Leopold-ville, 7. The Kassai River, 8. Bangala, 9. Basoko, 10. Lumani, 11. Stanley Falls. There are two "Military and Commercial Expeditions" on the Itimberi and Welle Rivers, and a third has just started.

Each one of these military districts is commanded by an officer of the Belgian Army, supported by other officers and non-commissioned officers. The "Commissaire of District" is of one of three classes, and needs not always be an army officer, for he deals with civil affairs only. All disputes and native *palavers* are settled by the military commander, and sometimes by the commissaire of the district, and their decision is final. When an offence has been committed against the State, the native may be fined, emprisoned or enslaved. In the Upper-Congo the State officials generally demand slaves for settling natives palavers. They promise to liberate these people after seven years service. As far as I have been able to investigate, this system of Government is unjust, capricious and absolutely cruel. There is scarcely one percent of the State officials, military and civil, who know the native language; and frequently the interpreter, an uneducated negro from Zanzibar or the East-Coast, knows little French, and puts questions indistinctly, or translates the testimony of the natives indifferently. I have seen this in the Supreme Court at Boma also. I called the attention of the Clerk of the Court to the poor French of the Interpreter, and he told me that, if that were all, it would not be so bad; but that the fellow was a *notorious liar* into the bargain! And yet upon this stammering patois hangs the bondage or liberty, the peace and property of many a native.

In addition to these military districts there are more than fifty (50) posts of from two to ten black soldiers in the Upper-Congo. They have no white commissioned officer, and act to suit their own fancy. They receive no supplies from the State, and are expected to levy tribute upon the natives. They seize fish, goats, fowls, eggs, vegetables &c. for their nourishment; and when the natives demur or refuse to be "spoiled," these black pirates burn their villages and confiscate their property. I have been an unwilling and mournfull witness to these atrocities. It is almost impossible for a traveller to buy food, [on] account [of] the ravages committed by these buccaneers of the State of Congo, who are guilty of murder, arson and robbery. Often the natives move their towns miles away rather than submit to the indignities inflicted by an unfeeling mercenary soldiery.

The entire military force of the State of Congo is less than three-thousand (3,000) men, and hundred of miles of the country is without a single soldier. In this country, destitute of a military police and semblance of constituted authority, the most revolting crimes are committed by the natives. They practice the most barbarous religious and funeral rites; they torture, murder and eat each other. Against these shocking crimes the State puts forth no effort; indeed it systematically abandons thousands of victims to the slaughter every year. Human hands and feet and limbs, smoked and dried, are offered and exposed for sale in many of the native village markets.

From the mouth of the Loumami-River to Stanley-Falls there are thirteen armed Arab camps; and in them I have seen many skulls of murdered slaves pendant from poles and over these camps floating their blood-red flag. I saw nowhere the Congo-State flag, and I know that it would be torn down if it were displayed among these ivory and slave raiders. Here the State has no authority, can redress no wrong, protect no life or property.

The tribes of the Congo are numerous and interesting people, and may be divided as follows: 1. The Mussurongo are on the Lower Congo River; 2. The Ki-Congo inhabit the Cataract Region; 3. The Ki-Têke or Batike people reside around Stanley-Pool and up as far as the mouth of the Kwa River; 4. Ki Bangi or Bobangi people extend from the mouth of the Kwa River to the mouth of the Mobangi River; 5. The Irebu (Kilolo?) or Balolo people occupy the banks of the Lulonga, Ruki and Ikelemba rivers; 6. The Lulanga, Bangala and Mekiba people speak the Bangala language; 7. The Upoto, N'Dobbe, Ebunda, Bumba and Jambinga people speak the Langa-Langa language, as far as the Itimberi River; 8. The Jalulema language is spoken as far as Basoko; 9. The Wakumu and Wakenia languages are spoken from Basoko to Stanley-Falls.

These various peoples are differentiated by their environs and occupations. In the Lower Congo, where the natives have been in contact with Europeans for centuries, felt the shock of the slave-trade and the degrading influence of rum, they are diminutive in form, obsequious, deceitful, untrustworthy, unmanly and unreliable. Their villages are the abodes of wretchedness, misery and common vice. Their huts, poorly constructed of bad material, and their uncleanness breed the most pestilential diseases, which often devastate whole communities of these hapless victims of their own filth.

Passing from the coast inland I found a slight improvement, a stronger and more active people, in the Cataract Region; and yet these pastoral people are surely falling under the destructive influence of poisonous liquor. Under the effect of this deadly liquor I found the old people looking older, and the young men weary and prematurely decaying; and villages, formerly the scenes of content and activity, at present rent by brawling disorders.

At Stanley-Pool, where the natives cannot obtain liquor I found them an industrious and prosperous people. They are fishermen and traders, and live in neat and comfortable villages. And as I continued my journey up the river, I noticed the native type improving in feature, size, complexion and even in character. Among the people around Bolobo, Bangala and Equator I beheld the most splendid types of physical manhood I had seen in any land or among any people I have travelled; I found them brave, frank and generous; but how long they will be able to keep this character if rum is once introduced among them, I cannot say. They have only been in contact with the white men for a few years, and thus far they are eager for trade, industrious and peaceable. And with practical missionary work, or industrialism, these people would soon become civilized.

From Iringi until some distance above Upoto, the natives are in a deep state of degradation. Their villages are built in circular form of grass and small bamboopoles, and their food is scanty and almost entirely vegetable. They suffer from cutaneous diseases; their eyes are jaundiced, and by constant intermarriage heartdisease is a tribal affliction. The women wear nothing but a string of beads around their loins, and the loss of life among infants is great, from lack of proper nursing and nourishment. The faces and bodies of these people are covered with the most revolting looking scars made with sharp knives. There is not one half square inch of space upon the face that is not cut and scarred; and often a piece of Ivory or Iron is passed through a hole in the upper lip or nose, and is worn as an ornament. Holes are made in the ears large enough to run an ordinary walking stick through, and large pieces of rope tied in them. The arms and breast are cut and tattooed, and around the neck and ankles are worn large brass and iron rings. These people practise human sacrifices; and I have examined the skulls of their victims in their villages, where they display them with an almost fiendish pleasure. From the mouth of the Aruwimi to the mouth of the Lumani river, there is quite a different people from those I had previously met with. They were a people without a country or a village. I called them Water-gypsies, for they live in large boats with their families. They fish and trade along the river with the natives. They are a strong, healthy and contented people, taking pleasure in their work, and with spirit to fight, when assailed by the more warlike tribes inhabiting the rivertowns.

I have noticed that wherever the African has sufficient food and labor, he presents a splendid type of man, tall, well and closely knit, muscular, agile and cheerful. He is also less cruel and superstitious.

I found a strange and striking variety of types. I have had among my carriers perfect types of the North-American Indian, the flat head, broad chin, large eyes, thin lips and wide mouth. Their hair is long, reaching below their shoulders, and which they always keep plaited in long braids. Their voice is shrill and far-reaching, and they run with the same skill and speed of the Indians, I have served against in Southwestern and Western America and Mexico.

I have come across the Japanese type, the eyes, head, face and size of body, identical with those of our eastern neighbours. I have seen tribes, destitute of every negroid characteristic, being light copper-color, with pronounced European features, a gentle and generous people.

As to the population in the Valley of the Congo, I would say it is many millions less than the figures furnished by H. M. STANLEY or the State of Congo. These figures give a population of from 49,000,000 to 51,000,000, while I give it as my honest and candid judgment that there are not more than 15,000,000 people in the entire country. I have travelled over the same route Mr. STANLEY took, and stopped at the same towns. I had the same or as good facilities for finding out the population, and with his book in my hand I endeavoured to test his figures. First of all it must be understood that the towns are numerous but thinly populated; and where he found ten thousand, (10,000) I found only 4,000 people, and so on in proportion.

Many of the towns, mentioned in his book on the Congo, have been moved away or destroyed by war or small pox epidemic. Nothing is so deceptive as estimating a population in a heathen country. The villages are often built along the river bank for miles, with small spaces between them. To see the people along the fronts of their villages creates the impression that the population is numerous; but when you begin your investigation you will find two hundred people in one village, one hundred and fifty in another, four hundred in another, and so on. In three miles of villages you may find two thousand (2,000) souls. Nothing concerning Africa is so constantly overestimated and exaggerated as its population, and I must warn lexicographers and map-makers that the population of Africa, as set down at 250,000,000, is pure and simple fiction. I do not believe it is 100,000,000, and no one will even know, until we shall be able to have a census by the European Powers occupying territory upon the African Continent, and then it will only be approximate. From Banana to Boma the Congo-country is composed of Islands, available for rice, coffee, and grazing; and from Boma to Matadi it is absolutely sterile. From Matadi to Leopoldville—the Cataract Region—there is but little good soil, and the vegetable life is small and precarious. Around Stanley-Pool there is some fertile land and it is cultivated by the natives to some extent. From the Pool through the Channel,—as I have decided to call it,—three days steaming, the country is perfectly barren. From the mouth of the Pool to the mouth of the Kassaï River the banks are steep and of white clay, and the channel narrow, through which rushes a current at 4 knots an hour. At the mouth of the Kassaï the high bluffs give way to low lands, fertile, open, green, wide and beautiful. At Bolobo and Lokolela, tobacco, beans, corn-manoic, &c. are raised in large quantities. On the Equator and at Bangala, nearly every vegetable found in Europe can be grown. The country continues fairly good until the Lumani river, and from thence to the seventh cataract (Stanley-Falls) it is poor. The Congo-country has been overestimated and its fertility exaggerated by the advertising agents of persons who wished to promote financial schemes. The commerce of the Congo has always been misrepresented. There are only two articles exported from the Upper-Congo, Ivory and Rubber, and these only in small quantities. I have no doubt but that many other valuable products of the country could be exported, and would find a ready market; but the native must be taught,—and he is a very conservative individual—to bring other things to the white trader. And if it require labor to put the new products before the trader, it will be a long time before it will be forth-coming.

There are five houses of the Dutch Trading Company between Stanley-Pool and Stanley-Falls; the Belgians have five; the French three. All the goods and supplies for trading purposes, which these Companies use, are carried from Matadi and Loango, two hundred and seventy and three hundred miles respectively, on the heads of natives. While it is true that the native does not care to work, that custom has made the African woman the producer while the man is the consumer, it should not be forgotten that within ten years or more seventy five thousand (75,000) blacks are engaged in the transport-system. This is one of the brightest and most significant pages in African history, and deserves our admiration and praise. These men make from three to four trips a year, 810 to 1,080 miles, and carry from 65 to 80 pounds burden. They are faithful and reliable, and without their service no trade could be conducted upon the Upper-Congo; neither missionary nor trader could exist. But while the transport system is admirable and adequate, it is also costly. Every load costs from £1 to £1.10. from Matadi to the Pool, and from Loango to Brazzaville. The carriers take up to the Pool bales of cloth, salt, powder, brass rods, beads, and canned food for the European traders and missionaries. They carry back to the Coast ivory and rubber. The transport is the great burden to commerce and missions at present, for it costs from ten to fifteen percent of the cost-price of goods to get them from the Coast to the Upper-Congo River. After all that is said about the fertility of African soil there is very little at present that an European can rely upon as food. He must import lard, butter, sardines, ham, sausages, corned-beef, tea, coffee, sugar, condensed milk, pickles, peaches, pears, strawberries, salt, pepper, crackers, flour, cheese, rice, macaroni, tapioca, spices &c. Flour, rice and sugar are heavy articles, and cost the consumer dearly. In fact all the articles I have enumerated have to be packed securely and are consequently bulky.

Last year the State of Congo sent 35,000 loads from Matadi to Leopoldville across the Cataract Region. It is hoped that the Congo-railway will remedy the difficulties of the transport-system; but this road is not yet built, nor will it be for some eight years to come. Even when completed it will not pay for years, until the native brings into the market some thing else besides Ivory and Rubber.

There must be organized industrialism by which cotton, rice, sugar, tobacco, coffee &c. can be cultivated for export.

In addition to the burdens of the transport system, the Congo-State has unwisely imposed burdensome taxes and duties upon the produce exported from the Congo. The duty on ivory of every quality is 2,000 francs = £80 per ton, enough to destroy the trade, and drive the trading companies into bankruptcy. The fact is, *the State of Congo is engaged in trade*, and while it taxes other traders exempts itself from all financial burdens, in direct violation of the provisions of the General-Act of the Conference of Berlin.

Timber is taxed to such an extent that a missionary cannot cut a stick three feet long without securing written permission, and even then a tax must be paid. The State steadfastly refuses to give a clear title to land; and every trader and missionary may be ousted by the railway company under the law of expropriation. Every servant, carrier and laborer, of whatsoever description, is taxed, and thus the State represses the spirit of progress and retards the development of the country. It is in a state of chronic controversy with the traders, and the most unfriendly relations subsist between them. No one has a voice in the Government. A carefully organized system of import-taxes has been established and goes into effect in Oct. 1890. Nothing in the history of political economy and tariff-legislation can equal these laws for their inequality, injustice and repressive character.

The State recruits its soldiers and employs its laborers on the East and West-coast of Africa; to transport them from the former coast costs £10 = $50 per capita, and to bring them from the latter coast costs £1 to £1.10/- = $5 to $7.

The soldiers serve three years, the workmen one year; and the loss by desertion, sickness, death and reshipment is about £12,000 = $60,000 per annum. The natives of the Congo serve in the transport corps because there are no Belgians to cruelly treat them; but they will not enter the service of the State. Kindness, firmness and justice to the natives would soon secure a large and reliable native labor force. But violence and injustice drive these poor children of nature away from the white man. Emigration cannot be invited to the Congo for a quarter of a century, and then only educated blacks from the Southern United States, who have health, courage, morals and means. They must come only in small companies, not as laborers, but as landed proprietors. One hundred families in ten years would be quite enough and not for twenty five years yet. *White labor can never hope to get a foot-hold here.*

The climate is too severe for northern people. There are the dry and the rainy season in the Lower-Congo, but above the Equator there is no dry, no rainy season; it rains at intervals all the time. I rather enjoyed the climate of the Equator more than the West-Africa climate. The climate above the Lumani and at Stanley-Falls is the severest I experienced. I have recorded a change of thirty degrees in the mercury of my thermometre at Stanley-Falls in one day of sixteen hours; and I have noted frequent changes of fifteen degrees. The rains fall frequently and the mists from the Falls are very heavy morning and evening. I found the five white men residing there either sick or convalescent.

Although the State of Congo promised the Powers of Europe to use all its abilities to suppress the slave-trade, the traffic goes on beneath its flag and upon its territory. At Stanley-Falls slaves were offered to me in broad day-light; and at night I discovered canoe loads of slaves, bound strongly together. When I complained of this I was told by the "Resident" of the Congo-State that he had no power to prevent it, which is quite true, for he had a garrison of thirty men of whom only seventeen were effectives.

But the State not only suffers the trade in slaves to continue, *it buys the slaves of natives*, and pays to its miilitary officers £3 per capita for every able-bodied slave he procures. Every military post in the Upper-Congo thus becomes a slave-market; the native is encouraged to sell slaves by the State, which is always ready to buy them. This buying of slaves is called "redemption," and it is said that after seven years the slave may have his liberty. But it is my opinion that these hapless creatures are the perpetual slaves of the State of Congo.

After thirteen years of occupation by the International Association and State of Congo, no map has been made of the Upper-Congo River; no school has been erected; no hospital founded and nothing contributed to science or geography. At first the Government was international in character, but of late years it has degenerated into a narrow Belgian Colony, *with a determined purpose to drive all other nations out of the Congo that are now represented by trade.* In a letter of instructions to the representative of the Government of the Republic of the United States at Berlin, the Secretary of State wrote on the 17th of October 1884: "As far as the administration of the Congo-Valley is concerned, this Government has shown its preference for a neutral control, such as is promised by the Free-States of the Congo, the nucleus of which has been already created through the organized efforts of the International Association. Whether the approaching Conference can give further shape and scope to this project of creating a great State in the heart of Western Africa, whose organization and administration shall afford a guarantee that it is to be held for all time, as it were, in trust for the benefit of all peoples, remains to be seen."

This singularly lucid statement carries with it a prophetic influence, and I clearly see how the promises and pledges of the Association and State have been violated. It would be vain to endeavour to hide the fact that the Congo-State is a Belgian colony as much as the Cape of Good Hope is an English Colony. The difference is that every body knew when England went to the Cape she intended to build a colony that should wear the British colonial stamp. Belgians invited the world to enjoy free-trade in the Congo, and now, after Englishmen, Frenchmen, Portuguese and Dutch have invested thousands of pounds in the venture, *they are to be taxed to death* by a purely Belgian Colonial Government. The mask is cast off and every provision of the General Act of the Conference of Berlin has been violated; and the written and sealed pledge made to the Government of the Republic of the United States, that no import- or export-duties would be levied, has long since been torn up and given to the winds. Please see Senate Executive Document No. 196, p.p. 348 and 355–357.

There is one ray of hope for the Congo, and that is in the character of the Christian Missions.

No foreign missionary field was ever so quickly occupied by Christian workers as the Congo. The American Baptist Missionary Union has eight stations, the English Baptists seven, and the Congo Bololo Mission three; Catholic missions three, one just abandoned, which made four, three Bishop-Taylor-missions, one "faithcure," "Simpson mission," two Swedish missions, twenty-seven (27) in all. Some of them are eminently useful, and several of them are conspicuously helpless. The missionaries have great influence with the natives, and they go and come among the fiercest cannibalistic tribes without fear of being molested. Whenever the friends at home, who support and regulate these missions, will add an industrial feature to each one of them, their efficiency will be increased tenfold.

My travels extended from the mouth of the Congo at Banana, where it empties into the South Atlantic, to its headwaters at the Seventh Cataract, at Stanley-Falls; and from Brazzaville, on Stanley-Pool, to the South Atlantic Ocean at Loango, I passed through the French-Congo, via Comba, Bouenza and Loudima. In four months, or in one hundred and twenty five days I travelled 3,266 miles, passing from Southwestern Africa to East Central Africa, and back to the sea. I camped in the bushes seventy-six times, and on other occasions received hospitality of traders, missionaries and natives. Of my eighty-five natives I lost not a life, although we sometimes suffered from fatigue, hunger and heat.

Although America has no commercial interests in the Congo it was the Government of the Republic of the United States which introduced this African Government into the sisterhood of States. It was the American Republic which stood sponsor to this young State, which has disappointed the most glowing hopes of its most ardent friends and most zealous promoters. Whatever the Government of the Republic of the United States did for the Independent State of Congo, was inspired and guided by noble and unselfish motives. And whatever it refrains from doing, will be on account of its elevated sentiments of humanity, and its sense of the sacredness of agreements and compacts, in their letter and spirit. The people of the United States of America have a just right to know *the truth*, the *whole truth* and *nothing but the truth*, respecting the Independant State of Congo, an absolute monarchy, an oppressive and cruel Government, an exclusive Belgian colony, now tottering to its fall. I indulge the hope that when a new Government shall rise upon the ruins of the old, it will be simple, not complicated; local, not European; international, not national; just, not cruel; and casting its shield alike over black and white, trader and missionary, endure for centuries.

AN IVORY CARAVAN

Le Congo Illustré 2 (1893) 43.

Reversing the direction of Conrad's (and Marlow's) first overland route (see "The Congo Diary," p. 159), this caravan is about to take, mainly, ivory from Stanley Pool (the Central Station) to Matadi (the Lower Station). Note the "Pilgrim" with his stave.

STANLEY FALLS

Johnston, Sir Harry. *George Grenfell and the Congo* (2 vols.) London: Hutchinson, 1908. I. 306. Photo by William Forfeitt.

Stanley Falls (Kurtz's Inner Station) is the culmination of the longest uninterrupted river journey possible up the Congo. This is the uppermost point reached by George Washington Williams and by Conrad (see p. 102 and p. 186).

JOHN HOPE FRANKLIN

[Williams's "Open Letter" to Leopold and the "Railway Report"] †

For a man of Williams's limited experience, delicate health, and uncertain financial support, a venture far into the African interior in 1890 was no mean undertaking. Yet on May 15 of that year, with a caravan of eighty-five men, this forty-year-old American set out to see all that he could by water as well as by land. Williams already knew a good deal about Henry M. Stanley, the intrepid explorer-journalist who had "found" Dr. David Livingstone in 1871. It was clear that Williams was attempting to second-guess Stanley regarding the railway; and he seemed to be vying with him in matters of exploration. Others also were taking a hard look at the Congo in 1890. If Williams did not meet them, he doubtless heard of them, and the mutual interests of these investigators gave his own mission added significance. Roger Casement, the British Foreign Service officer whose celebrated *Report* on the Congo more than a decade later would profoundly affect attitudes toward the Congo, was already an observer in 1890. Joseph Conrad, who would steadfastly resist numerous efforts to involve him in Congo reform, based his *Heart of Darkness* on his own experiences there in 1890. Even as he began his own journeys of exploration, Williams knew there was a major book to be written on what he found in the Congo.

Where possible, Williams used the Congo River mission and commercial steamers. The *Holland* seems to have been the one most frequently used. Since there were five Dutch Trading Company stations between Stanley Pool and Stanley Falls (Kisangani), and Williams depended on the Dutch for his mail as well as supplies, those houses proved to be good bases. The regular route of travel seemed to be the river, with regular excursions into the countryside. It was during such forays that Williams experienced the greatest difficulties. For two weeks, he wrote, "I had traveled through a country absolutely desititute of food. The courage of my men began to abate and it looked on several occasions, as if I would be compelled to execute one or two subordinate fellows who were endeavoring to bring on a mutiny. But with firmness and heroic suffering without a murmur I triumphed."

Williams's descriptions of the countryside were equally dramatic. "Sometimes I was crossing plains, which stretched days before me, as level as our own prairies, again I struggled for four days through the dense, dark and damp forest of Muyambu, where it rains every month of the year." He was fortunate when he encountered friendly people who offered him food and shelter if he "would honor them by remaining over night with them." Others, however, were hostile, denying him food and

† From *George Washington Williams: A Biography* (Chicago: The U of Chicago P, 1985), 192–95. Reprinted by permission.

warning him to move on. "But I never consented to go," he wrote. "I knew too well the virtue of my modern fire-arms; and I usually gave them to understand that I wanted food for my people and would pay for it, and if it were not forthcoming within one hour I would come and take it. Hungry men are usually heroes for the hour, and I always got food when there was any to be had. Brass-rods, three kinds of goods, knives and powder were the articles with which I bought food. . . . I am glad to say that I did not lose one of my 85 men, although several were sick. I think two may have died since we reached the coast, but after leaving my service."[1]

* * *

An important source of assistance and hospitality during the journey was the missions, which Williams visited regularly. There he secured not only important data regarding the treatment of the Africans by the Europeans but the kind of food and shelter that were quite rare on the Congo River and in the interior. One such mission was maintained at Bolobo by the Baptist Missionary Society of London, under the leadership of the Reverend George Grenfell. In June, Williams visited the mission and talked at length with Grenfell. Of the various reasons for Williams's being in the Congo, Grenfell thought an unannounced one the most important: "to hunt up reasons against the expatriation (or repatriotism is it?) of Negroes from the United States."[2] Apparently Grenfell thought no more of the idea than Williams, although to combat it was by no means Williams's major purpose in visiting Africa.

By the time Williams reached Bolobo, his largely negative impressions of the Congo were already formed. He did not hesitate to tell the missionaries there what he thought. "Lots of talk," Grenfell wrote in his diary. "Pessimistic mainly as regards the Congo." "I fancy he is not at all favorably disposed towards the [Congo] State, and may possibly paint things pretty black," he wrote his colleagues in London. For obvious reasons, Grenfell was hesitant about speaking out against the king of the Belgians. To London, however, he could comment on those dismaying things that Williams had an opportunity to see. "I wonder what he would say if he saw, as we did, nine slaves chained neck to neck in the State Station at Upoto and waiting for a steamer to carry them down to Bangala. . . . Or what would the Colonel say if he met, as we did, a big canoe with a State employee on board and were told they were out trying to buy slaves. . . . The evolving of a great free people out of the present chaos I fear will be a bitter process under the present administration, but even the best of governments and the wisest of administrations would need strong hands, and would often have to hit very hard."[3]

It was from Williams that Grenfell learned of the possibility of *conces-*

1. GWW to Robert H. Terrell, St. Paul de Loanda, Angola, October 14, 1890, Terrell Papers.
2. George Grenfell to A. H. Baynes, Bolobo, Congo State, June 23, 1890, Baptist Missionary Society Papers, London.
3. George Grenfell, Diary, March 2, 1889 to

August 1, 1890; George Grenfell to A. H. Baynes, Bolobo, Congo State, June 23, 1890; both in Baptist Missionary Society Papers. On the reluctance of Grenfell to criticize Leopold, see Sir Harry Johnston, *George Grenfell and the Congo*, 2 vols. (London, 1908), vol. 1, pp. 467–68.

sionnaire companies coming into existence in the Congo, where they would enjoy extensive privileges "in the development of the State."[4] Not all these companies would be Belgian; some might be German or from other countries. Williams was convinced that Henry Sanford had placed the idea of *concessionnaire* companies before the king as early as 1888. Grenfell was greatly disturbed by this information, not only because such companies were, he thought, in clear violation of the Act of Berlin proclaiming the Congo Free State, but also because they would subvert the independence of the State. Surely, he said, the Free State "has a firmer foundation than all this would seem to suggest." In any case, Grenfell confessed sadly, his circumstances were such that he did not "feel called upon to publicly question the action of the State."[5] News such as Williams brought would always make him a welcome guest at Bolobo.

Two months after Williams began his trip into the interior, he reached Stanley Falls. His observations along the way had to do with the climate, soil, topography, flora and fauna, and the people. From Stanley Pool to the mouth of the Kasai River, a distance of some one hundred miles, the banks were steep and of white clay, and the channel was narrow. From that point, the steep banks gave way to low lands, "fertile, open, green, wide and beautiful." This was the equatorial area, in which nearly every vegetable known in Europe could be grown. The country continued "fairly good" beyond the great bend of the river until the Lomani River. From there to the headwaters at Stanley Falls, a distance of about eighty-five miles, the land was poor. It was in this region that Williams found the climate most severe. At Stanley Falls he recorded a change of thirty degrees in a period of sixteen hours. It was, he concluded, much "too severe" for northern people. He encountered many human types in his journey to Stanley Falls, ranging from the industrious and prosperous tribes near Stanley Pool to those "in a deep state of degradation" from Iringi to Upoto. There were also great variations in size and appearance, from the "perfect types of the North-American Indian" among his carriers, to the water gypsies near the Lomani River, to the tall, dark, agile types around Bangala and the Equator.[6] Although not always pleased with what he saw, he felt he had seen enough to have a fairly clear notion of Africa.

Williams was of the opinion that the population of the Congo Free State was relatively sparse. Stanley had estimated it at somewhere between forty-nine and fifty million. This was a gross exaggeration, thought Williams, who judged it no more than fifteen million. "I have travelled over the same route Mr. STANLEY took, and stopped at the same towns. I had the same or as good facilities for finding out the population, and with his book in my hand I endeavoured to test his figures. First of all, it must be understood that the towns are numerous but thinly populated; and where he found ten thousand . . . I found only 4,000 people, and so on

4. Johnston, *Grenfell*, vol. 1, p. 445. [See p. 82, above—*Editor*.]
5. George Grenfell to A. H. Baynes (see note 2 above).
6. GWW *Report upon the Congo State*, pp. 11–13, 16–17, 20.

in proportion."[7] This was just one of the many areas in which Williams would disagree with Stanley's findings.

Despite the unfavorable climate, Williams remained at Stanley Falls for several days to rest, ruminate, and write. It was there that he wrote *An Open Letter to His Serene Majesty Leopold II* and *A Report on the Proposed Congo Railway* (reprinted below * * *). He also wrote Huntington, breaking the news to him that he had been disappointed with the "deceit, obtusiveness, ignorance and cruelty of the State of the Congo."[8]

The day he completed the railway report, he began the return journey. At Bolobo he disembarked from the *Holland* for another visit with Grenfell.[9] Proceeding to Stanley Pool from Bolobo, Williams took a new route to the sea through the French Congo.

GEORGE WASHINGTON WILLIAMS

An Open Letter to His Serene Majesty Leopold II, King of the Belgians and Sovereign of the Independent State of Congo †

Good and Great Friend,

I have the honour to submit for your Majesty's consideration some reflections respecting the Independant State of Congo, based upon a careful study and inspection of the country and character of the personal Government you have established upon the African Continent.

In order that you may know the truth, the whole truth, and nothing but the truth, I implore your most gracious permission to address you without restraint, and with the frankness of a man who feels that he has a duty to perform to *History, Humanity, Civilization* and to the *Supreme Being,* who is himself the "King of Kings."

Your Majesty will testify to my affection for your person and friendship for your African State, of which you have had ample practical proofs for nearly six years. My friendship and service for the State of Congo were inspired by and based upon your publicly declared motives and aims, and your personal statement to your humble subscriber:—humane sentiments and work of Christian civilization for Africa. Thus I was led to regard your enterprise as the rising of the Star of Hope for the Dark Continent, so long the habitation of cruelties; and I journeyed in its light and laboured in its hope. All the praisefull things I have spoken and

7. Ibid., p. 16. For Stanley's discussion of the population figures and other demographic features of the Congo basin, see Henry M. Stanley, *The Congo and the Founding of Its Free State,* 2 vols. (New York, 1885), vol. 2, chap. 37, esp. p. 364.
8. GWW to Collis P. Huntington, Stanley Falls,

Central Africa, July 16, 1890, Huntington Papers.
9. Grenfell Diary, July 29, 1890, Baptist Missionary Society papers.
† From John Hope Franklin, *George Washington Williams: A Biography* (Chicago: The U of Chicago P, 1985) 243–54. Reprinted by permission.

written of the Congo country, State and Sovereign, was inspired by the firm belief that your Government was built upon the enduring foundation of *Truth, Liberty, Humanity* and *Justice*.

It afforded me great pleasure to avail myself of the opportunity afforded me last year, of visiting your State in Africa; and how thoroughly I have been disenchanted, disappointed and disheartened, it is now my painfull duty to make known to your Majesty in plain but respectful language. Every charge which I am about to bring against your Majesty's personal Government in the Congo has been carefully investigated; a list of competent and veracious witnesses, documents, letters, official records and data has been faithfully prepared, which will be deposited with Her Britannic Majesty's Secretary of State for Foreign Affairs, until such time as an International Commission can be created with power to send for persons and papers, to administer oaths, and attest the truth or falsity of these charges.

I crave your Majesty's indulgence while I make a few preliminary remarks before entering upon the specifications and charges.

Your Majesty's title to the territory of the State of Congo is badly clouded, while many of the treaties made with the natives by the "Association Internationale du Congo," of which you were Director and Banker, were tainted by frauds of the grossest character. The world may not be surprised to learn that your flag floats over territory to which your Majesty has no legal or just claim, since other European Powers have doubtful claims to the territory which they occupy upon the African Continent; but all honest people will be shocked to know by what grovelling means this fraud was consummated.

There were instances in which Mr. HENRY M. STANLEY sent one white man, with four or five Zanzibar soldiers, to make treaties with native chiefs. The staple argument was that the white man's heart had grown sick of the wars and rumours of war between one chief and another, between one village and another; that the white man was at peace with his black brother, and desired to "confederate all African tribes" for the general defense and public welfare. All the sleight-of-hand tricks had been carefully rehearsed, and he was now ready for his work. A number of electric batteries had been purchased in London, and when attached to the arm under the coat, communicated with a band of ribbon which passed over the palm of the white brother's hand, and when he gave the black brother a cordial grasp of the hand the black brother was greatly surprised to find his white brother so strong, that he nearly knocked him off his feet in giving him the hand of fellowship. When the native inquired about the disparity of strength between himself and his white brother, he was told that the white man could pull up trees and perform the most prodigious feats of strength. Next came the lens act. The white brother took from his pocket a cigar, carelessly bit off the end, held up his glass to the sun and complaisantly smoked his cigar to the great amazement and terror of his black brother. The white man explained his intimate relation to the sun, and declared that if he were to request him to burn up his black brother's village it would be done. The third act was the gun trick. The white man took a percussion cap gun, tore the end of the paper which held the powder to the bullet, and poured the powder and paper into the gun, at the same time slipping the bullet into the sleeve of the left arm. A cap was placed upon the nipple of the gun, and the black brother was implored to step off ten yards and shoot at his white brother to demonstrate his statements that he was a spirit, and, therefore, could not be killed. After much begging the black brother aims the gun at his white brother, pulls the trigger, the gun is discharged, the white man stoops . . . and takes the bullet from his shoe!

By such means as these, too silly and disgusting to mention, and a few boxes of gin, whole villages have been signed away to your Majesty.

In your personal letter to the President of the Republic of the United States of America, bearing date of August 1st, 1885, you said that the possessions of the International Association of the Congo will hereafter form the Independent State of the Congo. "I have at the same time the honour to inform you and the Government of the Republic of the United States of America that, authorised by the Belgian Legislative Chambers to become the Chief of the new State, I have taken, in accord with the Association, the title of Sovereign of the Independent State of Congo." Thus you assumed the headship of the State of Congo, and at once organised a personal Government. You have named its officers, created its laws, furnished its finances, and every act of the Government has been clothed with the majesty of your authority.

On the 25th of February 1884, a gentleman, who has sustained an intimate relation to your Majesty for many years, and who then wrote as expressing your sentiments, addressed a letter to the United States in which the following language occurs:—"It may be safely asserted that no barbarous people have ever so readily adopted the fostering care of benevolent enterprise, as have the tribes of the Congo, and never was there a more honest and practical effort made to increase their knowledge and secure their welfare." The letter, from which the above is an excerpt, was written for the purpose of securing the friendly action of the Committee on Foreign Relations, which had under consideration a Senate Resolution in which the United States recognized the flag of the "Association Internationale du Congo" as the flag of a friendly Government. The letter was influential, because it was supposed to contain the truth respecting the natives, and the programme, not only of the Association, but of the new State, its legitimate successor, and of your Majesty.

When I arrived in the Congo, I naturally sought for the results of the brilliant programme:—"*fostering care*," "*benevolent enterprise*," an "*honest and practical effort*" to increase the knowledge of the natives "*and secure their welfare.*" I had never been able to conceive of Europeans, establishing a government in a tropical country, without building a hospital; and yet from the mouth of the Congo River to its head-waters, here at the seventh cataract, a distance of 1,448 miles, there is not a solitary hospital for Europeans, and only three sheds for sick Africans in the service of the State, not fit to be occupied by a horse. Sick sailors frequently die on board their vessels at Banana Point; and if it were not for the humanity of the Dutch Trading Company at that place—who have often opened their private hospital to the sick of other countries—many more might die. There is not a single chaplain in the employ of your Majesty's Government to console the sick or bury the dead. Your white men sicken and die in their quarters or on the caravan road, and seldom have christian burial. With few exceptions, the surgeons of your Majesty's government have been gentlemen of professional ability, devoted to duty, but usually left with few medical stores and no quarters in which to treat their patients. The African soldiers and labourers of your Majesty's Government fare worse than the whites, because they have poorer quarters, quite as bad as those of the natives; and in the sheds, called hospitals, they languish upon a bed of bamboo poles without blankets, pillows or any food different from that served to them when well, rice and fish.

I was anxious to see to what extent the natives had "*adopted the fostering care*" of your Majesty's "benevolent enterprise" (?), and I was doomed to bitter disappointment. Instead of the natives of the Congo "adopting the fostering care" of your Majesty's Government, they everywhere complain that their land has been taken from them by force; that the Government is cruel and arbitrary, and declare that they neither love nor respect the Government and its flag. Your Majesty's Government has sequestered their land, burned their towns, stolen their property, enslaved their women and children, and committed other crimes too numerous to mention in detail. It is natural that they everywhere shrink from "*the fostering care*" your Majesty's Government so eagerly proffers them.

There has been, to my absolute knowledge, no "*honest and practical effort made to increase their knowledge and secure their welfare.*" Your Majesty's Government has never spent one franc for educational purposes, nor instituted any practical system of industrialism. Indeed the most unpractical measures have been adopted *against* the natives in nearly every respect; and in the capital of your Majesty's Government at Boma there is not a native employed. The labour system is radically unpractical; the soldiers and labourers of your Majesty's Government are very largely imported from Zanzibar at a cost of £10 *per capita*, and from Sierre Leone, Liberia, Accra and Lagos at from £1 to £1/10.-*per capita*. These recruits are transported under circumstances more cruel than cattle in European countries. They eat their rice twice a day by the use of their fingers; they often thirst for water when the season is dry; they are exposed to the heat and rain, and sleep upon the damp and filthy decks of the vessels often so closely crowded as to lie in human ordure. And, of course, many die.

Upon the arrival of the survivors in the Congo they are set to work as labourers at one shilling a day; as soldiers they are promised sixteen shillings per month, in English money, but are usually paid off in cheap handkerchiefs and poisonous gin. The cruel and unjust treatment to which these people are subjected breaks the spirits of many of them, makes them distrust and despise your Majesty's Government. They are enemies, not patriots.

There are from sixty to seventy officers of the Belgian army in the service of your Majesty's Government in the Congo of whom only about thirty are at their post; the other half are in Belgium on furlough. These officers draw double pay,—as soldiers and as civilians. It is not my duty to criticise the unlawful and unconstitutional use of these officers coming into the service of this African State. Such criticism will come with more grace from some Belgian statesman, who may remember that there is no constitutional or organic relation subsisting between his Government and the purely personal and absolute monarchy your Majesty has established in Africa. But I take the liberty to say that many of these officers are too young and inexperienced to be entrusted with the difficult work of dealing with native races. They are ignorant of native character, lack wisdom, justice, fortitude and patience. They have estranged the natives from your Majesty's Government, have sown the seed of discord between tribes and villages, and some of them have stained the uniform of the Belgian officer with murder, arson and robbery. Other officers have served the State faithfully, and deserve well of their Royal Master.

Of the unwise, complicated and stupid dual Government of the State of Congo I cannot say much in this letter, reserving space for a careful examination of it in another place. I may say that the usefullness of many a Congo official is neutralised by having to keep a useless set of books. For example: an officer is in command of a station and he wishes to buy two eggs. He makes this entry in a ruled and printed book: "For nourishment bought two eggs for two Ntaka." In another book he must make this entry: "Two Ntaka gone out of the store." And in another book he must enter this purchase *seven times!* Comment upon such supreme folly is unnecessary. We need only feel compassion for the mental condition of the man in Brussels who invented this system, and deep sympathy with its victims in the Congo.

From these general observations I wish now to pass to specific charges against your Majesty's Government.

FIRST.—Your Majesty's Government is deficient in the moral, military and financial strength, necessary to govern a territory of 1,508,000 square miles, 7,251 miles of navigation, and 31,694 square miles of lake surface. In the Lower Congo River there is but one post, in the cataract region one. From Leopoldville to N'Gombe, a distance of more than 300 miles, there is not a single soldier or civilian. Not one out of every twenty State-officials know the language of the natives, although they are constantly issuing laws, difficult even for Europeans, and expect the natives to comprehend and obey them. Cruelties of the most astounding character are practised by the natives, such as burying slaves alive in the grave of a dead chief, cutting off the heads of captured warriors in native combats, and no effort is put forth by your Majesty's Government to prevent them. Between 800 and 1,000 slaves are sold to be eaten by the natives of the Congo State annually; and slave raids, accomplished by the most cruel and murderous agencies, are carried on within the territorial limits of your Majesty's Government which is impotent. There are only 2,300 soldiers in the Congo.

SECOND.—Your Majesty's Government has established nearly fifty posts, consisting of from two to eight mercenary slave-soldiers from the East Coast. There is no white commissioned officer at these posts; they are in charge of the black Zanzibar soldiers, and the State expects them not only to sustain themselves, but to raid enough to feed the garrisons where the white men are stationed. These piratical, buccaneering posts compel the natives to furnish them with fish, goats, fowls, and vegetables at the mouths of their muskets; and whenever the natives refuse to feed these vampires, they report to the main station and white officers come with an expeditionary force and burn away the homes of the natives. These black soldiers, many of whom are slaves, exercise the power of life and death. They are ignorant and cruel, *because* they do not comprehend the natives; they are imposed upon them by the State. They make no report as to the number of robberies they commit, or the number of lives they take; they are only required to subsist upon the natives and thus relieve your Majesty's Government of the cost of feeding them. They are the greatest curse the country suffers now.

THIRD.—Your Majesty's Government is guilty of violating its contracts made with its soldiers, mechanics and workmen, many of whom are subjects of other Governments. Their letters never reach home.

FOURTH.—The Courts of your Majesty's Government are abortive, unjust, partial and delinquent. I have personally witnessed and examined their clumsy operations. The laws printed and circulated in Europe "for the protection of the blacks" in the Congo, are a dead letter and a fraud. I have heard an officer of the Belgian Army pleading the cause of a white man of low degree who had been guilty of beating and stabbing a black man, and urging race distinctions and prejudices as good and sufficient reasons why his client should be adjudged innocent. I know of prisoners remaining in custody for six and ten months because they were not judged. I saw the white servant of the Governor-General, CAMILLE JANSSEN, detected in stealing a bottle of wine from a hotel table. A few hours later the Procurer-General searched his room and found many more stolen bottles of wine and other things, not the property of servants. No one can be prosecuted in the State of Congo without an order of the Governor-General, and as he refused to allow his servant to be arrested, nothing could be done. The black servants in the hotel, where the wine had been stolen, had been often accused and beaten for these thefts, and now they were glad to be vindicated. But to the surprise of every honest man, the thief was sheltered by the Governor-General of your Majesty's Government.

FIFTH.—Your Majesty's Government is excessively cruel to its prisoners, condemning them, for the slightest offences, to the chain gang, the like of which cannot be seen in any other Government in the civilised or uncivilised world. Often these ox-chains eat into the necks of the prisoners and produce sores about which the flies circle, aggravating the running wound; so the prisoner is constantly worried. These poor creatures are frequently beaten with a dried piece of hippopotamus skin, called a "chicote," and usually the blood flows at every stroke when well laid on. But the cruelties visited upon soldiers and workmen are not to be compared with the sufferings of the poor natives who, upon the slightest pretext, are thrust into the wretched prisons here in the Upper River. I cannot deal with the dimensions of these prisons in this letter, but will do so in my report to my Government.

SIXTH.—Women are imported into your Majesty's Government for immoral purposes. They are introduced by two methods, viz., black men are dispatched to the Portuguese coast where they engage these women as mistresses of white men, who pay to the procurer a monthly sum. The other method is by capturing native women and condemning them to seven years' servitude for some imaginary crime against the State with which the villages of these women are charged. The State then hires these women out to the highest bidder, the officers having the first choice and then the men. Whenever children are born of such relations, the State maintains that the woman being its property the child belongs to it also. Not long ago a Belgian trader had a child by a slave-woman of the State, and he tried to secure possession of it that he might educate it, but the Chief of the Station where he resided, refused to be moved by his entreaties. At length he appealed to the Governor-General, and he gave him the woman and thus the trader obtained the child also. This was, however, an unusual case of generosity and clemency; and there is only one post that I know of where there is not to be found children of the civil and military officers of your Majesty's Government abandoned to degradation; white men bringing their own flesh and blood under the lash of a most cruel master, the State of Congo.

SEVENTH.—Your Majesty's Government is engaged in trade and commerce, competing with the organised trade companies of Belgium, England, France, Portugal and Holland. It taxes all trading companies and exempts its own goods from export-duty, and makes many of its officers ivory-traders, with the promise of a liberal commission upon all they can buy or get for the State. State soldiers patrol many villages forbidding the natives to trade with any person but a State official, and when the natives refuse to accept the price of the State, their goods are seized by the Government that promised them "protection." When natives have persisted in trading with the trade-companies the State has punished their independence by burning the villages in the vicinity of the trading houses and driving the natives away.

EIGHTH.—Your Majesty's Government has violated the General Act of the Conference of Berlin by firing upon native canoes; by confiscating the property of natives; by intimidating native traders, and preventing them from trading with white trading companies; by quartering troops in native villages when there is no war; by causing vessels bound from "Stanley-Pool" to "Stanley-Falls," to break their journey and leave the Congo, ascend the Aruhwimi river to Basoko, to be visited and show their papers; by forbidding a mission steamer to fly its national flag without permission from a local Government; by permitting the natives to carry on the slave-trade, and by engaging in the wholesale and retail slave-trade itself.

NINTH.—Your Majesty's Government has been, and is now, guilty of waging unjust and cruel wars against natives, with the hope of securing slaves and women, to minister to the behests of the officers of your Government. In such slave-hunting raids one village is armed by the State against the other, and the force thus secured is incorporated with the regular troops. I have no adequate terms with which to depict to your Majesty the brutal acts of your soldiers upon such raids as these. The soldiers who open the combat are usually the bloodthirsty cannibalistic Bangalas, who give no quarter to the aged grandmother or nursing child at the breast of its mother. There are instances in which they have brought the heads of their victims to their white officers on the expeditionary steamers, and afterwards eaten the bodies of slain children. In one war two Belgian Army officers saw, from the deck of their steamer, a native in a canoe some distance away. He was not a combatant and was ignorant of the conflict in progress upon the shore, some distance away. The officers made a wager of £5 that they could hit the native with their rifles. Three shots were fired and the native fell dead, pierced through the head, and the trade canoe was transformed into a funeral barge and floated silently down the river.

In another war, waged without just cause, the Belgian Army officer in command of your Majesty's forces placed the men in two or three lines on the steamers and instructed them to commence firing when the whistles blew. The steamers approached the fated town, and, as was usual with them, the people came to the shore to look at the boats and sell different articles of food. There was a large crowd of men, women and children, laughing, talking and exposing their goods for sale. At once the shrill whistles of the steamers were heard, the soldiers levelled their guns and fired, and the people fell dead, and wounded, and groaning, and pleading for mercy. Many prisoners were made, and among them four comely looking young women. And now ensued a most revolting scheme: your Majesty's officers quarreling over the selection of these women. The commander of this murderous expedition, with his garments stained with innocent blood, declared, that his rank entitled him to the first choice! Under the direction of this same officer the prisoners were reduced to servitude, and I saw them working upon the plantation of one of the stations of the State.

TENTH.—Your Majesty's Government is engaged in the slave-trade, wholesale and retail. It buys and sells and steals slaves. Your Majesty's

Government gives £3 per head for able-bodied slaves for military service.
Officers at the chief stations get the men and receive the money when
they are transferred to the State; but there are some middle-men who
only get from twenty to twenty-five francs per head. Three hundred and
sixteen slaves were sent down the river recently, and others are to follow.
These poor natives are sent hundreds of miles away from their villages,
to serve among other natives whose language they do not know. When
these men run away a reward of 1,000 N'taka is offered. Not long ago
such a re-captured slave was given one hundred "chikote" each day until
he died. Three hundred N'taka-brassrod is the price the State pays for a
slave, when bought from a native. The labour force at the stations of
your Majesty's Government in the Upper River is composed of slaves of
all ages and both sexes.

ELEVENTH.—Your Majesty's Government has concluded a contract
with the Arab Governor at this place for the establishment of a line of
military posts from the Seventh Cataract to Lake Tanganyika, territory
to which your Majesty has no more legal claim, than I have to be Com-
mander-in-Chief of the Belgian army. For this work the Arab Governor
is to receive five hundred stands of arms, five thousand kegs of powder,
and £20,000 sterling, to be paid in several instalments. As I write, the
news reaches me that these much-treasured and long-looked for materials of war are to be discharged at Basoko, and the Resident here is to
be given the discretion as to the distribution of them. There is a feeling
of deep discontent among the Arabs here, and they seem to feel that
they are being trifled with. As to the significance of this move Europe
and America can judge without any comment from me, especially
England.

TWELFTH.—The agents of your Majesty's Government have misrepresented the Congo country and the Congo railway. Mr. H. M. STAN-
LEY, the man who was your chief agent in setting up your authority in
this country, has grossly misrepresented the character of the country.
Instead of it being fertile and productive it is sterile and unproductive.
The natives can scarcely subsist upon the vegetable life produced in
some parts of the country. Nor will this condition of affairs change until
the native shall have been taught by the European the dignity, utility
and blessing of labour. There is no improvement among the natives,
because there is an impassable gulf between them and your Majesty's
Government, a gulf which can never be bridged. HENRY M. STANLEY's
name produces a shudder among this simple folk when mentioned; they
remember his broken promises, his copious profanity, his hot temper,
his heavy blows, his severe and rigorous measures, by which they were
mulcted of their lands. His last appearance in the Congo produced a
profound sensation among them, when he led 500 Zanzibar soldiers
with 300 campfollowers on his way to relieve EMIN PASHA. They thought
it meant complete subjugation, and they fled in confusion. but the only
thing they found in the wake of his march was misery. No white man

commanded his rear column, and his troops were allowed to straggle, sicken and die; and their bones were scattered over more than two hundred miles of territory.

Emigration cannot be invited to this country for many years. The trade of the Upper Congo consists only of ivory and rubber. The first is very old and the latter very poor. If the railway were completed now, it would not be able to earn a dividend for ten or twelve years; and as I have carefully inspected the line of the proposed road, I give it as my honest judgment that it cannot be completed for eight years. This is due to the stock-holders; they should be undeceived. I am writing a report on the Congo Railway, and will not present any data in this letter upon that subject.

Conclusions

Against the deceit, fraud, robberies, arson, murder, slave-raiding, and general policy of cruelty of your Majesty's Government to the natives, stands their record of unexampled patience, long-suffering and forgiving spirit, which put the boasted civilisation and professed religion of your Majesty's Government to the blush. During thirteen years only one white man has lost his life by the hands of the natives, and only two white men have been killed in the Congo. Major BARTTELOT was shot by a Zanzibar soldier, and the captain of a Belgian trading-boat was the victim of his own rash and unjust treatment of a native chief.

All the crimes perpetrated in the Congo have been done in *your* name, and *you* must answer at the bar of Public Sentiment for the misgovernment of a people, whose lives and fortunes were entrusted to you by the august Conference of Berlin, 1884–1885. I now appeal to the Powers, which committed this infant State to your Majesty's charge, and to the great States which gave it international being; and whose majestic law you have scorned and trampled upon, to call and create an International Commission to investigate the charges herein preferred in the name of Humanity, Commerce, Constitutional Government and Christian Civilisation.

I base this appeal upon the terms of Article 36 of Chapter VII of the General Act of the Conference of Berlin, in which that august assembly of Sovereign States reserved to themselves the right "to introduce into it later and by common accord the modifications or ameliorations, the utility of which may be demonstrated experience."

I appeal to the Belgian people and to their Constitutional Government, so proud of its traditions, replete with the song and story of its champions of human liberty, and so jealous of its present position in the sisterhood of European States,—to cleanse itself from the imputation of the crimes with which your Majesty's personal State of Congo is polluted.

I appeal to Anti-Slavery Societies in all parts of Christendom, to Philanthropists, Christians, Statesmen, and to the great mass of people everywhere, to call upon the Governments of Europe, to hasten the close of the tragedy your Majesty's unlimited Monarchy is enacting in the Congo.

I appeal to our Heavenly Father, whose service is perfect love, in witness of the purity of my motives and the integrity of my aims; and to history and mankind I appeal for the demonstration and vindication of the truthfulness of the charges I have herein briefly outlined.

And all this upon the word of honour of a gentleman, I subscribe myself your Majesty's humble and obedient servant.

GEO. W. WILLIAMS.

Stanley Falls, Central Africa,
    July 18th, 1890.

"Prisoners"

Morel, Edmund D. *King Leopold's Rule in Africa*. London: Heinemann, 1904, 192.

This picture was taken at Boma (Conrad's and Marlow's first stop in Africa), where the death rate among "prisoners" ran to 70 percent. Note the Zanzibari guards, mentioned both in "The Congo Diary" (see p. 165) and in the story.

RAILROAD CONSTRUCTION

Le Congo Illustré 2 (1893)12.

Despite the poor quality of the photo, one can make out equipment and material scattered about and get some sense of the rugged terrain.

GEORGE WASHINGTON WILLIAMS

A Report on the Proposed Congo Railway †

Stanley Falls,
(Central Africa,)
July 16th 1890.

I inspected the route of the proposed Congo Railway and the country through which it is to pass, in May and June, but I judged it wise to withhold my views, until I should examine the Congo River, country and commerce, from Leopoldville to the headwater of the navigable Congo River at the seventh cataract, a distance of 1,068 miles.

A Congo railway has always been one of HENRY M. STANLEY's favourite schemes, but the stalwart common sense and commercial wisdom of Englishmen rejected his wild estimates, as was also the fate of his two volume advertisement of the possessions of the State of Congo. His scheme, as presented to the Conference of Berlin, was rejected and disowned as an American enterprise. The Sovereign of the Congo State and a few Belgian capitalists fell under the spell of MR. STANLEY's figures, so fearfully and wonderfully made, and the railway scheme for the Congo took definite shape.

On the 26th March, 1887, the Independent State of Congo granted a charter to the "Compagnie du Congo pour le Commerce et l'Industrie" for the surveying and building of a railway in the Congo country. The life of the charter was for ninety-nine years, and its terms the most liberal. The survey was to be completed within eighteen months, and a copy of it, with the cost of the work, was to be furnished to the Government of the State of Congo. * * * Nearly three and one half years have passed, and not one mile of the road-bed has been made, and only twenty miles of the survey completed. Of course the time will be extended.

The Difficulties with which the Congo Railway Company has to contend are almost insuperable. The first twenty miles of the proposed route present the real difficulties, while the remaining 250 miles furnish but comparatively slight obstructions. Matadi—in the Congo language *Stone*—richly deserves its name. It is but one aggregation of rocks piled one upon the other, in the wildest and most bewildering confusion. It is the most forbidding looking place in the Congo country. It occupies an important position at the head of the navigable waters of the lower Congo, and is situated about one hundred and ten (110) miles from the Atlantic Ocean. Although it is claimed that the river is navigable from Boma to Matadi by sea-going steamers, only one has ever ventured to ascend to

† From John Hope Franklin, *George Washington Williams: A Biography* (Chicago: U of Chicago P, 1985) 255–63. Reprinted by permission.

Matadi. On the 20th June, 1889, Captain J. W. MURRAY of the British steamship "Lualaba" went up, the Governor-General furnishing a bond covering the value of the vessel. I questioned Captain MURRAY on the 24th April last past, respecting the navigability of the thirty-five miles of river between Boma and Matadi; and while he admits that there are dangerous rocks, he also feels confident that there is water enough for European steamers, if they can once learn the channel. However, no other steamer has ventured to pass beyond Boma, where about one European steamer arrives each week. At present all supplies and goods for the railway company, the State stations and missions of the Upper Congo, are discharged at Banana or Boma and sent to Matadi by small draught steamers. This is an expensive and damaging system, since freight often remains exposed to the weather at Boma for weeks, there being no shelter; and the handling of it twice results in a great breakage. But this system, at present unavoidable, will, in my judgment, continue after the railway is completed, unless the State and the railway have the courage of their conviction, that the river *is* navigable between Boma, the Cape Salcity, and Matadi, the commercial entrepôt; and offer European steamers a guarantee of safe passage and free pilotage.

The terminal facilities at Matadi came under my observation first. Owing to the dangerous condition of the river bank, one or two large quays will be necessary for the transfer of freight to and from steamers and cars. After a careful study of all data bearing upon the question of tides there at Matadi, I conclude that the water rises from sixteen (16) to eighteen (18) feet, and that the volume and velocity of the river require works of unusual strength. And yet I saw a quay in process of construction at Matadi that would not endure one African season. It would be partially swept away and completely submerged.

I followed the surveyed route of the Congo railway from Matadi to the mouth of the Mpozo river,—about five miles. Every foot of this section is beset with difficulties: an ugly stream to bridge, cuts to dig, rocks to blast, a tunnel to bore, grades to make, culverts and masonry work to construct, nearly one thousand (1,000) feet above the bed of the River Congo, in sight of which the projected road is intended to pass until the river Mpozo, along whose left bank it is to pass for a short distance and then cross to the Mpalaballa-hill. This hill is 1,700 feet above sea level, and while the road may pass around or through it, it can never pass over it. The Mpozo is a turbulent stream, and it often rises from twelve to fifteen feet; and the bridge across its stormy bosom must be of ample size and strength. In the estimates of the Railway Company nine bridges are accounted for, and I have found twenty-six others of importance.

The young engineers who are employed upon the Congo railway have technical knowledge and zeal, but as Belgians they are deficient in that special experience of the weather phenomena of tropical countries, and there are many trials and disappointments awaiting them. A few years of experience might enable them to triumph over difficulties which no engineer unacquainted with African climate would master; but at the moment when experience is harvested, health fails or the term of service expires. New men come out to take the places of experienced men, and thus in the next eight years three distinct sets of engineers will have come and gone, sickness, death and expiration of term of service thinning their ranks.

Even after the road is completed it will require great care to keep it open during the rainy season.

The Labour System is difficult of solution, and the more I have studied it the more I am convinced that the railway company is pursuing an unwise policy in the recruitment and treatment of their workmen. In the estimates printed at Brussels early last year, the managers of this project declare their ability to secure many labourers in the cataract region, through which the road is to pass; but the harsh policy of the State towards the natives has produced in them a dread and suspicion of the white man. Thus the Company has been compelled to import labourers, like the State of the Congo, from the East and West Coast of the African Continent. From the East Coast come Zanzibar slaves, from the West Coast free Kroomen; the former for a term of years, the latter for one year. The compensation for the slave-labour is paid to their Zanzibar master, and the Kroomen get one shilling per day. I personally examined the food and quarters of these men, and as to the first, I am compelled to say it is deficient, in both quality and quantity; and, as to the second, it is just to declare that they are worse quartered than the natives, and that is saying a good deal. The food consists of two articles only: rice and a venerable dry fish; and the most general sickness is dysentery, of which malady a number die monthly. Added to bad food and poor quarters, the severe treatment bestowed upon these work-people is of such nature and frequency as to greatly impair their efficiency. They are beaten and kicked by their overseers upon the slightest provocation, and many run away. While I was carrying on my investigations near Matadi fifty Krooman ran away in one group, and every week these men are making desperate efforts to escape from the bondage of the railway company. The Krooman belong to the sea; and when they no longer behold its blue bosom nor smell its sweet waters, they droop and die. They were not intended to dig in the earth; but wherever they appear along the African continent, in factories or upon steamers, their labour has proved invaluable and their reputation for fidelity is unquestioned. The Congo has seen the first and the last of the Kroomen. They will count the moons upon a string, making a knot each month. When the twelfth knot is tied, they will return home to boycott the Belgium-Congo. It was thus they treated the Portuguese for ill-treating them, and neither love nor money can ever induce them to enter their service again. These black Irishmen of the West Coast have no flag to cover them, no language, no Government, but every year 5,000 of their number go from home to work with a united determination to serve their friends and shun their enemies.

The Zanzibar slaves are not useful on a railway, and they fall to their tasks with bitter reluctance.

The mechanics are composed of Belgians and black men from Sierra Leone and Accra. They receive the usual pay of men of their various handicrafts, and food and quarters are furnished by the railway company. The black men endure the climate and do excellent work of a certain kind; and where the white men are more skilful they are less useful because of their inability to endure the climate under the full stress their trades require. The loss by death falls more heavily upon the whites, and from Matadi to Stanley Falls their loss is 50 percent.

The road is to be narrow-gauged, 29½-inch wide, and single track; and its length from Matadi to Stanley Pool about 270 miles. It is proposed to run two trains per week in each direction, and as there will only be a daily service, it will require two days to perform the journey from Matadi to Stanley Pool. The half-way halting station will be at Kimpisi, with three other large stations, one at Loufou, Inkissi and Ntampa. There are to be five sections of little more than fifty miles each, with three halting places to each section for water and food.

The Estimates for the construction of such a road in such a country as the Congo must have been made with precipitous haste, and based upon insufficient data. * * * Even if these estimates were correct there is the vital question of the ability of the road to pay for itself. I know of no work, dealing along with the commerce of Africa, more unreliable and misleading than Mr. STANLEY's, "The Congo Free State." When he describes things and persons he displays the ability of an able correspondent. But the moment he attempts to deal with figures and trade, he becomes the veriest romancer. * * *

Modern history records nothing equal to the speculations of Mr. STANLEY, who has heretofore been regarded as a practical man. And while I have an interest in the civilisation of Africa equal to any person's, I cannot be silent, or suffer to pass unchallenged statements calculated to mislead and deceive the friends of humanity and civilisation. Mr. STANLEY's speculations—for they are nothing else—concerning the Congo may be, in part, realised within the next fifty or seventy-five years, but they are not available for the present. His figures as regards the population, towns and areas of the Congo, are no more deserving of confidence than his calculations about the commerce of the country. It is not an agreeable task to have to say these things of a man whose valour, perseverance, sufferings and triumphs have sent a thrill of admiration throughout the civilised world; but it is the stern duty of history to prevent error from being canonized instead of the truth, which must be written with an iron pen.

The plants of Mission stations and of tradinghouses and their steamers have already been or will be transported to the Upper Congo before the railway becomes a fact accomplished. By an organised industry for the preservation of Europeans, and the good of the natives, these Missions and tradinghouses will decrease the necessity of calling upon Europe for supplies; and the 40,000 native carriers in the zone, through which the railway is to pass, having once tasted the fruit of honest labour, will become suspicious and jealous of a railway, which would deprive them of those articles of European manufacture they now prize and enjoy. The result would become competition, and tradinghouses, which only receive goods every quarter, and make shipments in like periods of time, would find the transport system cheap enough and speedy enough to answer their business requirements. I examine all these questions knowing well that a successful financier, like a victorious soldier, must fight on both sides of his plans.

The projectors of the Congo Railway scheme have been too boastful and too profuse in their promises to the shareholders, and under these circumstances disappointment and confusion are sure to cover them, as heat follows light and the rising sun.

The Congo Railway ought to be built, and from the bottom of my heart I hope it will be. But capitalists and philanthropists must remember what I have declared, that it cannot be built for less than 40,000,000 francs, nor in less than eight years. By skillful and practical management, and with all the machinery employed in the construction of European and American railroads, the time could be reduced by two or three years. Meanwhile Africa needs the blessing of a practical labor system which, while it addresses itself to the soul, will not ignore the body, its earthly temple; and, while inculcating spiritual truths, will not fail to teach the native the primal lesson of human history: *For in the sweat of thy face shalt thou eat thy bread.*

GEO. W. WILLIAMS.

JOHN HOPE FRANKLIN

[Williams Ignored] †

A distinguished British foreign service officer, Roger Casement, was in the Congo at the same time Williams was there. With his experienced eye, he doubtless saw many of the things that Williams saw. Years later, in 1902, he wrote,

> I remember seeing in 1890 a letter written by an officer, directing one of the most important administrative districts of the Congo State, to a subordinate officer engaged in one of these . . . mancatching

† From John Hope Franklin, *George Washington Williams: A Biography* (Chicago: U of Chicago P, 1985) 255–63. Reprinted by permission.

raids. The object at that time was not military service. The Government needed porters for the transport of the many loads of equipment it was seeking to send to Stanley Pool, and being unwilling to pay the established rate fixed by Europeans collectively (missions and traders) as remuneration to the native porters the Congo Government compelled the carriage of its loads by force, giving an inferior wage to that paid by everyone else.[1]

Casement was all too familiar with the Congo State and its problems. In 1886–88 he had worked on various jobs in Henry Sanford's efforts to build up the transport system there. This involved one stint at Matadi and another at Equator on the upper congo. Before leaving, he also worked at a mission station as a lay helper for the Reverend W. Holman Bently.[2] When he returned in 1890 to serve as manager for the company that was to construct the railway from Matadi to Stanley Pool, he was doubtless familiar with some of the more unsavory features of Congolese policies. More than a dozen years later, as the British Foreign Office was preparing to "go public" in its criticisms of the Congo State, it turned to Casement, who had been there many times and who, in 1903, was his government's consul at Boma.

The reports Casement began to send from Boma to the Foreign Office in London indicate the nature and extent of the injustice that he saw in the administration of the Congo State. A Congolese could not sell the ivory he had carefully hoarded. His lands were not his own. He could not dispose of his produce in the open market. Indeed, the work of his own hands were not his.

> The very children he has begotten are born less to love their father and mother than to fear with that perfect fear, which casteth out all love, a distant being whom their 1,400 white oppressors term his sovereign. . . . All these things are not his, they belong to a 'Sovereign' he never saw, who rules him through an Administration of aliens—strangers in speech, thought, habit and home—who in turn make their will terribly felt by an armed and drilled force of 20,000 men—swift to anger and of great wrath.

In language similar to that used by Williams in the *Open Letter*, Casement expressed grave doubts regarding the validity of the titles by which Leopold claimed the lands of the Congo. The chiefs could not grant what they did not possess, and since they were merely the trustees of the tribal families, their public rights were "well defined and strictly limited by popular control." Consequently, Leopold's title to lands "granted" by the chiefs was, at best, cloudy.[3]

After a final, two-month inspection of the Upper Congo, Casement returned to London to write his report. Though outraged by what he

1. Roger Casement to the Foreign Secretary, the Marquis of Landsdowne, London, December 13, 1902, British Foreign Office Files, Africa, Confidential, Public Record Office.

2. Brian Inglis, *Roger Casement* (New York, 1973), pp. 28–31.

3. Ibid., February 15, 1903.

had seen, he was moderate in his utterances, thus adding force to what he said. The railway was efficient and convenient. The work force at Leopoldville was truly national, since the employees of the government there were drawn from nearly every part of the country. A hospital for Europeans "and an establishment designed as a native hospital are in charge of a European doctor. The open selling of slaves and the canoe convoys, which once navigated the Upper Congo, have everywhere disappeared."

Casement could make few other favorable statements about the Congo State. Many of his comments were similar to those that Williams had made thirteen years earlier. One wonders whether Casement had seen the *Open Letter* that had been discussed in England, Belgium, and France in 1891. The native hospital at Leopoldville was "an unseemly place" of three mud huts with the patients poorly attended. People in the riverside towns were forced to keep the government telegraph lines clear of undergrowth, for which they had received no payment for more than a year. When soldiers needed food or other supplies, they could require it of the local people, whose failure to comply would earn them a beating or imprisonment. The government could call upon a village, with no prior notice, to supply canoe paddlers, day laborers (male and female), timber gatherers, and woodcutters. Congolese were still subjected to terrible floggings with the "chicote," even for complaints about injustices they sought to make. It was the beatings, mutilations, and killings that distressed Casement the most. The cutting off of hands by government soldiers was a common form of mutilation. One young man's hands had been beaten off against a tree with the butt ends of rifles.[4]

As he had done in the case of Williams, King Leopold sought to discredit Casement even before the report was released. The two men had met in October 1900; the king told Casement, as he had told Williams in 1889, that his chief desire, then as always, was "the well-being and good government of the natives."[5] Three years later, on learning of the impending revelations in the Casement report, Leopold asked whether Casement was not the same British consul who had written the governor-general of the Free State in July 1901. In that letter, the king recalled, Casement had said, "Pray believe me, when I express now, not only for myself, but for my fellow-countrymen, in this part of Africa, our very sincere appreciation of your efforts to promote goodwill among all and to bring together the various elements in our local life." Leopold did not bother to place Casement's words in their proper context; Casement in fact was referring only to certain developments in the community of Boma and not to any general policy set forth by the king or his men.[6]

Although Casement had made no mention of Williams in his report, they had seen very much the same things and both were deeply moved by their experiences. If Casement was more restrained, it was perhaps

4. *Correspondence and Report from His Majesty's Consul at Boma Respecting the Administration of the Independent State of the Congo* (London, 1904),

p. 23, 26, 34, and passim.
5. Quoted in Inglis, *Roger Casement*, p. 56.
6. Ibid., pp. 75–76.

because diplomatic experience had taught him the virtue of understatement. Edmund D. Morel, who in 1904 was to found the Congo Reform Association at Casement's urging, saw in Casement and Williams similar sources of strength in a real reordering of conditions in the Congo. R. C. Phillips read portions of the *Open Letter* to a gathering in London in November 1890; and Morel said in 1902 that it "might have been written a few weeks, instead of eleven years ago. The state of affairs pictured by Colonel Williams has worsened instead of bettered. The evil is more widespread and the means of perpetuating it more extensive and more powerful."[7] Morel met Casement, before *The Report* was published. "From the moment our hands gripped and our eyes met," Morel wrote, "mutual trust and confidence were bred and the feeling of isolation slipped from me like a mantle. Here was a man indeed."[8]

Another person who plied the Congo in the summer of 1890, when Williams and Casement were there, was Joseph Conrad. Not yet the celebrated writer that he would become early in the next century, Conrad, an experienced seaman, had gone to the Congo in June 1890 to command the *Roi des Belges* for the up-river voyage. While some of his experiences are recorded in his novella, *Heart of Darkness*, the voyage affected most of his subsequent writings and, indeed, much of the remainder of his life. Although Williams and Conrad were on the river at the same time, they apparently did not meet. Conrad and Casement did, however. "Made the acquaintance of Mr. Roger Casement, which I should consider as a great pleasure under any circumstances and now it becomes a positive piece of luck," Conrad wrote in his diary. "Thinks, speaks well, most intelligent and very sympathetic."[9]

Conrad was almost mesmerized by the Congo country and especially the river, as indeed were many other sojourners there. "Going up that river," he wrote, "was like travelling back to the earliest beginnings of the world, when vegetation rioted on the earth and the big trees were kings." Conrad also had to confront the reality of the present. There was the disgusting spectacle of the inefficiency of Leopold's Congo. Marlow, in *Heart of Darkness*, was revolted by wrecked vessels on the river, "a railway truck lying there on its back," a "stack of rusty nails," and other "pieces of decaying machinery."[1] He was also revolted by the exploitation of the Congolese by the king and his men. It was not necessary that Conrad admire the Congolese or greatly respect them—and it is to be doubted that he did—in order to be outraged by some practices he saw

7. Morel, *Affairs of West Africa*, p. 320. See also his *King Leopold's Rule in Africa* (New York, 1905), p. 104. The account of the reading from the *Open Letter* in a London meeting is repeated in his *Red Rubber*, 4th ed. (London, 1919), p. 40.

8. Quoted in Inglis, *Roger Casement*, p. 79. See also a memorandum by E. D. Morel, "Origin of British Interest in Congo Reform," a manuscript in the Morel Collection, London School of Economics.

9. "The Congo Diary," in Joseph Conrad, *Tales of Hearsay and Last Essays* (London, 1955), p. 161.

[See p. 159, below—*Editor.*]

1. The problem of inefficiency in the Congo is discussed in Hunt Hawkins, "Conrad's Critique of Imperialism in *Heart of Darkness*," PMLA 94 (March 1979): 286–99.

2. In his article, "The Issue of Racism in *Heart of Darkness*," *Conradiana* 14, no. 3(1982): 163–71, Hunt Hawkins argues that Conrad was not a racist. For an opposing view, see Chinua Achebe, "An Image of Africa," *Massachusetts Review* 18 (Winter 1977): 782–94. [See pp. 251–62, below—*Editor.*]

in 1890.[2] He wrote Casement that he thought it "an extraordinary thing that the conscience of Europe, which seventy years ago had put down the slave trade on humanitarian grounds, tolerates the Congo State today. It is as if the moral clock had been put back many hours. . . . In the old days England had in her keeping the conscience of Europe. . . . But I suppose we are busy with other things—too much involved in great affairs to take up the cudgels for humanity, decency and justice." Conrad declined to join the fight to reform the Congo. After all, he pleaded, he was "only a wretched novelist" and surely not the man Casement needed.[3]

Thus, of all the 1890 observers and critics of Leopold's rule in the Congo—Grenfell the missionary, Casement the diplomat, Conrad the novelist, Williams the reporter, and doubtless others—only Williams saw fit to make his unfavorable views widely known immediately. The others had their own reasons for remaining silent at the time; and in due course they would all express their disapproval with varying degrees of fervor. When they did speak out, not one mentioned Williams's *Open Letter* or his other reports. The Williams file at the British Foreign Office was thick, thanks to the detailed dispatches from Brussels by Lord Vivian and Martin Gosselins. Casement could have used it to advantage, but he gives no credit to Williams. Grenfell knew more about misrule in the Congo than Williams would ever know; and he indicated as much after his first meeting with Williams in 1890. Nevertheless, he remained quiet for another dozen years. He even accepted appointment by Leopold to serve on a commission of missionaries to watch over and protect native interests, though he conceded that the commission was a farce.[4] In 1903, Casement sharply criticized Grenfell's acquiescence in the king's rule, pointing out that Grenfell's own "garrison district is the severest condemnation of state rule."[5] By that time, Grenfell was having rather stormy sessions with the governor-general of the Congo, who upbraided him for the mildly worded protests he had begun to utter.[6]

It took courage for Williams to write the *Open Letter* in 1890. As an extremely ambitious man, he must have counted the costs of such a disclosure. Collis P. Huntington, his benefactor, would obviously be distressed to read in the *Open Letter* the indictments against the man with whom he hoped to have a number of intimate business arrangements in the Congo. Yet Williams seemed never to falter in his determination to expose the king. The man of "flexible values" of a decade earlier was, by 1890, a person of considerable moral strength.

After the Congo Reform Association was organized in 1904, a verita-

3. Conrad's letter to Casement is quoted in Inglis, *Roger Casement*, p. 92. Conrad continued to be sympathetic and even wrote a letter for publication. For a discussion of his role in Congo reform, see Hunt Hawkins, "Joseph Conrad, Roger Casement, and the Congo Reform Movement," *Journal of Modern Literature* 9, no. 1 (1981): 65–80.
4. Johnston, *George Grenfell*, vol. 1, pp. 467–68.
5. Roger Casement, "Diary, Wednesday August

5, 1903," British Home Office; in custody of the Public Record Office.
6. Johnston, *George Grenfell*, vol 1, p. 467. During these years the *Baptist Missionary Magazine* did not mention GWW's criticisms and "remained a steady admirer of both the Congo country and its government." David Lagergren, *Mission and State in the Congo* (Uppsala, 1970), p. 106.

ble crusade against conditions in the Congo was conducted by people
such as E. D. Morel and Sir Harry Johnston in Britain and Lyman
Abbott and G. Stanley Hall in the United States.[7] Except for the reading
of the *Open Letter* at a London meeting in 1890, one searches in vain
for any mention of Williams. Williams's eloquent indictment had certainly been taken seriously in Brussels. If later critics, as William K.
Parmenter claims,[8] did not know of it, they were ignorant of an important chapter in the history of the Congo State.

JOHN DeCOURCY MacDONNELL

[The Visionary King]†

Nothing is more clear to the student of the history of Africa than the
definite purpose which animated all King Leopold's legislation from the
commencement of his rule over the Congo through all the changing
years to the present moment. That purpose has ever been to secure the
prosperity of the wide realm of the Congo and of its inhabitants. It is
clearly shown and clearly observed in every decree the sovereign of the
Congo has made. All that has been done in the Congo rests on the
King's sole authority. In accepting the sovereignty of the Independent
State King Leopold faced the greatest problem and undertook the weigh-
tiest responsibility of our age, but he faced it unfettered. The diploma-
tists who sat at the Congress of Berlin seem to have looked to no more
than the interests of foreign traders and, in a somewhat vague way, the
protection against slavery of the native races of Africa. It is well for mankind that the sovereign of the Congo looked farther, and that his views
were wise.

King Leopold undertook to protect the native races from the raids of
slave traders, and he undertook to free them from slavery; he undertook
to open up Equatorial Africa to trade, and to establish a settled government in it; but these undertakings, great though they were, were but the
least part of his task. Besides them, he had to regulate his government
so that trade and industry would flourish profitably in the land in the
future, and he had to educate and to civilise the negroes. Politicians and
pamphleteers who deal only with the present moment are apt to overlook
these, the main, points of King Leopold's great undertaking; but it is
with regard to them, and not to any passing need, that King Leopold's
rule in Africa and his legislation for the Congo must be judged.

7. See, for example, the monthly issues of the
Official Organ of the Congo Reform Association for
the years 1905–7.
8. William K. Parameter, "The Congo and Its
Critics, 1880–1913," unpublished Ph.D. disser-
tation, Harvard University, 1952, p. 149.
† From *King Leopold II: His Rule in Belgium and
the Congo* (London, 1905) 162–63.
  MacDonnell (1869–1915), an Irishman and
Celtic scholar, was a Belgian civil servant.

RICHARD HARDING DAVIS

[His Brother's Keeper]†

After one has talked with the men and women who have seen the atrocities, has seen in the official reports that those accused of the atrocities do not deny having committed them, but point out that they were merely obeying orders, and after one has seen that even at the capital of Boma all the conditions of slavery exist, one is assured that in the jungle, away from the sight of men, all things are possible. Merchants, missionaries, and officials even in Leopold's service told me that if one could spare a year and a half, or a year, to the work in the hinterland he would be an eye-witness of as cruel treatment of the natives as any that has gone before, and if I can trust myself to weigh testimony and can believe my eyes and ears I have reason to know that what they say is true. I am convinced that to-day a man, who feels that a year and a half is little enough to give to the aid of twenty millions of human beings, can accomplish in the Congo as great and good work as that of the Abolitionists.

Three years ago atrocities here were open and above-board. For instance. In the opinion of the State the soldiers, in killing game for food, wasted the State cartridges, and in consequence the soldiers, to show their officers that they did not expend the cartridges extravagantly on antelope and wild boar, for each empty cartridge brought in a human hand, the hand of a man, woman, or child. These hands, drying in the sun, could be seen at the posts along the river. They are no longer in evidence. Neither is the flower-bed of Lieutenant Dom, which was bordered with human skulls. A quaint conceit.

The man to blame for the atrocities, for each separate atrocity, is Leopold.

KING LEOPOLD II

[The Sacred Mission of Civilization]*

Our refined society attaches to human life (and with reason) a value unknown to barbarous communities. When our directing will is implanted among them its aim is to triumph over all obstacles, and results which could not be attained by lengthy speeches may follow philanthropic influence. But if, in view of this desirable spread of civilisation, we count

† From *The Congo and the Coasts of Africa* (New York: Charles Scribner's Sons, 1907) 44–47. Davis (1864–1916) was a renowned, world-traveling journalist.
* From Guy Burrows, *The Land of the Pigmies* (London, 1898) 286.
The title for this selection is the title of a pamphlet prepared in 1953 by the Belgian government for presentation to the members of the U.N.

Le Congo Illustré 2 (1893)80.

Many ironic details can be noted in this official Belgian propaganda allegory of Europe in Africa, but especially interesting are the steam-engine boiler and the steamer in the background.

UPSTREAM NATIVES AND THE *Roi des Belges*

Le Congo Illustré 2 (1893)91.

This artist's touch-up of a photograph by M. F. De Muese reflects more closely Conrad's actual experiences on the River Congo than it does his artistic rendering of Marlow's experiences. See "The Congo Diary" (p. 159) and "Up-river Book" (p. 167).

upon the means of action which confer upon us dominion and the sanction of right, it is not less true that our ultimate end is a work of peace. Wars do not necessarily mean the ruin of the regions in which they rage; our agents do not ignore this fact, so from the day when their effective superiority is affirmed, they feel profoundly reluctant to use force. The wretched negroes, however, who are still under the sole sway of their traditions, have that horrible belief that victory is only decisive when the enemy, fallen beneath their blows, is annihilated. The soldiers of the State, who are recruited necessarily from among the natives, do not immediately forsake those sanguinary habits that have been transmitted from generation to generation. The example of the white officer and wholesome military discipline gradually inspire in them a horror of human trophies of which they previously had made their boast. It is in their leaders that they must see living evidence of these higher principles, taught that the exercise of authority is not at all to be confounded with cruelty, but is, indeed, destroyed by it. I am pleased to think that our agents, nearly all of whom are volunteers drawn from the ranks of the Belgian army, have always present in their minds a strong sense of the career of honour in which they are engaged, and are animated with a

THE *Roi des Belges*

Le Congo Illustré 3 (1894) 21.
The *Roi des Belges* undergoing repair at Kinchasa-Stanley Pool. Note the pilot-house and tunnel.

THE *Roi des Belges*

Le Mouvement Geographique 8 (1891) 113.

The *Roi des Belges* underoing repair at Kinchasa-Stanley Pool. Note that the super-structure has been removed, exposing the vertical boiler.

pure feeling of patriotism; not sparing their own blood, they will the more spare the blood of the natives, who will see in them the all-powerful protectors of their lives and their property, benevolent teachers of whom they have so great a need.

A Map of Zaire
1987

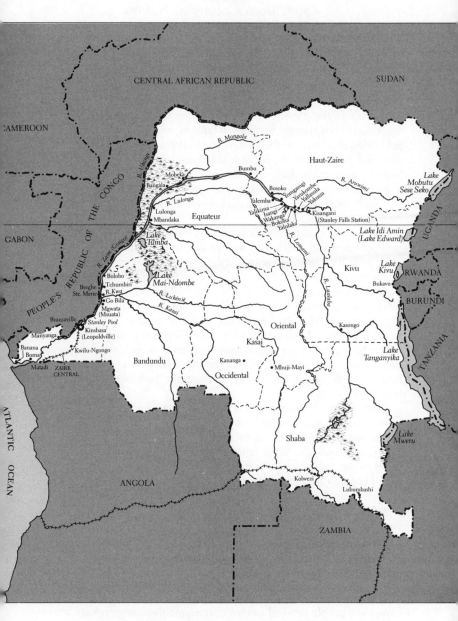

LYNNE RICE

Zaire, from Colony to Nation:
A Brief History, 1908 to 1987†

The "Congo," the Zaire of today, still harbors that "heart of darkness" uncovered by Joseph Conrad. The names of places and the faces of leaders have changed over the years, but the underlying reality of outside forces lusting for power remains the same. From the time of King Leopold's rule to the present, the history of the Congo can be traced as a movement from tyranny to chaos to tyranny and chaos combined. Leopold ruled absolutely in the Congo, so absolutely that, as Maurice Hennessy notes on page 81, he was able to bequeath his so-called Independent State to Belgium in 1895. At the time of his death in 1908, the Free State became the Belgian Congo and remained under Belgian domination until 1960, when the demand for independence could no longer be denied.

For five years following independence, the people of the Congo struggled unsuccessfully with and against one another to forge a political order to fit their own needs and further their own interests at home and in Africa. Almost from the beginning, however, international political forces tried to shape that struggle for their own ends. The outcome, in 1965, was the installation as president of Joseph-Desiré Mobutu, later to call himself Mobutu Sese Seko. Mobutu remains in power today, supported by the United States and other Western nations. But Zaire, despite the enormous economic potential of its natural resources, is ineptly run, looted by its own government, heavily in debt, and unable even to feed its people: within the country, support for the Mobutu dictatorship is fast eroding away.

With an attitude that remains in evidence today, Europe and the United States in 1908 assumed without question that the fate of this African people would and should be determined by the political powers of the day. It was, perhaps, to be expected that when Belgium assumed control with the announced intention of righting the wrongs perpetrated by King Leopold's regime, no ceremony was observed in the Congo, merely an announcement posted in the capitol in Leopoldville (Kinshasa), which proclaimed Belgian sovereignty over all territories within the Independent State of Congo, effective November 15, 1908.

Under Belgian rule, the actual center of governing power remained in Brussels. Within the Congo, improving communications favored concentration of power in the Government-General in Leopoldville (Kinshasa), the Central Station of Conrad's story. Resumption of free international trade and the apparent end of outright exploitation of the Congolese people satisfied foreign critics, and the Congo reform movement was abandoned. The stated Belgian policy of the time emphasized the duties of colonial rule: Belgium would bring to the Congo technical progress, improved living conditions, and the Christian religion (Slade 1–7). Economic gains for Belgium were rarely mentioned. But, despite its proclaimed adherence to a doctrine of indirect rule, the Belgian administration found its economic priorities incompatible with any real autonomy for local African leadership.

From the beginning, Belgian authority within the Congo rested on the apparently unassailable alliance of state, private companies, and the Church (Slade 12). The laws of the state mandated the cultivation of certain crops; taxes were still collected in the form of obligatory labor or forced trade of produce needed by the people for their own use; racial discrimination was institutionalized; and the Congolese people required administrative authorization to move from place to place within the country. Except for the Catholic seminaries, secondary education was unavailable, and primary education was left entirely in the hands of the Church, which also served as an agency for the transmission of European values. Capitalist interests controlled the lives of workers in large-scale agriculture and mining. Thousands of Congolese were transplanted miles from their traditional homelands by the *Union Minière du Haut-Katanga*, the largest mining conglomerate. Miners were well provided for, as a matter of good business, but here as elsewhere the system overall left very little room for African initiative or social mobility (Slade 4, 9, 29, 34). A study of the Bashu tribe located near the Uganda border suggests that, in the rural areas, occupation by the new Belgian colonizers was followed by social disruption and economic decline caused by forced movement to larger consolidated villages. African perception of the changes imposed by the Belgian administration, at least in those areas newly colonized after the takeover, differed substantially from reports of growing economic prosperity recorded by Belgian officials (Packard 76–77).

World War I and the period that followed contributed little to the growth of political consciousness in the Congo. Rural labor shortages caused by the forced movement of workers to centers of European economic development in the 1920's and a financial crisis resulting from the depression of the 1930's were weathered without any noticeable change in the mood of the population. The occasional regional or religious uprisings that did occur seemed isolated incidents, unconnected to any general anticolonial sentiment (Young 1984 77). The apparatus of colonial government remained intact, too entrenched for either ruler or subject to imagine it could be dismantled (Slade 2).

But World War II brought unforeseen and irreversible changes. With the Belgian government's attention focused of necessity on the war in Europe, the management of the Congo was left to the resident colonial administrators. Because their numbers were much reduced and their attention concentrated on the production of resources needed for the war, their personal contact with the Congolese diminished. At the same time, the demand for compulsory labor increased. This led to further social disorientation and rural economic decline as large numbers of people moved to the cities to meet labor needs. Under these pressures, sporadic strikes and demonstrations broke out. Though they were quickly and violently put down, these outbreaks were a sign that Africans had begun to feel, however tenuously, their collective strength. European prestige, already damaged, broke down further after the war with the return of Congolese troops who had served in other parts of the world, seen different relationships between black and white, and absorbed wartime propaganda against Nazi racial doctrines (Slade 8–17).

Nationalism, considered as the explicit demand for African political rights and self-determination, came late to the Belgian territories. The first public claim for independence in the Congo appeared only in 1956. The Belgian government's rigid control and resistance to political activism on the part of anyone in the colony, European or Congolese, were largely responsible for the delay. African political parties were altogether forbidden before 1958, and restricted until 1959. Belgium maintained, from the first, a policy designed to isolate the Congo: very few Africans were permitted to travel or to attend schools abroad, and strict censorship was enforced. The aim of the colonial government was to avoid political disturbance and pursue a policy of gradual technical progress and material improvement. Peaceful discussions of economic and political emancipation would come—at some unforeseen time in the future. But Africa was not content to wait. The only result of Belgium's obstinacy was that when the demand for independence came, the Congolese were without the trained leadership and political experience needed for successful self-rule (Slade 1–2, 6).

In the immediate postwar era, only a few Congolese were aware of the political unrest in other parts of Africa. These were the *évolués*, townspeople who had received more education, could speak French, and were comparatively well off—the middle class whose creation had been encouraged by Belgian policy. As a result, they could no longer fit comfortably into the traditional African structures at the same time that they were becoming increasingly proud of their identity as Africans. Even though they rejected total assimilation by the alien Western culture, they still had a desire for a life-style comparable to that of the Belgians who lived among them—but they became increasingly aware of the bars to its achievement. In an attempt to respond to these dissatisfactions, the Belgian government half-heartedly instituted a series of legal reforms aimed at removing social and economic discrimination (Slade 11–32).

Shifts in the political climate within Belgium also contributed to the ferment in Africa, as when in 1954, the long-standing Catholic government was replaced by a Liberal/Socialist coalition that objected to and sought to weaken the Catholic Church's monopoly over African education (Slade 33–35). Business interests in the Congo opposed the policy of the new government, fearing, and thereby contributing to, the breakdown of the alliance of state, Church, and capital. Africans, enlisted by

Belgian political parties in this factional dispute in Europe, discovered both the lack of unity in Belgium and the power of their own organized political opinion in Belgium and at home (Slade 40–45).

Thus, the evolution and spread of *évolué* discontent was accompanied by a growing political consciousness. Its first overt manifestation was the 1956 publication by a group in Leopoldville of the *Manifeste de Conscience Africaine*, which called for the institution of greater political liberties over a thirty-year timetable. Abako, a cultural organization of the Bakongo tribal group in the Leopoldville area, headed by tribal leader Joseph Kasavubu, responded with a manifesto that called for "immediate independence." Even the Catholic Church, in the process of redefining its African role, announced its support for this ill-defined emancipation. Already made evident by these two, separate manifestos was what was to become a major line of division in the politics of the Congo. While the *Conscience Africaine* called for the formation of one strong national party, Abako, because it was a group with basically ethnic and regional loyalties, urged the formation of several political parties and would go on to waver between the call for a separate republic in the Lower Congo region and the call for the formation of a federalist national government with strong regional autonomy (Young 1984 707–9).

When Belgian restrictions were finally removed in 1958, political parties sprang up across the territory. They tended to form alliances along the nationalist/federalist split that had appeared earlier. One pole was dominated by the *Movement National Congolais—Lumumba* (MNC/L), founded and headed by Patrice Lumumba, who had been actively criticizing the Belgian government and the Congo's European community since the 1940's. Lumumba's party called for immediate independence, national unity, and a strong central government. On the federalist side, Abako was joined by the *Confederation des Associations Ethniques du Katanga* (Conakat), a party formed and headed by Moise Tshombe, whose family held the chiefship of the Lunda, a prominent tribe in Katanga. Conakat membership included Europeans, and the party had strong ties with the West. Its chief loyalty was to Katangese economic interest, but, if it was to be part of a Congolese nation, Conakat favored a loose federalist system with strong regional autonomy. The Belgian administration supported the formation of a "center" party, the *Parti National du Progrès* (PNP), which claimed to represent five million Congolese (a claim not reflected in the eventual 1960 election results) who desired independence without civil disobedience or violence. The PNP allied itself with Conakat (Slade 46, 59–66).

A three-day riot began on January 4, 1959, when the administration sought to disperse a crowd that had gathered for an Abako political meeting; the riot left the government's plan for a gradual movement toward independence outdated before its publication only a week later. The plan was further invalidated by the surprise broadcast on the same day of a speech by Belgian king Baudouin, which contained a pledge to lead the Congo to independence "without undue precipitation or interminable delay." By mid-1959, politicization, which had begun in the cities, spread to the rural areas, and the Belgian administration was fast losing control. By the end of 1959, Belgium had come to the conclusion that only by granting immediate independence could they hope to retain any influence in the Congo (Young 1984 711).

In January and February of 1960, a Round Table Conference of Belgian and Congolese political representatives was held in Brussels to discuss independence. The date agreed upon was June 30, 1960, with national and provincial elections scheduled for May. The Belgian Parliment approved, and a provisional constitution was signed on May 19 by King Baudouin. In the elections that followed, the left-wing MNC-Lumumba emerged as the strongest party in both the central and the provincial assemblies (Ingham 316). The diversity of political aims and loyalties in the Congo, however, made it impossible for Lumumba to form a government with himself as prime minister until he agreed to the nomination of his political rival, Abako's Joseph Kasavubu, as president. Even then, Lumumba's government received only five more votes than the bare minimum required for confirmation (Young 1984 711–13).

Confusion followed. Problems that had been submerged by the flurry of political activity surrounding the elections surfaced immediately. Both the armed forces and the bureaucracy were still, in their upper echelons, almost entirely European. The new leaders had accepted a plan for Africanization of the officer corps that would require a decade or more for implementation; the soldiers were not content to wait. On July 4, 1960, mutiny broke out in Kinshasa, and mutinous conditions existed all across the country. Lumumba's efforts at appeasement were unavailing. In the wake of the mutiny, European administrators gave way to panic and fled, leaving the administrative structure in the hands of previously unpromoted, and therefore inexperienced, Congolese bureaucrats. Moise Tshombe, now provincial president in Katanga, took advantage of the disruption in Kinshasa to declare Katanga an independent state on July 11. There, Belgian troops came to the aid of their protégé. A gendarmerie was formed with the aid of Belgian officers, and Belgian functionaries were ordered to remain at their posts. Although public and private support by these Belgians made the secession possible, Belgian government aid was refused, and the new state was not accorded official recognition by any country, including Belgium (Young 1984 711–720).

The intervention of Belgian troops in Katanga proved only a first step toward the internationalization of the Congo crisis. By July 14, 1960, the Congolese government had requested United Nations forces, American troops, and Soviet supervision (Young 1984 722). An international force, sent by the UN in response to this request, remained in the country until June 1964, but its effectiveness was hampered by UN Charter provisions that called for it to keep the peace without intervening in internal affairs or trying to influence the resolution of constitutional discord. Further, Soviet and American conflict within the UN organization, and the lack of a clearly legitimate center of authority within the

Congo during part of its stay, added to the force's difficulties in carrying out its assignment. As a result of these restrictions, they could offer Lumumba no relief in his struggle against secessionist Katanga and other rebels. By August, the United States had concluded that it could not dominate Lumumba and had begun to support political factions seeking his overthrow and using the CIA to hatch plots for his assassination. In Africa, however, Ghana's president Kwame Nkrumah, later defeated by a military coup run by the CIA, exerted all the diplomatic machinery at his command to keep Lumumba in power. When Lumumba discovered that UN forces would not be able to aid him in his attempt to stabilize the internal political situation, he requested and received Soviet aid (Young 1984 722–23).

At this point, the Congolese government disintegrated. President Kasavubu, on the basis of an ambiguous provision in the constitution, dismissed Lumumba from the office of prime minister on September 5. Lumumba responded by announcing the removal of Kasavubu. Parliament was convened and annulled the actions of both men. On September 14, Colonel Joseph Mobutu, former journalist and employee of the Congo Information Service in Brussels immediately prior to independence, seized power with UN approval. Mobutu and the UN then chose to recognize Kasavubu's position, but not Lumumba's. Western support, especially that of Belgium and the United States, was far more effective than anything the Soviets could provide for Lumumba (Young 1984 721). UN troops surrounded his house to "protect" him. When he later escaped and attempted to join his supporters in Kisangani (formerly Stanley Falls, the Inner Station of *Heart of Darkness*), he was captured, taken to Katanga, and murdered. (Young 1984 721).

The start of 1961 saw the Congo torn into rival camps. Supporters of Lumumba, who had regrouped in Kisangani under former Lumumba vice-premier Antoine Gizenga and claimed to be the only legal government, exercised some influence over Orientale and Kivu provinces. Kasavubu and Mobutu held an uncertain authority in the provinces of Leopoldville and Equateur. Katanga had proclaimed itself an independent state with Tshombe at its head, while in South Kasai, Albert Kalonji refused allegiance to either Gizenga or Kasavubu. With the administration paralyzed, the army in shambles, and the country suffering from the presence of international rivalries, prospects for the future of the unified Congo looked very dim (Ingham 316).

Throughout 1961–62, President Kasavubu attempted to salvage the nation. In July 1961, Parliament was reconvened with the UN as a mediator, and except for members of Conakat, representatives from all the provinces attended. Kasavubu was able to form a new government with Cyrille Adoula, former trade-union leader and strong supporter of UN and American policy, as a compromise candidate for prime minister. Parliament then turned to the task of drafting a new constitution. Attempts to end the Katanga secession dominated this period, but failed as Tshombe played a game of agreeing to rejoin the nation whenever he felt threatened and backing out when an immediate crisis ended. In August, UN forces, under pressure from New York headquarters, joined in the struggle against Katanga. There, on September 18, UN Secretary-General Dag Hammarskjöld was killed in a plane crash on his way to meet Tshombe in the hope that an agreement that would end the conflict could be reached. Fighting continued off and on, however, until late in 1962, when UN troops exceeded their instructions and pressed on to a decisive victory. On July 14, 1963, Tshombe finally declared an end to the Katanga secession (Young 1984 723–4).

Even with the period of Katangese secession finally at an end, the country remained politically fragmented. On September 30, President Kasavubu dissolved Parliament, which had been unable to reach agreement on a new constitution, and appointed a representative commission to take up the task, with the assistance of the UN. In October, Premier Adoula's government began to operate with full legislative powers, but over a country with severe economic problems and an ineffective army— a country in which regional autonomy was fact if not law. The new constitution, recommended in 1964, to some degree institutionalized that informal federalism (Young 1984 724–5).

Faced with increasing disorder, Premier Adoula's government was unable to take control. Tshombe, from his exile in Madrid, forged a policy designed to attract factions across the political spectrum. He succeeded in attracting President Kasavubu, who, in July 1964, invited Tshombe to form a government with him. Within a short time, anti-Tshombe elements, dominated by a faction still loyal to the policies formulated by Lumumba, rebelled against this new government. African countries, troubled by the return of Tshombe and his reintroduction of Europeans into the administration, refused aid. The government was supported, however, by Belgium and the United States. Their support led to a worldwide controversy when, together, they launched a paratrooper operation to rescue Europeans held hostage by the revolutionary national government proclaimed on September 5 in the Lumumbist capital at Kisangani. The country's African neighbors were deeply offended by the unstated assumption that European lives were of more value than African lives (Young 1984 725–26).

Although the main force of the rebellion was broken by the close of 1964 when the U.N. forces left, sporadic outbreaks continued throughout 1965. Government attempts to restore authority resulted in massacres that matched those of the rebels, and, although opposition was finally wiped out, recovery was slow. The months of fighting had destroyed communications networks and caused crop losses that led to serious food shortages in some areas (Ingham 317).

Elections to the National Assembly were scheduled in March 1965 under the new constitution. When Parliament was convened in the following September, Tshombe, whose new party had gained a majority, challenged Kasavubu for the office of president, and Kasavubu dismissed him from his post as prime minister. When Kasavubu failed in his attempt to gain parlimentary approval for a new government without Tshombe, the military intervened and installed General Joseph-Desiré Mobutu as president on November 25, 1965 (Young 1984 729–30).

Mobutu began his presidency by disbanding all existing political organizations. In the late 1960's, a new political order emerged, built around a single national party, the *Mouvement de la Revolution* (MPR), which was fused with all organizations in the State, from youth movements to trade unions. A national ideology, "authenticity," was proclaimed, a rejection of past European cultural influences in favor of African heritage. In 1971, under this policy, all names in the country (places and people) were changed: the Congo became the Republic of Zaire, and Joseph Mobutu became Mobutu Sese Seko—Mobutu Himself Forever. When the constitution was revised in 1974, it declared the MPR Zaire's sole institution; the State became, legally, a mere appendage of the party. The party's chief (Mobutu) automatically held the presidency and was given direct control as well as effective appointment power over all organs of government. At this time, "authenticity" became "Mobutism": the words and writings of the president constituted the official doctrine of the country (Young 1984 732–33). From then on, Mobutu Sese Seko has never been seen in public without a leopardskin cap and his carved staff, the traditional symbols of kingship.

Concentration of power in his own hands is the organizing principle behind Mobutu's methods. Potential rivals are allowed access to government positions but encouraged by the system to exploit them for personal gain (Kestin 103, 105). Those in the upper echelons of the political and economic fields, especially Mobutu himself, have been able to amass large fortunes. Any opposition is quickly neutralized. Often, return to favor is possible, but only for the properly chastened. Occasionally, removal is permanent or even deadly (Turner 126–27).

In a system so thoroughly personalized, catastrophic policy errors are a constant possibility (Young 1978 174). In pursuing his dream of a leadership position among developing African nations, Mobutu concentrated resources on development of the mining industry to the detriment of other areas of the economy with the result that the sharp fall in copper prices in 1973 hit much harder than was necessary. Also in 1973, Mobutu instituted a policy of "zairianization" (followed later by "radicalization"), under which economic enterprises were turned over directly or indirectly to party loyalists. Often they were merely stripped of their assets—no attempt was made to operate them. By 1976, when the failure of these policies was acknowledged and former owners invited to return, the economy was in ruins (Turner 124–25). For a stark, bleak picture of these troubled times, see the novel by V. S. Naipaul, *The Bend in the River* (1979), which is set in the town that grew up where Kurtz's trading station was located, then Stanley Falls, now Kisangani.

Internal conditions resulting from these and other policies left Zaire vulnerable to external threats and pressures. In 1977–78, the *Front National pour la Liberation du Congo* (FNLC), a force descended from the old Katangese gendarmerie, twice invaded the Shaba province from its base in neighboring Angola with the aim of overthrowing the Mobutu government. The Zairian army, which had in the past shown itself disloyal and inept despite massive infusions of foreign military aid (Turner 124–25), was reinforced by Moroccan troops and repelled the 1977 invasion (Shaba I) easily. By 1978, however, when the Shaba II invasion took place, the conflict had become a center point for international tensions. Although the primary motivation for the invasions came from the FNLC's opposition to conditions within Zaire, the United States saw Shaba II as an extension of aggressive Soviet-Cuban interventions in other parts of Africa (Young 1978 181–82). Zaire also attracted support of several European, African, and Middle Eastern nations and even China (Young 1978 169–70). Efforts at a peaceful settlement of differences between Angola and Zaire after Shaba I were hampered by continuing Angolan and Cuban support of the FNLC and by Zaire's continued support of the *Uniao Nacional para a Independicial Total de Angola* (UNITA) and other Angolan movements in their attempts to destabilize the Angolan government. The Shaba II invasion, which followed the failure of these efforts, had far more serious consequences (Zartman 132–37). Thousands were killed during the FNLC occupation, the reconquest by French and Belgian troops with logistical support from the United States, and the Zairian "pacification" that followed. This time, FNLC forces reached the mining center of Kolwezi, which had the result of crippling the country's vital mining industry for months. Zaire's rail connection across Angola to the coast was severed, and, in 1984, had still not been renewed.

At first, there had seemed reason to hope for stability and economic recovery under Mobutu's regime: post-independence disorder was brought to an end, the country reunited, the national debt erased, inflation brought under control, and real wages began to rise. Support for Mobutu was widespread among a people for whom memories of violence and upheaval were still fresh (Young 1978 170–71). By 1973–74, however, the picture had changed, and today Zaire's situation is uncertain: the debt to foreign banks has topped five billion dollars (interest payments alone reached one billion dollars in 1984) (Kestin 100, 101, 103); corruption is entrenched at all levels; millions of dollars have been wasted on ill-conceived public works projects (Turner 124–25); and the infrastructure necessary to support a prosperous agricultural sector has deteriorated seriously, and no effort is being made to restore it (Young 1978 175). At present, 60 percent of the country's food must be imported. Food shortages, impoverishment, and demoralization have pushed political unrest in the capital to a critical level, and conditions are little better for the rest of the population (Kestin 106, 110).

On December 7, 1986, Edward A. Gargan, former *New York Times* correspondent in West Africa, reported in the Sunday Magazine Section that in contrast to the traditional responsibilities upheld by village chiefs, President Mobutu does not believe "that he is accountable to his people.

In fact, in a continent plagued by what may seem to be an unfair number of corrupt leaders, Mobutu presides over a country where corruption
has reached dizzying new heights. Mobutu himself has assembled an
extraordinary fortune—one plundered from Africa's third-poorest country, a land with an annual per capita gross national product of $140. He
owns chateaus in Brussels, Paris and near Lausanne. He has homes in
Nice, Venice and Spain. He controls vast agricultural plantations in
Zaire and has interests in virtually every major foreign company operating in his country. It is impossible to quantify precisely the dimensions
of Mobutu's wealth, although in Kinshasa, the capital, $5 billion is often
mentioned as 'a nice round number.' "

Mobutu continues to hold power in part because of his pervasive network of internal control and the fading but still extant fears within Zaire
of another period of violence like that which follow independence.
Externally, Mobutu is propped up by European and American economic and political interests. He appeals skillfully and successfully to
Western fears of another Shaba invasion, of the Soviet-Cuban threat,
and of the disastrous consequences to Western creditors should the regime
collapse. The West has demanded political reforms in return for aid, but
the reforms have been more show than substance (Young 1978 178–
79). In 1983, economic reforms mandated by the International Mone-
tary Fund caused some optimism in the West, but, although they have
somewhat limited large-scale corruption (Blackburn 52), their impact on
the general population has been largely negative (Kestin 106–10). The
gulf between the privileged and the impoverished has continued to grow,
social tension has increased, and the potential for violence is high. The
legitimacy of the Mobutu government continues to erode, and its survival, although not impossible, is far from certain (Young 1978 176,
178–79, 183).

Works Cited

Blackburn, Peter. "Mobutu is Turning Turbulent Zaire into an Island of Stability." *Business
    Week*, December 17, 1984: 52 +.
Great Britain, Naval Intelligence Division. *The Belgian Congo*. Geographical Handbook Series.
    Oxford: Navel Intelligence Division, 1944.
Ingham, Kenneth. "Congo (Kinshasa)." *Encyclopedia Britannica*. 1973 ed.
Kestin, Hesh. "God and Man in Zaire." *Forbes* 132 (1985): 100–110.
Packard, Randall. *Chiefship and Cosmology: An Historical Study of Political Competition.*
    Bloomington: Indiana UP, 1981.
Slade, Ruth M., and Marjory Taylor. *The Belgian Congo*. 2nd ed. London: Oxford UP, 1961.
Turner, Thomas. "Mobutu's Zaire: Permanently on the Verge of Collapse?" *Current History* 80
    (1981): 124 +.
Young, M. Crawford. "Zaire, Rwanda and Burundi." *The Cambridge History of Africa*. Ed.
    Michael Crowder. 8 vols. Cambridge: Cambridge UP, 1984.
———. "Zaire: The Unending Crisis." *Foreign Affairs* 57 (1978): 169–85.
Zartman, I. William. *Ripe for Resolution: Conflict and Intervention in Africa*. New York: Oxford
    UP, 1985.

Conrad in the Congo

> On the 14th of August, 1879, I arrived before the mouth of this river to ascend it, with the novel mission of sowing along its banks civilised settlements, to peacefully conquer and subdue it, to remould it in harmony with modern ideas into National States, within whose limits the European merchant shall go hand in hand with the dark African trader, and justice and law and order shall prevail, and murder and lawlessness and cruel barter of slaves shall for ever cease.
> —HENRY M. STANLEY, 1885

> Night-time. We are slowly ascending the river. There are a few lights in the distance on the left bank; a bush fire on the horizon; at our feet the terrifying thickness of the waters.
> —ANDRÉ GIDE, 1927

MURIEL C. BRADBROOK

[Conrad: A Biographical Sketch] †

In the history of English literature there has never been anything like the history of Joseph Conrad; nor, so far as I am aware, has there been anything like him in any other European literature. He was a Pole of the landowning class, who became a Marseilles gun-runner at twenty, an English master mariner at twenty-nine, and one of the great English novelists at thirty-eight. Born in 1857, his childhood was darkened by the savage repressions which Tsarist Russia inflicted on the Poles after the abortive rebellion of 1863. His father, as a leader of the Polish people, was imprisoned and exiled; his mother, who elected to share the exile, was treated with ruthless barbarity and died in 1865. His father, a dying man, returned to Cracow in 1868 and died the next year. He had been a poet, a dramatist, and a translator of Hugo, de Vigny [1] and Shakespeare.

Konrad Korzeniowski was urged to seek his fortune abroad by his guardian and uncle, Tadeusz Bobrowski: but none of the family approved of his plan to be a sailor. However, in 1874, Joseph Conrad went to Marseilles, and here he became engaged in gun traffic for the Carlist

† From *Joseph Conrad: Poland's English Genius* (New York: Cambridge UP, 1941) 5–6. Reprinted by permission. Unless indicated otherwise, annotations are by the editor.

1. Victor Hugo (1802–85) and Alfred Victor de Vigny (1797–1863), French writers.

party in Spain. Here also he met two people who were to count for more than anything as inspiration to his literature, whose portraits he drew agai: and again—a lovely Basque girl, whose name is unknown,[2] and Dominic Cervoni, the Corsican sailor.[3] Conrad sailed also to the West Indies and to Istanbul; and it was not until 1878 that he landed at Lowestoft, having joined an English vessel. Till 1894 he sailed in English ships with the one interlude of his Congo adventure in 1890; and though his original romantic impulse had sprung from a reading of Marryat,[4] his efficiency was recognised by the usual certificates from that very unromantic body, the Board of Trade, in 1880, 1883 and 1886, when he took his master's "ticket". The story of his seafaring life is told in his books. He sailed in Australian wool-clippers, traders in Malaya and the Gulf of Siam, and in Mediterranean and home waters. It was only in 1889 that Conrad began his first novel,[5] and not till five years later that he finally gave up the sea. He had a long struggle as an author, for though he was soon recognised by such people as Edward Garnett and Henry James, there was little money in his work, and for nearly twenty years he lived in poverty. Then came prosperity but also the Great War, agonising to Conrad: his son was in the British Army, his feelings triply engaged by his triple fidelity to England, France and Poland. Finally, after a few years of success and ease, he died suddenly in 1924, at the age of sixty-six.

JOSEPH CONRAD

Geography and Some Explorers †

The voyages of the early explorers were prompted by an acquisitive spirit, the idea of lucre in some form, the desire of trade or the desire of loot, disguised in more or less fine words. But Cook's three voyages are free from any taint of that sort.[1] His aims needed no disguise. They were scientific. His deeds speak for themselves with the masterly simplicity of a hard-won success. In that respect he seems to belong to the single-minded explorers of the nineteenth century, the late fathers of militant geography whose only object was the search for truth. Geography is a science of facts, and they devoted themselves to the discovery of facts in the configuration and features of the main continents.

2. Identified as Paula de Somogyi by Jerry Allen, *The Thunder and the Sunshine* (New York, 1958), but denied by Jocelyn Baines, *Joseph Conrad: A Critical Biography* (London, 1960). Frederick R. Karl, *Joseph Conrad: The Three Lives* (New York, 1979), takes a middle stance.
3. The story is told most directly in *The Arrow of Gold* [Bradbrook's note].
4. Captain Frederick Marryat (1792–1848), British naval officer and novelist, who wrote *Mr. Midshipman Easy* and other stories of the sea.

5. *Almayer's Folly*.
† From *Last Essays*, ed. Richard Curle (London: J. M. Dent & Sons, Ltd., 1926) 10–17. Reprinted by permission. Annotations by the present editor.
1. Captain James Cook (1728–79), supported by the Admiralty and the Royal Society, made three trips around the world, 1768–71, 1772–75, and 1776–79, with the special purpose of exploring and charting the South Pacific. Cook was killed in the Hawaiian Islands, February 14, 1779.

It was the century of landsmen investigators. In saying this I do not forget the polar explorers, whose aims were certainly as pure as the air of those high latitudes where not a few of them laid down their lives for the advancement of geography. Seamen, men of science, it is difficult to speak of them without admirative emotion. The dominating figure among the seamen explorers of the first half of the nineteenth century is that of another good man, Sir John Franklin,[2] whose fame rests not only on the extent of his discoveries, but on professional prestige and high personal character. This great navigator, who never returned home, served geography even in his death. The persistent efforts extending over ten years to ascertain his fate advanced greatly our knowledge of the polar regions.

As gradually revealed to the world this fate appeared the more tragic in this, that for the first two years the way of the *Erebus* and *Terror* expedition seemed to be the way to the desired and important success, while in truth it was all the time the way of death, the end of the darkest drama perhaps played behind the curtain of Arctic mystery.

The last words unveiling the mystery of the *Erebus* and *Terror* expedition were brought home and disclosed to the world by Sir Leopold McClintock, in his book, "The Voyage of the Fox in the Arctic Seas." It is a little book, but it records with manly simplicity the tragic ending of a great tale. It so happened that I was born in the year of its publication. Therefore, I may be excused for not getting hold of it till ten years afterwards. I can only account for it falling into my hands by the fact that the fate of Sir John Franklin was a matter of European interest, and that Sir Leopold McClintock's book was translated, I believe, into every language of the white races.

My copy was probably in French. But I have read the work many times since. I have now on my shelves a copy of a popular edition got up exactly as I remember my first one. It contains the touching facsimile of the printed form filled in with a summary record of the two ships' work, the name of "Sir John Franklin commanding the expedition" written in ink, and the pathetic underlined entry "All well." It was found by Sir Leopold McClintock under a cairn[3] and it is dated just a year before the two ships had to be abandoned in their deadly ice-trap, and their crews' long and desperate struggle for life began.

There could hardly have been imagined a better book for letting in the breath of the stern romance of polar exploration into the existence of a boy whose knowledge of the poles of the earth had been till then of an abstract formal kind as mere imaginary ends of the imaginary axis upon which the earth turns. The great spirit of the realities of the story sent me off on the romantic explorations of my inner self; to the discov-

---

2. Sir John Franklin (1786–1847) in 1845 led an exploring party in the *Erebus* and *Terror* in search of the Northwest passage. Franklin died while the ships were ice-bound from April 1846 to September 1848, at which point the crews tried their luck on foot. None survived. See *Heart of Darkness*, p. 8.

3. A marker formed by piling stones.

ery of the taste of poring over maps; and revealed to me the existence of
a latent devotion to geography which interfered with my devotion (such
as it was) to my other schoolwork.

Unfortunately, the marks awarded for that subject were almost as few
as the hours apportioned to it in the school curriculum by persons of no
romantic sense for the real, ignorant of the great possibilities of active
life; with no desire for struggle, no notion of the wide spaces of the
world—mere bored professors, in fact, who were not only middle-aged
but looked to me as if they had never been young. And their geography
was very much like themselves, a bloodless thing with a dry skin covering a repulsive armature of uninteresting bones.

* * *

Thus it happened that I got no marks at all for my first and only paper
on Arctic geography, which I wrote at the age of thirteen. I still think
that for my tender years it was an erudite performance. I certainly did
know something of Arctic geography, but what I was after really, I suppose, was the history of Arctic exploration. My knowledge had considerable gaps, but I managed to compress my enthusiasm into just two
pages, which in itself was a sort of merit. Yet I got no marks. For one
thing it was not a set subject. I believe the only comment made about it
to my private tutor was that I seemed to have been wasting my time in
reading books of travel instead of attending to my studies. I tell you,
those fellows were always trying to take my scalp. On another occasion
I just saved it by proficiency in map-drawing. It must have been good, I
suppose; but all I remember about it is that it was done in a loving spirit.

I have no doubt that star-gazing is a fine occupation, for it leads you
within the borders of the unattainable. But map-gazing, to which I became
addicted so early, brings the problems of the great spaces of the earth
into stimulating and directing contact with sane curiosity and gives an
honest precision to one's imaginative faculty. And the honest maps of
the nineteenth century nourished in me a passionate interest in the truth
of geographical facts and a desire for precise knowledge which was extended
later to other subjects.

For a change had come over the spirit of cartographers. From the
middle of the eighteenth century on the business of map-making had
been growing into an honest occupation, registering the hard-won
knowledge, but also in a scientific spirit recording the geographical ignorance of its time. And it was Africa, the continent out of which the
Romans used to say some new thing was always coming, that got cleared
of the dull imaginary wonders of the dark ages, which were replaced by
exciting spaces of white paper. Regions unknown! My imagination could
depict to itself there worthy, adventurous and devoted men, nibbling at
the edges, attacking from north and south and east and west, conquering
a bit of truth here and a bit of truth there, and sometimes swallowed up
by the mystery their hearts were so persistently set on unveiling.

Among them Mungo Park, of western Sudan, and Bruce, of Abyssi-

nia,[4] were, I believe, the first friends I made when I began to take notice—
I mean geographical notice—of the continents of the world into which
I was born. The fame of these two had already been for a long time
European, and their figures had become historical by then. But their
story was a very novel thing to me, for the very latest geographical news
that could have been whispered to me in my cradle was that of the
expedition of Burton and Speke, the news of the existence of Tanganyika
and of Victoria Nyanza.[5]

I stand here confessed as a contemporary of the Great Lakes. Yes, I
could have heard of their discovery in my cradle, and it was only right
that, grown to a boy's estate, I should have in the later sixties done my
first bit of map-drawing and paid my first homage to the prestige of their
first explorers. It consisted in entering laboriously in pencil the outline
of Tanganyika on my beloved old atlas, which, having been published
in 1852, knew nothing, of course, of the Great Lakes. The heart of its
Africa was white and big.

                              *   *   *

It must not be supposed that I gave up my interest in the polar regions.
My heart and my warm participation swung from the frigid to the torrid
zone, fascinated by the problems of each, no doubt, but more yet by the
men who, like masters of a great art, worked each according to his temperament to complete the picture of the earth. Almost each day of my
schoolboy life had its hour given up to their company. And to this day I
think that it was a very good company.

Not the least interesting part in the study of geographical discovery
lies in the insight it gives one into the characters of that special kind of
men who devoted the best part of their lives to the exploration of land
and sea. In the world of mentality and imagination which I was entering
it was they and not the characters of famous fiction who were my first
friends. Of some of them I had soon formed for myself an image indissolubly connected with certain parts of the world. For instance, western
Sudan, of which I could draw the rivers and principal features from
memory even now, means for me an episode in Mungo Park's life.

It means for me the vision of a young, emaciated, fair-haired man,
clad simply in a tattered shirt and worn-out breeches, gasping painfully
for breath and lying on the ground in the shade of an enormous African
tree (species unknown), while from a neighbouring village of grass huts

4. Mungo Park (1771–1806), Scottish explorer of
the Niger. Park's account of his first trip, Travels
in the Interior of Africa, was published in 1799 and
immediately proved popular. He drowned in the
Niger while on a second exploration.

James Bruce (1730–94) was also a Scottish
explorer in Africa who wrote in retirement Travels
to Discover the Source of the Nile in the Years 1768–
73. 5 volumes, 1790.

5. Sir Richard Francis Burton (1821–90), known
for his translation of the "Arabian Nights" (The
Thousand Nights and a Night, 16 volumes, 1885–

86), was an adventurer who set the pattern for
Stanley, Lawrence, and their kind. The Foreign
Office and Royal Geographical Society commissioned Burton in 1856 to search for the sources of
the Nile and to map what Burton called the "huge
white blot" of Central Africa. In February he discovered Lake Tanganyika, and his assistant, Capt.
J. H. Speke, discovered Victoria Nyanza. The discovery of these and the other Great Lakes drew
David Livingstone into his own search for the
sources of the Nile.

a charitable black-skinned woman is approaching him with a calabash[6] full of pure cold water, a simple draught which, according to himself, seems to have effected a miraculous cure. The central Sudan, on the other hand, is represented to me by a very different picture, that of a self-confident and keen-eyed person in a long cloak and wearing a turban on his head, riding slowly towards a gate in the mud walls of an African city, from which an excited population is streaming out to behold the wonder—Doctor Barth, the protégé of Lord Palmerston, and subsidized by the British Foreign Office, approaching Kano, which no European eye had seen till then, but where forty years later my friend Sir Hugh Clifford, the Governor of Nigeria, travelled in state in order to open a college.[7]

I must confess that I read that bit of news and inspected the many pictures in the illustrated papers without any particular elation. Education is a great thing, but Doctor Barth gets in the way. Neither will the monuments left by all sorts of empire builders suppress for me the memory of David Livingstone. The words "Central Africa" bring before my eyes an old man with a rugged, kind face and a clipped, gray moustache, pacing wearily at the head of a few black followers along the reed-fringed lakes towards the dark native hut on the Congo headwaters in which he died, clinging in his very last hour to his heart's unappeased desire for the sources of the Nile.

That passion had changed him in his last days from a great explorer into a restless wanderer refusing to go home any more. From his exalted place among the blessed of militant geography and with his memory enshrined in Westminster Abbey, he can well afford to smile without bitterness at the fatal delusion of his exploring days, a notable European figure and the most venerated perhaps of all the objects of my early geographical enthusiasm.

Once only did that enthusiasm expose me to the derision of my schoolboy chums. One day, putting my finger on a spot in the very middle of the then white heart of Africa, I declared that some day I would go there. My chums' chaffing was perfectly justifiable. I myself was ashamed of having been betrayed into mere vapouring. Nothing was further from my wildest hopes. Yet it is a fact that, about eighteen years afterwards, a wretched little stern-wheel steamboat I commanded lay moored to the bank of an African river.

6. A gourd.
7. Heinrich Barth (1821–65), German explorer, and author of *Travels and Discoveries in North and Central Africa*, 1857, visited Kano in Northern Nigeria in 1851 and 1854. The 3rd Viscount Palmerston (1784–1865), statesman and champion of empire, was prime minister from 1855 until his death. Sir Hugh Clifford (1866–1941), a lifetime civil servant, was governor of Nigeria from 1919–25. He was author of several books, the first of which, *Studies in Brown Humanity* (about Malaya), was favorably reviewed by Conrad in the April 1898 *Academy*. The two then became and remained friends. See Clifford's review of the *Youth* volume (*The Spectator*, November 29, 1902).

JOSEPH CONRAD

["When I Grow Up I Shall Go *There*"] †

It was in 1868, when nine years old or thereabouts, that while looking at a map of Africa of the time and putting my finger on the blank space then representing the unsolved mystery of that continent, I said to myself with absolute assurance and an amazing audacity which are no longer in my character now:

"When I grow up I shall *go there*."

And of course I thought no more about it till after a quarter of a century or so an opportunity offered to go there—as if the sin of childish audacity was to be visited on my mature head. Yes. I did go there: *there* being the region of Stanley Falls which in '68 was the blankest of blank spaces on the earth's figured surface.

JOSEPH CONRAD

Extracts from Correspondence, January 16 to June 18, 1890 *

16th January, 1890
[letterhead: The British and
Foreign Transit Agency. Barr,
Moering & Co., Shipping and
Custom House Agents, 36,
Camomile Street, London, E.C.]

My Dear Uncle.[1]

I have just had a letter from Kazimierówka,[2] in which, in reply to my inquiry, Uncle Tadeusz tells me that you are living in Brussels and gives me your address. I am terribly sorry that I did not know this earlier, as I

---

† From *A Personal Record* (London: J. M. Dent & Sons, Ltd., 1912) 13. Reprinted by permission.
* From *The Collected Letters of Joseph Conrad, Volume I, 1861–1897*, ed. Frederick R. Karl (also: General Editor) and Laurence Davies (Cambridge: Cambridge UP, 1983) 33–34, 36, 41, 48, 49, 50–51, 51–53, 55–56, 57. Reprinted by permission of the General Editor, the Estate of Joseph Conrad, and the Cambridge University Press. Annotations by the present editor.
1. Alexander Poradowski, first cousin of Conrad's maternal grandmother, was, like Conrad's father, an exile from Poland after the abortive revolution of 1863. He died February 7, 1890, but not before

Conrad was able to see him again and meet his wife Marguerite, daughter of a distinguished scholar who was for a time the archivist to Belgium's royal family. Madame Poradowska, the "aunt" of *Heart of Darkness*, because of her family's position had many friends within the royal government. Moreover, from the 1880's on, she gained some minor fame as an author in her own right. In both respects, she was a beneficient spirit to Conrad at this stage in his careers as seaman and writer.
2. In the then, as now, Russian Ukraine, but formerly a part of Poland; the home of Conrad's uncle and guardian, Tadeusz Bobrowski.

was in Brussels in October last year.[3] It is possible, however, that before long I shall have to visit Brussels again. The object of this scrawl to you is to remember myself to the relation whose great kindness to me in Cracow[4] I have certainly not forgotten. I do not ask whether you will permit me to visit you—for I permit myself not to doubt it; but I would very much like to be certain that you are in Brussels and that I shall be able to find you there in the course of the next month.

I returned to London six months ago after a three years' absence. Of these three years I spent one among the islands of the Malay Archipelago, after which I spent two years as master of an Australian vessel in the Pacific and Indian Oceans. I am now more or less under contract to the 'Société Belge pour le Commerce du Haut Congo' to be master of one of its river steamers. I have not signed any agreement, but Mr. A. Thys, the director of that Company, has promised me the post. Whether he will keep his promise and when he will send me to Africa, I do not yet know; it will probably be in May.

I intend to visit Uncle Tadeusz soon; that is to say I want to, and he also wants me to; but he says that it is difficult during the winter. I am expecting a letter from him in a few days' time, which will decide the matter. If I do go home it will be via Hamburg—returning via Brussels. If, however, my visit is postponed I shall nevertheless be going to Brussels in March in connection with the post in the Congo. Therefore in any case I shall have to pleasure of seeing you, my dear Uncle, and of making myself known to Aunt Poradowska whom I only know from that portrait of her which you had with you in Cracow.

In the meantime, my dear Uncle, a most cordial embrace from your affectionate relation and servant,

Konrad Korzeniowski.
A letter care of Messrs. Barr Moering will always find me.

Tuesday, 4 February 1980
[London]

My dear Aunt,

Many thanks for your card. I am leaving London tomorrow, Friday, at 9 a.m. and should arrive in Brussels at 5.30 p.m. I shall therefore be with you at about six. Believe me, with the liveliest gratitude, your very affectionate nephew and very devoted servant

Conrad Korzeniowski

3. Conrad had gone to Brussels to be interviewed by Albert Thys (1832–1913) for the position of captain of a river steamer on the Congo. In December 1888, Thys had founded the Trading Company of the Upper Congo, which was, under the terms of the Berlin agreement, an illegal *commissionaire* company. Thys has been described as a long-time "henchman" of Leopold in Congo affairs.
4. Conrad's childhood home and the prerevolutionary home of Poradowski.

10 March 1890
Kazimierówka

My dear Aunt,

Only yesterday I received your letter of 15 February, through the agency of our good Aunt Gabrielle. The delay is explained by our absence from Kazimierówka, to which we returned yesterday after an excursion in the immediate area that lasted ten days.

Many thanks for the kind memory you carry of me. My admiration and friendship for you are increased by a feeling of deep gratitude for the goodness you show me. The thought of seeing you again in Brussels will console me when the time to part from my uncle arrives. I leave him on 15 April, and I will have the happiness of seeing you on the 23rd of the same month, if all goes well.

* * *

I ask your pardon for such a short letter. The post leaves today and I have received a pile of letters which must be answered promptly. I believe that my recommendation to the Company of the Congo was not strong enough and that the matter will not succeed at all. That vexes me a little.

To our next meeting, dear Aunt—soon, for time goes quickly. I kiss your hands, and I embrace you warmly. Your affectionate nephew

C. Korzeniowski

14 April 1890
Kazimierówka

My dear Aunt,

I have received your kind and charming letter, and this proof of friendship you give me in concerning yourself with my African plans touches me more than I can express. Many thanks for your kind attention. With impatience I await the moment when I shall be able to kiss your hands while thanking you in person.

I am leaving my uncle's in four days. I have some visits to make on the way (among others, one of forty-eight hours to Lublin) so that I shall not be in Brussels until the 29th of this month.—Then we shall talk of your plans to visit Poland and your future projects, which interest me a good deal—as you can well believe.[5]

Have you received my last letter? I wonder. I have some doubts now. Did I understand you correctly? Has my reply offended you? In reading it, please think of the deep attachment I feel for you and also for the memory of my poor dear Uncle Alexander. So be indulgent, my dear and kind aunt.

---

5. Madame Poradowska planned to visit her late husband's (and Conrad's) relatives in Lublin, Poland, during the summer of 1890.

Au revoir, then, for the time being. We have visitors and I have just escaped for a moment to write these few words. They are calling for me!

I kiss your hands. Your very devoted friend and nephew
                                                    J.C. Korzeniowski

                                        London, 2nd May, 1890.

My dear Maryleczka.[6]

I could not write any sooner. I have been extremely busy and in fact still am so. In four days' time I am sailing to the Congo, and I have to prepare myself for a three years' stay in Central Africa. You can, therefore, imagine how precious each minute is to me. I hope that your Mother is better now and that you, my dear, will soon be writing to me. Probably your letter will be too late to find me in Europe, but it is certain to be forwarded to me. Do not be surprised by the delay in getting a reply; no one can tell where your letter will eventually catch up with me.

                        *   *   *

                                        Your loving,
                                        K. N. Korzeniowski.

                                        London, 6th May, 1890

Maryleczka dear,

I am sailing in an hour. As soon as the photographs are ready I shall send a letter.

                        *   *   *

                                        Your loving,
                                        K. N. Korzeniowski.

                                        15 May 1890
                                        Teneriffe

My dear little Aunt,

What if I were to begin by telling you I have so far avoided the fever! What if I could assure you all my letters will start with this good news! Well, we shall see! In the meanwhile I am comparatively happy, which is all one can hope for in this wicked world. We left Bordeaux on a rainy day.[7] Dismal day, a not very cheerful departure, some haunting memories, some vague regrets, some still vaguer hopes. One doubts the future. For indeed—I ask myself—why should anyone believe in it? And, con-

---

6. Maria Bobrowska, one of the cousins whom   7. Around May 10.
Conrad had visited in Lublin.

sequently, why be sad about it? A little illusion, many dreams, a rare flash of happiness followed by disillusionment, a little anger and much suffering, and then the end. Peace! That is the programme, and we must see this tragi-comedy to the end. One must play one's part in it.

The screw turns and carries me off to the unknown. Happily, there is another me who prowls through Europe, who is with you at this moment. Who will get to Poland ahead of you. Another me who moves about with great ease; who can even be in two places at once. Don't laugh! I believe it has happened. I am very serious. So don't laugh. I allow you, however, to say: 'What a fool he is!' This is a concession. Life is composed of concessions and compromises.

* * *

I kiss your hands and commend myself to your heart.

Your very devoted
Conrad

Freetown, Sierre Leone,
22nd May, 1890.

My dearest Karol![8]

It is just a month today since you were scandalized by my hurried departure from Lublin. From the date and address of this letter you will see that I have had to be pretty quick, and I am only just beginning to breathe a little more calmly. If you only knew the devilish haste I had to make! From London to Brussels, and back again to London! And then again I dashed full tilt to Brussels! If you had only seen all the tin boxes and revolvers, the high boots and the tender farewells; just another handshake and just another pair of trousers!—and if you knew all the bottles of medicine and all the affectionate wishes I took away with me, you would understand in what a typhoon, cyclone, hurricane, earthquake—no!—in what a universal cataclysm, in what a fantastic atmosphere of mixed shopping, business, and affecting scenes, I passed two whole weeks. But the fortnight spent at sea has allowed me to rest and I am impatiently waiting for the end of this trip. I am due to reach Boma on the 7th of next month and then leave with my caravan to go to Léopoldville.[9] As far as I can make out from my 'lettre d'instruction' I am destined to the command of a steamboat, belonging to M. Delcommune's[1] exploring party, which is being got ready. I like this prospect very much, but I know nothing for certain as everything is supposed to be kept secret. What makes me rather uneasy is the information that 60 per cent. of our Company's employees return to Europe before they have completed

---

8. Another cousin, Karol ("Charles") Zagórski.
9. Conrad actually arrived on June 12, took a steamer to Matadi, where he departed by foot on June 28 for Leopoldville and Kinshasa on Stanley Pool, where he arrived in the morning of August 2.
1. Alexandre Delcommune (1855–1922), who wrote a book on his twenty years in Africa. In 1890 he headed an expedition, the "Eldorado Exploring Expedition" of *Heart of Darkness*, up the Kassai River for the new Katanga Company, for which Conrad was to have been the captain of the river steamer.

even six months' service. Fever and dysentery! There are others who are sent home in a hurry at the end of a year, so that they shouldn't die in the Congo. God forbid! It would spoil the statistics which are excellent, you see! In a word, there are only 7 per cent. who can do their three years' service. It's a fact! To tell the truth, they are French! Des nevrosés! (C'est très chic d'être nevrosé[2]—one winks and speaks through the nose.) Yes! But a Polish nobleman, cased in British tar! What a concoction! Nous verrons![3] In any case I shall console myself by remembering— faithful to our national traditions—that I looked for this trouble myself.

When you see—with the help of a microscope, no doubt—the hieroglyphics of my handwriting. you will, I expect, wonder why I am writing to you? First, because it is a pleasure to talk to you; next, because, considering the distinguished personage who is penning this autograph, it ought to be a pleasure to you too. You can bequeath it to your children. Future generations will read it with admiration (and I hope with profit). In the meantime, trêve de bêtises![4]

I kiss my dear uncle's and aunt's hands, and your wife's too. I forget none of you, but can't write the whole list because this abominable lamp is going out.

Yours very affectionately
K. N. Korzeniowski.

10 June 1890
Libreville, Gabon

Dear Little Aunt,

This being the last port of call before Boma, where my sea-voyage ends, I am beginning this letter here at the moment of leaving so as to continue it during the passage and end it the day of my arrival in Boma, where of course I am going to post it.

No new events. As to feelings, also nothing new, and there is the trouble. For, if one could unburden oneself of one's heart, one's memory (and also—one's brain) and obtain a whole new set of these things, life would become perfectly diverting. As this is impossible, life is not perfectly diverting. It is abominably sad! * * *

While awaiting the inevitable fever, I am very well. In order to make my existence even slightly bearable, I need letters, many letters. From you, among others. Do not forget what I am telling you, dear and kind little Aunt.

After my departure from Boma, there may be an extended silence. I shall be unable to write until Léopoldville. It takes twenty days to go there, on foot too! How horrible!

You will probably write to my uncle; it was your intention, I believe.

---

2. "Such neurotics! (Very fashionable to be neurotic. . . .)"

3. "We shall see!"

4. . . . no more of this foolishness!"

It would be kind if you would give him news of me. For example, that you saw me in Brussels, that I was well in body and spirit. This will give him pleasure and make him easier about my fate. He is very fond of me, and I grow as tender as an old fool when I think of him. Forgive this weakness. When do you return to Brussels? What are your future plans? Tell me all about it in your letter and sit at your desk only when you have a strong inclination to chat with 'the absent one'. 'The absent one' will be my official name in future. I shall be very happy to know that nobody is worrying you; that you work with an untroubled free spirit. I await your new work with curiosity and impatience. You must send it to me. Agreed? I have learned that my company has a sea-going ship and probably will build others. If I could obtain the command of one, that would be much better than the river. Not only is it healthier; there is always the chance of returning to Europe at least every year. When you return to Brussels, I beg you to let me know if any ships of this sort are being built so that I can enter my request. You can learn this through M. Wauters,[5] whereas I, in the depths of Africa, will have no news. I am sure you will do that for me.

Au revoir, dear Aunt. I love and embrace you.

C. Korzeniowski

18 June 1890
Matadi

Thank you! Many thanks, dear Aunt, for your kind and charming letter, which met me at Boma. Only my dear little Aunt could think up such splendid surprises. Has it given me pleasure?! I have a good mind to say No in order to punish you for having asked, for having seemed to doubt it!

I leave tomorrow on foot.[6] Not an ass here except your very humble servant. Twenty days of safari. Temperature very bearable here and health very good. I shall write as soon as possible. Now I embrace you very heartily and kiss the hand that wrote the words which made me very happy the day before yesterday. Your very loving nephew and devoted servant

Conrad

5. A. J. Wauters was the general secretary for all the Belgian companies operating in the Congo and was editor of two periodicals that furnish detailed information on all activities within the Free State, the *Mouvement Geographique* and the *Congo Illustré*.

6. Frederick Karl questions the date of this letter because "The Congo Diary" indicates that Conrad left Matadi on June 28, arriving in Kinshasa on August 2.

ZDZISŁAW NAJDER

[Introduction to "The Congo Diary" and the "Up-river Book"] †

Conrad's stay in the Congo (12 June–4 December 1890) is one of the most important periods of his life. Even if we question as excessive the claim of his first biographer, G. Jean-Aubry, that the journey to the Congo shaped Conrad's philosophical outlook,[1] we must recognize the enormous physical and moral impact of these six months. Conrad signed in Brussels a contract to serve for three years as an officer on river steamboats belonging to the Société Anonyme pour le Commerce du Haut-Congo. He left Europe full of energy and thrilling expectations, with ideas about a "civilizing mission."[2] He returned gravely ill, never to regain fully his good health, disillusioned, with memories to be used later in his most famous story, "Heart of Darkness," and in another bitter denunciation of colonialism, "An Outpost of Progress."

From this period there survive a few letters and also a unique document, the so-called "Congo Diary." The manuscript consists of two notebooks. The first, untitled, is an actual diary, kept by Conrad during his trek from Matadi to Kinshasa between [28] June and 1 August. This part was published (with errors and rather spotty annotation) by Richard Curle in 1926 and included in the volume *Last Essays*. The second, entitled by Conrad "Up-river Book" and commenced on board the steamer *Roi des Belges* on 3 August 1890, does not preserve the form of a diary—there are only four dates, although it spans sixteen days—and contains almost exclusively notes, instructions and sketches concerning navigation up the Congo, at that time a not-too-frequented and only recently explored river. The second notebook was not published by Curle because, according to him, "it has no personal or literary interest."[3] This I believe is an exaggerated statement; still, since Curle's verdict, no Conrad scholar seems to have looked into the "Up-river Book."

The Congo notes constitute one of Conrad's earliest writings in English and reflect, if not his command of the language (his third), then at least his characteristic difficulties with it. These would come from two sides at once: from the Polish, which was his native language, the only one he used daily for his first seventeen years, and the one in which in 1890 he wrote most of his letters; and from the French, which he learned as a child, mastered during his stay in France in 1874–78 and, of course, used in the Congo. And his difficulties were threefold: choice of words, spelling, and grammar, particularly syntax.

† From *Congo Diary and Other Uncollected Pieces*, ed. Zdzisław Najder (New York: Doubleday, 1978) 1–6. Reprinted by permission of the editor.
1. G. Jean-Aubry, *Joseph Conrad: Life and Letters*, 2 vols., London, 1926, vol. I, pp. 141–43. [See p. 195, below—*Editor*.]

2. Tadeusz Bobrowski to Conrad, 24 June 1890, Zdzisław Najder, ed., *Conrad's Polish Background*, Oxford University Press, 1964, p. 129.
3. Richard Curle, Introduction to "The Congo Diary," Joseph Conrad, *Last Essays*, p. 159.

156 BACKGROUNDS AND SOURCES

Spelling mistakes are, of course, both most obvious and most trivial. Usually, not only in the notebooks, but in Conrad manuscripts in general, they stemmed from a similarity between an English and a French (differently spelled) word; and so he would write "ressemble" for "resemble," "mentionned" for "mentioned," and so on. Some, like the persistent "lays" and "laying" for "lies" and "lying" (found also, for instance, in a letter to Garnett of 15 March 1895), arise from the intricacies of English conjugation. The really exotic ones, like "andulating" for "undulating," can be explained only by reference to the rules of Polish spelling and pronunciation.

In his choice of words, Conrad would sometimes fail to realize the difference of meaning between similar-looking French and English words: hence "accidented" in the sense of "uneven." In grammar, the pressure of Polish seems to have been stronger throughout his writing career.[4] "There is 3 islands" is, of course, a Gallicism; but "much more trees" is a mistake Poles habitually tend to commit. Syntactically flabby sentences, like the one beginning "The looks of the whole establishment . . ." (27 June) sound perfectly normal in Polish, which is a much more inflected and therefore cohesive language.

The diary proper has been used as a source of biographical information and, even more frequently, compared with "Heart of Darkness" for purposes of psychological and factual interpretation of the story. I shall not discuss the parallelisms here, as the ground seems to have been pretty well covered—and also because I am afraid that paying excessive attention to such analogies may be detrimental to a fuller understanding of the story. It may distract us from seeing what it essentially is: not a relation about places and events, but a symbolic presentation of moral and ideological problems. It may also hamper our recognition that Marlow is not the author's mouthpiece, but one of the two main characters of the story, a co-hero, whose point of view is markedly different from the authorial perspective and whose attitudes are even subjected to irony. Generally, the fact that we assume to know much about the personal background of "Heart of Darkness" encourages biographical and psychoanalytic approaches to the tale—which would greatly displease Conrad himself. More important than any autobiographical echoes are the allusions, conscious or not, to literary tradition and, more broadly, to the history of ideas—to the Aeneid, to Dante, to the legends about Alexander the Great.[5]

4. Cf. Arthur P. Coleman, "Polonisms in the English of Conrad's *Chance*," *Modern Language Notes*, XLVI (Nov. 1931), pp. 463–68.
5. On analogies with the *Aeneid* see Lillian Feder, "Marlow's Descent into Hell," *Nineteenth-century Fiction*, IX (March 1955), pp. 280–92. On analogies with Virgil and Dante see Robert O. Evans, "Conrad's Underworld," *Modern Fiction Studies*, II (May 1956), pp. 56–62. Both texts are reprinted in *The Art of Joseph Conrad: A Critical Symposium*, ed. R. W. Stallman, Michigan State University Press, 1960.

The parallel with Alexander the Great has not been so far noticed, although several important elements of the legends about his death resemble significantly the story of Kurtz. Alexander demanded to be paid the homage due to a god, and killed Callisthenes, who refused to do so. When he fell ill with malaria, he had himself carried on a litter to attend sacrifices. His soldiers thronged to see him and pay him tribute. Although greatly weakened, he wanted to be honored and deluded himself about his recovery. The night before he died, he crawled out on all fours from his palace

The origins of the two notebooks are different. The "Up-river Book" is written for an obvious and practical purpose: Conrad was expecting to command a steamboat on the Congo and therefore put down data and instructions concerning the best passages, dangerous shallows and snags, wooded places where fuel could be collected, visibility, orientation points, etc. These notes are made from a precise location—the bridge; for a specific purpose—to be used when navigating the boat on the next up-river trip; and for private use—they are in English, although everybody around spoke French. (Conrad served on French ships only as a young apprentice and certainly felt more at ease using English nautical terminology.)

The reasons for keeping the first notebook, the diary proper, are less evident. The practical importance of these jottings is limited: only information concerning distances and directions, and perhaps a few names of people and places, could conceivably be of any future use; these account for only 5 per cent of the text. Most of the remarks have either descriptive or strictly personal content: "Kinzilu rushing in. A short distance from the mouth fine waterfall. Sun rose red—from 9h a.m. infernally hot day. Harou very little better. Self rather seedy. Bathed."

I believe Conrad made these notes with the intention of using them later to refresh his memory. He had by that time written a few chapters of *Almayer's Folly* and was beginning to learn that his imagination must be firmly supported by his own reminiscences—or by studying the reminiscences of others. There are indications that, while on board the *Vidar* (August 1887–January 1888), he also took notes, later used in his Malayan novels.[6] Contrary to Curle's opinion, I think it is highly probable that the Congo diary was not the only one Conrad ever kept: after all, we know for certain that he used to make extensive notes when preparing for and writing his books.[7] As a beginning author and realizing well the thematic possibilities offered by his African journey, he apparently wished to put down some distinct and concrete impressions—in order to be able later to bolster his memories with hard data. After arriving at Kinshasa he was, by turn, either too busy or too sick to continue.

Such a purpose in writing the diary would explain the limitations of its content. Some critics have noted that Conrad's remarks do not contain any condemnation, any expression of resentment against atrocities which he must have observed—if we are to believe "Heart of Darkness"—during his stay in Matadi and on his walk to Kinshasa. We do not have to assume that the sequence of events in "Heart of Darkness" follows precisely the sequence of Conrad's own experiences. But any-

to drown himself in the Euphrates, hoping that his body would be lost and people would believe that he had disappeared like an immortal god. But his wife traced him and brought him back to die in bed. Kurtz is also the object of a cult, takes part in human sacrifices, falls ill with fever, accepts last tributes when carried on a stretcher, tries to escape—on all fours—back to his worshipers, is captured

and dies in bed; etc., etc.
6. Jocelyn Baines, *Joseph Conrad: A Critical Biography*, London, 1960, p. 90.
7. E.g., the notes discovered by Norman Sherry (*Times Literary Supplement*, 25 June 1970). Conrad frequently mentions making notes for planned novels in his letters to his literary agent, James B. Pinker.

way, a closer look at the notes shows that—apart from the first two entries, covering fifteen days and rather bitter in tone—there are no general statements there, only specific, detailed remarks. For the purpose of future remembering they were sufficient, and the only pertinent, material.

The descriptions contained in "Heart of Darkness" may not in particular cases be confirmable either by reference to Conrad's diary or by other reports; sometimes, when subjected to a piecemeal verification, they may even appear incredible. But the overall picture of the Congo presented by the story is supported by much contemporary evidence. Thus a letter, written by an unidentified correspondent just a few months after Conrad had crossed the same territory and reporting the impressions of passengers on the same *Roi des Belges*, strikingly confirms Conrad's assessments: "The country is ruined. Passengers in the steamer *Roi des Belges* have been able to see for themselves that from Bantja, half a day's journey below our factory at Upoto, to Bumba inclusive, there is not an inhabited village left—that is to say four days' steaming through a country formerly so rich, to-day entirely ruined."[8]

The first notebook is an obviously interesting document which acquires even greater biographical value when read in conjunction with the letters written by Conrad at that time to Poland and France. Publishing the "Up-river Book" may, however, need justification. I believe it is worth printing for several reasons. It allows us to witness Conrad at work, using the idiom of his profession—a quite different language from the rather flowery English of his early novels. It reminds us that shapes and colors were the things to which his occupation made his most sensitive. And it provides additional insight into the private factual background of "Heart of Darkness": the importance of securing timber, the feeling of constant tension and insecurity and isolation. The officers on the small (15-ton) steamer were completely preoccupied with navigation and at the same time absolutely cut off from and ignorant of life on the shores of the enormous river.

Curle's statement to the contrary, I think that Conrad did look into his notebooks when writing "Heart of Darkness." Apart from several fragments of the diary proper echoing on pages 23–24, there are two passages which read like excerpts from the "Up-river Book": "I saw an islet, a mere grassy hummock of bright green in the middle of the stream. It was the only thing of the kind, but as we opened the reach more I perceived it was the head of a long sandbank or rather a chain of shallow patches stretching down the middle of the river. . . . I sheered her well inshore, the water being deepest near the bank as the sounding-pole informed me" (p. 44).

Curle is also mistaken in his belief that "we cannot discover where it [the "Up-river Book"] was ended. The last place mentioned is Lulanga." The second part of this notebook is subtitled "from Equator to Bangala"

8. Quoted in Edmond D. Morel, *Red Rubber*, Manchester-London, 1906, p. 40.

and it is at Bangala—later renamed Nouvelle Anvers—that Conrad stopped writing, on August 19 in the evening.

Why did he interrupt making his notes? There are two possible explanations: one, that he got sick (we know that before the end of the up-river journey he had three attacks of tropical fever);[9] the other, that he either was told or resolved himself that he would not command a vessel on the Congo.

The text published here is based on the original manuscripts of the two Congo notebooks, both now in the Houghton Library, Harvard University. Various brief entries in the first notebook, some of them dating from as late as 1893, which do not form a continuation of the *Congo Diary*, have been left out. J. Miłobędzki, who published the notebooks in a Polish journal, *Nautologia* (Gdynia, 1972, No. 1 [antedated, in fact 1974]), with a valuable introduction and footnotes, included some of these scribblings.

JOSEPH CONRAD

The Congo Diary †

Arrived at Matadi on the 13th of June, 1890.[1]

Mr. Gosse, chief of the station (O.K.) retaining us for some reason of his own.[2]

Made the acquaintance of Mr. Roger Casement,[3] which I should consider as a great pleasure under any circumstances and now it becomes a positive piece of luck.

Thinks, speaks well, most intelligent and very sympathetic.

Feel considerably in doubt about the future. Think just now that my life amongst the people (white) around here cannot be very comfortable. Intend avoid acquaintances as much as possible.

Through Mr. R.C. have made the acquain[tan]ce of Mr. Underwood, the Manager of the English Factory (Hatton & Cookson) in Kalla Kalla. Av[era]ge com[merci]al hearty and kind. Lunched there on the 21st.

24th. Gosse and R.C. gone with a large lot of ivory down to Boma. On G.['s] return to start to up the river. Have been myself busy packing ivory in casks. Idiotic employment. Health good up to now.

9. Conrad to Marguerite Poradowska, 26 September 1890, *Letters of Joseph Conrad to Marguerite Poradowska, 1890–1920,* ed. John A. Gee and Paul J. Sturm, Yale University Press, 1940, p. 16. [See p. 188, below—*Editor.*]

† From *Congo Diary and Other Uncollected Pieces,* ed. Zdzisław Najder (New York: Doubleday, 1978) 7–16. Reprinted by permission of the editor.

1. An important colonial station about forty miles up from Boma at the mouth of the Congo. Conrad arrived there by boat, on his way to take up the command of a river steamship in Kinshasa.

2. The recently nominated director of Matadi station of the Société Anonyme pour le Commerce du Haut-Congo.

3. This future Irish nationalist leader (1864–1916) was at the time employed by the Société as supervisor of a planned railway, connecting Matadi with Kinshasa. He had been to the Congo before, in 1887. Later he became British Vice-Consul for the Congo and in 1903 prepared a widely publicized report on atrocities committed by Belgian colonialists. [See also pp. 120–125, above—*Editor.*]

Wrote to Simpson,[4] to Gov. B.,[5] to Purd.,[6] to Hope,[7] to Capt. Froud,[8] and to Mar.[9] Prominent characteristic of the social life here: people speaking ill of each other.

Saturday, 28th June. Left Matadi with Mr. Harou[1] and a caravan of 31 men. Parted with Casement in a very friendly manner. Mr. Gosse saw us off as far as the State station.

First halt, M'poso. 2 Danes in Comp[a]ny.[2]

Sund[ay], 29th. Ascent of Pataballa sufficiently fatiguing. Cramped at 11h a.m. at Nsoke River. Mosquitos.[3]

Monday, 30th. To Congo da Lemba after passing black rocks long ascent. Harou giving up. Bother. Camp bad. Water far. Dirty. At night Harou better.

Tuesday, 1st. Left early in a heavy mist, marching towards Lufu River. Part route through forest on the sharp slope of a high mountain. Very long descent. Then market place from where short walk to the bridge (good) and camp. V.[ery] G.[ood] Bath. Clear river. Feel well. Harou all right. 1st chicken, 2 p.[m.]. No sunshine today.

Wednesday, 2nd July.
Started at 5:30 after a sleepless night. Country more open. Gently andulating[4] hill. Road good in perfect order. (District of Lukungu.) Great market at 9:30, bought eggs and chickens[!].

Feel not well today. Heavy cold in the head. Arrived at 11 at Banza Manteka. Camped on the market place. Not well enough to call on the missionary.[5] Water scarce and bad. Camp[in]g place dirty. 2 Danes still in Company.

Thursday, 3rd July.
Left at 6 a.m. after a good night's rest. Crossed a low range of hills and entered a broad valley, or rather plain with a break in the middle. Met an off[ic]er of the State inspecting; a few minutes afterwards saw at a camp[in]g place the dead body of a Backongo. Shot? Horrid smell.

4. James H. Simpson, of the Australian shipowning firm Henry Simpson & Sons, to which the barque *Otago* belonged, commanded by Conrad between January 1888 and March 1889 (his only command).
5. Tadeusz Bobrowski (1829–94), his maternal uncle and guardian.
6. R. Curle suggests that it was "captain Purdy, an acquaintance of Conrad" (*Last Essays*, p. 161). Nothing, however, is known about this person. William Purdu of Glasgow served, as first mate, together with Conrad on *Loch Etive* in 1880. (J. Allen, *The Sea Years of Joseph Conrad*, New York, 1965, p. 318.)
7. George Fountaine Weare Hope, Conrad's friend in London, businessman and ex-seaman.

8. The Secretary of London Ship-Master Society.
9. Marguerite Poradowska (1848–1937), widow of his cousin Aleksander Poradowski. She helped Conrad in obtaining his position in the Congo. The letter is dated June 18.
1. Prosper Harou, an agent of the Société, who arrived from Europe on the same boat as Conrad.
2. Many Scandinavians served as officers on the Society's steamboats. Cf. N. Sherry, *Conrad's Western World*, Cambridge, 1971, pp. 17–91.
3. Always spelled thus in the diary.
4. Several times spelled so in the diary. The beginning "u" in "undulating" is pronounced like the Polish "a."
5. Charles E. Ingham, author of *Congo Reading Book*, 2 vols., London, 1890–91.

Crossed a range of mountains, running NW–SE by a low pass. Another broad flat valley with a deep ravine through the centre. Clay and gravel. Another range parallel to the first mentioned, with a chain of low foothills running close to it. Between the two came to camp on the banks of the Luinzono River. Camp[in]g place clean. River clear Gov[ernmen]t Zanzibari[6] with register. Canoe. 2 danes camp[in]g on the other bank. Health good.

General tone of landscape gray-yellowish (dry grass), with reddish patches (soil) and clumps of dark-green vegetation scattered sparsely about, mostly in steep gorges between the high mountains or in ravines cutting the plain. Noticed Palma Christi—Oil palm. Very straight, tall and thick trees in some places. Name not known to me. Villages quite invisible. Infer their existence from cal[a]bashes suspended to palm trees for the "malafu." Good many caravans and travellers. No women unless on the market place.

Bird notes charming. One especially, a flute-like note. Another kind of "boom" ressembling[7] the very distant baying of a hound. Saw only pigeons and a few green parrouquets; very small and not many. No birds of prey seen by me. Up to 9 a.m. sky clouded and calm. Afterwards gentle breeze from the N[or]th generally and sky clearing. Nights damp and cool. White mists on the hills up about halfway. Water effects very beautiful this morning. Mists generally raising before sky clears.

Section of today's road.
[a drawing: section of the day's march]
General direction NNE–SSW
Distance—15 miles.

Friday, 4th July.

Left camp at 6h a.m. after a very unpleasant night. Marching across a chain of hills and then in a maze of hills. At 8:15 opened out into an andulating plain. Took bearings of a break in the chain of mountains on the other side. Bearing NNE. Road passes through that. Sharp ascents up very steep hills not very high. The higher mountains recede sharply and show a low hilly country. At 9:30 market place.

At 10h passed R. Lukanga and at 10:30 camped on the Mpwe R.

Today's march. Direction NNE½N. Dist[an]ce 13 miles.

[section of the day's march]

Saw another dead body lying by the path in an attitude of meditative repose.

In the evening three women of whom[8] one albino passed our camp. Horrid chalky white with pink blotches. Red eyes. Red hair. Features very Negroid and ugly. Mosquitos. At night when the moon rose heard shouts and drumming in distant villages. Passed a bad night.

6. The Congo Free State frequently employed Zanzibaris as soldiers or policemen.

7. After the French *ressemblant*.

8. "Which" crossed out.

Saturday, 5th July.

Left at 6:15. Morning cool, even cold and very damp. Sky densely overcast. Gentle breeze from NE. Road through a narrow plain up to R. Kwilu. Swift-flowing and deep, 50 yds. wide. Passed in canoes. After[war]ds up and down very steep hills intersected by deep ravines. Main chain of heights running mostly NW–SE or W and E at times. Stopped at Manyamba. Camp[in]g place bad—in hollow—water very indifferent. Tent set at 10:15.

Section of today's road. NNE Distance 12 m.

[a drawing]

Today fell into a muddy puddle. Beastly. The fault of the man that carried me. After camp[in]g went to a small stream, bathed and washed clothes. Getting jolly well sick of this fun.

Tomorrow expect a long march to get to Nsona, 2 days from Man-yanga. No sunshine today.

Sunday, 6th July.

Started at 5:40. The route at first hilly, then after a sharp descent traversing a broad plain. At the end of it a large market place. At 10h sun came out.

After leaving the market, passed another plain, then walking on the crest of a chain of hills passed 2 villages and at 11h arrived at Nsona. Village invisible.

Section of day's march.

[a drawing]

Direction about NNE.

Distance—18 miles.

In this camp (Nsona) there is a good camp[in]g place. Shady. Water far and not very good. This night no mosquitos owing to large fires lit all round our tent.

Afternoon very close. Night clear and starry.

Monday, 7th July.

Left at 6h after a good night's rest on the road to Inkandu, which is some distance past Lukungu Gov[ernmen]t station.

Route very accidented.[9] Succession of round steep hills. At times walking along the crest of a chain of hills.

Just before Lukunga our carriers took a wide sweep to the southward till the station bore N[or]th. Walking through long grass for 1½ hours. Crossed a broad river about 100 feet wide and 4 deep. After another ½ hour's walk through manioc plantations in good order, rejoined our route to the Ed[1] of the Lukunga Sta[ti]on. Walking along an andulating plain towards the Inkandu market on a hill. Hot, thirsty and tired. At 11h arrived in the M[ar]ket place. About 200 people. Business brisk. No

---

9. From the French *accidenté*—uneven, rough, hilly.   1. Mistake for "East."

water. No camp[in]g place. After remaining for one hour, left in search of a resting place.

Row with carriers. No water. At last, about 1½ p.m., camped on an exposed hillside near a muddy creek. No shade. Tent on a slope. Sun heavy. Wretched.

[section of the day's march]

Direction NE by N.

Distance—22 miles.

Night miserably cold. No sleep. Mosquitos.

Tuesday, 8th July.

Left at 6h a.m.

About ten minutes from camp left main gov[ernmen]t path for the Manyanga track. Sky overcast. Road up and down all the time. Passing a couple of villages.

The country presents a confused wilderness of hills land slips on their sides showing red. Fine effect of red hill covered in places by dark-green vegetation.

½ hour before beginning the descent got a glimpse of the Congo. Sky clouded.

Today's march—3h.

[section of the day's march]

General direction N by E.

Dist[an]ce 9½ miles.

Arrived at Manyanga at 9h a.m.

Received most kindly by Messrs. Heyn[2] & Jaeger. Most comfortable and pleasant halt.

Stayed here till the 25th.[3] Both have been sick. Most kindly care taken of us. Leave with sincere regret.

			(Mafiesa)
Fridy 25th	Nkenghe		LEFT
Sat. 26	Nsona		Nkendo
Sun. 27	Nkandu		LUASI
Mon. 28	Nkonzo		(Nkoma)
Tue. 29	Nkenghe		Nzungi
Wed. 30	Nsona		Inkissi
Thur. 31	Nkandu	mercredi	Stream
Fri. 1 Aug.	Nkonzo		Luila
Sat. 2	Nkenghe		Nselenba
Sun. 3	Nsona		
Mon. 4	Nkandu		
Tue. 5	Nkonzo		
Wed. 6	Nkenghe[4]		

2. The new chief of the Society's station at Manyanga.

3. Conrad never fully explained the reasons for this protracted stay.

4. Local names of the days of the "week," designated according to marketplaces.

Friday, the 25th July, 1890.
Left Manyanga at 2½ p.m. with plenty of hammock carriers. H. lame and not in very good form. Myself ditto but not lame. Walked as far as Mafiela and camped—2h.

Saturday, 26th.
Left very early. Road ascending all the time. Passed villages. Country seems thickly inhabited. At 11h arrived at large market place. Left at noon and camped at 1h p.m.
[section of the day's march with notes]
a camp—a white man died here—market—govt. post—mount—croco- dile pond—Mafiesa
    Gen. direction E½N—W½S.
    Sun visible at 8 am. Very hot. Distance—18 miles.

Sunday, 27th.
Left at 8h am. Sent luggage carriers straight on to Luasi and went ourselves round by the Mission of Sutili.
Hospitable reception by Mrs. Comber. All the missio[naries] absent.
The looks of the whole establishment eminently civilized and very refreshing to see after the lots of tumble-down hovels in which the State and Company agents are content to live—fine buildings. Position on a hill. Rather breezy.
Left at 3h pm. At the first heavy ascent met Mr. Davis, miss[ionary] returning from a preaching trip. Rev. Bentley[5] away in the South with his wife.
This being off the road, no section given. Distance traversed about 15 miles. General direction ENE.
At Luasi we get on again on to the Gov[ernmen]t road.
Camped at 4½ pm. With Mr. Heche in company.
Today no sunshine.
Wind remarkably cold. Gloomy day.

Monday, 28th.
Left camp at 6:30 after breakfasting with Heche.
Road at first hilly. Then walking along the ridges of hill chains with valleys on both sides. The country more open and there is much more trees[6] growing in large clumps in the ravines.
Passed Nzungi and camped 11h on the right bank of Ngoma, a rapid little river with rocky bed. Village on a hill to the right.
[section of the day's march]
    General direction ENE.
    Distance—14 miles.
    No sunshine. Gloomy cold day. Squalls.

___

5. Rev. W. Holman Bentley, author of *Pioneer- ing in the Congo*, London, 1900.   6. From the Polish *wiele więcej drzew.*

Tuesday, 29th.

Left camp at 7h after a good night's rest. Continuous ascent; rather easy at first. Crossed wooded ravines and the river Lunzadi by a very decent bridge.

At 9h met Mr. Louette escorting a sick agent of the Comp[an]y back to Matadi. Looking very well. Bad news from up the river. All the steamers disabled. One wrecked.[7] Country wooded. At 10:30 camped at Inkissi.
[section of the day's march]

General direction ENE.

Dist[an]ce—15 miles.

Sun visible at 6:30. Very warm day.

Inkissi River very rapid, is about 100 yards broad. Passage in canoes. Banks wooded very densely and valley of the river rather deep but very narrow.

Today did not set the tent but put up in Gov[ernmen]t shimbek.[8] Zanzibari in charge—very obliging. Met ripe pineapple for the first time. On the road today passed a skeleton tied up to a post. Also white man's grave—no name. Heap of stones in the form of a cross.

Health good now.

Wednesday, 30th.

Left at 6 a.m. intending to camp at Kinfumu. Two hours' sharp walk brought me to Nsona na Nsefe. Market. ½ hour after, Harou arrived very ill with billious [sic] attack and fever. Laid him down in Gov[ernmen]t shimbek. Dose of Ipeca.[9] Vomiting bile in enormous quantities. At 11h gave him 1 gramme of quinine and lots of hot tea. Hot fit ending in heavy perspiration. At 2 p.m. put him in hammock and started for Kinfumu. Row with carriers all the way. Harou suffering much through the jerks of the hammock. Camped at a small stream.

At 4h Harou better. Fever gone.
[section of the day's march with notes]
wooded—camp—grass—Nsona a Nsefe—wood stream—open—wood—Lulufu River—a remarkable conical mountain bearing NE visible from here—Inkissi.

General direction NE by E.

Distance—13 miles.

Up till noon, sky clouded and strong NW wind very chilling. From 1 h pm to 4h pm sky clear and very hot day. Expect lots of bother with carriers tomorrow. Had them all called and made a speech which they did not understand. They promise good behaviour.

Thursday, 31st.

Left at 6h. Sent Harou ahead and followed in ½ an hour. Road presents several sharp ascents and a few others easier but rather long. Notice

7. The *Florida* was wrecked on July 18, but was refloated and brought back to Kinshasa in five days. (N. Sherry, p. 41.)
8. Word differently spelled in various African languages and dialects; a few huts occuped by people of the same employment (e.g., railway builders).
9. Ipecacuanha, an herb medicine against dysentery.

in places sandy surface soil instead of hard clay as heretofore; think, however, that the layer of sand is not very thick and that the clay would be found under it. Great difficulty in carrying Harou. Too heavy. Bother. Made two long halts to rest the carriers. Country wooded in valleys and on many of the ridges.

Section of today's road.

[a drawing]

At 2:30 pm reached Luila at last and camped on right bank. Breeze from SW.

General direction of march about NE½E.

Distance est[imated]—16 miles.

Congo very narrow and rapid. Kinzilu rushing in. A short distance up from the mouth fine waterfall.

Sun rose red—from 9h a.m. Infernally hot day.

Harou very little better.

Self rather seedy. Bathed. Luila about 60 feet wide. Shallow.

Friday, 1st of August 1890.

Left at 6:30 am after a very indifferently passed night. Cold, heavy mists. Road in long ascents and sharp dips all the way to Mfumu Mbé.

After leaving there, a long and painful climb up a very steep hill; then a long descent to Mfumu Kono where a long halt was made. Left at 12:30 p.m. towards Nselemba. Many ascents. The aspect of the country entirely changed. Wooded hills with openings. Path almost all the afternoon thro' a forest of light trees with dense undergrowth.

After a halt on a wooded hillside reached Nselemba at 4h 10m p.m.

[section of the day's march]

Put up at Gov[ernmen]t shanty.

Row between the carriers and a man stating himself in Gov[ernmen]t employ, about a mat. Blows with sticks raining hard. Stopped it. Chief came with a youth 13 suffering from gunshot wound in the head. Bullet entered about an inch above the right eyebrow and came out a little inside. The roots of the hair, fairly in the middle of the brow in a line with the bridge of the nose. Bone not damaged apparently. Gave him a little glycerine to put on the wound made by the bullet on coming out. Harou not very well. Mosquitos. Frogs. Beastly. Glad to see the end of this stupid tramp. Feel rather seedy. Sun rose red. Very hot day. Wind S[ou]th.

General direction of march—NE by N.

Distance—about 17 miles.

JOSEPH CONRAD

Up-river Book †

Commenced 3. Aug[u]st 1890
S.S. "Roi des Belges"

On leaving—from A after passing the two islands steer for clump—high tree, two isl[and] points. Sandy beach.

[Two sketches with contours of land and islands, marked: N°I, A, trees, sandy, point, bay, foul, and stones]

N°II Steer for inside sandy point, then keep out (about East by the sun). As you approach coast breaks out into islands—B Steer for end marked B. *From position C. a further point visible*. C. Steer for sandbank II, behind hazy clumps of trees visible on a point of land. No islands visible. Left bank island presents appearance of mainland. Bank II covered at H[igh] W[ater]. Come up right to the bank I. Pass near islet y. Leave bank II on on port side. Steer for sandy path on S[ou]th shore.

N°III.IV.

Position D. Point *a* looks low now. S[ou]th side sandbank cov[ered] at H[igh] W[ater].

The opening narrows. Point *a* advancing. Position E.

Low land and outlying sandbanks a little to port. Steering for a little square white patch. Stick on it. Pass close to the sands—*Cautiously!*

N°V. (and also IV)

Position F. ENE. Patch about ESE—Pass along sand shore not far from point △ steering well in. Island X on the starboard side and generally kept ahead. On the port side (left bank) extensive and dangerous sand bank. 1½ foot *(Capt. Coch)* [1] As you proceed in point ⊙ seems closed in with island X and apparently no passage. Further on it opens again. A small grassy patch marks the end of point ⊙ High hills right ahead looming behind island X.

† From *Congo Diary and Other Uncollected Pieces*, ed. Zdzisław Najder (New York: Doubleday, 1978) 17–38. Reprinted by permission of the editor.

1. Ludwig Rasmus Koch (1865–1906), a Dane, captain of the *Roi des Belges* (N. Sherry, *Conrad's Western World*, Cambridge, 1971, p. 400).

Come right up to the island, then steer along shore to the point ⊙ a little on the port bow as from *position F.a.* Coming up to a white patch after opening a small channel cutting X in two. A small island app[arent]ly closes the passage. When nearing the end of X *must* keep close and steer into the bay 8 getting the clump of trees on the port side. Going out the highest mountain will be right ahead—always keep the high mountain ahead crossing over to the left bank. To port of highest mount a low black point. Opposite a long island stretching across. The shore is wooded.

V.Va.

As you approach the shore the black point and the island close in together—No danger. Steering close to the mainland between the island and the grassy sandbank, towards the high mount[ain]s steering close to the left bank *of the river all the time. Entered.*

VI. On left bank wooded point.

Right valley. 1st Reach nearly north.

2nd Reach about NNE.

Left bank. Wooded point.

3d Reach the same and wooded point.

4th Reach NbyE.

Point III. Stones off.

IV. Before getting abreast there is a rocky shoal ⅓ out. 9 hours after entering the river sighted "2 sago-trees point" not at all remarkable. Low flat at the foot of the hills. The appearance of point VI is bushy. Rather low. Round slope behind as per sketch.

Just before coming up to p[oin]t VI got bottom at 6 feet stones. Hauled out. Point VII called "Sandstone Pt." with a small ledge of rock outside of it.

Before closing with it cross over to the right bank.

Moored to—grassy Beach backed by trees. 25 Miles from the entrance—5ʰ30.

4th Aug. VII This reach is about *E.* Shortly after leaving, point A opens out double in peculiar shape. Off point VIII long stone ridge. Point A has a small sand-spit covered at full river. Right below the point there is a small sandbank along the shore. Wooding place. May get in between sandbank and the shore. After passing A point in the middle of the river there is a rocky ledge now above water. Covered at F[ull] W[ater]. River rather narrow. Steering well off the right bank.

Snake tree point has a ledge of rock lying well off. To give a wide berth.

Here begins a reach about NE (by the sun). On the left bank many palms visible.

After passing Sn[ake] Tree point on the left bank entrance to Black River—A remark[ab]le clump little further on *R. bank*—*Point C.*

Off point C. *cross over.* On the left bank on point XI one palm rather conspicuous when coming up. After turning point C. you open up a remarkable point running from high mountains called point Licha. Wooding place. (6h am.) On the right bank past point C. sandy beaches to be met often. On left bank a little past XI point there is a market place. Rocky shoals near in shore.

From Licha point up. VIII

From Licha—crossing over to right bank where there is outcrop of rock. Small sandy beach near.

Left 6:15

Bearing Licha	S15°W	} Time
Point O	S25°W	} 6:35
Point XII.	N48°E	} h.m.
Point D.	N34°E	} 6:35/
Point F	N36°E	7:15

Rate about 3½ miles per *h*

After leaving Licha keep in the middle

B[earing] T[ime]
G. N33°E 9ʰ20ᵐ
Pt XIII 8:15
Pt XIV from
p[o]s[itio]n
b[earing]
NEbyN½[N]

bearing from p[oin]t XII.
opposite XII rocky cliff with
ledges extending.
After point XII indented shore with a low
shore with a low flat
running at the foot of the
hills. After passing XIII
rocky sweep—this reach
is NEbyN.—Steer by the left bank
2 low points with many palms
in the bight.

Point H
at 10ʰ50ᵐ

An island in the middle
of the bight.

Before closing with G
point small S[and] B[ank] parallel
to the shore—pass[age] inside(?)

IX

Pt XV bore ⎫
NEbyN½N ⎪
from x pᵗ ⎬
Pᵗ K bore ⎪
NNE from ⎪
Isᵈ 3 ⎭
Islet N 3
at 10ʰ50ᵐ

good wooding place.

After passing 1ˢᵗ island open up a point and
sight a long and a very small island. Island No. 2
long wooded. Small islet No. 3—This reach is
NEbyN nearly.

Between Is[lan]d No. 2 and No. 3 rocky
ledges and no passage. From abreast P[oin]t H
it seems as if Is. 3 was abreast Point XIV. The
NW End of Is[lan]d 2 has a palm grove—The
island lays NW–SE.

All along right shore small beaches—and dead
wood on most of them. After passing point XIV
a long stretch of low land on left bank with
islands (very small). A remarkable clump
of trees as per chart and many palm trees on
the low shore.

Island N 4
at Noon.
Island No 4
to
Point M
NEbyE
2ʰ30ᵐ p.m.

This stretch of low land continues for a long
time with many palms.

General appearance light green.

Long reach with a regular sweep on the left
bank from Island No. 4 2½ up.

X. This Reach is *NEbyN*. Directly after
passing p[oin]t M. on the right shore rocky shoals
extending good way out.

Afterwards same appearance. Hills to water's
edge with small sandy beaches.

Over p[oin]t XVI curious yellow path on a
hill.

Steering a little over on the right bank
side. On the other side villages on slope of hill.
After point N another p[oin]t forming a high
plain.

At N 3ʰ45ᵐ

A little further ridge of rocks. Before coming
to high plain p[oin]t N° 2 is a wooding place.
P[oin]t bore NEbyN at 4ʰ25ᵐ from high plain
P[oin]t N°2. Abreast point XVII at 5ʰ10ᵐ length
of reach 5½ m. The new reach about NE½N.
Abreast point XVII a long parallel ridge of rocks
well off the shore.

Off Point P a long rocky ridge extending into
the river (from here in one day to Kichassa down
stream. 12 hours steaming).

All the time keeping over to the French shore.

Hills on left shore present a reddish appearance. All the right bank fringed with trees. At the small beach near Point P at 5^h50^m—moored—Wooding places—Villages on the opposite bank.

Point P. 6^h0^m
End of point Bankap
bore NEbyN from
mid[d]le of the river.
A little past P^t P.
7^h45 at point XVIII

Left. Cross over from the beach below the Point P.

Here commences a reach about *NE*.

After rounding P[oin]t P. there is a wooding place. Narrow beach.

From there steer a little over where there is a small island not app[aren]t. No passage. After that keep nearly in the middle.

All that shore is a low flat fringed by trees backed by low hills. Bordered by reefs.

Steer in the middle—till abreast p[oin]t Q. then a little over to the right bank—

from Camp
to
XVIII–6 miles
16¾

XI After p[oin]t XVIII a [sic] invisible sandbank stretches along the right shore. Keep off nearly in center.

Bankab–NEbyN
Point R from mi[d]dle NNE. On pt Bankab two high trees—one broad another less spreading.

Pt XVIII at 7^h45^m
times
from XVIII
Reach—NEbyN½N.
to pt R. at 9^ham
from XVIII to R.
1^h45^m or say 6 miles.
NEbyN ½N.
Bankab Pt 9^h15^m
Ganchu bore N½W

About 1 hour after passing pt XVIII—passing the wooded false points rocks extend out into the river. P[oin]t Q bearing about N[or]th and Bankab about NNE.

On nearing p[oin]t Bankab on French shore to the N[or]th [of] p[oin]t Q small island/N°6/and long sandbank over which from the middle of the river you see Ganchu P[oin]t bearing about NbyE. The islet N°6 has a few trees and a dead palm on it. Opp[osi]te on same shore in a ravine small vill[ag]e. Round Bank[ab] in back curr[ent].

When rounding Bankab keep on Right side and enter the current sweeping out of the bight cautiously and end on nearly.

(On coming down follow the current round the bight.)

When about the middle of the open snatch steer right across to clear Ganchu's Point. Pass the point cautiously. Stones. Then steer straight for P[oin]t XIX. Along the left shore below the point stretches of a sandbank ressembling a beach but covered at F[ull] W[ater].

Pt XIX at 10^h40^m
Pt S bore N.

From p[oin]t XIX cross over a little of a small beach on the opposite side by compass about NbyW½W.

This short Reach is about *NNE*. Next short Reach is about NEbyN½N

Keeping a little over on the right shore. On the left bank bushes growing down to the water. Right shore low, undulating. Wooded (Coming down from S the false XIX point should be alone visible).

Pt.S. *at Noon* 12[h].

Pt XX bore N½E.

Entrance of River Kassai. NEbyN.

Point on right bank white patch bore N½W.

Next pt to S. N¾W.

XII. Entrance to Kassai rather broad. On S[ou]th side a bright beach with a spreading dead tree above it mark the mouth.

At the Cath[oli]c mission moor alongside the head of the beach.

From P[oin]t S to Mission. NNE.1[h]

Made fast at 1[h] p.m.

Pt XX. bore N5°W

Left the mission at 2½—In the bight between the miss[ion] and P[oin]t XX rocky ledges. Off P[oin]t XX a stony ridge partially cover[e]d at high water.

From XX.
Pt T. bore NbyE½E at 3[h]20[m] p.m.

Off Pt XX at 3[h]20[m] making it about 2[h] from the Pt S.

After passing P[oin]t XX follow the left shore at some distance to the p[oin]t with the grassy slope about NNE. From there cross over towards point T. Sandbank always covered in the bight. Current easy in the middle.

Off Point T at 5[h]25

Probably there is a passage between the sand and the left bank.

Point XXI bore N¾E

This reach about N. (Stopped at 5[h]45[m].)

Left stopping place at 7[h] am.

On Right bank—from stopping place sighted a dark-green p[oin]t—a long spit of sand cov[ere]d at full water with high rocks also cov[ere]d at very full water.

On *left shore* a sandb[an]k always covered extends ⅓[d] into the river.

Got soundings below the dark-green P[oin]t

bearing NbyWest. P[oin]t XXI bore NEbyE. 3
fth and 4 fth[2]

[Proceeding up you open the Lawson River
Entrance][3] Opening Lawson River with sandbank across the mouth and rocks stretching off.
Further a long cut beach. P[oin]t XXI gets
indistinct on nearer approach. No danger on
that side.

A small rocky ledge on the point Past Pt XXI
at[4] This reach about NbyE. After passing P[oin]t
XXI—R[i]g[h]t bank low scrubby and trees.
Sm[all] hills. To the left higher hills with bare
tops and a belt of forest halfway up from the
water's edge. At P[oin]t U—Wooding places.
Caution The landing must be approached cautiously on account of stones and snags. Round
P[oin]t U cautiously. When entering the reach
keep rather on the outer edge of the current
following the right shore. Sandbank on left shore
not visible.

From 3 fath[oms] position the P[oin]t XXII
bears NEbyE. The middle of uncovered S[outh]
B[an]k bears about N½E.

A spit with 1½ fth at less than ½ full river
extends towards U high land. On rounding
P[oin]t XXII give a wide berth. There is [sic] 2
stony ledges of which the outer one is cov[ere]d
at full river. This reach about NEbyN. Before
passing Mission P[oin]t you open out false p[oin]t
W which is not noticeable. Also a point on the
left shore. Coast in perfect semicircle sand,
swamp and trees—hills opened out there. A few
high thin trees dispersed in that stretch.

As you near the end of the semicircle the
M[ission] marked in sketch disappears.

From the same place Island N 7 bore
N¾E.—from point (Eng[lish] Mission)[5] at
Grenfell p[oin]t—at *4^h* p.m.

When passing the dangerous sandbank called
mission sands keep close in with M[issi]on Point
and have the island either on port bow or starboard quarter till you clear M[issi]on Point.
[A sketch with contours of shore, islands, a

XIII

2. Soundings, in fathoms.
3. This sentence lightly crossed out. Lawson River
is named Mbali on newer maps.

4. Time not entered.
5. Bolobo, a mission established in 1886 by the
well-known missionary George Grenfell.

sandbank and the ship's track represented by a
dotted line etc. Islands (or parts of the mainland) numbered: 8, 9 and 10. A point on No.
10 marked B.]

NE   EbyN   NEbyE   NE
Square little beach ahead △
and bore Sth   NNW   *Nth*
          From Pt B.   *Island 11*
                              careful of
                              snags opposite the dead tree
Passage inside island 10 at full water.

Passage inside small islet off 2 Palm P[oin]t
at full water. When must keep close inshore
keep close to Island 12—over a bank with 2

Koch's passage

fath. After passing Is[lan]d 12 steer for bush on
end of the long island.

From there for bush point on the M[ai]n land
follow cut bank, then cross over towards low
island.

XIV

Sandbank right across after approaching in—
steer along it towards the tree on it and pass
between it and the M[ai]nland (when nearing
1 fth. to 1½ fth.).

Steer in middle of passage and then for XXIV
p[oin]t following the bight of the shore. From
p[oin]t XXIV steer between two small islands
keeping over to starboard. Soundings in 1, 1½,
1 fath—variable. Bolobo village. Landing place.
A few minutes after passing the mission keep
out a little into the river.

This reach from the mission is about NE.
Follow the right bank, the courses being from
NE till you open the bend of low shore. Then
P[oin]t of M[ai]nland bearing NEbyE and small
island bearing EbyNth.

Steer in the bend a little watching for edge
of sandbank. Leave the small island on
St[arboar]d side. Sandbanks on both sides with
spits across the course. After nearing island 12
another small island is seen to be left to
starb[oar]d. General direction of land from there
is ENE. After passing the island keep at
mod[era]te distance off.

XV

When app[roa]ch[in]g long islands there is a
bank with 1 fth at ½ full. Close in a little with
the main.

After passing steep round bank steer in with

the bend. When off the swamp spit all the islands on the southern bearing seem one land.

XV*a*   Arrived at stopping place at 5ʰ30ᵐ. Village.

Left stopping place at 6 am. Steering for P[oin]t XXV keep in with the bend. Remarkable. Islands.

XVI   Island bearing NE. Square clump light green. Follow the island *15th* shore all the time— remarkable palm—second small island, then steer for little grassy inlet.

Soundings in 1½ and 1 fth. Course about ENE. Leave grassy islet on St[arboar]d hand and steer in 1½ to 2 fth for island bearing ENE N° 16.

XVII   Follow the shore of island N° 16 on an NE½E course. *Mind the snags* along island N° 16.

Cross over well before getting to Pool P[oin]t.

Cross to where higher trees begin.

When nearing M[ai]nland p[oin]t you will see the open passage between Is[lan]d 17 and 18.

XVIII   The entrance to the Oubangi is barred on the up-river side by extensive sandbanks. The opposite Congo shore forms a ½ circle from the F[ren]ch mission⁶ to P[oin]t XXVI.

When rounding P[oin]t XXVI the current is very strong. Rocks off the p[oin]t. Sandbank stretching close from the N[or]th towards it always covered but impassable at any state of the river. Inside the bight steer close in to guard against dangerous snags. Rounding the points pretty close you sight to port the commencement of a long island called Flat Is[lan]d. Proceeding on pass the village of Pressinbi then Irebu.

Sharp bend in the shore where the mouth of the R[iver Oubangui] is. From elbow cross over to the flat island avoiding S[and]b[an]ks and snags—then where a few palms form clump cross over again and follow main shore.

Rounding another point still follow main shore at times only 2 to 1½ fath[oms] water. Otherwise passage not intricate. Otherwise keep generally by the line indicated on the chart.

6. At Irebu, opposite the mouth of the Ubangi.

After leaving Irebu there is no wooding place for some time.

XXIII. and A. Thursday—14th Aug[u]st. Left stopping place at 6.10^m.

Pass outside the sm[all] islet in the first bend after leaving. The general direction since yesterday[7]

Entering the next narrow reach keep on but at a little dist[an]ce from left shore—Snags— This reach is safe across (Koch). A succession of canal-like bends. The shore covered with dense forest right down to water's edge.

The river opens suddenly disclosing more islands.

XXIV After rounding the last P[oin]t of the narrow part of the channel lies SE. Then ahead you have 3 islands looking at first like one. As you near the point opposite them they open out. Off that point sandbank runs over to the islands—go over it. XXV.

Then a wide bight of the main shore is entered. On the P[or]t side many islands presenting varied aspects from different places. The general direction is NE½N about.

Keep pretty well on the main shore watching for snags all along.

On the port side extensive sandbanks partly visible but mostly covered at ½ F[ull] W[ater]. Both shores heavily timbered with dense undergrowth. After sighting a long island and following it for some time you enter a NbyE reach, then you enter a narrow passage between two islands NEbyE. At the end of short passage islands in sight again and the river broadens out. A broad stretch where the course is about NE½E. All islands seen from the broad passage are now shut together into one. XXVI

Entering another broad expansion of the river follow cautiously the courses set on the chart XXVI V[i]ll[a]ge of Ikongo—Bad. XXVII Rounding the next 2 points there is another broad stretch comparatively free of sandb[an]ks. Steer from p[oin]t to p[oin]t on the main shore having always the islands on your p[or]t hand. General direction about *NE*.

XVII

Main shore less thickly overgrown now—
Islands all heavily timbered. After passing Lower
Mission Point a small bay *with* stones in it.
Beaches coloured *red*. After passing 2 more
points you sight the Am[erican] Mission[8] in the
bottom of a small bight. Hardly vis[i]ble. A big
dead tree marks it exactly.

II Part
in N[or]th Lat[itu]de from Equator to Bangala

*Charts in Nth Lat^{de} Saturday—16th Aug^{st},
1890–7^h30^m*

Left Equator[ville]—Follow the bank. Short
distance round the first point pass State Station.

River narrowed by islands. App[arent]ly no
sandbanks. After passing the 2^d point the next
reach broadens out. Courses: NNE–NE and
ENE.

After passing a point with tall trees you open
out a reach about E.

A low point of land without trees bearing east
marks the appr[oa]ch of Berouki R[iver][9]

The other bank of the Berouki is covered with
forest growth, Two sm[all] islands mark the
entrance of the south arm of the delta. Steering
about NE close to two small islands to port of
you you app[roa]ch the point of the second arm
of the Berouki delta.

Steer close to it pass[in]g over 3 fth., the next
reach being NbyW very nearly.

Soon another branch of the delta is passed.
Very narrow.

The NbyW reach ends at a low point after
pass[in]g a sm[all] clearing and a one-limbed
tree. Pass small river II N. The next reach opens
on about the same width, two small islands
forming the bend. Direction N[or]th.

River perhaps a little wider in this reach—
The same appearance of the banks. Dense
growth of bushes and not very tall trees of a
dark green tint. On the port side S[and]b[ank]
visible before reach. Point. After passing the
point a straight reach due North, not very long.

8. At Bolenge.   9. Usually: Ruki, or Rouki, River.

⅔ds up pass over the S[and]B[ank]. Sound[in]gs
in 2.1 fath and 4 feet. Steer right in shore
minding the snags.

Snags to be looked out for all the way here.

Rounding the point by a fine large tree and
then 2 palms enter a short reach NbyE.

After a point another long reach NbyE. Some
small islands open out on the port side. *II N
(A)*. Long reach to a curved point. Great quantity of dangerous snags along the starb[oar]d
shore. Follow the slight bend of the shore with
caution. The middle of the channel is a
S[and]B[ank] always covered.

The more northerly of the 2 islands has its
lower end bare of trees covered with grass a[nd]
light-green low bushes, then a low flat, and the
upper end is timbered with light trees of a darker
green tint. A long sandbank unc[overe]d at ½
Full stretches in to the S[ou]th[war]d. No passage inside the islands.

After rounding the point a broad reach opens
out towards NNE.

On the port side some small islands. Starboard shore makes a great sweep to the next
point.

The middle of this expansion of the river is
fouled by extensive sands always covered (Koch).

Follow the bend of the shore keeping pretty
well in but not to brush the bank.

Both shores uniform dark-green forest. When
nearing the limit point of the reach you will
close with some sm[all] islands. Leave them to
port. S[and]B[ank] between the islands and the
point. Keeping to starboard you get over it in
2.1. fath. Broad bend follows. The direction of
the short reach being NNE.

In the bend itself extensive sandbank to be
left to port side. Patches on this bank uncovered at ½ F[ull] water.

The channel is pretty wide: there is no
necessity in shaving the starboard bank to[o]
close. After this a straight long reach on N½E
bearing. Keep nearly in the middle but more
to starboard. St[arboar]d side islands divided by
very narrow channels on port app[a]r[en]tly one
island only. Usual app[earan]ce of dense vegetation dow[n] to water's edge. N[or]th End

sm[all] S[and]B[an]k. 2 fth At the N[or]th end
sharp bend and the broad sweep—NbyE to
NEbyN and N.

To starb[oar]d wide branch dividing islands
before mentionned[1] from m[ai]n land.

IV N

Next reach NNE nearly—Follow the
Starb[oar]d side now M[ai]n L[and]d river
broad—some app[earan]ce On Starb[oar]d side
pass a little narrow branch opening island again.
This reach ends like the last by a straight shore
across its upper end where there is a [word
omitted] of triangular expansion. Next reach
nearly North—after passing the limit point reach
nearly north.

A small double island green on the Starb[oar]d
side.

V.N. After this first more islands open up with
pretty broad channels between, through which
the back shore can be seen—River very broad
here. All the islands are laying [sic] on a line
of bearing about NbyE from the last point.
Point ahead on a bearing ½ a point more
northerly.

[A sketch of a reach of the river]

Many large snags along the shores of the
islands. Bush and trees to the water's edge.
After passing a narrow island take the channel
where there is a small islet with a conspicuous
tree in the middle of it.

This channel is at first NE then gradually
sweeps up to NbyE and narrows greatly.

After coming out of it you enter a broad
expanse with an islet about East and two
larger islands with passage between about
NNE. [A sketch representing a reach of the
river]

This expanse is bounded to the Eastward by
the M[ai]nland.

Heavy sandb[an]ks show between the
further northern and the upper eastern
islands.

The passage is narrow mostly NNE with a
slight easterly bend on its upper end nearly
NEbyN.

1. After the French *mentionné*.

The main land is seen right across when coming out to the N[orthw]ard.

Passage clear.

VI N.

Main Land runs nearly N and S. Almost opp[osi]te the Is[lan]d Pass[a]ge there is a wooding place.

Rounding the N[or]th point of the first straight stretch there is a 2[d] elbow and then again a straight N[or]th stretch. To Port there is 3 islands[2] on the bend and another long island further up with some more behind it. On Main shore after passing a dead stem with a few palms growing near it there is a point with a rocky ledge off it.

The northern expansion of this expansion is perceived with islets and islands. The course is between these and the M[ai]n L[an]d. Off the m[ai]n shore there are rocky ledges under water in several places.

Rocks when the little N[orth]ern islet bears North going along the shore. Many villages on this shore. Leaving all the islands on the Port side cross the mouth of the Loulanga R[iver][3] and steer along m[ai]n shore the reach lying about NbyW½W.

It presents a narrow appearance.

[A sketch of a reach of the river. A dotted line represents the track of the riverboat. One side marked: Shallow S.B., islet; the other side marked: A grassy plain with large trees on the bank; the dotted line marked: *NNW*.]

Loulanga R[iver] and French Factory. Direction *NE*. first reach.

Entering, islet to port. Keep mod[era]te dist[ance] from Star[boar]d shore.

River turns northerly.

To starb[oar]d low circular island. Passage behind. In this back channel is the factory.

Approaching landing mind the stones High bank. Make fast to a tree there. Small, bad land[in]g place. Arr[ived] at F[rench] F[actory] 8[h]15[m] *VII N.* Left the F[rench] F[actory] 12[h]45[m] (the back island passage through *Lulanga*).

Leaving the F[ren]ch F[acto]ry steer NNE

---

2. From the French *Il y a trois isles.*   3. Correctly: Lulonga.

when clear of round islet facing it and then
NNW to enter the narrow channel between two
wooded Is[lan]ds, Lulanga left on the starb[oar]d
side. Extensive sandbanks to port of you. Pass
over in 2 fath or perhaps 9 feet at ½ full water.

The first reach narrow—about NbyW.

Keep in the middle. A short bend NbyE.
Nth.VII. The back passage.

[Sketch of a reach with a dotted line representing the boat's track on which following courses
are marked: NNW, NWbyN, and N; and
soundings in fathoms: 2, and 2. Left shore
marked: SB., Grass bank, Bush, and Tresa.
Starboard shore marked: grassbank]

The next reach is about NWbyN.

A straight due North—A long bend. Come
over to P[or]t Side—snags almost in the middle
of passage. A reach due N[or]th.

Another stretch NbyE.

Pass channel to Starb[oar]d leading to Baringu—sand beach facing it stretch towards
NbyW Water shallows to 9 and 7 feet.

[Three consecutive pages with sketches forming a rough outline chart of the Lulonga Passage together with sketches on pp. 58 and 61,
and then 67 and 69. The dotted line marked:
N, N, NbyE, NbyW, NE, NNE, NE, NbyE,
and NNE. The bank on the Port Side marked:
Grass bk, Bush, Sm beach, Grass, grass. The
Starboard Side marked: Snags, To Baringu,
Grass swampy, Swamp grass, High bushed point
2^h30^m]

A reach to NE follows. Grassy banks.

Off port bank sand shallows.

After rounding that point channels branch
off. Follow the more easterly. Small islet in it.

A long straight about NbyE½E.

Passage broadens out with islands coming in
sight.

[A sketch of a part of the Lulonga Passage. The
boat's track marked: N½E. On Port Side: 3^h30^m.
On the Starboard Side: S Bank, S-B, and
soundings in fathoms: 2, 2, and 2.]

Steering for a small island bearing N[or]th.
Leave it on St[arboar]d Side.

Towards the upper end of it cross over to port
avoiding snags Follow the Port shore.

In the elbow must go close in to avoid extensive S[and] B[an]k stretching right in from the island.

Before passing the two small islets get soundings in 2 fath. and less. Keep well inshore. Mind the snags.

A Broad straight NbyE nearly
[The last part of the Lulonga Passage. A dotted line marked: NbyE to NNE. On the Port Side: Snags. Soundings in fathoms: 2, 2, 2, 1, 1, 2, 2, 2, 2. On the Starboard Side: S-Bks.]

When following it must close over to port, avoiding however sunken trees. Passing over tails of the great sandb[an]k with less than one fath[om] up to 2 fath. soundings.

Arriving at the end of this straight cross over on a NE course and enter the main route up the river.

End of Lulanga Pass.

VII.N.

Long NE½N reach; pretty straight. Island to port in a bend of the shore. Off it 2 S[and] B[an]ks on opposite shore with 2 fath at ½ full. Steering along the starb[oar]d bank. Many snags stranded well off the shore.

The point closing this reach on the Port Side has a high tree on it.

After passing this there is a broad straight channel at the end of which no point is seen.

The broad channel runs NbyW.

Sandbanks. Take the narrow channel.

Directly inside camp[in]g place. Indifferent wood.

VIII.N.

A narrow reach about NEbyN.

Left camp at South end of it at 6ʰa.m.

Curve to the NNE and a little broader reach. The reach expands in a NEbyE direction. To Port several islands and a small islet bushy on one end, low on the other. Follow the M[ai]n Land on the Starb[oar]d side. Great many snags lining the shore. On the Port Side probably shallow water (K[och]).

At the end of this broad long stretch appear 2 islands.

The little islet to port has a long S[and] B[an]k on its southern end.

The main shore runs Northeasterly. The next point to port after pass[in]g the islet has an extensive SE uncovered in places at ½ F[ull] stretching away along shore to next small island. From here an island appears in the middle of river bear[in]g *NNE*.

Steering nearly for it. After passing second islet to port the river opens out to starboard into islands laying [sic] NE and SW nearly or a little more Easterly.

Steer for the middle island about NbyE½E, then into the broad reach on its port side leaving it to Starb[oar]d.

Taking this route the M[ai]n Land of the right bank is left and course taken to left or north bank. (This is not the usual course, not safe to follow at less than ½ full water).

IX.N.

Keep a little nearer to the middle island than to the islands on your Port side. Proceeding cautiously must feel your way in 12 to 8 feet water. The shore on the port side is the North Bank of the river.

Snags along but not much off. After passing two little islands you sight a dead trunk of a tree and villages begin. In many places cut bank. Excellent wooding places up to the point and in the great bend. (10^h50) *Left 11:30* Rounding the 1st point after the dead tree you open the 2nd point bearing ab[ou]t NE where this reach ends. To Starb[oar]d several islands of which two are prominent. Land backing there in a semicircle at a great distance—M[ai]nLand on the S[ou]th Bank not visible.

The river very broad here. Follow close in the bend as there is a large sandbank between the island and the main shore.

Nearing the P[oin]t sounding in 12 to 10 feet (at ½ F.W.)

Mind a very bad snag nearly off the point. After a bit of straight shore and a small point ab[ou]t ENE open out 2 small islets come in sight. Steer along the m[ai]n shore. When pass[in]g the islets much caution and good look out—sandbanks.

[A sketch: the boat's track on a bend of the river and soundings in feet. Also marked: Village,

IX.N.

X.N.

184 BACKGROUNDS AND SOURCES

SB Cov. ½ F. less 3 feet] Islet N°19.

Following the bend—when approaching the P[oin]t SandB[an]k extends from islet to St[arboar]d. A snag stranded on outer edge— pass between the shore and the snag. Another S[and]B[ank] on the point and snags off it. Must steer very close to the bank which is steep to.

River expands broadly here. The general direction of the main shore to the end of the expansion is ENE nearly. For some consider- able distance the Starb[oar]d shore is low and grassy. After rounding the shutting in point leave the broad reach and follow the mainland by a narrower channel laying [sic] about NEbyN and turning towards the NE or more easterly still. Coming out of this channel again into the broad part a great number of islands come in sight.

Steer carefully amongst sand bank watching for the edges. Cross over to the island and back to where 2^d village down is. At big clearing cross over again and enter another back passage. Sound[in]gs in 10 to 6 feet. Many snags and some of them right in the fairway.

Between a long low island and the main sandb[an]ks across with less than 6 feet water over them the passage rather intricate from islet N°19.

The north[er]n end of that pass[a]ge has a S[and]B[an]k with 10–6 feet of water at ½ F.W.

Coming out of it you follow a broad stretch on a NEbyE½E course (about) and then keep off the broad channel to the NE between the m[ai]nland and an island.

Passage narrow—where it broadens 2 islets in the bend. One of them has a thin tall dead tree with one green branch on it. It looks like a flagstaff with a bough tied up to it at right angles. Steering in always keep closer to the main shore. Good many nasty snags all along.

After passing the second of the 2 islets you may notice a third—small. The main shore runs NEbyE. On the Starb[oar]d side many islands close together form an almost contin[u]ous shore.

The channel is not deep from 10 to 6 feet of water some little distance up after passing the 2^d of two islets.

After that no soundings in *12* feet.

Several small islets on the Starb[oar]d side.

On the islands on the Starb[oar]d side good many dead palms.

Further on a sandbank right across: *6–10 feet*.

At large clearing stopped. Firewood. Snags.

XIII. Left at 6ʰ30ᵐ A straight reach NE½N. When approaching the P[oin]t (to Port) ending the straight steer over to the other side to avoid sandbank.

XIII. N.

On starb[oar]d side small islets in the bights of the shore, which is composed of long islands overlapping each other and appearing like one land when steaming up the river.

Round in back again in 9 feet of water.

Following the main shore care should be taken to avoid snags which are stranded right along it in great quantities. *2ᵈ reach* before coming to end of it cross over to the island 20. Right close in to the upp[e]r end—in 9 to 5 feet. Sandbank off the main shore. Pass close point on starb[oar]d side and steer to leave next island on starb[oar]d side *nearly* in midchannel. Sandbank on the m[ai]n shore—Cross over to upper end of vill[a]ge clearing. Follow the shore—Opposite sm[a]ll beach in isl[an]d to starb[oard] sound[in]gs 9 feet. After passing this, steer off the m[ai]n shore and steer across in 9 to 5 feet to leave the sm[a]ll islet to port. Keep nearly in the middle when entering the pass[a]ge, then steer rather over to starb[oar]d shore (big island). *Snags*. Coming out of the back channel you sight a very [word missed] clearing bearing N[or]th. Steer a little below it passing over 10 feet sound[in]gs. When nearing the bank water deepens.

Follow the cut bank pretty close. Safe. No snags there—Half round reach following in a EbyN direction. Forest. Snags again. Keep a little out. A long small islet hardly noticeable before coming to the closing P[oin]t on P[or]t side. *Sound[in]gs 10 feet*.

Another bend where you keep nearly in the middle. *10 feet S[oun]d[in]gs* in one place.

This bend terminates in a NE direction.

There is now a double channel—one broad about EbyN, another narrow nearly NE. Leave

the island to starb[oard] and follow its inner shore
to take the narrow p[assa]ge. Sound[in]gs 9 to 5
feet.

This passage is between the m[ai]n land on
Port side and 2 islands on starb[oar]d. Where
the 1st is[lan]d finishes there is a sandbank.
Steering close in to the islands in s[ou]nd[ing]s
10 to 5 feet—Steer over to M[ai]n shore and
back again. All the way about 7 feet of water.
Less in places.

After leaving this narrow passage and rounding the point another similar passage presents
itself—Keep nearly in the middle where 7 *to* 9
feet water are obtained at ½ F[ull] W[ater].

Another narrow passage presenting the same
features, only a little narrower. About 10 feet
of water—Passage ends on an Eastern bearing.

Coming out of this last the main stream is
entered. River broadens. This is the upper end
of the northern bank passage.[4]

XV.

JOSEPH CONRAD

[Stanley Falls, Early September 1890] †

Everything was dark under the stars.[1] Every other white man on board
was asleep. I was glad to be alone on deck, smoking the pipe of peace
after an anxious day. The subdued thundering mutter of the Stanley
Falls hung in the heavy night air of the last navigable reach of the Upper
Congo, while no more than ten miles away, in Reshid's camp just above
the Falls, the yet unbroken power of the Congo Arabs slumbered uneasily. Their day was over.[2] Away in the middle of the stream, on a little

4. *Roi des Belges* crossed the Equator in the morn-
ings of August 16. She arrived the same day at the
mouth of the Lulonga, leaving on August 17 early
afternoon. Then there are two overnight stops
mentioned, and by the evening of August 19 the
boat must have reached Bangala (or Nouvelle-
Anvers, N 1'36" E19'07")—as indicated in the title
of the second part of the Up-river Book.
†.From "Geography and Some Explorers," *Last
Essays*, ed. Richard Curle (London: J. M. Dent &
Sons, Ltd., 1926) 17. Reprinted by permission.
Annotations by the present editor.
1. Conrad arrived in Kinshasa, the port for Leopoldville at Stanley Pool, on August 2 only to find
that his ship, the *Florida*, was one of those that
had been reported disabled on July 29 (see "Congo
Diary," p. 165). To learn the river while the ship
was being repaired, Conrad was assigned on August

3 as second in command to Captain Koch of the
S.S. *Roi des Belges*, which left Kinshasa on August
4 for a relief trip up the river all the way to Stanley
Falls, where it arrived September 1. On board with
Conrad was Camille Delcommune (1859–92), the
Acting Manager for the Trading Company of the
Upper Congo and the brother of Alexandre, to
whose Katanga exploring party Conrad had been
assigned, in Brussels, as Captain.
2. Reshid was the nephew of the halfcaste Arab
Tipu-Tipu who ruled central Africa by force.
Although Stanley had in the name of King Leopold made Tipu-Tipu the "governor" of the Stanley Falls area in 1887, by 1890 Tipu's incessant
slaving and ivory raids had so incensed philanthropic and commercial interests alike that they for
once joined power.

island nestling all black in the foam of the broken water, a solitary little light glimmered feebly, and I said to myself with awe, "This is the very spot of my boyish boast."

A great melancholy descended on me. Yes, this was the very spot. But there was no shadowy friend to stand by my side in the night of the enormous wilderness, no great haunting memory, but only the unholy recollection of a prosaic newspaper "stunt"[3] and the distasteful knowledge of the vilest scramble for loot that ever disfigured the history of human conscience and geographical exploration. What an end to the idealized realities of a boy's daydreams! I wondered what I was doing there, for indeed it was only an unforeseen episode, hard to believe in now, in my seaman's life. Still, the fact remains that I have smoked a pipe of peace at midnight in the very heart of the African continent, and felt very lonely there.[4]

JOSEPH CONRAD

Extracts from Correspondence, September 24 and 26, 1890 †

Kinshasa,
Stanley Pool,
Congo.
24th September, 1890.

My dear Maryleczka,

Your letter and the photograph reached me today and I hasten to write and explain to you the long interruption in our correspondence.

I have been on the river Congo, some 2,000 versts[1] from the coast where the post office is, so I could neither send nor get news from Europe. I was pleased to get your letter although at the same time it saddened me slightly. I have lived long enough to realize that life is full of griefs and sorrows which no one can escape, nevertheless I cannot help feeling sad at the thought that people whom I love must suffer, and are suffering. It is nonetheless pleasing to get a proof of the trust you place in me by writing openly about your worries. Indeed, I do not deserve to have a

3. Stanley and Livingstone.

4. The manager was evidently anxious to return to Kinshasa because the agent at the Stanley Falls Station, Georges Antoine Klein, a Frenchman who had been in the Congo since early in 1889, was extremely weakened by dysentery; however, Klein died on board on September 21 and was buried at Bolobo, at Grenfell's mission. Captain Koch also had fallen ill, and on September 6 Camille Delcommune wrote Conrad a note giving him temporary command of the *Roi des Belges*, which, pulling two barges probably full of ivory, returned to Kinshasa on Stanley Pool under Conrad, arriving September 24.

† From *The Collected Letters of Joseph Conrad, Volume I, 1861–1897*, ed. Frederick R. Karl (also: General Editor) and Laurence Davies (Cambridge: Cambridge UP, 1983) 57–58 and 61–63. Reprinted by permission of the General Editor, the Estate of Joseph Conrad, and the Cambridge University Press. Annotations by the present editor.

1. A Russian *verst* is about two-thirds of an English mile.

place in your hearts—for I am practically a stranger to you—nevertheless the affectionate words you have written are most precious to me. I shall carefully preserve them in my heart, and the photograph will be in my album so that I can glance each day at my dear little sister.

* * *

I am very busy with all the preparations for a new expedition to the River Kassai.[2] In a few days I shall probably be leaving Kinshasa again for a few months, possibly even for a year or longer. Thus you must not be surprised if you get no sign of life from me for a long time.

* * *

Do not forget about me amidst all the new events in your life. I embrace you most warmly.

Your always loving brother,
K. N. Korzeniowski.

26 September 1890
Kinshasa

Dearest and best of Aunts!

I received your three letters together on my return from Stanley Falls, where I went as a supernumerary on board the vessel *Roi des Belges* in order to learn about the river. I learn with joy of your success at the Academy, which, of course, I never doubted. I cannot find words sufficiently strong to make you understand the pleasure your charming (and above all kind) letters have given me. They were as a ray of sunshine piercing through the grey clouds of a dreary winter day; for my days here are dreary. No use deluding oneself! Decidedly I regret having come here. I even regret it bitterly. With all of a man's egoism, I am going to speak of myself. I cannot stop myself. Before whom can I ease my heart if not before you?! In speaking to you, I am certain of being understood down to the merest hint. Your heart will divine my thoughts more quickly than I can express them.

Everything here is repellent to me. Men and things, but men above all. And I am repellent to them, also. From the manager in Africa[3] who has taken the trouble to tell one and all that I offend him supremely, down to the lowest mechanic, they all have the gift of irritating my nerves—so that I am not as agreeable to them perhaps as I should be. The manager is a common ivory dealer with base instincts who considers himself a merchant although he is only a kind of African shop-keeper. His name is Delcommune. He detests the English, and out here I am naturally regarded as such. I cannot hope for either promotion or salary increases while he is here. Besides, he has said that promises made in

---

2. This was to be the Alexandre Delcommune Katanga expedition to which Conrad had been assigned in Brussels. But the assignment was not honored by the brothers Delcommune, and the *Florida* left, without Conrad, under the command of another on October 17.

3. Camille Delcommune.

Europe carry no weight here if they are not in the contract. Those made to me by M. Wauters are not. In addition, I cannot look forward to anything because I don't have a ship to command. The new boat will not be completed until June of next year, perhaps. Meanwhile, my position here is unclear and I am troubled by that. So there you are! As crowning joy, my health is far from good. *Keep it a secret for me*—but the truth is that in going up the river I suffered from fever four times in two months, and then at the Falls (which is its home territory), I suffered an attack of dysentery lasting five days. I feel somewhat weak physically and not a little demoralized; and then, really, I believe that I feel homesick for the sea, the desire to look again on the level expanse of salt water which has so often lulled me, which has smiled at me so frequently under the sparkling sunshine of a lovely day, which many times too has hurled the threat of death in my face with a swirl of white foam whipped by the wind under the dark December sky. I regret all that. But what I regret even more is having tied myself down for three years. The truth is that it is scarcely probable I shall see them through. Either someone in authority will pick a groundless quarrel in order to send me back (and, really, I sometimes find myself wishing for it), or I shall be sent back to Europe by a new attack of dysentery, unless it consigns me to the other world, which would be a final solution to all my distress! And for four pages I have been speaking of myself! I have not told you with what pleasure I have read your descriptions of men and things at home.[4] Indeed, while reading your dear letters I have forgotten Africa, the Congo, the black savages and the white slaves (of whom I am one) who inhabit it. For one hour I have been happy. Know that it is not a small thing (nor an easy thing) to make a human being happy for an *entire hour*. You can be proud of having succeeded. And so my heart goes out to you with a burst of gratitude and the most sincere and most profound affection. When will we meet again? Alas, meeting leads to parting—and the more one meets, the more painful the separations become. Such is Fate.

Seeking a practical remedy to the disagreeable situation which I have made for myself, I conceived of a little plan—still up in the air—in which you could perhaps help me. It appears that this company, or another affiliated with it, will have some ocean-going vessels (or even has one already). Probably that great (or fat?) banker who rules the roost where we are concerned will have a large interest in the other company. If someone could submit my name for the command of one of their ships (whose home port will be Antwerp) I would be able to get away for a day or two in Brussels when you are there. That would be ideal! If they wanted to call me home to take command, I would naturally pay the cost of coming back myself. This is perhaps not a very practicable idea, but if you return to Brussels in the winter, you could learn through M. Wauters what the chances are. Isn't that so, dear little Aunt?

* * *

4. At Lublin, in Poland.

I urge you by all the gods to keep secret from *everybody* the state of my health, or else my uncle will certainly hear of it. I must finish. I leave within an hour for Bamou,[5] by canoe, to select trees and have them felled for building operations at the station here. I shall remain encamped in the forest for two or three weeks, unless ill. I like the prospect well enough. I can doubtless have a shot or two at some buffaloes or elephants. I embrace you most warmly. I shall write a long letter by the next mail.[6]

Your affectionate nephew
J.C.K.

G. JEAN-AUBRY

[Marguerite Poradowska's Letter to Albert Thys] †

We have no direct evidence of the causes of his rupture with Camille Delcommune, but we have an indirect one of the greatest value; it is a letter addressed by a cousin of Conrad's on November 29th, 1890, from Lublin (Poland) to the Director of the Société du Haut-Congo in Brussels, and which contains the following passages:—

. . . I received a letter from Mr. Conrad Korzeniowski himself, who has just returned from Stanley Falls after two months' navigation on the up-river. . . . He tells me that his health is greatly affected, and he feels utterly demoralized. Further, the steamer of which he is to take command will not be ready before June, perhaps, and the Director, M. Delcommune, told him plainly that he was not to expect either promotion, or an increase in his salary, as long as he will be in the Congo. He also added that the promises made in the contract, and the promises which you were kind enough to make him are indeed not stated in the contract.

Mr. Korzeniowski's position, therefore, is as false as it can be, which is aggravated by these fevers and dysentery, which have greatly weakened him. Mr. Korzeniowski's family is naturally worried to hear this news; we all hoped that he would be able to stand the climate, but another voyage might destroy his health for always. You can understand that we are all very anxious, and that is why the family has asked me to write to you for advice so that we may know how to get this poor young man out of this dreadful position.

---

5. Thirty miles west of Kinshasa.
6. No letter survives, but Conrad went on his lumber expedition and returned to Kinshasa by October 19, by which time he had received no command and decided to leave Africa. In the meantime, his "aunt," Marguerite Poradowska,
once again tried to pull strings in Brussels, this time by letter from Poland.
† From G. Jean-Aubry, *Joseph Conrad in the Congo* (London: William Heinemann, Ltd., 1926) 70–72.

There is some means, which Mr. Conrad submitted himself in his letter, asking me to speak to you about it (as he thinks I am already back in Brussels). It appears that the Cie. Commerciale du Congo (or another affiliated firm) owns a steamer which makes the trip between Banana and Antwerp. It is even said that this society owns several other steamers.

If Mr. Conrad could obtain the command of one of these steamers it would mean that the solution of the problem is ready found, as at sea there will be no more fever nor dysentery. He has asked me, therefore, to beg you to kindly submit his name for the command of one of these steamers which starts from Antwerp. He adds that if he were called back for this purpose he would be prepared to bear himself the expenses of the return voyage. . . . It is sad to think that a capable man such as Mr. Conrad Korzeniowski, who has been used to commanding steamers for fifteen years, should be reduced to this subordinate position, and should be exposed to such fatal disease.

You seemed to have taken an interest in Mr. C. Korzeniowski, and during my stay in Brussels I was able to form an opinion of your kindness, and I hope that you will not withdraw your support, but that, on the contrary, you will advise him as to the steps he should take.

G. JEAN-AUBRY

[Letter from Conrad's Uncle] †

* * * Some weeks later, when he was about to reach Europe, his uncle, Thadée Bobrowski, wrote to him on December 27th, 1890:—

On the 24th I received your letter dated October 19th, from Kinchassa, which informs me of the unfortunate end of your expedition to the Congo and your return to Europe. Mme. Marguerite (Poradowska) informed me also of it from Lublin, where she heard it through the Director of the Company, to whom she had written for news of you.

. . . Although you assure me that the first sea breeze will give you back your health, I found your writing so changed—which I attribute to fever and dysentery—that since then my thoughts are not at all happy. I never hid from you that I was not partisan to your African project. I remained faithful to my principle to leave everybody to be happy in their own way.

See a specialist on tropical diseases immediately, for our doctors here know nothing on the subject, and I have not even the possibility of telling you to come and rest here.

Tell me also the state of your finances, so that perhaps I may help you to the extent of my means.

† From G. Jean-Aubry, *Joseph Conrad in the Congo* (London: William Heinemann, Ltd., 1926) 72.

JOSEPH CONRAD

[Two Final Notes] †

I call to mind * * * a specially awkward turn of the Congo between Kinshasa and Leopoldville—more particularly when one had to take it at night in a big canoe with only half the proper number of paddlers. I failed in being the second white man on record drowned at that interesting spot through the upsetting of a canoe. The first was a young Belgian officer, but the accident happened some months before my time, and he, too, I believe, was going home; not perhaps quite so ill as myself— but still he was going home. I got round the turn more or less alive, though I was too sick to care whether I did or not, and, always with "Almayer's Folly"[1] amongst my diminishing baggage, I arrived at that delectable capital Boma, where before the departure of the steamer which was to take me home I had the time to wish myself dead over and over again with perfect sincerity.[2]

* * *

An Outpost of Progress is the lightest part of the loot I carried off from Central Africa, the main portion being of course the *Heart of Darkness*. Other men have found a lot of quite different things there and I have the comfortable conviction that what I took would not have been of much use to anybody else. And it must be said that it was but a very small amount of plunder. All of it could go into one's breast pocket when folded neatly. As for the story itself it is true enough in its essentials. The sustained invention of a really telling lie demands a talent which I do not possess.

ALBERT J. GUERARD

[From Life to Art] *

Heart of Darkness is the most famous of [Conrad's] personal short novels: a *Pilgrim's Progress* for our pessimistic and psychologizing age. "Before the Congo I was just a mere animal."[1] The living nightmare of 1890 seems to have affected Conrad quite as importantly as did Gide's

† From *A Personal Record* (London: J. M. Dent & Sons, Ltd., 1912) 14. And from "Author's Note," *Tales of Unrest* (London: J. M. Dent & Sons, Ltd., 1921) x. Selections reprinted by permission. Annotations by the editor.
1. Conrad began his career as a writer quite unpremeditatedly one morning in London while looking for a ship in 1889. He continued to work on his manuscript during his visit to his Uncle Tadeusz early in 1890 and had seven chapters with

him in the Congo.
2. Conrad went by canoe from Kinshasa to Leopoldville, by caravan from Leopoldville to Matadi, by boat from Matadi to Boma, and by steamship from Boma to Europe, leaving December 4.
* From *Conrad the Novelist*, 33–38. Cambridge, Mass. Copyright 1958 by the Fellows of Harvard College. Reprinted by permission. Copyright, 1986, by Albert C. Guerard. Annotations by the editor.
1. See below, p. 195.

Congo experience thirty-six years later.[2] The autobiographical basis of the narrative is well known, and its introspective bias obvious; this is Conrad's longest journey into self. But it is well to remember that *Heart of Darkness* is also other if more superficial things: a sensitive and vivid travelogue, and a comment on "the vilest scramble for loot that ever disfigured the history of human conscience and geographical exploration."[3] The Congo was much in the public mind in 1889, when Henry Stanley's relief expedition found Emin Pasha (who like Kurtz did not want to be rescued),[4] and it is interesting to note that Conrad was in Brussels during or immediately after Stanley's triumphant welcome there in April 1890. This was just before he set out on his own Congo journey. We do not know how much the Georges Antoine Klein who died on board the *Roi des Belges* resembled the fictional Kurtz, but Stanley himself provided no mean example of a man who could gloss over the extermination of savages with pious moralisms which were very possibly "sincere."

Heart of Darkness thus has its important public side, as an angry document on absurd and brutal exploitation. Marlow is treated to the spectacle of a French man-of-war shelling an unseen "enemy" village in the bush, and presently he will wander into the grove at the first company station where the starving and sick Negroes withdraw to die. It is one of the greatest of Conrad's many moments of compassionate rendering. The compassion extends even to the cannibal crew of the *Roi des Belges*. Deprived of the rotten hippo meat they had brought along for food, and paid three nine-inch pieces of brass wire a week, they appear to subsist on "lumps of some stuff like half-cooked dough of a dirty lavender colour" which they keep wrapped in leaves. Conrad here operates through ambiguous suggestion (are the lumps human flesh?) but elsewhere he wants, like Gide after him, to make his complacent European reader *see*: see, for instance, the drunken unkempt official met on the road and three miles farther on the body of the Negro with a bullet hole in his forehead.[5] *Heart of Darkness* is a record of things seen and done. But also Conrad was reacting to the humanitarian pretenses of some of the looters precisely as the novelist today reacts to the moralisms of cold-war propaganda. Then it was ivory that poured from the heart of darkness; now it is uranium. Conrad shrewdly recognized—an intuition amply developed in *Nostromo*—that deception is most sinister when it becomes self-deception, and the propagandist takes seriously his own fictions. Kurtz "could get himself to believe anything—anything." The benevolent rhetoric of his seventeen-page report for the International Society for the

2. See *Travels in the Congo*, Paris, 1927 and New York, 1929.
3. See above, p. 187.
4. Emin Pasha, an agent of the Egyptian government, was perfectly content to sit in the center of Africa and amass large amounts of ivory. Naturally the commercial interests of Europe became "concerned" and started a private subscription to finance

his relief—and the relief of his ivory.
5. Compare "The Congo Diary," above, p. 165. Conrad did not use the skeleton tied to a post that he saw on Tuesday, July 29. It might have seemed too blatant or too "literary" in a novel depending on mortuary imagery from beginning to end [from Guerard's note].

Suppression of Savage Customs was meant sincerely enough. But a deeper sincerity spoke through his scrawled postscript: "Exterminate all the brutes!" The conservative Conrad (who found Donkin[6] fit to be a labor leader) speaks through the journalist who says that "Kurtz's proper sphere ought to have been politics 'on the popular side.' "

* * *

In any event, it is time to recognize that the story is not primarily about Kurtz or about the brutality of Belgian officials but about Marlow its narrator. To what extent it also expresses the Joseph Conrad a biographer might conceivably recover, who in 1898 still felt a debt must be paid for his Congo journey and who paid it by the writing of this story, is doubtless an insoluble question. I suspect two facts (of a possible several hundred) are important. First, that going to the Congo was the enactment of a childhood wish associated with the disapproved childhood ambition to go to sea, and that this belated enactment was itself profoundly disapproved, in 1890, by the uncle and guardian.[7] It was another gesture of a man bent on throwing his life away. But even more important may be the guilt of complicity, just such a guilt as many novelists of the Second World War have been obliged to work off. What Conrad thought of the expedition of the Katanga Company of 1890–1892 is accurately reflected in his remarks on the "Eldorado Exploring Expedition" of *Heart of Darkness*: "It was reckless without hardihood, greedy without audacity, and cruel without courage. . . . with no more moral purpose at the back of it than there is in burglars breaking into a safe." Yet Conrad hoped to obtain command of the expedition's ship even after he had returned from the initiatory voyage dramatized in his novel. Thus the adventurous Conrad and Conrad the moralist may have experienced collision. But the collision, again as with so many novelists of the second war, could well have been deferred and retrospective, not felt intensely at the time.

6. In *The Nigger of the "Narcissus."*
7. See *Life and Letters*, I, 137 [from Guerard's note].

Writing the Story

G. JEAN-AUBRY

[From Sailor to Novelist] †

Conrad's health was affected during all the rest of his life by his African expedition. He suffered from attacks of the gout which made his life an intermittent martyrdom. But, on the other hand, it is a not unlikely supposition that this journey to the Congo and its unfortunate consequences gave us the greater writer. * * * The illness which he brought back from the Congo, by limiting his physical activity and confining him to his room for several months, obliged him to withdraw into himself, to call up those memories with which his life, though he was only thirty-five, was already extraordinarily full, and to try to estimate their value both from the human and the literary point of view. * * * It may be said that Africa killed Conrad the sailor and strengthened Conrad the novelist.

EDWARD GARNETT

[Art Drawn from Memory] *

I agree with M. Jean-Aubry that Conrad's Congo experiences were the turning-point in his mental life and that its effects on him determined his transformation from a sailor to a writer. According to his emphatic declaration to me, in his early years at sea he had "not a thought in his head." "I was a perfect animal," he reiterated, meaning, of course, that he had reasoned and reflected hardly at all over all the varieties of life he had encountered. The sinister voice of the Congo with its murmuring undertone of human fatuity, baseness and greed had swept away

† From *Life and Letters* (London: William Heinemann, Ltd., 1927), I, 141–42. Reprinted by permission of J. M. Dent & Sons, Ltd.
*From "Introduction," *Letters from Conrad 1895–1924* (London: The Nonesuch Press, 1928) xii, xviii–xix. Reprinted by permission.
  Edward Garnett (1865–1937), essayist and dramatist, as a reader for the publishing house of Fisher

Unwin "discovered" Conrad in 1894. After successfully arguing for the publication of Conrad's first work, *Almayer's Folly*, Garnett convinced Conrad that he should forsake the sea to become a writer. They remained lifelong friends. See Garnett's review of the *Youth* volume (*The Academy*, December 6, 1902) and Conrad's reaction (*Letters from Conrad*, pp. 187–88).

the generous illusions of his youth, and had left him gazing into the heart of an immense darkness.

* * *

Great quickness of eye was one of Conrad's gifts. I remember while sitting one evening with him in the Café Royal I asked him, after a painted lady had brushed haughtily past our table, what he had specially noticed about her. "The dirt in her nostril," he replied instantly. On this acute sense rested his faculty of selecting the telling detail, an unconscious faculty, so he said. I remarked once of the first draft of *The Rescue*, that as a seaman he must have noted professionally the details of the rainstorm at sea described in Chapter III. Conrad denied this, and asserted that all such pictures of nature had been stored up unconsciously in his memory, and that they only sprung into life when he took up the pen. That Conrad's memory had extraordinary wealth of observation to draw on I had an illuminating proof in *Heart of Darkness*. Some time before he wrote this story of his Congo experience he narrated it at length one morning while we were walking up and down under a row of Scotch firs that leads down to the Cearne.[1] I listened enthralled while he gave me in detail a very full synopsis of what he intended to write. To my surprise when I saw the printed version I found that about a third of the most striking incidents had been replaced by others of which he had said nothing at all. The effect of the written narrative was no less sombre than the spoken, and the end was more consummate; but I regretted the omission of various scenes, one of which described the hero lying sick to death in a native hut, tended by an old negress who brought him water from day to day, when he had been abandoned by all the Belgians. "She saved my life," Conrad said; "the white men never came near me." When on several occasions in those early years I praised his psychological insight he questioned seriously whether he possessed such a power and deplored the lack of opportunities for intimate observation that a sailor's life had offered him. On one occasion on describing to him a terrible family tragedy of which I had been an eye-witness, Conrad became visibly ill-humoured and at last cried out with exasperation: "Nothing of the kind has ever come my way! I have spent half my life knocking about in ships, only getting ashore between voyages. I know nothing, nothing! except from the outside. I have to guess at everything!" This was of course the artist's blind jealousy speaking, coveting the experiences he had not got, and certainly he could have woven a literary masterpiece out of the threads I held, had he known the actors.

1. The Cearne was Garnett's home in Surrey. This incident took place in early September 1898 [Editor].

RICHARD CURLE

[His Piercing Memory] †

He never kept any notes, and even his Congo diary, which gives so
many hints for *Heart of Darkness*, survived only by chance and was, as
I gather from Mrs. Conrad (who told me she had retrieved it from the
waste-paper basket), never consulted by Conrad when writing that story.

* * *

This story was serialized in *Blackwood's Magazine* between February
and April, 1899, and I remember Conrad telling me that its 40,000
words occupied only about a month in writing. When we consider the
painful, slow labour with which he usually composed, we can perceive
how intensely vivid his memories of this experience must have been,
and * * * how intensely actual. But then the notebook only goes to
prove the almost self-evident contention that much of Conrad's work is
founded upon autobiographical remembrance. Conrad himself wrote of
this story in his Author's Note [1917] to * * * the *Youth* volume in
which it appeared: *"Heart of Darkness* is quite as authentic in fundamentals as *Youth* . . . it is experience pushed a little (and only a little)
beyond the actual facts of the case."

* * *

No other diary of Conrad's is extant, and I am very sceptical as to
whether he ever kept another. He was not at all that type of man, and
his piercing memory for essentials was quite sufficient for him to recreate
powerfully vanished scenes and figures for the purposes of his work.

FORD MADOX FORD

[The Setting] *

Heart of Darkness is a tale told *viva voce* by a ship's captain on the
deck of a cruising yawl, to a Director of Companies, a Lawyer, and an
Accountant, all of whom followed the sea to the extent of taking week-
end cruises in the *Nellie*—the cruising yawl. They formed the society in
which Conrad lived at Stamford-le-Hope [1] while, having left the sea but

† From *The Last Twelve Years of Joseph Conrad* by
Richard Curle. Copyright © 1928 by Doubleday
and Company Inc. P. 67. Reprinted by permission
of the publisher. And from "The Congo Diary,"
Last Essays, ed. Richard Curle (London: J. M.
Dent & Sons, Ltd., 1926) 158, 160. Reprinted by
permission.
* From "Heart of Darkness," *Portraits from Life* by
Ford Madox Ford. Copyright © 1936 and 1937 by
Ford Madox Ford. Pp. 59–60. Reprinted by per-
mission of Houghton Mifflin Company and Janice
Biala.

Ford Madox Ford (Hueffer) (1873–1939),
English poet, novelist, and critic, knew Conrad
intimately and collaborated with him on three
books, the first of which was begun in the fall of
1898.
1. In Essex, from September 1896 to September
1898 [Editor].

living near its verge, he was still quivering with his attempt, with the aid of the Director, the Lawyer, and the Accountant, to float a diamond mine in South Africa. For Conrad had his adventures of that sort, too— adventures ending naturally in frustration. And since, while waiting for that financial flotation to mature, he floated physically during week-ends in the company of those financiers on the bosom of that tranquil water-way, he really believed that all the bankers, lawyers, and accountants of the obscure square mile of city upstream were also seamen, or so near it as made no difference. He emerged, of course, from that conviction, but the tragedy was that, by the time he came to see life more collec-tively and less as a matter of Conway-trained[2] and steadfast individuals heroically fighting August northwesters, the unseeing and malignant destiny that waits on us writers set him in such circumstances as robbed him of the leisure in which *Youth* and *Heart of Darkness* could be writ-ten. For those two stories were written and re-written and filed and thought over and re-thought over by a leisured mind of a rare literary common sense.

*   *   *

While he was still under the spell of sea-following and the hypnotism of mariners, he did his best and, as it were, cleanest work. For I think it is to *Youth*, *Heart of Darkness*, and the matchless *Nigger of the "Narcis-sus"* that those epithets must be ascribed, leaving *Almayer* and *The Out-post of Progress* to be considered as his prentice work.

JOSEPH CONRAD

Extracts from Correspondence, July 22, 1896, to December 3, 1902 †

22[d] July. 96.
Ile Grande[1]
par Lannion

Dear Mr Unwin.[2]

    * * * Bad or good I cannot be ashamed of what is produced in perfect single mindedness—I cannot be ashamed of those things that are like

2. The *Conway* was an Admiralty training ship [Editor].
† From *The Collected Letters of Joseph Conrad, Volume I, 1861–1897*, ed. Frederick R. Karl (also General Editor) and Laurence Davies (Cambridge: Cambridge UP, 1983) 293–94. *Volume II, 1898–1902* (1986) 129–30, 132–33, 133, 139–140, 145–46, 146, 146, 147, 148, 149–50, 150, 151, 152, 155, 152, 153, 161–62, 162–63, 157–58, 164–65, 174–75, 406–7, 415–18, 459–60, 460–61. Reprinted by permission of the General Editor, the

Estate of Joseph Conrad, and the Cambridge University Press. Annotations by the present editor.
1. An island off Lannion on the northern coast of Brittany, where Conrad lived for six months after he married Jessie George, age twenty-three, on March 24, in London.
2. T. Fisher Unwin (1845–1935), publisher of *Almayer's Folly* (1895), *An Outcast of the Islands* (1896), *Tales of Unrest* (1898), was also the pub-lisher of the magazine *Cosmopolis*, in which "An Outpost of Progress" appeared June–July 1897.

fragments of my innermost being produced for the public gaze.

* * * But I should like to sell them. If you think I am greedy then consider I am greedy for very little after all. And if you knew the wear and tear of my writing you would understand my desire for some return. I writhe in doubt over every line.—I ask myself—is it right?—is it true?—do I feel it so?—do I express all my feeling? And I ask it at every sentence—I perspire in incertitude over every word!—Perhaps you will smile over all this fuss. But I am sure You will not smile unkindly. After all it is my work. The only lasting thing in the world. People die—affections die—all passes—but a man's work remains with him to the last.

—You will soon receive a story for the *Cosmo*. * * *

—It is a story of the Congo. There is no love interest in it and no woman—only incidentally. The exact locality is not mentioned. All the bitterness of those days, all my puzzled wonder as to the meaning of all I saw—all my indignation at masquerading philanthropy—have been with me again, while I wrote. The story is simple—there is hardly any description. The most common incidents are related—the life in a lonely station on the Kassai. I have divested myself of everything but pity—and some scorn—while putting down the insignificant events that bring on the catastrophe. Upon my word I think it is a good story—and not so gloomy—not fanciful—alas! I think it is interesting—some may find it a bore! * * * Yours very faithfully

Jph Conrad.

[letterhead: Pent Farm][3]
13th December 1898

Dear Mr Blackwood.[4]

I owe you a great many thanks for the *Maga*[5] which reaches me with a most charming regularity. In truth it is the only monthly I care to read, and each number is very welcome, though each is a sharp jog to my conscience. And yet, God knows, it is wide-awake enough and daily avenges the many wrongs my patient publishers suffer at my hands.

And this is all I can say unless I were to unfold for the nth time the miserable tale of my inefficiency. I trust however that in Jany I'll be able to send you about 30000 words or perhaps a little less, towards the Vol: of short stories.[6] Apart from my interest it is such a pleasure for me to appear in the *Maga* that you may well believe it is not laziness that keeps me back. It is, alas, something—I don't know what—not so easy to overcome. With immense effort a thin trickle of MS is produced—and that, just now, must be kept in one channel only lest no one gets anything and I am completely undone.

3. In Kent, where Conrad had moved in October and lived until 1907.
4. William Blackwood was the fifth editor of the famed *Blackwood's Magazine*, established 1817 in Edinburgh as a monthly literary journal.
5. The nickname for *Blackwood's Magazine*.

6. Agreed to in May or June 1898 on the strength of the just-completed *Youth* and eighteen pages of "Jim: A Sketch," which turned out to be *Lord Jim*. (See below, p. 212, n. 3, and Kimbrough essay, p. 406.)

* * *

Well. I only wanted you to know I am alive and not utterly lost to sense of my shortcomings. Accept my best wishes for the coming year. It is near enough already to make sinners of my sort think about turning over a new leaf and so on. I hope you will like my new leaves however belated they may be. I am dear Mr Blackwood always Yours faithfully

Jph Conrad.

[letterhead: Pent Farm]
[18 December 1898]

My dearest Garnett.[7]

I was glad to see thy fist.

* * *

Now I am at a short story for B'wood which I must get out for the sake of the shekels.

* * *

Ever Yours

Jph. Conrad

[letterhead: Pent Farm]
21/12/98

Dear Mr Meldrum[8]

The heartiest wishes to you and yours from us both. I trust next year we shall be able to foregather often.

* * *

Excuse hurried scrawl but I've left all my Xmas letters to the last and have a dozen more to write tonight. With kindest regards Always faithfully yours

Jph. Conrad.

I am writing something for *Maga* a tale (short) in the manner of *Youth*, to be ready in a few days.

[letterhead: Pent Farm]
31/12/98

Dear Mr Blackwood.

Come this moment to hand is your good le[t]ter whose kind wishes, believe me, I reciprocate with all my heart.

Your proposal delights me.[9] As it happens I am (and have been for

---

7. Edward Garnett (1868–1937) as a reader for Unwin "discovered" Conrad when he read and championed *Almayer's Folly*. He quickly became Conrad's advisor and friend. (See p. 195, above.)
8. Blackwood's literary advisor in London, on Paternoster Row.
9. On December 30, 1898, Blackwood invited Conrad to contribute to "*Maga*'s thousandth number," the February 1899 issue.

the last 10 days) working for *Maga*. The thing is far advanced and would have been finished by this only our little boy fell ill, I was disturbed and upset and the work suffered. I expect to be ready in a very few days. It is a narrative after the manner of *youth* told by the same man dealing with his experiences on a river in Central Africa. The *idea* in it is not as obvious as in *youth*—or at least not so obviously presented. I tell you all this, for tho' I have no doubts as to the *workmanship* I do not know whether the *subject* will commend itself to you for that particular number. Of course I should be very glad to appear in it and shall try to hurry up the copy for that express purpose, but I wish you to understand that I am prepared to leave the ultimate decision as to the date of appearance to your decision after perusal.

The title I am thinking of is *"The Heart of Darkness"* but the narrative is not gloomy The criminality of inefficiency and pure selfishness when tackling the civilizing work in Africa is a justifiable idea. The subject is of our time distinc[t]ly—though not topically treated. It is a story as much as my *Outpost of Progress* was but, so to speak 'takes in' more—is a little wider—is less concentrated upon individuals. I destine it for the vol: which is to bear Your imprint. Its lenght [sic] will be under 20,000 words as I see it now. If suitable and you wish to curtail it a couple of pars: could be taken out—from the proof, perhaps.

There is also the question of McClure securing copyright in the States. They bungled the *Youth* affair and I am not in a position to despise the almighty dollar—as yet.

All I can do is hurry up. Meantime many thanks for thinking of me.

Friendly greetings to Your Nephew.[1] I am delighted to be remembered by him.

> I am dear Mr Blackwood, most
> sincerely yours
> Jph. Conrad.

> [letterhead: Pent Farm]
> 2 Jan 1899

Dear Mr Meldrum.

I enclose here a letter from Mr Blackwood and a note (at the back of my reply).

This will make it clear to You how matters are. I am very pleased Mr B'wood thought of me; but his letter coming just now makes it difficult for me to do what I intended doing—or at least I fancy so.

I began the story for Maga 10 days ago. It would have been finished Yesterday had it not been our boy fell ill (he is better now) and thus knocked on the head my peace of mind and, say, inspiration. At any rate there is a delay. Now my intention was to ask Mr Blackwood to let

---

1. George Blackwood, influential in, and later to head, the firm.

me have £40 before the 10th Jan. on the *general* account of my short stories (ser & book). The story would have covered the sum or more; but now the story is not quite ready and my necessity remains all the same. Still I would have asked for the cheque had it not been for this extremely pleasant letter. I don't want M^r B'wood to think I am taking advantage of his ouverture *[sic]*. In this difficulty real or fancied may I ask you whether you could arrange for me with Mr B'wood. The story shall be in your hands shortly it will be about 20000 words (at the agreed rate for serial it would be about £50). My necessity is not a matter of life or death but of the very greatest inconvenience of which I would fain be relieved by your good offices. If you think I could ask Mr B'wood without gross indecency please mediate. I've just written to him and don't want to fire off another letter. And you can put a better look on the thing.

If you want to refer to the story its title so far is *The Heart of Darkness*. A Central Afr: narrative in the manner of Youth—told by the same man. It would stand dividing into two instalments.

I would like you particularly to read the story and the type shall go to London. As I write this one in pencil my wife *must* type, herself or I would send you the *MS* of what is ready. A mere shadow of love interest just in the last pages—but I hope it will have the effect I intend. With our kindest regards to Mrs Meldrum and yourself

I am most faithfully yours
Jph. Conrad.

[Pent Farm]
Tuesday. [3 January 1899]

My dear Hueffer.[2]

Just a word of thanks. The story I told you of holds me. It grows like the genii out of the bottle in the Tale. Won't be done till *Sat*. Till then I am distracted.

With kindest regards to You both from us two.

Ever Yours
Jph. Conrad.

Pent Farm
Tuesday. [3 January 1899]

My dear Wells.[3]

* * * I haven't looked into the W[heels] of C[hance] yet. I can't till I am done with my infernal tale. It grows like the genii from the bottle in the Arabian Tale. Seventy pages—pencil pencil—since I saw you. Also the boy has been ill. My wife's kind regards to Mrs Wells and you. She

2. Ford Madox Ford (1873–1939), whom Conrad met in 1898, in Kent. They quickly became friends and collaborators. (See p. 197, above.)

3. H. G. Wells (1866–1946), the novelist, wrote favorable reviews of *Almayer* and *Outcast*; he and Conrad became friends while living in Kent.

wants to know how you got home. Anyway let me know how you are. I fancy I shall turn up at Granville St[?] before long.

Your

Conrad.

[letterhead: Pent Farm]
6th Jan 1899

Dear Mr Blackwood

Thanks very much for the cheque for £40 (on account of short stories) which I received to-day.

I am, dear Sir always faithfully yours
Jph. Conrad.

P.S. I assure you I appreciate your prompt readiness. I am—alas! not so prompt. Still to morrow I shall send off about 12,000 of *H. of D* to Mr Meldrum. I shall also request him to have a copy typewritten on my ac^t to hand to *McClure*.[4]

Lots more of the story is written—not typed, and in a few days shall be despatched. I am afraid it will be too long for one n°

It has grown upon me a bit—and anyhow the value is in the detail.

J. C.

Pent Farm.
Stanford. near Hythe.
Kent
6th Jan. 1899 (?)

Dear Madame,[5]

* * * Only a word in all haste, for I am extremely busy: in the middle of a piece of work waiting and impatiently waited for because it should have been finished in November and is still there—on my table.

My best wishes to you and all yours.* * *

Always your very faithful servant,
Conrad Korzeniowski

[letterhead: Pent Farm]
Monday. [9 January 1899]

Dear Mr Meldrum.

I send you pp. *1 to 35* typed of *The Heart of Darkness* and from 35 (typed) it goes on to p. 58 of Manuscript.

4. Robert McClure, of S. S. McClure Company, Conrad's American publisher. Because McClure had failed to get an American copyright on *Youth* before it appeared in *Maga*, the *Atlantic Monthly* was not able to carry out its plan to take it. Conrad was understandably upset that when *Outlook* (New York) reprinted *Youth* in October, in the absence of international copyright, he did not get a cent. However, McClure's secured the rights on "The Heart of Darkness" (the serial title) before the February number of *Maga* and published it in 1903 in the first American edition of the *Youth* volume.
5. Baroness de Brunnow, a friend from the days of Conrad's youth in Cracow, Poland.

pp 58 to 90

which is all written up to yesterday. I am awfully sorry to send the pencil *MS* but my wife is not well enough to go on and I want you to have the first half of the story at once. May I ask you to have *the whole* typed out on my acc/t in at least 2 copies. One for Mr McClure and one for *Maga*. The type *from the MS* should be corrected by me before going to printers so You perhaps will let me have that portion for that purpose as soon as ready.

I had a friendly letter and cheque £40 from Mr Blackwood. I am in doubt as to the 1000th N°. There will be no time for US. Copyright. And I can't forego a penny. Are you angry with me for the bother I am giving? I am working under difficulties and that's the truth. Thanks.

.   Apologies. Cordially Yours
                                        Joseph Conrad.

PS Where MS. illegible let them leave blank spaces I can fill up when correcting.

Stephen left for Europe I hear.

                                        Pent Farm.
                                        12th Jan. 1899.

Dear Mrs. Bontine,[6]

* * * Pardon this hurried scrawl. I am finishing in a frightful hurry a story for *B'wood* and it's an immense effort.

With many things I am, dear Mrs. Bontine, always your most faithful and obedient servant.

                                        [letterhead: Pent Farm]
                                        13th Jan 99.

My dear Stephen.[7]

I am more glad than I can say to hear of you being here at last. * * *
I intended to wire myself to-day inquiring. Well that's all over now. I know where to locate you when I think of you—which is often—very. I've been nearly dead and several times quite mad since you left. This is no joke it is the sober truth. I haven't been able to write and felt like cutting my throat. Not a ghost of a notion in my head, not a sentence under the pen. Well. Never mind. It's a little better now. * * * I am coming to see you directly I finish a rotten thing I am writing for B'wood. It *is* rotten—and I can't help it. All I write is rotten now. I am pretty well decayed myself. I ought to be taken out and flung into a dusthole—

6. Mother of Robert Bontine Cunninghame Graham (see note 6, below). The letter is not signed.
7. Stephen Crane (1871–1900) and Conrad had met in October 1897. See the Norton Critical Edition of *The Nigger of the "Narcissus,"* ed. R. Kimbrough.

along with the dead cats—by heavens! Well. Enough. I don't want to bore you into a faint in your first week in Merry England.

Ever yours

Conrad

[letterhead: Pent Farm]
13 Jan 99.

My dear Garnett

* * *

Ah If I could only write! If I could write, write, write! But I can not. No 50 gs. will help me to that.[8] However I am turning out some rotten stuff for B.wood's 1000th N°. Been asked to! Honours will never cease. 'House' wrote autograph! Ah will you—says I. Thereupon I cram them with rubbish. As soon as I turn out the last line I shall come to town for a couple of days. Must see you. Also others. Let me know where You perch. Where You hop too.

Ever Yours

Jph. C.

[Pent Farm]
[13 January 1899][9]

Dear Sirs.

I have marked (on the last page p65) the place where the first instalment might end.

It would be about *half* of the whole story or perhaps a little more.

I shall hurry up the rest as fast as I can. Excuse this scrap of paper and the pencil.

In great haste
Yours faithfully
Jph. Conrad.

---

8. The *Academy*, a literary review, had awarded Conrad a prize of fifty guineas for his five, collected *Tales of Unrest* (1898).
9. Both Frederick Karl and William Blackburn, ed., *Joseph Conrad: Letters to William Blackwood and David S. Meldrum* (Durham, N.C., 1958), p. 45, date this letter February 7, 1899. I have redated it January 13, 1899. Conrad's letters to Ford and Wells on January 3, to Blackwood on January 6, and to Meldrum on January 9 all refer to the first ninety pages of manuscript, which covered the first installment. The page 65 referred to here clearly refers to the balance of the manuscript (pages 58–90), which Meldrum had had typed and sent back to Conrad for correction. The thirty-five pages (manuscript pages 1–58) that Mrs. Conrad had typed Meldrum had already sent to Edinburgh. Notice that here Conrad refers to the story as if it will appear in two installments. Some time toward the end of January, Conrad sent through Meldrum to Blackwood a part of this second (and "final") installment of the story. At that time, the plan was still to run "The Heart of Darkness" (the serial title) in two parts, February and March, but when Conrad finished the "balance of the story" on February 6, he felt that that balance would be too long for merely one more number and wired Meldrum asking that the story be extended into a third number (April). (See n. 3, p. 206, below.)

[letterhead: Pent Farm]
13 Jan 99.

My dear Mr Meldrum.

* * *

I shall come up as soon as *H of D* is finished. I've sent the balance of type to Ed:[1] I am infinitely grateful to you for your patience with me. Believe me most sincerely yours

Jph. Conrad.

[letterhead: Pent Farm]
Monday [16 January 1899]

Dear Mr Meldrum.

Pardon my brutally bad behaviour. Of course I would be delighted and it is very good of you to ask me. As soon as I am done with the *H of D* I shall write you and the day after call on you in Paternoster Row. It will be before end of this month for certain.[2]

The thing has grown on me. I don't think it will be bad.

With very kind regards

Most sincerely Yours

Jph. Conrad.

[letterhead: Pent Farm]
8th Feby 1899

Dear Mr Blackwood.

Thanks very much for your wire. It put my mind at ease for I felt the balance of the story was a little long for one instalment.[3] For the rest I was pretty well to time with it; only 24 hours late and this solely through missing the post by some ten minutes.

I got letters from various people who seem to like the thing, so far.

I was delighted with the number. Gibbon especially fetched me quite. But everything is good. Munro's verses—excellent, and Whibley very interesting—very appreciative very fair. I happen to know Rimbaud's verses.

I must own that I regret the old type. One misses the familiar aspect of the pages when opening the familiar cover. I am "plus royaliste que le roi"—more conservative than Maga.

I am glad to see that the majority (in fact all) of the people for whose opinion I care seem to think I am on the right track in my work for Maga. When talking with Mr Meldrum about the forthcoming volume

1. This refers to the now-lost, revised, typed version of manuscript pages 58–90.
2. They met on January 30.
3. That is, for a second installment only. Note that the February issue of *Maga* had already been published and that Conrad was receiving reactions and that he goes on to describe to Blackwood his delight with the whole number.

he seemed to agree with my idea of keeping to that line. I call it idea but probably it is a necessity. When I sit down to write for you I feel as if in a friendly atmosphere, untrammeled—like one is with people that understand, of whom one is perfectly sure. It is a special mood and a most enjoyable one.

Well, I must go on with the wretched novel [4] which seems to have no end and whose beginning I declare I've forgotten. It is a weird sensation; the African nightmare feeling I've tried to put into H of D is a mere trifle to it. Believe me, dear Sir, always very faithfully yours

Jph. Conrad.

[letterhead: Pent Farm]
Wednesday. [8 February 1899]

Dear Mr Meldrum.

I had a wire from Mr B'wood advising me that the story is to go into three numbers.

I've send [sic] the completed MS. to Edinburgh direct, by Tuesdays morning post. [5]

I think it will be 40000 words. The first inst[mt] was about 14000 (27 pages) and the two others should run to 12000 each. I had £40 on account and (oppressed by my usual impecuniosity) would like to have the balance at once (£50–60). If you remember our conversation you may perhaps guess why I am so anxious.

Pardon me for invading your home with my business. I won't offend again.

I like the story, tho' it is terribly bad in places and falls short of my intention as a whole. Still I am glad I wrote it.

With kindest regards
very faithfully yours
Jph. Conrad.

[Pent Farm]
8 Feb[r] 99.

Cherissime ami. [6]

I am simply in the seventh heaven to find you like the H of D so far. You bless me indeed. Mind you don't curse me by and bye for the very same thing. There are two more instalments in which the idea is so wrapped up in secondary notions that You—even You!—may miss it.

---

4. *The Rescue.*
5. February 7, 1899.
6. R. B. Cunninghame Graham (1852–1936), Scottish writer, aristocrat, and socialist, who wrote Conrad an enthusiastic letter in the summer of 1897 when *An Outpost of Progress* first appeared.

Although the two quickly became and remained close friends, the difference between them is signaled by the fact that when Conrad refused in 1903 to support Roger Casement's work in the Congo, he forwarded the appeal to Cunninghame Graham. (See above, p. 159, n. 3.)

And also You must remember that I don't start with an abstract notion.

I start with definite images and as their rendering is true some little effect is produced. So far the note struck chimes in with your convictions—mais après? There is an après.[7] But I think that if you look a little into the episodes you will find in them the right intention though I fear nothing that is practically effective. Somme toute c'est une bête d'histoire qui aurait pu être quelque chose de très bien si j'avais su l'écrire.[8]

* * *

[letterhead: Pent Farm]
12th Febr. 1899.

Dear Mr Blackwood.

The delay in acknowledging your kind letter and enclosure arises from the fact that in Stanford we have no Sunday post and I was not in time for the Sat: night's mail.

Thanks very much for what you send and still more for what you say. The cheque for £60 now received and the previous one of £40 on account of the same tale *(H of D)* will probably overpay it as I do not think it will run to 40000 words. I did write that number or even more but I've been revising and compressing the end not a little.[9] The proof of the second instalment I kept only twelve hours—not knowing but it might have been wanted at once. I marked a place—on p. 24— where a break is, at least, practicable. If it does not commend itself to your judgment there may be a better place, somewhere within the last inst[t] of typed MS, I've sent to Edinburgh on Tuesday last. My own MS copy is in such confusion and moreover so unlike the final 'type' that I could not venture on its authority to indicate any final sentence or paragraph for the ending of part 2[d].

I am delighted to hear you like the story. Very good of You to write me when so painfully indisposed. I trust the attack has not been severe. Mine always are and I am subject to them at least once a year.[1]

I wonder what you will think of the end of the story. I've been writing up to it and it loomed rather effective till I came to it actually. Still I am not altogether dissatisfied with the manner of it; but of course one cannot judge one's own *fresh* work—at any rate.

* * *

Pardon the lenght *[sic]* of this letter and pray believe me always yours faithfully

Jph. Conrad.

---

7. "—but later on? There is a sequel."

8. "In short, it is a silly story which might have been something quite fine if I had known how to write it." The entire letter (Karl II, 157–61) is a powerful statement of Conrad's peculiar, personal politics.

9. Conrad took advantage of the extension of the story into three parts to rewrite the ending. It is not possible to tell when he actually finished this last revision of the manuscript.

1. The gout.

[letterhead: Pent Farm]
Sunday evening [12 March? 1899]

Dearest Jack[2]

* * * The finishing of *H of D* took a lot out of me. I haven't been
able to do much since.

Ever Yours

Conrad.

Pent Farm
10 Avril 1902.

Mon cher Davry,[3]

* * *

The Blackwood volume will contain: first, *Youth: a narrative* (In giving you the title of *Falk* in the Heinemann volume as *Falk: a narrative*,
I was wrong. It's *Falk: A Reminiscence.*); second, *Heart of Darkness*; and
third, a story I am now in the middle of composing, whose title is *The
End of the Tether*, at the end of one's resources, in other words. That's
the idea, but the title looks stupid. Nearly 75,000 words in all. One and
two have already appeared in *Blackwood's Magazine*. Three will appear
shortly. One and two are told in the first person by Marlow—the gentleman who, if you recall, narrates *Lord Jim*. One, the story of a ship on
fire at sea. Two happens in the Belgian Congo. A wild story of a journalist who becomes manager of a station in the interior and makes himself worshipped by a tribe of savages. Thus described, the subject seems
comic, but it isn't. Three, written in the third person, is rather sentimental. It is about an old captain. At present it has neither head nor
tail. That's it.

With that I give you a very cordial handshake and go to bed.

Yours truly.

[letterhead: Pent Farm]
31 May 1902

Dear Mr Blackwood.

Directly on my return I sit down to thank you for your very kind and
patient hearing. That the occasion was painful to me (it is always painful

2. John Galsworthy (1867–1933), British novelist
and dramatist, who was at this time Conrad's
neighbor. They remained lifelong friends.
3. Henry-Durand Davray (1873–1944), man of
letters who translated Conrad, and other "contemporary" authors, into French. The letter is not
signed.

to be 'asking') makes your friendly attitude the more valuable: and to say this is the primary object of my letter. But there is something more.[4]

* * *

I know exactly what I am doing. M[r] George Blackwood's incidental remarks in his last letter that the story is not fairly begun yet is in a measure correct but, on a large view, beside the point. For, the writing is as good as I can make it (first duty), and in the light of the final incident, the whole story in all its descriptive detail shall fall into its place—acquire its value and its significance. This is my method based on deliberate conviction. I've never departed from it. I call your own kind self to witness and I beg to instance Karain—Lord Jim (where the method is fully developed)—the last pages of Heart of Darkness where the interview of the man and the girl locks in—as it were—the whole 30000 words of narrative description into one suggestive view of a whole phase of life and makes of that story something quite on another plane than an anecdote of a man who went mad in the Centre of Africa. And Youth itself (which I delight to know you like so well) exists only in virtue of my fidelity to the idea and the method.

* * *

This is my creed. Time will show. And this you may say is my over-weening conceit. Well, no. I know well enough that I know nothing. I should like to think that some of my casual critics are in the possession of that piece of information about themselves. Starting from that knowledge one may learn to look on with some attention—at least. But enough of that.

Believe me, dear M[r] Blackwood in all trust and confidence yours

Jph. Conrad.

[letterhead: Pent Farm]
2 December 1902

My dear Clifford[5]

This is indeed a most gorgeous appreciation. I am delighted with all you say and am made really happy by your sympathy. I got the cutting this morning, on the last day of my forty-fourth year, and thus it becomes a noble birthday offering which I am inexpressibly proud to receive.

I would fain persuade myself that I deserve all you say but I can't succeed in that. I am only happy to think that there is *something* in my work which could have appealed to You to that extent.

---

4. Conrad had wanted to see Blackwood about money matters and to complete the plans for the *Youth* volume. During the conference held that morning, he must have felt that his artistic aims and abilities were being questioned through some expression of uncertainty over how effective *The End of the Tether* (only partially completed, but that part already in the hands of the "House") might be. The whole, long letter (Karl II, 415–18) should

be read to understand how seriously Conrad regarded his standing and his integrity as an artist. 5. Sir Hugh Clifford (1866–1941), colonial administrator, had written early favorable reviews of Conrad's writing, as had Conrad of Clifford's. Clifford had just reviewed the *Youth* volume in the *Spectator*, November 29, 1902: 827–29, with special praise for *Heart of Darkness*.

What however I know I deserve (tho' you glide gently even tenderly over the point) are your remarks as to the style. I am glad you absolve me from affectation.

Style is a matter of great concern to me as you know; and perhaps my very anxiety as to the proper use of a language of which I feel myself painfully ignorant produces the effect of laboured construction: whereas as a matter of striving my aim is simplicity and ease. I begin to be afraid I'll never achieve it; thus I shall lose myself in a wilderness of endeavour unilluminated by knowledge.

What I am afraid of is: verbiage. Not so much the superfl[u]ous sentence as the superfluous word is my bugbear. You may smile perhaps at this pretence of conciseness; yet (as the French jurymen) "upon my honour and my conscience" that's what I am trying for. The treatment of the subject may be long; there may be too many phrases:—but the phrases should be without excrescences, almost bare.

The trouble is that I have no skill in tracking out of my principle.

However I must stop these confidences. Thanks! from the bottom of my heart. With kindest regards from us both for Mrs Clifford and yourself. Gratefully always yours

Jph. Conrad.

[letterhead: Pent Farm]
3 December 1902

My Dear Señora[6]

I ought to have answered your letter before this; but I have been plunged in a torpor so profound that even your attack on my pet Heart of Darkness could do no more than make me roll my eyes ferociously. Then for another day I remained prone revolving thoughts of scathing reply. At last—I arose and . . .

Seriously—I don't know that you are wrong. I admit that your strictures are intelligible to me; and every criticism that is intelligible (a quality by no means common) must have some truth in it, if not the whole truth. I mean intelligible to the author of course. As I began by saying—yours is to me; therefore I, in a manner, bear witness to its truth, with (I confess) the greatest reluctance. And, of course, I don't admit the whole of your case. What I distinctly admit is the fault of having made Kurtz too symbolic or rather symbolic at all. But the story being mainly a vehicle for conveying a batch of personal impressions I gave the rein to my mental laziness and took the line of the least resistance. This is then the whole Apologia pro Vita Kurtzii—or rather for the tardiness of his vitality.

My indignation having been (at first) fulgurant my gratitude for all the charming things you say so well in commendation of your servant burns

6. Elsie Hueffer (1876–1924), novelist and translator, married to Ford Madox Ford.

with a steady and unalterable glow. Indeed, pray believe me, your letter
has given me a very great pleasure; and I thank you for writing it; for to
write to an author who sends his book is—generally—an odious task.

I may say then "Au revoir a bientôt." I shall bring the cuttings[7] with
me. Most of them are unintelligible to me and consequently contain no
truth. Jessie sends her love. Believe me always faithfully yours,

Jph. Conrad.

FORD MADOX FORD

[The Ending] †

I will add some further notations as to the passage I have quoted from
Heart of Darkness.[1] It has always seemed to me—and still seems—one
of the most perfect passages of prose in the language and it has for me a
certain added significance from the fact that it must have been the first
passage of Conrad's prose to which I ever paid minute and letter-by-
letter consideration. He had come to stop with me at the Pent,[2] and had
there received the proofs of the story in one or another of its stages.[3] And
being worried over—and above all having the leisure to attend to—his
closing passages, it was the last paragraph to which he first invited me to
pay attention.

We must have argued over it for three whole days, going from time
to time over the beginning and the body of the story, but always at the
back of the mind considering that last paragraph and returning to it to
suggest one or another minute change in wording or in punctuation.

If you will take the trouble to look back to the passage as I have quoted
it, you will see that it begins, 'We have lost the first of the ebb.' Actually,
in the copy from which I am quoting—Doubleday, Doran's Malay edition of 1928—the last paragraph begins, 'Marlow ceased and sat apart,
indistinct and silent, in the pose of a meditating Buddha. Nobody moved
for a time,' and then continues with the Director's speech.

In the original version, those last two sentences stood apart, the word
'time' ending the paragraph. And we tried every possible juxtaposition
of those sentences, putting 'No one moved for a time' in front of Mar-

7. Press clippings.

† From "Heart of Darkness," *Portraits from Life* by
Ford Madox Ford. Copyright © 1936 and 1937 by
Ford Madox Ford. Pp. 61–63. Reprinted by per-
mission of Houghton Mifflin Company and Janice
Biala.

1. The last three sentences of the story.

2. Ford's home in Kent.

3. Probably the proofs for the projected Blackwood volume of three stories, only two of which,
Youth and *Heart of Darkness*, were completed. The
third was to have been *Lord Jim*, but as the fall of

1899 and winter of 1900 passed *Jim* got to be so
long that Blackwood decided that he would have
to issue it separately as a novel after its serial
appearance in *Maga*. Although Conrad returned
proof on *Heart of Darkness* by the end of February
1900 and it was in plates by the middle of May,
the *Youth* volume did not appear until late 1902,
with *The End of the Tether* as the third story. No
extant version of the story has a last paragraph such
as Ford describes. See also Ford, *Joseph Conrad*
(Boston, 1924), 168–71.

low's ceasing; running that sentence up to the end of the last paragraph
of speech; cutting it out altogether—because the first principle of the
technique of Conrad and myself at that time was that you should never
state a negative. If nobody moves, you do not have to make the statement; just as, if somebody is silent, you just do not record any speech of
his, and leave it at that.

However, the negative statement got itself left in at the end, I suppose
as a matter of cadence, though I remember suggesting the excision of
'for a time'—a suggestion that Conrad turned down because that would
have made the statement too abrupt and dramatic. The last paragraph
of a story should have the effect of what musicians call a coda—a passage
meditative in tone, suited for letting the reader or hearer gently down
from the tense drama of the story, in which all his senses have been shut
up, into the ordinary workaday world again.

In the interest of that tranquillity, either Conrad or I suggested the
use of the adjectival-participle form in the last clause of the paragraph.
I can't remember which of us it was, because we changed our position
morning by morning, according as the one or the other of us had got up
feeling the more French. We never read anything but French in those
days, but sometimes Conrad, and less often I, would have a British reaction. . . . And to make that passage classic English prose, you would
have to put it:

> . . . the tranquil waterway, leading to the uttermost ends of the
> earth, flowing sombre under an overcast sky, seemed to lead into
> the heart of an immense darkness.

Or, since Conrad—or, in the alternative, I—might object to the asso-
nance of 'flowing' and 'leading':

> the tranquil waterway, leading to the uttermost ends of the earth,
> flowed sombre under an overcast sky, seemed to lead into the heart
> of an immense darkness.

Which last would be the version I should today adopt, as being, with its
punctuation and all, the most tranquilly classic.

But I suppose that, in the end, we both of us got up one morning
feeling unbridledly and unrepentantly Gallic—and so you have only one
comma and a French dash for punctuation of the whole sentence and
the relatively harsh 'seemed,' instead of the tender 'seeming.'[4]

---

4. For yet another version, see the reproduction of manuscript p. 99 on p. 217.

CONRAD'S MANUSCRIPT OF *HEART OF DARKNESS* †

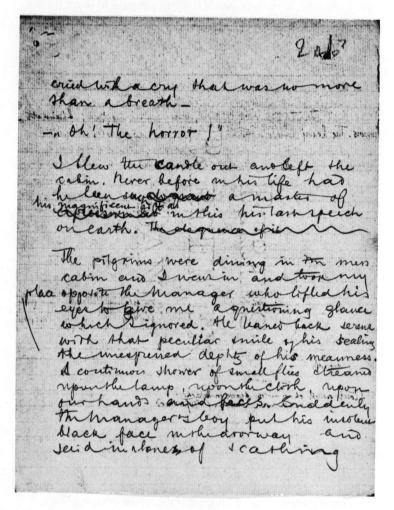

"Oh! The horror!"

†Courtesy of Yale University Library

Contempt —

—" Mistah Kurtz — he dead."

All the pilgrims rushed out
to see. I remained and went on with
my dinner. I believe I was considered
brutally callous. However I did
not eat much. There was
a lamp in there — light — don't
you know — and outside it was
so beastly, beastly dark. I
went no more near the remarkable
man who had so unhesitatingly
pronounced a judgment upon
the adventures of his soul on this
earth. The voice was gone. What else
had been there? The pilgrims buried something next
day in a muddy hole.

"Mistah Kurtz—he dead."

whisper all around us in a whisper that seemed to swell menacingly like the first whisper of a rising wind. "Oh! the horror!"

— His last word — to live with." She murmured. "Don't you understand I loved him — I loved him."

I pulled myself together and spoke slowly.

— "The last word he pronounced was — your name."

I heard a light sigh and then my heart stood still ~~stopped~~ ~~dead~~ exulting and terrible by the cry of inconceivable triumph and of unspeakable pain. ~~He said~~ ~~him~~ "I knew it — I was sure!" . . . She knew. She was sure. It seemed to me the house would collapse, the heavens would fall upon my head. But nothing happened. The heavens do not fall for such a trifle. Would they have fallen, I wonder, if I had rendered Kurtz justice.

"The last word he pronounced was—your name."

99

He wanted only justice

Hadn't he said he wanted only
justice? But I couldn't. I could
not tell her. It would have
~~been too dark too dark. It~~
~~would have been too dark of that~~
~~looking.~~
been too dark — too dark altogether.

Marlow ceased and sat apart in the pose of a meditating Buddha.
~~The men slept.~~ Nobody moved for
a time. "We have lost the first of
the ebb," said the Director suddenly.
I looked around. The offing was
barred by a black bank of
clouds and the ~~only waterway~~ tranquil
waterway that leading to the uttermost
ends of the earth flowing sombre
under an overcast sky seemed
to lead into the heart of an
immense darkness.

The End

. . . into the heart of an immense darkness.

Conrad on Life and Art

Most of the working truths on this earth are humble, not heroic; and there have been times in the history of mankind when the accents of heroic truth have moved it to nothing but derision.

—1912

My task which I am trying to achieve is, by the power of the written word, to make you hear, to make you feel—it is above all, to make you *see*.

—1897

[Fidelity: Four Notes] †

Those who read me know my conviction that the world, the temporal world, rests on a few very simple ideas; so simple that they must be as old as the hills. It rests notably, among others, on the idea of Fidelity. At a time when nothing which is not revolutionary in some way or other can expect to attract much attention I have not been revolutionary in my writings. The revolutionary spirit is mighty convenient in this, that it frees one from all scruples as regards ideas. Its hard, absolute optimism is repulsive to my mind by the menace of fanaticism and intolerance it contains. No doubt one should smile at these things; but, imperfect Aesthete, I am no better Philosopher. All claim to special righteousness awakens in me that scorn and anger from which a philosophical mind should be free.

* * *

"Work is the law. Like iron that lying idle degenerates into a mass of useless rust, like water that in an unruffled pool sickens into a stagnant and corrupt state, so without action the spirit of men turns to a dead thing, loses its force, ceases prompting us to leave some trace of ourselves on this earth." The sense of the above lines does not belong to me. It may be found in the note-books of one of the greatest artists that ever lived, Leonardo da Vinci. It has a simplicity and a truth which no amount of subtle comment can destroy.

The Master who had meditated so deeply on the rebirth of arts and sciences, on the inward beauty of all things,—ships' lines, women's faces—

† From "A Familiar Preface" (1912), *Conrad's Prefaces*, ed. Edward Garnett (London: J. M. Dent & Sons, Ltd., 1937) 208. From "Tradition" (1918) and "Well Done" (1918), *Notes on Life and Let-* *ters* (London: J. M. Dent & Sons, Ltd., 1921) 194–95, 189–91. Selections reprinted by permission of the publisher.

and on the visible aspects of nature was profoundly right in his pronouncement on the work that is done on the earth. From the hard work of men are born the sympathetic consciousness of a common destiny, the fidelity to right practice which makes great craftsmen, the sense of right conduct which we may call honour, the devotion to our calling and the idealism which is not a misty, winged angel without eyes, but a divine figure of terrestrial aspect with a clear glance and with its feet resting firmly on the earth on which it was born.

And work will overcome all evil, except ignorance, which is the condition of humanity and, like the ambient air, fills the space between the various sorts and conditions of men, which breeds hatred, fear, and contempt between the masses of mankind and puts on men's lips, on their innocent lips, words that are thoughtless and vain.

* * *

It is my deep conviction, or, perhaps, I ought to say my deep feeling born from personal experience, that it is not the sea but the ships of the sea that guide and command that spirit of adventure which some say is the second nature of British men. I don't want to provoke a controversy (for intellectually I am rather a Quietist) but I venture to affirm that the main characteristic of the British men spread all over the world, is not the spirit of adventure so much as the spirit of service. I think that this could be demonstrated from the history of great voyages and the general activity of the race. That the British man has always liked his service to be adventurous rather than otherwise cannot be denied, for each British man began by being young in his time when all risk has a glamour. Afterwards, with the course of years, risk became a part of his daily work; he would have missed it from his side as one misses a loved companion.

The mere love of adventure is no saving grace. It is no grace at all. It lays a man under no obligation of faithfulness to an idea and even to his own self. Roughly speaking, an adventurer may be expected to have courage, or at any rate may be said to need it. But courage in itself is not an ideal. A successful highwayman showed courage of a sort, and pirate crews have been known to fight with courage or perhaps only with reckless desperation in the manner of cornered rats. There is nothing in the world to prevent a mere lover or pursuer of adventure from running at any moment. There is his own self, his mere taste for excitement, the prospect of some sort of gain, but there is no sort of loyalty to bind him in honour to consistent conduct. I have noticed that the majority of mere lovers of adventure are mightily careful of their skins; and the proof of it is that so many of them manage to keep it whole to an advanced age. You find them in mysterious nooks of islands and continents, mostly red-nosed and watery-eyed, and not even amusingly boastful. There is nothing more futile under the sun than a mere adventurer. He might have loved at one time—which would have been a saving grace. I mean loved adventure for itself. But if so, he was bound to lose this grace very soon. Adventure by itself is but a phantom, a dubious shape without a heart.

*   *   *

The successive generations that went out to sea from these Isles went out to toil desperately in adventurous conditions. A man is a worker. If he is not that he is nothing. Just nothing—like a mere adventurer. Those men understood the nature of their work, but more or less dimly, in various degrees of imperfection. The best and greatest of their leaders even had never seen it clearly, because of its magnitude and the remoteness of its end. This is the common fate of mankind, whose most positive achievements are born from dreams and visions followed loyally to an unknown destination. And it doesn't matter. For the great mass of mankind the only saving grace that is needed is steady fidelity to what is nearest to hand and heart in the short moment of each human effort. In other and in greater words, what is needed is a sense of immediate duty, and a feeling of impalpable constraint. Indeed, seamen and duty are all the time inseparable companions. It has been suggested to me that this sense of duty is not a patriotic sense or a religious sense, or even a social sense in a seaman. I don't know. It seems to me that a seaman's duty may be an unconscious compound of these three, something perhaps smaller than either, but something much more definite for the simple mind and more adapted to the humbleness of the seaman's task. It has been suggested also to me that this impalpable constraint is put upon the nature of a seaman by the Spirit of the Sea, which he serves with a dumb and dogged devotion.

Those are fine words conveying a fine idea. But this I do know, that it is very difficult to display a dogged devotion to a mere spirit, however great. In everyday life ordinary men require something much more material, effective, definite, and symbolic on which to concentrate their love and their devotion. And then, what is it, this Spirit of the Sea? It is too great and too elusive to be embraced and taken to a human breast. All that a guileless or guileful seaman knows of it is its hostility, its exaction of toil as endless as its ever-renewed horizons. No. What awakens the seaman's sense of duty, what lays that impalpable constraint upon the strength of his manliness, what commands his not always dumb if always dogged devotion, is not the spirit of the sea but something that in his eyes has a body, a character, a fascination, and almost a soul—it is his ship.

[The Cruel Sea] †

The love that is given to ships is profoundly different from the love men feel for every other work of their hands—the love they bear to their houses, for instance—because it is untainted by the pride of possession. The pride of skill, the pride of responsibility, the pride of endurance there may be, but otherwise it is a disinterested sentiment. No seaman

† From *The Mirror of the Sea* (1905) 136–37.

ever cherished a ship, even if she belonged to him, merely because of the profit she put in his pocket. No one, I think, ever did; for a ship-owner, even of the best, has always been outside the pale of that senti-ment embracing in a feeling of intimate, equal fellowship the ship and the man, backing each other against the implacable, if sometimes dis-sembled, hostility of their world of waters. The sea—this truth must be confessed—has no generosity. No display of manly qualities—courage, hardihood, endurance, faithfulness—has ever been known to touch its irresponsible consciousness of power. The ocean has the conscienceless temper of a savage autocrat spoiled by much adulation. * * *

[The Faithful River] †

The estuaries of rivers appeal strongly to an adventurous imagination. This appeal is not always a charm, for there are estuaries of a particularly dispiriting ugliness: lowlands, mudflats, or perhaps barren sandhills without beauty of form or amenity of aspect, covered with a shabby and scanty vegetation conveying the impression of poverty and uselessness. Some-times such an ugliness is merely a repulsive mark. A river whose estuary resembles a breach in a sand rampart may flow through a most fertile country. But all the estuaries of great rivers have their fascination, the attractiveness of an open portal. Water is friendly to man. The ocean, a part of Nature farthest removed in the unchangeableness and majesty of its might from the spirit of mankind, has ever been a friend to the enter-prising nations of the earth. And of all the elements this is the one to which men have always been prone to trust themselves, as if its immens-ity held a reward as vast as itself.

From the offing the open estuary promises every possible fruition to adventurous hopes. That road opens to enterprise and courage invites the explorer of coasts to new efforts towards the fulfilment of great expec-tations. The commander of the first Roman galley must have looked with an intense absorption upon the estuary of the Thames as he turned the beaked prow of his ship to the westward under the brow of the North Foreland. The estuary of the Thames is not beautiful; it has no noble features, no romantic grandeur of aspect, no smiling geniality; but it is wide open, spacious, inviting, hospitable at the first glance, with a strange air of mysteriousness which lingers about it to this very day. The navi-gation of his craft must have engrossed all the Roman's attention in the calm of a summer's day (he would choose his weather), when the single row of long sweeps (the galley would be a light one, not a trireme) could fall in easy cadence upon a sheet of water like plate-glass, reflecting faithfully the classic form of his vessel and the contour of the lonely shores close on his left hand. I assume he followed the land and passed through what is at present known as Margate Roads, groping his careful

† From *The Mirror of the Sea* (1905) 100–103.

way along the hidden sandbanks, whose every tail and spit has its beacon
or buoy nowadays. He must have been anxious, though no doubt he
had collected beforehand on the shores of the Gauls a store of information from the talk of traders, adventures, fishermen, slave-dealers, pirates—
all sorts of unofficial men connected with the sea in a more or less
reputable way. He would have heard of channels and sandbanks, of
natural features of the land useful for sea-marks, of villages and tribes
and modes of barter and precautions to take: with the instructive tales
about native chiefs dyed more or less blue, whose character for greedi-
ness, ferocity, or amiability must have been expounded to him with that
capacity for vivid language which seems joined naturally to the shadiness
of moral character and recklessness of disposition. With that sort of spiced
food provided for his anxious thought, watchful for strange men, strange
beasts, strange turns of the tide, he would make the best of his way up,
a military seaman with a short sword on thigh and a bronze helmet on
his head, the pioneer post-captain of an imperial fleet. Was the tribe
inhabiting the Isle of Thanet[1] of a ferocious disposition, I wonder, and
ready to fall, with stone-studded clubs and wooden lances hardened in
the fire, upon the backs of unwary mariners?

Amongst the great commercial streams of these islands, the Thames
is the only one I think open to romantic feeling, from the fact that the
sight of human labour and the sounds of human industry do not come
down its shores to the very sea, destroying the suggestion of mysterious
vastness caused by the configuration of the shore. The broad inlet of the
shallow North Sea passes gradually into the contracted shape of the river;
but for a long time the feeling of the open water remains with the ship
steering to the westward through one of the lighted and buoyed passage-
ways of the Thames, such as Queen's Channel, Prince's Channel, Four-
Fathom Channel; or else coming down the Swin from the north. The
rush of the yellow flood-tide hurries her up as if into the unknown between
the two fading lines of the coast. There are no features to this land, no
conspicuous, far-famed landmarks for the eye; there is nothing so far
down to tell you of the greatest agglomeration of mankind on earth
dwelling no more than five-and-twenty miles away, where the sun sets
in a blaze of colour flaming on a gold background, and the dark, low
shores trend towards each other.

[The World of the Living] †

This story, which I admit to be in its brevity a fairly complex piece of
work, was not intended to touch on the supernatural.[1] Yet more than
one critic has been inclined to take it in that way, seeing in it an attempt
on my part to give the fullest scope to my imagination by taking it beyond

1. The Isle of Thanet lies off Kent in Southeast
England [Editor].
† From "Author's Note," The Shadow Line (Lon-

don: J. M. Dent & Sons, Ltd., 1920) ix–x.
Reprinted by permission.
1. The Shadow Line [Editor].

the confines of the world of the living, suffering humanity. But as a matter of fact my imagination is not made of stuff so elastic as all that. I believe that if I attempted to put the strain of the supernatural on it it would fail deplorably and exhibit an unlovely gap. But I could never have attempted such a thing, because all my moral and intellectual being is penetrated by an invincible conviction that whatever falls under the dominion of our senses must be in nature and, however, exceptional, cannot differ in its essence from all the other effects of the visible and tangible world of which we are a self-conscious part. The world of the living contains enough marvels and mysteries as it is; marvels and mysteries acting upon our emotions and intelligence in ways so inexplicable that it would almost justify the conception of life as an enchanted state. No, I am too firm in my consciousness of the marvellous to be ever fascinated by the mere supernatural, which (take it any way you like) is but a manufactured article, the fabrication of minds insensitive to the intimate delicacies of our relation to the dead and to the living, in their countless multitudes; a desecration of our tenderest memories; an outrage on our dignity.

[To Make You See] †

A work that aspires, however humbly, to the condition of art should carry its justification in every line. And art itself may be defined as a single-minded attempt to render the highest kind of justice to the visible universe, by bring to light the truth, manifold and one, underlying its ever aspect. It is an attempt to find in its forms, in its colours, in its light, in its shadows, in the aspects of matter and in the facts of life, what of each is fundamental, what is enduring and essential—their one illuminating and convincing quality—the very truth of their existence. The artist, then, like the thinker or the scientist, seeks the truth and makes his appeal. Impressed by the aspect of the world the thinker plunges into ideas, the scientist into facts—whence, presently, emerging they make their appeal to those qualities of our being that fit us best for the hazardous enterprise of living. They speak authoritatively to our common-sense, to our intelligence, to our desire of peace or to our desire of unrest; not seldom to our prejudices, sometimes to our fears, often to our egoism—but always to our credulity. And their words are heard with reverence, for their concern is with weighty matters; with the cultivation of our minds and the proper care of our bodies: with the attainment of our ambitions: with the perfection of the means and the glorification of our precious aims.

It is otherwise with the artist.

Confronted by the same enigmatical spectacle the artist descends within himself, and in that lonely region of stress and strife, if he be deserving

†The Preface (1897), *The Nigger of the "Narcissus,"* (New York: Norton, 1979) 145–48. Reprinted by permission. Annotations by the editor.

and fortunate, he finds the terms of his appeal. His appeal is made to our less obvious capacities: to that part of our nature which, because of the warlike conditions of existence, is necessarily kept out of sight within the more resisting and hard qualities—like the vulnerable body within a steel armour. His appeal is less loud, more profound, less distinct, more stirring—and sooner forgotten. Yet its effect endures forever. The changing wisdom of successive generations discards ideas, questions facts, demolishes theories. But the artist appeals to that part of our being which is not dependent on wisdom; to that in us which is a gift and not an acquisition—and, therefore, more permanently enduring. He speaks to our capacity for delight and wonder, to the sense of mystery surrounding our lives: to our sense of pity, and beauty, and pain: to the latent feeling of fellowship with all creation—and to the subtle but invincible, conviction of solidarity that knits together the loneliness of innumerable hearts: to the solidarity in dreams, in joy, in sorrow, in aspirations, in illusions, in hope, in fear, which binds men to each other, which binds together all humanity—the dead to the living and the living to the unborn.

It is only some such train of thought, or rather of feeling, that can in a measure explain the aim of the attempt, made in the tale which follows,[1] to present an unrestful episode in the obscure lives of a few individuals out of all the disregarded multitude of the bewildered, the simple, and the voiceless. For, if there is any part of truth in the belief confessed above, it becomes evident that there is not a place of splendour or a dark corner of the earth that does not deserve, if only a passing glance of wonder and pity. The motive, then, may be held to justify the matter of the work; but this preface, which is simply an avowal of endeavour, cannot end here—for the avowal is not yet complete.

Fiction—if it at all aspires to be art—appeals to temperament. And in truth it must be, like painting, like music, like all art, the appeal of one temperament to all the other innumerable temperaments whose subtle and resistless power endows passing events with their true meaning, and creates the moral, the emotional atmosphere of the place and time. Such an appeal to be effective must be an impression conveyed through the senses; and, in fact, it cannot be made in any other way, because temperament, whether individual or collective, is not amenable to persuasion. All art, therefore, appeals primarily to the senses, and the artistic aim when expressing itself in written words must also make its appeal through the senses, if its high desire is to reach the secret spring of responsive emotions. It must strenuously aspire to the plasticity of sculpture, to the colour of painting, and to the magic suggestiveness of music— which is the art of arts. And it is only through complete, unswerving devotion to the perfect blending of form and substance; it is only through an unremitting never-discouraged care for the shape and ring of sentences that an approach can be made to plasticity, to colour; and the light of magic suggestiveness may be brought to play for an evanescent

---

1. *The Nigger of the "Narcissus."*

instant over the commonplace surface of words: of the old, old words, worn thin, defaced by ages of careless usage.

The sincere endeavour to accomplish that creative task, to go as far on the road as his strength will carry him, to go undeterred by faltering, weariness, or reproach, is the only valid justification for the worker in prose. And if his conscience is clear, his answer to those who, in the fulness of a wisdom which looks for immediate profit, demand specifically to be edified, consoled, amused; who demand to be promptly improved, or encouraged, or frightened, or shocked, or charmed, must run thus:—My task which I am trying to achieve is, by the power of the written word, to make you hear, to make you feel—it is, before all, to make you *see*. That—and no more, and it is everything. If I succeed, you shall find there according to your deserts: encouragement, consolation, fear, charm—all you demand and, perhaps, also that glimpse of truth for which you have forgotten to ask.

To snatch in a moment of courage, from the remorseless rush of time, a passing phase of life, is only the beginning of the task. The task approached in tenderness and faith is to hold up unquestioningly, without choice and without fear, the rescued fragment before all eyes and in the light of a sincere mood. It is to show its vibration, its colour, its form; and through its movement, its form, and its colour, reveal the substance of its truth—disclose its inspiring secret: the stress and passion within the core of each convincing moment. In a single-minded attempt of that kind, if one be deserving and fortunate, one may perchance attain to such clearness of sincerity that at last the presented vision of regret or pity, of terror or mirth, shall awaken in the hearts of the beholders that feeling of unavoidable solidarity; of the solidarity in mysterious origin, in toil, in joy, in hope, in uncertain fate, which binds men to each other and all mankind to the visible world.

It is evident that he who, rightly or wrongly, holds by the convictions expressed above cannot be faithful to any one of the temporary formulas of his craft. The enduring part of them—the truth which each only imperfectly veils—should abide with him as the most precious of his possessions, but they all: Realism, Romanticism, Naturalism, even the unofficial sentimentalism (which like the poor,[2] is exceedingly difficult to get rid of), all these gods must, after a short period of fellowship, abandon him—even on the very threshold of the temple—to the stammerings of his conscience and to the outspoken consciousness of the difficulties of his work. In that uneasy solitude the supreme cry of Art for Art, itself, loses the exciting ring of its apparent immorality. It sounds far off. It has ceased to be a cry, and is heard only as a whisper, often incomprehensible, but at times and faintly encouraging.

Sometimes, stretched at ease in the shade of a roadside tree, we watch the motions of a labourer in a distant field, and after a time, begin to wonder languidly as to what the fellow may be at. We watch the move-

2. John 12.8.

ments of his body, the waving of his arms, we see him bend down, stand up, hesitate, begin again. It may add to the charm of an idle hour to be told the purpose of his exertions. If we know he is trying to lift a stone, to dig a ditch, to uproot a stump, we look with a more real interest at his efforts; we are disposed to condone the jar of his agitation upon the restfulness of the landscape; and even, if in a brotherly frame of mind, we may bring ourselves to forgive his failure. We understood his object, and, after all, the fellow has tried, and perhaps he had not the strength—and perhaps he had not the knowledge. We forgive, go on our way—and forget.

And so it is with the workman of art. Art is long and life is short,[3] and success is very far off. And thus, doubtful of strength to travel so far, we talk a little about the aim—the aim of art, which, like life itself, is inspiring, difficult—obscured by mists. It is not in the clear logic of a triumphant conclusion; it is not in the unveilng of one of those heartless secrets which are called the Laws of Nature. It is not less great, but only more difficult.

To arrest, for the space of a breath, the hands busy about the work of the earth, and compel men entranced by the sight of distant goals to glance for a moment at the surrounding vision of form and colour, of sunshine and shadows; to make them pause for a look, for a sigh, for a smile—such is the aim, difficult and evanescent, and reserved only for a very few to achieve. But sometimes, by the deserving and the fortunate, even that task is accomplished. And when it is accomplished—behold!—all the truth of life is there: a moment of vision, a sigh, a smile—and the return to an eternal rest.

Books †

Of all books, novels, which the Muses should love, make a serious claim on our compassion. The art of the novelist is simple. At the same time it is the most elusive of all creative arts, the most liable to be obscured by the scruples of its servants and votaries, the one pre-eminently destined to bring trouble to the mind and the heart of the artist. After all, the creation of a world is not a small undertaking except perhaps to the divinely gifted. In truth every novelist must begin by creating for himself a world, great or little, in which he can honestly believe. This world cannot be made otherwise than in his own image: it is fated to remain individual and a little mysterious, and yet it must resemble something already familiar to the experience, the thoughts and the sensations of his readers. At the heart of fiction, even the least worthy of the name, some sort of truth can be found—if only the truth of a childish theatrical ardour in the game of life, as in the novels of Dumas the father. But the

3. Attributed to Hippocrates, fifth century B.C.
† From "Books" (1905), *Notes on Life and Letters*, 6–10. Annotations by the editor.

fair truth of human delicacy can be found in Mr. Henry James's novels; and the comical, appalling truth of human rapacity let loose amongst the spoils of existence lives in the monstrous world created by Balzac.[1] The pursuit of happiness by means lawful and unlawful, through resignation or revolt, by the clever manipulation of conventions or by solemn hanging on to the skirts of the latest scientific theory, is the only theme that can be legitimately developed by the novelist who is the chronicler of the adventures of mankind amongst the dangers of the kingdom of the earth. And the kingdom of this earth itself, the ground upon which his individualities stand, stumble, or die, must enter into his scheme of faithful record. To encompass all this in one harmonious conception is a great feat; and even to attempt it deliberately with serious intention, not from the senseless prompting of an ignorant heart, is an honourable ambition. For it requires some courage to step in calmly where fools may be eager to rush. As a distinguished and successful French novelist once observed of fiction, "C'est un art *trop* difficile."[2]

It is natural that the novelist should doubt his ability to cope with his task. He imagines it more gigantic than it is. And yet literary creation being only one of the legitimate forms of human activity has no value but on the condition of not excluding the fullest recognition of all the more distinct forms of action. This condition is sometimes forgotten by the man of letters, who often, especially in his youth, is inclined to lay a claim of exclusive superiority for his own amongst all the other tasks of the human mind. The mass of verse and prose may glimmer here and there with the glow of a divine spark, but in the sum of human effort it has no special importance. There is no justificative formula for its existence any more than for any other artistic achievement. With the rest of them it is destined to be forgotten, without, perhaps, leaving the faintest trace. Where a novelist has an advantage over the workers in other fields of thought is in his privilege of freedom—the freedom of expression and the freedom of confessing his innermost beliefs—which should console him for the hard slavery of the pen.

* * *

Liberty of imagination should be the most precious possession of a novelist. To try voluntarily to discover the fettering dogmas of some romantic, realistic, or naturalistic creed in the free work of its own inspiration, is a trick worthy of human perverseness which, after inventing an absurdity, endeavours to find for it a pedigree of distinguished ancestors. It is a weakness of inferior minds when it is not the cunning device of those who, uncertain of their talent, would see to add lustre to it by the authority of a school. Such, for instance, are the high priests who

1. Alexandre Dumas (1802–70), French novelist, author of *The Three Musketeers* and *The Count of Monte-Christo*.

Henry James (1843–1916), American novelist, friend and neighbor of Conrad when *Heart of Darkness* was written, became a British citizen at the outbreak of World War I.

Honoré de Balzac (1799–1850), French novelist, whose incomplete work of philosophical fiction, *The Human Comedy*, runs to forty volumes.

2. "It is much too difficult an art."

have proclaimed Stendhal for a prophet of Naturalism.[3] But Stendhal himself would have accepted no limitation of his freedom. Stendhal's mind was of the first order. His spirit above must be raging with a peculiarly Stendhalesque scorn and indignation. For the truth is that more than one kind of intellectual cowardice hides behind the literary formulas. And Stendhal was preeminently courageous. He wrote his two great novels, which so few people have read, in a spirit of fearless liberty.

It must not be supposed that I claim for the artist in fiction the freedom of moral Nihilism. I would require from him many acts of faith of which the first would be the cherishing of an undying hope; and hope, it will not be contested, implies all the piety of effort and renunciation. It is the God-sent form of trust in the magic force and inspiration belonging to the life of this earth. We are inclined to forget that the way of excellence is in the intellectual, as distinguished from emotional, humility. What one feels so hopelessly barren in declared pessimism is just its arrogance. It seems as if the discovery made by many men at various times that there is much evil in the world were a source of proud and unholy joy unto some of the modern writers. That frame of mind is not the proper one in which to approach seriously the art of fiction. It gives an author—goodness only knows why—an elated sense of his own superiority. And there is nothing more dangerous than such an elation to that absolute loyalty towards his feelings and sensations an author should keep hold of in his most exalted moments of creation.

To be hopeful in an artistic sense it is not necessary to think that the world is good. It is enough to believe that there is no impossibility of its being made so. If the flight of imaginative thought may be allowed to rise superior to many moralities current amongst mankind, a novelist who would think himself of a superior essence to other men would miss the first condition of his calling. To have the gift of words is no such great matter. A man furnished by a long-range weapon does not become a hunter or a warrior by the mere possession of a fire-arm; many other qualities of character and temperament are necessary to make him either one or the other. Of him from whose armoury of phrases one in a hundred thousand may perhaps hit the far-distant and elusive mark of art I would ask that in his dealings with mankind he should be capable of giving a tender recognition to their obscure virtues. I would not have him impatient with their small failings and scornful of their errors. I would not have him expect too much gratitude from that humanity whose fate, as illustrated in individuals, it is open to him to depict as ridiculous or terrible. I would wish him to look with a large forgiveness at men's ideas and prejudices, which are by no means the outcome of malevolence, but depend on their education, their social status, even their professions. The good artist should expect no recognition of his toil and no admiration of his genius, because his toil can with difficulty be appraised and his genius cannot possibly mean anything to the illiterate who, even

3. Stendhal, pen name of Marie-Henri Beyle (1783–1842), French novelist and critic, author of *The Red and the Black* and *The Charterhouse of Parma*.

from the dreadful wisdom of their evoked dead, have, so far, culled nothing but inanities and platitudes. I would wish him to enlarge his sympathies by patient and loving observation while he grows in mental power. It is in the impartial practice of life, if anywhere, that the promise of perfection for his art can be found, rather than in the absurd formulas trying to prescribe this or that particular method of technique or conception. Let him mature the strength of his imagination amongst the things of this earth, which it is his business to cherish and know, and refrain from calling down his inspiration ready-made from some heaven of perfections of which he knows nothing. And I would not grudge him the proud illusion that will come sometimes to a writer: the illusion that his achievement has almost equalled the greatness of his dream. * * *

[Fiction Is Human History] †

All creative art is magic, is evocation of the unseen in forms persuasive, enlightening, familiar and surprising, for the edification of mankind, pinned down by the conditions of its existence to the earnest consideration of the most significant tides of reality.

Action in its essence, the creative art of a writer of fiction may be compared to rescue work carried out in darkness against cross gusts of wind swaying the action of a great multitude. It is rescue work, this snatching of vanishing phases of turbulence, disguised in fair words, out of the native obscurity into a light where the struggling forms may be seen, seized upon, endowed with the only possible form of permanence in this world of relative values—the permanence of memory. And the multitude feels it obscurely too; since the demand of the individual to the art is, in effect, the cry, "Take me out of myself!" meaning really, out of my perishable activity into the light of imperishable consciousness. But everything is relative, and the light of consciousness is only enduring, merely the most enduring of the things of this earth, imperishable only as against the short-lived work of our industrious hands.

When the last aqueduct shall have crumbled to pieces, the last airship fallen to the ground, the last blade of grass have died upon a dying earth, man, indomitable by his training in resistance to misery and pain, shall set this undiminished light of his eyes against the feeble glow of the sun. The artistic faculty, of which each of us has a minute grain, may find its voice in some individual of the last group, gifted with a power of expression and courageous enough to interpret the ultimate experience of mankind in terms of his temperament, in terms of art. I do not mean to say that he would attempt to beguile the last moments of humanity by an ingenious tale. It would be too much to expect—from humanity. I doubt the heroism of the hearers. As to the heroism of the artist, no doubt is necessary. There would be on his part no heroism. The artist

† From "Henry James: An Appreciation" (1905), *Notes on Life and Letters*, 13–17.

in his calling of interpreter creates (the clearest form of demonstration) because he must. He is so much of a voice that, for him, silence is like death; and the postulate was, that there is a group alive, clustered on his threshold to watch the last flicker of light on a black sky, to hear the last word uttered in the stilled workshop of the earth. It is safe to affirm that, if anybody, it will be the imaginative man who would be moved to speak on the eve of that day without to-morrow—whether in austere exhortation or in a phrase of sardonic comment, who can guess?

For my own part, from a short and cursory acquaintance with my kind, I am inclined to think that the last utterance will formulate, strange as it may appear, some hope now to us utterly inconceivable. For mankind is delightful in its pride, its assurance, and its indomitable tenacity. It will sleep on the battlefield among its own dead, in the manner of an army having won a barren victory. It will not know when it is beaten. And perhaps it is right in that quality. The victories are not, perhaps, so barren as it may appear from a purely strategical, utilitarian point of view. . . . These warlike images come by themselves under the pen; since from the duality of man's nature and the competition of individuals, the life-history of the earth must in the last instance be a history of a really very relentless warfare. Neither his fellows, nor his goods, nor his passions will leave a man alone. In virtue of these allies and enemies, he holds his precarious dominion, he possesses his fleeting significance; and it is this relation in all its manifestations, great and little, superficial or profound, and this relation alone, that is commented upon, interpreted, demonstrated by the art of the novelist in the only possible way in which the task can be performed: by the independent creation of circumstance and character, achieved against all the difficulties of expression, in an imaginative effort finding its inspiration from the reality of forms and sensations. That a sacrifice must be made, that something has to be given up, is the truth engraved in the innermost recesses of the fair temple built for our edification by the masters of fiction. There is no other secret behind the curtain. All adventure, all love, every success is resumed in the supreme energy of an act of renunciation. It is the uttermost limit of our power; it is the most potent and effective force at our disposal on which rest the labours of a solitary man in his study, the rock on which have been built commonwealths whose might casts a dwarfing shadow upon two oceans. Like a natural force which is obscured as much as illuminated by the multiplicity of phenomena, the power of renunciation is obscured by the mass of weaknesses, vacillations, secondary motives and false steps and compromises which make up the sum of our activity. But no man or woman worthy of the name can pretend to anything more, to anything greater. * * * The earth itself has grown smaller in the course of ages. But in every sphere of human perplexities and emotions, there are more greatnesses than one—not counting here the greatness of the artist himself. Wherever he stands, at the beginning or the end of things, a man has to sacrifice his gods to his passions or his passions to his gods. That is the problem, great enough, in all truth, if approached in the spirit of sincerity and knowledge.

In one of his critical studies, published some fifteen years ago, Mr. Henry James claims for the novelist the standing of the historian as the only adequate one, as for himself and before his audience.[1] I think that the claim cannot be contested, and that the position is unassailable. Fiction is history, human history, or it is nothing. But it is also more than that; it stands on firmer ground, being based on the reality of forms and the observation of social phenomena, whereas history is based on documents, and the reading of print and handwriting—on second-hand impression. Thus fiction is nearer truth. But let that pass. A historian may be an artist too, and a novelist is a historian, the preserver, the keeper, the expounder, of human experience.

[The Symbolic Character of Fiction] †

Some critics have found fault with me for not being constantly myself. But they are wrong. I am always myself. I am a man of formed character. Certain conclusions remain immovably fixed in my mind, but I am no slave to prejudices and formulas, and I shall never be. My attitude to subjects and expressions, the angles of vision, my methods of composition will, within limits, be always changing—not because I am unstable or unprincipled but because I am free. Or perhaps it may be more exact to say, because I am always trying for freedom—within my limits.

Coming now to the subject of your inquiry, I wish at first to put before you a general proposition: that a work of art is very seldom limited to one exclusive meaning and not necessarily tending to a definite conclusion. And this for the reason that the nearer it approaches art, the more it acquires a symbolic character. This statement may surprise you, who may imagine that I am alluding to the Symbolist School of poets or prose writers. Theirs, however, is only a literary proceeding against which I have nothing to say. I am concerned here with something much larger. But no doubt you have meditated on this and kindred questions yourself.

So I will only call your attention to the fact that the symbolic conception of a work of art has this advantage, that it makes a triple appeal covering the whole field of life. All the great creations of literature have been symbolic, and in that way have gained in complexity, in power, in depth and in beauty.

I don't think you will quarrel with me on the ground of lack of precision; for as to precision of images and analysis my artistic conscience is at rest. I have given there all the truth that is in me; and all that the critics may say can make my honesty neither more nor less. But as to

1. "The Art of Fiction." James and Conrad admired each other's work greatly—and not only because they were good friends [Editor].
† From a letter to Barrett H. Clark, May 14, 1918, in G. Jean-Aubry, Life and Letters (London: Wil-

liam Heinemann, Ltd., 1927) II 204–5. Reprinted by permission of J. M. Dent & Sons, Ltd.
    Clark (1890–1953), drama editor, translator, and critic.

"final effect" my conscience has nothing to do with that. It is the critic's affair to bring to its contemplation his own honesty, his sensibility and intelligence. The matter for his conscience is just his judgment. If his conscience is busy with petty scruples and trammelled by superficial formulas then his judgment will be superficial and petty. But an artist has no right to quarrel with the inspirations, either lofty or base, of another soul.

[Explicitness Is Fatal to Art] †

I have this morning received the article for the *Blue Peter*.[1] I think I have given you already to understand the nature of my feelings. Indeed, I spoke to you very openly, expressing my fundamental objection to the character you wished to give to it. I do not for a moment expect that what I am going to say here will convince you or influence you in the least. And, indeed, I have neither the wish nor the right to assert my position. I will only point out to you that my feelings in that matter are at least as legitimate as your own. It is a strange fate that everything that I have, of set artistic purpose, laboured to leave indefinite, suggestive, in the penumbra of initial inspiration, should have that light turned on to it and its insignificance (as compared with, I might say without megalomania, the ampleness of my conceptions) exposed for any fool to comment upon or even for average minds to be disappointed with. Didn't it ever occur to you, my dear Curle, that I knew what I was doing in leaving the facts of my life and even of my tales in the background? Explicitness, my dear fellow, is fatal to the glamour of all artistic work, robbing it of all suggestiveness, destroying all illusion. You seem to believe in literalness and explicitness, in facts and also in expression. Yet nothing is more clear than the utter insignificance of explicit statement and also its power to call attention away from things that matter in the region of art.

There, however, I am afraid we will never agree. Your praise of my work, allied to your analysis of its origins (which really are not its origins at all, as you know perfectly well), sounds exaggerated by the mere force of contrast. I wouldn't talk like this if I did not attach a very great value to everything you write about me and did not believe in its wide influence. It isn't a matter of literary criticism at all if I venture to point out to you that the dogmatic, ex-cathedra tone that you have adopted in your article positively frightens me. * * * It is generally known that you are my intimate friend, that the text carries an air of authority and that a lot of dam-fools will ascribe to me the initiative and the sanction of all the

† From a letter to Richard Curle (April 24, 1922) in *Conrad to a Friend* by Richard Curle. Pp. 112–14. Copyright © 1928 by Doubleday & Company, Inc. Reprinted by permission of the publisher.
1. Richard Curle, "Joseph Conrad in the East." Curle (b. 1883) became interested in Conrad in

1912 when he wrote his first of many critical appraisals of Conrad's work. The two met and became close friends. See Curle's *The Last Twelve Years of Joseph Conrad*, Garden City, N.Y., 1928 [*Editor*].

views and facts expressed. And one really could not blame them if they thought and said that I must have wanted all those facts disclosed.

[My Manner of Telling] †

I am returning you the article[1] with two corrections as to matters of fact and one of style.

As it stands I can have nothing against it. As to my feelings that is a different matter; and I think that, looking at the intimate character of our friendship and trusting to the indulgence of your affection, I may disclose them to you without reserve.

My point of view is that this is an opportunity, if not unique then not likely to occur again in my lifetime. I was in hopes that on a general survey it could also be made an opportunity for me to get freed from that infernal tale of ships, and that obsession of my sea life which has about as much bearing on my literary existence, on my quality as a writer, as the enumeration of drawing-rooms which Thackeray frequented could have had on his gift as a great novelist. After all, I may have been a seaman, but I am a writer of prose. Indeed, the nature of my writing runs the risk of being obscured by the nature of my material. I admit it is natural; but only the appreciation of a special personal intelligence can counteract the superficial appreciation of the inferior intelligence of the mass of readers and critics. Even Doubleday was considerably disturbed by that characteristic as evidenced in press notices in America, where such headings as "Spinner of sea-yarns—master-mariner—seaman writer" and so forth predominated. I must admit that the letterpress had less emphasis than the headings; but that was simply because they didn't know the facts. That the connection of my ships with my writings stands, with my concurrence I admit, recorded in your book is, of course, a fact. But that was biographical matter, not literary. And where it stands it can do no harm. Undue prominence has been given to it since, and yet you know yourself very well that in the body of my work barely one-tenth is what may be called sea stuff, and even of that, the bulk, that is *Nigger* and *Mirror*, has a very special purpose, which I emphasize myself in my Prefaces.

* * *

My manner of telling, perfectly devoid of familiarity as between author and reader, [is] aimed essentially at the intimacy of a personal communication, without any thought for other effects. As a matter of fact, the thought for effects is there all the same (often at the cost of mere directness of narrative) and can be detected in my unconventional grouping and perspective, which are purely temperamental and wherein almost

† From a letter to Richard Curle (July 14, 1923) in *Conrad to a Friend* by Richard Curle. Copyright © 1928 by Doubleday & Company, Inc. Pp. 147–50. Reprinted by permission of the publisher.

1. A review article of the Dent Uniform Edition of Conrad's works for the London *Times Literary Supplement*. Doubleday had just published the Concord Edition in America [Editor].

all my "art" consists. That, I suspect, has been the difficulty the critics
felt in classifying it as romantic or realistic. Whereas, as a matter of fact,
it is fluid, depending on grouping (sequence) which shifts, and on the
changing lights giving varied effects of perspective.

It is in those matters gradually, but never completely, mastered that
the history of my books really consists. Of course the plastic matter of
this grouping and of those lights has its importance, since without it the
actuality of that grouping and that lighting could not be made evident
any more than Marconi's electric waves could be made evident without
the sending-out and receiving instruments. In other words, without
mankind, my art, an infinitesimal thing, could not exist.

ARTHUR SYMONS

[Every Novel Contains Autobiography] †

This is one of his confessions. "May there not emerge at last the vision
of a personality; the man behind the books so fundamentally dissimilar
as for instance, *Almayer's Folly* and *The Secret Agent*—and yet a coherent justifiable personality both in its origin and in its actions?" In 1907
he wrote to me, thanking me for my "rejected address to the public on
behalf of his art, and for the warm, living sincerity of my impression and
of my analysis." He confesses that "fourteen years of honest work are not
gone for nothing. A big slice of life that, which I may say is not altogether lost. There has been in all the time not ten minutes of amateur-
ishness. That is the truth. For the rest I may say that there are certain
passages in your article which have surprised me. I did not know that I
had 'a heart of darkness' and 'an unlawful soul.' Mr. Kurtz had—and I
have not treated him with easy nonchalance. Believe me, no man ever
paid more for his lines than I have. But then I possess an inalienable
right to the use of all my epithets. The fact is that I am really a much
simpler person. Death is a fact—and violent death is a fact too. In the
simplicity of my heart I tried to realize these facts when they came in.
Do you really think that Flaubert gloated over the death bed of Emma,
or the death march of Mâtho, or the last moments of Félicité?[1] I've
never looked into myself. There was no time in these years to turn my
head away from the table. There are whole days when I did not know
whether the sun shone or not. And, after all, the books are there! As for
the writing of novels, delightful or not, I have always approached my
task in the spirit of love for mankind. And I've rather taken it seriously.
But I stand outside and feel grateful to you for the recognition of the

†From Arthur Symons, *Notes on Joseph Conrad:
With Some Unpublished Letters*. Copyright 1925
by Arthur Symons and Myers & Co. Pp. 15–18.
Reprinted by permission.

1. Gustave Flaubert (1821–80), French novelist,
author of *Madame Bovary*, (Emma) *Salammbô*
(Mathô), and *Un Coeur Simple* (Felicité). [*Editor*].

work—not the man. Once the last page is written the man does not count. He is nowhere." * * *

"One thing that I am certain of, is that I have approached the object of my task, things human, in a spirit of piety. The earth is a temple where there is going on a mystery play childish and poignant, ridiculous and awful enough in all conscience. Once in I've tried to behave decently. I have not degraded the quasi religious sentiment by tears and groans: and I have been amused and indifferent, I've neither grinned nor gnashed my teeth. In other words I've tried to write with dignity, not only out of regard of myself, but for the sake of the spectacle, the play with an obscure beginning and an unfathomable *dénouement*. I don't think this has been noticed. It is your penitent beating the floor with his forehead and the ecstatic worshippers at the rails that are obvious to the public eye. The man standing quietly in the shadow of the pillar if noticed at all runs the risk of being suspected of sinister designs. As I wrote to a friend I have been quarrying my English out of a black night, working like a coal miner in his pit. For fourteen years now I have been living as if in a cave without echoes. If you come shouting gloriously at the mouth of the same you can't really expect me to pretend I am not there."

Conrad wrote: "I know that a novelist lives in his work. He stands there, the only reality in an invented world, amongst imaginary things, happenings and people. Writing about them, he is only writing about himself. Every novel contains an element of autobiography—and this can hardly be denied, since the creator can only explain himself in his creations."

CRITICISM

ROBERT F. HAUGH

[*Heart of Darkness:* Problem for Critics] †

Conrad's "Heart of Darkness" first appeared as a serial in *Blackwood's Magazine* for February, March, and April, 1899 [and] * * * received a mixed critical press. The story was taken by some as an attack upon Belgian colonial methods in the Congo; as a moral tract; and as a study in race relationships. *The Bookman* called it "a symbolic picture of the inborn antagonisms of two races, the white and the black." *The Spectator*, without indicating that it understood the story any better, praised the moral tone. Most of the other contemporary reviewers read it as a criticism of Belgian colonialism, an issue that remained alive until Conrad's death and got attention in his obituary notices.

Nearly three years after its initial magazine appearance, "Heart of Darkness" appeared in book form as one of the stories in the volume entitled *Youth*. Edward Garnett, Conrad's discoverer and friend in the publishing house of Fisher Unwin, came closer than anyone else up to that time. He wrote a review for *The Academy and Literature* for December 6, 1902, in which he said:

> A most amazing, consummate piece of artistic diablerie—an analysis of the white man's morale when let loose from European restraint, and planted down in the tropics as an "emissary of light" armed to the teeth to make trade profits out of subject races. The gulf between the white man's system and the black man's comprehension of its results—the unnerved, degenerating whites staring all day and every day at the heart of darkness which is alike meaningless and threatening to their own creed and conception of life—

Conrad was aware of certain obscurities in "Heart of Darkness," although he was quite willing to receive praise from those he puzzled. He wrote to Garnett: "My dearest fellow, you quite overcome me. And your brave attempt to grapple with the fogginess of H. of D., to explain what I myself tried to shape blindfold, as it were, has touched me profoundly." Conrad heard from his friend Cunninghame Graham, after the first installment had appeared, and warned him in reply:

> I am simply in the seventh heaven to find you like H. of D. so far. You bless me indeed. Mind you don't curse me bye and bye for the same thing. There are two more installments in which the idea is so wrapped up in secondary notions that you—even you—may miss it. And you must remember also that I don't start with an abstract

† From *Joseph Conrad: Discovery in Design* by Robert F. Haugh. Copyright 1957 by University of Oklahoma Press. Pp. 35–40. Reprinted by permission.

notion. I start with definite images and as their rendering is true some little effect is produced.

No doubt many have missed the idea in "Heart of Darkness" and many have cursed Conrad for it. But as many have loved him for the wrong reasons. The fogginess in Conrad has been most memorably pointed out by E. M. Forster in *Abinger Harvest* [New York, 1936], reprinting his review of Conrad's *Notes on Life and Letters*. Forster meant his remarks to apply to Conrad generally:

> What is so elusive about him is that he is always promising to make some general philosophical statement about the universe, and then refraining in a gruff declaimer . . . there is a central obscurity, something noble, heroic, inspiring half-a-dozen great books, but obscure! Obscure! Misty in the middle as well as at the edges, the secret cask of his genius contains a vapour rather than a jewel; and that we needn't try to write him down philosophically, because there is, in this direction, nothing to write. No creed, in fact.

These impassioned mixed metaphors of Mr. Forster, which have been parroted many times, themselves veil the nature of the obscurity—which may be a fault in the viewer rather than in the object. Another who says, finally, that "Heart of Darkness" is one of Conrad's greatest, but who quotes the above sentiments from E. M. Forster, is F. R. Leavis. In *The Great Tradition* [London, 1948], Leavis recognizes that " 'Heart of Darkness' is, by common consent, one of Conrad's best things—an appropriate source for the epigraph of *The Hollow Men*: 'Mistah Kurtz—he dead.' " But the ultimate judgment of Mr. Leavis is drawn from Forster: the "disconcerting weakness or vice" by which the "Heart of Darkness" is marred. It remains to him a story obscure in its meanings, further damaged by an "adjectival and worse than supererogatory insistence upon 'unspeakable rites,' 'monstrous passions,' 'inconceivable mystery' and so on." My feeling about both Leavis and Forster is that they find a variety of metaphysical melodrama here; that they do not really understand the images and actions of the story. With a better understanding of what Conrad intends, objections to his language disappear.

Those who find in "Heart of Darkness" primarily a protest at colonial policies can read with ease and clarity, untroubled by ambiguities. Joseph Warren Beach says:

> Kurtz is a personal embodiment, a dramatization, of all that Conrad felt of futility, degradation, and horror in what the Europeans in the Congo called "progress," which meant the exploitation of the natives by every variety of cruelty and treachery known to greedy man. Kurtz was to Marlow, penetrating this country, a name, constantly recurring in people's talk, for cleverness and enterprise. . . . The blackness and mystery of his character tone in with the savage mystery of the Congo, and they develop *pari passu* with the

atmosphere of shadowy horror. This development is conducted cumulatively by insensitive degrees, by carefully correlated new items, new intimations; and all this process is controlled through the consciousness of Marlow. Thus we have a triumph of atmospheric effect produced with the technique of the limited point of view, a story in a class with "The Fall of the House of Usher" and "The Turn of the Screw." [*The Twentieth-Century Novel*, New York, 1932.]

We can agree with Mr. Beach if we concede that the Conrad who wrote "Heart of Darkness" is different, not only in conceptual interests, but in technical methods, from the Conrad who wrote *Lord Jim* and *The Nigger of the Narcissus*. But the assumption of centrality in the story of social and economic commentary, and the assumption of a straightforward narrative pattern, are inadequate to extract the meaning from Conrad anywhere, and especially from "Heart of Darkness."

Finally, there is Paul Wiley, in his *Conrad's Measure of Man* [Madison, Wis., 1954], who finds the myth of the fall from innocence throughout Conrad, and who makes of Kurtz the man driven from the Garden of Eden. The awkwardness here is that a Christian myth leaves so much unexplained at important moments in the story, as it does elsewhere in Conrad. When Marlow went back to the ring of fire in the jungle to get Kurtz that night before they started back to civilization, he found that Kurtz had kicked himself loose from heaven and hell: "There was nothing above or below him." Only Kurtz himself, demonic being, can be invoked. This is not within the conceptual framework of Christianity. Kurtz has become pre-Christian, primal energy, demiurge. And he is capable of utterly destroying the ethical man, Marlow. Kurtz has no relationship with the Christian Satan. The Christian Satan has many ethical referents; he is a necessary and even cherished figure, often contemplated. Not so with Kurtz, whose "horror" is unthinkable. The Christian Satan is very much thinkable, a vital member of the moral household more real to many than Christ. He helps to define morality, and is brought forth upon every occasion to be examined for object lessons. Kurtz's horror is "too dark—too dark altogether" to be looked at. The enigma in "Heart of Darkness" is here; if we are to understand the story we must deal adequately with that "darkness" and its meaning. And what are these "surface truths" that Marlow finds saving, but which Kurtz can never find?

These enigmas cannot be resolved by a spot analysis of Kurtz at the very moment of his death. "Heart of Darkness" is an "epiphany" story, in the sense used by James Joyce, who introduced the term into literary criticism. "Epiphany" is a rather surprising word, the way Joyce uses it. The word comes from the language of salvation; it is the revelation of divinity, a "showing forth" of the Lord. The surprise in Joyce is that the structure is used again and again to reveal spiritual isolation. Its use is closer to Freud than to Christianity. That is, it describes the use of successive images in a non-causal, or a non-dramatic relationship; rather in a free associational appearance. Joyce sets up tangent structures—tangent, not parallel—curved shapes of idea or experience which touch and curve away. It is the calculus of art—the relationship of two curved shapes in motion. In *Dubliners*, Joyce uses the method again and again. For instance, in "Clay" he sets up small, unrelated (dramatically) relationships so ordered that as the warmth of the story increases, the terror grows that little Maria is to be cast out of human fellowship—even the tiny circle that she enjoys—and then she will die. Joyce did not invent the technique; he merely supplied the name by which it may be identified. Flaubert and Chekhov, both very dear to Conrad, were using this non-dramatic method long before Joyce.

The agent for the epiphanies in "Heart of Darkness" is Marlow, who is very much more than the "limited viewpoint" that J. W. Beach has him. He is a brother to Kurtz, identified with him in the climax of the story, impelled by the powerful attraction of the man—or demon—to something in himself, to search him out in the darkness. He must follow his demon to the nether regions, to the heart of darkness, take the talisman from his lips, and return to the city. Only the talisman turns out to be "The horror!" and it is too dark to contemplate. So Marlow takes back the word "love" to deliver, the truth being too dark for the Intended. It is not too dark for Marlow, though, nor for others with totems powerful enough to withstand its evil energies.

* * *

The true talisman was not carried back to the Intended. Her saving illusions could not have borne the demonic words; but then neither could many of those fidelities—surface truths—that we encountered on our way up the river. To Marlow [Kurtz] was a hero who had shown him the limits of the mortal spirit; and the situations penetrating into the human condition became more illuminating the closer we came to Kurtz's darkness. His remarkable energies, his stature, his amazing appeal to fellow humans in his moments of darkest savagery, the very magnificence of his plunge into the pit of the universe, all these showed Marlow a moral universe, dark though it was. Emerson's line: "Yawns the pit of the Dragon, Lit by rays from the Blest" indicates the nature of this final, blinding illumination: "that could not see the light of the candle, but was wide enough to penetrate all the hearts of the universe." This is why, to Marlow, Kurtz is a true hero; a vision downward, dark, may be as true as a vision upward into the light. * * * Conrad's hero may leap high into the rarefied air as does Jim, or plunge deep into the darkness of the pit as does Kurtz; in his remarkable actions he defines the mortal condition, and in his last moment of vision he sees all the scheme of the universe; and we share it in a moment of tragic exaltation. But for most of us fidelity to household gods is the clue to "how to be"; our leaky boilers hold us to surface truths, even as we learn the meaning of life from the moral adventurers who go to their deaths at the far rims of the universe.

ALBERT J. GUERARD

The Journey Within †

Conrad, * * * like many novelists today, was both drawn to idealism and repelled by its hypocritical abuse. "The conquest of the earth, which mostly means the taking it away from those who have a different complexion or slightly flatter noses than ourselves, is not a pretty thing when you look into it too much. What redeems it is the idea only. An idea at the back of it, not a sentimental pretence but an idea; and an unselfish belief in the idea. . . ." Marlow commits himself to the yet unseen agent partly because Kurtz "had come out equipped with moral ideas of some sort." Anything would seem preferable to the demoralized greed and total cynicism of the others, "the flabby devil" of the Central Station. Later, when he discovers what has happened to Kurtz's moral ideas, he remains faithful to the "nightmare of my choice." In *Under Western Eyes* Sophia Antonovna makes a distinction between those who burn and those who rot, and remarks that it is sometimes preferable to burn. The Kurtz who had made himself literally one of the devils of the land, and who in solitude had kicked himself loose of the earth, burns while the others rot. Through violent not flabby evil he exists in the moral universe even before pronouncing judgment on himself with his dying breath. A little too much has been made, I think, of the redemptive value of those two words—"The horror!" But none of the company "pilgrims" could have uttered them.

The redemptive view is Catholic, of course, though no priest was in attendance; Kurtz can repent as the gunman of [Graham Greene's] *The Power and the Glory* cannot. "Heart of Darkness" (still at this public and wholly conscious level) combines a Victorian ethic and late Victorian fear of the white man's deterioration with a distinctly Catholic psychology. We are protected from ourselves by society with its laws and its watchful neighbors, Marlow observes. And we are protected by work. "You wonder I didn't go ashore for a howl and a dance? Well, no—I didn't. Fine sentiments, you say? Fine sentiments be hanged! I had no time. I had to mess about with white-lead and strips of woolen blanket helping to put bandages on those leaky steam-pipes." But when the external restraints of society and work are removed, we must meet the challenge and temptation of savage reversion with our "own inborn strength. Principles? Principles won't do." This inborn strength appears to include restraint—the restraint that Kurtz lacked and the cannibal crew of the *Roi des Belges* surprisingly possessed. The hollow man, whose evil is the evil of *vacancy*, succumbs. And in their different degrees the pilgrims

† From *Conrad the Novelist* by Albert J. Guerard. Copyright 1958 by The President and Fellows of Harvard College. Copyright 1987 by Albert J. Guerard. Pp. 35–48. Reprinted by permission of the author.

and Kurtz share this hollowness. "Perhaps there was nothing within" the manager of the Central Station. "Such a suspicion made one pause— for out there there were no external checks." And there was nothing inside the brickmaker that papier-mâché Mephistopheles, "but a little loose dirt, maybe."

As for Kurtz, the wilderness "echoed loudly within him because he was hollow at the core." Perhaps the chief contradiction of "Heart of Darkness" is that it suggests and dramatizes evil as an active energy (Kurtz and his unspeakable lusts) but defines evil as vacancy. The primitive (and here the contradiction is only verbal) is compact of passion and apathy. "I was struck by the fire of his eyes and the composed languor of his expression . . . This shadow looked satiated and calm as though for the moment it had had its fill of all the emotions." Of the two men- aces—the unspeakable desires and the apathy—apathy surely seemed the greater to Conrad. Hence we cannot quite believe the response of Marlow's heart to the beating of the tom-toms. This is, I think, the story's minor but central flaw, and the source of an unfruitful ambiguity: that it slightly overdoes the kinship with the "passionate uproar," slightly undervalues the temptation of inertia.

* * *

Substantially and in its central emphasis "Heart of Darkness" con- cerns Marlow (projection to whatever great or small degree of a more irrecoverable Conrad) and his toward and through certain facets or potentialities of self. F. R. Leavis seems to regard him as a narrator only, providing a "specific and concretely realized point of view."[1] But Mar- low reiterates often enough that he is recounting a spiritual voyage of self-discovery. He remarks casually but crucially that he did not know himself before setting out, and that he likes work for the chance it pro- vides to "find yourself . . . what no other man can ever know." The Inner Station "was the farthest point of navigation and the culminating point of my experience." At a material and rather superficial level, the journey is through the temptation of atavism. It is a record of "remote kinship" with the "wild and passionate uproar," of a "trace of a response" to it, of a final rejection of the "fascination of the abomination." And why should there not be the trace of a response? "The mind of man is capable of anything—because everything is in it, all the past as well as all the future." Marlow's temptation is made concrete through his expo- sure to Kurtz, a white man and sometime idealist who had fully responded to the wilderness: a potential and fallen self. "I had turned to the wilder- ness really, not to Mr. Kurtz." At the climax Marlow follows Kurtz ashore, confounds the beat of the drum with the beating of his heart, goes through the ordeal of looking into Kurtz's "mad soul," and brings him back to the ship. He returns to Europe a changed and more know- ing man. Ordinary people are now "intruders whose knowledge of life

1. *The Great Tradition* (London, 1948) 183.

was to me an irritating pretence because I felt so sure they could not possibly know the things I knew."

On this literal plane, and when the events are so abstracted from the dream-sensation conveying them, it is hard to take Marlow's plight very seriously. Will he, the busy captain and moralizing narrator, also revert to savagery, go ashore for a howl and a dance, indulge unspeakable lusts? The late Victorian reader (and possibly Conrad himself) could take this more seriously than we; could literally believe not merely in a Kurtz's deterioration through months of solitude but also in the sudden reversions to the "beast" of naturalistic fiction. Insofar as Conrad does want us to take it seriously and literally, we must admit the nominal triumph of a currently accepted but false psychology over his own truer intuitions. But the triumph is only nominal. For the personal narrative is unmistakably authentic, which means that it explores something truer, more fundamental, and distinctly less material: the night journey into the unconscious, and confrontation of an entity within the self. "I flung one shoe overboard and became aware that that was exactly what I had been looking forward to— a talk with Kurtz." It little matters what, in terms of psychological symbolism, we call this double or say he represents: whether the Freudian id or the Jungian shadow or more vaguely the outlaw. And I am afraid it is impossible to say where Conrad's conscious understanding of his story began and ended. The important thing is that the introspective plunge and powerful dream seem true; and are therefore inevitably moving.

Certain circumstances of Marlow's voyage, looked at in these terms, take on a new importance. The true night journey can occur (except during analysis) only in sleep or in the waking dream of a profoundly intuitive mind. Marlow insists more than is necessary on the dreamlike qualify of his narrative. "It seems to me I am trying to tell you a dream— making a vain attempt, because no relation of a dream can convey the dream-sensation, that commingling of absurdity, surprise, and bewilderment in a tremor of struggling revolt . . ." Even before leaving Brussels Marlow felt as though he "were about to set off for the centre of the earth," not the center of a continent. The introspective voyager leaves his familiar rational world, is "cut off from the comprehension" of his surroundings; his steamer toils "along slowly on the edge of a black and incomprehensible frenzy." As the crisis approaches, the dreamer and his ship move through a silence that "seemed unnatural, like a state of trance"; then enter (a few miles below the Inner Station) a deep fog. "The approach to this Kurtz grubbing for ivory in the wretched bush was beset by as many dangers as though he had been an enchanted princess sleeping in a fabulous castle."[2] Later, Marlow's task is to try "to break the spell" of the wilderness that holds Kurtz entranced.

2. The analogy of unspeakable Kurtz and enchanted princess may well be an intended irony. But there may be some significance in the fact that this once, the double is imagined as an entranced feminine figure.

The approach to the unconscious and primitive may be aided by a savage or half-savage guide, and may require the token removal of civilized trappings or aids; both conceptions are beautifully dramatized in Faulkner's "The Bear." In "Heart of Darkness" the token "relinquishment" and the death of the half-savage guide are connected. The helmsman falling at Marlow's feet casts blood on his shoes, which he is "morbidly anxious" to change and in fact throws overboard.[3] * * * Here we have presumably entered an area of unconscious creation; the dream is true but the teller may have no idea why it is. So too, possibly, a psychic need as well as literary tact compelled Conrad to defer the meeting between Marlow and Kurtz for some three thousand words after announcing that it took place. We think we are about to meet Kurtz at last. But instead Marlow leaps ahead to his meeting with the "Intended"; comments on Kurtz's megalomania and assumption of his place among the devils of the land; reports on the seventeen-page pamphlet; relates his meeting and conversation with Kurtz's harlequin disciple—and only then tells of seeing through his binoculars the heads on the stakes surrounding Kurtz's house. This is the "evasive" Conrad in full play, deferring what we most want to know and see; perhaps compelled to defer climax in this way. The tactic is dramatically effective, though possibly carried to excess: we are told on the authority of completed knowledge certain things we would have found hard to believe had they been presented through a slow consecutive realistic discovery. But also it can be argued that it was psychologically impossible for Marlow to go at once to Kurtz's house with the others. The double must be brought on board the ship, and the first confrontation must occur there. * * * The incorporation and alliance between the two becomes material, and the identification of "selves."

Hence the shock Marlow experiences when he discovers that Kurtz's cabin is empty and his secret sharer gone; a part of himself has vanished. "What made this emotion so overpowering was—how shall I define it— the moral shock I received, as if something altogether monstrous, intolerable to thought and odious to the soul had been thrust upon me unexpectedly." And now he must risk the ultimate confrontation in a true solitude and must do so on shore. "I was anxious to deal with this shadow by myself alone—and to this day I don't know why I was so jealous of sharing with any one the peculiar blackness of that experience." He follows the crawling Kurtz through the grass; comes upon him "long, pale, indistinct like a vapor exhaled by the earth." ("I had cut him off cleverly . . .") We are told very little of what Kurtz said in the moments that follow; and little of his incoherent discourses after he is brought back to the ship. "His was an impenetrable darkness. I looked at him as you

---

3. Like any obscure human act, this one invites several interpretations, beginning with the simple washing away of guilt. The fear of the blood may be, however, a fear of the primitive toward which Marlow is moving. To throw the shoes overboard would then mean a token rejection of the savage, not the civilized-rational. In any event, it seems plausible to have blood at this stage of a true initiation story.

peer down at a man who is lying at the bottom of a precipice where the sun never shines"—a comment less vague and rhetorical, in terms of psychic geography, then it may seem at a first reading. And then Kurtz is dead, taken off the ship, his body buried in a "muddy hole." With the confrontation over, Marlow must still emerge from environing darkness, and does so through that other deep fog of sickness. The identification is not yet completely broken. "And it is not my own extremity I remember best—a vision of grayness without form filled with physical pain and a careless contempt for the evanescence of all things—even of this pain itself. No. It is his extremity that I seem to have lived through." Only in the atonement of his lie to Kurtz's "Intended," back in the sepulchral city, does the experience come truly to an end. "I laid the ghost of his gifts at last with a lie . . ."

Such seems to be the content of the dream. If my summary has even a partial validity it should explain and to an extent justify some of the "adjectival and worse than supererogatory insistence" to which F. R. Leavis (who sees only the travelogue and the portrait of Kurtz) objects. I am willing to grant that the unspeakable rites and unspeakable secrets become wearisome, but the fact—at once literary and psychological—is that they must remain *unspoken*. A confrontation with such a double and facet of the unconscious cannot be reported through realistic dialogue. * * * When Marlow finds it hard to define the moral shock he received on seeing the empty cabin, or when he says he doesn't know why he was jealous of sharing his experience, I think we can take him literally . . . and in a sense even be thankful for his uncertainty. The greater tautness and economy of "The Secret Sharer" comes from its larger conscious awareness of the psychological process it describes; from its more deliberate use of the double as symbol. And of the two stories I happen to prefer it. But it may be the groping, fumbling "Heart of Darkness" takes us into a deeper region of the mind. If the story is not about this deeper region, and not about Marlow himself, its length is quite indefensible. But even if one were to allow that the final section is about Kurtz (which I think simply absurd), a vivid pictorial record of his unspeakable lusts and gratifications would surely have been ludicrous. I share Mr. Leavis' admiration for the heads on the stakes. But not even Kurtz could have supported many such particulars.

"I listened on the watch for the sentence, for the word that would give me the clue to the faint uneasiness inspired by this narrative that seemed to shape itself without human lips in the heavy night-air of the river." Thus one of Marlow's listeners, the original "I" who frames the story, comments on its initial effect. He has discovered how alert one must be to the ebb and flow of Marlow's narrative, and here warns the reader. But there is no single word; not even the word *trance* will do. For the shifting play of thought and feeling and image and event is very intricate. It is not vivid detail alone, the heads on stakes or the bloody shoes; nor only the dark mass of moralizing abstraction; nor the dramatized psychological intuitions apart from their context that give "Heart of Darkness" its brooding weight. The impressionist method—one cannot leave this story without subscribing to the obvious—finds here one of its great triumphs of tone. The random movement of the nightmare is also the controlled movement of a poem, in which a quality of feeling may be stated or suggested and only much later justified. But it is justified at last.

The method is in important ways different from that of *Lord Jim*, though the short novel was written during an interval in the long one, and though Marlow speaks to us in both. For we do not have here the radical obfuscations and sudden wrenchings and violent chronological ambiguities of *Lord Jim*. Nor are we, as in *Nostromo*, at the mercy of a wayward flashlight moving rapidly in a cluttered room. "Heart of Darkness" is no such true example of spatial form. Instead the narrative advances and withdraws as in a succession of long dark waves borne by an incoming tide. The waves encroach fairly evenly on the shore, and presently a few more feet of sand have been won. But an occasional wave thrusts up unexpectedly, much farther than the others: even as far, say, as Kurtz and his Inner Station. Or, to take the other figure: the flashlight is held firmly; there are no whimsical jerkings from side to side. But now and then it is raised higher, and for a brief moment in a sudden clear light we discern enigmatic matters to be explored much later. Thus the movement of the story is sinuously progressive, with much incremental repetition. The intent is not to subject the reader to multiple strains and ambiguities, but rather to throw over him a brooding gloom, such a warm pall as those two Fates in the home office might knit, back in the sepulchral city.

Yet no figure can convey "Heart of Darkness" in all its resonance and tenebrous atmosphere. The movement is not one of penetration and withdrawal only; it is also the tracing of a large grand circle of awareness. It begins with the friends on the yacht under the dark above Gravesend and at last returns to them, to the tranquil waterway that "leading to the uttermost ends of the earth flowed sombre under an overcast sky—seemed to lead into the heart of an immense darkness." For this also "has been one of the dark places of the earth," and Marlow employs from the first his methods of reflexive reference and casual foreshadowing. The Romans were men enough to face this darkness of the Thames running between savage shores. "Here and there a military camp lost in a wilderness like a needle in a bundle of hay—cold, fog, tempests, disease, exile, and death—death skulking in the air, in the water, in the bush." But these Romans were "no colonists," no more than the pilgrims of the Congo nineteen hundred years later; "their administration was merely a squeeze." Thus early Marlow establishes certain political values. The French gunboat firing into a continent anticipates the blind firing of the pilgrims into the jungle when the ship has been attacked. And Marlow hears of Kurtz's first attempt to emerge from the wilderness long before he meets Kurtz in the flesh, and wrestles with his reluctance to leave. Marlow returns again and again, with increasing irony, to Kurtz's benevolent pamphlet.

The travelogue as travelogue is not to be ignored; and one of Roger Casement's consular successors in the Congo (to whom I introduced "Heart of Darkness" in 1957), remarked at once that Conrad certainly had a "feel for the country." The demoralization of the first company station is rendered by a boiler "wallowing in the grass," by a railway truck with its wheels in the air. Presently Marlow will discover a scar in the hillside into which drainage pipes for the settlement had been tumbled; then will walk into the grove where the Negroes are free to die in a "greenish gloom." The sharply visualized particulars suddenly intrude on the somber intellectual flow of Marlow's meditation: magnified, arresting. The boilermaker who "had to crawl in the mud under the bottom of the steamboat . . . would tie up that beard of his in a kind of white serviette he brought for the purpose. It had loops to go over his ears." The papier-mâché Mephistopheles is as vivid, with his delicate hooked nose and glittering mica eyes. So too is Kurtz's harlequin companion and admirer, humbly dissociating himself from the master's lusts and gratifications. "I! I! I am a simple man. I have no great thoughts." And even Kurtz, shadow and symbol though he be, the man of eloquence who in this story is almost voiceless, and necessarily so—even Kurtz is sharply visualized, an "animated image of death," a skull and body emerging as from a winding sheet, "the cage of his ribs all astir, the bones of his arm waving."

This is Africa and its flabby inhabitants; Conrad did indeed have a "feel for the country." Yet the dark tonalities and final brooding impression derive as much from rhythm and rhetoric as from such visual details: derive from the high aloof ironies and from a prose that itself advances and recedes in waves. "This initiated wraith from the back of Nowhere honoured me with its amazing confidence before it vanished altogether." Or, "It is strange how I accepted this unforeseen partnership, this choice of nightmares forced upon me in the tenebrous land invaded by these mean and greedy phantoms." These are true Conradian rhythms, but they are also rhythms of thought. The immediate present can be rendered with great compactness and drama: the ship staggering within ten feet of the bank at the time of the attack, and Marlow's sudden glimpse of a face amongst the leaves, then of the bush "swarming with human limbs." But still more immediate and personal, it may be, are the meditative passages evoking vast tracts of time, and the "first of men taking possession of an accursed inheritance." The prose is varied, far more so than is usual in the early work, both in rhythm and in the movements from the general to the particular and back. But the shaped sentence collecting and fully expending its breath appears to be the norm. Some of the best passages begin and end with them:

> Going up that river was like traveling back to the earliest beginnings of the world, when vegetation rioted on the earth and the big trees

were kings. An empty stream, a great silence, an impenetrable forest. The air was warm, thick, heavy, sluggish. There was no joy in the brilliance of sunshine. The long stretches of the waterway ran on, deserted, into the gloom of overshadowed distances. On silvery sandbanks hippos and alligators sunned themselves side by side.

The insistence on darkness, finally, and quite apart from ethical or mythical overtone, seems a right one for this extremely personal statement. There is a darkness of passivity, paralysis, immobilization; it is from the state of entranced languor rather than from the monstrous desires that the double Kurtz, this shadow, must be saved. In Freudian theory, we are told, such preoccupation may indicate fear of the feminine and passive. But may it not also be connected, through one of the spirit's multiple disguises, with a radical fear of death, that other darkness? "I had turned to the wilderness really, not to Mr. Kurtz who, I was ready to admit, was as good as buried. And for a moment it seemed to me as if I also were buried in a vast grave full of unspeakable secrets. I felt an intolerable weight oppressing my breast, the smell of the damp earth, the unseen presence of victorious corruption, the darkness of an impenetrable night."

It would be folly to try to limit the menace of vegetation in the restless life of Conradian image and symbol. But the passage reminds us again of the story's reflexive references, and its images of deathly immobilization in grass. Most striking are the black shadows dying in the greenish gloom of the grove at the first station. But grass sprouts between the stones of the European city, a "whited sepulchre," and on the same page Marlow anticipates coming upon the remains of his predecessor: "the grass growing through his ribs was tall enough to hide his bones." The critical meeting with Kurtz occurs on a trail through the grass. Is there not perhaps an intense horror behind the casualness with which Marlow reports his discoveries, say of the Negro with the bullet in his forehead? Or: "Now and then a carrier dead in harness, at rest in the long grass near the path, with an empty water-gourd and his long staff lying by his side."

All this, one must acknowledge, does not make up an ordinary light travelogue. There is no little irony in the letter of November 9, 1891, Conrad received from his guardian after returning from the Congo, and while physically disabled and seriously depressed: "I am sure that with your melancholy temperament you ought to avoid all meditations which lead to pessimistic conclusions. I advise you to lead a more active life than ever and to cultivate cheerful habits."[4] Uneven in language on certain pages, and lacking "The Secret Sharer" 's economy, "Heart of Darkness" nevertheless remains one of the great dark meditations in literature, and one of the purest expressions of a melancholy temperament.

4. *Life and Letters* I.148.

CHINUA ACHEBE

An Image of Africa: Racism in Conrad's *Heart of Darkness* †

In the fall of 1974 I was walking one day from the English Department at the University of Massachusetts to a parking lot. It was a fine autumn morning such as encouraged friendliness to passing strangers. Brisk youngsters were hurrying in all directions, many of them obviously freshmen in their first flush of enthusiasm. An older man going the same way as I turned and remarked to me how very young they came these days. I agreed. Then he asked me if I was a student too. I said no, I was a teacher. What did I teach? African literature. Now that was funny, he said, because he knew a fellow who taught the same thing, or perhaps it was African *history*, in a certain Community College not far from here. It always surprised him, he went on to say, because he never had thought of Africa as having that kind of stuff, you know. By this time I was walking much faster. "Oh well," I heard him say finally, behind me: "I guess I have to take your course to find out."

A few weeks later I received two very touching letters from high school children in Yonkers, New York, who—bless their teacher—had just read *Things Fall Apart*. One of them was particularly happy to learn about the customs and superstitions of an African tribe.

I propose to draw from these rather trivial encounters rather heavy conclusions which at first sight might seem somewhat out of proportion to them. But only, I hope, at first sight.

The young fellow from Yonkers, perhaps partly on account of his age but I believe also for much deeper and more serious reasons, is obviously unaware that the life of his own tribesmen in Yonkers, New York, is full of odd customs and superstitions and, like everybody else in his culture, imagines that he needs a trip to Africa to encounter those things.

The other person being fully my own age could not be excused on the grounds of his years. Ignorance might be a more likely reason; but here again I believe that something more willful than a mere lack of information was at work. For did not that erudite British historian and Regius Professor at Oxford, Hugh Trevor Roper, also pronounce that African history did not exist?

If there is something in these utterances more than youthful inexperience, more than a lack of factual knowledge, what is it? Quite simply it is the desire—one might indeed say the need—in Western psychology to set Africa up as a foil to Europe, as a place of negations at once remote

† An amended version (1987) of the second Chancellor's Lecture at the University of Massachusetts, Amherst, February 18, 1975; later published in *The Massachusetts Review*, 18 (1977): 782–94.

Reprinted by permission of the author and *The Massachusetts Review*, © 1977, The Massachusetts Review, Inc.

and vaguely familiar, in comparison with which Europe's own state of
spiritual grace will be manifest.

This need is not new; which should relieve us all of considerable
responsibility and perhaps make us even willing to look at this phenomenon dispassionately. I have neither the wish nor the competence to
embark on the exercise with the tools of the social and biological sciences but more simply in the manner of a novelist responding to one
famous book of European fiction: Joseph Conrad's *Heart of Darkness*,
which better than any other work that I know displays that Western
desire and need which I have just referred to. Of course there are whole
libraries of books devoted to the same purpose but most of them are so
obvious and so crude that few people worry about them today. Conrad,
on the other hand, is undoubtedly one of the great stylists of modern
fiction and a good story-teller into the bargain. His contribution therefore falls automatically into a different class—permanent literature—
read and taught and constantly evaluated by serious academics. *Heart of
Darkness* is indeed so secure today that a leading Conrad scholar has
numbered it "among the half-dozen greatest short novels in the English
language."[1] I will return to this critical opinion in due course because
it may seriously modify my earlier suppositions about who may or may
not be guilty in some of the matters I will now raise.

Heart of Darkness projects the image of Africa as "the other world,"
the antithesis of Europe and therefore of civilization, a place where man's
vaunted intelligence and refinement are finally mocked by triumphant
bestiality. The book opens on the River Thames, tranquil, resting,
peacefully "at the decline of day after ages of good service done to the
race that peopled its banks." But the actual story will take place on the
River Congo, the very antithesis of the Thames. The River Congo is
quite decidedly not a River Emeritus. It has rendered no service and
enjoys no old-age pension. We are told that "Going up that river was
like travelling back to the earliest beginnings of the world."

Is Conrad saying then that these two rivers are very different, one
good, the other bad? Yes, but that is not the real point. It is not the
differentness that worries Conrad but the lurking hint of kinship, of
common ancestry. For the Thames too "has been one of the dark places
of the earth." It conquered its darkness, of course, and is now in daylight
and at peace. But if it were to visit its primordial relative, the Congo, it
would run the terrible risk of hearing grotesque echoes of its own forgotten darkness, and falling victim to an avenging recrudescence of the
mindless frenzy of the first beginnings.

These suggestive echoes comprise Conrad's famed evocation of the
African atmosphere in *Heart of Darkness*. In the final consideration his
method amounts to no more than a steady, ponderous, fake-ritualistic
repetition of two antithetical sentences, one about silence and the other
about frenzy. We can inspect samples of this on pages 36 and 37 of the

1. Albert J. Guerard, Introduction to *Heart of Darkness* (N.Y.: New American Library, 1950) 9.

present edition: a) *It was the stillness of an implacable force broo* *an inscrutable intention* and b) *The steamer toiled along slowly edge of a black and incomprehensible frenzy.* Of course there is a cious change of adjective from time to time, so that instead of *inscr* *ble*, for example, you might have *unspeakable*, even plain *mysterious* etc., etc.

The eagle-eyed English critic F. R. Leavis drew attention long ago to Conrad's "adjectival insistence upon inexpressible and incomprehensible mystery." That insistence must not be dismissed lightly, as many Conrad critics have tended to do, as a mere stylistic flaw; for it raises serious questions of artistic good faith. When a writer while pretending to record scenes, incidents and their impact is in reality engaged in inducing hypnotic stupor in his readers through a bombardment of emotive words and other forms of trickery much more has to be at stake than stylistic felicity. Generally normal readers are well armed to detect and resist such underhand activity. But Conrad chose his subject well—one which was guaranteed not to put him in conflict with the psychological pre-disposition of his readers or raise the need for him to contend with their resistance. He chose the role of purveyor of comforting myths.

The most interesting and revealing passages in *Heart of Darkness* are, however, about people. I must crave the indulgence of my reader to quote almost a whole page from about the middle of the story when representatives of Europe in a steamer going down the Congo encounter the denizens of Africa.

> We were wanderers on a prehistoric earth, on an earth that wore the aspect of an unknown planet. We could have fancied ourselves the first of men taking possession of an accursed inheritance, to be subdued at the cost of profound anguish and of excessive toil. But suddenly as we struggled round a bend there would be a glimpse of rush walls, of peaked grass-roofs, a burst of yells, a whirl of black limbs, a mass of hands clapping, of feet stamping, of bodies swaying, of eyes rolling under the droop of heavy and motionless foliage. The steamer toiled along slowly on the edge of a black and incomprehensible frenzy. The prehistoric man was cursing us, praying to us, welcoming us—who could tell? We were cut off from the comprehension of our surroundings; we glided past like phantoms, wondering and secretly appalled, as sane men would be before an enthusiastic outbreak in a madhouse. We could not understand because we were too far and could not remember, because we were travelling in the night of first ages, of those ages that are gone, leaving hardly a sign—and no memories.
>
> The earth seemed unearthly. We are accustomed to look upon the shackled form of a conquered monster, but there—there you could look at a thing monstrous and free. It was unearthly and the men were. . . . No they were not inhuman. Well, you know that was the worst of it—this suspicion of their not being inhuman. It

v to one. They howled and leaped and spun and
but what thrilled you was just the thought of
yours—the thought of your remote kinship
ionate uproar. Ugly. Yes, it was ugly enough,
ough you would admit to yourself that there
raintest trace of a response to the terrible frank-
noise, a dim suspicion of there being a meaning in it
you—you so remote from the night of first ages—could comprehend.

Herein lies the meaning of *Heart of Darkness* and the fascination it holds over the Western mind: "What thrilled you was just the thought of their humanity—like yours. . . . Ugly."

Having shown us Africa in the mass, Conrad then zeros in, half a page later, on a specific example, giving us one of his rare descriptions of an African who is not just limbs or rolling eyes:

> And between whiles I had to look after the savage who was fireman.
> He was an improved specimen; he could fire up a vertical boiler.
> He was there below me and, upon my word, to look at him was as
> edifying as seeing a dog in a parody of breeches and a feather hat
> walking on his hind legs. A few months of training had done for
> that really fine chap. He squinted at the steam-gauge and at the
> water-gauge with an evident effort of intrepidity—and he had filed
> his teeth too, the poor devil, and the wool of his pate shaved into
> queer patterns, and three ornamental scars on each of his cheeks.
> He ought to have been clapping his hands and stamping his feet on
> the bank, instead of which he was hard at work, a thrall to strange
> witchcraft, full of improving knowledge.

As everybody knows, Conrad is a romantic on the side. He might not exactly admire savages clapping their hands and stamping their feet but they have at least the merit of being in their place, unlike this dog in a parody of breeches. For Conrad things being in their place is of the utmost importance.

"Fine fellows—cannibals—in their place," he tells us pointedly. Tragedy begins when things leave their accustomed place, like Europe leaving its safe stronghold between the policeman and the baker to take a peep into the heart of darkness.

Before the story takes us into the Congo basin proper we are given this nice little vignette as an example of things in their place:

> Now and then a boat from the shore gave one a momentary contact
> with reality. It was paddled by black fellows. You could see from
> afar the white of their eyeballs glistening. They shouted, sang; their
> bodies streamed with perspiration; they had faces like grotesque
> masks—these chaps; but they had bone, muscle, a wild vitality, an
> ergy of movement that was as natural and true as the surf

along their coast. They wanted no excuse for being there. They were a great comfort to look at.

Towards the end of the story Conrad lavishes a whole page quite unexpectedly on an African woman who has obviously been some kind of mistress to Mr. Kurtz and now presides (if I may be permitted a little liberty) like a formidable mystery over the inexorable imminence of his departure:

> She was savage and superb, wild-eyed and magnificent. . . . She stood looking at us without a stir and like the wilderness itself, with an air of brooding over an inscrutable purpose.

This Amazon is drawn in considerable detail, albeit of a predictable nature, for two reasons. First, she is in her place and so can win Conrad's special brand of approval and second, she fulfills a structural requirement of the story: a savage counterpart to the refined, European woman who will step forth to end the story:

> She came forward all in black with a pale head, floating toward me in the dusk. She was in mourning. . . . She took both my hands in hers and murmured, "I had heard you were coming." . . . She had a mature capacity for fidelity, for belief, for suffering.

The difference in the attitude of the novelist to these two women is conveyed in too many direct and subtle ways to need elaboration. But perhaps the most significant difference is the one implied in the author's bestowal of human expression to the one and the withholding of it from the other. It is clearly not part of Conrad's purpose to confer language on the "rudimentary souls" of Africa. In place of speech they made "a violent babble of uncouth sounds." They "exchanged short grunting phrases" even among themselves. But most of the time they were too busy with their frenzy. There are two occasions in the book, however, when Conrad departs somewhat from his practice and confers speech, even English speech, on the savages. The first occurs when cannibalism gets the better of them:

> "Catch 'im," he snapped with a bloodshot widening of his eyes and a flash of sharp teeth—"catch 'im. Give 'im to us." "To you, eh?" I asked; "what would you do with them?" "Eat 'im!" he said curtly. . . .

The other occasion was the famous announcement:

> "Mistah Kurtz—he dead."

At first sight these instances might be mistaken for unexpected acts of generosity from Conrad. In reality they constitute some of his best assaults. In the case of the cannibals the incomprehensible grunts that had thus far served them for speech suddenly proved inadequate for Conrad's purpose of letting the European glimpse the unspeakable craving in their hearts. Weighing the necessity for consistency in the portrayal of the dumb brutes against the sensational advantages of securing their conviction by clear, unambiguous evidence issuing out of their own mouth Conrad chose the latter. As for the announcement of Mr. Kurtz's death by the "insolent black head in the doorway" what better or more appropriate *finis* could be written to the horror story of that wayward child of civilization who willfully had given his soul to the powers of darkness and "taken a high seat amongst the devils of the land" than the proclamation of his physical death by the forces he had joined?

It might be contended, of course, that the attitude to the African in *Heart of Darkness* is not Conrad's but that of his fictional narrator, Marlow, and that far from endorsing it Conrad might indeed be holding it up to irony and criticism. Certainly Conrad appears to go to considerable pains to set up layers of insulation between himself and the moral universe of his history. He has, for example, a narrator behind a narrator. The primary narrator is Marlow but his account is given to us through the filter of a second, shadowy person. But if Conrad's intention is to draw a *cordon sanitaire* between himself and the moral and psychological malaise of his narrator his care seems to me totally wasted because he neglects to hint however subtly or tentatively at an alternative frame of reference by which we may judge the actions and opinions of his characters. It would not have been beyond Conrad's power to make that provision if he had thought it necessary. Marlow seems to me to enjoy Conrad's complete confidence—a feeling reinforced by the close similarities between their two careers.

Marlow comes through to us not only as a witness of truth, but one holding those advanced and humane views appropriate to the English liberal tradition which required all Englishmen of decency to be deeply shocked by atrocities in Bulgaria or the Congo of King Leopold of the Belgians or wherever.

Thus Marlow is able to toss out such bleeding-heart sentiments as these:

> They were dying slowly—it was very clear. They were not enemies, they were not criminals, they were nothing earthly now, nothing but black shadows of disease and starvation lying confusedly in the greenish gloom. Brought from all the recesses of the coast in all the legality of time contracts, lost in uncongenial surroundings, fed on unfamiliar food, they sickened, became inefficient, and were then allowed to crawl away and rest.

The kind of liberalism espoused here by Marlow/Conrad touched all the best minds of the age in England, Europe and America. It took different forms in the minds of different people but almost always managed to sidestep the ultimate question of equality between white people and black people. That extraordinary missionary, Albert Schweitzer, who sacrificed brilliant careers in music and theology in Europe for a life of service to Africans in much the same area as Conrad writes about, epitomizes the ambivalence. In a comment which has often been quoted Schweitzer says: "The African is indeed my brother but my junior brother." And so he proceeded to build a hospital appropriate to the needs of junior brothers with standards of hygiene reminiscent of medical practice in the days before the germ theory of disease came into being. Naturally he became a sensation in Europe and America. Pilgrims flocked, and I believe still flock even after he has passed on, to witness the prodigious miracle in Lamberene, on the edge of the primeval forest.

Conrad's liberalism would not take him quite as far as Schweitzer's, though. He would not use the word *brother* however qualified; the farthest he would go was kinship. When Marlow's African helmsman falls down with a spear in his heart he gives his white master one final disquieting look.

> And the intimate profundity of that look he gave me when he received his hurt remains to this day in my memory—like a claim of distant kinship affirmed in a supreme moment.

It is important to note that Conrad, careful as ever with his words, is concerned not so much about *distant kinship* as about someone *laying a claim* on it. The black man lays a claim on the white man which is well-nigh intolerable. It is the laying of this claim which frightens and at the same time fascinates Conrad, ". . . the thought of their humanity—like yours. . . . Ugly."

The point of my observations should be quite clear by now, namely that Joseph Conrad was a thoroughgoing racist. That this simple truth is glossed over in criticisms of his work is due to the fact that white racism against Africa is such a normal way of thinking that its manifestations go completely unremarked. Students of *Heart of Darkness* will often tell you that Conrad is concerned not so much with Africa as with the deterioration of one European mind caused by solitude and sickness. They will point out to you that Conrad is, if anything, less charitable to the Europeans in the story than he is to the natives, that the point of the story is to ridicule Europe's civilizing mission in Africa. A Conrad student informed me in Scotland that Africa is merely a setting for the disintegration of the mind of Mr. Kurtz.

Which is partly the point. Africa as setting and backdrop which eliminates the African as human factor. Africa as a metaphysical battlefield devoid of all recognizable humanity, into which the wandering European enters at his peril. Can nobody see the preposterous and perverse arrogance in thus reducing Africa to the role of props for the break-up of one petty European mind? But that is not even the point. The real question is the dehumanization of Africa and Africans which this age-long attitude has fostered and continues to foster in the world. And the question is whether a novel which celebrates this dehumanization, which depersonalizes a portion of the human race, can be called a great work of art. My answer is: No, it cannot. I do not doubt Conrad's great talents. Even *Heart of Darkness* has its memorably good passages and moments:

The reaches opened before us and closed behind, as if the forest had stepped leisurely across the water to bar the way for our return.

Its exploration of the minds of the European characters is often penetrating and full of insight. But all that has been more than fully discussed in the last fifty years. His obvious racism has, however, not been addressed. And it is high time it was!

Conrad was born in 1857, the very year in which the first Anglican missionaries were arriving among my own people in Nigeria. It was certainly not his fault that he lived his life at a time when the reputation of the black man was at a particularly low level. But even after due allowances have been made for all the influences of contemporary prejudice on his sensibility there remains still in Conrad's attitude a residue of antipathy to black people which his peculiar psychology alone can explain. His own account of his first encounter with a black man is very revealing:

> A certain enormous buck nigger encountered in Haiti fixed my conception of blind, furious, unreasoning rage, as manifested in the human animal to the end of my days. Of the nigger I used to dream for years afterwards.[2]

Certainly Conrad had a problem with niggers. His inordinate love of that word itself should be of interest to psychoanalysts. Sometimes his fixation on blackness is equally interesting as when he gives us this brief description:

> A black figure stood up, strode on long black legs, waving long black arms. . . .

as though we might expect a black figure striding along on black legs to wave white arms! But so unrelenting is Conrad's obsession.

As a matter of interest Conrad gives us in A *Personal Record* what amounts to a companion piece to the buck nigger of Haiti. At the age of sixteen Conrad encountered his first Englishman in Europe. He calls him "my unforgettable Englishman" and describes him in the following manner:

> "(his) calves exposed to the public gaze . . . dazzled the beholder by the splendor of their marble-like condition and their rich tone of young ivory. . . . The light of a headlong, exalted satisfaction with the world of men . . . illumined his face . . . and triumphant eyes. In passing he cast a glance of kindly curiosity and a friendly gleam of big, sound, shiny teeth . . . his white calves twinkled sturdily."[3]

2. Jonah Raskin, *The Mythology of Imperialism* (N.Y.: Random House, 1971) 143.
3. Bernard C. Meyer, M.D., *Joseph Conrad: A*

Psychoanalytic Biography (Princeton: Princeton UP, 1967) 30

Irrational love and irrational hate jostling together in the heart of that talented, tormented man. But whereas irrational love may at worst engender foolish acts of indiscretion, irrational hate can endanger the life of the community. Naturally Conrad is a dream for psychoanalytic critics. Perhaps the most detailed study of him in this direction is by Bernard C. Meyer, M.D. In his lengthy book Dr. Meyer follows every conceivable lead (and sometimes inconceivable ones) to explain Conrad. As an example he gives us long disquisitions on the significance of hair and hair-cutting in Conrad. And yet not even one word is spared for his attitude to black people. Not even the discussion of Conrad's antisemitism was enough to spark off in Dr. Meyer's mind those other dark and explosive thoughts. Which only leads one to surmise that Western psychoanalysts must regard the kind of racism displayed by Conrad as absolutely normal despite the profoundly important work done by Frantz Fanon in the psychiatric hospitals of French Algeria.

Whatever Conrad's problems were, you might say he is now safely dead. Quite true. Unfortunately his heart of darkness plagues us still. Which is why an offensive and deplorable book can be described by a serious scholar as "among the half dozen greatest short novels in the English language." And why it is today perhaps the most commonly prescribed novel in twentieth-century literature courses in English Departments of American universities.

There are two probable grounds on which what I have said so far may be contested. The first is that it is no concern of fiction to please people about whom it is written. I will go along with that. But I am not talking about pleasing people. I am talking about a book which parades in the most vulgar fashion prejudices and insults from which a section of mankind has suffered untold agonies and atrocities in the past and continues to do so in many ways and many places today. I am talking about a story in which the very humanity of black people is called in question.

Secondly, I may be challenged on the grounds of actuality. Conrad, after all, did sail down the Congo in 1890 when my own father was still a babe in arms. How could I stand up more than fifty years after his death and purport to contradict him? My answer is that as a sensible man I will not accept just any traveller's tales solely on the grounds that I have not made the journey myself. I will not trust the evidence even of a man's very eyes when I suspect them to be as jaundiced as Conrad's. And we also happen to know that Conrad was, in the words of his biographer, Bernard C. Meyer, "notoriously inaccurate in the rendering of his own history."[4]

But more important by far is the abundant testimony about Conrad's savages which we could gather if we were so inclined from other sources and which might lead us to think that these people must have had other occupations besides merging into the evil forest or materializing out of

4. Meyer, p. 30.

260 CHINUA ACHEBE

it simply to plague Marlow and his dispirited band. For as it happened, soon after Conrad had written his book an event of far greater consequence was taking place in the art world of Europe. This is how Frank Willett, a British art historian, describes it:

> Gaugin had gone to Tahiti, the most extravagant individual act of turning to a non-European culture in the decades immediately before and after 1900, when European artists were avid for new artistic experiences, but it was only about 1904–5 that African art began to make its distinctive impact. One piece is still identifiable; it is a mask that had been given to Maurice Vlaminck in 1905. He records that Derain was 'speechless' and 'stunned' when he saw it, bought it from Vlaminck and in turn showed it to Picasso and Matisse, who were also greatly affected by it. Ambroise Vollard then borrowed it and had it cast in bronze. . . . The revolution of twentieth century art was under way![5]

The mask in question was made by other savages living just north of Conrad's River Congo. They have a name too: the Fang people, and are without a doubt among the world's greatest masters of the sculptured form. The event Frank Willett is referring to marked the beginning of cubism and the infusion of new life into European art, which had run completely out of strength.

The point of all this is to suggest that Conrad's picture of the peoples of the Congo seems grossly inadequate even at the height of their subjection to the ravages of King Leopold's International Association for the Civilization of Central Africa.

Travellers with closed minds can tell us little except about themselves. But even those not blinkered, like Conrad with xenophobia, can be astonishing blind. Let me digress a little here. One of the greatest and most intrepid travellers of all time, Marco Polo, journeyed to the Far East from the Mediterranean in the thirteenth century and spent twenty years in the court of Kublai Khan in China. On his return to Venice he set down in his book entitled *Description of the World* his impressions of the peoples and places and customs he had seen. But there were at least two extraordinary omissions in his account. He said nothing about the art of printing, unknown as yet in Europe but in full flower in China. He either did not notice it at all or if he did, failed to see what use Europe could possibly have for it. Whatever the reason, Europe had to wait another hundred years for Gutenberg. But even more spectacular was Marco Polo's omission of any reference to the Great Wall of China nearly 4,000 miles long and already more than 1,000 years old at the time of his visit. Again, he may not have seen it; but the Great Wall of China is the only structure built by man which is visible from the moon![6] Indeed travellers can be blind.

5. Frank Willett, *African Art* (N.Y.: Praeger, 1971) 35–36.
6. For the omission of the Great Wall of China, I am indebted to *The Journey of Marco Polo* as recreated by artist Michael Foreman, published by *Pegasus Magazine*, 1974.

As I said earlier Conrad did not originate the image of Africa which we find in his book. It was and is the dominant image of Africa in the Western imagination and Conrad merely brought the peculiar gifts of his own mind to bear on it. For reasons which can certainly use close psychological inquiry the West seems to suffer deep anxieties about the precariousness of its civilization and to have a need for constant reassurance by comparison with Africa. If Europe, advancing in civilization, could cast a backward glance periodically at Africa trapped in primordial barbarity it could say with faith and feeling: There go I but for the grace of God. Africa is to Europe as the picture is to Dorian Gray—a carrier onto whom the master unloads his physical and moral deformities so that he may go forward, erect and immaculate. Consequently Africa is something to be avoided just as the picture has to be hidden away to safeguard the man's jeopardous integrity. Keep away from Africa, or else! Mr. Kurtz of *Heart of Darkness* should have heeded that warning and the prowling horror in his heart would have kept its place, chained to its lair. But he foolishly exposed himself to the wild irresistible allure of the jungle and lo! the darkness found him out.

In my original conception of this essay I had thought to conclude it nicely on an appropriately positive note in which I would suggest from my privileged position in African and Western cultures some advantages the West might derive from Africa once it rid its mind of old prejudices and began to look at Africa not through a haze of distortions and cheap mystifications but quite simply as a continent of people—not angels, but not rudimentary souls either—just people, often highly gifted people and often strikingly successful in their enterprise with life and society. But as I thought more about the stereotype image, about its grip and pervasiveness, about the willful tenacity with which the West holds it to its heart; when I thought of the West's television and cinema and newspapers, about books read in its schools and out of school, of churches preaching to empty pews about the need to send help to the heathen in Africa, I realized that no easy optimism was possible. And there was, in any case, something totally wrong in offering bribes to the West in return for its good opinion of Africa. Ultimately the abandonment of unwholesome thoughts must be its own and only reward. Although I have used the word *willful* a few times here to characterize the West's view of Africa, it may well be that what is happening at this stage is more akin to reflex action than calculated malice. Which does not make the situation more but less hopeful.

The Christian Science Monitor, a paper more enlightened than most, once carried an interesting article written by its Education Editor on the serious psychological and learning problems faced by little children who speak one language at home and then go to school where something else is spoken. It was a wide-ranging article taking in Spanish-speaking children in America, the children of migrant Italian workers in Germany, the quadrilingual phenomenon in Malaysia, and so on. And all this while the article speaks unequivocally about language. But then out of the blue sky comes this:

> In London there is an enormous immigration of children who speak Indian or Nigerian dialects, or some other native language.[7]

I believe that the introduction of dialects which is technically erroneous in the context is almost a reflex action caused by an instinctive desire of the writer to downgrade the discussion to the level of Africa and India. And this is quite comparable to Conrad's withholding of language from his rudimentary souls. Language is too grand for these chaps; let's give them dialects!

In all this business a lot of violence is inevitably done not only to the image of despised peoples but even to words, the very tools of possible redress. Look at the phrase *native language* in the *Science Monitor* excerpt. Surely the only *native* language possible in London is Cockney English. But our writer means something else—something appropriate to the sounds Indians and Africans make!

Although the work of redressing which needs to be done may appear too daunting, I believe it is not one day too soon to begin. Conrad saw and condemned the evil of imperial exploitation but was strangely unaware of the racism on which it sharpened its iron tooth. But the victims of racist slander who for centuries have had to live with the inhumanity it makes them heir to have always known better than any casual visitor even when he comes loaded with the gifts of a Conrad.

WILSON HARRIS

The Frontier on Which *Heart of Darkness* Stands †

I read Chinua Achebe's article on Joseph Conrad with much interest and some sympathy. My sympathy rests on an appreciation of his uneasiness in the face of biases that continue to reinforce themselves in post-imperial western establishments. Perhaps the West does have the bad conscience Achebe attributes to it and is seeking, therefore, some assuagements of its guilt.

There are certainly writers, novelists, reporters, as he indicates, who seem predisposed to see nothing but bankruptcy in the Third World and one wonders in what unconscious degree perhaps the West may desire such bankruptcy—cultural and political—to become a fact of history, whereby it may justify its imperial past by implying that imperial order, across centuries of colonialism, was the only real support the modern world possessed, the only real governance the Third World respected.

7. *Christian Science Monitor*, November 25, 1974, 11.
† From *Research on African Literatures* 12(1981):

86–92. © 1981 by the University of Texas Press. Reprinted by permission.

Achebe's essay on "the dehumanisation of Africa and Africans" by "bloody racists" is, therefore, in the light of western malaise and postimperial hangover, a persuasive argument, but I am convinced his judgement or dismissal of *Heart of Darkness*—and of Conrad's strange genius—is a profoundly mistaken one. He sees the distortions of imagery and, therefore, of character in the novel as witnessing to horrendous prejudice on Conrad's part in his vision of Africa and Africans.

As I weighed this charge in my own mind, I began to sense a certain incomprehension in Achebe's analysis of the pressures of form that engaged Conrad's imagination to transform biases grounded in homogeneous premises. By form I mean the novel form as a medium of consciousness that has its deepest roots in an intuitive and much, much older self than the historical ego or the historical conditions of ego dignity that binds us to a particular decade or generation or century.

The capacity of the intuitive self to breach the historical ego is the life-giving and terrifying objectivity of imaginative art that makes a painting or a poem or a piece of sculpture or a fiction endure long beyond the artist's short lifetime and gives it the strangest beauty or coherence in depth.

This interaction between sovereign ego and intuitive self is the tormenting reality of changing form, the ecstasy as well of visionary capacity to cleave the prison house of natural bias within a heterogeneous asymmetric context [1] in which the unknowable God—though ceaselessly beyond human patterns—infuses art with unfathomable eternity and grace.

I believe that this complex matter may arouse incomprehension in Africa where, by and large, tradition tends towards homogeneous imperatives. In South America where I was born this is not the case. The crucial hurdle in the path of community, if community is to create a living future, lies in a radical aesthetic in which distortions of sovereign ego may lead into confessions of partiality within sovereign institutions that, therefore, may begin to penetrate and unravel their biases, in some degree, in order to bring into play a complex wholeness inhabited by other confessing parts that may have once masqueraded themselves as monolithic absolutes or monolithic codes of behavior in the old worlds from which they emigrated by choice or by force.

It is in this respect that I find it possible to view *Heart of Darkness* as a frontier novel. By that I mean that it stands upon a threshold of capacity to which Conrad pointed though he never attained that capacity himself. Nevertheless, it was a stroke of genius on his part to visualize an original necessity for distortions in the stases of appearance that seem

1. *Asymmetric context* implies that the unknowable God mediates between all structures. Thus if one were to say "the sun is a rose" one would visualize—in asymmetric context—an inimitable or unstructured mediation existing between *sun* and *rose*. Both *sun* and *rose*, therefore, are partial signatures of—partial witnesses to—a universal principle of mediation, a universal principle of light beyond capture or structure. That principle of mediation at the heart of all metaphor may only be perceived as an *untameable* force mediating between *sun* and *rose*.

Symmetric context on the other hand would imply a binding locality or materiality or physicality in which *sun* and *rose* are *tameable* extensions or symmetric inversions of each other.

sacred and that cultures take for granted as models of timeless dignity.

There is a dignity in liberal pretensions until liberalism, whether black or white, unmasks itself to reveal inordinate ambitions for power where one least suspects it to exist.

The novel form Conrad inherited is the novel form in which most writers, black and white, write today. For comedy of manners is the basis of protest fiction, fiction of good guys and bad guys, racist guys and liberal guys. Comedy of manners is the basis of realism that mirrors society to identify refinements of behavior that are social or antisocial, heroic or antiheroic. All this is an oversimplification perhaps, but it may help to complement what is less obvious in this analysis.

The novel form Conrad inherited—if I may restate my theme in a more complex way—was conditioned by a homogeneous cultural logic to promote a governing principle that would sustain all parties, all characterizations, in endeavoring to identify natural justice, natural conscience behind the activity of a culture.

It was with such works of disturbing imagination as Edgar Alan Poe's *Arthur Gordon Pym* and James Hogg's *Confessions of a Justified Sinner,* both published in the 1830s, Melville's *Benito Cereno,* in the middle of the nineteenth century, and Conrad's *Heart of Darkness,* at the beginning of the twentieth century, that the logic of human-made symmetry or absolute control of diversity, the logic of benign or liberal order, disclosed hideous biases within a context of heterogeneous bodies and pigmentations. For the truth was that the liberal homogeneity of a culture becomes the ready-made cornerstone upon which to construct an order of conquest, and by degrees "The horror! The horror!" was intuitively manifest. Conquest is the greatest evil of soul humanity inflicts upon itself and on nature.

Such an admission—such a discovery that sacred human stasis may come to shelter the greatest evil—is a catastrophe for the liberal ego-fixated mind. In it, nevertheless, lies a profound creation myth that may begin to nourish a capacity for meaningful distortion of images through which to offset or transform the hubris of apparently sacred order and to create, by painful and yet ecstatic degrees, a profound, complex, and searching dialogue between confessing and confessional heterogeneous cultures that are no longer the monolithic or absolute civilizations they once were in Africa, China, Europe, India, or the Americas in the fourteenth century and fifteenth century before the circumnavigation of the globe and the fall of ancient America. Creation myth is a paradox. It is a vision of catastrophe and of coherence in depth *nevertheless* within or beneath the fragmented surfaces of given world orders. It is a vision of mysterious regeneration that apprises us of our limits and in so doing awakens a capacity to dream beyond those limits, a capacity for infinite conception of life and of humility, a capacity for complex risk, creativity, and dialogue with others through and beyond institutions inhibited by, or based on, the brute conquest of nature from which creation has recoiled again and again over long ages to leave us and our antecedents bereft and yet intensely aware of the priceless gift of being that begins all over again in the depths of animate perception.

The most significant distortion of imagery in *Heart of Darkness* bears upon Kurtz's liberal manifesto of imperial good and moral light. In that manifesto or consolidation of virtues the "Exterminate all the [alien] brutes" becomes inevitable. Thus Conrad parodies the notion of moral light that devours all in its path—a parody that cuts to the heart of paternalism with strings attached to each filial puppet. (The invasion of Afghanistan in the year of Machiavellian politics 1980 is a late-twentieth-century version of paternal Kurtz in which the virtues of the Soviet monolith make no bones about the symmetry of Communist power to encircle the globe.)

At no point in his essay does Achebe touch upon the crucial parody of the proprieties of established order that mask corruption in all societies, black and white, though this is essential, it seems to me, to a perception of catastrophe behind the dignified personae monoliths wear. (And, in this context, one is not speaking only of conquistadorial monoliths but of mankind the hunter whose folklore is death; mankind the ritualist who sacrifices female children to maintain the symmetry of males, or mankind the priest who once plucked the heart from the breast of a living victim to feed the sun.)

These distortions of the human mask (hunter, priest, ritualist) set their teeth upon African characters like an initiation ceremony at the heart of the Bush to bite deep as well into the European conquistador/butcher/businessman Kurtz.

Kurtz's manifesto, liberal manifesto, affected Marlow as follows:

> All Europe contributed to the making of Kurtz, and by and by I learned that most appropriately the International Society for the Suppression of Savage Customs had entrusted him with the making of a report for its future guidance. And he had written it too. I've seen it. I've read it. . . . Seventeen pages of close writing. He had found time for it. . . . He began with the argument that we whites, from the point of development we had arrived at, "must necessarily appear to them [savages] in the nature of supernatural beings—we approach them with the might of a deity," and so on, and so on. "By the simple exercise of our will we can exert a power for good practically unbounded," etc. etc. From that point he soared and took me with him. . . . It gave me the notion of an exotic Immensity ruled by an august Benevolence. It made me tingle with enthusiasm. . . . It was very simple and at the end of that moving appeal to every altruistic sentiment it blazed at you luminous and terrifying like a flash of lightning in a serene sky: "Exterminate all the brutes!" The curious part was that he had apparently forgotten all about that valuable postscriptum because later on when he in a sense came to himself, he repeatedly entreated me to take good care of "my pamphlet." . . .

    In this context of parody it is possible, I think, to register a foreboding
about the ultimate essence of *Heart of Darkness* and to sense an exhaustion of spirit that froze Conrad's genius and made it impossible for him
to cross the frontier upon which his intuitive imagination had arrived.
Achebe does not appear to have given any thought to this matter in his
essay. My view is that parody tends to border upon nihilism, a fact all
too clear in modern fiction and drama. Parody is the flag of the death of
god, the death of faith, and without faith imaginative art tends to freeze
and cultivate a loss of soul. Perhaps god has been so conditioned by
homogeneous or tribal idols that freedom of spirit seems a chimera.
When I speak of the necessity for faith I am not referring therefore to
cults of idolatry but to a conviction written into the stars as into one's
blood that creation is a priceless gift beyond human formula or calcula-
tion of Faustian will.

    Conrad's despair is so marked that one is conscious of infinite deso-
lation within the very signals he intuitively erects that bear upon a radical dialectic of form. His parody—like Beckett's parody—remains
formidable because it cuts to the bone and heart of liberal complacency.
The transition beyond parody that humanity needs neither Beckett nor
Conrad fulfills.

    I am convinced myself that there is a movement of transition in some
complex areas of twentieth century literature beyond parody but such an
exploration would require another essay. I shall give, however, two
examples that may suggest a groping transition. First of all, Wole Soyinka's masterpiece *The Road* is influenced, I am sure, by Conrad in
that the unscrupulous professor is psychically related to Kurtz with the
profound distinction that the professor's faith in "the chrysalis of the
Word"[2] prepares him for a descent into the fertility of the African mask,
so that he sustains in himself the wound that kills those who exist in the
depths of place and time. He is, as it were, the involuntary metaphysic
that illumines outcast humanity within the dissolution of the mask or
persona conferred by the savage god, Ogun, in contradistinction to Kurtz's
totalitarian loss of soul within the rigidity of the mask conferred by the
hubris of material bias.

    My second example of possible transition through and beyond post-
Conradian legacies is a remarkable asymmetric American fiction by the
black writer Jean Toomer in his book *Cane*, published in 1923, which
comprises a series of half-fictions, half-plays shot through by stream of
consciousness and lyrical moments as well as by short interludes or poems.

    The characters appear implicitly clothed in property and landscapes
they wear like bizarre roots and masks to suggest an unfreedom of personality locked in polarizations. This perception is psychic rather than
behavioristic and, therefore, it may begin to undermine the polarizations since it is capable of seeing them not for what they appear to be—
forms of strength—but for what they essentially are—fragmentations of

2. Wole Soyinka, *The Road* (London: Oxford University Press, 1965), p. 45.

a community dangerously divided within itself against itself. Paradoxically this psychic apprehension begins to grope for coherence in depth that needs to be grasped ceaselessly by imagery that points through itself, beyond itself, into a visionary comedy of wholeness that can never be structured absolutely. Indeed, where adamant property binds flesh and blood *Cane* is a revelation of bitterness and conflict since it evokes memories of the auction block on which persons were bought and sold, metaphorically nailed to the cross, as it were, as pieces of property.

I must confess, in bringing this article to a close, that I was rather surprised when Achebe quoted F. R. Leavis in support of his thesis. Leavis of all people! Leavis, as far as I am aware, possessed no sympathy whatever for imaginative literature that fell outside of the closed world of his "great tradition."

I would question Leavis's indictment of Conrad for an addiction to the adjective. The fact of the matter is that the intuitive archetypes of sensation and nonsensation by which Conrad was tormented are not *nouns*. They are qualitative and infinite variations of substance clothed in nouns. Nouns may reveal paradoxically, when qualified, that their emphasis on reality and their inner meaning can change as they are inhabited by variable psychic projections born of the mystery of creation. There is a *woodenness* to *wood*, there is also a *gaiety* to *wood* when it is stroked by shadow or light that turns *wood* into a mask worn by variable metaphysical bodies that alter the content within the mask. The livingness of wood is the magic of carven shapes that act in turn upon the perceiving eye and sculpt it into a window of spirit.

Marlow's bewilderment at the heart of the original forest he uneasily penetrated reveals unfinished senses within him and without him, unfinished perceptions that hang upon veils within veils.

> The *living* trees, lashed together by the creepers and every *living* bush of the undergrowth, might have been changed into *stone*, even to the *slenderest* twig, to the *lightest* leaf. It was not sleep—it seemed unnatural, like a state of trance. Not the *faintest* sound of any kind could be heard. You looked on amazed and began to suspect yourself of being *deaf*—then the night came suddenly and struck the *blind* as well. About three in the morning some large fish leaped and the *loud* splash made me jump as though a gun had been fired. When the sun rose there was a *white* fog, very warm and clammy, and more *blinding* than the night. . . . [A] cry, a very loud cry as of infinite desolation soared slowly in the *opaque* air. It ceased. A complaining clamour, modulated in savage discords, filled our ears.

At this stage I would like to add to the considerations I have already expressed by touching on the issue of "music" in imaginative literature.

The loud cry and clamor as of an orchestra at the heart of the Bush that come as a climax in the quotation from *Heart of Darkness* are of interest in the context of the human voice breaking through instruments

of stone and wood and other trance formations to which the human
animal is subject. Indeed it is as if the stone and wood *sing*, so that in
mirroring hard-hearted dread and rigid desolation they suffer at the same
time a disruption or transformation of fixed bias within themselves.

I am not suggesting that Conrad extends this notion into a profound
discovery of new form or radical aesthetic but it is marginally yet significantly visible in the passage I have quoted.

Caribbean writers and poets have been interested in the ground of
music in fiction and poetry. Edward Brathwaite, Derek Walcott, and
others have complex approaches to music. I have intuitively explored in
novels organic metaphors of music. In a recent article[3] I confessed to
some of these intuitive archetypes and in particular to the pre-Colum-
bian bone flute as a trigger of organic capacity to release a diversity of
sombre or rock-hard images in alliance or attunement with phenomenal
forests, walking trees, butterfly motifs within singing bodies of evolutionary hope in the midst of legacies of conquest and catastrophe.

I am reminded now, as I write this, of Beethoven's late quartets in
which he wrestled with "the intolerable muteness" (as Anton Ehrenzweig puts it) "of a purely instrumental music; he tries to make the
instruments sing in a human way. . . . In the end the human voice
itself must break in as a symbol of extreme disruption in order to obey a
more profound logic."[4]

FRANCES B. SINGH

The Colonialistic Bias of *Heart of Darkness* †

It is a truth universally acknowledged that *Heart of Darkness* is one of
the most powerful indictments of colonialism ever written. Why this is
so can be explained by reference to Conrad's own life. As a child Conrad
was a victim of Russia's colonialistic policies toward Poland. On account
of his father's revolutionary activities on behalf of Polish freedom, he,
his mother, and his father were exiled to Siberia. When Conrad grew
up he chose to follow the sea as a career because he felt it would provide
him with the sense of openness, freedom, and democracy he had not
been able to feel in his childhood. Ironically the profession which he
thought would take him away from the horror of colonialism often brought
him closer to it.

Heart of Darkness grows out of one of Conrad's brushes with colonialism. In 1890 Conrad was given command of a river steamer plying
among the trading stations set up by the Belgians along the Congo River.
At that time the Belgian Congo was the most ruthlessly exploited region

3. Wilson Harris, "The Enigma of Values," *New
Letters*, 40, 1 (1973), 141–49.
4. Anton Ehrenzweig, *The Hidden Order of Art*

(London: Paladin, 1970), p. 219.
†From *Conradiana* 10(1978): 41–54. Reprinted by
permission.

in the whole African continent, and what made the exploitation worse was that it went on under the cover of brotherhood and philanthropy. Conrad's experiences there form the basis of *Heart of Darkness*. In 1902 he said that its story was "mainly a vehicle for conveying a batch of personal impressions," and in the "Author's Note" to *Youth and Two Other Stories*, he described it as "experience pushed a little (and only very little) beyond the actual facts of the case."[1] However Conrad does not tell the story directly; it is narrated by a character called Marlow.

Marlow's impressions of colonialism fall into three classes. The first type is a direct, straightforward attack and is exemplified in his descriptive analysis of the Roman colonization of ancient Britain:

> They grabbed what they could get for the sake of what was to be got. It was just robbery with violence, aggravated murder on a great scale, and men going at it blind. . . . The conquest of the earth, which mostly means the taking it away from those who have a different complexion or slightly flatter noses than ourselves, is not a pretty thing when you look into it too much.

The second is ironic and is well illustrated by his references to the "noble cause," the "jolly pioneers of progress," and the "improved specimen" who was his fireman. His tone is also ironic as he comments on Kurtz's report for the International Society for the Suppression of Savage Customs: " 'The peroration was magnificent, though difficult to remember, you know. It gave me the notion of an exotic Immensity ruled by an august Benevolence.' " Marlow combines the attack direct with the attack through irony in his description of the Eldorado Exploring Expedition to heighten the immorality of its intentions:

> This devoted band called itself the Eldorado Exploring Expedition and I believe they were sworn to secrecy. Their talk however was the talk of sordid buccaneers. It was reckless without hardihood, greedy without audacity, and cruel without courage. There was not an atom of foresight or of serious intention in the whole batch of them, and they did not seem aware these things are wanted for the work of the world. To tear treasure out of the bowels of the land was their desire, with no more moral purpose at the back of it than there is in burglars breaking into a safe. Who paid the expenses of the noble enterprise I don't know. . . .

The third and most important type of comment uses metaphor to lash out against colonialism. Thus Brussels is likened to a "whited sepulchre," and the offices of the trading company which runs the steamers on the Congo to "a house in a city of the dead." The African natives, victims of Belgian exploitation, are described as "shapes," "shadows," and "bundles of acute angles," so as to show the dehumanizing effect of coloni-

---

1. Quoted by Jocelyn Baines, *Joseph Conrad: A Critical Biography* (London: Weidenfeld & Nicholson, 1960), p. 227; Joseph Conrad, *Youth and Two Other Stories* (Garden City, N.Y.: Doubleday, Page & Co., 1923), p. xi. [*See also*, p. 3, *above—Editor.*]

alistic rule on the ruled. Kurtz becomes "an animated image of death carved out of old ivory," a "voice" and a "shadow," suggesting the loss of personality that colonialism effects on the rulers.

Of all the suggestive metaphors used in the story, however, there is nothing like the title itself. On one level it indicates merely the geographical location of the Belgian Congo and the color of its inhabitants. On another it refers to the evil practices of the colonizers of the Congo, their sordid exploitation of the natives, and suggests that the real darkness is not in Africa but in Europe, and that its heart is not in the breasts of black Africans but in all whites who countenance and engage in colonialistic enterprise. While on the first level the metaphor has a direct, factual, and straightforward application, on the second it is ironic, for what is apparently black is really white, and what is apparently white is really black.[2] These two levels, therefore, correspond structurally to the first two classes into which Marlow's observations on colonialism fall. What unites these two interpretations of the metaphor is the fact that they are both based on real phenomena: the ethnography of the Congo, the nature and consequence of empire-building.

There is also a third level to the metaphor, and it is psychological in meaning. Marlow introduces the story of his experiences in Africa by philosophizing on the life led by the Roman colonizers of ancient Britain.

> Land in a swamp, march through the woods, and in some inland post feel the savagery, the utter savagery, had closed round him,— all that mysterious life of the wilderness that stirs in the forest, in the jungles, in the hearts of wild men. There's no initiation either into such mysteries. He has to live in the midst of the incomprehensible which is also detestable. And it has a fascination too, that goes to work upon him. The fascination of the abomination—you know. Imagine the growing regrets, the longing to escape, the powerless disgust, the surrender—the hate.

According to Marlow the colonizers became psychologically depraved because, being cut off from the norms of civilization, they turned to the lawless jungle. Marlow implies that his trip upriver into the geographical heart of ethnographically darkest Africa represents a similar experience: that his voyage is a voyage through the dark backward and abysm of time into the inner heart of darkness, the utterly savage state of being that existed before civilization tamed the unconscious with its absolute desire for egotistic self-fulfillment by means of moral restraints:

> Going up that river was like travelling back to the earliest beginnings of the world, when vegetation rioted on the earth and the big trees were kings. . . . you thought yourself bewitched and cut off

2. Both Bruce K. Stark, "Kurtz's Intended: The Heart of *Heart of Darkness*," *Texas Studies in Literature and Language*, 16 (1974), pp. 537, 539 and Eloise K. Hay, *The Political Novels of Joseph* *Conrad* (Chicago: University of Chicago Press, 1963), p. 134, agree with this position but interpret the story as a whole differently.

for ever from everything you had known once—somewhere—far away—in another existence perhaps. . . . And this stillness of life did not in the least resemble a peace. It was the stillness of an implacable force brooding over an inscrutable intention. It looked at you with a vengeful aspect.

Thus Marlow uses the unknown, remote, and primitive Africa as a symbol for an evil and primeval force, something similar to what E. M. Forster was to do later through the Marabar Caves in A *Passage to India*.

By giving these three interpretations of the metaphor, "heart of darkness," Marlow pushes it to its limit. The question is, did Marlow push it too far? For the story also carries suggestions that the evil which the title refers to is to be associated with Africans, their customs, and their rites. Marlow talks, for example, of their "unspeakable rites" and the "satanic litany" of Kurtz's followers. Furthermore he uses words like *brutal, monstrous, vengeful, implacable, inscrutable, evil, accursed, hopeless, dark,* and *pitiless* so constantly in talking about Africa that the people of Africa begin to be tinged by the qualities that these words connote. Thus the woman who comes abreast of the steamer is described in terms of the wilderness: "She stood looking at us without a stir and like the wilderness itself, with an air of brooding over an inscrutable purpose." The sentence recalls Marlow's earlier observation that the stillness of the jungle was the "stillness of an implacable force brooding over an inscrutable intention," which "looked at you with a vengeful aspect." By describing the woman in terms of the wilderness, Marlow transfers its evil qualities to her, and she becomes the personification of the spirit of the jungle: "the fascination of the abomination."

Marlow does, no doubt, declare from time to time that he is not qualified to judge Africans: "The prehistoric man was cursing us, praying to us, welcoming us—who could tell?" The question mark at the end is a confession of his lack of understanding and his refusal to pass judgment. But his language elsewhere leaves no doubt as to what his judgment is. While it is all very well for Marlow to suggest that those who deny the principles of civilization in themselves and those who use those principles to destroy the lives of others both possess hearts of darkness, it is not correct to locate the source of the psychological heart of darkness in Africans. As Marlow was well aware, the Africans were more sinned against than sinning, for it was they who were being exploited and not the other way around.

Put another way the historical and the psychological levels of the metaphor work against each other. Historically Marlow would have us feel that the Africans are the innocent victims of the white man's heart of darkness; psychologically and metaphysically he would have us believe that they have the power to turn the white man's heart black. That is, Marlow equates the primitive with the evil and physical blackness of Africans with a spiritual darkness. The physical is confused with the metaphysical, the literal with the metaphorical. But one cannot have it both ways. Marlow's feeling that Kurtz became depraved by turning to "the forest, to the bush, towards the gleam of fires, the throb of drums, the drone of weird incantations" as another man may catch a cold from getting caught in a storm is just a kind of transference of moral responsibility. Africa and Africans are his scapegoat for the existence of the powers of darkness in the white man and through him the heart of darkness which was first associated with the West gets reassociated with Africa.

Specifically Marlow believes Kurtz to have "taken a high seat amongst the devils of the land" because of his participation in certain tribal ceremonies which seem to have involved human sacrifice, cannibalism, and head-hunting. Marlow, however, refuses to become enlightened about the significance of these customs, remaining transfixed by the surface horror they generate for the European. He calls them "unspeakable," says on one occasion, "I don't want to know anything of the ceremonies used when approaching Mr. Kurtz," and believes as an article of faith that Kurtz will be "utterly lost" if he participates in a certain ceremony. His refusal to try to understand the significance of the rites of the Africans stems from his conviction that what he will be told will support his feeling that they are abominations. But by believing that these actual rites, the customs of the same people whom the Belgians were exploiting, are exercises in evil and that knowledge of them should be suppressed, Marlow is, in effect, a member of that colonialistic front for which Kurtz wrote, the International Society for the Suppression of Savage Customs. And as long as he refuses to understand their true significance, as long as he finds them to be a living example of the depths to which man can sink, as long as he believes they should be suppressed, then he has cried, along with every colonizer before and since, "Exterminate all the brutes."

Thus Marlow's sympathy for the oppressed blacks is only superficial. He feels sorry for them when he sees them dying, but when he sees them healthy, practising their customs, he feels nothing but abhorrence and loathing, like a good colonizer to whom such a feeling offers a perfect rationalization for his policies. If blacks are evil then they must be conquered and put under white man's rule for their own good.[3] Marlow is trying to have it both ways, anti-colonialistic and anti-depravity, but as long as he associates the life of depravity with the life of blacks then he can hardly be called anti-colonial. He may sympathize with the plight of blacks, he may be disgusted by the effects of economic colonialism, but because he has no desire to understand or appreciate people of any culture other than his own, he is not emancipated from the mentality of a colonizer.

After Marlow lands on the coast he walks into a shady grove where he sees black men dying. He is appalled by the sight, and the language he uses to recount the experience indicates his horror:

3. This was the excuse given for enslaving Africans by a fifteenth century Portuguese writer. See Katherine George, "The Civilized West Looks at Primitive Africa," in Ashley Montagu, ed., *The Concept of the Primitive* (New York: Free Press, 1968), p. 181.

They were dying slowly—it was very clear. They were not enemies,
they were not criminals, they were nothing earthly now, nothing
but black shadows of disease and starvation lying confusedly in the
greenish gloom. Brought from all the recesses of the coast in all the
legality of time contracts, lost in uncongenial surroundings, fed on
unfamiliar food, they sickened, became inefficient, and were then
allowed to crawl away and rest.

The slow ponderousness of the sentences engraves on the mind the terrible sight of people who have been stripped of their humanity by colonialism. His use of the phrase "became inefficient," however, raises a
doubt as to the orientation of his sympathies. Earlier when Marlow was
talking about the Roman colonization of Britain he had said that whereas
the Romans could not help but succumb to "the savagery, the utter
savagery . . . all that mysterious life of the wilderness that stirs in the
forest, in the jungles, in the hearts of wild men," the Englishman would
not succumb, because he possessed the great virtue of "efficiency." If
the comment about the Romans is used as a gloss on the description of
the "inefficient" blacks then it would seem that they are morally and
physically inferior to those who can remain efficient in spite of the jungle. In *Heart of Darkness*, the most efficient people are colonizers like
the Manager of the Central Station and the Accountant at the Outer
Station.

Marlow proceeds in his description of the grove of death by focussing
on one young man: "The man seemed young—almost a boy—but you
know with them it's hard to tell." At one stroke, through the use of the
word "them," he dissociates himself from the people whose tragedy is
unfolding in front of his eyes. The use of the word "them" is significant
as well if we recall its use in *Lord Jim*, which dates from the same period
as *Heart of Darkness*. In *Lord Jim*, Marlow asks over and over again if
Jim was "one of us," meaning the morally upright and honest people of
the world, or "one of them," meaning the corrupt, dishonest, and cow-
ardly people of the world. If we assume that the Marlow of *Heart of
Darkness* is using the pronoun "them" in the same way he uses it in
Lord Jim, then we can only conclude that he finds blacks to be morally
inferior to himself and his friends, the "us" of the story.

Marlow travels upstream with a crew of cannibals. His attitude toward
their cannibalism reveals his condescension, fear, ignorance, and contempt. He says that they are "fine fellows," but immediately qualifies
this observation by adding, "in their place." He says he admires them
because they do not eat human flesh on board the ship, but adds that
this restraint surprised him‘ "these chaps . . . had no earthly reason for
any kind of scruple. Restraint! I would just soon have expected restraint
from a hyena prowling amongst the corpses of a battlefield." Thus while
he admits they possess restraint he cannot figure out why. The reason,
of course, is because he never completely grants them human status: at
best they are a species of superior hyena. Marlow's ignorance here with

respect to the habits of cannibals in noteworthy. One might have condoned it in an ordinary sailor, but Buddha-like Marlow, we were promised, was different, open and responsive to the "changing immensity of life"; and what he should have realized, if he had really kept his eyes and mind open, was that cannibals do not eat human flesh out of greed or lust or even as a dietary staple, but to commemorate an important occasion connected with the well-being of their society.[4] That is, a society in which cannibalism has ritual significance cannot possibly be a symbol for a lawless and bestial one. All primitive ritual, no matter how shocking it may appear to an outsider, is, in the words of Johan Huizinga, "sacred play . . . fecund of cosmic insight and social development."[5] The anthropologist Stanley Diamond is even more explicit: "Even ritualized cannibalism . . . recognizes and directly confronts the concrete humanity of the subject."[6]

As Marlow talks about the cannibals, prejudice and fear get woven into his narrative. Here is his report of the conversation he had with his cannibal headman about the tribesmen on the shore:

> "Aha!" I said, just for good fellowship's sake. "Catch 'im," he snapped with a bloodshot widening of his eyes and a flash of sharp teeth—"catch 'im. Give 'im to us." "To you, eh?" I asked; "what would you do with them?" "Eat 'im!" he said curtly, and leaning his elbow on the rail looked out into the fog in a dignified and profoundly pensive attitude.

Again if Marlow had been the kind of person who noticed things he would have seen that cannibals do not eat human flesh so casually and kill so indiscriminately—unfairly and inhumanely, from the cannibal's point of view—by the powerful rifles the white men on board Marlow's ship would have used. The idea, rather, as anthropologists tell us, is to kill the opponent in such a way that it proves the prowess of the one who does the killing and gives the other person a chance to defend himself and prove his manliness as well, because there is no point in eating a man unless his strength, courage, and heroism will pass into the person who killed him. Therefore hand-to-hand combat without any weapon at all is generally regarded as the noblest and most honorable form of combat.[7]

On the trip upstream Marlow catches glimpses of villages in which ceremonial rites are being performed. His reaction indicates how closed he is to a non-English experience, and how superior he feels to the people who are involved in these rites:

4. See, for example, Stanley Diamond, "The Search for the Primitive," in Montagu, pp. 134–35; George, p. 185. On what Conrad's imagination made of cannibalism, see Jerome Zuckerman, "The Motif of Cannibalism in The Secret Agent," Texas Studies in Literature and Language, 10 (1968), 295–99; and Albert C. Yoder, "Oral Artistry in Conrad's Heart of Darkness: A Study in Oral Aggression," Conradiana, 2 (1969–70), 65–78.

5. Johan Huizinga, Homo Ludens: A Study of the Play-Element in Culture (Boston: Beacon, 1955), p. 24, quoted in Diamond, p. 134.

6. Diamond, p. 134.

7. Diamond, p. 135.

We were cut off from the comprehension of our surroundings; we glided past like phantoms, wondering and secretly appalled, as sane men would be before an enthusiastic outbreak in a madhouse. . . . It was unearthly and the men were. . . . No they were not inhuman. Well, you know that was the worst of it—this suspicion of their not being inhuman. It would come slowly to one. They howled and leaped, and spun, and made horrid faces, but what thrilled you was just the thought of their humanity—like yours—the thought of your remote kinship with this wild and passionate uproar. Ugly. Yes, it was ugly enough, but if you were man enough you would admit to yourself that there was in you just the faintest trace of a response to the terrible frankness of that noise, a dim suspicion of there being a meaning in it which you—you so remote from the night of first ages—could comprehend.

Note how Marlow qualifies his assertions. The men are human, but they are madmen performing mad rites; a little further on in the text these mad rites will degenerate into a "fiendish row." A kinship does exist between the men on the shore and the men on the boat, but it is ugly because the black men personify in themselves and reawaken in the whites through their practices the destructive powers of the Unconscious. But there is no indication that apart from what Marlow says these rites are being performed so as to invoke the dark powers. Therefore if Marlow is feeling the call of the wild in these ceremonies it is because he has invested them with it in the first place. It is as if Marlow, not being able to cope with his guilt feelings about possessing unsocial drives and urges, transfers them to a perfectly innocent, though apparently fearsome, group of people, and labels them as devotees of the powers of darkness because (1) that way he can get out of thinking that they and he are both human, (2) that way he can blame somebody else for his own problems, and (3) the connection between physical blackness and psychical darkness is only too easy to make and believe in.

Marlow goes on to say that if the wild rites of the villagers appeal to us than that appeal must be quenched by what he refers to as "inborn strength," though earlier he had offered devotion to duty, efficiency, and a sense of responsibility as equally acceptable antidotes. In this particular case Marlow resists the temptation to go ashore by devoting himself to his job:

You wonder I didn't go ashore for a howl and a dance? Well, no— I didn't. Fine sentiments, you say? Fine sentiments be hanged! I had no time. I had to mess about with white-lead and strips of woollen blanket helping to put bandages on those leaky steam-pipes— I tell you. I had to watch the steering and circumvent those snags and get the tin-pot along by hook or by crook.

By turning to work and responsibility and duty, by turning to white-lead and strips of woolen blanket, however, Marlow is turning to some symbols and beliefs of Western civilization whose political, cultural, and economic necessities brought colonialism into being.

This is damning enough, but it becomes ironic when we realize that Marlow, for all his superior attitudes, is not at all superior to the blacks. Like a tribesman he possesses talismans to ward off evil, only he calls them devotion to duty, efficiency, and a sense of responsibility. Incidentally the physical manifestation of his devotion to his job, the strips of woolen blanket hastily tied to leaky steam-pipes, looks perilously similar to his "very second-rate" helmsman's impromptu magic "charm, made of rags, tied to his arm."

Before Marlow reaches Kurtz he comes across that enigmatic figure, the harlequin Russian sailor. Marlow scorns him because he is simple and has swallowed everything that Kurtz told him unquestioningly, from the nobility of life to the fact that the heads on the poles surrounding Kurtz's house belonged to rebels. It seems at first sight that Marlow's disbelief in this story is a blow against colonialism, but as the heads were taken in an inter-tribal war about which Marlow wants to know nothing, they may very well have belonged to rebels. There is no reason for Marlow to feel superior to the Russian: in this matter, the latter may know more than him. Certainly his attitude toward the tribesmen is far more intelligent than Marlow's: "They are simple people," he says, and leaves it at that. Now the Russian is merely a white version of those other children of nature in *Heart of Darkness*, the black tribesmen, and Marlow's condescending attitude toward him shows up the weakness of his general attitude toward the blacks: it is not justified by the facts of the case. I suggest further that the only reason Marlow doesn't associate the Russian too with the powers of darkness is because he has a white skin, for as the Russian himself recognizes, he belongs to Africa and its people.

Marlow reaches Kurtz and sides with him as the lesser of two evils because Kurtz recognizes his own depravity on his deathbed. Of what, however, did that depravity consist? According to Marlow Kurtz's depravity consisted of a terrible egotism which made him seek gratification for various lusts in "unlawful" ways. These "unlawful" ways, however, seem to be nothing more than Kurtz's adoption of the customs of an African tribe. So what Marlow implies is that Kurtz's tribalization is a symbol of his depravity. From the little we see of Kurtz's followers, though, there is nothing to suggest that they are depraved. Rather they appear as protective, simple and unselfconscious—far better specimens of humanity than the white people of *Heart of Darkness*.

Kurtz's tribalization, therefore, can be seen as a rejection of the materialism of the West in favor of a simpler and more honest way of life. Certainly from the point of view of the African tribesman Kurtz has done nothing abominable in recognizing the virtues of his way of life. And from the point of view of some modern anthropologists, who believe that only by becoming a part of another culture can one understand and appreciate it, Kurtz is an enlightened individual, far more advanced than his contemporaries in his thinking about primitive societies.

The problem with Kurtz, which Marlow doesn't realize, is not that Kurtz went native, but that he did not go native enough, for Kurtz perverted the customs of the tribe, making them a means to a deplorable end—namely, keeping the ivory flowing and colonialism a profitable venture for his employers—and he never assumed the positive virtues of the tribe.[8] Thus the adoption of the tribal way of life is the wrong symbol for Kurtz's depravity. Marlow picks it because he does not differentiate between tribal customs and evil practices.

Kurtz's last words are "The horror! The horror!" and for Marlow the horror being referred to is the blackness of Kurtz's soul. But there is more to this blackness than meets Marlow's eye. I have just argued that Kurtz's depravity consisted not in giving in too much to the tribal way of life but in not giving in enough. If that is the case I would suggest that contrary to Marlow's implication the "horror" refers first to what Kurtz has done to the blacks and only secondarily to what he has done to himself, since the latter is only the effect, and not the cause of the former. Consequently the full application of Kurtz's last words would not only be to himself but also to men like Marlow who seemed to hate colonialism but really lived by its values and associated the practices of the blacks with the road to perdition.

The other famous line in the story, "Exterminate all the brutes!" is capable of a similar extended interpretation. Marlow takes the word "brutes" to refer to the Africans and interprets the fact that the sentence comes at the end of a document written to suggest a better way of approaching the less developed as meaning that Kurtz became more savage than the so-called savages. But Marlow's interpretation is tinged by a colonialistic bias. Given that Kurtz became one with an African tribe and learned to understand the meaning of their customs, his words may be taken to mean that the only way Africa could develop would be if the real brutes or savages, the colonizers, were removed. What Kurtz developed in the jungle, therefore, was not an "unlawful soul," but historical foresight.

To what extent, though, are Marlow's attitudes Conrad's? If it can be established that Conrad had different attitudes from Marlow on colonialism and evil, then *Heart of Darkness* would be Conrad's *Modest Proposal*, in that the author would be arguing something different from what his persona was preaching. Furthermore by showing Marlow's terms as limited, Conrad would be making the larger point that those who see others as less than human are themselves dehumanized by their own vision. On the other hand if Conrad shares Marlow's prejudices then

8. For a similar interpretation see Stephen A. Reid, "The 'Unspeakable Rites' in *Heart of Darkness*," in Marvin Mudrick, ed., *Conrad: A Collection of* *Critical Essays* (Englewood Cliffs: Prentice-Hall, 1966), pp. 52–54.

278 FRANCES B. SINGH

Heart of Darkness was written, consciously or unconsciously, from a colonialistic point of view.

It is possible that on two points Conrad dissociated himself from Marlow, namely his attitude to work and his attitude toward the Intended. Through Kurtz Conrad depicted the "total bankruptcy of the work ethic [for] it is consistently his [i.e. Kurtz's] industriousness and indefatigability that are emphasized."[9] This would seem to indicate that Conrad realized that Marlow's belief in the all-saving power of work was a limited one. With regard to the Intended, critics have noted that she is really "the horror," but because Marlow has an idealized conception of women, he is not able to see the truth.[1]

At first glance it also looks as if the narrator who frames Marlow's story represents a more comprehensive point of view than Marlow, for his role is to interpret the meaning of the tale and give it a universal significance. However, the meaning he draws from it is ultimately no different from Marlow's. At the beginning of *Heart of Darkness*, he is an upholder of English colonialism, calling the English "bearers of a spark from the sacred fire." At the end he realizes that the Thames leads "into the heart of an immense darkness," meaning that English colonizers are as evil as any other, and that those who set forth on colonialistic enterprises, no matter how nobly they were conceived, lose themselves in the process. Thus it would seem that the narrator, unlike Marlow, is a true critic of colonialism. But insofar as his strictures are based on the experiences of men like Kurtz then they just boil down to this: that inside every white man there is a black man, who is evil, and that to become, as Kurtz literally did, the black man, constitutes depravity.

On evil, Marlow reflects Conrad's attitude. In 1912 Conrad wrote of Dostoyevsky's *The Brothers Karamazov:* "It sounds to me like some fierce mouthings from prehistoric ages."[2] The statement shows that Conrad associated the primitive ("prehistoric ages") with the bestial ("mouthings"). As I have discussed earlier Marlow, too, makes this association between the primitive and the bestial when he talks about his cannibal crew; it is implied again when he describes the speech of the tribesmen as "amazing words that resembled no sounds of human language."

On colonialism too Marlow projects Conrad's ideas. In 1899 Conrad wrote about the Boer War in a letter to a cousin: "That they—the Boers—are struggling in good faith for their independence cannot be doubted; but it is also a fact that they have no idea of liberty, which can only be found under the English flag all over the world."[3] That is, Conrad sympathized with the Boers' struggle for independence, but he also believed that they were not capable of achieving much on their own. This ambiv-

9. Avrom Fleishman, *Conrad's Politics: Community and Anarchy in the Fiction of Joseph Conrad* (Baltimore: Johns Hopkins, 1967), p. 106.
1. See, for example, Gerald B. Kauvar, "Marlow as Liar," *Studies in Short Fiction*, 5 (1968), 290–92; Addison C. Bross, "The Unextinguishable Light of Belief: Conrad's Attitude Toward Women,"
Conradiana, 2 (1969–70), 39–46; James Ellis, "Kurtz's Voice: The Intended as 'The Horror!'" *English Literature in Transition*, 19 (1976), 105–10; Stark, pp. 535–55.
2. Baines, p. 360.
3. Baines, p. 238.

alent attitude toward the Boers is reflected in Marlow's attitude toward the blacks. He sympathizes with their plight when he stumbles into the grove of death, but finds nothing of value in their culture of "unspeakable rites," "satanic" litanies and "fiendish" rows.

Ambivalent, in fact, is probably the most accurate way to sum up Conrad's attitude toward colonialism. In 1899 he wrote both that "England alone sends out men . . . with . . . a transparent sincerity of feeling" and that "intentions will, no doubt count for something [i.e. when colonizing nations have to face the Day of Judgment], though, of course, every nation's conquests are paved with good intentions.[4] He could talk ironically of Kipling's accounts in a newspaper which "spoke much of the rights and duties of civilization, of the sacredness of the civilizing work, and extolled the merits of those who went about bringing light and faith and commerce to the dark places of the earth,"[5] but he could also write in a different key, as in his letter to *Blackwood's Magazine*: "The title I am thinking of is '*The Heart of Darkness*' but the narrative is not gloomy. The criminality of inefficiency and pure selfishness when tackling the civilizing work in Africa is a justifiable idea."[6] But if a work is to be called truly anti-colonial then such ambivalence is not permissible, for it compromises the position. The compromises that Marlow makes, as when he fights off identification with the blacks or when he tells lies about Kurtz to prevent the civilized Western world from collapsing,[7] stem from Conrad's own inability to face unflinchingly the nature of colonialism.

In 1906 Conrad wrote an essay entitled "The Weight of the Burden" in which he makes colonialism into a religion, calling it a "sacred fire."[8] In *Heart of Darkness*, Marlow also uses the rhetoric of religion to justify colonialism: "What redeems it is the idea only. An idea at the back of it, not a sentimental pretence but an idea; and an unselfish belief in the idea—something you can set up and bow down before, and offer a sacrifice to. . . ." Marlow, it is true, makes a distinction between the right type of worship, as exemplified in this quotation, and the wrong type, which is practiced by the Belgian colonizers: "They wandered here and there with their absurd long staves in their hands like a lot of faithless pilgrims bewitched inside a rotten fence. The word 'ivory' rang in the air, was whispered, was sighed. You would think they were praying to it." This distinction is absent in the remark of Conrad. But the presence of the distinction does not reduce the significance of the fact that Marlow, like Conrad, sees colonialism in religious terms which can legitimize it.

What can we conclude on the basis of this evidence? It seems to me that although Conrad was to some extent aware of some of the limitations of Marlow's attitudes and pointed them up in the story, he was not

4. Quoted by Fleishman, p. 98; quoted by Hay, p. 128.
5. Hay, p. 119.
6. Hay, p. 120.
7. Hay, pp. 135–36.
8. Quoted by Robert F. Lee, *Conrad's Colonialism* (The Hague: Mouton, 1969), p. 19.

sensitive to all of them. In fact he transferred the most important ones to Marlow, who therefore becomes his mouthpiece in the story for them.

Nevertheless although I have argued in this essay that Marlow's ethnocentricity leads him to side with the colonizers against the Africans and that this approach is shared by Conrad as well, I do not wish to suggest that Conrad intended *Heart of Darkness* as a vindication of colonialistic policies or that the story should be removed from the canon of works indicting colonialism. Rather my aim has been to illuminate the problem he ran into when he attempted to indict colonialism. My argument has been based on modern views of anthropology according to which the term primitive describes a type of communal structure and does not refer "historically [to] an inchoate time of cultural origins or psychiatrically [to] the period when supposed 'primary processes' were directly expressed."[9]

However Conrad was a man of his times, and as such, reflected the current anthropological position which held that primitive people were morally inferior to civilized ones. At the time he was writing *Heart of Darkness* he was reading the anthropologist Eduard von Hartmann, who was one of the more enlightened anthropologists of the day because he recognized the important role the unconscious plays in human affairs. He was also ahead of his times in that he believed that not all primitive societies were inferior to civilized ones. However he did not believe that the Africans were among the primitive elect; for him they were an inferior and doomed people.[1] Apparently Conrad, through Marlow, conflated Hartmann's theory of the unconscious with his belief about Africans, so as to intensify the psychological theme of the story. The colonialistic bias of *Heart of Darkness* is a by-product of this conflation. Insofar as it is a by-product rather than the intended one of the story, it reveals the limitations of Conrad's notions rather than the existence of a reactionary and racist streak in him. Nevertheless for the modern reader his limitations reduce the significance of his achievement as a psychologist and a moralist, ironically turning a story that was meant to be a clear-cut attack on a vicious system into a partial apology for it, and a study of the depths in all men into an excuse for their existence.

C. P. SARVAN

Racism and the *Heart of Darkness* †

As I have shown elsewhere,[1] Conrad's setting, themes, and his triumph in writing major literature in his third language, have won him a special

9. Diamond, p. 109.
1. See John E. Saveson, "Conrad's View of Primitive Peoples in *Lord Jim* and *Heart of Darkness*," *Modern Fiction Studies*, 16 (1970), 174–75.

† From *The International Fiction Review* 7(1980): 6–10. Reprinted by permission.
1. "Under African Eyes," *Conradiana*, 8 (1976), 233–39.

admiration in the non-European world. "The African writer and Joseph Conrad share the same world and that is why Conrad's world is so familiar. Both have lived in a world dominated by capitalism, imperialism, colonialism." [2] But African readers are also checked by, and disconcerted at, works such as *The Nigger of the "Narcissus"* and *Heart of Darkness*. The case against the latter was most strongly made by Chinua Achebe in the course of a lecture titled "An Image of Africa," delivered at the University of Massachusetts on the 18th of February 1975. [3] He argued that Conrad sets up Africa "as a foil to Europe, a place of negations . . . in comparison with which Europe's own state of spiritual grace will be manifest." Africa is "the other world," "the antithesis of Europe and therefore of civilization, a place where man's vaunted intelligence and refinement are finally mocked by triumphant bestiality." Achebe commented on Conrad's comparison of the Congo and the Thames, and also alleged that the contrast made between the two women who loved Kurtz one African, the other European, is highly prejudiced. Any sympathy expressed for the sufferings of the black African under colonialism, argued Achebe is a sympathy born of a kind of liberalism which whilst acknowledging distant kinship, repudiates equality. Conrad, continued Achebe, is a "racist"—and great art can only be "on the side of man's deliverance and not his enslavement; for the brotherhood and unity of all mankind and not for the doctrines of Hitler's master races or Conrad's 'rudimentary souls.' " Achebe concluded his attack on *Heart of Darkness* by describing it as "a book which parades in the most vulgar fashion prejudices and insults from which a section of mankind has suffered untold agonies and atrocities in the past and continues to do so in many ways and many places today. I am talking about a story in which the very humanity of black people is called in question. It seems to me totally inconceivable that great art or even good art could possibly reside in such unwholesome surroundings."

I shall in the following pages attempt to narrowly limit myself to an examination of the charge of racism brought against Conrad's *Heart of Darkness*. Let us begin with the fictional Marlow whose story was once heard and is now related by a fictional narrator. "It might be contended . . . that the attitude to the African. . . . is not Conrad's but that of his fictional narrator, Marlow. . . . [But] Marlow seems to me to enjoy Conrad's complete confidence." Marlow's portrait is drawn with quiet irony and, at times, a mocking humor which denotes "distance" between

2. Ngugi Wa Thiong'o, "Writers in Politics," *Busara*, 8, No. 1 (1976), 5. Previously known as James Ngugi, he is the author of four novels (*Weep Not, Child*, 1964; *The River Between*, 1965; *A Grain of Wheat*, 1967; *Petals of Blood*, 1977), a play (*The Black hermit*, 1968) and a collection of essays (*Homecoming*, 1972).
3. *The Chancellor's Lecture Series: 1974–75*, University of Massachusetts at Amherst, pp. 31–43. Chancellor Bromery in introducing Achebe said *inter alia*, "The Scottish Arts Council has this year awarded him their second annual Neil Gunn International Fellowship. The Modern Language Association of America has voted Professor Achebe an honourary fellowship in their Association. . . . His first novel, *Things Fall Apart*, brought him to world-wide attention and acclaim. . . . His works have now been translated into twenty languages and his literary reputation is secure" (p. 29). I am grateful to Professor Achebe for sending me a copy of his lecture.

creator and character. For example, he is described as resembling an idol and he sits like a European Buddha without the lotus. Marlow claims to be deeply, almost pathologically averse to telling lies but we find that he prevaricates at least twice within this tale. He condemns the Roman conquest and contrasts it with the "superior" European colonialism:

> What saves us is efficiency—the devotion to efficiency. But these chaps were not much account really. They were no colonists, their administration was merely a squeeze. . . . They were conquerors, and for that you only want brute force—nothing to boast of, when you have it, since your strength is just an accident arising from the weakness of others. They grabbed what they could. . . . It was just robbery with violence, aggravated murder on a great scale. . . . The conquest of the earth, which mostly means the taking it away from those who have a different complexion or slightly flatter noses than ourselves, is not a pretty thing when you look into it too much. What redeems it is the idea only. An idea at the back of it, not a sentimental pretence but an idea; and an unselfish belief in the idea. . . .

A long quotation but necessary in that it again separates author from character. Significantly, this "idea" is presented in ambiguous "pagan" terms as "something you can set up, and bow down before, and offer a sacrifice to." What is more, the rest of the story shows that the European colonial conquest, contrary to Marlow's claims, was much worse than that of the Romans. One remembers that harrowing description of men waiting to die: "Black shapes crouched, lay, sat between the trees, leaning against the trunks, clinging to the earth, half coming out . . . in all the attitudes of pain, abandonment, and despair. . . . They were not enemies, they were not criminals. . . ." Immediately after this description, Marlow meets the elegant, perfumed, "hairdresser's dummy" and confesses that he "respected his collars," the collars of a man who comes out "to get a breath of fresh air," indifferent to the despair and death by which he is surrounded. It may be argued that Marlow is here speaking with irony and the description "hairdresser's dummy" may appear to make Marlow's attitude to the dummy as clear and unequivocal. But Marlow continues with unmistakable admiration that "in the great demoralisation of the land he kept up his appearance. That's backbone." He kept up *appearances*, and that points to one of the important thematic significances of this work, namely, the discrepancy between appearance and reality; between assumption and fact; between illusion and truth. Thus it is not correct to say that Marlow has Conrad's complete confidence, and even more incorrect to say that Conrad believed Europe to be in a state of grace. The glorious sailors proudly cited by Marlow were pirates and plunderers. This ironic distance between Marlow and Conrad should not be overlooked though the narrative method makes it all too easy. Nor can Conrad's very forceful criticisms of colonialism be lightly passed over as weak liberalism. What ships unload in

Africa are soldiers and customhouse clerks: the one to conquer and the other to administer and efficiently exploit. The cannon pounds a continent and "the merry dance of death and trade goes on." This "rapacious and pitiless folly" attempts to pass itself off as philanthropy, and to hypocritically hide its true nature under words such as enemies, criminals, and rebels. The counterparts of enemies, criminals, and rebels are the emissaries of light, such as Kurtz!

As a critic has pointed out, "Africa *per se* is not the theme of *Heart of Darkness*, but is used as a locale symbol for the very core of an 'accursed inheritance'."[4] At the risk of oversimplification, the story may be seen as an allegory, the journey ending with the sombre realization of the darkness of man's heart. But it may prove emotionally difficult for some to follow the allegory when it is thought that Conrad, casting about for an external parallel, for a physical setting to match the inner darkness, chose Africa. An argument may be constructed as follows: to the Romans, the people of Britain were barbarians; now when the Europeans come to Africa, the Africans in comparison seem savage, but deep down in the European breast there still lurks the old savagery. "It is not the differentness that worries Conrad but the lurking hint of kinship, of common ancestry . . . if [the Thames] were to visit its primoridal relative, the Congo, it would run the terrible risk of hearing grotesque, suggestive echoes of its own forgotten darkness, and falling victim to an avenging recrudescence of the mindless frenzy of the first beginnings." When the Romans looked down upon the people of Britain, and the Europeans upon "natives," it was because they felt they had achieved a much higher civilization than the people they were confronting and conquering. The contempt was not on grounds of race itself, and Conrad suggests that Europe's claim to be civilized and therefore superior, needs earnest reexamination. The reference in *Heart of Darkness* is not to a place (Africa), but to the condition of European man; not to a black people, but to colonialism. The crucial question is whether European "barbarism" is merely a thing of the historical past. Surely the contrast between savage African and "civilized" European, in the light of that greedy and inhuman colonialism, is shown to be "appearance" rather than reality. The emphasis, the present writer would suggest, is on continuity, on persistence through time and peoples, and therefore on the fundamental oneness of man and his nature. If a judgment has to be made, then uncomplicated "savagery" is better than the "subtle horrors" manifested by almost all the Europeans Marlow met on that ironic voyage of discovery. When Marlow speaks of the African in European service as one of the "reclaimed," it is grim irony for he has been reclaimed to a worse state of barbarism. Left to itself, Africa has a "greatness" that went "home to one's very heart." As Marlow begins his story, the light changes as though "stricken to death by the touch of that gloom brooding over a crowd of men": yet the gloom is very much over the Thames as well.

4. Robert Lee, *Conrad's Colonialism* (The Hague: Mouton, 1969), p. 49.

The Thames as "a waterway leading to the uttermost ends of the earth" is connected with and therefore a part of those uttermost ends. The river signifies what is abiding in nature, in man, and in the nature of man, even as "the sea is always the same" and foreign shores and foreign faces are veiled not by mystery but by ignorance.

The immaculately dressed, fastidious, and sensitive hairdresser's dummy, a representative of civilized Europe and a part of the colonial machinery, is totally insensitive to the suffering he helps to cause and by which he is surrounded. (His extreme cleanliness is perhaps to be seen as compulsive, an attempt to keep clean in the midst of that moral dirt.) Even in the case of Kurtz, one must remember that all Europe had "contributed" to his making. As for pagan rites and savage dances, the Europeans with "imbecile rapacity" were "praying" to ivory, that is, to materialism, and one red-haired man "positively danced," bloodthirsty at the thought that he and the others "must have made a glorious slaughter" of the Africans in the bush.[5] The alleged primitiveness of the boilerman only serves to show the similarity between his *appearance* and the *actions* of the "civilized."

Achebe also noted that Kurtz's African mistress is the "savage counterpart to the refined, European woman." But the European woman is pale and rather anemic whilst the former, to use Conrad's words, is gorgeous, proud, superb, magnificent, tragic, fierce, and filled with sorrow. She is an impressive figure and, importantly, her human feelings are not denied. The contrast, however, is not simply between these two, but between Kurtz's African mistress on the one hand, and Marlow's aunt and Kurtz's "Intended" on the other. The aunt glibly believes that he who goes to the Congo is "a lower sort of apostle": "She talked about 'weaning those ignorant millions from their horrid ways.' " The hairdresser's dummy, we recall, was first taken to be "a sort of vision." The same ignorance and the same illusions are found at the end, in Kurtz's Intended. After all, he was also one of those apostles. The darkness which is often mentioned refers not only to the darkness within man, to the mysterious and the unpredictable, but also to ignorance and illusions: it is significant that as Marlow talks with Kurtz's Intended, the "darkness deepened." The African woman faces the truth and endures the pain of her dereliction, whilst the illusions of the two European women are also the fond illusions of European society.

This is not to claim that Conrad was free of all prejudice, nor to deny that he has wholly resisted the temptation to use physical appearance and setting as indicators of nonphysical qualities.[6] Conrad reflects to

5. Compare Mark Twain, *More Tramps Abroad*, London, 1897, pp. 137–38: "There are many humorous things in the world; among them, the white man's notion that he is less savage than the other savages."

6. Compare Shiva Naipaul, "Zambia's Compromise with the West," *Spectator*, 11 June 1977, p. 11: "Now and then, in a clearing in the bush, there is the fleeting apparition of a village of mud huts. Women, squatting in the shade, look up expressionlessly from their labours; squads of naked children, shouting, arms flailing, come rushing over the beaten brown earth to wave. . . . The wilderness closes in again. . . . Nothing indicates that you have made any progress."

some degree the attitudes of his age, and his description of the fireman as a dog in a parody of breeches, is cruel. On the one hand, in terms of technological progress, the gap between London and the Congo was immense; on the other, though it is extreme to say that Conrad called into question the very humanity of the African, one's perspective and evaluation of this work need alteration.

In a conversation with me,[7] Ngugi Wa Thiong'o accepted some of Achebe's criticisms but felt he had overlooked the positive aspect, namely, Conrad's attack on colonialism. The skulls stuck on poles outside Kurtz's house, Wa Thiong'o said, was the most powerful indictment of colonialism. No African writer, he continued, had created so ironic, apt, and powerful an image: ironic when one considers that Kurtz and many others like him had come to "civilize" the non-European world; apt when one recalls what they really did. But Wa Thiong'o also observed that though Conrad (having experienced the evils of Czarist imperialism) castigates Belgian atrocities, he is much milder in his criticisms of British imperialism. This ambivalence, concluded Professor Wa Thiong'o, compromised Conrad's otherwise admirable stand. Leonard Kibera (Kenyan novelist, short story writer, critic, and teacher) wrote informally to me as follows: "I study *Heart of Darkness* as an examination of the West itself and not as a comment on Africa. Many Africans do get turned off Conrad because they feel he used the third world so totally as a background against which he examined Western values and conduct that the people in Africa and Asia are no more than caricatures. I do not object to this and appreciate the fact that in Conrad there is not that Joyce Cary, Graham Greene pretension of understanding the third world."[8] Nadine Gordimer writing on another famous European in Africa states that Livingstone, reassessed, emerges as a fallible human being.[9] Conrad too was not entirely immune to the infection of the beliefs and attitudes of his age, but he was ahead of most in trying to break free.

MIKE WILMINGTON

Worth the Wait: *Apocalypse Now* †

Brando's face. The face of Colonel Kurtz in *Apocalypse Now*. The face that looks out at you from its sheltering cocoon of darkness, its envelope of night. It's a lumpy face: drawn and yellow and tallowy, and there's something horrible in the eyes. . . . And the hands move slowly, caressingly along the bald scalp, as water drips down from the bowl that the hands have held with a communicant's reverence. . . . And all around is the gathering darkness, the jungle cries, the sounds of the wind crac-

7. University of Nairobi, 19 July 1977.
8. Letter dated 7 April 1977.
9. *Contrast* 30(1973): 82.

† From *Madison Press Connection*, October 19, 1979. Reprinted by permission of the author.

kling the fronds, mist steaming up from the river. There is no expression on that face, none at all. It's as blank as stone, as the green idol that stands outside, where weeds crack and writhe through the stairways, where corpses are swaying in the breeze, skulls, entrails, bones, all the remnants of the night. Disease and smoke and perspiration seep out of the walls. And that face simply stares at you, and it's like eyes gazing out from a pool of ash. . . .

The face of Death. Of the Apocalypse.

There's been so much controversy about *Apocalypse Now* that I better situate myself on the film right now. I think it's a staggering movie, an overwhelming, overpowering experience—yet both times when I walked out of it, I had this strange, empty, bereaved feeling. It wasn't a feeling that had any connection with the Vietnam War itself, because, in fact, the movie operates less as a document about the war than as a phantasmagoria, a surreal reflection on things past. When Coppola started *Apocalypse Now* over four years ago, he said he wanted it to be like one of Ken Russell's movies, and he selected Vittorio Storaro, Bernardo Bertolucci's regular cameraman, to get a dreamlike floating quality out of the visuals.

At the center of *Apocalypse Now*, symbolized by Kurtz's face, shining in the shadows, there's a certain moral confusion, an irresolute wavering, a mistiness, a philosophical intangibility. I'm not so sure this is bad. The first two hours of the movie are so spectacular, so concrete, that this odd, muted ending (and Coppola remarked in *Rolling Stone* that he wanted the ending to be even more undefined) seems somehow appropriate. In *Apocalypse Now*, after all, we are traveling, just as Conrad did, to the lower region of the soul—unexplored territory. It might have been obscene to be more sure about what those regions concealed.

As almost everyone knows by now, *Apocalypse Now*, is perhaps the great "obsessional" movie project of our time. Coppola embarked on the film more than four years ago, after buying the original script from John Milius, and originally scheduling George Lucas to direct it. He took it over himself in the wake of his quantum jump in prestige after *The Conversation* took the Grand Prize at Cannes and both *Godfather* movies won Oscars. And since then, it seemed, he's been going slowly out of his mind. Some weird psychodrama kept unfolding almost daily in the pages of *Variety* and the other trade journals, all of it revolving around the volcano that the *Apocalypse* project had become. Actors were hired, actors were fired. A stock company was set up and dissolved. Typhoons delayed the production. The lead actor, Martin Sheen, suffered both a nervous breakdown and a heart attack. Forty-five million dollars were slowly consumed. Brando proved as mysterious, as intransigent as ever. The shooting, the editing, the mixing dragged on interminably. What was the name of the film? *Apocalypse Now?* Or, *Apocalypse Whenever?*

When *Apocalypse Now* finally surfaced in an incomplete version and shared another Cannes Grand Prize with the Volker Schloendorff adaptation of *The Tin Drum,* a substantial number of writers and reporters had consigned Coppola to the insane asylum. And, indeed, in his brief appearance in last spring's Oscar Show (to present the "Best Director" award to Michael Cimino for *The Deer Hunter*) he seemed to be, well, babbling. This hostility has carried over into more than a few reviews of the movie—reviews which attack Coppola's sanity and responsibility, the movie's budget, accuracy, morality and politics.

Granted, *Apocalypse Now* became Coppola's obsession. (At one point he told George Lucas and John Milius that they were next in line to take over the movie if he died on location.) Granted, it is pretentious and wildly ambitious. Granted, it is probably not as great a work of art as Conrad's *Heart of Darkness.* Granted, it is not a true picture of Vietnam. But it is a staggering achievement.

Purely on the level of cinematography and action direction, it takes your breath away. Every sequence, every minute, every frame churns with violence and beauty. When Kilgore's helicopters come sweeping in over the waves in an early sequence, Wagner's "Ride of the Valkyries" pouring like a mad dirge from the loudspeakers, death and destruction raining down on the Vietcong-held villagers while the combat pilots crack jokes, and three of them prepare to catch the pipeline and go surfing in the center of this inferno, in the middle of the firebombing— it's such an insanely appropriate nightmare, such a deadly, crystal-clear metaphor for the entire adventure of warfare (war as it seems to impressionable kids) that it explodes inside you on several levels. Robert Duvall as Kilgore—stripping off his jacket and scarf, and preparing to plunge into the waves, ignoring the explosions around him, and grinning happily over the distant smell of napalm as it incinerates a forest (and its inhabitants)—is the macho adventurer gone wild, a crazed Leatherstocking.

Insanity is probably a metaphor for the entire film. Death, destruction, sex—everything winds out on this grand lunatic scale. And watching it all is the ultimate passive, tormented, almost "hipster" observer: Willard, played by Martin Sheen as the man tortuously following all the tracks toward the center of the cavern—toward the "Termination, with extreme prejudice" of the mad Green Beret, Kurtz, toward the mystery at the End of the River, toward what may, in fact, be himself. (Coppola has confirmed that the meaning of the copy of Frazer's *The Golden Bough* in Kurtz's headquarters is the legend of the Fisher King who dies and is replaced by his conquerer—in this case the Fisher King is Kurtz and his replacement, Willard.)

The USO show, the night-bombing, everything in the movie keeps plunging toward some crazy paroxysm, until, abruptly, the "heroes" shoot down an unarmed family in a sampan—shoot them down brutally, relentlessly, as if it were the final answer in a cold equation. And you know that the insanity is somehow endemic . . . not contained in Kurtz, not contained in Kilgore, not contained in Willard, or the U.S. Army, or the policymakers who have set this Engine of Destruction in motion.

But that the insanity is somehow universal, and that to gaze on it is somehow to gaze at The Truth. (Which is one reason, I suppose that the movie has been attacked philosophically. There is something deeply nihilistic at its center.)

I don't think *Apocalypse Now* should be approached as an analysis of the Vietnam conflict. Obviously, that's something it was never intended to be—not when John Milius, a political conservative and Vietnam hawk, originally wrote it, and not when Coppola, a political liberal and dove, began reshaping it. The "horror" of which Kurtz speaks at the end is not something which can be so easily categorized (and the movie twists in on itself at this point, like a collapsible labyrinth, since "The horror" is a direct quotation from *Heart of Darkness*, and since one of the poems Brando pores over intently is T. S. Eliot's "The Hollow Men," which has as its epigraph another direct quotation, "Mistah Kurtz—he dead"). It's not about anything that direct. It's a search—a search through the bloody holocaust that is our nightmare of Vietnam (rather than its reality), a search through all the myths and motifs of Western literature and movies, a search along a glistening river surrounded by shadows, a search toward death and dissolution.

Probably Coppola, articulate as he sometimes seems, could not explain what that search was meant to find. The goal of an obsession is never really clear, most of all to the obsessed. But what Coppola and his associates—Milius, Michael Herr, Storaro, Brando, Sheen, Robert Duvall, and all the others—managed to pull from those Philippine jungles and that series of withering catastrophes is so startling and fascinating and hypnotic that its flaws seem miniscule. The fate of the gambler, the man who takes the mad plunge, is to appear ridiculous. Coppola has certainly risked that—and much, much more—by fashioning this grandiose, scintillating nightmare. But, for me, his triumphs overmatch his catastrophes. *Apocalypse Now* is an infernally magnificent film—beautifully obsessive, beautifully mad.

ROBERT LaBRASCA

Two Visions of "The horror!" †

By the time *Apocalypse Now* was completed, it was little more than inspired by Joseph Conrad's novella *Heart of Darkness*. Conrad was never mentioned in the picture's credits, which is probably as it should be: Conrad would not likely have been flattered by the association—his themes having been deserted for a thinner, more "intellectual," less resonant vision. But it may be worthwhile to lay one against the other, not to

† From *Madison Press Connection*, November 17, 1979. Revised 1986. Reprinted by permission of the author. © Copyright 1986, Robert La Brasca.

measure *Apocalypse Now* as cinematic art (that's another matter entirely), but to get an idea what the vision really is, bearing in mind that one work is the product of a single consciousness in reflection, while the other required an army of creative minds, functionaries and drudges, along with $31 million of the world's resources.

Heart of Darkness was the work of a Pole (born Josef Konrad Nalecz Korzeniowski) writing in 1898 in his third language. He was an adventurer who had spent 20 years at sea before immersing himself in the literary profession. Somehow, all that wandering about the earth, his national displacement (he'd lived most of his teen years in Russian exile with his nationalist parents), and the sudden lurch—in his 30s—from plying the sea to furious writing give special weight to his work, add credence to the notion that he wrote down what his mind saw clearly, rather than what his prose could adequately decorate. This applies especially to *Heart of Darkness*, some eighty pages of slightly enhanced reminiscence of a journey Conrad had made eight years before up the Congo River. It remains one of the most haunting tales in modern literature— a trip by sea, land and river steamer, straight to the desperate void at the core of the human soul.

Conrad's vehicle for the journey is his narrator, Marlow, a seaman who recites the anecdotes on the deck of a pleasure yacht at anchor in the mouth of the Thames. Marlow is the most worldly of men, possessed of a bitter wit, an ounce of humility—not much more—and a vivid, insistent rhetorical style. There is nothing cryptic in his words; he speaks with the authority and clarity of someone who has glimpsed the *facts* of what others might only gossip about. Conrad paints him buddhalike, as if instilled with the wisdom of successive lives, but he is primarily an eloquent voice, one filled beneath the sarcasm with humanity. As he recalls his "inconclusive experiences," he unrelentingly judges the European mission of "progress" in Africa as a transparent disguise for greed.

"The conquest of the earth," Marlow explains, "which mostly means the taking it away from those who have a different complexion or slightly flatter noses than ourselves, is not a pretty thing when you look into it too much." Marlow predicts early on in his narrative the gradual exposure of "a flabby, pretending, weak-eyed devil of a rapacious and pitiless folly." It is the devil of what has come to be called "colonialism" or "imperialism," and is summed up in "blind ambition." It is incarnate in the man who becomes the object of Marlow's pilgrimage: Mr. Kurtz.

Kurtz is the other anchor of the book: a "remarkable man," a painter, a poet, a musician, an orator—"a universal genius," the very flower of European civilization. This, at least, is what Marlow, as he travels upriver, hears of the man—and that Kurtz is a boon to his employers, shipping out more ivory than any other agent on the river. As we encounter with Marlow the succession of petty, avaricious Europeans who populate the "civilized" outposts, we begin to yearn with him for the presence—the words—of Kurtz. Amid the grotesque oppression of the mysterious, defeated natives, the flies, the heat, and the jackals bearing the flag of progress, Kurtz becomes a vestige of hope.

And finally, after death visits the steamer and we emerge from an opaque fog (a Dantean passage to an inner world), we approach at last the citadel of Kurtz's empire: a shed bulging at the seams with ivory, a clearing filled with battalions of unquestioningly obedient Africans, and the shack of the "universal genius" surrounded by a crude row of posts, holding high the severed heads of "rebels." The man himself appears: "an animated image of death carved out of old ivory," diseased, delirious, nearly eaten alive by the jungle and his own ambition. Kurtz, acquiescing to threats and coercion from Marlow, departs on the steamer where, sinking toward death, he rants, "My Intended, my ivory, my station, my river. . . ." And Marlow responds in an aside, "[E]verything belonged to him. It made me hold my breath in expectation of hearing the wilderness burst into a prodigious peal of laughter that would shake the fixed stars in their places."

Kurtz issues the feeble cry, "The horror! The horror!" and the man of vision, of poetry, the "emissary of pity, and science, and progress" is gone. The jungle closes 'round.

There's more, but that's the guts of it: a tale whose darkness perpetually illuminates the grim emptiness at the limit of personal and national ambition, the vanity of power's claim to civilization, and the frail evil that lurks in even the *best* of its emissaries. *Heart of Darkness* virtually predicts Vietnam.

Now Coppola has brought us *Apocalypse Now*, the end product of five years of his life—a powerful movie, a technical triumph, a tour de force of style, and so much less than the little book that gave it the spark of birth. Coppola removed Marlow, the lens through which every dimension of Conrad's darkness was made vivid, and gave us Willard, an inarticulate assassin lacking the empathetic quality that might have made him engaging and the irony that would have made the distance comfortable. He replaced "Kurtz's last disciple," Conrad's foolish but still credible innocent, with Dennis Hopper as a burned-out photographer who seems a virtual refugee from the Manson family—thus eliminating the last character witness and leaving poor Kurtz (Marlon Brando) to speak for himself. Coppola diminished the spell of the jungle—the surrounding, encroaching darkness—and gave us instead a claustrophobic sense of the river, interrupted frequently by an almost carnival atmosphere.

All of this might be forgiveable, even praiseworthy, if in the end the film had its own center from which these new elements radiated, or toward which they converged. But it doesn't—or its gravity isn't strong enough to hold them all.

Somewhere in the colossal process of this project, Coppola lost the unity; he found himself making two pictures instead of one. Most of the episodic journey upriver in Vietnam is straightforward action footage, but its content is bizarre: consumer America dropped like phosphorous bombs into simple agrarian villages and wild forests—Jimi Hendrix in the trenches, water skiing on the Mekong, Playboy bunnies lowered from helicopters under sideshow lights. It's a brilliant updating and figurative translation of Conrad's vision to Vietnam, and it works.

But then . . .

As we approach Kurtz, things begin to go awry, because Coppola was apparently never able to decide who Kurtz was—victim, hero or madman—or what to do with him. It's almost as if Conrad's "universal genius"/"hollow sham" had come back to haunt the production—demanding a larger role, exerting his unyielding will, without knowing precisely his own intention. And the director, it seems, tried to cover for the confusion with a flourish of style: grotesque, deathly tableaus; shadowy figures; everywhere drifting smoke and dramatic, stagey lighting. The final segment, culminating in the ritual killing of Kurtz intercut with the bloody ceremonial sacrifice of a bull, is masterfully done, but it's also puffed up. We get Brando reading from T. S. Eliot's "The Hollow Men" with Jessie Weston's *From Ritual to Romance* and James Frazer's *The Golden Bough* on the coffee table, so to speak—hints of deep stuff, credentials for admission to the Academy.

Is there any more to it than that?

Ancient, archetypal regicide is the obvious notion ((hence, Weston and Frazer), implying the succession of Willard to the throne (a suggestion that Coppola's ultimate ending seems to want to retract). The king is dead; long live the king! But of what? Of all this carnage to no purpose?

In Conrad, Kurtz was at least driven by greed for ivory and the ambition "to have kings meet him at railway stations," but Coppola offers us only some vague issue of human will, of absolutely raw power—an ideology of terrorism plain and simple. Coppola's Kurtz (or is this the Kurtz of John Milius, the original screenwriter, whose later credits include *Conan the Barbarian* and *Red Dawn?*) has come to the crystalline revelation that there is some ultimate truth in the willingness to employ absolutely ruthless means in the accomplishment off one's will. It is a sociopathic insight and, unfortunately, the strongest viewpoint articulated in the film.

I've heard it argued that this is brilliant fascist art, woven closely around themes that can also be found in Nazi mysticism. The argument goes something like this: the unity of *Apocalypse Now* centers around that abstract question of Will, intertwined with the Grail legend. Symbols are scattered throughout to tip us off that the Will is an abstract, something out there, beyond history, beyond ethics, virtually beyond human context. But you could also map it as a liberal anti-war picture—with its sympathetic images of Vietnamese villagers and ruthless portrayal of the military, the obvious madness of Kurtz, and Willard's apparent choice to return to his own world after slaying the tyrant. It's probably neither and tries to be apolitical, though the political and moral questions linger like the bodies hanging from the trees around Kurtz's compound. Coppola seems to poke at them now and then as the picture approaches its end, unsure whether he should bury them or leave them to rot where they hang.

In light of what Coppola told *Rolling Stone* interviewer Greil Marcus, if he'd had his way, this might have been the best fascist document of all time. He wanted an idealized image of Kurtz—"a Gauguin figure, with mangoes and babies"—but Brando wanted no part of it. That kind of presentation of Kurtz would have made him more sympathetic, and probably more believable. The director also wanted a different ending on the picture. He wanted it ambiguous, with the possibility left open that Willard stayed to inherit Kurtz's domain—which would have left the viewer with that question of choice, of power (perhaps wondering, "Will we have the guts to nuke the gooks next time?").

Coppola submitted to Brando—he couldn't have him walking off the set—and swallowed an ending he didn't want. He probably did so because creditors were hounding him and he needed to get the $31 million back. "If I feel that I'm a real lone opinion," he told Marcus, "and I don't feel disposed to really fight for it, I'll go with what the bright people I have working with me are saying: . . . everyone wanted—even the computers wanted" the ending we ultimately saw, an ending Coppola told Marcus he considered "a lie." The ending on *Apocalypse Now* is the one that would have been the right answer on "Family Feud," the one the computers told him the majority of preview audiences preferred.

Later, when it looked like *Apocalypse* was going to make its money back, Marcus met with Coppola again, and the director had decided the ending was right, even it *was* "a little bit of a lie."

Many of his changes from Conrad are understandable. Coppola couldn't, for instance, use greed as a central motive because Vietnam wasn't as surfacely simple as that. Henry Kissinger's idea of "our interests" was something vaguer than ivory, and, in a way, Kurtz's abstract engagement with the question of will is an appropriate analogy for the motive of our involvement in Southeast Asia. But Coppola doesn't expose the folly of American ambition there; he ennobles it in the mullings of Brando's Kurtz—and I wonder why.

Could it be that in five years of struggling with this project—risking his fortune, getting sick with jungle rot, and trying to maintain authority over platoons of Hollywood types and primitive Ifugao tribesmen by the hundreds—Coppola found himself identifying with Conrad's Kurtz? Coppola was, after all, off on his own, risking his future—his ambitious plans for Zoetrope Studios—on something that was constantly getting out of hand. As Kurtz was point man for the ivory trade, Coppola was an agent of the movie industry. And, as Kurtz embodied the spirit of a parasitic enterprise, Coppola's film betrays the ambiguities of Hollywood: the enormous technical and sensual power of film, the desire of many of its artisans to turn that into something like art, and the business and marketing factors that perpetually militate against any fully realized achievement.

WILLIAM M. HAGEN

Heart of Darkness and the Process of Apocalypse Now †

Toward the end of Apocalypse Now we reach that supremely Conradian moment when Willard, the Marlow figure, confronts the object of his journey, Colonel Kurtz. Does he come to rescue Kurtz and, in so doing, test himself? If Francis Ford Coppola had chosen to follow Joseph Conrad here, he might have gotten some desperately needed U.S. military assistance.[1] But that was not the kind of script conclusion the director of The Godfather and Godfather II had planned for his war epic.

Still, Coppola underscores the significance of the meeting by altering his style. When Willard is taken into the temple for the first time, the whole pace of the film slows down, as if in imitation of the ponderous immensity of Brando. Brando-Kurtz slowly emerges into the light and pats water on his gleaming bald head, in a kind of ritual cleansing. The camera holds the shots for a much longer period than usual, allowing movement to be dictated by the actors rather than by focusing in or editing. Dialogue too proceeds at a much slower pace, with pauses occurring within sentences as well as between them. Questions are left hanging for a few extra beats, even when there is nothing particularly threatening about them. Of course, the pace has been slackening ever since the Do Lung Bridge sequence, but this scene is so slow it borders on worship. Brando is meant to be mythic, the still center of darkness, worshipped and self-worshipping, capable of every atrocity including self-annihilation through his double. Willard is so affected by the atmosphere of disorder and stasis, that he has to force himself to kill Kurtz. Through lighting, camera angles, and cross-cutting, the murder itself is transformed into a kind of dance in and out of darkness, creating a visual-aesthetic experience quite as isolated as the slow-motion destruction of a Sam Peckinpah film. The acquiescence of Kurtz and the preliminary appearance of Willard out of black water make the whole affair a kind of rite of rebirth-initiation into the world of Kurtz through slaying of the king.

With the exception of the rather abrupt thematic cross-cuts between the murder and the ritual killing of a caribou, the encounters are quite stunning and organic . . . visually. We could perhaps accept the deliberate departure from Conrad's novel if the director did not also seek to build in the psychological-moral dimensions of Heart of Darkness. His

†From Conradiana 13(1981): 45–54. Reprinted by permission.

1. Lawrence Suid, "Hollywood and Vietnam," Film Comment, 15 (September–October 1979), 22.

WILLIAM M. HAGEN

characters may be caught in a ritual of death and rebirth, but he wants them to have depth all the same. He wants viewers to confront the immensity of this war one more time. Above all, he wants to explain everything through Kurtz. So Coppola picks up Kurtz' last words and tries to build a structural theme for the last portion of the film. By the time we hear "The horror!" for the last time, in a memory replay, we are likely to have worked up that fine wrath normally reserved for all those who quote outrageously out of context.

Conrad's Kurtz mouths his last words as a message to himself and, through Marlow, to the world. He has not really explained himself to Marlow before this final exclamation. Through Marlow's summary and moral reactions, we come to a sense of the possibilities of meaning rather than definite meaning. The message is more Marlow's and the reader's than it is Kurtz'. By contrast, Coppola's Kurtz precisely defines "horror"; the only way we can make his definition our message is to see his horror and enact his definition with Willard. The way to judgment lies through vicarious violence. Judgment is self-judgment.

The problem with even this transaction is that Willard seems almost unmoved by his experience. He certainly expresses no moral judgment. The worst he says is that he sees "no method" in Kurtz's operations. This statement may strike the reader of Conrad as uncomfortably similar to the Station Manager's amoral judgment of Kurtz' atrocities as merely "unsound" or bad for company business. The separation of reason from civilized morality, the fragmentation of the self so typical of the techno-crat, causes Marlow to prefer the nightmare of Kurtz. Better to commit atrocities passionately than to account them wrong on grounds of effi-ciency. Like Dante—whose traditional moral hierarchy he reflects—Marlow can summon up a measure of sympathy for those who succumb to their emotions or appetites and reserve unmeasured scorn for those who pervert reason. Within the film, only the general at the briefing and Chef show the rational or emotional repugnance toward Kurtz; Wil-lard, the professional soldier, is more than halfway friendly with this horror. After Chef joins the heads and Willard becomes part of the hor-ror, we may realize that the whole point of the scenes at the Kurtz com-pound is to make the audience confront Kurtz' horror without moral mediation. From the very beginning, the shots of the compound were carefully filled with more separate images and actions, especially around the edges of the frame, than the eye could integrate. The eye was always kept moving and focussing on different parts of the screen. We did not have Marlow's field glasses or his sensibility to distance us or focus in sympathetically; we were entrapped and overwhelmed in an amoral medium range. Thus, instead of judgment or self-judgment, we are likely to come away from this perceptual overdose with the feeling that it has been a bad trip, and nothing more.

Others have compared and contrasted the film to Conrad's novel.[2]

2. Especially noteworthy are Marsha Kinder's "The Power of Adaptation in *Apocalypse Now*," *Film Quarterly*, 33 (Winter 1979–80), 12–20, and the articles published in *Conradiana* 13, 1 (1981).

After all of the analyses, however, one may be moved to wonder just what the director-writer had in mind with regard to *Heart of Darkness*, or what process led from the novel to such a mixture of visual spectacle and moral-intellectual vacuity.

The program handed out at the screenings of the 70-mm print of *Apocalypse Now* gives the following script credits: "Written by John Milius and Francis Coppola; Narration by Michael Herr." Nowhere in the formal credits is Joseph Conrad or *Heart of Darkness* mentioned. The novel is briefly referred to in the program's log: "September 3, 1976. Marlon Brando arrives. He reads *Heart of Darkness* and shaves his head for the Col. Kurtz role." Within the film itself, the novel is not accorded reference equal to *The Golden Bough* or T. S. Eliot's poetry; it is not recited as quotation or included among the books in the bibliographic pan toward the end of the film. Of course, for the cognizant, there are plenty of lines, or echoes of lines, as well as the unmentioned epigraph to Kurtz' favorite poem, "The Hollow Men."

In point of fact, Conrad's name originally appeared in the screen credits, but was removed after one of the listed writers protested through the Screen Writer's Guild. Coppola is quite candid about the three texts that contributed to the final script: the novel, Michael Herr's *Dispatches*— originally published as a series of *Esquire* articles—and John Milius' script, entitled *Apocalypse Now*, which built some of its passages from Herr's book and *Heart of Darkness*. The script itself went through several phases: the original 1969 script by Milius, collaborative revisions during preproduction period (1975–76), Coppola's revisions during production, and Herr's narration, added after shooting was completed in 1977.

To read the statements regarding *Heart of Darkness* by the two main architects of the script, Milius and Coppola, is to confront a tangle of high intentions, self-delusion, and probably self-protection. It is harder to verify what Milius says about his original script or its collaborative revision because, apart from two fragments in *Film Comment* (July–August 1976), nothing has been published. In an interview included with the script fragments, he claims to have used *Heart of Darkness* "in an allegorical sense."[3] Kurtz went up the river with a military mission and a moral mission: he was to turn the tribesmen into a fighting force and bring them "democracy and Western civilization."[4] He succeeds admirably in the first mission at the cost of the second mission and his own civilized sanity. Milius depicts him as having made sense of the war by embracing tribal values:

> [To Willard] We revel in our own blood; we fight for glory, for
> land that's under our feet, gold that's in our hands,
> women that worship the power in our loins. I summon
> fire from the sky. Do you know what it is to be a white
> man who can summon fire from the sky?[5]

3. "John Milius Interviewed by Richard Thompson," *Film Comment*, 12 (July–August 1976), 15.
4. Milius, 15.

5. " 'Apocalypse Now' Script Extracts," *Film Comment*, 12 (July–August 1976), 14.

Milius meant for the audience to confront the tribalization of Americans in the very first scene of the original script. That scene depicts the colonel's team members ambushing a column of Viet Cong. G.I.'s emerge from the jungle, one by one, dressed and painted like savages. The camera records the scene from the point of view of the victims: the audience is variously blasted by a shotgun, incinerated by a flame-thrower, and scalped by an American wearing a peace sign on his helmet. Quite apart from the Kurtz behind the spooky voice on the tape recording and the ghostlike images of the photos, then, this was to be the reality Willard moved toward. As opposed to the film, this was madness with enough method for a professional soldier to admire. Willard's journey was to be an odyssey, with adventures that threatened to delay or divert him from his mission, while revealing the purposelessness of our war effort. Encounters with a surfing colonel (Cyclops), Playboy bunnies in a downed helicopter (Sirens), the Do Lung Bridge sequence (visit to underworld for further instruction?), and a meal at an old French plantation (Circe? Lotus-eaters?) would make grand scenes and trigger an analysis of his own role in the war.

The jungle was to have the force of the environment in *Bridge on the River Kwai*, becoming more powerful and primeval as Willard approached the Kurtz compound. Willard's line in the film—"Even the jungle wanted him dead"—picks up a theme ennunciated by Kurtz in Milius' script. He shows Willard a rotting hole in his side and points to the insects swarming around him: "The beast of the jungle did the rest. I haven't long to go. . . . the only justice will be had by the beasts. . . . Theirs will be final, and we will have made no more mark on this jungle than a stone thrown into an ocean."[6] Even though this may sound like Conrad merged with *Lord of the Flies* one assumes that the Milius script would have stressed the surroundings as a means of initiation to Kurtz' world rather than as a green backdrop out of which pop tigers, banners, tracer bullets, and arrows.[7] Certainly the above-mentioned opening establishes the jungle and swamp first; the ambushers emerge from underwater and behind foliage.

Given the opening view of savage Americans, the inefficiency of the official war effort, and the power of the jungle, the conversion of Willard to Kurtz' side in Milius' script would seem inevitable. They would join forces and die together. Coppola apparently agreed that some conversion to Kurtz' position was the more logical conclusion, but bowed to audience surveys which indicated a preference for Willard alive and faithful to his original mission. One speculates some problems, however, since Willard was to have undergone psychological change during his journey. Was this change to be represented only by a change of allegiance? His late assertion that he kills because "it feels so good," delivered to

6. "Script Extracts," 14.
7. For an excellent example of how well film can show the impact of the environment on civilized man, I recommend Werner Herzog's *Aguirre, the Wrath of God* (1973), with Klaus Kinski playing the conquistador whose mind and morality disintegrate in the presence of a vast jungle which both conflicts with and objectifies his boundless ambition.

Kurtz in the Milius script would seem appropriate at any point in the script for a man "who exists only because of the war." Perhaps he merely joins the more efficient war. At any rate, the self-doubting, guilt-ridden Willard, established in the first scene of the film, is Coppola's creation.

On the other hand, Milius' Kurtz definitely seems more of a piece than Brando-Coppola's Kurtz. If the jungle environment were actually established as a force, if Kurtz' other lines were as strong as those in the published fragment, if we can imaginatively fill out Kurtz by using the comparison Milius makes to the Paul Newman character in Milius' previous film, *The Life and Times of Judge Roy Bean*, then Milius' Kurtz would have gone down (with Willard) in a blaze of apocalyptic glory. We would probably have been spared Kurtz' unearned realization of "The horror! The horror!" whispered to us in stereo or sexophonic (70-mm version) sound.

One must be careful, however, not to use a speculated script to construct "the film that might have been." It is quite evident that Milius established much of the plot and most of the lavish scenes in the first half of the film, all of which constitute a major variance from the method of *Heart of Darkness*. Milius says he wanted the spectator "to see the exhilaration of it all . . . the horror of it all: you're going right into the war with no holds barred."[8] Certainly his first scene preserves no Conradian mental and moral distance from the action. The direct approach to the war, as a series of perceptual traumas that threaten to reduce the mind to passivity owe as much to the acid journalism of Michael Herr's *Dispatches* filtered through a sensibility fascinated with war as to what Stanley Kauffmann calls Coppola's "apparent sense that the world is seen most truthfully when it is seen as spectacle."[9] If Milius' Kurtz was more of a piece, he was more a piece of this action, living in splendor with wives, babies, and few doubts.

Coppola was quite dissatisfied with the conception of Willard in the original script. Although Milius claims that his script was not political, Coppola saw the whole thing as "a political comic strip" up to and including the end.

> Attila the Hun [i.e., Kurtz] with two bands of machine-gun bullets around him, taking the hero Willard by the hand. . . . Willard converts to Kurtz's side; in the end, he's firing up at the helicopters that are coming to get him, crying out crazily.[1]

He decided to "take the script much more strongly in the direction of *Heart of Darkness*—which was, I know, opening a Pandora's box."[2] In particular, one can see problems in his conception of Willard, whom he felt was "literally zero" in Milius' script. He wanted to "psychologize" Willard, following Conrad's lead, but "In no way could he get in the

8. Milius, 15.
9. "Coppola's War," *The New Republic*, 181 (15 September 1979), 24.

1. "An Interview with Francis Coppola," *Rolling Stone* (1 November 1979), 52–53.
2. Coppola, 53.

298   WILLIAM M. HAGEN

way of the audience's view of what was happening, of Vietnam."[3] The
latter statement certainly reveals that Coppola never understood the role
of Marlow in the novel. By the same token, I think his instincts were
right: one cannot have a spectacle vicariously experienced and an experience filtered through a narrator who has changed mentally and morally
as a result of that experience. Scenes which enlarge our sense of a real
world, as in the picaresque novel, usually do so at some expense to
character; scenes which enlarge or create a crisis for the character who
is our vantage point are often not fully objectified. Would the helicopter
assault have been as effective if the camera had been restricted to Willard's vantage point? Would Conrad's Kurtz have seemed as powerful if
Marlow had faithfully recorded all that he said? Some film theorists
would add that Coppola's instincts were right even if he *had* understood
the role of Marlow because film redeems material reality or its immediate perception more naturally than consciousness. Critics who bemoan
the medium's tendency to reduce Conrad to exotic scenes and large
characters, to present his work as primarily romantic, might be tempted
to agree. At any rate, Coppola's problem was that he wanted it both
ways: he wanted the exhilarating episodes of Milius and he wanted the
psychological dimension of Conrad's Marlow. Michael Herr's method
of grabbing all the experience one can get in the great trip of life would
not help him achieve a balance. So he went into production with this
problem, hoping that a good actor might help him resolve it. He had
hopes that "the part would play the person."[4] The role of Willard was
offered to Steve McQueen, Al Pacino, James Caan, Jack Nicholson,
and Robert Redford. Since the problem of Willard was also the problem
of Kurtz, many of the same actors were offered the Kurtz role. Apparently, only in the editing room would Coppola realize the results of such
contrary impulses—a film with radically different styles in its different
parts.

During the shooting of *Apocalypse Now*, Eleanor Coppola, the director's wife, began keeping a journal which was to help her make a documentary film of the production. Whether the documentary was completed
or not, she drops all mention of it about mid-way through the journal,
where personal and family problems increasingly enter. The journal itself,
published by Simon and Schuster under the title of *Notes*, unfortunately, is too fragmentary and begins too late in the process to offer
much information on specific script decisions that moved the film closer
to or farther away from *Heart of Darkness*.

What it does reveal is just how many script decisions were deferred
till production was actually underway. Coppola the director shot scenes
by day, while Coppola the writer rewrote scenes by night. Throughout,
he hoped that important elements of plot, character, and theme could
achieve conceptual clarity during the process of production. For instance,
although he was sure enough about the Willard part to fire Harvey Keitel

3. Coppola, 53.
4. Eleanor Coppola, *Notes* (Simon and Schuster: New York, 1979), p. 157.

because he projected too strongly, he apparently did not realize that Sheen's Willard was verging toward nonentity till late in the picture. At that point, probably after Sheen's physical breakdown rendered him unable to reshoot extensively, Coppola made the decision to have Michael Herr work up the voice-over narration to fill out the character. Even if Conrad's Marlow suggested this method, it was not part of the original script. For another more extreme instance, Notes presents Brando as having virtual veto power over his lines and character. "Francis hadn't been able to write a scene that Marlon thought was really right."[5] He arrived without having read Heart of Darkness: he and Coppola had to work out the character, almost in front of the cameras. Coppola re-scripted some scenes after viewing the footage of those very scenes. The isolation of Brando-Kurtz from his men, enshrined in his temple compound, is as much due to the problems of working out character on a two-week time schedule as it is to any thematic intention. In the original Milius script and in Coppola's mind he might have been integrated into that part of the film fashioned by "Heart of Darkness and me,"[6] but Notes and the interview make it clear that the anxious director and his overweight, opinionated star conceived and filmed the character at almost the same time. "As soon as Brando started to improvise, Frances could begin to direct, that is, see the direction the scene should go."[7] It is not surprising that the character has more physical and visual presence than psychological power. The cinematographer, Vittorio Storaro, was more deliberate in planning his effects.

Some critics have suggested that Notes itself should be regarded as a kind of publicity release. (Did husband, who suggested the journal become a book, also suggest changes? Certainly he filled out some details.) Throughout the journal, the director displays self-doubts about his product, while maintaining the highest esteem for his sources, Conrad's novel and our corporate Vietnam experience. The self-doubt, later displayed in the test showings of different versions of the film, rather artfully becomes Coppola's own journey into darkness during the process of filmmaking. The open-ended approach to script fits right in, or course. Almost two months into production, early in the journal, the director's wife sets up a thematic connection that becomes prevalent in the book:

> Willard and Kurtz are not resolved. . . . Now he [Frances Coppola] is struggling with the themes of Willard's journey into self and Kurtz' truths that are in a way themes he has not resolved within himself, so he is really going through the most intense struggle to write his way to the end of the script and understand himself on the way.[8]

> More and more it seems like there are parallels between the character of Kurtz and Francis. There is the exhilaration of power in the face of losing everything.[9]

5. Notes, p. 138.
6. Coppola, 53.
7. Notes, p. 138.

8. Notes, p. 43.
9. Notes, p. 44.

Later, as Sheen settles into his muted Willard and Brando is due to arrive, the resolution of Kurtz becomes the primary problem. Rereading Conrad does not help Coppola: "The ideas of what Kurtz represents are so big that when you try to get a handle on them they are almost undefinable."[1] Unfortunately, his decision to use a star for the Kurtz role and his own realistic proclivities push him in the direction of defining, whereas Conrad is careful to suggest. Where specific outlines are not credible, the character, like his compound, is presented as too large to be contained in the frame. Isolated bigness and hollowness are the result: a huge temple honeycombed with small barren rooms, a large body with a shining oval head, a rhetoric that echoes more than it means.

The director's journey becomes a personal journey for the whole crew, for his family, especially for this wife, who wants to create something herself. Still later, when Sheen collapses, Coppola seems to collapse too and begins talking about divorce. Finally, the creative journey is connected to the war: "there was no simple solution to the script. Just as there was no simple right answer as to why we were in Vietnam."[2] In the program notes, Coppola ties it all together, projecting the journey as an audience catharsis as well:

> Over the period of shooting, this film gradually made itself; and curiously, the process of making the film became very much like the story of the film. . . .
> I, like Captain Willard, was moving up a river. . . .
> It was my thought that if the American audience could look at the heart of what Vietnam was really like . . . they would be only one small step away from putting it behind them.

Coppola's statements here may strike us as pretentious and self-serving, but I tend to think that he has made the common mistake of artists who imagine that the experience of the audience and the stature of the artwork can somehow be predicted by the anguish of the creative process. In wanting to improve the Milius script, especially after the Do Lung Bridge sequence, he turned to *Heart of Darkness* and the somewhat improvisatory method itself. However, by not working out the precise relation of *Heart of Darkness* to the conception of the film in script form, Coppola insured a less faithful adaptation. In a process of conceptualization *and* production, different script considerations externalize as physical factors and personalities. Without a firm script or a director with a firm conception, group spontaneity can all-too-easily give way to anxiety and competition. Costly sets, actors, sound engineers, a tribe of extras, stocks of explosives, a meticulous cinematographer (who wants to organize by shot frames rather than by scenes) directly or indirectly pressure the director to help fill in the blank places of the script. In such a situation, the medium may have more voices than the message.

Ironically, although Coppola wanted to draw the greatness of the film

1. *Notes*, p. 127.　　2. *Notes*, p. 130.

from the greatness of the novel, the section of the film most like *Heart of Darkness* is the weakest because he makes the rather romantic assumption—which is, in fact, a misreading of the novel—that experience itself will immediately dictate certain discoveries. He forgets the years of reflection Marlow has given to his experience, the "recollection in tranquility" that Wordworth argued must follow "the spontaneous overflow of powerful emotions" if they are to be shaped into art. Although one may shuffle the scenes around like cards,[3] although sound or narration may be added, the scenes themselves cannot be done again; celluloid is much less tractable than words.

I tend to see *Apocalypse Now* as a failed masterpiece, another instance of the fact that the production-editing process cannot bear too much of the conceptual load in a feature film.[4] Coppola needed something definite to improvise *against*. I would reluctantly speculate that his film would have achieved greater unity if he had relied more on Milius' scripted version of *Heart of Darkness* than the novel itself.

E. N. DORALL

Conrad and Coppola: Different Centres of Darkness †

When a great artist in one medium produces a work based on a masterpiece in the same or another medium, we can expect interesting results. Not only will the new work be assessed as to its merits and validity as a separate creation, but the older work will also inevitably be reassessed as to its own durability, or relevance to the new age. I am not here concerned with mere adaptations, however complex and exciting they may be, such as operas like *Otello, Falstaff* and *Béatrice et Bénédict*, or plays like *The Innocents* and *The Picture of Dorian Gray*. What I am discussing is a thorough reworking of the original material so that a new, independent work emerges; what happens, for example, in the many Elizabethan and Jacobean plays based on Roman, Italian and English stories, or in plays like *Eurydice, Antigone* and *The Family Reunion*, which reinterpret the ancient Greek myths in modern terms. In the cinema, in many ways the least adventurous of the creative arts, we have been inundated by adaptations, some so remote from the original works as to be, indeed, new works in their own right, but so devoid of any merit that one cannot begin to discuss them seriously. But from time to time an intelligent and independent film has been fashioned from the

3. *Notes*, p. 263.
4. Apropos are Coppola's remarks to an assistant towards the end of the production of *The Godfather*: "Do you still want to direct films? Always remember three things: have the definitive script ready before you begin to shoot. There'll always be some changes, but they should be small ones. Second, work with people you trust and feel secure

with. Third, make your actors feel very secure so they can do their job well. . . . I've managed to do none of these things on this film." Ira Zuckerman, *The Godfather Journal* (New York: Manor Books, 1972), p. 122.
† From *Southeast Asian Review of English* 1(1980): 19–27, Reprinted with permission of the author and editors.

original material. At the moment I can recall only the various film treat-
ments of Hemingway's *To Have and Have Not*. But now, in Francis
Coppola's recent Vietnam war film, *Apocalypse Now*, based on Joseph
Conrad's *Heart of Darkness*, we have a worthy addition to this category
which may well set the standard by which all other cinematic re-crea-
tions will henceforth be judged.

Conrad's novella, one hardly needs reminding, is the account of a
journey from Brussels to the heart of the Congo which partially resembles one made by Conrad himself in 1890. His narrator, Marlow,
employed by a colonial company to captain a river steamboat, sails in a
steamer down the west coast of Africa to the mouth of the Congo, then
continues in a smaller boat to a town thirty miles higher up the river
(Matadi), from which he travels overland to the Central Station (the
town of Kinchasa at Stanley Pool) and finally into the heart of darkness
to the Inner Station (at Stanley Falls). The novella soon becomes a series
of impressionistic vignettes exposing the brutalities of colonial, and particularly Belgian colonial rule. In 'the city that always makes me think
of a whited sepulchre' (Brussels) Marlow is given his commission, in a
house with 'grass sprouting between the stones' guarded by two sinister
women who 'knitted black wool feverishly.' Down the coast of Africa he
passes a French man-of-war subduing a native rebellion; 'In the empty
immensity of earth, sky, and water, there she was, incomprehensible,
firing into a continent.' More vivid impressions await him in the town
thirty miles up-river. 'I came upon a boiler wallowing in the grass,' 'an
undersized railway truck lying there on its back with its wheels in the air
. . . as dead as the carcass of some animal.' A chain-gang of emaciated
blacks passes him; he nearly falls into 'a vast, artificial hole . . . the
purpose of which I found it impossible to divine;' he enters a grove like
'the gloomy circle of some Inferno,' in which 'black shadows of disease
and starvation' are slowly dying. On the overland route to the Central
Station there are 'paths, paths, everywhere; a stamped-in network of paths
spreading over the empty land, through long grass, through burnt grass,
through thickets, down and up chilly ravines, up and down stony hills
ablaze with heat; and a solitude, a solitude, nobody, not a hut.' Marlow
passes 'several abandoned villages' and hears the beat of far-off drums at
night, 'a sound weird, appealing, suggestive, and wild. . . .' After fifteen
days he arrives at the Central Station, where the exposure of colonialism
continues. The Company's agents wander 'here and there with . . . absurd
long staves in their hands like a lot of faithless pilgrims bewitched inside
a rotten fence,' and finally a band called the Eldorado Exploring Expedition passes through; 'To tear treasure out of the bowels of the land was
their desire, with no more moral purpose at the back of it than there is
in burglars breaking into a safe.' The cumulative power of these impressions is intensified when counterpointed by the theme of the mysterious
Mr. Kurtz, the agent of the Inner Station, who is first mentioned in the
up-river town. As Marlow proceeds on his journey Kurtz grows in mystery and grandeur, his gigantic 'singleness of purpose' condemning the

sordid selfishness of the other colonial agents. At the Central Station Marlow is told that he will have to take his boat to the Inner Station and bring back Kurtz, who is very sick. As he proceeds to the heart of the 'mighty big river . . . resembling an immense snake uncoiled, with its head in the sea, its body at rest curving afar over a vast country and its tail lost in the depths of the land,' Marlow broods over the 'strange rumours' of Kurtz's unorthodox behaviour, which fascinates him as it embarrasses everyone else. And so the novella moves to its climax, with Kurtz gradually engulfing the atrocities of the other agents in his own immense horror.

Coppola's film is similarly structured. His narrator, Captain Willard, on leave from the battlefront, is given his mission at the very beginning of the film, to locate and eliminate the famous Colonel Kurtz who, after murdering four South Vietnamese officers under his command, has taken his men over the border into Cambodia, where they are indiscriminately killing Vietcong, South Vietnamese and Cambodians. This is 'totally beyond the pale of any acceptable conduct,' Willard is told. And so he journeys up the Nung, 'a river which [like the Congo] snakes across the land like a main circuit cable' to the border and beyond, studying Colonel Kurtz's dossier en route while a vast panorama of the Vietnam war unrolls before him. In the first episode he meets the eccentric Colonel Kilgore who refuses to let the war interfere with his favourite sport, surfing. Kilgore (the syllables taken separately describe the man) is prepared to attack a Vietcong-controlled village at the mouth of the Nung river not really because Willard and his boat need to get through but because the waves at that point have a six-foot peak which is ideal for surfing. In the film's most memorable scene the village is attacked by helicopters flying to the music of 'The Ride of the Valkyries' and demolished by napalm bombs as Kilgore's boys ride the nearby surf. 'I love the smell of napalm in the morning,' Kilgore says wistfully. 'It smells . . . like . . . victory.' In other episodes Willard encounters a tiger in the jungle while looking for mangoes, attends a striptease show for thousands of GI's which abruptly ends when the soldiers rush onto the stage to manhandle the artistes, meets another boat the occupants of which are searched for weapons and massacred in a moment of panic, arrives at the furthest point in Vietnam, 'the arsehole of the world,' where a demoralised group of GI's rebuild a bridge every morning which the Vietcong demolish every night, and finally penetrates into Cambodia where, in an attack on the boat by Kurtz's followers, two of the crew are killed, one of them, the helmsman, by an arrow through his body. And, as in the novella, between these episodes, Willard continues reading Kurtz's dossier and allows the Colonel's personality to penetrate and absorb his own.

Throughout the journey other, minor parallels to the novella occur. Willard is told that an earlier passenger on the boat blew his brains out; in *Heart of Darkness* Marlow's predecessor Fresleven was killed by natives, and a former passenger on the little steamer to Matadi hanged himself because of the sun 'or the country perhaps.' The attack on the boat by

Kurtz's men and the manner of the helmsman's death are common to the novella and the film. The press photographer whom Willard meets in Colonel Kurtz's camp speaks almost exactly like the Russian Marlow meets in Mr. Kurtz's Station. 'He made me see things—things. . . . Now—just to give you an idea—I don't mind telling you, he wanted to shoot me too one day;' the words are Conrad's but, in content and rhythm, might just as well have come from Coppola's script. The two Kurtzes, especially, often act and speak alike. Both have asked to be sent to their assignment; both are impressively bald (surely a symbolic touch); both are happy with the agent sent to end their jungle existence. 'I was to have the care of his memory,' says Marlow in words almost identical with those Colonel Kurtz uses when he asks Willard to represent him faithfully to his son in America. When the manager of the Central Station complains that Kurtz's method is 'unsound,' Marlow asks, 'Do you . . . call it "unsound method?" ' 'Without doubt,' he [exclaims] hotly. 'Don't you?' . . . 'No method at all,' Marlow murmurs. In the film Colonel Kurtz asks pointedly, 'Are my methods unsound?' And Willard replies, 'I don't see any method, sir.' Later, another comment, 'But his soul was mad,' is repeated by the photographer in the film, 'The man's clear in his mind but his soul is mad.' Eventually Marlow hazily explains what happened to Mr. Kurtz. 'There was nothing either above or below him—and I knew it. He had kicked himself loose of the earth. Confound the man! he had kicked the very earth to pieces.' The laconic Willard puts it more simply, 'He broke from all that [human society], and then he broke away from himself.' In both novella and film, Kurtz is little more than a voice (in the film he is barely visible), which instructs Marlow-Willard for some days and finally expires after muttering the now famous last words.

So much for the similarities between the novella and the film. They are numerous—the same 'story' and structure, and some parallel characters, incidents and expressions. It is strange, therefore, not to find Conrad's name among the film's credit titles. But *Apocalypse Now* is also a work of art in its own right, and from the beginning this too is apparent, despite the resemblances to *Heart of Darkness*. The steamboat which takes Willard up the Nung river is far more important than the boat which Marlow captains from the Central to the Inner Station. Coppola's riverboat is a modern Ship of Fools and its four-man crew, two blacks and two whites, the helmsman, the clown, the coward and the sportsman are innocents caught in a conflict they know nothing about. In *Heart of Darkness*, apart from Marlow, no one develops or elicits our sympathy, as distinct from our liking. In the film, however, there is some development of character. The helmsman Philips becomes increasingly hostile towards Willard till, at the moment of death, he tries to strangle him. The other black, Clean, is friendly and carefree, and his death, while listening to a tape of his mother pleading with him to come back home in one piece, is the film's most poignant moment. The coward, Chef, also develops; shattered by his encounter with a tiger early in the film and still frightened when he has to search another boat for weapons, he has, by the end, gained enough courage to stand by Willard in his encounter with Kurtz. If Lance, the surfer is less alive than the others, it is because he is intended to be the shallowest personality of the four. Thus two perspectives of the Vietnam War are offered in the film— the events seen from the riverboat and the life of the characters on that boat.

But it is only at the climax, when Marlow and Willard confront Kurtz, that *Heart of Darkness* and *Apocalypse Now* part company and develop differently. I think we must be specific, if we are to appreciate Conrad's novella fully, as to the nature of Kurtz's ultimate degradation, which can only be hinted at but never bluntly stated. Identifying it correctly will also enable us to defend Conrad's style against F. R. Leavis' famous accusation, that the "adjectival insistence upon inexpressible and incomprehensible mystery" has a muffling rather than a magnifying effect. We remember, of course, that there is much excessively colourful writing in Conrad's earliest novels, *Almayer's Folly* and *An Outcast of the Islands*. But in *The Nigger of the 'Narcissus'* he had shown his ability to write more directly and powerfully when his subject required it. Is the gross over-writing of *Heart of Darkness* then a backward step, or did *that* subject demand *that* particular style? The vagueness and 'adjectival insistence' are found mainly in Marlow's descriptions of 'darkness' and of Kurtz's degradation. 'Everything belonged to him—but that was a trifle. The thing was to know what he belonged to, how many powers of darkness claimed him for their own.' Kurtz presides 'at certain midnight dances ending with unspeakable rites, which—as far as I reluctantly gathered from what I heard at various times—were offered up to him— do you understand?—to Mr. Kurtz himself.' Kurtz would go on long expeditions; 'mostly his expeditions had been for ivory;' he would 'disappear for weeks; forget himself amongst these people—forget himself— you know.' When Marlow eventually identifies the 'round carved balls' on posts before Kurtz's station as human heads, he makes his most revealing comment, 'They only showed that Mr. Kurtz lacked restraint in the gratification of his various lusts, that there was something wanting in him—some small matter which, when the pressing need arose, could not be found under his magnificent eloquence.' That Kurtz massacred the natives, stole ivory and was worshipped as a god are all bluntly stated by Marlow. What then could he do beyond these things that, in 1899 (when Conrad wrote *Heart of Darkness*) Marlow could only allude to as 'unspeakable rites' and 'various lusts'? Surely we are meant to conclude that Kurtz, who set out for Africa carrying the light of European civilization at its brightest, came face to face, like other post-Darwinian heroes before him, with the essential animal nature of man, over which civilization is mere clothing, and that then, with his typical ruthless honesty, he cast off his ideals and humanity and dared to live at the other extreme, as the total animal Darwin and the Naturalists said he really was; he tore down the facade behind which the other colonialists sheltered, and converted metaphor into brutal fact, not only devouring Africa, as they did, but, very specifically, devouring Africans. It is this 'horror' that cannot be directly stated but which, disguised behind the most impressive and justified verbiage in Conrad's works, provides a fitting climax to the earlier colonial brutalities and also gives *Heart of Darkness* that mysterious grandeur which has fascinated so many readers. And this is the tragedy of Kurtz. Daring to face the consequences of his nature, he loses his identity; unable to be totally beast and never again able to be fully human, he alternates between trying to return to the jungle and recalling in grotesque terms his former idealism. 'Kurtz discoursed. A voice! a voice! It rang deep to the very last. It survived his strength to hide in the magnificent folds of eloquence the barren darkness of his heart. Oh, he struggled, he struggled. . . . The shade of the original Kurtz frequented the bedside of the hollow sham whose fate it was to be buried presently in the mould of primeval earth. But both the diabolic love and the unearthly hate of the mysteries it had penetrated fought for the possession of that soul satiated with primitive emotions, avid of lying fame, of sham distinction, of all the appearances of success and power.' Inevitably Kurtz collapses, his last words epitomizing his experience, 'The horror! The horror!'

There are a few human heads in Colonel Kurtz's camp in Cambodia—but they do not seem to be particularly important. Certainly they are not as conspicuous as the dozens of complete dead bodies lying around. Colonel Kurtz's problem is basically a military one, for *Apocalypse Now*, we must remember, is a film about war, not colonization. Colonel Kurtz had been an ideal commander, destined to rise in the military hierarchy, till an event occurred which altered his whole life. Sent to supervise the inocculation of children in a village, he was horrified to learn that the Vietcong later broke in and cut off every inoculated arm. Colonel Kurtz then faced his own darkness, that a war can be fought successfully only *if* one learns to come to terms with 'horror and moral terror' ('Horror and moral terror must be your friends,' he tells Willard); one can win *if* one eliminates all human feeling in favour of total ruthlessness. Colonel Kurtz has accepted the challenge of the 'if'. (He had revealed to the news photographer that 'if' is the middle word of 'life'.) Unlike the other commanders who hypocritically claim they are fighting for the preservation of civilization while annihilating whole villages by napalm bombs, Kurtz has bravely cast off the trappings of civilization and turned himself and his men into pure fighting machines. He can therefore rightly boast that he is beyond the timid lying morality of his colleagues. As the news photographer explains to Willard, there are no 'fractions' (that is, mingled emotions) in Kurtz's make-up; there is only the totality of love or hate. Willard can appreciate this because, earlier in the film, after the accident that killed all the natives in a boat suspected of carrying hidden weapons, he had commented sadly, 'We cut them up with guns and then give them a band aid.' By the time he reaches Kurtz, Willard is convinced that the American army in Vietnam is totally confused in its motives, while Kurtz is admirably if insanely single-minded in his actions. As early as the Kilgore episode Willard had noted, 'If that's how Kilgore fought the war, I wonder what they had against Kurtz.' And so he determines to decide for himself whether to kill Kurtz or join him, which in fact is what his predecessor had done.

Kurtz, however, has other plans for Willard; that is why he has allowed him to reach his camp alive. Like his namesake in *Heart of Darkness* he has discovered that the consequence of rejecting his humanity to live and fight like an animal is that life has become meaningless and empty. He has faced the challenge of darkness only to be engulfed by it. At this point Coppola introduces into his film the anthropomorphic theories of Sir J. G. Frazer's *The Golden Bough*, Jessie Weston's persuasive though irritatingly repetitive *From Ritual to Romance*, and T. S. Eliot's *Poems*, books which we see, like signposts, in Kurtz's library. Indeed Coppola makes him read 'The Hollow Men' to stress the point. Kurtz is now the sick god of his tribe, that notorious bore the Fisher King, and he desperately needs the Quester to execute him and free his paralysed people.[1] So Willard is carefully groomed for this role which he finally enacts. Some facile symbolism prepares us for the dénouement. Early in the film a chaplain conducts a holy communion service on the battlefield while the camera mounts to take in a helicopter overhead with a cow dangling from it. In the very next scene Kilgore and his men dine off the roasted beast. This intrusive symbol of the scapegoat dying for the life of the community is repeated at the end of the film when Willard executes Kurtz at the same moment that Kurtz's soldiers kill another animal in a ritual ceremony. But Willard does not become Kurtz's successor. Instead he sails away, leaving Kurtz's men to be wiped out by an airstrike from Saigon which we know is imminent. This attack probably was to have been the noisy ending Coppola at one time envisaged for his film. Fortunately he preferred a quieter one; now, as Willard's boat moves downstream, we hear Kurtz's final words again, 'The horror! The horror!'

This excursion into anthropomorphism accounts for another significant difference between *Heart of Darkness* and *Apocalypse Now*. In the novella, as I have already mentioned, there is an increase in tension and interest when we move from the atrocities of the colonialists to the mysterious evil world of Kurtz. This is because, whether it is narrating action or reporting speech, the novel comes to us through the medium of words, words which can be equally exciting as vehicles of action or description. In *Heart of Darkness* the vague and massive words which present Kurtz's evil are more impressive and exciting, because of what they hide, than the precise words which describe the colonial atrocities earlier on. The reader moves willingly from the evil he understands to the evil he can only guess at. On the screen, however, there is a greater gulf between action and speech, for the former comes to us directly, as in real life,

---

1. The most relevant section of Frazer's book seems to be "The Killing of the Divine King"; in Miss Weston's book, see chapters ii and iv particularly.

without needing words to convey it. We *see*, and we do not need to be *told*. Consequently a first viewing of *Apocalypse Now* can be a bewildering, even exhausting experience. For we suddenly realize that here is a film which begins with considerable action and then declines steadily towards the slow, muted final episode in Kurtz's camp. Has something gone wrong with the planning? Has Kilgore, brilliantly played by Robert Duvall, struck us so forcibly with his lunacy that nothing afterwards is as exciting? Or is this movement from action to discussion, from noise to virtual silence deliberate on Coppola's part? When we consider Coppola's rejection of Conrad's cannibal climax in favour of a rather clumsily contrived ritual sacrifice, the answer becomes clear. *Apocalypse Now* is designed from the first to move towards extinction. *Of course* the lunacy of Kilgore and the other commanders is more terrifying than Kurtz's comparatively rational solution to the problem of warfare. It is far more sickening to see supposedly civilized men burning whole villages without any qualms than to see declared savages killing each other. In a taped message to his colleagues Kurtz taunts them, 'What do they call it when the assassins accuse the assassin?' What he accomplishes in the film is to strip them of their grotesque facade of civilization, to embody in himself the spirit of pure, uncompromising warfare, and then bravely to submit to the inevitable resulting emptiness. If you want war, then fight it thoroughly, and this is what will happen to you. It can only end in a longing for extinction. With Kurtz dies his army and, by implication, all warmongers. In this sense he is fully the scapegoat, dying not that others may live but that they may see that they too must follow him into destruction. Rarely has a work of art appeared in any medium which moves so steadily and daringly from life to death.[2] And of a new world emerging from the old, there is not the slightest hint.

There remains one major difference between *Apocalypse Now* and its source. So far, the *Heart of Darkness* we have been describing could have been written by any pessimistic novelist at the end of the last century, one may even insist, by any novelist except Joseph Conrad. For what makes a novel a Conrad novel is the presence in it of the Conrad hero, that powerful moral force struggling for survival in a disintegrating world. By 1900 perceptive thinkers had long predicted the chaos to come, the breakdown of established religious, political and social systems which our century has experienced. But at that time 'the centre' still held. Darwinism, Marxism and anarchism may have eaten into the framework of society but outwardly the churches and empires stood as strong as ever. The most advanced writers only warned of the coming desolation and each was able to offer a personal solution to the catastrophe. For Conrad the world may be falling to pieces but the individual hero can remain intact, a moral force personified. Whether he survives or dies, he is true to himself, and his integrity is a kind of triumph. *Heart of Darkness* has two typical Conrad heroes, three if we accept the chief

2. Structurally, the film resembles Gustav Mahler's extraordinary *Third Symphony* and, to a lesser extent, his *Ninth* and *Tenth*; also, of course, Tchaikovsky's *Pathétique*.

accountant at the up-river station. Perhaps we should. He is not a moral character but Marlow 'respected the fellow. Yes. I respected his collars, his vast cuffs, his brushed hair. His appearance was certainly that of a hairdresser's dummy, but in the great demoralisation of the land he kept up his appearance. That's backbone. His starched collars and got-up shirt-fronts were achievements of character.' The Russian who owns the book *An Inquiry into some Points of Seamanship* is clearly a Conrad hero. 'For months—for years—his life hadn't been worth a day's purchase—and there he was gallantly, thoughtlessly alive, to all appearance indestructible solely by the virtue of his few years and of his unreflecting audacity. I was reduced into something like admiration—like envy. . . . If the absolutely pure, uncalculating, unpractical spirit of adventure had ever ruled a human being, it ruled this be-patched youth.' It is Marlow, however, who provides the answer to Kurtz and the colonialists. The latter are clearly despicable; Kurtz is admirable in his original idealism and his daring to abandon it and live according to what he conceives to be his true nature; but for Marlow there is a better way. 'You wonder I didn't go ashore for a howl and a dance? Well, no—I didn't. Fine sentiments, you say? Fine sentiments be hanged! I had no time. I had to mess about with white-lead and strips of woollen blanket helping to put bandages on those leaky steam-pipes—I tell you.' 'The earth for us is a place to live in, where we must put up with sights, with sounds, with smells too, by Jove!—breathe dead hippo so to speak and not be contaminated. . . . [Y]our strength comes in, the faith in your ability for the digging of unostentatious holes to bury the stuff in—your power of devotion not to yourself but to an obscure, back-breaking business.' Throughout the novella Marlow insists on the power of efficiency, doing the job one is paid for to the best of one's ability, as a means of conquering darkness. Towser or Towson, the author of the manual on seamanship had demonstrated this. 'Not a very enthralling book, but at the first glance you could see there a singleness of intention, an honest concern for the right way of going to work which made these humble pages . . . *luminous with another than a professional light*' (emphasis added). If *Heart of Darkness* is, as some critics claim, an account of an exploration conducted by Marlow into the heart of man, from his *superego* through the *ego* into the *id*, then its conclusion is that man can surmount the bestiality of the *id* by finding order and integrity within himself (the *ego*) and demonstrating this by worthwhile and responsible action (the *superego*). Indeed, for many critics, *Heart of Darkness* is about Marlow the saved, not Kurtz the damned; it is the story of how to survive the approaching horror.

But *Heart of Darkness* has another positive force than its heroes. Enveloping the horror of Kurtz is the Congo Free State of Leopold II, totally corrupt though to all appearances established to last for a long time. But beyond this travesty of colonial enlightenment, mightier and nobler in every way, is the British Empire, for Conrad the best government the world had ever seen. On the map Marlow sees in the Brussels

office 'there was a vast amount of red—good to see at any time because
one knows that some real work is done there.' In the novella the British
Empire still stands firm, testifying to man's ability to conquer darkness
with a workable system. Marlow is concerned to remind his British audience on the cruising yawl *Nellie* that their empire came out of darkness
and must always struggle to remain free of it. Thus, in 1900, all is not
yet lost. 'If England to itself do rest but true' and continues to produce
heroes, there is some hope for mankind against the imminent catastrophe.

In the 1970's no such illusions are admissible. No responsible artist
would dare to advocate the U.S.A. or any other country as the answer
to today's chaotic world. Arguably too, the established religions have
also failed. But it comes as a shock to realize that Coppola, an American
director, cannot even offer us the traditional American hero, that seemingly imperishable if necessarily 'renewed' Adam, who is always turning
up in American books and films, in Vietnam itself only a year ago as the
Deer Hunter. In *Apocalypse Now* there are no safe frameworks—no noble
nation, no valid faith, no pioneers. The riverboat is a ship of fools, not
heroes. The self-reliant Russian of the novella has become the syco-
phantic news photographer drugged by Kurtz's ideas. And Willard is no
Marlow. At the very beginning he says, 'There is no way of telling his
[Kurtz's] story without telling my own, and if his story is a confession,
so is my own.' What he means is that his personality has been absorbed
into Kurtz's till he is fashioned into a tool, the necessary executioner and
guardian of his victim's reputation. Critics who berated the actor Martin
Sheen for portraying Willard as a mere puppet missed the point of the
role. In a film enacting the extinction of a ruthless colonel and his army,
and therefore the extinction of all warmongers and their armies, Willard
is Everyman, ourselves, deprived of our individuality till we are mere
instruments of higher powers. We are clearly meant to identify with
Willard, to see with his eyes and think his thoughts; and the great shock
of the film is that this journey on the river of human nature leads us
with Willard into the hollow heart of Colonel Kurtz. In Coppola's film,
unlike Conrad's novella, there is only the darkness. What the novelist
warned against and in some measure provided for has arrived. We are
in the great Last Day of the Apocalypse.

Heart of Darkness has withstood the test of time. It endures and will
probably always endure. Of its age, it speaks to all ages which, in a
nutshell, are surely the essentials of a great work of art. It may be too soon
to pronounce definitely on *Apocalypse Now*. In this discussion I have
not been concerned to review it purely as a film and will not therefore
deal with its many other merits, especially the cinematography—for once
an Oscar was intelligently awarded. Is it a masterpiece or, as most critics
seem to think, *almost* a masterpiece? Certainly it is an impressive film
by any standards. But I think we can already confidently assert that,
whatever its eventual stature, in two respects at least, its extraordinary
structure and its total commitment to today's reality, Coppola's film is

worthy to stand as 'a new creation' beside the Conrad novella from which it derives.

IAN WATT

[Impressionism and Symbolism in *Heart of Darkness*]†

In the tradition of what we are still calling modern literature, the classic status of *Heart of Darkness* probably depends less on the prophetic nature of Conrad's ideas[1] than on its new formal elements. These new narrative elements reflect both the general ideological crisis of the late nineteenth century and the literary innovations which accompanied it; but there are other and more direct reasons for considering them. Many readers of *Heart of Darkness* have found it rather obscure, and in particular, obscure in its answer to questions that would have been normal to ask, and easy to answer, in the case of most nineteenth-century fiction; questions such as: What is the heart of darkness? What does Kurtz actually do and why don't we see him doing it? What does it matter to Marlow, and why doesn't he tell the Intended? These questions about *Heart of Darkness* all receive answers, but only in terms of its own formal presuppositions. This qualification would actually apply to almost any literary work, but the terms of *Heart of Darkness* are especially difficult to decipher.

Conrad provides us with very little critical guidance. This is no doubt partly because of the intuitive way he wrote. As Edward Crankshaw put it, Conrad "seems to have worked in a state of semi-blindness, calculating as the need arose, crossing his bridges as they came, living, so to speak, from hand to mouth."[2] This mingling of the intuitive and the calculating in Conrad's mode of fictional creation was probably too complicated for him to describe, even perhaps to recall; and so he leaves us with miscellaneous critical explanations which are always incomplete, often unhelpful, sometimes wayward, and yet in their own way psychologically convincing. In this Conrad offers a total contrast to Henry James, whose prefaces are so conscious, logical, and comprehensive that as descriptions of what actually happened they seem too good to be true.

Conrad's most helpful comment on the method of *Heart of Darkness* occurs very early in the story, where the primary narrator explains that the meanings of Marlow's tales are characteristically difficult to encompass:

† From *Conrad in the Nineteenth Century* (Berkeley and Los Angeles: U of California P, 1979) 168–200, 249–53. Used by permission of the University of California Press. These pages have been selected, titled, and edited by Robert Kimbrough with the kind permission of Ian Watt.

1. Watt's preceding discussion was called "Ideological Perspectives" [*Editor*].
2. Edward Crankshaw, *Joseph Conrad: Some Aspects of the Art of the Novel*, 1936 (New York, 1963), p. 10.

The yarns of seamen have a direct simplicity, the whole meaning of which lies within the shell of a cracked nut. But Marlow was not typical (if his propensity to spin yarns be excepted) and to him the meaning of an episode was not inside like a kernel but outside, enveloping the tale which brought it out only as a glow brings out a haze, in the likeness of one of these misty halos that, sometimes, are made visible by the spectral illumination of moonshine.

The passage suggests at least three of the distinctive elements in *Heart of Darkness*. First of all there is the duplication of narrators; and the first one, who begins and ends the story in his own voice, feels called on to explain that the second one, Marlow, goes in for a very special kind of storytelling, which has two distinctive qualities. These two qualities are suggested metaphorically, and may be roughly categorised as symbolist and impressionist: the abstract geometry of the metaphor is symbolist because the meaning of the story, represented by the shell of the nut or the haze around the glow, is larger than its narrative vehicle, the kernel or the glow; but the sensory quality of the metaphor, the mist and haze, is essentially impressionist.

I

Impressionism

Mist or haze is a very persistent image in Conrad. It appeared as soon as he began to write: there was an "opaline haze" over the Thames on the morning when he had recalled Almayer; and the original Olmeijer had first come into Conrad's view through the morning mists of Borneo. In *Heart of Darkness* the fugitive nature and indefinite contours of haze are given a special significance by the primary narrator; he warns us that Marlow's tale will be not centered on, but surrounded by, its meaning; and this meaning will be only as fitfully and tenuously visible as a hitherto unnoticed presence of dust particles and water vapour in a space that normally looks dark and void. This in turn reminds us that one of the most characteristic objections to Impressionist painting was that the artist's ostensive "subject" was obscured by his representation of the atmospheric conditions through which it was observed. Claude Monet, for instance, said of the critics who mocked him: "Poor blind idiots. They want to see everything clearly, even through the fog!" [3] For Monet, the fog in a painting, like the narrator's haze, is not an accidental interference which stands between the public and a clear view of the artist's "real" subject: the conditions under which the viewing is done are an essential part of what the pictorial—or the literary—artist sees and therefore tries to convey.

A similar idea, expressed in a similar metaphor, occurs twenty years later in Virginia Woolf's classic characterization of "Modern Fiction" (1919). There she exempts Conrad, together with Hardy, from her

3. Quoted by Jean Renoir in *Renoir, My Father*, trans. Randolph and Dorothy Weaver (Boston and Toronto, 1958), p. 174.

objections to traditional novels and those of her Edwardian contemporaries, H. G. Wells, Arnold Bennett, and John Galsworthy.[4] Her basic objection is that if we "look within" ourselves we see "a myriad impressions" quite unrelated to anything that goes on in such fiction; and if we could express "this unknown and uncircumscribed spirit" of life freely, "there would be no plot, no comedy, no tragedy, no love interest or catastrophe in the accepted style, and perhaps not a single button sewn on as the Bond Street tailors would have it." For, Virginia Woolf finally affirms, "Life is not a series of gig lamps symmetrically arranged; life is a luminous halo, a semi-transparent envelope surrounding us from the beginning of consciousness to the end."

The implications of these images of haze and halo for the essential nature of modern fiction are made somewhat clearer by the analogy of French Impressionist painting, and by the history of the word impressionism.

As a specifically aesthetic term, "Impressionism" was apparently put into circulation in 1874 by a journalist, Louis Leroy, to ridicule the affronting formlessness of the pictures exhibited at the Salon des Indépendants, and particularly of Claude Monet's painting entitled "Impression: Sunrise." In one way or another all the main Impressionists made it their aim to give a pictorial equivalent of the visual sensations of a particular individual at a particular time and place. One early critic suggested that "l'école des yeux" would be a more appropriate designation for them than "Impressionists";[5] what was new was not that earlier painters had been blind to the external world, but that painters were now attempting to give their own personal visual perceptions a more complete expressive autonomy; in the words of Jean Leymarie, what distinguished the French Impressionists was an intuitive "response to visual sensations, devoid of any theoretical principle."[6] It was this aim which, as E. H. Gombrich has said, allots the Impressionist movement a decisive role in the process of art's long transition from trying to portray what all men know to trying to portray what the individual actually sees.[7]

The history of the words "impression" and "impressionism" in English embodies a more general aspect of the long process whereby in every domain of human concerns the priority passed from public systems of belief—what all men know—to private views of reality—what the individual sees. Beginning with the root meaning of "impression"—from *premere*, to "press" in a primarily physical sense, as in the "impression" of a printed book—the *Oxford Dictionary* documents a semantic flow towards meanings whose status is primarily psychological. The meaning of impression as "the effect produced by external force or influence on the senses or mind" was apparently established as early as 1632; and afterwards it proceeded to reflect the process whereby, from Descartes

4. *The Common Reader* (London, 1938), pp. 148–49.
5. Jacques Lethève, *Impressionnistes et Symbolistes devant la presse* (Paris, 1959), p. 63.
6. Jean Leymarie, *Impressionism*, trans. J. Emmons, 2 vols. (Lausanne, 1955), vol. 2, p. 28.
7. E. H. Gombrich, *The Story of Art*, 12th ed. (London, 1972), p. 406.

onwards, the concentration of philosophical thought upon epistemological problems gradually focussed attention on individual sensation as the only reliable source of ascertainable truth. The most notable single name connected with the process is probably that of David Hume, who opened A *Treatise of Human Nature* (1739–1740) with the ringing assertion, "All the perceptions of the human mind resolve themselves into two distinct kinds, which I shall call *IMPRESSIONS* and *IDEAS*." He had then attributed greater "force and violence" to impressions, as opposed to ideas, which he defined as merely the "less lively perceptions" which occur when we reflect on our original sense-impressions.[8] It was in protest against this empirical tradition in philosophy that the first English usage of "impressionism" occurred. In 1839 John Rogers, an eccentric word-coiner who entitled his attack on popery *Antipopopriestian*, wrote an ironical panegyric of the two main English prophets of "universal doubt": "All hail to Berkeley who would have no matter, and to Hume who would have no mind; to the Idealism of the former, and to the *Impressionism* of the latter!"[9]

It is appropriate that the word "impressionism" should be connected with Hume, since he played an important part in making the psychology of individual sensation supplant traditional philosophy as the main avenue to truth and value. One incidental result of this in the romantic and post-romantic period was that the religious, imaginative, emotional and aesthetic orders of being became increasingly private, a trend which in the course of the nineteenth century led both to the Aesthetic movement and to Impressionism. The most influential figure here is Walter Pater. In the famous "Conclusion" to *The Renaissance* (1868–1873), for instance, he speaks of how every person enclosed in "the narrow chamber of the individual mind" can directly experience only "the passage and dissolution of impressions, images, sensations"; these are "unstable, flickering, inconsistent," and the individual mind is therefore condemned to keep "as a solitary prisoner its own dream of a world."

This epistemological solipsism became an important part of the cultural atmosphere of the nineties; but by then the main English usage of the term "impressionism" was in reference to the French school of painters, and to their English counterparts who came to the fore with the foundation of the New English Art Club in 1886.[1] As in France, the term was very quickly extended to ways of writing which were thought to possess the qualities popularly attributed to the painters—to works that were spontaneous and rapidly executed, that were vivid sketches rather than detailed, finished, and premeditated compositions.[2] The literary use of the term remained even more casual and descriptive; although

8. Bk I, "Of the Understanding," Pt. 1, sect. i.
9. 2nd ed. (New York, 1841), p. 188.
1. See Holbrook Jackson, "British Impressionists," in *The Eighteen-Nineties* (London, 1939), pp. 240–50.
2. See *OED*, and Todd K. Bender, "Literary Impressionism: General Introduction," in *Preliminary Papers for Seminar #8*, distributed for the Modern Language Association Annual Meeting, 1975 (University of Wisconsin, Madison, 1975), 1–21.

Stephen Crane was widely categorised as an "impressionist," [3] and in 1898 a reviewer of Conrad's first collection of short stories, *Tales of Unrest*, described him as an "impressionistic realist," [4] there was little talk of impressionism as a literary movement until considerably later.

It was Ford Madox Ford who gave wide currency to the view that he and Conrad, like Flaubert and Maupassant, had been writers of impressionist fiction. This view was expounded in Ford's 1913 essay "On Impressionism," which sees the distinctive trait of "the Impressionist" as giving "the fruits of his own observations alone"; [5] but it is Ford's memoir of Conrad which gives his fullest account of literary impressionism. The memoir was published after Conrad's death, and so we do not know whether Ford's statement there that Conrad "avowed himself impressionist" [6] would have been contradicted by Conrad if communication had been possible. Garnett immediately registered an emphatic protest, [7] but later critics such as Joseph Warren Beach [8] and Edward Crankshaw [9] applied the term to Conrad, and he is now ensconced in literary history as an impressionist.

Conrad certainly knew something about pictorial and literary impressionism, but the indications are that his reactions were predominantly unfavourable. [1] Conrad's tastes in painting, as in music, were distinctly old-fashioned; he apparently disliked Van Gogh and Cézanne, and the only painter he ever mentioned as a model for his own writing was the peasant realist Jean-François Millet: in a letter to Quiller-Couch, Conrad wrote "it has been my desire to do for seamen what Millet (if I dare pronounce the name of that great man and good artist in this connection) has done for peasants." [2] As to literary impressionism, at the very least Conrad probably read a mildly derogatory article on "The Philosophy of Impressionism," which appeared in *Blackwood's Magazine* in May 1898, [3] and presumably knew Garnett's view of Stephen Crane as an artist of "the surfaces of life."

Conrad's own references to Crane's impressionism suggest that he shared Garnett's unsympathetic view of it. Thus, speaking of Crane's story, "The Open Boat," Conrad writes: "He is *the only* impressionist and *only* an impressionist." [4] This was in 1897, and Conrad's sense of the limitations of impressionism apparently hardened later; thus in 1900 he praised the

3. By Edward Garnett, for instance, in a 1898 essay reprinted in *Friday Nights* (London, 1922).
4. Cited by Bruce E. Teets and Helmut Gerber, eds., *Joseph Conrad: An Annotated Bibliography of Writings About Him* (De Kalb, Ill., 1971), p. 16.
5. Reprinted in *Critical Writings of Ford Madox Ford*, ed. Frank MacShane (Lincoln, 1964), p. 37.
6. *Joseph Conrad: A Personal Remembrance* (London: Duckworth, 1924), p. 6.
7. *Nation and Athenaeum* 36 (1924), 366–68.
8. In *The Twentieth-Century Novel* (New York, 1932), Conrad and Lawrence are categorised under Impressionism; Joyce comes under Post-Impressionism, Virginia Woolf under Expressionism.

9. Crankshaw writes: "The label will do as well as any other" (*Joseph Conrad*, p. 9).
1. Conrad visited Marguerite Poradowska in the Paris apartment of her cousin, Dr. Paul Gachet, close friend of Van Gogh and Cézanne, and found his collection "nightmarish" (René Rapin, ed., *Lettres de Joseph Conrad à Marguerite Poradowska* [Geneva: Droz, 1966] 87).
2. Zdzisław Najder, "Joseph Conrad: A Selection of Unknown Letters," *Polish Perspectives* 13 (1970): 32.
3. By C. F. Keary, no. 991, pp. 630–36.
4. *Letters from Conrad, 1895 to 1924* (London: Nonesuch Press, 1928), p. 107.

316   IAN WATT

"focus" of some Cunninghame Graham sketches, and added: "They are much more of course than mere Crane-like impressionism."[5] Conrad was to pay much more favourable public tributes to Crane later; but his early private comments make it clear that, much like Garnett, he thought of impressionism as primarily concerned with visual appearances. This is confirmed by Conrad's usage of the term in *The Mirror of the Sea* (1906). He writes there of a sailor asking "in impressionistic phrase: 'How does the cable grow?' "; here "impressionistic" can only mean describing how things look as opposed to stating what is "really happening."

* * *

Heart of Darkness is essentially impressionist in one very special and yet general way: it accepts, and indeed in its very form asserts, the bounded and ambiguous nature of individual understanding; and because the understanding sought is of an inward and experiential kind, we can describe the basis of its narrative method as subjective moral impressionism. Marlow's story explores how one individual's knowledge of another can mysteriously change the way in which he sees the world as a whole, and the form of *Heart of Darkness* proposes that so ambitious an enterprise can only be begun through one man trying to express his most inward impressions of how deeply problematic is the quest for—to use Pater's terms—"an outer world, and of other minds." There is a certain kinship between the protagonist of Pater's *Marius the Epicurean* (1885) and Marlow, who comes to believe something fairly close to the "sceptical argument" of Marius; since "we are never to get beyond the walls of this closely shut cell of one's own personality," it follows that "the ideas we are somehow impelled to form of an outer world, and of other minds akin to our own, are, it may be, but a day dream."[6] *Heart of Darkness* embodies more thoroughly than any previous fiction the posture of uncertainty and doubt; one of Marlow's functions is to represent how much a man cannot know; and he assumes that reality is essentially private and individual—work, he comments, gives you "the chance to find yourself. Your own reality—for yourself, not for others—what no other man can ever know. They can only see the mere show, and never can tell what it really means."

The other most distinctively impressionist aspect of Conrad's narrative method concerns his approach to visual description; and this preoccupation with the problematic relation of individual sense impressions to meaning is shown most clearly in one of the minor innovations of his narrative technique.

Long before *Heart of Darkness* Conrad seems to have been trying to find ways of giving direct narrative expression to the way in which the consciousness elicits meaning from its perceptions. One of the devices that he hit on was to present a sense impression and to withhold naming it or explaining its meaning until later; as readers we witness every step

5. C. T. Watts, ed., *Joseph Conrad's Letters to R. B. Cunninghame Graham* (Cambridge: Cambridge UP, 1969), p. 130.
6. Pater, *Marius the Epicurean*, pp. 106, 110.

by which the gap between the individual perception and its cause is belatedly closed within the consciousness of the protagonist.

* * *

This narrative device may be termed delayed decoding, since it combines the forward temporal progression of the mind, as it receives messages from the outside world, with the much slower reflexive process of making out their meaning. Through this device—here used somewhat crudely—the reader participates in the instantaneous sensations, and is "made to see" [what a character may *not* see at that moment.]

* * *

By the time Conrad came to write *Heart of Darkness*, then, he had developed one narrative technique which was the verbal equivalent of the impressionist painter's attempt to render visual sensation directly. Conrad presented the protagonist's immediate sensations, and thus made the reader aware of the gap between impression and understanding; the delay in bridging the gap enacts the disjunction between the event and the observer's trailing understanding of it. In *Heart of Darkness* Conrad uses the method for the most dramatic action of the story, when Marlow's boat is attacked, just below Kurtz's station. Marlow, terrified of going aground, is anxiously watching the cannibal sounding in the bows just below him: "I was looking down at the sounding-pole and feeling much annoyed to see at each try a little more of it stick out of that river, when I saw my poleman give up the business suddenly and stretch himself flat on the deck without even taking the trouble to haul his pole in."

Marlow's initially inexplicable visual impression is accompanied by his irritation at an apparently gratuitous change in the normal order of things. Here, however, the effect is duplicated: "At the same time the fireman, whom I could also see below me, sat down abruptly before his furnace and ducked his head. I was amazed." Only now does the cause of these odd changes in posture begin to emerge: "Then I had to look at the river mighty quick because there was a snag in the fairway. Sticks, little sticks, were flying about, thick; they were whizzing before my nose, dropping below me, striking behind me against my pilot-house." But it is only when Marlow has finished attending to his duty as captain, and negotiated the next snag, that his understanding can finally decode the little sticks: "We cleared the snag clumsily. Arrows, by Jove! We were being shot at!"

Meanwhile the pilgrims, and, to Marlow's fury, even his helmsman, have started "squirting lead" into the bush. Marlow is navigating and catching occasional glimpses of "vague forms of men" through the shutterhole of the pilot-house, when his attention is suddenly deflected:

> Something big appeared in the air before the shutter, the rifle went overboard, and the man stepped back swiftly, looked at me over his shoulder in an extraordinary, profound, familiar manner, and fell upon my feet. The side of his head hit the wheel twice, and the

end of what appeared a long cane clattered round and knocked over a little camp-stool. It looked as though after wrenching that thing from somebody ashore he had lost his balance in the effort. The thin smoke had blown away, we were clear of the snag, and looking ahead I could see that in another hundred yards or so I would be free to sheer off away from the bank, but my feet felt so very warm and wet that I had to look down. The man had rolled on his back and stared straight up at me; both his hands clutched that cane. It was the shaft of a spear. . . . He looked at me anxiously, gripping the spear like something precious, with an air of being afraid I would try to take it away from him.[7]

A third sudden and unfamiliar action is enacted through the protagonist's consciousness, and the delay in his decoding of it makes the reader simultaneously experience horror and sardonic amusement. Amusement, because we feel a certain patronising contempt for those who do not understand things as quickly as we do, and because there is a gruesome comedy in the mere visual impression of the helmsman's "air of being afraid I would try to take [the spear] away from him." This macabre note has already been prepared for: if the poleman lies down, and then the fireman sits down, it is only natural that Marlow should assume that the dead helmsman's recumbent posture must be just a third example of the crew's deserting their duty just for their personal safety.

Still, the passage is obviously not primarily comic. Conrad's main objective is to put us into intense sensory contact with the events; and this objective means that the physical impression must precede the understanding of cause. Literary impressionism implies a field of vision which is not merely limited to the individual observer, but is also controlled by whatever conditions—internal and external—prevail at the moment of observation. In narration the main equivalents to atmospheric interference in painting are the various factors which normally distort human perception, or which delay its recognition of what is most relevant and important. First of all, our minds are usually busy with other things—Marlow has a lot to do just then, and it is only natural that he should be annoyed by being faced with these three new interferences with his task of keeping the boat from disaster. Secondly, our interpretations of impressions are normally distorted by habitual expectations—Marlow perceives the unfamiliar arrows as familiar sticks. Lastly, we always have many more things in our range of vision than we can pay attention to, so that in a crisis we may miss the most important ones—in this case that the helmsman has been killed. Conrad's method

7. Beerbohm hit off Conrad's use of delayed decoding for the climax of his story. The protagonist is "silenced by sight of what seemed to be a young sapling sprung up from the ground within a yard of him—a young sapling tremulous, with a root of steel" (A Christmas Garland, London 1950, p. 133). The closest analogy seems to be this passage, although Jocelyn Baines says that "Max Beerbohm based his witty parody of Conrad in A Christmas Garland" on "Karain" and "The Lagoon" (Jocelyn Baines, Joseph Conrad: A Critical Biography [London: Weidenfeld and Nicholson, 1960] 190) and Addison C. Bross argues, in "Beerbohm's 'The Feast' and Conrad's Early Fiction," (Nineteenth-Century Fiction 26 [1971]: 329–36), for "An Outpost of Progress" as a closer source.

reflects all these difficulties in translating perceptions into causal or conceptual terms. This takes us deeply into the connection between delayed decoding and impressionism: it reminds us, as Michael Levenson has said, of the precarious nature of the process of interpretation in general; and since this precariousness is particularly evident when the individual's situation or his state of mind is abnormal, the device of delayed decoding simultaneously enacts the objective and the subjective aspects of moments of crisis. The method also has the more obvious advantage of convincing us of the reality of the experience which is being described; there is nothing suspiciously selective about the way it is narrated; while we read we are, as in life, fully engaged in trying to decipher a meaning out of a random and pell-mell bombardment of sense impressions.

The attempt to transcribe the process of individual perception was one of the most widely diffused tendencies in all the arts during the period between 1874, the date of the first Impressionist exhibition in Paris, and 1910, the date of the exhibition of new painting in London for which Roger Fry coined the term Post-Impressionism. Conrad's device of delayed decoding represents an original narrative solution to the general problem of expressing the process whereby the individual's sensations of the external world are registered and translated into the causal and conceptual terms which can make them understandable to the observer and communicable to other people. More generally, Marlow's emphasis on the difficulty of understanding and communicating his own individual experience aligns *Heart of Darkness* with the subjective relativism of the impressionist attitude. Nevertheless, it is very unlikely that Conrad either thought of himself as an impressionist or was significantly influenced by the impressionist movement. Conrad wanted to pay as much attention to the inside as to the outside, to the meaning as to the appearance; and this is one of the reasons why, in the last analysis, he is so different both from the French Impressionists and from Pater, Crane, or Ford.

Behind this difference is another which gives a unique quality to the impressionist elements in Conrad. For Conrad, the world of the senses is not a picture but a presence, a presence so intense, unconditional, and unanswerable that it loses the fugitive, hypothetical, subjective, and primarily aesthetic qualities which it usually has in the impressionist tradition. Ramon Fernandez, in one of the very few indispensable essays on Conrad, remarks that his way of describing the external world is the exact opposite of traditional narrative description such as Balzac's: Conrad's art, he writes, "does not trace the reality before the man, but the man before the reality; it evokes experiences in their subjective entirety because the impression is the equivalent of the entire perception, and because the whole man experiences it with all the powers of his being." Conrad's "great originality," Fernandez concludes, "is to have applied this impressionism to the knowledge of human beings."[8]

8. "L'Art de Conrad," *Nouvelle Revue française* 12 (1924): 732; conveniently available in English in *The Art of Joseph Conrad*, ed. Robert W. Stallman (East Lansing, Mich., 1960), pp. 8–13.

II
Symbolism

In the narrator's description of Marlow's unseamanlike conduct as a storyteller, the symbolist aspect derives from the main geometrical feature of the illustration. It is based on the contrasted arrangements of two concentric spheres. In the first arrangement, that of the typical seaman's yarn, the direction given our minds is, to use a term from Newtonian physics, "centripetal": the story, the narrative vehicle, is the shell, the larger outside sphere; it encloses a smaller sphere, the inner kernel of truth; and as readers of the yarn we are invited to seek inside it for this central core of meaning. Marlow's tales, on the other hand, are typically "centrifugal": the relation of the spheres is reversed; now the narrative vehicle is the smaller inside sphere; and its function is merely to make the reader go outside it in search of a circumambient universe of meanings which are not normally visible, but which the story, the glow, dimly illuminates. This subordinate yet necessary role of the story was made even clearer in the manuscript, which included the two phrases here italicised: "the meaning of an episode was not inside like a kernel but outside *in the unseen*, enveloping the tale which *could only bring* it out as a glow brings out a haze."[9]

The outer sphere of larger meaning, then, is presumably infinite, since, unlike the husk of a nut, the haze lacks any ascertainable circumference; but to be visible the haze needs the finite glow; and so the two together constitute a symbol in Carlyle's view of it: "the Infinite is made to blend itself with the Finite, to stand visible, and as it were, attainable there."[1]

When Virginia Woolf speaks of the aim of modern fiction as the expression of life seen as "a luminous halo, a semi-transparent envelope," and proceeds to applaud Conrad for conveying this "unknown and uncircumscribed spirit," her words, like those of Conrad's narrator, suggest an analogy both to Carlyle and to later symbolist theories of literature. But Virginia Woolf's views of modern fiction, as we have seen, are also consistent with the general impressionist position; both her terms and those of Conrad's narrator, in fact, imply something like a symbiotic relationship between the symbolist and impressionist perspectives.

There is some doubt, however, whether either impressionism or symbolism stand for meanings which are sufficiently clear to be worth using. The case of symbolism is particularly obstinate, because the term is used much more widely, and with less reference to any specific historical movement. The issue can perhaps best be approached by considering two general questions: first, why did no one talk about literature as symbolic until the last century or so? And second, why have so many modern critics assumed that their main task is to find symbolic meanings in whatever literature they find worth discussing?

9. I am indebted to Dave Thorburn, and Marjorie Wynne of the Beinecke Library, for sending me a copy of the holograph. [See p. 9, above—*Editor.*]
1. *Sartor Resartus*, Bk. 3, ch. 3, p. 158.

Historically, the impressionist and symbolist tendencies are alike in being antitraditional assertions of the private individual vision. In this they are essentially reflections of much vaster changes, which first became apparent in the romantic period, and took more urgent forms during the intellectual crisis of the late nineteenth century, a crisis by now most familiar to literary history in its twin manifestations of the death of God and the disappearance of the omniscient author.

In its simplest terms, symbolism involves a process whereby particular objects or events are attributed some larger, nonliteral meaning. This larger meaning is connected to its verbal sign either by arbitrary convention or by a natural extension of its normal properties. The use of the fixed conventional kind of symbolism—the apple of discord, for instance—was hardly a problem before the romantic period, because everything in the outside world was widely agreed to constitute a fixed order, in which each item had its appropriate religious, moral, or social role: the connection between the object and its meaning was public and established—most obviously in mythology and allegory; and the fixed and public quality of these established linkages is indicated by the fact that the earliest sense of the word "symbol" was "a creed or confession of faith" (OED).

In the romantic period, and by a historical process broadly parallel to that which led to the impressionist effort to render an individual visual representation of the external world, many poets felt impelled to discard symbols of a fixed and conventional kind, and instead to assign their own personal symbolic meanings to natural objects, to mountains, birds and flowers. These meanings began from the properties of the object, but they were often taken further by the writer's imagination.[2] In its extreme form, the correspondence between the particular, literal object and its imagined symbolic meaning was of a mystical or esoteric kind, as often in Blake; more commonly the meaning, while not hermetic, extended far beyond the inherent representativeness of the object; and that meaning was based on the assumption that the poet had privileged access to previously unknown immanent connections between the external world and spiritual reality.

* * *

Neither Baudelaire, nor the most famous of what have come to be called the French Symbolist poets—Verlaine, Rimbaud and Mallarmé—called themselves Symbolists; nor did the painters, Gustave Moreau (1826–1898), Puvis de Chavannes (1824–1898), and Odilon Redon (1840–1916). The ideas and much of the vocabulary of Symbolism, however, had been worked out long before the movement was named,

---

2. In this very summary and simplified account I am particularly indebted to Frank Kermode, *Romantic Image* (London, 1957), M. H. Abrams, *Natural Supernaturalism: Tradition and Revolution in Romantic Literature* (New York, 1971), Marcel Raymond, *De Baudelaire au Surréalisme* (rev. ed., Paris, 1969), and Jean-Jacques Mayoux, *Vivants piliers: le roman anglo-saxon et les sym-* boles (Paris, 1960). Tzvetan Todorov's comprehensive analysis in *Théories du symbole* (Paris, 1977) appeared too late to be used. Its first six chapters place the changing nature of the symbol during the romantic period in the more general perspective of the breakdown of the Western tradition of rhetoric.

322 IAN WATT

as it belatedly was in poetry when Jean Moréas wrote his manifesto in 1886, and in painting at the Cafe Volpini exhibition in 1889.[3]

* * *

In the nineties, England was very much more receptive to foreign literature and philosophy than it had been earlier in the Victorian period;[4] in many circles Mr. Podsnap's "Not British" had become a term, no longer of anathema, but of acclamation. As a result, Symbolism, like Impressionism, was much in the air; and so, quite apart from his own wide reading in French, there can be no doubt that, by the time he wrote *Heart of Darkness*, Conrad could hardly have avoided knowing something about the French Symbolists. * * * [Still,] it is virtually certain that whatever similarities may exist between Conrad and the French Symbolists are not the result of any direct literary influence on Conrad or of his doctrinal adhesion. * * * There is, however, much in Conrad's letters which suggests that he shared many of the basic attitudes of the French Symbolists. These attitudes may be summarily divided into two categories: the ontological—the kinds of basic reality, knowledge, or vision, which literature seeks beyond the "bundle of fragments" offered by the external world; and the expressive—the characteristic formal methods by which the reader is induced to seek this vision beyond the work's overt statements.

* * *

Heart of Darkness, then, belongs to a specifically symbolic tradition of fiction, and it is the only one of Conrad's novels which does. As to his theoretical position on the symbolic nature of the novel, and on the French Symbolists, Conrad expressed himself most directly, though not unambiguously, in a letter of 1918. In answer to a critic who had written to him about the "final effect" of a work of art, Conrad maintained the general position that "All the great creations of literature have been symbolic." "A work of art," he explained, "is very seldom limited to one exclusive meaning and not necessarily tending to a definite conclusion. And this for the reason that the nearer it approaches art, the more it acquires a symbolic character. This statement may surprise you, who may imagine that I am alluding to the Symbolist School of poets or prose writers. Theirs, however, is only a literary proceeding against which I have nothing to say. I am concerned here with something much larger."[5]

Conrad casually dissociates himself from the French Symbolists, not in order to say anything against their "literary proceedings," but to affirm a "much larger" view: that great works of art do not necessarily "tend to definite conclusions"; and that the extent of their "symbolic character" is directly proportional to the quality of their art.

It is possible that Conrad's use of the word symbolic here may mean no more than that in the greatest works of literature the characters and

3. See Jean Leymarie, *Impressionism*, vol. 2, pp. 86–88, and Guy Michaud, *Message poétique du symbolisme* (Paris, 1947), pp. 165, 123–24, 143–44.
4. See Christophe Campos, *The View of France:*

From Arnold to Bloomsbury (London, 1965), especially pp. 164–73.
5. G. Jean-Aubry, *Joseph Conrad: Life and Letters* (London: Heinemann, 1927), II, 205.

their destinies stand for much more than their particular selves and actions, and are representative of more universal feelings and situations. This would be a variant of the commonest usage of "symbolic" as meaning "widely representative"; and it would then carry the idea that all the components of the novel should have wider and more general implications. But Conrad seems to be implying something more: only a larger meaning for symbolic, surely, would justify his assumption that his statement may be found "surprising"; and the essence of his statement is presumably that the quality of art is proportional to its range of symbolic meanings. Such a view, of course, would be consistent both with the image of the glow and the haze, and with the general intention of the French Symbolists. But Conrad's letter is sufficiently obscure to allow of some doubt; and so as regards *Heart of Darkness*, the only real test must be that of its actual narrative practice. One passage, whose symbolism has been given conflicting interpretations, seems especially appropriate.

On his way to receive his appointment from the trading company, Marlow goes through

> A narrow and deserted street in deep shadow, high houses, innumerable windows with venetian blinds, a dead silence, grass sprouting between the stones, imposing carriage archways right and left, immense double doors standing ponderously ajar. I slipped through one of these cracks, went up a swept and ungarnished staircase, as arid as a desert, and opened the first door I came to. Two women, one fat and the other slim, sat on straw-bottomed chairs knitting black wool. The slim one got up and walked straight at me—still knitting with downcast eyes—and only just as I began to think of getting out of her way, as you would for a somnambulist, stood still, and looked up. Her dress was as plain as an umbrella cover, and she turned round without a word and preceded me into a waiting-room. I gave my name, and looked about.

Marlow is ushered into the presence of the director, and then

> In about forty-five seconds I found myself again in the waiting room with the compassionate secretary who full of desolation and sympathy made me sign some document. I believe I undertook amongst other things not to disclose any trade secrets. Well, I am not going to.
>
> I began to feel slightly uneasy. You know I am not used to such ceremonies and there was something ominous in the atmosphere. It was just as though I had been let into some conspiracy—I don't know—something not quite right, and I was glad to get out. In the outer room the two women knitted black wool feverishly. People were arriving and the younger one was walking back and forth introducing them. The old one sat on her chair. Her flat cloth slippers were propped up on a foot-warmer and a cat reposed on

her lap. She wore a starched white affair on her head, had a wart
on one cheek, and silver-rimmed spectacles hung on the tip of her
nose. She glanced at me above the glasses. The swift and indifferent
placidity of that look troubled me. Two youths with foolish and
cheery countenances were being piloted over and she threw at them
the same quick glance of unconcerned wisdom. She seemed to know
all about them and about me too. An eerie feeling came over me.
She seemed uncanny and fateful. Often far away there I thought of
these two, guarding the door of Darkness, knitting black wool as for
a warm pall, one introducing, introducing continuously to the
unknown, the other scrutinizing the cheery and foolish faces with
unconcerned old eyes. "*Ave!* Old knitter of black wool. *Morituri te
salutant.*" Not many of those she looked at ever saw her again—
not half—by a long way.

Several critics have made the two knitters a primary basis for a large-
scale symbolic interpretation of *Heart of Darkness* in which Marlow's
whole journey becomes a version of the traditional descent into hell,
such as that in the sixth book of Virgil's *Aeneid*,[6] and in Dante's *Inferno*.
This kind of critical interpretation assumes that the symbolic reference
of the verbal sign must be closed rather than open, and that it arises, not
from the natural and inherent associations of the object, but from a
preestablished body of ideas, stories, or myths. The present passage certainly makes symbolic reference to associations of this kind: Marlow presents his own experience in the general perspective of the pagan and
Christian traditions of a journey to the underworld: this is made sufficiently explicit when he talks of the knitters "guarding the door of Darkness," and of the two youths "being piloted over." But this is not the
only symbolic reference of the passage, nor the most important; and
there is no reason to assume that the movement from the literal to the
symbolic must be centripetal. Only some such assumption could have
impelled one critic to assert that there is a "close structural parallel between
Heart of Darkness and *Inferno*," and proceed to equate the company
station with Limbo and the central station with the abode of the fraudulent, while making Kurtz both a "traitor to kindred" and a Lucifer.[7]

One obvious practical objection to this kind of symbolic interpretation
is that it alerts our attention too exclusively to a few aspects of the narrative—to those which seem to provide clues that fit the assumed unitary
and quasi-allegorical frame of symbolic reference. This leads us to inter-
rogate the text only in those terms, and to ask such questions as: Why
does Conrad give us only *two* fates? Which one is Clotho the spinner?
and which Lachesis the weaver? Did the Greeks know about knitting
anyway? Where are the shears? What symbolic meaning can there be in
the fact that the thin one lets people *in* to the room and then *out* again—
a birth and death ritual, perhaps? Lost in such unfruitful preoccupa-

6. Lillian Feder, "Marlow's Descent into Hell,"   7. Robert O. Evans, "Conrad's Underworld,"
Nineteenth-Century Fiction 9 (1955): 280–92.   *Modern Fiction Studies* 2 (1956): 59;60.

tions, our imaginations will hardly be able to respond to the many other symbolic clues in the passage, or even to the many other meanings in those details which have secured our attention.

In fact a multiplicity of historical and literary associations pervades the scene in the anteroom; and this multiplicity surely combines to place the two knitters in a much more universal perspective. There is, most obviously, the heartless unconcern manifested throughout the ages by the spectators at a variety of ordeals that are dangerous or fatal to the protagonists. This unconcern is what the fates have in common with the two other main historical parallels evoked in the passage—the French *tricoteuses* callously knitting at the guillotine, and the Roman crowds to whom the gladiators address their scornful farewell in Marlow's rather pretentious interjection: "Ave! Old knitter of black wool, *Morituri te salutant."*

Within the context of *Heart of Darkness* as a whole the function of these three examples of symbolic reference is local and circumscribed; like Marlow's earlier historical allusions to Drake and Franklin they are dropped as soon as made; they are not intended to link up with other allusions into a single cryptographic system which gives the main symbolic meaning of the work as a whole. One reason for this is surely that any continuing symbolic parallel would undermine the literal interest and significance of the narrative at every compositional level, from the essential conflict of the plot, to the details of its narrative presentation.

The present passage, then, gives clear evidence of how Conrad aimed at a continuous immediacy of detail which had symbolic reference that was primarily of a natural, open, and multivocal kind. Marlow presents a highly selective but vivid series of details; they are for the most part given as raw and unexplained observations, and the autonomy and isolation of each particular image seems to impel the reader to larger surmise. There is, for instance, the approach of the thin knitter who "got up and walked straight at me—still knitting with downcast eyes—and only just as I began to think of getting out of her way, as you would for a somnambulist, stood still, and looked up. Her dress was as plain as an umbrella cover."

If we submit ourselves to the evocative particularity of these intensely visualised details, their symbolic connotations take us far beyond our primary sense of the fateful, uncanny, and impassive atmosphere of the scene; we are driven to a larger awareness of a rigid, mechanical, blind, and automatised world. If we attempt to explain the sources of this awareness we can point to the way that the thin knitter does not speak to Marlow, nor even, apparently, see him; her movements are unrelated to other human beings. The knitter's appearance increases this sense of the nonhuman; her shape recalls an umbrella and its tight black cover; there has been no effort to soften the functional contours of its hard and narrow ugliness with rhythmic movements, rounded forms, or pleasing colours. It is not that the knitter reminds us of the classical Fates which really matters, but that she is herself a fate—a dehumanised death in life to herself and to others, and thus a prefiguring symbol of what the trading company does to its creatures.

Some of the images in the passage are representative in a limited and mainly pictorial way; the older knitter, for example, with her wart and her flat cloth slippers, becomes a stark visual image of physical and spiritual deformity combined with imperturbable self-complacence. But there is another, larger, and to some extent contrary, tendency, where the extreme selectivity of Marlow's memory draws our attention to his state of mind at the time. For instance, when Marlow comments about the tycoon: "He shook hands I fancy," his uncertainty suggests that his consciousness was occupied with other matters. Marlow omits much that would certainly be mentioned in an autobiography, or a naturalist novel; we are not, for instance, given the details of Marlow's contract, or the name of the people. This omission of proper names is a particularly typical symbolist procedure—in Maeterlinck, for instance, or in Kafka. The general reason for the strategy is clear: most of the details about the narrative object are omitted, so that what details remain, liberated from the bonds and irrelevancies of the purely circumstantial and contingent, can be recognised as representatives of larger ideas and attitudes.

Marlow despecifies the tycoon to reveal his essence; he calls him merely a "pale plumpness" because big bureaucrats typically eat too much, don't exercise outdoors, are featureless and somewhat abstract. But there is another essence involved in the situation; if Marlow so often despecifies the external and the factual aspects of the scene, it is because his own hierarchy of attention at the time was primarily internal and moral; what Marlow was actually registering with benumbed incredulity was his spiritual reaction to being initiated into the most universal and fateful of modern society's rites of passage—the process whereby the individual confronts a vast bureaucracy to get a job from it.

Marlow begins his rite of passage with a representative ecological sequence: approach through unfamiliar streets and arid staircases; passive marshalling from waiting room to grand managerial sanctum; and, forty-five seconds later, a more rapid return thence through the same stages, with a delayed and demoralising detour for medical examination. The sequence of routinised human contacts is equally typical: the impassive receptionists; the expert compassion of the confidential secretary; the hollow benevolence of the plump tycoon; the shifty joviality of the clerk; and the hypocritical pretences of the medical examiner.

Marlow registers but rarely comments; and we are thus left free to draw our deductions about the symbolic meanings of the passage. They are multiple, and they are not expounded but suggested; consequently our interpretative priorities will depend on our literary imagination as readers, and on our own way of conceiving reality.

One possible direction of larger symbolic reference concerns the implicit view of civilisation suggested in the passage. Some of the details of the scene suggest the way Marx saw one result of modern capitalism as the turning of people into mere objects in a system of economic relations;

human beings become things and so their personal relationships take on a "spectral objectivity."[8] This interpretation is also consistent with Max Weber's related view that modern bureaucratic administration brings with it "the dominance of a spirit of formalistic impersonality."[9] Since both these interpretations find some support in the literal meanings of the passage, as well as in other parts of *Heart of Darkness*, they can reasonably be regarded as tributes to Conrad's power not only to penetrate the essential moral meaning of the institutions of the modern world, but to communicate that meaning symbolically.

The passage also implies a good deal about the unspoken subjective meaning of the ordeal for Marlow. When the scene ends we can look back and see that Marlow is left with a sense of a doubly fraudulent initiation: the company has not told him what he wants to know; but since Marlow has been unable to formulate the causes of his moral discomfort, much less ask any authentic question or voice any protest, his own tranced submission has been a betrayal of himself. These implications prefigure what we are to see as one of the larger and more abstract themes of the story—the lack of any genuinely reciprocal dialogue; even Marlow cannot or does not speak out. In this passage, for instance, Marlow's most extended dialogue at the company's offices is with the doctor. In part it merely typifies this particular aspect of bureaucratic initiation: the formulaic insult ("Ever any madness in your family?"); the posture of disinterested devotion to scientific knowledge (measuring Marlow's cranium); and the pretendedly benevolent but actually both impractical and deeply disquieting counsel ("Avoid irritation more than exposure to the sun"). Such details might be said to operate partly in a centripetal way, since they point to specific later issues in the narrative—to Kurtz's skull and those on his fenceposts, and to the physical and mental collapse of Kurtz and Marlow at the end; but the details also have larger and more expansive centrifugal overtones. The horrors of the modern secular hell are not merely the affronting mumbo-jumbo of the medical priesthood; Marlow has illumined the haze which hangs like a pall over the society of which the doctor, the clerk, the knitters and the pale plumpness are the symbolic representatives; and we are led outwards to discern the ramifying absences of human communion.

We are left with an overpowering sense of Marlow's fateful induction into the vast overarching network of the silent lies of civilisation. No one will explain them—not the servants of the company certainly, if only because the jobs of the personnel depend on their discretion; the great corporate enterprise has no voice, yet Marlow cannot help attributing moral meanings and intentions to all the tangible manifestations of the power which controls his life.

The absence of shared understanding exists at an even higher level of

8. The phrase, "gespenstische Gegenständlichkeit," is that of Georg Lukács (*Existentialismus oder Marxismus?* [Berlin, 1951]), p. 41, summarising one aspect of Marx's view of reification.

9. Max Weber, *The Theory of Social and Economic Organisation*, trans. A. M. Henderson and Talcott Parsons (New York, 1947), p. 340.

abstraction. Marlow hardly knows the meaning of what is happening to him; there is no Virgil in sight, much less a Beatrice; and no one even seems aware that the problem exists. Later the narrative reveals that this gap extends throughout Marlow's world; we go from the silent, lethal madness of the trading company to that of the civilisation for which it stands; Marlow is confronting a general intellectual and moral impasse whose narrative climax is enacted when he is forced to lie to the Intended; and this gap, in turn, can be seen in a wider historical and philosophical perspective as a reflection of the same breakdown of the shared categories of understanding and judgment, as had originally imposed on Conrad and many of his contemporaries the indirect, subjective, and guarded strategies that characterised the expressive modes of Symbolism.

One could argue that the distinctive aim, not only of Conrad but of much modern literature, is not so much "to make us see," but, somewhat more explicitly, "to make us see what we see"; and this would ultimately involve a view of narrative in which every detail is inherently symbolic. The reader and the critic of such literature, therefore, must assume that since each individual text generates its own symbolic meaning, only a primary commitment to the literal imagination will enable him to see the larger implications of all the particularities which confront him. Thus in the present scene the knitters suggest many ideas which are essentially generalised forms of the literal or inherent qualities which Marlow has recorded; and each of these symbolic meanings can in turn be extended in a centrifugal way to a larger understanding of the world Conrad presents. The opposite kind of critical reading starts from an esoteric interpretation of particular objects—the knitters are "really" the fates—and combines them into a centripetal and cryptographic interpretation which is based, as in allegory, on a single and defined system of beliefs, and is largely independent of the literal meanings of the details presented and of their narrative context. But the primary narrator's image has warned us against proceeding as though there is a single edible kernel of truth hidden below the surface; and it is surely curious, even saddening, to reflect that, out of the dozen or more studies of the scene with the knitters, none has interpreted it as part of a larger symbolic vision of the great corporation and its civilisation.

The modern critical tendency to decompose literary works into a series of more or less cryptic references to a system of non-literal unifying meanings is in large part a misguided response to a very real problem in the interpretation of much modern literature.

Many of the characteristics of that literature can be seen as the result of the convergence of the symbolist and impressionist traditions. The two movements were largely parallel manifestations in the *avant garde* ferment which affected all the arts during the last three decades of the nineteenth century; and this fusion of the impressionist and symbolist tendencies continued into the twentieth century. The Imagist movement, for instance, is primarily a development of the impressionist tendency, as Ford's connection with it suggests, but Imagism also had strong ties with the English symbolist poets. In his 1913 Imagist Manifesto, Ezra Pound, who was in part reacting against what he considered the vagueness of both impressionist and symbolist art, nevertheless telescoped the primary emphasis of both tendencies when he defined his literary objective, the image, as "that which presents an intellectual and emotional complex in an instant of time," and went on to make the ringing polemic affirmation "the natural object is always the *adequate* symbol."[1]

Pound's dual principles suggest how the impressionist and symbolist emphases combined to form the basis of the characteristic expressive idiom not only of modern poetry but of modern narrative prose. The same two emphases, for example, underlie Marvin Mudrick's almost pardonable hyperbole that "After *Heart of Darkness*, the recorded moment—the word—was irrecoverably symbol."[2] "The recorded moment," with its emphasis on immediate sensation, is primarily impressionist, and so is Mudrick's subsequent analysis of how Conrad developed "the moral resources inherent in every recorded sensation."

The need to derive moral meaning from physical sensation partly arises from the fact that both the impressionists and the symbolists, as has already been noted, proscribed any analysis, prejudgment, or conceptual commentary—the images, events, and feelings were to be left to speak for themselves. This laid a particular burden on the writer's power of expression, since his objects alone had to carry a rich burden of suggested autonomous meanings. The symbolist method therefore begins by making the same descriptive demand as that of impressionism: the writer must render the object with an idiosyncratic immediacy of vision, which is freed from any intellectual prejudgment or explanatory gloss; and the reader must be put in the posture of actively seeking to fill the gaps in a text which has provoked him to experience an absence of connecting meanings.

* * *

If Conrad belongs to the symbolist tradition it is only in a limited, eclectic, and highly idiosyncratic way; even if one accepts in some very general sense the view that modern literature is mainly a continuation of the symbolist tradition[3] and waives the until now insuperable difficulties of definition,[4] there seems little to be gained by categorising Conrad, along with Proust, Kafka, Joyce, Mann, and Faulkner, as a symbolist

1. "A Stray Document," in *Make It New: Essays* (London, 1934), pp. 336–37. On Pound's view of the relationship of imagism to impressionism, see Herbert N. Schneidau, *Ezra Pound: The Image and the Real* (Baton Rouge, La., 1969), pp. 34–35.
2. "The Originality of Conrad," *Hudson Review* 11 (1958): 553.
3. Influentially propounded by Edmund Wilson in *Axel's Castle: A Study of the Imaginative Literature of 1870–1930* (New York, 1931).
4. In his *The Symbolist Aesthetic in France: 1885–1895*, 2nd ed. (Oxford, 1968), A. G. Lehmann concludes that "the terms 'literary symbol' and 'symbolist' are terms which, introduced and fortified by a series of mischances, should never have been allowed to remain in usage" (p. 316).

novelist,[5] especially if this is taken to involve dissociating him from the impressionist tradition to which he is more commonly assigned. The particular case of *Heart of Darkness*, however, is somewhat different; its narrative technique in most respects typifies, and indeed anticipates, the general expressive idiom of modern literature; but its plot, its themes, and some of the evidence about its intentions are closer to some of the central features of the French symbolist movement than any of Conrad's other works.

Its plot contains some very untypical elements of adventure and melodrama, but it is nevertheless based on a simple symbolic quest, in which the various forms of "darkness" which Marlow encounters have as many possible meanings as the blue flower in Novalis. The essence of the action is a process of expanded moral awareness; as Marlow says, his journey was significant only because it "seemed somehow to throw a kind of light on everything about me—and into my thoughts."

The structure of *Heart of Darkness* is very largely based on naturally symbolic actions and objects: the plot—a journey, a death, and a return; the characters—Kurtz, or the helmsman; the incidents—Marlow's interview for the job, or the grove of death; the material objects—the rivets, the staves of the pilgrims, the heads on the posts; the scene—the Thames and the Congo; the atmosphere—light and darkness. In all these elements the symbolic meaning of objects and events is established through the expansion of their inherent properties, and they have a structural, rather than a merely illustrative, function.

The analogy is equally close as regards subject matter. *Heart of Darkness* shares many of the characteristic preoccupations and themes of the French Symbolists: the spiritual voyage of discovery, especially through an exotic jungle landscape, which was a common symbolist theme, in Baudelaire's "Le Voyage" and Rimbaud's "Bâteau ivre," for instance; the pervasive atmosphere of dream, nightmare, and hallucination, again typical of Rimbaud; and the very subject of Kurtz also recalls, not only Rimbaud's own spectacular career, but the typical symbolist fondness for the lawless, the depraved, and the extreme modes of experience.

More generally, we surely sense in *Heart of Darkness* Conrad's supreme effort to reveal, in Baudelaire's phrase about Delacroix, "the infinite in the finite."[6] This intention is suggested in Conrad's title. The Symbolist poets often used titles which suggested a much larger and more mysterious range of implication than their work's overt subject apparently justified—one thinks of the expanding effect of T. S. Eliot's *The Waste Land*, for example, or of *The Sacred Wood*. This centrifugal suggestion was sometimes produced by an obtrusive semantic gap—a coupling of incongruous words or images that force us to look beyond our habitual

5. These are all, for instance, classified as "romantic symbolists" in William York Tindall's *The Literary Symbol* (New York, 1955), p. 3. Mark Schorer described *Heart of Darkness* as "that early but wonderful piece of symbolist fiction" in his classic essay "Technique as Discovery" (*The World We Imagine* [New York, 1968], p. 19).

6. *Oeuvres complètes*, ed. Ruff (Paris, 1968), p. 404.

expectations; there is, for instance, the initial puzzling shock of the titles of two of the great precursive works of symbolism which appeared in 1873, Rimbaud's *Une Saison en enfer*, and Tristan Corbière's "Les Amours jaunes."

Compared with the particularity of Conrad's earlier and more traditional titles, such as *Almayer's Folly* or *The Nigger of the "Narcissus"*, *Heart of Darkness* strikes a very special note; we are somehow impelled to see the title as much more than a combination of two stock metaphors for referring to "the centre of the Dark Continent" and "a diabolically evil person." Both of Conrad's nouns are densely charged with physical and moral suggestions; freed from the restrictions of the article, they combine to generate a sense of puzzlement which prepares us for something beyond our usual expectation: if the words do not name what we know, they must be asking us to know what has, as yet, no name. The more concrete of the two terms, "heart," is attributed a strategic centrality within a formless and infinite abstraction, "darkness"; the combination defies both visualisation and logic: How can something inorganic like darkness have an organic centre of life and feeling? How can a shapeless absence of light compact itself into a shaped and pulsing presence? And what are we to make of a "good" entity like a heart becoming, of all things, a controlling part of a "bad" one like darkness? *Heart of Darkness* was a fateful event in the history of fiction; and to announce it Conrad hit upon as haunting, though not as obtrusive, an oxymoron as Baudelaire had for poetry with *Les Fleurs du Mal*.

* * *

III
Conclusions

Conrad's frequent use of the word illusion is a sign of a philosophical scepticism which would obviously inhibit him from attempting to define the intellectual basis of his own practical human commitments; but this does not undermine, and indeed it may even strengthen, the conviction that although the sceptical mind knows that all ideological structures are really illusions, they may in practice be necessary restraints upon human egoism, laziness, or despair.

Marlow's behaviour in *Heart of Darkness* reflects this dual attitude. His awareness of the fragility and the intellectual hollowness of civilisation inhibits him in his dealings with others; his usual comportment is one of sceptical passivity; even his sympathy is uneasy and reserved, as in the scene with the Intended. Her grandiose illusions about Kurtz gradually force Marlow to go from taut acquiescence to more positive violation of the truth. Thus when the Intended stops her eulogy of Kurtz with "But you have heard him. You know!" Marlow replies, "Yes, I know." Then, "with something like despair in [his] heart," he bows his head before the Intended's "great and saving illusion that shone with an unearthly glow in the darkness, in the triumphant darkness from which

I could not have defended her—from which I could not even defend myself."

The lie to the Intended, then, is both an appropriately ironic ending for Marlow's unhappy quest for truth, and a humane recognition of the practical aspects of the problem: we must deal gently with human fictions, as we quietly curse their folly under our breath; since no faith can be had which will move mountains, the faith which ignores them had better be cherished.

At the end of the scene we are left wondering whether it is worse that the ideals of the Intended should continue in all their flagrant untruth, or that Marlow should have been unable to invoke any faith in whose name he could feel able to challenge them. To put the alternatives in terms of the main symbolic polarity of *Heart of Darkness* as a whole: which perspective is more alarming? that people such as the Intended should be so blinded by their certitude of being the bearers of light that they are quite unaware of the darkness that surrounds them? or, on the other hand, that those who, like Marlow, have been initiated into the darkness, should be unable to illumine the blindness of their fellows to its omnipresence?

In the early part of the narrative, the main effect of Conrad's light-dark imagery was to break down many of its associated conventional antitheses in the domain of human values; we move into a world where there are no longer any easy and complacent distinctions between black and white, and there are no longer any simple choices to be based upon them, like a preference for light or dark beer. In the first section, Marlow's European conception of blackness as inferior or evil is undermined when he finds no moral darkness in the black inhabitants of Africa, but is forced to link many of the traditional negative connotations of darkness with the colour white. In *Heart of Darkness* it is the white invaders, for instance, who are, almost without exception, embodiments of blindness, selfishness, and cruelty; and even in the cognitive domain, where such positive phrases as "to enlighten," for instance, are conventionally opposed to negative ones such as "to be in the dark," the traditional expectations are reversed. In Kurtz's painting, as we have seen, "the effect of the torchlight on the face was sinister"; the steamboat's final approach to the inner station, which is the goal of Marlow's quest, involves passing through an immobilising "white fog . . . more blinding than the night"; and this oxymoron is repeated in the later variant of "the blind whiteness of the fog."

Until Marlow confronts the Intended, the general development of the ramifying symbolic contrasts between light and darkness has been fairly easy to transpose into the terms which define the intellectual perspective that he has acquired as a result of his Congo experience. It can be summarised along the following lines: the physical universe began in darkness, and will end in it; the same holds for the world of human history, which is dark in the sense of being obscure, amoral, and without purpose; and so, essentially, is man. Through some fortuitous and inexplicable development, however, men have occasionally been able to bring light to this darkness in the form of civilisation—a structure of behaviour and belief which can sometimes keep the darkness at bay. But this containing action is highly precarious, because the operations of darkness are much more active, numerous, and omnipresent, both in society and in the individual, than civilised people usually suppose. They must learn that light is not only a lesser force than darkness in power, magnitude, and duration, but is in some way subordinate to it, or included within it; in short, that the darkness which Marlow discovers in the wilderness, in Kurtz and in himself, is the primary and all-encompassing reality of the universe.

Marlow says of his voyage up the river that they "penetrated deeper and deeper into the heart of darkness". There is a very traditional literal basis for this identification of the African wilderness with the "heart of darkness";[7] the wilderness is by definition an extreme example of a place where the light of civilisation has not come; and Africa, for this and other reasons, long figured in European thought as the Dark Continent. But Marlow also gives the wilderness much larger metaphysical connotations. It is an actively malign force; and it is also, Marlow senses, impenetrable to human thought, because it has a primal inclusiveness which confounds the categories which man has constructed as the basis of his civilisation.

Kurtz has internalised the spiritual meaning of the wilderness. Marlow's references to him assume the established equation of darkness with evil, as in such phrases as "a dark deed" for a crime, and "the prince of darkness" for the devil; and Marlow twice applies the term "heart of darkness" to Kurtz. In the first example he merely speaks of "the barren darkness of his heart", but in a later passage he merges Kurtz and the wilderness into a single living presence. The passage occurs when Marlow, on his way to the Intended, suddenly sees his vision of Kurtz: "The vision seemed to enter the house with me—the stretcher, the phantom-bearers, the wild crowd of obedient worshippers, the gloom of the forests, the glitter of the reach between the murky bends, the beat of the drum regular and muffled like the beating of a heart, the heart of a conquering darkness".

There is nothing particularly new in the idea that darkness is the primal reality to which all else in the world is posterior in origin and subordinate in power. In the Judaeo-Christian tradition, for example, the idea is embodied at the cosmic level in the book of Genesis, where "darkness was upon the face of the earth" in the beginning of things. The Western religious tradition as a whole makes light not the rule but the exception; it is the result of a beneficent divine intervention, which may be temporary and is certainly not bestowed unconditionally.

This transcendental view of the world is very difficult to embody in

7. For the general historical background of European conceptions, see Philip Curtin, *Image of Africa* (Madison, Wisc., 1964), and on the fictional tradition, G. D. Killam, *Africa in English Fiction* (Ibadan, 1968), especially pp. 8–11.

narrative, although the general aim was common enough in the nine-teenth century, as in Melville's symbolic use of blackness.[8] In *Heart of Darkness* this quasi-transcendental perspective is most obviously appar-ent in its language: such words as "unspeakable," "inconceivable," "inscrutable," and "nameless" are really an attempt—on the whole unsuccessful—to make us go beyond the limits of ordinary cognition, to transcend what Conrad or anybody else really knows. The ensuing sense of rhetorical strain is particularly marked in the passages dealing with Kurtz, where Marlow uses the language of ethical absolutes, although there is no reason to believe that he accepts any conceptual structure on which they might depend. For instance, Marlow makes the moral judg-ment that Kurtz was "beguiled . . . beyond the bounds of permitted aspirations", although he has no belief in the existence of anyone empowered to issue or deny such permits.

In the last pages of *Heart of Darkness* there is a final variation on the values associated with whiteness and light. Back in the sepulchral city, the Intended's fireplace has "a cold and monumental whiteness"; her "fair hair" and "pale visage" seem "surrounded by an ashy halo"; her eyes "glitter." In the falling dusk, the Intended, all in mourning black, dedicates her soul, "as translucently pure as a cliff of crystal," to the memory of Kurtz; to Marlow her "great and saving illusion" shines with "an unearthly glow"; and, although the Intended is illumined by "the unextinguishable light of belief and love," Marlow tells us that "with every word spoken the room was growing darker."

Light has been degraded to a cold and artificial brightness—it can no longer combat darkness; while whiteness has become some diseased albino mutation, capable, no doubt, of producing the cold phosphorescent glow of idealism, but sick and pallid indeed compared with the other tragic and heroic woman whom Kurtz abandoned in the heart of darkness. We seem to have moved from a realisation of the overwhelming power of darkness in the psychological, moral, and spiritual realm, to a larger and intangible change of a metaphysical kind, in which light seems to have a peculiar affinity with unnaturalness, hypocrisy, and delusion, and to be quite as contrary to the positive values of human life as the worst manifestations conventionally attributed to darkness.

How far some such conceptual rendition of the symbolic implications of light and darkness constitutes the main thematic burden in *Heart of Darkness* as a whole depends very largely on how much weight we give to the implications of the imagery, as opposed to other aspects of the novel. If some of the more intangible and abstract of the novel's general concerns are singled out for separate analytic consideration, they cer-tainly tend, in the very process of making its thought seem more consis-tent than it is, to make its purport more negative. Thus Hillis Miller, only a part of whose complex argument can be touched on here, pre-sents Conrad as unremittingly nihilist in his basic vision of reality: "the

8. See Harry Levin, *The Power of Blackness: Hawthorne, Poe, Melville* (New York, 1958).

heart of darkness is the truth," he writes; it means "the absorption of all forms in the shapeless night from which they have come"; and compared to its power all man's intellectual fabrications, the whole "realm of reason and intention is a lie."[9]

Heart of Darkness is Conrad's most direct expression of his doubts about the foundations of human thought and action, and its mode of narration reflects this. The subjective, questioning, and inconclusive way in which the story is told has led Tzvetan Todorov to move from the implications of "the derisory nature of knowledge" and Marlow's inability to understand Kurtz, to see *Heart of Darkness* as implying the impossibility of expressing the essential reality of human experience in fiction.[1]

But these negative views are surely too absolute: Marlow's tale, and the story as a whole, are not entirely, or even mainly, self-referential— its sepulchral city and its Africa are seen through Marlow's eyes, but they are places full of real horrors. What makes reading *Heart of Darkness* so unforgettable is surely the harrowing power with which Conrad convinces us of the essential reality of everything that Marlow sees and feels at each stage of his journey. Nor can Conrad's social and moral purport be regarded as ultimately nihilist, as Hillis Miller argues; Marlow's positives—work and restraint, for instance—make a less impressive appearance in the narrative than do all the negatives which he discovers; but Marlow's defences are firmly present in the stubborn energy and responsibility of his daily activities. Of course, no very flattering or sanguine view of man's behaviour and prospects emerges from *Heart of Darkness*, and it must have seemed grotesquely pessimistic to its original readers. It surely seems a good deal less so eighty years later, except to those who have had a very blinkered view of the century's battlefields. In any case, neither Conrad nor Marlow stands for the position that darkness is irresistible; their attitude, rather, is to enjoin us to defend ourselves in full knowledge of the difficulties to which we have been blinded by the illusions of civilisation.

Marlow had begun his narrative by saying "And this also . . . has been one of the dark places of the earth." His story ends when night has fallen in the sepulchral city, and he stops telling it with his face hidden by the same darkness on the Thames. There is a further formal symmetry when, in the last brief paragraph, the primary narrator reappears.

He sees Marlow in "the pose of a meditating Buddha." A very odd sort of Buddha, to be sure: one who actively applies himself to the practical truths of the secular world, and who, if he still awaits enlightenment, is no more sanguine about its advent than the protagonists of *Waiting for Godot*. But the reference to Buddha is justified in one respect:

9. *Poets of Reality*, p. 33. My general reading of "darkness" is indebted to his. See also Royal Roussel, *The Metaphysics of Darkness: A Study in the Unity and Development of Conrad's Fiction* (Baltimore and London, 1971).
1. Tzvetan Todorov, "Connaissance du vide," especially pp. 151, 153–54.

Marlow's narrative is essentially a self-examining meditation. *Heart of Darkness* is not, like "Youth" or *Lord Jim*, the act of a raconteur; it is the act, rather, of a man who stumbled into the underworld many years ago, and lived to tell its secrets, although not until much later. Then, mysteriously, the right occasion presented itself: a time and a place that supply both the evocative atmosphere, and the stimulus of an audience with whom Marow has enough identity of language and experience to encourage him to try to come to terms at last with some of his most urgent and unappeased moral perplexities through the act of sharing them.

When Marlow has finished, no one moves. The captain finally breaks the silence on a practical note: "We have lost the first of the ebb." It is a tribute of a sort; Marlow's tale has "arrested, for the space of a breath" the punctual hands of a few yachtsmen. But the turn of the tide is also a reminder of the endless and apparently meaningless circularity of the physical and the human world on every time scale, from that of the daily round to that of evolutionary history. This circularity is finally enacted in the fictional setting and the larger meaning of the tale itself. The river, which had been serenely luminous at the beginning, is now dark; and this becomes the occasion for another tribute. Marlow has not only learned and endured; he has also, it would seem, changed the way that the primary narrator, at least, sees the Thames; for when he raises his head, the narrator's vision, now coloured by the expansive power of Marlow's primary symbol, discovers that "the tranquil waterway . . . seemed to lead into the heart of an immense darkness."

ROBERT S. BAKER

[Watt's Conrad]†

Literary impressionism, as practiced by Joseph Conrad, was a technique that endeavored to fix and shape randomly flowing experience according to Jamesian formal standards, an art of keen and conspicuous craft that resulted in a series of early masterpieces like *Heart of Darkness* and *Lord Jim*, where scene and sensation were skillfully blended. Despite what could be called its rationalized execution, it was not productive of thematic orderliness, nor of a narrative so smooth-surfaced as to yield its meaning without the reader's active engagement, indeed, his necessary recognition that Conrad's art was one of dramatized reticence rather than omission. Conrad's endeavor to refine and extend the forms of fiction was, in part, an endorsement of James's earlier effort to defend the aesthetic status of the novel, and, at the same time, an expression of Conrad's own peculiar sensitivity to the illogicality, intransigence, and

† From *Contemporary Literature* 22 (1981): 116–26. Copyright, 1981, by The University of Wisconsin Press. Revised by the author, 1986. Reprinted by permission.

complexity of human experience. "I am modern," he wrote, "and I would rather recall Wagner the Musician and Rodin the Sculptor who both had to starve a little in their day—and Whistler the Painter who made Ruskin the Critic foam at the mouth with scorn and indignation. They too have arrived. They had to suffer for being 'new.' "

The question of Conrad's modernity remains a vexing issue, entangled in the perfervid rhetoric of his "Preface" to *The Nigger of the "Narcissus*," and complicated by the ambiguous nature of his debt to figures like Henry James and Walter Pater, as well as the snarled cat's cradle of implication contained in the term "impressionism." After all, Conrad criticized Stephen Crane as "the *only* impressionist and *only* an impressionist," and observed of his own work that he was not of the avant-garde but, rather, somewhere in the rear, not the principal but merely a spear-carrier, dispiritedly plodding "in the beaten track" and fated to repeat "the old formulas of expression." Yet he read Pater, customarily addressed James in his letters as "Cher Maître," and, in some sense, was conscious of aesthetic aims that broke with traditional stylistic conventions, aims that still seem best defined as "impressionist." Conrad was always prepared to go against the grain, to pursue an impressionist technique in the first half of *Lord Jim* and come near to abandoning it in large stretches of the second. In some works this style of dramatizing the complexity and shifts of human feeling and perception is muted and attenuated, while in others it becomes an assertive display of technique remarkable for its ability to convey the romantic skepticism that lay at the heart of Conrad's work. In this regard Marlow was his greatest achievement, Conrad's most characteristic protagonist, whose eternally troubled consciousness was caught up in the hopeless endeavor of maintaining a rigid code in a world that permitted anything but the shallow assurances of an unbending morality. The latter was never an unexamined framework for Marlow or, of course, for Conrad himself; and in his finest work it was wedded to a Pyrrhonist epistemology and an idiom of nuance and irony sensitively adapted to the interplay of moral and phychological impulse that comprised Conrad's essential subject: an idiom, moreover, in which words were regarded as poetically exploitable, malleable, and subtle, yet on the narrative level were repeatedly dismissed as powerless in the face of an unassimilable "reality."

If Conrad is a skeptical empiricist whose intellectual affiliations and stylistic practice can be traced back to David Hume, he remains, at least for Ian Watt, the most rational of empiricists. In *Conrad in the Nineteenth Century* (1979), Watt has, in large measure, restricted himself to those critical readings that can be sanctioned by biographical evidence, systematically resisting any suggestion that Conrad created a body of work notable for its complex interweaving of mutually enriching strands of meaning. The nub of the issue is Watt's simplistic notion that the text is accessible to something called "the literal imagination," a meaningless term that simply cloaks a bias in favor of plot summary and "a literal reading of the work." Watt's position is polemical, an ostensibly tonic revision aimed at redressing the balance in favor of a more elementary, even transparent Conrad. But the attempt to dispel the romantic mists and critical excesses of some Conrad critics in order to reveal an artist of a more austerely classical cast of mind is dearly purchased by Watt, despite the chorus of praise that has greeted the publication of the book, an enthusiastic outburst ranging from Alfred Kazin's claim that it will "sweep the field" to Edward Said's inflated assessment ("one of the great critical works produced since the 1950s").

Watt's book is the first installment of a projected two-volume work, an ambitious study undertaken in response to the exigent fact that "we are further than ever from anything like a consensus in our views of the basic character of Conrad's achievement." This is nonsense as anyone even superficially familiar with recent Conrad criticism would have to concede. Conrad studies are not in a state of disarray, while the consensus regarding Conrad's literary achievement is, by and large, congruent with Watt's. The novels he has selected for examination and reassessment are those that have been generally agreed upon as comprising the major canon, a fact supported by the extraordinarily derivative quality of Watt's book. The value of *Conrad in the Nineteenth Century* lies principally with Watt's analysis of certain aspects of Conrad's style: in particular, his taxonomic approach to the various rhetorical devices that collectively constitute Conrad's impressionism. Watt skillfully identifies and catalogues a number of narrative usages repeatedly employed by Conrad in the fiction of the 1890s, focusing on four works competed by 1900: *Almayer's Folly*, *The Nigger of the "Narcissus," Heart of Darkness*, and *Lord Jim*. In the chapter on *Lord Jim*—the most successful in the book—he defines and illustrates Conrad's adoption of a number of either Jamesian or uniquely Conradian strategies including "scenic presentation," "Progression d'effet," "chronological looping," "delayed decoding," as well as analepsis and prolepsis, all of which collectively testify to Conrad's modernity, his innovative approach to the art of fiction, and his determined aim never to abrogate the realistic surface of experience. Watt is equally good on Conrad's relationship with James and has written some of the finest pages I can remember reading on the various bonds of intimacy and affiliation between Marlow and Jim.

His scrupulous attention to Conrad's narrative technique, however, is not matched by an equally sensitive alertness to Conrad's figurative style. Much of this flows from Watt's critical prejudices, and influences his handling of the intellectual background of Conrad's early work. He claims that literary critics are suspicious of what he calls "the history of ideas approach," a grossly unwarranted generalization, as the torrent of books spilling from university presses over the past twenty-five years so massively testifies. The difficulty lies with Watt's use of philosophical or broadly critical sources or influences. He exhibits no holistic grasp of late nineteenth-century intellectual history; indeed, he offers not a richly sustained synthesis of the intellectual presuppositions and operative ideas discernible throughout the period but rather a series of unrelated improvisations, often pertinent but equally often thinly conceived, sketchily analyzed, and manifestly strained in their connection with Conrad. In brief, this is often (but not always) intellectual history of the potted variety, too insistently pluralist as a consequence of its empiricist premises. Conrad is, admittedly, a notoriously difficult writer to deal with; the surviving evidence of his reading is fragmentary, even casually oblique. Watt, however, introduces a series of figures that seem either unrelated to Conrad or, where a connection could be richly probed, are too often encapsulated in brief sketches lacking in force and depth. The reader is confronted with Durkheim on anomie, Balfour Stewart on entropy, George Simmel on social conflict, and Gustave Le Bon on crowd dynamics, as well as more predictable figures like Darwin, Schopenhauer, Marx, Spencer, Ibsen, Flaubert, and Nietzsche. For many of these authors there is no evidence linking them with Conrad—not necessarily an objection—but they do not figure in anything more than a synoptic index to Conrad's work. Durkheim's concept of anomie is not handled with sufficient cogency to convince this reader that it sheds significant light on *The Nigger of the "Narcissus,"* although the connection is potentially an interesting one.

But too often the "history of ideas approach" as practiced by Watt is oddly meretricious. A typical instance occurs in the chapter on *Heart of Darkness*—the most uneven chapter in the book—where Watt initially claims that the "moral trajectory" of Kurtz's life embodies a paradox "similar" to Schopenhauer's concept of Cain as a tragic figure. But after a paragraph on this comparison, Watt lamely concludes that Kurtz is "hardly a real parallel to Schopenhauer's Cain," leaving the reader perplexed as to why the comparison was introduced in the first place. Similarly, Watt very suggestively introduces Balfour Stewart's work on entropy but confines it to the opening pages of *Heart of Darkness*, never establishing its manifest connections with the novella as a whole. Sections of chapter four are very good indeed, the succinctly sketched essays "The Nineties and the Savage God" and "Evolution and Imperialism" being especially pertinent to Conrad. But the lengthy critical reading, polemically impoverished by Watt's dogmatic faith in literalist surface interpretation, injects a peculiarly niggardly note that misconstrues Conrad's use of incrementally developed motifs as well as his allusions to Classical and Christian myth intended to structure and extend the meaning of *Heart of Darkness*. Watt apparently believes that the autonomy of the text is in some way compromised by symbolism and myth, that much previous criticism of Conrad has weakened the effect of the literal narrative by diverting the reader's attention away from a tenor transparently clear. Such a simplistic approach does not work well with Conrad, as Watt's doggedly shallow reading of *Heart of Darkness* demonstrates.

To begin with, Watt's account of Conrad's novella is beset with a confusion of aims that often results in outright contradiction. Rejecting the idea of interwoven levels of significance, he confines himself to the political theme, handing out praise and blame to those critics who do or do not subscribe to his blinkered literalism. A typical instance of the methodological confusion that skews much of his criticism is his attack on the construction T. S. Eliot placed upon Kurtz's ostensibly penitential last words. Eliot is misguided, Watt argues, in conceiving of Kurtz's final words as an inclusive judgment "on the essential depravity of man and his civilization," when in fact the object of Kurtz's verdict "is surely himself and what he has done." This could be dismissed as simpleminded were it not for the fact that Watt has repeatedly stressed Kurtz's universal significance, observing only a few pages earlier that "Kurtz's mind" is dramatized by Conrad as "acting out the whole past of human barbarism," essentially Eliot's point, while in a paragraph immediately following the one in which Eliot is berated for his universalizing proclivities, Watt maintains that Kurtz is a "Faustian" figure, as if Faust is not a broadly emblematic type transcending the merely individual. Similarly, Watt earnestly raps the knuckles of those deluded Conradians who have insisted on the presence of allusions to Classical or Christian myth in *Heart of Darkness* (despite his own persiflage on Cain), dismissing the work of Lillian Feder and Robert O. Evans in an unconvincing argument aimed at overturning the notion that Conrad has intentionally used the Classical Fates in the novella. Watt's account of Marlow's initiation into the Belgian Trading Company in its offices in Brussels is an instructive example of his lack of critical discrimination and critical tact, a polemical reductiveness in the service of an idiosyncratic theory of literary meaning. Bent on denying the clear textual allusions to the three Fates, Clotho, Lachesis, and Atropos, neglecting Marlow's pun on the word fate ("uncanny and fateful"), as well as the black dresses of the two women linking them to Kurtz's Intended "all in black" and the black woman Marlow saw on the banks of the river during his attempt to rescue Kurtz, and pretending to ignore how Conrad deliberately invokes the specific functions of all three of the Fates in *Heart of Darkness*, he frets over the possibility of nuance and allusion: "Why," he complains, "does Conrad give us only *two* fates? Which is Clotho the spinner? and which Lachesis the weaver? Did the Greeks know about knitting anyway? Where are the shears?" This would be comic were it not for the fact that he denigrates the work of two critics who have significantly contributed to our comprehension of *Heart of Darkness*. Watt, who evidently believes that the shears must be literally present, cannot make the imaginative leap to perceive the analogy between knitting and weaving! But it turns out that the "literal imagination" has a card up its sleeve, a joker proclaiming that the seated figure knitting black wool is, *mirabile dictu*, one of "the French *tricoteuses* callously knitting at the guillotine." But where is the guillotine? Where are the tumbrils? And where is Louis the Sixteenth? Is he Marlow? Is he Kurtz? Or is it all a matter of King Charles's head? Far worse, however, Watt proceeds to invoke that *deus ex machina*, the literal text, claiming that "the older knitter, for example, with her wart and her flat cloth slippers," becomes "a stark visual image of physical and spiritual deformity." Watt, inspired by "the literal imagination," is a critic who can perceive Chaos and Old Night in a wart, and who experiences Kierkegaardian dread at that most terrifying of spectres, a pair of flat slippers. To attempt to discredit the work of Feder and Evans on such perversely banal grounds as these is comically unpersuasive. But more is at stake here than significance of the initial scene in the company offices. Watt frets, rhetorically, that he cannot discover Atropos, the third Fate, a conscious lapse that reveals how far Watt is willing to go in order to deny that Conrad's political and ideological themes might entail (as they always do) other assumptions and coexist with other levels of meaning.

The third Fate, Atropos, is the black woman who stretches out her arms towards the steamer in which Kurtz lies. Her arms send out shadows that function as the Atropian shears; Kurtz dies shortly after. But Conrad is not a Spenserian allegorist and feels no need to equip her with a pair of huge glittering shears. But to refuse to see the black woman as Atropos (Watt claims she is an emblem of healthy physicality because Conrad once saw a black woman who struck him so—so much for the "literal imagination") is to raise other, profounder issues. If she is associated with Kurtz's fate, what precisely is it? This question leads inevitably to a much wider interplay of symbolic associations, including the black woman's relationship with Kurtz's Intended and Conrad's fascination with the psychological double. Despite the amount of work that has been done on this subject, the reader will find no mention of it in Watt's book—as if Conrad was not the author of The Secret Sharer, or as if the double was not a significant feature of Dostoevsky and Dickens, and so part of the nineteenth century proclaimed in the title of Watt's book. But Watt's nineteenth century is a selective affair and Dickens, whose work contains so much that could be profitably applied to Conrad's, gets short shrift in Watt's study.

Watt, nevertheless, does concede that Kurtz is psychopathic and does write two or three pages on Conrad and Freud; but faced with Conrad's part of cryptic allusion and supple ambiguities, he insists that Conrad be ineluctably clear and, consequently, adheres to the surface narrative of Heart of Darkness. The political reading he offers is tedious because it is so well known; no one needs to be told that Conrad's novella is an attack on European imperialism. But this is what Watt does for page after tedious page of plot summary. His antipathy to allusive suggestion, to delicate shadings of meaning and muted but compelling hints of a wider and richer design, tentatively conceived and gracefully insinuated into the surface narrative, explains much of Watt's uneasiness with Conrad's impressionism. Historical or biographical corroboration is only one test of a text's meaning, and to remain so resolutely and predictably on the surface of a work so meticulously and subtly structured is to evade, not illuminate, Conrad's masterpiece.

The section of chapter four that focuses on Kurtz's Intended founders as a consequence of this self-imposed limitation. Why Kurtz's fiancee is never given a Christian or surname; why she physically resembles Kurtz (her "forehead, smooth and white" mirroring Kurtz's "lofty frontal bone"); why she is presented as essentially a "voice" (like Kurtz); why she is insistently linked to death, entropy, the jungle, to "cruel and absurd mysteries," and to the company as well; why she assumes the same posture as the black woman; these are some of the insistently intertwined strands of implication that cannot be dismissed as a shibboleth existing only in the minds of a few perversely dogmatic critics. Watt simply ignores them.

Marlow, at the outset of *Heart of Darkness*, endorses imperialism if it is energized by an "idea," an informing vision that one can "set up, and bow down before, and offer a sacrifice to. . . ." He confronts the brutal results of imperialism in the Congo, but his principal goal is to discover the "idea" proclaimed by the voice of Kurtz, but not traced to its source until he returns to the apartment of Kurtz's Intended. Here he genuflects to the "unearthly glow" of her sinister faith, thereby establishing a subtle complicity with Kurtz. And when he informs her that Kurtz's last utterance was, in fact, her name (a name deliberately emphasized by Conrad as a result of its notable absence, in favor of an abstract noun), the reader remembers only the words "The horror! The horror!" Just as Kurtz's small sketch in oils of the sinister white woman is linked to the portrait of the Intended that Marlow brings with him to her apartment in Brussels, the conjunction of her enigmatic name and Kurtz's self-condemnation is a pivotal bond that draws all three together in a web of complicity. The Intended is Kurtz's heritage, his idea, the source of the momentum energizing his mistaken mission; in short, his intention. She appears to symbolize an over-wrought cerebrality stretched to the breaking point and turned back on itself, a selfless ideal turned entropically fanatical. Kurtz has collapsed under a Promethean imperative, first shared then rejected, but finally tentatively forgiven by Marlow. He has found his "idea" and he does bow down to it and sacrifices the truth into the bargain.

Watt never examines the English tradition of romantic Prometheanism in Blake, Shelley, Byron, and Wordsworth, an oversight that helps to explain his neglect of Coleridge and, in particular, the "Rime of the Ancient Mariner," one of the few texts that we know Conrad read and used, not only repeatedly alluding to it in *Nostromo* and *The Shadow-Line* but drawing on it for *Heart of Darkness* as well. In the latter, the traditional romance narrative structure of withdrawal, transformation, and return is strenuously insisted upon by Conrad, and not determined by the need of magazine publication as Watt argues. Like the Mariner, Marlow returns to another wedding guest (both of whom never enter the kirk), having traveled full circle, but rendered "helpless," transformed but not completely enlightened, a condition stressed by Conrad, who introduces his narrator as a Buddha "without a lotus-flower"—the symbol of achieved wisdom.

The Intended stands at the end of Marlow's journey much as she stood at the origin (geographical and ideological) of Kurtz's. And just as she is lied to by Marlow and abandoned by Kurtz, her ambiguous marginality marks the limits of Conrad's incomplete emancipation from the middle-class, Eurocentric values attacked in *Heart of Darkness*. At the outer boundary of the text's horizon, she functions as a device of ideological closure, permitting Marlow a face-saving form of compromise in which he masks a secret horror of the "truth" from the full light of day in a sentimental scene shot through with ironies. Marlow's journey is essentially one of a progressively politicized but sceptical epigone in search of a master (the example of the Russian harlequin both paralleling and contrasting with Marlow's exigent desires to encounter the "voice" of his "enchanted princess"). His journey turns on the notion of Kurtz's uniquely endowed status and the "voice" that will proclaim and finally formulate its legitimacy in some traditional, totalizing vision. Yet, according to Marlow, Kurtz's first and last words consist of references to the Intended. When the reader finally encounters Kurtz, he is no Promethean idealist but a "pitiful Jupiter," the traditional antagonist of Prometheus, and almost his first recorded utterance is "my Intended" (it is preceded by "my ivory" but Marlow immediately revises this by quoting the full exclamation, placing "my Intended" before "my ivory"). Marlow later informs the Intended herself that Kurtz's last words were, in fact, her "name." References to the Intended, then, actual or imputed, carefully frame Marlow's encounter with Kurtz and his "echo," forgrounding her role as the symbolic context for Kurtz's experience and Marlow's ostensible enlightenment. The first and last words of the narrative's apocalyptic voice, then, are enclosed by references to this enigmatic figure. The reader, of course, remembers that, first, she is never named and second, that Kurtz's last words were "The horror! The horror!" presumably an act of self-judgment in the form of a liberating confession of spiritual bankruptcy that links the idealized Intended with Kurtz's nadir of narcissistic excess.

In *Heart of Darkness*, only Marlow and Kurtz have names (excepting the dead Freshleven and the incompletely identified Towser or Towson, the author of the harlequin's lost book on seamanship). It is an atomized world of metonymies where characters are reduced to their functions, or reified individuals, of brick makers, station managers, road repairmen, accountants, company spies, alienists, and of the Intended. Her role as a disembodied "voice," the crystal "echo" to Kurtz's Narcissus, ties her to Kurtz much as she is motifically sutured to the woman in Kurtz's painting. Both female figures are images of Kurtz's intentions, both are blind, both associated with the torches and haloes of traditional Promethean iconography, and just as the illumination of the allegorical figure's torch casts a "sinister" light, the blaze of blinded idealism that elicits from Marlow his concluding act of helpless genuflexion is described as "unearthly" and "ashy." But the Intended finally outplays and proble-

matizes the codes on which *Heart of Darkness* seems to rely. In the final
scene, the external setting of her house is carefully associated with the
company offices while the interior is evoked in terms of the Congo wilderness. Her voice merges with Kurtz's with whom she also shares the
broad forehead as an emblem of cerebrality. Her gestures are pointedly
linked to those of the black woman when she assumes the same pose as
Kurtz's queen at the moment of his death—thereby connecting her to
Atropos, the third fate. Her gestures and her situation suggest something
more than an image of pathos and innocence just as Marlow's lie is not
simply a tender gesture, but rather a white lie that suppresses a dark
truth. It is the final act that dramatizes Marlow's inability to deal with
Kurtz's allegory (the painting being a subtle form of self-criticism achieved
by Kurtz before his final surrender) and the report with its post-scriptum
which Marlow suppresses (the central lie of *Heart of Darkness*). The lie
to the Intended is a weak ethical act that preserves an illusion as well as
Marlow's ironically qualified "intimacy" with Kurtz.

Indeed, it is Marlow's perplexed moral resistance to and his unre-
solved complicity with Kurtz that creates the fertile complications of his
discourse. It is Marlow who confidently states at the outset of his narrative that despite the clear and overwhelming corruption of imperialism,
it can be "redeemed" by means of it informing "ideas," and that such
an idea should be bowed down before and sacrificed to. This informing
idea is the subject of Kurtz's painting, the cerebralized intentions and
intellectual accomplishments energizing the Promethean imperative itself
(and associated with Kurtz as poet, painter, musician, journalist, political leader, etc.). Marlow, however, having signed his "document . . .
not to disclose any trade secrets" perseveres in his loyalty to Kurtz, condemning his actions (and dissociating himself from the besotted Russian)
yet persisting in his attempt to penetrate to the voice of that saving idea,
to locate it, defend it, worship it, and sacrifice the truth to it if necessary.
He finds it not in the voice of the degenerate Kurtz nor even in the cry
of self-judgment, "The horror! The horror!" but in Kurtz's European
"echo," whom Marlow calls "My Destiny," a repetition of Kurtz's "My
Intended" but now perceived fatalistically. Kurtz dies blind, unable to
perceive the candle Marlow holds before him; the woman in the painting cannot see the sinister light cast by her torch. Marlow, just prior to
his interview with the Intended, accepts his "common fate," confesses
his lack of a "clear perception of what he wanted" and bows before the
"ashy halo" of the former's "unextinguishable light" despite his awareness of the encroaching shadows of Kurtz's reality that fill the room.

In *Heart of Darkness*, the forbidden and base energies of irrational
darkness proceed directly from the conscious rational idealism that functions as their very denial. The Intended is the symbol of a fatally corrupted European culture, and Marlow cannot surrender his allegiances
to such an "idea." It is this ideological contradiction, only incompletely
formulated in Conrad's text, that accounts for at least this reader's sense
of ideological shadows at war behind the opulent phonetic obscurities of

Marlow's narrative. The fatally divided allegiances of a narrator who both admired the British imperial red in the map of colonized Africa, but who also preferred his maps "blank" at the centre, recur in the semic organization of his narrative which oscillates between the conflicting codes of a Promethean idealism beyond recuperation and a politicized need to confront the reasons why. In this regard Jameson's concept of the political unconscious is as pertinent to an assessment of Marlow's acts of suppression as the conventionally Freudian.

BRUCE JOHNSON

Conrad's Impressionism and Watt's "Delayed Decoding" †

Ian Watt's careful probing of Conrad's "impressionism" in *Conrad in the Nineteenth Century*, despite its canny ability to capture the flavor of time and place, leads us nonetheless to slight one of historic impressionism's most important aspects: the participation of so many of these artists—including Conrad—in the original Lockean sense of both the word *impressionism* and the extended epistemology it implies.[1] Popular art history usually asserts that instead of painting a tree, the impressionist painted the effect of a tree on a particular sensibility; Lewis Mumford somewhere uses just that phrase, "the effect of a tree," to note impressionism's shift from object to affect. In the same historical shorthand, expressionism then becomes the objectification of powerful emotions emerging from that now no-longer-screening but originating sensibility. In Stephen Crane we can sometimes see the entire process in a single sentence.

Joseph Conrad, however, saw even in his first two novels that for the writer as for the painter there could be no such bald act as "painting a tree." As E. H. Gombrich and other art historians have shown, the aesthetic tradition and its models largely determine how a tree or anything else is represented. Albrecht Dürer's strange woodcut of a largely imagined rhinoceros is decisive for other artists even after they have seen the real thing in Africa two hundred years later.[2] The painter who attempts "objectively" to "paint a tree" at least begins with what his culture and his aesthetic traditions prepare him and allow him to see. There is in short no easy, "realist" alternative to impressionism; the impressionist, as Conrad apparently understood the term, seeks not only to render "the

† From *Conrad Revisited: Essays for the Eighties*, ed. Ross C Murfin (University: The U of Alabama P, 1985) 51–70. Reprinted by permission.
1. See Ian Watt, *Conrad in the Nineteenth Century* (Berkeley and Los Angeles: University of California Press, 1979), pp. 169–80. Watt too sees the origin of the word in the context of Locke and Hume (cf. p. 171) but would probably not agree that the Lockean sense persists and helps to place Conrad in the mainstream of historic impressionism.
2. E. H. Gombrich, *Art and Illusion: A Study in the Psychology of Pictorial Representation* (Princeton, N.J.: Princeton University Press, 1969), pp. 81–82.

effect of a tree," with all the emotional and visual peculiarities of the individual point of view, but to remind the reader continually that what he might easily and readily assume to be "objectively" the tree is actually the result of complex cultural prejudices. And those preconceptions, he knew, work in the viewer and reader even less obviously than the unique personal peculiarities of his point of view. We can agree that in matters of visual art Conrad was conservative and far less well informed than many of his friends. Surely, however, it does not in any event follow that a literary impressionist would be instictively attracted to impressionist painting; Conrad certainly was not. Yet his affinities with impressionist art lie deeper than oil paint and canvas in an epistemology that he recognized as both modern and revolutionary. In the awareness that there is no "realist" alternative to impressionism, that all complaisant norms are normal with a vengeance, Conrad had not jumped but dove head first into the twentieth century.

I raise the question of Ian Watt's creation of the phrase "delayed decoding"[3] partly so that I may stand on his shoulders (as I and so many others have often done before) and partly because the phrase leads naturally to his conclusion that "it is very unlikely that Conrad either thought of himself as an impressionist or was significantly influenced by the impressionist movement." Unlike so much of Watt's analysis in this book, that particular claim serves only to isolate Conrad from one of the most important aspects of early modernism. Readers of Conrad need not have read *Conrad in the Nineteenth Century* to surmise that by "delayed decoding" Watt means those moments—such as the attack on the steamer in *Heart of Darkness*—when the narrator sees and feels events without, at first, being able to name or explain them. Of all things Watt says about the process of these observations, the one quality he does not elicit seems to me the most important for connecting Conrad not only with impressionism but with epistemological currents at the turn of the century broader even than that movement.

In discussing "delayed decoding" in connection with Conrad's impressionism, we ought to recognize that the original undecoded observation ("Sticks, little sticks were flying about," to quote an appropriate example from *Heart of Darkness*) is terribly valuable to Conrad and not really undesirable temporary misunderstanding so much as an unmediated observation. In meticulously recording these uninterpreted or minimally interpreted observations—and they are often visual—Conrad reflects one of the original purposes of impressionism: to return to the most aboriginal sensation before concepts and rational categories are brought to bear. ("Arrows, by Jove! We were being shot at!")

There was an enduring Lockean impulse behind much early impressionist painting that required removing a good many of the mediating intellections in favor of the only irreducible sensation the painter had: the way it "seemed" to him. In painting, such a move often meant the

---

3. See Watt, *Conrad in the Nineteenth Century*, pp. 175–79. [See pp. 316–17, above—*Editor.*]

deemphasis of drawing and perspective (both insistently intellectual abstractions, particularly as they appeared in French neoclassical painting) in favor of color and light and veils of atmosphere, the elimination of narrative elements in favor of the moment, and so on toward the accomplishment of unintellectualized immediacy, or at least the illusion of it. Parallel developments took place in philosophy, largely in Edmund Husserl's early work from roughly 1900 to 1913, in the *Logische Untersuchungen* and *Ideen I.*[4]

Husserl suggested that a "presuppositionless" philosophy had to trust the impression, not because it was in Locke's sense primary sensation which one could trust more than secondary ideas (and more than ideas based on ideas, the risk increasing toward the birth of "notions"), but because one could not challenge the simple claim that "this is the way it seemed to me." To the accusation that the individual had been mistaken, that "facts" later discovered or explanations later deduced had shown him to be wrong, the individual human consciousness might answer with Ford Madox Ford's narrator Dowell in *The Good Soldier*, "Isn't it true to say that for nine years I possessed a goodly apple?" For Husserl the subjective impression was the only trustworthy beginning for an ultimate grasp of essences. Although Husserl rather quickly moves toward an esoteric mediation on these impressions, his mood at the turn of the century, at the very moment *Lord Jim* was being published, is similar to Conrad's: to press back to the way it seemed ("but my feet felt so very warm and wet that I had to look down") is to have puzzling access to truths largely obscured after the organizing concepts and causes and explanations have been imposed, after what is warm and wet becomes blood, death, attack, the natives' fear of losing Kurtz, and, finally, their fear of losing God—after little sticks become arrows and an absurdly treasured cane the shaft of a deadly spear. But to suggest that the intellections, the causes and categories and explanations, are somehow the "truth" encoded in the original sensation is to ignore an important aspect of the impressionist impulse and movement. The unexplained feeling of "warm and wet" is as true and valuable to Conrad as the concept "attack"—a concept, by the way, that the story subsequently shows to be genuinely imponderable. An examination of other instances of Conrad's "delayed decoding" shows that the "explanations" are no more encoded in the original subjective sensation than a French neoclassical canvas would be in Monet's impressionist rendering of the scene.

Furthermore, when Watt says that "Conrad wanted to pay as much attention to the inside as to the outside, to the meaning as to the appearance," he is adopting a separation that to Husserl would have been discouragingly reminiscent of Kant's *noumenal* and *phenomenal* and to many impressionists would have ignored the meaning *in* the impression. There

4. A word of caution: the best way to understand *Logische Utersuchungen* is to turn immediately to part 2, "The Fundamental Phenomenological Outlook," in *Ideen*, published first in 1913. The full strategic objectives of the earlier work are nearly impossible to see without this later "introduction." See Edmund Husserl, *Ideas: General Introduction to Pure Phenomenology*, trans. W. R. Boyce Gibson (New York: Macmillan, Collier Books, 1962).

is a strong sense in which Husserl's long argument in *Logische Unter-suchungen* is directed against just such a separation of meaning and appearance in those disciplines based upon an inadequate sense of how consciousness exists. Far more important than grasping Husserl's argu-ment, however, must be the critic's sense that there is something in the *Zeitgeist* that produces both Husserl's and impressionism's defense of subjectivity against the increasingly strident claims of science to reveal-ing in an orgy of "objectivity" the "inside" of Nature.

Thus, however much Conrad's impressionism may suggest relativity and even indeterminacy—no single view of Lord Jim having any real priority or authority over other equally coherent views—it also partici-pates in the other crucial component of historic impressionism: a belief long-lived and probably stemming originally from the climate of Locke and Hume that the impression, the impress upon the mind of immedi-ate sensual impulses, lies closer to the origin of meaning than the oper-ation of subsequent thought. Clearly the relativism in impressionistic practice is prominent in Conrad's fiction, but the other historic compo-nent emerges at crucial moments and occasionally becomes a potent symbolic entrance to the most difficult meaning of the work. Although Conrad can, of course, no longer believe in anything like a Lockean model of consciousness, he shares with that intellectual climate a pas-sion for the origins of consciousness.

In a remarkable essay written in 1883 for a small exhibition of paint-ings by Pissarro, Degas, and Renoir, the poet Jules Laforgue emphasizes just the point I am making, that impressionism consists of returning the eye to, in his words, a "primitive" state where what the mind has learned can be stripped away from what the "natural eye" can truly apprehend: "a natural eye forgets tactile illusions and their convenient dead-lan-guage of line and acts only in its faculty of prismatic sensibility." "No line, light, relief, perspective, or chiaroscuro, none of those childish classifications." [5] Although the notion of primitive, original "impres-sion" is no longer Lockean or derived immediately from Hume, the new Young-Helmholtz theory of color vision and the famous Weber's or Fechner's law for measuring the intensity of sensation allow a nine-teenth-century scientific version of the same basic metaphor for the mind. The impressionists invariably believe, as Jules Laforgue does, that their painting has returned to what the eye intrinsically does in its natural or primitive state, before it has been reshaped by what the tactile senses know and what all kinds of intervening intellection may demand as the proper emphasis of painting. Such demands may even call for an histor-ical motif as the structuring aesthetic principle (not, say, a patch of coastal water in the sunlight but the death of Socrates or the oath of the Horatii). In short, all the new scientific and quasi-scientific theories of color and

5. Jules Laforgue, "Impressionism," in "Impres-sionism: The Eye and the Poet," trans. William Jay Smith, *Art News* 55 (1956): 43–45. Reprinted in Linda Nochlin, *Impressionism and Post-Impres-sionism, 1874–1904: Sources and Documents* (Englewood Cliffs, N.J.: Prentice-Hall, 1966), pp. 14–20; these quotations pp. 16 and 17.

vision that inform impressionism only serve to confirm the impressionist's intuition that he has reached back to some kind of original seeing, and that such perception offers a kind of truth quickly eroded with the impositions of reason and the special perceptions of other senses, particularly of the tactile sense.

There seems little reason to believe that Conrad's "delayed decoding" departs in any important way from this general impressionist practice. Of course not all of Conrad's main instances of "delayed decoding" depend quite so much on the eye as those in *Heart of Darkness*. But virtually all of them imply not so much an initial misunderstanding that will subsequently "clear up" as they do an initial unguarded perception whose meaning may be far more revealing to the reader than the subsequent "decoding." The fact that arrows seem at first to be "little sticks" may reveal more about the ambiguous attitude of Kurtz's natives toward these intruders, and about Kurtz's functioning among them as a god, than the subsequently official and rather self-limiting definition of this very complex set of events and feelings as, simply, an "attack." One of the main points of the journey upriver is that increasingly almost nothing can confidently be "read"; traditional meanings and traditional names no longer function, and along with the "pilgrim" who is no real pilgrim we cry out, "Good God! What is the meaning. . . ."

In such an atmosphere there can be no secure decoding—largely because there has been no sense of meaning encoded. The metaphor of coding and decoding erodes. As Marlow soon notes, there was more "desperate" grief than threat in "this savage clamour that had swept by us on the river-bank." Of the arrows themselves, neither Marlow nor the reader knows whether they are poisoned or, as they seem, "wouldn't kill a cat." Francis Ford Coppola in *Apocalypse Now* obviously thinks the arrows are *essentially* "little sticks" because he has his Marlow-assassin call out something like "These are little sticks! They're just trying to scare us!" All the familiarity that Conrad employs in describing the death of the helmsman, the *impression* of the helmsman's death, constitutes not a misunderstanding that must subsequently be straightened out with identifications such as "spear," "blood," and "death" in place of "a long cane," something "warm and wet," and the intimate gesture of the helmsman clutching "that cane." On the contrary, the "impression" apparently contained for Conrad a truth not available once the intellect and its categories of cause and effect had begun to work in Marlow: that violent death instantly becomes a paradoxically intimate experience, in which the very instrument of death may well seem a personal possession, "like something precious," the victim "afraid I would try to take it away from him." We are not invited to suppose that in this last impressionistic supposition Marlow has been wildly wrong, that no victim would regard the instrument of his certain death as a precious personal possession. Most assuredly the text is haunted by the possibility that the rapidly dying helmsman (suddenly confronted by the most irrevocably personal event of his life) might paradoxically feel just this way. Even the apparent temporary validity of the explanation that this is largely a violent attack is finally undercut when the "angry and warlike yells" stop instantly and are replaced by a "tremulous and prolonged wail of mournful fear and utter despair." If we cannot tell whether this is an attack in any ordinary sense of the word—despair more than anger, an act of worship perhaps more than anything—the apparently misguided first impressions become peculiarly authoritative.

In order to confirm my sense that Conrad's use of this device is not only impressionistic in a way that owes a good deal to the larger aesthetic movement but also peculiarly revealing of the novel's guiding epistemology, we need to move on to a later instance in *The Secret Agent*. Throughout this novel we recognize that the border between organic and inorganic is continually blurred and violated. The street that Mr. Verloc enters on his way to the embassy "in its breadth, emptiness, and extent . . . had the majesty of inorganic nature, of matter that never dies." "And the thick police constable, looking a stranger to every emotion, as if he, too, were part of inorganic nature, surging apparently out of a lamppost took not the slightest notice of Mr. Verloc." This is the novel, after all, in which Mrs. Verloc imagines that "after a rainlike fall of mangled limbs the decapitated head of Stevie lingered suspended above, and fading out slowly like the last star of a pyrotechnic display." Certainly it is by no means clear that this ontological blurring is always impressionistic in the sense of the "primitive" or "natural eye" mentioned by Laforgue, but many readers have felt that it is indeed the peculiar "Lebenswelt" of this novel.

In the scene I should like to discuss, Winnie has just stabbed Verloc in what paradoxically might appear to be merely a decorous extension of their "respectable home life." "To the last its decorum had remained undisturbed by unseemly shrieks and other misplaced sincerities of conduct." As Winnie leans over the couch on which Verloc, quietly dead, reclines, she looks "at the clock with inquiring mistrust. She had become aware of a ticking sound in the room." The reader has no way of knowing, almost until Winnie does, that the ticking sound is no mechanical measure of abstract time but the dripping of Verloc's blood. As the interval between drops or "ticks" diminishes, and the sound approaches that of a continual flow of life's blood, "as if the trickle had been the first sign of a destroying flood," we recognize that all the symbolic suggestiveness of the attack on Greenwich mean time here intersects with the ontological blurring of the inanimate and animate, abstract time with the time measured by drops of human blood, time and human life finally measured in the same medium; and this intersection is permeated with the flood allusion, the cleansing flood that brings no new covenant and on the contrary a "free" Winnie. It is appropriate that having fully identified the sound, she flees the room by giving the table a push "as though it had been alive." Verloc's round hat, which had earlier sought the cover of the table like some fugitive cat or dog, becomes a hat again when the table is moved and rocks "slightly on its crown in the wind of her flight."

In short, the original illusion, that the dripping blood had been the even ticking of the clock, provides not a random misunderstanding that is subsequently cleared up but a stunning preparation for all the symbolic complication available when we connect with the murder of Verloc the role that abstract, measured time has played in this novel. Somehow the relationship of these rational, order-giving abstractions (Greenwich standard time) with anarchy and with the passions that actually create the illusions of ideal order have not crystalized until Winnie's confusion of the ticking clock with the dripping blood; it is less a confusion than a fusion, a fusion of the inanimate and animate that has haunted the text from the beginning. A good case can be made for saying that the crisis of the novel lies not in Stevie's demolition or even in the moment of the stabbing but only in these imagistic reflections by Winnie on both murders.

It strikes me that a good part of Conrad's "delayed decoding" resembles the attempt of Hemingway and before him of Mark Twain to recognize that there is no such thing as an isolated and meaningful fact or event or object. Meaning, as William Barrett argues in his book *Time of Need* while discussing Hemingway and other moderns, is a function of connectedness.[6] The meaning we see in an apparently discreet moment or event depends on the conceptual and emotional "net" we use to capture it. (This metaphor is Iris Murdoch's in her first novel called *Under the Net* and probably derives from her reading in phenomenology and her experience of Wittgenstein at Oxford.) Tom Sawyer's literary expectations and the Grangerfords' code of the blood feud are two such compelling systems of meaning that they begin to affect what one can see in the first place. We may recognize in the kind of critical analysis appropriate to these writers a congruence of Gestalt psychology with early phenomenology, both of them products of the period from roughly 1900 to 1913 or '14, although in American literature and in William James and Charles Peirce we find many anticipations of such epistemological analysis.[7] Melville himself develops a similar technique for *Moby Dick* and there are clearly enough reasons in the special plight of mid-nineteenth-century American consciousness to explain why this technique of "I look, we look, ye look" may have been an American talent even before it became Husserl's. The influence from William James to Husserl is slowly and recently becoming clear, were one to pursue this rather elegant transatlantic connection. In any event, Stephen Crane was himself immersed in the awareness; one can see it emerging from the wooden naturalism of *Maggie: A Girl of the Streets* and, despite Conrad's private

6. William Barrett, *Time of Need: Forms of Imagination in the Twentieth Century* (New York: Harper and Row, 1973), pp. 64–83.
7. See Avrom Fleishman's prescient application

of Charles Peirce to some of Conrad's effects in *The Secret Agent*, "The Criticism of Quality: Notes for a Theory of Style," *University Review* 33 (1966): 3–10.

undervaluing of Crane's impressionism in *The Red Badge of Courage*, watch its flowering in that novel.

The point is that having understood how preconceived "nets" of meaning instantly trap an event, sight, sound, comment, alleged "fact" or what have you, the fledgling phenomenologist begins to relish two basic maneuvers. First, to reveal how what seemed to be a random impression (say, the apparent ticking of a clock) was in truth instantly ensnared in a matrix of connectedness, could not perhaps have even been perceived had not an appropriate net been already present and active. Can we even *perceive* what is essentially unconnected or meaningless? Clocks and time are, after all, a very important preoccupation for Conrad in this novel, for the reader of *The Secret Agent*, and for Winnie, who in caring "nothing for time" indicates the author's deep involvement with it. Another author or character might instantly have attributed another meaning to the measured sound, as any Gestalt psychologist would argue.

The second fascination for the beginning phenomenologist lies in the possibility that there may be a kind of pristine though not necessarily innocent perceiving outside the nets, that one may cultivate a certain talent for lifting them; *aletheia*, which William Barrett translates as "unhiddenness," may be a different sort of truth from that suggested by the German *wahr*, connected with "*bewahren*, to guard or preserve."[8] While not actually participating in Husserl's cry of "Zu den Sachen selbst!" an important vein of literary impressionism, certainly in part Conrad and Crane, participates in this phenomenological urgency that is so broadly characteristic of the turn of the century. (Husserl's search for a "presuppositionless" philosophy begins, I repeat, with *Logische Untersuchungen* in 1900 and runs in its pure early form to *Ideen I* in 1913.)

Conrad is anxious to recreate those rather rare moments when we perceive something that is either genuinely outside the usual nets and must subsequently be contained (as a sudden, surprising occurrence may be) or, more likely, when we perceive something that only appears to be pristine in this way. In brief, it is vital to Conrad's moral sense that he reveal again and again the value of this phenomenological perceiving (on those rare occasions when it may be possible) and—the more likely occasion—that he show his readers how perception usually depends on the preconceptions, the emotional and intellectual Gestalten that make the perception possible in the first place. Thus "delayed decoding" is an important part of both Conrad's and Crane's larger experiments with these preconceptions, of their attempts to reveal how perception depends on Gestalten that may be as manic and overt as the Swede's regarding the Wild West in Crane's "The Blue Hotel" or as subtly pervasive and controlling as Henry Fleming's sense of war as heroic struggle and epic denouement (even though positively "Greeklike struggle," Henry imag-

8. Barrett, *Time of Need*, pp. 72–74.

ines, was probably a thing of the past). Henry retains enough of this preconception to be singularly disappointed that in seeing him off to war his mother says "nothing whatever about returning with his shield or on it." As *The Red Badge of Courage* develops, Henry's controlling assumptions wax and wane; new variations of the "epic struggle" mind-set emerge and are immediately challenged by events that Henry is usually not prepared to receive. Most especially, the central issue in his mind, whether he shall be courageous or a coward, is in its very dichotomous stiffness a function of his epic mind-set. We need not go on to show that in this kind of analysis *The Red Badge* is a virtuoso performance that had begun with the perceptions of Maggie in *Maggie: A Girl of the Streets* and, interestingly enough, may have entered the mainstream of literary impressionism from the crisis to which Crane brought naturalistic assumptions in that novel. As a would-be naturalist in *Maggie*, Crane had seen that if environment determines character (as the colon in the novel's title insists), environment is a perceived thing: to Maggie, Pete is "a knight," to cite only one extreme instance of this truth.

Conrad gives Lord Jim a mind-set that he may very well have learned from watching Crane's performance in *The Red Badge*, though to reviewers who pointed out similarities and suggested an influence on *The Nigger of the "Narcissus,"* Conrad answered that he had not read *The Red Badge* until after *The Nigger* had been finished. As I said in an article many years ago, his sensitivity to the alleged influence from the younger master may have led him to experiment with his own memory, even though he admired Crane and his work.[9] Although in letters Conrad disparaged Crane's "impressionism" as largely a taste for striking metaphors, Conrad's own Lord Jim begins his career so full of the assumptions, so equipped with the screens and blinders of "light" adventure stories that his conception of heroism and heroic honor will never change. These "thoughts . . . full of valorous deeds" were "the best parts of life, its secret truth, its hidden reality." The crew of the *Patna* did not matter; "Those men did not belong to the world of heroic adventure." His measure of life is "a hero in a book." It is my sense—though critics have always disagreed on the issue—that this screen of heroic adventure, this special set of colored glasses, continues right through the end of the novel, determining how Jim imagines he can use Patusan, Jewel, Brown, and determining to the end his conception of both heroism and redemption. In a world where most people seek their experience through the medium of such Gestalten, moments of phenomenological "unhiddenness," *aletheia*, become especially precious to the author, though the author may well make his character regard them as mistakes, or as confusion later to be decoded with conventional or traditional categories and explanations. Many of these perceptions will subsequently (in the course of the text) be shown to have been no unhiddenness at all but to have been generated by preconceptions so subtle and so much a part of the culture that

9. Bruce Johnson, "Joseph Conrad and Crane's *Red Badge of Courage*," *Papers of the Michigan Academy of Science, Arts, and Letters* 48 (1963): 649–55.

neither character nor reader or even author could initially have detected the net. William Bonney has shown how Conrad works endlessly with the rubrics of traditional romance in this regard, and how the expectations of readers steeped in such Western romance epistemology are deliberately aroused and then undercut.[1]

No doubt both Conrad and Crane were skeptical about the possibility that any such true "unhiddenness" existed. Yet many passages in their work testify to a curiosity about such possibilities. When Henry Fleming has run from the battle, his mind frantically experiments with variations of an anthropomorphized Nature, of an intention in Nature. He trips and stumbles, and so Nature, he momentarily feels, is inimical to his flight. When, moments later in relative quiet, he throws a pine cone at a squirrel and watches it flee, Nature, he concludes, is teaching him one of its laws: that it is only natural to flee danger. Finally, still exploring the feeling that he may only have acted naturally and that this now-benevolent Nature has conducted him to a "chapel" of trees in the forest in order that he find a measure of peace in its bosom, he discovers in the "chapel" near where the altar would have been, a "thing," the corpse of a soldier with ants "trundling some sort of a bundle along the upper lip" and "venturing horribly near to the eyes." In the midst of anthropomorphic preconceptions and emotional presuppositions that turn almost anything into intentions and tall trees into a chapel, he finds this moment of *aletheia*, the unhidden revelation that Nature is indifferent process. The eyes may be window to the soul, but not to ants about their natural business.

Crane's rhetoric is as busy in the image of the ants as it had been in the other details of Henry's flight from battle, and of course Henry's "red badge of courage" might also be recognized as a red badge of cowardice if the circumstances of his head wound were known. Yet Crane's intention in the title is not simply ironic but to play, rather, upon the epistemological implications of the word *badge*. Nothing is a badge absolutely. Only relative to a particular mind-set, to a presupposed web of connectedness, can something signify in the manner suggested by the word *badge*. Thus questions that critics have vigorously debated about whether Crane intends us to feel that Henry has in some sense "redeemed" his earlier flight or has been both coward and hero in so short a time are all subsumed in these larger epistemological interests. Concerned as he may be to push his absurdist view of man's place in the cosmos (epitomized by the waving tourists on the beach in the "The Open Boat," a story that Conrad found "fundamentally interesting"), Crane is far more interested in problems of perception and signification that are central to historic impressionism.

My pleasure in Conrad's approach to these issues comes both from impressions such as those during the "attack" in *Heart of Darkness* and from such moments as the dripping blood mistaken for the ticking clock in *The Secret Agent*. Whether the "unhiddenness" is only illusory, with, in fact, potent presuppositions already at work selecting and filtering, as they are in Winnie's mind, or the perception is genuinely phenomenological, Conrad seems willing to suspend the kind of barely sublimated rhetoric that we often find at similar moments in Stephen Crane. He is so much a student of what the world might be were it perceived even for a moment outside these nets that he willingly suspends rhetoric that might have tempted him. Carried to a kind of reductio ad absurdum, a similar technique characterizes, in theory at least, the novels of Alain Robbe-Grillet or the inexplicably lingering camera work in *Last Year at Marienbad*. In Conrad, such experiments reveal their turn-of-the-century tentativeness, but they nonetheless participate in a phenomenological sensitivity densely entangled by the first few years of the century with the practice and theory of impressionism.

The principal strategy of Husserl's work from 1900 to just before the war is to suggest that subjective impression, far from being the antagonist of scientific, objective observation, is the *only* unimpeachable perception and provides the high road to true essences. To a cultural historian in the 1980s, Husserl's use of the impression may seem a particularly odd and Germanic defense of the value of subjectivity. But impressionism had already schooled itself (as Laforgue's essay suggests) in the proper methods for divesting one's perception of presuppositions arising from senses other than sight, "tactile illusions and their convenient dead language of line," to cite only one example.

Impressionism's passion to return to the "primitive eye" is no doubt involved in the larger taste of all early modernism for analysis in terms of origins, in *The Waste Land* no less than in Frazer, Freud, and Marx. When all kinds of orthodox foundations have crumbled, the suspicion has usually been that they were not fundamental enough to stand, that one had not gone down to bedrock. Since the entire impetus of *Heart of Darkness* is toward such origins, in morality ("restraint"), language, and consciousness itself, it would be very unusual indeed if these instances of unrehearsed perception were not at some level in Conrad's mind analogous to his destination upriver, to the "primitive" form of things, which turns out not to be necessarily savage at all. As in most elements of this story the putatively "civilized" becomes the most genuinely savage, so "civilized" perception, where items are duly registered in nets of traditional or customary signification at once, can readily become a form of violence. Marlow begins to see in this pristine way only when the steamer has very symbolically entered fog and seems about to lose all moorings, all sense of direction; Marlow himself by this time has come to suspect the conventional moorings of "civilization" (particularly as to language) in precisely the sense that he has seen these nets used with the utmost violence to define the "enemies" of "progress" and of "civilization." He is prepared for the risk of seeing in this naïve way.

Claude Monet is reported to have said:

When you go out to paint, try to forget what objects you have before you—a tree, a house, a field, or whatever. Merely think, here is a little square of blue, here an oblong of pink, here a streak of yellow, and paint it just as it looks to you, the exact color and shape, until it gives your own naïve impression of the scene before you.

He said he wished he had been born blind and then had suddenly gained his sight so that he could have begun to paint in this way without knowing what the objects were that he saw before him.[2]

In this revolutionary comment we of course recognize a continuation of the modernist impulse to purge art of extraneous rhetoric and to move toward "pure" art; but the comment also implies a phenomenological flavor not unlike Husserl's "bracketing," the famous *epoché* necessary to wrest a thing from the nets of tradition, convention, and even existence. As would Husserl, Conrad approaches the so-called "attack" with an openness and a respect for the truly apodictic (the compellingly *present* to the viewer) that does not initially seek explanations or theories but follows the spirit of Wittgenstein's admonition: "Describe, don't explain." The few comparisons (the helmsman holding the "cane" as though someone might try to take it from him) are not offered primarily as explanations or theories about what has happened but as the sort of imaginative flexibility with the immediate experience that Husserl recommended in order to intensify the looking. The true spirit of *epoché* refused to establish quickly and prejudically hierarchies of what might be very real, less real, or not so real about the experience.[3] The *epoché* is to be found elsewhere in impressionism and early modernism, and represents a generosity about subjective experience, a refusal to constrict it with preconceived theories about what is "real" or even about the nature of subjectivity itself. The associations Marlow makes with the puzzling events before his eyes serve only to open him to the experience, to make him see more intently and with fewer prejudgments than he or the reader can usually manage. We do not await the "true" explanation of all these strange actions so much as we recognize subsequently the value of such looking, such perception, when confronted with the spectacle of Marlow's experience of Kurtz. Clearly Conrad feels we must be prepared for this kind of perceiving before we arrive at our destination. Like the Accountant, the Lawyer, and the Director of Companies, we are too well equipped with ready-made judgments that immediately constrict our ability to perceive. Husserl does not pull the idea of *epoché* out of thin air but out of the rich context of an increasingly positivist nineteenth century. Of course the maneuver is in Monet made in the name of optical integrity, but had it been made in the name of an equivalent integrity for all the senses and for the act of perception in general the effect and the spirit would be very similar to Conrad.

2. Lilla Cabot Perry, "Reminiscences of Claude Monet from 1889 to 1909," *American Magazine of Art* 18 (1927): 119–25. Reprinted in Nochlin, *Impressionism and Post-Impressionism*, pp. 35–36; this quotation p. 35.

3. See Don Ihde, *Experimental Phenomenology* (New York: G. P. Putnam's Sons, 1979), p. 36 and, indeed, all of chapter 2.

In this peculiar and virtually unnoticed coincidence of impressionism and phenomenology at the turn of the century, a cultural historian has a unique opportunity for uncovering an aspect of early modernism that probably has not yet been given a name. If Kurtz and Marlow have not also "been born blind" and then suddenly gained their sight, they are assuredly among those early moderns who have found it necessary to work toward the primordial origins of consciousness, in the manner of those other pioneers (surely John Locke among them) who feel required to do so at the beginning of any new "period" in human consciousness.

When the little sticks begin flying two hours after the "cotton-wool" fog has lifted (that time when to let go the bottom would have meant being "absolutely in the air—in space"), Conrad offers us not confused seeing, but a "freshness of sensory perception" that William Barrett in describing Hemingway's story "Big Two-Hearted River" has called the "morning of the world." [4] The whole episode of the fog and the "attack" is introduced by Marlow's puzzlement at the cannibal crew's "restraint"— his astonishment that in their hunger they do not simply eat the "pilgrims." ("Restraint! What possible restraint? Was it superstition, disgust, patience, fear—or some kind of primitive honour?") This restraint is to him a "greater mystery" than the "inexplicable note of desperate grief in this savage clamour that had swept by us on the river-bank behind the blind whiteness of the fog." The reader's mind is invited to substitute one "mystery" for another and finally to regard even the "attack" (the pilgrims' word) as all but imponderable in abstract terms: "What we afterwards alluded to as an attack was really an attempt at repulse. The action was very far from being aggressive; it was not even defensive in the usual sense; it was undertaken under the stress of desperation and in its essence was purely protective."

The only things we can rely on in this devolution of abstract, traditional language and categories are the utterly fresh, sensory perceptions, now somehow freed from the conventional expectations that might have persisted in Conrad's audience, had not all of us by now gone so far upriver toward, to use Conrad's phrase, "the beginnings of time." And of course what we are ultimately left with is the utterly fresh sensuous impression of Kurtz, largely as a voice, beyond any of the abstractions that might have kept this presence from us or have screened it in conventional ways. It has, in short, been necessary to create the morning of the world because, whether he is corrupt or heroic or both, that is where this character stands. We can now begin to create afresh whatever abstractions we may design to contain Kurtz, but always with the sure sense that we have experienced for a moment the world all but emptied of them.

4. Barrett, *Time of Need*, pp. 77, 79.

GARRETT STEWART

Lying as Dying in *Heart of Darkness* †

> It is indeed impossible to imagine our own death; and whenever we
> attempt to do so we can perceive that we are in fact still present as
> spectators.
>
> Freud, "Our Attitude towards Death"

Lying is dying. So says Marlow, and so Conrad is out to demonstrate,
even at the expense of his own narrator. "There is a taint of death, a
flavour of mortality in lies," Marlow announces early in *Heart of Darkness*, but the final words he quotes from himself in the novel—his consoling statement to Kurtz's devoted fiancée that her lover expired uttering
her name—constitute his own lie about a dying man's last words. Thus
lie's fatal taint makes rot even of a man's deathbed integrity. It infects
and cancels that unflinching power of speech at mortality's point of no
return which Conrad calls in *Lord Jim* the "triumph" of expression "in
articulo mortis" (p. 233; Ch. xli),[1] his own expression evoking the English
word "articulation" as well as the Latin idiom for "turning point." The
full import of Marlow's self-indicting charity is bound to elude us if the
imagery of death has not been carefully logged. *Heart of Darkness* is the
deviously mapped quest for a sequestered space beyond geographical
coordinates, a recessed sector of the soul to which only death, firsthand
or secondhand, can guarantee passage. Negotiating the further transit
from Kurtz's renowned deathbed utterance to Marlow's appended lie
(itself, as I try to show, an indirect death scene), detecting the continuity
between main plot and coda, is one of the most troublesome maneuvers
in Conrad studies. Yet taking the scent of lie's taint, as it emanates from
the symbolic corpses and metaphoric decay that litter the course of the
story, is the best way of tracing Conrad's equation of death and deceit.
Whether political, moral, or psychological, mendacity is the most mortal of sins, against ourselves and others. Although Marlow equivocates,
Conrad is there behind him to warn us that the lies of Western idealism
mislead us to death.

The plot of *Heart of Darkness* is in part a political autopsy of imperialist myths. A level-headed seaman named Marlow, teller of his own
tale, journeys to the Congo as steamer captain for a European trading
company; hears rumors about another agent of the company, an eloquent mastermind named Kurtz; later discovers that the man has submitted to, rather than suppressed, the natives' savagery, with its hints of
cannibalism and sexual license; finally meets up with Kurtz, remaining
by his side to hear the man's deathbed judgment on his own degeneracy
and diabolism; and then returns to Europe to lie about Kurtz's "worthy"
end in order to give the man's fiancée something to live for and with.

† From *PMLA* 95 (1980): 319–31. Reprinted by
permission.

1. Conrad, *Lord Jim*, ed. Thomas C. Moser (New
York: Norton, 1968).

Marlow's trek toward Kurtz, first by water, then by land, is made now in the wake of a generalized epidemic of death, now in the footsteps of walking specters: a dead march to the heart of a defunct and festering ideal of European superiority. Though the novel's "adjectival insistence,"[2] which so famously annoyed F. R. Leavis, centers nowhere more relentlessly than on permutations of "dark" and "deadly," "tenebrous" and "moribund," the effect is one not so much of morbid atmospherics as of moral asperity, an attack on death-dealing imperialist motives and the truths they obscure.

Heart of Darkness harkens back to origins. It suggests that a naked exposure of the human ego, unshielded by civilization and its self-contents, to a world of savagery presumed to be far beneath it is, in the long evolutionary run, only a baring of the soul to the most primally rooted human impulses. To plumb the native is to come up against the innate, apart from all cultural or racial demarcations. Even before Marlow begins his African narrative proper, he ruminates that the Thames, on which he and his fellow seamen are traveling, has also been, as far back as the Roman colonization, "one of the dark places of the earth." Apropos of the story to come, this initial sense of a primordial blackness triggers an association, more than gratuitous, with "death skulking in the air, in the water, in the bush. They must have been dying like flies here." In Roman England under the pall of colonization, yes, just as in Africa, where Marlow found everywhere "the merry dance of death and trade . . . in a still and earthly atmosphere as of an overheated catacomb," where trade rivers were "streams of death in life."

Beyond the sinister topography of the African landscape, which lays bare the inevitable brutality of imperialism as itself a mode of death, Marlow has also faced his own private demise in an embodied omen. On leaving the company offices in Europe, he must pass by those black-garbed, knitting women, the sibylline harpies and harbingers of death, to whom departing agents seem to sense as the appropriate valediction *"Morituri te salutant"*. As one about to die, or narrowly to skirt his own death, Marlow shortly after encounters two European predecessors, predeceased, on his way to what he calls (recalling a metaphor from its grave) the "dead center" of Africa. First he hears reports of the anonymous Swedish captain who "hanged himself on the road"—no one knows exactly why, but no one is surprised—and later he learns certain details about an earlier Nordic fatality, the Dane Fresleven, who was Marlow's immediate predecessor in the post of company agent and who was conveniently murdered by a representative of the jungle so that Marlow could step "into his shoes." Marlow, sensing the mortal stakes in his adventure and unwilling to content himself with the mere report of Fresleven's death, searches out the corpse in the jungle, become by now a skeletal memento mori with grass growing through its ribs.

Marlow therefore achieves in life what the rest of us receive from such

2. Leavis, *The Great Tradition* (London, 1948; rpt. New York: New York Univ. Press, 1964), p. 177.

stories as the one he spins: he procures an intuition of his own end in the doom of a surrogate. Yielding us the "warmth which we never draw from our own fate,"[3] or in Conrad the chill of recognition, the death scene is art's perpetual bequest to life, though its insights may too easily be forfeited. One of the chief motives for a death scene in literature is thus in *Heart of Darkness*, and never more so than with the final death of Kurtz, devolved on a character within the fiction, indeed the narrator, who gravitates to the death of the Other, first with the nameless Swede and much more urgently with the murdered Fresleven and then twice later, as we will see, to savor the extremity otherwise unavailable to consciousness. The reader, through character—as Marlow, through rumored dooms, skeletons, finally dying men—comes within the safe proximity of his or her own end, a death by imaginative proxy. To vary Shakespeare, in art we ruminate our ruin at one remove, as Marlow's mortuary agenda so complexly exemplifies up to, and even after, his own feverish brush with death following immediately on the death of Kurtz.

Kurtz himself is introduced as the barely living fulfillment of the mortal fate of Marlow as contemplated through his double, Fresleven—though such thoughts hover at the level of mere foreboding, without as yet any explicit parallel between Marlow and Kurtz, except that they are both European agents in Africa. When Kurtz makes his long-delayed appearance Marlow describes him too, like Fresleven, as a skeleton, "the cage of his ribs all astir, the bones of his arms waving". In a scene that looks forward to the remarkable epiphany in *The Magic Mountain* where Hans Castorp sees latent within him, by way of an X ray, his own corpse, Kurtz as breathing skeleton keeps company with the remains of Fresleven as a death's-head memento mori. As Kurtz emerges from his blankets "as if from a winding-sheet," his moribund condition is also personally retributive, an oblique revenge on himself, as arch imperialist, for those untended dying natives in that "grove of death" Marlow had earlier come on, all of whom were reduced to skeletal "bundles of acute angles." In tandem with this ironic reprisal for Kurtz—the witherer withered—is another symbolic pattern of poetic justice, for Kurtz has also been shriveled to an image of the precious corrupted element, the cold ivory, in which he has traded and debased his humanistic ideals. The mania for this dead bone strikes Marlow from the first as having a "taint of imbecile rapacity" like (as with lying for that matter) "a whiff from some corpse", and when Kurtz appears on the scene to personify that greed, his all-but-fossilized being seems like "an animated image of death carved out of old ivory."

Even before Kurtz's first onstage appearance a premature and precipitous description of him as a breathing corpse broke into Marlow's chronological narrative, providing a glimpse of the story's haunted destination. Marlow cannot keep down the need to tell his auditors in advance that

3. Walter Benjamin, "The Storyteller," *Illuminations*, ed. Hannah Arendt, trans. Harry Zohn (New York: Schocken Books, 1969), p. 101.

the visionary encounter with genius he had gone in search of would never be more than spectral—the eviscerated Kurtz reduced, by the time Marlow first sees him, to a disembodied voice in a "disinterred body." Exploring Marlow's preoccupation with Kurtz *as voice* leads us to recognize the logic of such a premature intrusion, for it argues the deepest logic of the novel's first full-dress death, which frames this premonition, the wordless end of a subtly partial doppelgänger for Marlow and Kurtz together in the former's native helmsman. Marlow can share in Kurtz's slaying self-knowledge because "it"—what was left of the man, his neutered "shade" or "wraith"—"it could speak English to me. The original Kurtz had been educated partly in England." Thus Conrad quietly implicates England, and Marlow as Englishman, in Kurtz's European hubris and diseased idealism—and of course implicates himself, too, as British-educated master of nonnative English eloquence. I introduce Conrad's famed English, not just Marlow's expert story-telling, because the local stress on the risks and responsibilities of rhetorical power seems to broaden outward into a comment on the dark expressiveness that brings us the story in the first place.

Marlow admits that his grandiose expectations of Kurtz center on the man's vocal eloquence, for "I had never imagined him as doing, you know, but as discoursing. . . . The man presented himself as a voice," possessing as his only "real presence" the "gift of expression, the bewildering, the illuminating, the most exalted and the most contemptible, the pulsating stream of light or the deceitful flow from the heart of an impenetrable darkness." Marlow realizes the double nature of language, its power to illuminate and ennoble but also to corrupt, and he imagines Kurtz as a disembodied annuciation of this very duality. Kurtz's wasted person when finally encountered bears out this sense of him as language incarnate, for his flesh has withered to the bone, leaving only a speaking soul, a direct effluence from the heart of darkness. And it is a death scene, as so often in literature, that will finally put to the ironic test this power of eloquence. It is important to note, also, that we have a piece of transcribed as well as merely rumored eloquence that ties Kurtz not only to Marlow as a speaking "presence" but again to Conrad, this time as author. Before returning to the narrative of the trip upriver, Marlow slows to summarize a report Kurtz had written for the International Society for the Suppression of Savage Customs; even here the dangerous underside of rhetorical flourish is apparent: "It was eloquent, vibrating with eloquence, but too high-strung . . . a beautiful piece of writing. . . . It made me tingle with enthusiasm. This was the unbounded power of eloquence—of words—of burning nobel words . . . the magic current of phrases." Kurtz exposes the danger of the verbal genius that delivers him to us as a prose incarnation, for at the end of his manuscript he had scrawled into view that darkheartedness which, like his greatness, is charged by the current of his magniloquence, though rendered now in a sudden truncation of all burning and burnished phrase: "Exterminate all the brutes!" Rhetorical sonority in a moral vacuum boils down to a curt, criminal injunction, and the dream of piercing eloquence that Conrad shares with Marlow, especially in this most "high-strung" and over-wrought story, and that both share with Kurtz, an eloquence obsessively stressed in this digression, stands confessed in its essential emptiness. Voice must mean what it delivers, and even Marlow as narrator here—though not Conrad, who is an ironic step or two to the side—protests too much in his brooding reiterations.

To follow Conrad more deeply into the relation of voice to death and darkness, we must note the strategic location of this digression on Kurtzian verbal virtuosity. Closing off the intrusive reverie, Marlow writes: "No, I can't forget him, though I am not prepared to affirm the fellow was exactly worth the life we lost in getting to him." He is referring to his murdered helmsman, a man of no words at all lanced to death in a native attack meant to keep the rescue party from removing Kurtz. "I missed my late helmsman awfully—I missed him even while his body was still lying in the pilot-house." Despite Marlow's deep-seated racism, death solidifies the sense of human commonality, for stabbed through the side, the otherwise negligible "fool-nigger" suddenly "looked at me over his shoulder in an extraordinary, profound, familiar manner, and fell upon my feet." It is the "familiarity" of a soul that knows its own death in the common body. The nameless savage, civilized only enough to enable him to serve the mechanical function of steering, has no English in which to voice the mysteries of his injury and his death. Yet even untutored mortality has its voiceless eloquence: "I declare it looked as though he would presently put to us some question in an understandable language, but he died without uttering a sound. . . . Only in the very last moment as though in response to some sign we could not see, to some whisper we could not hear, he frowned heavily. . . ." Death speaks to, but not through, him an unspeakable something, the whisper of incommunicable revelation, and the resulting frown "gave to his black death-mask an inconceivably sombre, brooding, and menacing expression"—that last noun used in only one of its senses and awaiting completion in the articulate death of Kurtz. Kurtz too has his facial expressions carved in the death mask seemingly hewn of his coveted ivory, but he dies vocally transmitting, as well as receiving, the "whisper" from beyond. The moment of death for the helmsman is precisely marked by a transition in the prose across one of Conrad's most stunning flourishes of the "gift of expression." In this jungle world where death is so treacherously slurred with life, where the landscape itself evinces a Coleridgean "life-in-death," the syllabic momentum of Conrad's studied euphony smooths and blurs one noun into its stretched sibilant antonym, the stare of life into the blank of death: "The lustre of inquiring *glance* faded swiftly into vacant *glassiness*" (my italics). But one death, so vividly imagined and so final, immediately leans forward to become the preview of another.

Almost at once, by a deviously pertinent non sequitur, Marlow adds to the pilgrim at his side: "And by the way, I suppose Mr. Kurtz is dead as well by this time." So begins the frenetic early digression on Kurtz and on the fear of a lost opportunity for an audience with him, imagined only as an audition of his voice in the aftermath of the helmsman's voiceless demise. Just as Marlow is changing the subject—or is he?—from one certain death to a probable one, he is tearing off the shoes filled with the blood of the helmsman who fell at his feet, imploring but mute, as if in a last brotherly supplication. Certainly we are to recall the dead Fresleven and Marlow, on that earlier captain's death, stepping "into his shoes." Now it would seem that Marlow's own life's blood has been shed into them in a symbolic blood brotherhood with his pilot that amounts to a sudden doubling at the point of death. If we assume Conrad is preoccupied with such secret sharing as part of a coherent symbolism in this story, we must begin to range and discriminate Marlow's dead or dying doppelgängers. At first almost a matter of statistical survey or impersonal backdrop, then slowly driven home, even internalized, the surrogate deaths gather step by step toward an excruciating revelation.

En route, the death of the helmsman is an important and rarely discussed middle term. Immediately after the conjecture of Kurtz's probable death, Marlow returns to the death of the pilot to suggest a closer tie than expected between himself and his helmsman: ". . . for months I had him at my back—a help—an instrument. It was a kind of partnership. He steered for me—I had to look after him." One is brawn, physical instrumentality, the other percipience and concern; one muscle, the other mind; and death serves to distinguish, but at the same time to bond, them "like a claim of distant kinship affirmed in a supreme moment." When we note later that the same phrase, "supreme moment," is used for Kurtz's death, we have the parallel unmistakably confirmed. Providing a cool head to Kurtz's tortured soul, Marlow pilots for Kurtz as the helmsman has done before for Marlow. The psychological crux here is a vexing crisscross of doubles that lingers in the imagination until it sorts itself into shape. Though allegory may seem too bald a term for the nested subtleties of Conrad's elusively apportioned psychology, some appreciation of pattern is essential.

If Kurtz is the heart or soul of darkness repressed beneath the accretions and delusions of civilization, what is Marlow's relation, obsessive as it is, to Kurtz? As organizing and expressive consciousness, passionately desirous of the Kurtzian eloquence so as better to tell the Kurtzian secrets, Marlow is mind—we might say ego or even superego—to an id identified with those dark lusts in the jungle. When Kurtz tries to return to the jungle, Marlow must prevent him. Mind must detect and control the unconscious atavistic urges, repress the regressive. This is what Marlow indirectly admits when he has caught up with the escaping Kurtz in the underbrush: "Soul! If anybody ever struggled with a soul I am the man." Of course many have had such conflicts, but usually with their own soul. In the psychic scheme of this novel, however, all things external seem to radiate from Marlow as percipient center, even the jungle incantation in this very scene, for "I confounded the beat of the drum with the beating of my heart and was pleased at its calm regularity." But only Kurtz knows the true rhythms of that native darkness and embodies them symbolically as the objectified buried interior of Marlow's consciouness. In the introduction to a joint edition of this novel and *The Secret Sharer*, Albert Guerard points out that Conrad's departure from such classics of doppelgänger fiction as Poe's *William Wilson* and Dostoevsky's *The Double* reflects a shift away from the pattern whereby "the second selves of the heroes are embodiments of the accusing conscience."[4] Instead, the Conradian double tends to embody a "more instinctive, more primitive, less rational self," a relation in which the helmsman certainly stands—and falls—to Marlow. So too with Kurtz in relation to Marlow, though at the last moment the unconscious life does seem to spew forth a voiced conscience, accusatory and horrible. Interested also in the doppelgänger, Richard Ellmann has suggested that we might go outside the narrative to see Kurtz as a shearing off of one part of Conrad, whose Polish name Korzeniowski abbreviates by transliteration to Kurtz.[5] When Conrad in *Heart of Darkness* decided to test such delvings and divisions of self against its ultimate cancellation in death, however, he inserted the helmsman as the middle term that would help render such death in its twin definition—physical mortality as well as the closure of consciousness—and thus augmented the allegory of his terminal partnerings.

The helmsman, Kurtz, and Marlow form a triangle of body and soul equidistant from the overseeing mind. A mere "instrument" of the white imperialist, yet a physical tool rather surprisingly missed when his awareness has vacated the body, the helmsman is the animal, or preconscious, side of Marlow, primitive but no more initiated into darkness, perhaps, than Marlow. His going is the death of the body, mortality at its lower common factor, in which the "distant kinship" claimed for the first time is merely the fraternity of those who, born for death, are thus, regardless of color, human. Death democratizes as it levels, the corpse of the Other becoming the body of a brother. First a skeleton in tall grass, now a bodied but speechless demise, soon the death throes of an almost incorporeal eloquence: these are the stages of Marlow's face-to-face confrontation with mortality, one on one, or one on naught.

For this confrontation, the "whisper" that registers as a glint in the helmsman's eye must eventually be given voice, even if it is "The horror! The horror!" that Kurtz "cried in a whisper." Like spiritual corpses before him in Dickens, George Eliot, and Hardy, Kurtz dies offstage just moments after his last words. (We must wait for the manager's black servant to stick his head in the cabin door and say—with "scathing contempt" but, because of his untrained grammar, without the verb of being that lends paradox to most predications of death—"Mistah Kurtz—he dead.") Direct representation of demise would be redundant for this

4. Guerard, Introd., Heart of Darkness and The Secret Sharer, Signet Classic ed. (New York: New American Library, 1950), p. 11.

5. Ellmann, *Golden Codgers: Biographical Speculations* (New York: Oxford Univ. Press, 1973), p. 18.

"disinterred" wraith, whose terminal disease had long before done its worst.

The symptoms of Kurtz's jungle fever are, like the words that punctuate its final stage, a direct tapping of spiritual essence. Though understated in its allegorical causation, his is one of those classic deaths of the literary tradition whose etiology wavers between physiology and symbolism. Not only did he live a spiritual death, but the death he dealt to others returns to him with the gruesome suitedness of his physical end. We have watched allusions accumulate from the start to the traditional effect that as he has slain, so he is laid low; as he lusted, so death covets him. When we first see him he is wasted to the inanimate matter of his obsession, his face an ivory death mask; the maker of skeletons and corpses, he is collapsed now to a heap of bone. Morally as well as bodily the jungle has claimed him, and its endemic death now overmasters him by punitive reversal: Africa "had taken him, loved him, embraced him, got into his veins, consumed his flesh, and sealed his soul to its own by the inconceivable ceremonies of some devilish initiation." His terminal sickness is merely the pathological insignia of his soul's disease. Kurtz dies lingeringly of a fever contracted at the heart of the primordial. Something he encounters there meets no resistance, immunological or spiritual; it first inflames, then gradually emaciates him, eating him up from within. This contact is one of the overdetermined weddings of medicine and morality against which, once they become more than a literary figuration, Susan Sontag rails so passionately in *Illness as Metaphor*.[6] They are, of course, the very lifeblood of classic fictional dying, where dramatic sense must be made from the onset of mortal absence.

With just this purpose in mind, Marlow comes to the death of Kurtz with expectations fashioned by myth or literature or both: "Did he live his life again," Marlow asks in one of the clichés of extinction, "in every detail of desire, temptation, and surrender during that supreme moment of complete knowledge?" Kurtz himself has another mortuary formula haltingly in mind just before the end, not Marlow's "drowning man archetype" but another facile parallel between life and its end: "I withdrew quietly, but I heard him mutter, 'Live rightly, die, die. . . .' I listened. There was nothing more." To such swallowed clichés has Kurtz's superb rhetorical gift dwindled. We struggle to recognize a stuttered version, caught in Kurtz's throat, of some balked orthodox formula like "Live rightly, die rightly," or "Live rightly, die nobly," as the manuscript originally had it. Only the converse (if any such formulaic correspondence) could be true for Kurtz, and full fictional honesty demands that, live however you have chosen to live, the fact is simple that you die, not crystallizing your raison d'être but canceling it. Kurtz, knowing this no doubt, cannot get beyond the predication of death—"die, die," the broken record of a broken soul. Yet he is still struggling to sum up in his scorching last words, "The horror! The horror!" The whispered

6. Sontag, *Illness as Metaphor* (New York: Farrar, 1978).

repetition raises for us an even more teasing question: Why twice? Is there a thanatological recipe present here too? "He had summed up— he had judged. 'The horror!' " Both summation and judgment are comprehended in that single word, repeated in Kurtz's actual words once for each—the horror that has been perpetrated, the horror that descends as judgment, either in this pitiless and empty death or in whatever damnation there could be to come. Not until the coda of the novel, when the horror is deceitfully expurgated only to grin from the very depths of its denial, will the full doubleness of its reference be implicitly whispered.

Contaminated by the "horror," Marlow himself shortly falls ill and nearly gets himself buried along with Kurtz, but instead of focusing on his own near death, Marlow insists that "It is his [Kurtz's] extremity that I seem to have lived through." The idiomatic preposition "through" reminds us that only another's death can be undergone without finality, lived up to the moment of and worked past to its other side. And this is for Marlow, of course, not displacement or evasion, at least the first time around, for Kurtz's soul is not some phenomenon entirely removed from him. Allegorically, if we may say so, Kurtz *as soul* represents—below the level of the still-repressive consciousness for which Marlow *as mind* has stood—the buried anguish and guilt of Marlow's own soul, as the helmsman had earlier stood for, and in the stead of, Marlow's bodily self in his multistaged encounter with oblivion. In his book on Conrad's relation to autobiographical narrative, Edward W. Said suggests that *Heart of Darkness* exaggerates the entire first-person mode to a crisis point, where the reportorial or ruminative impulse no longer has the benefit of retrospect. Drawing on Schopenhauer, Said writes that the "only possible meeting between thought and action is in death, the annihilation of both. For the mind to accept death as a solution of the difficulty would be to accept the devastating irony that permits the destruction of the consciousness, the only faculty capable of enjoying the solution."[7] Conrad's early tales instead, according to Said, "posit a compromise in which the agent usually dies . . . and the reflecting mind continues still uncertain, still in darkness." The mind, miraculously sustained beyond the symbolic death of body and soul, remains puzzled with the potentially creative questioning of artistic distance. Again we must note the emphasis on voice, on the articulated end of experience that provides the matter of reflection. Kurtz's death before the eyes and especially the ears of Marlow is best read as the death not of a man alongside a man but of a tragic agonist in the presence of a receptive, if finally too timid, interpreter. One student of Conrad has suggested that Kurtz evokes "from the sensitive Marlow feelings akin to the traditional emotions of pity and terror."[8] Death is cathartic; it boasts the revelatory "compression" (Marlow's own term) of literature pitched to its "supreme moment," where

7. Said, *Joseph Conrad and the Fiction of Autobiography* (Cambridge: Harvard Univ. Press. 1966), p. 113.

8. Paul L. Wiley, "Conrad's Skein of Ironies," originally published in Kimbrough [1963], p. 226.

the consciousness, of reader or audience or here "partner," can move, instructed but unconsumed, through the death of the Other.

If this weathering of death by a double were advanced as a *modus moriendi* in life, however, rather than in tragic art, a basic premise of existentialism, as phrased in emphatic italics by Heidegger, would be directly violated, for *"No one can take the Other's dying away from him"* (Heidegger's italics).[9] Death is undeflectably one's own, for its "end" has a teleological component that is irreducibly private, the coming from potential into presence, always final, of being's fullness—for Kurtz that complete, and completely recognized, "horror," a corruption damningly one's own even while universalized. Kurtz therefore projects the latent predilection of the human race for darkness, a prepossession that when ripened to completeness becomes the very definition of death, the end (to vary Heidegger's "being-toward-death") of a tragic being-toward-darkness. In a characteristic run of ontological argot, Heidegger sums up the principle of mortal individuality by saying that "coming-to-an-end implies a mode of Being in which the particular *Dasein* [roughly "Being"] simply cannot be represented by someone else" (p. 286). Yet what is true existentially, true to life, cannot be true to art, or art would fail us precisely where we most need the intervention of a shaping consciousness. Art's tragic figures must die for us, and for Marlow in our place.

The notion that Kurtz elicits from Marlow the "traditional emotions of pity and terror" that, say, Kurtz or Faust or any other tragic figure evokes in us as audience is developed at some length in Murray Krieger's valuable chapter on Conrad in *The Tragic Vision*. For Krieger, *"Heart of Darkness* is effective as an ideal archetype of the literature of the tragic vision, giving us an exemplary version of the relations between representatives of the ethical and of the tragic realms." By his "relation to Marlow," that is, Kurtz becomes in his fatally concentrated self-revelation "an allegory of the role that the visionary and the literature in which he figures are to play for those of us who are interested but not ourselves committed totally."[1] Marlow is entirely aware, too, of the role he has assigned to his articulate double as doomed visionary, even as we note how throttled and nihilistic is Kurtz's so-called tragic recognition. Death by proxy, terminal vantage through a ritual scapegoat, may be entirely a literary invention, but it is one Marlow tries hard to validate from his experience, for it alone offers him a model of death with understanding, however horrible, to contrast with the nonepiphanic pallor of his own approach to the brink:

> I was within a hair's-breadth of the last opportunity for pronouncement, and I found with humiliation that probably I would have nothing to say. This is the reason why I affirm that Kurtz was a remarkable man. He had something to say. He said it. . . . True,

9. Martin Heidegger, *Being and Time*, trans. John Macquarrie and Edward Robinson (1927; rpt. New York: Harper, 1962), p. 284.

1. Krieger, *The Tragic Vision: Variations on a Theme in Literary Interpretation* (New York: Holt, 1960), p. 155.

he had made that last stride, he had stepped over the edge, while I
had been permitted to draw back my hesitating foot. And perhaps
in this is the whole difference; perhaps all the wisdom, and all truth,
and all sincerity, are just compressed into that inappreciable moment
of time in which we step over the threshold of the invisible.

Marlow, the moral consciousness who dips into the heart of tragic darkness but returns on guard, thus embodies what Krieger calls "the ethical
resistance to the tragic" in which "moral strength resides." I should like
soon to qualify this statement, for the tragedy in *Heart of Darkness* and
the irony seem more pervasive than Krieger believes, Marlow's admirable "restraint" more like repression and delusion. Nevertheless, Krieger's
point about the central dichotomy between moral percipience and tragic
vision is well taken. It suggests that the order of art attempts to soften
existential extremity by molding it to understanding and, further, that
death by proxy may be taken as a test case for the entire narrative and
dramatic enterprise, the knowing voice transmitting visionary experience
into the receptive mind as the essential transaction of all fictional tragedy.

   If Marlow is no more than an eavesdropper on tragedy, our mediator
between visionary depths and the everyday, then the considerable number of critics who find him receiving Conrad's unqualified assent, even
in his supposedly benign final lie, would be correct. Marlow, who aligns
lies and death in his own mind, knows better. On any reading of the
novel, one understands Marlow's awe at Kurtz's deathbed pronouncement, but why should the Marlow of majority opinion be at all dismayed
that he too, no more than nearing that "last opportunity" for statement,
could not muster Kurtz's extremity of self-judgment? Why should a man
of complex ethical sensitivity who has "kept his head" through demonic
tribulations feel diminished by comparison with a life so singlemindedly
surrendered to blackness that a reverberating disyllable, like Keats's "for-
lorn," can toll its retribution? Or we can put the question another way:
In this allegory of "homo duplex"—to use the term that Edward Said
fitly borrows from Conrad's letters[2]—how lightly can we afford to take a
doubling of the climactic denomination, "The horror! The horror!"?
Not only a dead echo within the soul but a resonance with the darkness
outside, in another dichotomy not only summation but also judgment,
this doubleness seems further to indict both parties at the scene, Kurtz
as well as Marlow—passing judgment on the former's exaggeratedly
depraved soul, but only as it concentrates the potential horror of "all the
hearts that beat in the darkness."

   And perhaps there is one final doubling of "the horror" to consider,
when Marlow lies to Kurtz's Intended that "The last word he pronounced was—your name." That we never know her name, so awk-
wardly withheld from the reader, that indeed her title "Intended" seems
to incarnate in her all the original Kurtz's best blind intentions, admits

2. Said, *Beginnings: Intention and Method* (New York: Basic Books, 1975), pp. 104, 130.

her even more readily than otherwise into the sphere of his searing universal revelation: the horror in me (as Kurtz might have said), the horror in all, even in her, the nameless abstract ideal. A lie that would liquidate the tragedy, Marlow's fib exposes the lie of idealism that generates it. Marlow himself, however, has a lesser motive in mind when he falsifies Kurtz's death. Criticism often senses something vaguely contaminating as well as consoling about this lie, but what is *mortal* about it goes undiscussed. As I hope now to show, Marlow's last words about Kurtz's last words are the death knell of his own tragic apprehension, the squandering of Kurtz's delegated revelation on a squeamish deceit. They signal, in fact, some measure of the very death of self Marlow thought he had slipped past, for that "flavour of mortality" in lies leaves its acrid taste throughout the last scene.

Given what we know of Marlow's ultimate attitude toward the Congo experience, the surprise is that criticism can so widely persist in thinking Marlow's whitewashing capitulation merely a white lie, a sacrificial violation of his own spiritual insight out of humanist charity. When he pontificates early on about lie's taint, the point is hammered home as a personal revulsion. Lying "appalls me"; it is "exactly what I hate and detest in the world"; it "makes me miserable and sick like biting into something rotten would." One must doubt whether it could be simply for the solace of another that he later submits himself to his spiritual death. His strict ethical theorem, the equation of death with lying, is even in the early context no stray remark, for it threads untruth to death in the causal nexus of the European experience in Africa. What dying and lying have in common is that they both induce decay, the psychic moribundity and physical decomposition visible everywhere on that colonized landscape we traverse on our way to the death of Kurtz. The novel's largest lie is the one that premises its experience: the ultimately self-revenging hubris of imperial impulse. The question is what degree of collusion in this untruth Marlow, long its implicit critic, ultimately allows himself to take comfort in.

Against the muddied tide of critical opinion, Eloise Knapp Hay, writing about the political novels of Joseph Conrad, has helped us to see how the political self-deception of Marlow serves to discredit him as a morally reliable narrator.[3] For though we read the novel as a progressive disclosure of European delusions in Africa, we must recall that Marlow's words of introduction are uttered from the vantage of retrospect, uttered and thus undercut. Having seen the darkness at the heart of Europe's colonizing onslaughts, he can still say, with a combination of political acuity and idealistic confusion: " 'The conquest of the earth, which mostly means the taking it away from those who have a different complexion or slightly flatter noses than ourselves, is not a pretty thing when you look into it too much. What redeems it is the idea only. An idea at the back of it, not a sentimental pretence but an idea; and an unselfish belief in

3. Hay, *The Political Novels of Joseph Conrad: A Critical Study* (Chicago: Univ. of Chicago Press, 1963); see esp. Hay's treatment of Marlow's lie, pp. 150–54.

the idea—something you can set up, and bow down before, and offer a sacrifice to. . . .' He broke off." Despite his witnessing to the inevitable corruption that comes from white imperialism, Marlow would seem to be saying that without "selfishness" Kurtz could have succeeded, and yet the very claim is demolished by the religious imagery of bowing and sacrificing. Idealism degrades itself to idol worship, as we know from the perverse exaltation and adoration of Kurtz in the jungle, his ascent to godhead.

The inbred spoilage of an ennobling ideal was also sketched out with the first jungle victim we heard about in any detail, the Danish captain Fresleven, who began as "the gentlest, quietest creature that ever walked on two legs." Yet he was murdered by a native while "mercilessly" beating an African chief over some misunderstanding about two black hens. After all, Marlow says without surprise, "[H]e had been a couple of years already out there engaged in the noble cause, you know, and he probably felt the need at last of asserting his self-respect in some way." Thus is the nobility of the white man's grand burden sapped and trivialized. Marlow's parenthetical "you know" (such things taken for granted by us far-thinking Europeans) teeters uneasily between sarcasm and apologetics; Marlow himself is unsure how to feel about his beloved idealism, however fine and selfless, when it can be so readily undermined, here and of course with Kurtz, by eruptions of the ego in sadistic self-assertion. Indeed Kurtz seemed at first the very embodiment of this "noble cause," but too much its incarnation in the long run, too little its acolyte. If Kurtz somewhere held to any glimmer of his original "idea," he must have lost sight of it entirely amid the blackness of his end. Does Marlow mean to imply, however, that Kurtz is the kind of "sacrifice" the idea deserves? Surely Kurtz died in the name of his idea's death, not its perpetuation, died at the hands of his own traitorous neglect of the ideal. There are, Marlow is so far right, purposes in themselves commendable, but when they are implemented by persons in power the danger is always that others will be sacrificed to the ghost of idealism's grandeur, cannibalized by its rhetoric and its personal magnetism. Bowing down tends to surrender vigilance. In line with the imagery of adoration, Marlow himself is twice described in the prologue as an inscrutably effigy, first with a posture and complexion that "resembled an idol" and later, just before his defense of imperialism, with "the pose of a Buddha preaching in European clothes and without a lotus-flower." His own person partially incarnates that idolatry masquerading as an almost religious truth—in another key, Kurtz's idealism turned demonic—which is the monitory center of his tale. Though Marlow knows the evils of white suppression at first hand, he represses them far enough from consciousness to leave continued space for the European idealism he still shares with "the original Kurtz."

Recognizing this, we are a far cry from the sympathetic treatment given Marlow's lie about Kurtz's sustained greatness in the most recent, and on this point not untypical, book about Conrad: "Marlow's lie to her, strain as we may, obstinately remains an ordinary white lie, a humane expression of compassion without devious moral implications and by no stretch of the imagination can we regard it as evincing a form of corruption of his part."[4] H. M. Daleski is thus taking direct issue, and he means to, with Conrad's own statement that in "the last pages of *Heart of Darkness* . . . the interview of the man and the girl locks in—as it were—the whole 30,000 words of narrative description into one suggestive view of a whole phase of life, and makes of that story something quite on another plane than an anecdote of a man who went mad in the Centre of Africa."[5] To side with Conrad against many of his critics in this is to note, for one thing, Marlow's often discussed view of women as cocooned dreamers whom a touch of reality would wilt. Though on the one hand this helps explain his eagerness to protect the Intended from the truth, on the other hand Marlow should have learned better—given another woman he has met—by the time he sees Kurtz's fiancée. When the Intended wails her disbelief in Kurtz's absolute absence, Marlow joins her silently in this faith in the man's perpetuity: "I saw him clearly enough then. I shall see this eloquent phantom as long as I live." But his specter is, to use Conrad's suggestive language, "locked in" also to Marlow's haunted vision of the Intended and of another dark woman superimposed on her image, Kurtz's black consort from the jungle: ". . . and I shall see her too, a tragic and familiar Shade resembling in this gesture another one, tragic also and bedecked with powerless charms, stretching bare brown arms over the glitter of the infernal stream, the stream of darkness." When this sentence is followed immediately by the Intended's ambiguous intuition about Kurtz's death, the feminine pronoun itself is rendered ambiguous by the narrative's overlapping of two spectral images, as if the black (or brown) soul mate is whispering a cryptic truth through the tremulous voice of the white woman's delusion. We have just heard about the tragic African shade, and then: "She said suddenly very low, 'He died as he lived.' " Two "she"s obtain, one obtruding from the past, to reinforce both the Intended's myth and at the same time the darker reality that Kurtz's "tenebrous" consort in the jungle had no reason to doubt as he was torn from her.

Marlow has seen two colors of the feminine heart and thus of the human heart artificially construed as Other. But the Intended carries her savage sister inside her, just as Marlow envelops Kurtz. Dark truth lurks beneath blanching delusion, and both women, copresent in the narrator's mind's eye, are emanations of Marlow as well as of Kurtz. Marlow's early allusion to Brussels as "a city that always makes me think of a whited sepulchre" comes entirely clear only after we have grown to recognize Kurtz as the personified corpse of the *civis* and its hypocrisy; Marlow, returned to the "sepulchral city" as if for entombment himself, washes it the whiter with the bleach of deceit in the course of his lying

4. Daleski, *Joseph Conrad: The Way of Dispossession* (London: Faber and Faber, 1977), p. 75.
5. Letter to his publishers, William Blackwood,

31 May 1902; quoted by Daleski, p. 73 [and, above, p. 210—*Editor*].

interview with the Intended. We now see his previous remark about
defending female illusions more clearly too as the self-protective gesture
to which he briefly admits even during his much earlier allusion to the
Intended: "Did I mention a girl? Oh, she is out of it—completely. They—
the women I mean—are out it—should be out of it. We must help them
to stay in that beautiful world of their own, *lest ours gets worse*" (my
emphasis on Marlow's revealing afterthought). When Marlow reflects at
the end, in his own final words to us, that the alternative to his lie
"would have been too dark—too dark altogether," he is speaking not
only on her behalf but on his own, in rebuttal to the tragic truth vouch-
safed to him in Kurtz's death and repressed in Marlow's own approach
to that end, as well as being repressed, by timid necessity, in his subsequent return to civilization.

Marlow repeatedly describes his experience in Africa, and especially
with Kurtz, as a "nightmare," and this is never more telling a metaphor
than in Marlow's drawing back from the ultimate fate of Kurtz. Psychological truism has it that we never dream our own death, even in the
worst of nightmares—that we always wake to consciousness within an
inch or so of the abyss. So with Marlow's nightmare. We can neither
dream nor, according to Freud, even force ourselves to imagine with
any cogency our own demise. Marlow, therefore, must wake up from
another's fatal nightmare just in the nick of time's tilting over into eternity. Only later is the lie of idealism unconsciously resurrected from its
own death scene in order to be traded on as the barter of return, the
inevitably exacted price of repatriation to the European community.
Kurtz's revelation is a sweeping death sentence, the end point of an
asymptotic nighmare that Marlow holds off in order to come back and
go on. Kurtz's abject but profound darkness dims to a "grey skepticism"
in Marlow that is not only the trivialization but the very ticket of return.

If, back at the sepulchral hub of Europe, the Intended's dark counter-
specter, that feminine apparition from our savage source, might only be
held to a shadowy depth that does not impinge so remorselessly on consciousness, the woman of Faith might still manage to embody for Marlow an ideal he could "bow down before," offer his own misguided and
mortal "sacrifice" to in the form of that deadly lie. As he said earlier of
Kurtz: "I laid the ghost of his gifts at last with a lie." These gifts of insight
into darkness must be laid to rest, or else Marlow would have nothing
left to revere. Kurtz's revelation of "the horror" is fatally incompatible
with genuflection. Since we know that Marlow's own idollike person
seems an outward sign of such internalized idealism, internalized at the
expense of full truth, we sense the reflexivity: "bowing my head before
the faith that was in her, before that great and saving illusion that shone
with an unearthly glow in the darkness, in the triumphant darkness from
which I could not have defended her—from which I could not even
defend myself." With devious valor, however, he attempts this self-defense,
and by preserving such a feminine dreamworld he hopes to prevent his

own from "getting worse," making good the psychic parallelism in "defended her . . . defend myself." For Marlow (to risk again the boxing off of a more expressive complexity) is ultimately homo quadruplex, a wholeness reified into the mental powers of assimilation (as well as repression) played off against lower and would-be higher functions: mind against body in the helmsman, heart or soul in Kurtz, and finally a supervening and repressive Faith in the Intended. In this fourfold "allegory," eventually unfolded, she represents pure idealist intentionality preserved against the corrosive truth of experience, but preserved by being interred along with the buried truth in a sarcophagal unreality.

Daleski follows his critique of Conrad's coda with this sentence: "Consequently, it is difficult for us to make any meaningful connection between the lie and death." But we are now in a position to make this connection amid the metaphors of spiritual deadliness and posthumous defeatism that litter the coda as much as they do the tale itself. Marlow's untruth is lethal precisely because it kills the meaning of a death. There is a corollary to the proposition that lying is a kind of dying. Truth, even grasped only in death, is a defiance of death, a notion hallowed in British fiction's treatment of demise. Kurtz's self-realization, about the "horror" his life and death would have epitomized, rendered his image deathless in the mind, a perennial admonishing phantom, except that the lie kills it. Partly to abet Marlow in this homicidal denial, two of the most trusted mortuary formulas of fiction, each a version of death by epitome, are invoked with some verbal and thematic deviousness in connection with Kurtz's death, one early, one late. When Marlow realizes that the name Kurtz, meaning "short" in German, is belied by the man's considerable height, he says—as if forgetting (because wanting to, no doubt) the cauterizing truth telling of Kurtz's last utterance—that "the name was as true as everything else in his life—and death." Marlow's own retrospective account seems colored, obscured, by the late meliorating lie eventually summoned to slay Kurtz's black epiphany. Marlow does, however, recognize the "true" consonance of Kurtz's life and death in another sense, for the persistent specter of Kurtz's ghost calls up this postmortem observation: "He lived then before me, he lived as much as he had ever lived . . . a shadow darker than the shadow of the night." Ghostliness is at one with his ghastly aura in life. There is further evidence in the coda that Conrad, if not Marlow, has the mortuary tradition in literature specifically in mind, with its often rigorous equations between death and identity. When, hoping for solace, the Intended clutches at the time-tested heroic prescription, "He died as he lived," Marlow's mock iteration, "His end . . . was in every way worthy of his life," not only secretly reverses the moral judgment implicit in her faith, even as he preserves some of that faith for her and for himself, but helps us see the additional irony to which Marlow, in the throes of untruth, is no doubt blinded. The epitomizing apothegm of death is traditionally phrased with a change in tense—"He died as he *had* lived"—with pluperfect brought to perfection (in the existential sense) in the preterit. The Intended, however, has unwittingly summarized the nature of a corrupt life coextensive with death and equivalent to it: the long-pending end of a man who, again, "died as he lived." Living a lie of moral superiority, lies being deadly, Kurtz died *while* he lived ("as" in this sense), his death scene true to life in its very deadliness. What Céline would call "death on the installment plan" is, however, a truth about Kurtz that is itself sabotaged and assassinated.

An equally mordant telescoping of tense arrests us in the most curious passage in this coda, where Marlow seems more than usually aware that his words may fail to capture his only half-glimpsed purpose: "For her he had died only yesterday. And by Jove, the impression was so powerful that for me too he seemed to have died only yesterday—nay this very minute. I saw her and him in the same instant of time—his death and her sorrow—I saw her sorrow in the very moment of his death. Do you understand? I saw them together—I heard them together." Her black-draped mourning is Kurtz's darkness visible; her untarnished faith is the lie overlaying his fatal eloquence. For her Kurtz died yesterday, while for Marlow, who somewhere knows the truth, he dies in the instant, every instant, of her deluded mourning, in which Marlow now colludes. The faith Marlow so sustains, in and through its feminine vessel, is a faith that kills, that denies the tragic content of the death scene—as if Kurtz himself had not inched over the edge into revelation. And so in Marlow's mind's-eye vision—a palimpsest of mourning superimposed on simultaneous death—Kurtz's *present* deathbed, symbol of the present murder of his very meaning, and the Intended's immolation on the bier of his memory are, after all, "locked together." They give us death's poisonous aftertaste in the mouth of untruth. If this is an even bleaker reading of the story's denouement than usual, at least it seeks to respect the tragic potential of the previous climax, the legacy of insight willed by a cruel but lucid death.

For in the Intended's dedication to Kurtz's misunderstood and ideal-ized shade there is, we come finally to see, a heart-denying lie that is equivalent to the death it euphemizes, a lie that rests at the heart of the death it originally causes. In short, such faith in moral supermen breeds the death of its own heroic avatars in their all too human incarnations. Marlow cannot separate the black of Kurtz's end from that of his finan-cée's mourning, because he uses her suffering as an excuse to deflect the full import of the former tragedy, reducing it to futile pathos. This vicious circle is imaged as an almost hallucinatory superimposition, her contin-uing grief over and above her idol's recurring death. And it renders vis-ible the link between death and delusion just before the sustaining lie is tendered. If we can answer affirmatively Marlow's "Do you under-stand?" then this appalling double image becomes the symbolic config-uration of death as lie incarnate, corpse and killing delusion seen in line with the same vanishing point, spiritual negation zeroing in on a void.

JULIET McLAUCHLAN

The "Value" and "Significance" of *Heart of Darkness* †

Must we interpret *Heart of Darkness* "in the light of the final incident" in order to see the story's coherence, worth, and essential meaning? Or not? Recent consideration of some of the more representative yet divergent critical views has prompted this fresh attempt to answer the basic question. The starting point must be Conrad's own words: ". . . in the light of the final incident, the whole story . . . shall fall into place—acquire its value and its significance."[1]

It has been claimed by a recent critic that Conrad "bungled the scene,"[2] and from time to time others have challenged its success.[3] The very extent of critical disagreement has itself convinced many readers and students that it is useless to go on trying to link the ending meaningfully to the story as a whole: since interpretations differ so radically, Conrad must have failed to do what he thought he was doing. Yet uneasy doubts persist. Suppose Conrad did succeed. Suppose we are missing the whole point of the story. After a glance at some relevant criticism I shall argue for the success of the scene in Conrad's terms.

Something akin to the supposed "botching of the end of 'Heart of Darkness' "[4] seems to be implicit in the dismissive notion that Kurtz's savage consort "has no status in the essential fable. Nor has the other woman."[5] Such a view can only discourage serious consideration of the final scene, as may views which imply that the Intended has no metaphorical or symbolic significance but is just a young woman bereft, to whom Marlow lies to "preserve the 'saving illusion' of another."[6] Marlow's lie is then seen as "analogous to that of Captain Allistoun's to Jimmy . . . to give her 'something to live with.' "[7]

Such views are clearly at odds with the notion that, since the Intended's "home is a graveyard," Kurtz is to be seen as "degraded, exalted, tragic" while "Brussels is civilised, hypocritical, dead."[8] On a very much deeper note: "the light" if taken with its usual positive connotations has become so "degraded" by the time the scene occurs, that it is a mere "cold and artificial brightness" capable of imparting no more than:

† From *Conradiana* 15 (1983): 3–21. Reprinted by permission.

1. *Joseph Conrad: Letters to William Blackwood and David S. Meldrum*, ed. William Blackburn (Durham: Duke University Press, 1958), p. 154 [and, above, p. 210—*Editor*].
2. H. M. Daleski, *Joseph Conrad: The Way of Dispossession* (London: Faber, 1977), p. 76.
3. See for example, Thomas Moser, *Joseph Conrad: Achievement and Decline* (Hamden, Connecticut: Archon Books, 1966), p. 79; F. R. Leavis, *The Great Tradition* (London: Chatto and Windus, 1948), p. 181; Eloise Knapp Hay, *The Political Novels of Joseph Conrad* (Chicago: University of Chicago Press, 1963), pp. 149–53.
4. Daleski, p. 24.
5. J. I. M. Stewart, *Joseph Conrad* (London: Longman, 1968), p. 230.
6. Jocelyn Baines, *Joseph Conrad: A Critical Biography* (London: Weidenfeld and Nicolson, 1969), p. 230.
7. Daleski, p. 74. Daleski goes on to differentiate Marlow's lie from the captain's because of Marlow's horror of lying.
8. C. B. Cox, *Joseph Conrad: The Modern Imagination* (London: Dent, 1974), pp. 58, 57.

JULIET MCLAUCHLAN

the cold phosphorescent glow of idealism, but sick and pallid indeed
compared with the other tragic and heroic woman whom Kurtz
abandoned in the heart of darkness . . . [we have] moved from a
realisation of the *overwhelming* power of darkness in the psychological, moral and spiritual realm, to a larger and intangible change
of a metaphysical kind, in which light seems to have a peculiar
affinity with unnaturalness, hypocrisy, and delusion, and [even] *to
be quite as contrary to the positive values in human life as the worst
manifestations conventionally attributed to darkness.*[9]

I have italicized words which seem to me to be indefensible: true, Conrad's method often involves reversing expectations with regard to the
value of light (most strikingly in *Nostromo*) but I hope to demonstrate
that he is doing something else at the end of *Heart of Darkness*.[1]

A very recent critic has argued: "Lying is dying. So says Marlow, and
. . . Conrad is out to demonstrate [this] even at the expense of his own
narrator." Following Marlow's experience of Kurtz's death, Marlow's
"appended lie" is "an indirect death scene" for Marlow himself. Despite
his unequivocal statements about "the taint of death" and "the flavour
of mortality in lies":

the final words he quotes from himself in the novel . . . constitute
his own lie about a dying man's last words. Thus [sic] lie's fatal
taint makes rot even of a man's deathbed integrity. [Further] Marlow's last words about Kurtz's last words are the death knell of his
own tragic apprehension, the squandering of Kurtz's delegated revelation onto a squeamish deceit . . . Marlow's untruth is lethal
precisely because it kills the meaning of a death. [Marlow uses the
suffering of the Intended] to deflect the full import of the former
tragedy . . . reducing it to futile pathos.

In a sense the whole view of this critic is based upon the assertion that:
"Whether political, moral, or psychological, mendacity is the most mortal of sins, against ourselves and others."[2] Through the gradual development of my own argument it will be clear why I reject this view as
simply too narrow to illuminate the tale *in toto* through consideration of
its final scene. I shall from time to time take issue with other specific
points from this essay.

Further critical views point towards what I hope to demonstrate.
Although I feel especially indebted to these critics, I make no claim that
any of them would agree wholly with my own approach. Without Marlow's lie "the passionate devotion of the Intended would be shattered,

9. Ian Watt, *Conrad in the Nineteenth Century*
(Los Angeles and London: University of California
Press, 1980), pp. 251–52. It seems presumptuous
to take issue with any of Watt's views, given the
all-round contribution to Conrad criticism which
is represented by his monumental chapter on this
story. I shall do so, however, on a few crucial points
which bear closely upon the argument of this essay.

[A selection from Watt's book appears on pp. 311–
36 in this volume—*Editor*.]
1. Juliet McLauchlan, *Conrad: Nostromo* (London, 1969), pp. 15–18.
2. Garrett Stewart, "Lying as Dying in *Heart of
Darkness*," PMLA, 95 (1980), 319–31. [This essay
appears on pp. 358–74 in this volume—*Editor*.]

and one of the few islands of naïve idealism in the world would be conquered."[3] "As Kurtz's savage consort symbolizes the soul of the jungle, Kurtz's fiancée . . . symbolizes the soul of civilization. By lying to Kurtz's Intended, Marlow presents civilization with a slender ray of light with which to keep back the darkness."[4] Marlow's "feeling of infinite pity [is not only] compassion for the fragility of the woman's illusions [but] for the fragility of the civilization . . . however corrupt and hollow, the best of which the girl represents . . . [she] represents all the best of Kurtz's ideals—all the best of what he has 'intended' for the world as well as for himself . . . [Marlow is then] a barrier between the degraded and the exalted . . . [his function lies in] maintaining the part of civilization worth saving [and], however tenuously, man's humanity."[5] The Intended and the savage woman are, respectively, "the embodiment of light" and "the embodiment of darkness."[6] The "light of visionary purpose" is of some lasting value, as is the "positive illusion" which Marlow lies to save.[7]

These views all suggest the presence of a pattern of imagery similar to that which Conrad actually develops throughout *Heart of Darkness*. The culmination in the final scene makes it possible to clarify five major aspects of the story: first, the symbolic function of the Intended herself; second, the nature of Kurtz's "victory," resulting as it does from a sustained inner conflict; third, the nature and extent of Kurtz's debasement; fourth, some aspects of Marlow's "choice of nightmares";[8] fifth, the relationship between, on the one hand, ideas and ideals, and on the other, the words used to express them. Not only has Conrad successfully handled the final scene, he has embodied in *Heart of Darkness* a theme which no one since Shakespeare has presented with such power: the upward and downward potential of man.

It is the downward potential which has most often fascinated readers and critics. Indeed they have become so fascinated by the "abomination" of human debasement, as suggested so disturbingly in Kurtz, that they have largely ignored clear implications of humanity's upward potential. Yet it is "the two extremes that can exist within the human mind"[9] which Marlow must penetrate and comprehend.[1] When Marlow is trying to clarify his sense of the savages' "humanity," of "remote kinship with this wild and passionate uproar," of the "faintest trace of a response to the terrible frankness of that noise," of "a dim suspicion of

3. C. T. Watts, *Conrad's Heart of Darkness: A Critical and Contextual Study* (Milan: Ugo Mursia, 1977), p. 122.
4. Ted E. Boyle, "Marlow's Lie," in *Heart of Darkness*, ed. Robert Kimbrough (New York: Norton, 1971), p. 243. See also Boyle's *Symbol and Meaning in the Fiction of Joseph Conrad* (The Hague: Mouton, 1965), for fuller discussion.
5. Kenneth A. Bruffee, "The Lesser Nightmare," in Kimbrough [1971], pp. 236–38. The phrases given here do not do justice to the complexities of this fine article.
6. Florence H. Ridley, "The Ultimate Meaning

of *Heart of Darkness*," *NCF*, 18 (1963), pp. 43–53. The entire article merits critical attention.
7. Jacques Berthoud, *Joseph Conrad: The Major Phrase* (Cambridge: Cambridge University Press, 1978), p. 63.
8. Juliet McLauchlan, "The 'Something Human' in *Heart of Darkness*," *Conradiana*, 9 (1977), 115–25 discusses Marlow's choice from a different standpoint.
9. Walter Wright in Kimbrough [1971], p. 241.
1. Daleski, pp. 52 and 54 shows clearly that "penetrate" and "sight" are synonymous with the insight which Marlow gradually gains.

there being a meaning in it which you—you so remote from the night of first ages—could comprehend," he asks "And why not?" explaining that the mind of man can thus "comprehend" because it contains "all the past as well as all the future." Although the "triumphant darkness" conquers Kurtz *almost* entirely, Marlow has to see at the end that the conquest must not be accepted as final for "all the future" of humanity: a qualified "victory" has been won, and any hope for humanity's future will depend upon preservation of "the light of visionary purpose." In this sense, then, "the light" remains a positive value, not itself "degraded," yet, as will be seen, presented in such ways as to qualify severely any sense of its practical power or efficacy.

Light in a positive sense is made to focus consistently upon the figure of the Intended—or rather upon her soul, but the first reference to "the girl" as "out of it" comes almost as an aside during that remarkable outburst in which Marlow first reveals something of the nature and extent of Kurtz's debasement. Up to this point in the narrative, Kurtz has remained essentially a puzzle for Marlow's auditors, for the reader, and for Marlow himself within the chronology of the story. As a "gifted crea-ture" and, especially, as "a man who had come out equipped with moral ideas of some sort" Kurtz has piqued Marlow's curiosity: would, or could, such a man succeed?—if so, how would he comport himself? There has been a further puzzle in Marlow's first "distinct glimpse." He seems to have "seen" Kurtz, as it were, when Kurtz has turned back and is again "setting his face towards the depths of the wilderness." Ominous doubt is suggested: "*Perhaps* he was just simply a fine fellow who stuck to his work for its own sake" (my italics). There is a further ominous note in the noxious uncle's advice to the manager to leave Kurtz "to this"—to the unspecified but probably fatal effects of the wilderness. There is doubt, yes, but nothing to prepare auditors or reader for the shock of that shat-tering image of an exhumed corpse mouthing the words, "My Intended":

> You should have heard the disinterred body of Mr. Kurtz saying, "My Intended." You would have perceived directly then how com-pletely she was out of it.

Suddenly we become aware of some abject failure on the part of Kurtz, some bitter disillusionment on the part of Marlow. And Kurtz's Intended must indeed be "out of it" whether the word refers to a real fiancée or to Kurtz's intentions. At the end of his passionate outburst, Marlow sums up Kurtz as "not common" and declares that Kurtz not only "had the power to charm or frighten rudimentary souls into an aggravated witch-dance in his honour [but] . . . had conquered one soul in the world that was neither rudimentary nor tainted with self-seeking."

The first part of that extract is finely expressive of an essential aspect of Kurtz's debasement, which consists in his "getting himself adored" by his primitive followers. At the opposite extreme, through his idealistic eloquence, he has won a human soul, pure, selfless, mature. Following Marlow's later account of Kurtz's death and his partial assessment of

Kurtz's "victory" he recalls having heard "a long time after . . . the echo of his magnificent eloquence thrown to me from a soul as translucently pure as a cliff of crystal." When Marlow finds himself in the presence of the Intended, these qualities resonate fully for the reader, reinforcing a sense of her selflessness and "translucent" purity of soul. Marlow's first sight of her comes through her photograph, and her beauty strikes him less forcibly than her "beautiful expression" which seems to him not at all dependent upon pose or "manipulation of [external] light." Her face, with its "delicate shade of truthfulness" reveals that she is "ready to listen without mental reservation, without suspicion, without a thought for herself." How can these qualities (which are presented quite without irony) be associated with hypocrisy, or with any related negatives? The Intended is, however, blind to what Kurtz really is. Why? I return to this below but mention here that her illusory view has recently been explained and, to some extent, excused in terms of the social background: "merely by allotting women a leisure role, society has in effect excluded them from discovering reality; so it is by no choice or fault of hers that the Intended inhabits an unreal world."[2] There is clearly an element of truth in this, but to conclude that Marlow could not have "conveyed the truth about Kurtz to her, because she is armoured by the invincible credulity produced by the unreality of the public rhetoric" is to apply to the Intended words which apply perfectly to Marlow's aunt, not to the girl.[3] It is an error to assume that both women are "out of it" in the same way. To do so is to fail to take into account the positive value in the Intended's "mature capacity for fidelity, for belief, for suffering," her devoted adherence to the ideals which Kurtz has expressed. The aunt is, indeed, "out of it" because of her "invincible credulity" and the sentimental pretence of her utterly trivial nature. The Intended must be categorized quite differently: as "such a thunderingly exalted creature as to be altogether deaf and blind to anything but heavenly sights and sounds." To live, in that way, remote from all reality, in a state of total illusion, is not, of course, in Conradian terms a valuable or workable approach to living—in this way she is "out of it."

Throughout the whole scene with the Intended the imagery works to intensify a sense that the value of the Intended is subject to grave limitations. Great beauty of body and soul are portrayed in surroundings of growing darkness and isolation from any other human being: "Since his mother died I have had no one—no one . . ."; "The dusk was falling"; "The room was growing darker"; "The darkness deepened"; towards that "conquering darkness" against which Marlow comes to feel there is only the defence of a lie. In the midst of the gloom and loneliness (intensified by the fact that she is in mourning) there shines only the gold of her hair and her pale haloed brow, "illumined by the unextinguishable light of belief [which is not, of course, knowledge] and love." It is the inner light of her heart and soul which must not be extinguished; the great and "saving illusion" *even though illusory*, must be allowed to survive. The glow is "unearthly" precisely because all it represents has not been brought down to earth, and probably never will be, for the word "illusion" (as so consistently used by Conrad) is crucial: illusions are not enough to live by, but humanity cannot live without them—and in this story humanity has no future without them. Marlow has realized the need to save "another soul"—the soul of civilization. The "cliff of crystal" is a fine image for the remoteness of the beautiful idea: of gem-like clarity and brightness, its very form is such as to suggest something unreal and unattainable in human terms. Once again, we "see" the Intended as "out of it." Conrad's or Marlow's misogyny is often invoked to explain this, but misogyny is just not the point. Trying to penetrate the "impenetrable darkness" of Kurtz, Marlow has had to "peer down [as] at a man who is lying at the bottom of a precipice where the sun never shines." Infinitely high above shines the cliff of crystal. In this fine contrast, Conrad's touch is very sure. Both extremes are remote from the fully human, which must dwell between, working doggedly at the task in hand, and even breathing "dead hippo"—but upwards humanity must continue to look and strive.

Surrounding the Intended, and pervading the scene, there is even more ominous and less hopeful imagery. Details in the description of the street, the house, and the furniture suggest death and burial. In every sense Kurtz's intentions must be seen as dead and entombed; so it is appropriate that the Intended should be depicted as shut in, cut off, dead to and for the rest of the world and its normal activities.

Before proceeding further, we can come to terms (at least partially) with a large claim which Marlow has made early in the story: "What redeems it [the conquest of the earth] is the idea only. An idea at the back of it, not a sentimental pretence but an idea; . . . something you can set up, and bow down before, and offer a sacrifice to. . . ." *Can* any idea, or ideal, be felt to be redemptive, given the darkness which has to be contemplated in this tale? Redemptive of what? Certainly not redemptive of the actual situation in any practical way, whether it be in the corrupt civilization of the sepulchral city, or still less in the wilderness, where people are made to slave and die by the emissaries of such "civilization." Marlow, "the moral man"[4] (mature humanity) has to learn finally that, however debased the human may become, human nature has also the capacity and the need to look towards exalted ideals in aspiration and worship—with less sense here of a "dubious idolatry"[5] than of humanity's often inexplicable willingness to make sacrifices, even the ultimate sacrifice, in the service of an ideal. Ideals themselves are not invalidated by even the gravest human failure to make them the reality of human experience.

On that practical, human level Kurtz has failed completely. Yet from the standpoint of the final scene it is possible to assess the meaning and value of his "victory." A key approach is to see that "without some eth-

---

4. Berthoud, p. 61.   5. Berthoud, p. 43.

ical belief, Kurtz's judgment would have no logical basis":[6] some sense of moral values must survive within Kurtz to enable him to judge himself. Significantly, during the scene itself Marlow:

> saw her and him in the same instant of time—his death and her sorrow—I saw her sorrow in the very moment of his death. Do you understand? I saw them together—I heard them together. She had said with a deep catch of the breath, "I have survived," while my strained ears seemed to hear distinctly, mingled with her tone of despairing regret, the summing-up whisper of his eternal condemnation.

All that Kurtz had intended, or persuaded himself that he intended, survives here, embodied physically, before Marlow's eyes. During that "supreme moment of complete knowledge" when Kurtz has seen and judged his abysmal fall from his intentions, he has *experienced* the "horror" precisely because he, too, sees "together" his intentions and his failure. In an ordinary metaphorical sense, a person is said to be wedded to his work, to that into which he puts his heart and soul. Instead of thus wedding himself to his Intended, Kurtz has espoused the wilderness. The vision of Kurtz which accompanies Marlow into the house of the Intended is associated with "the beat of the drum . . . like the beating of a heart, the heart of a conquering darkness." Kurtz's heart has come to beat to the beat of that heart. Betraying the soul of civilization, his soul has come to be possessed by the soul of the wilderness.

Despite this, Kurtz has continued to the end to talk of his "ideas" and "plans," of his "Intended." Because of this, and because Marlow has himself seen "together" the horror of Kurtz's failure and the loftiness of his intentions, we can now see the nature of the "struggle" within Kurtz's tormented soul, a struggle which culminates in his "eternal condemnation." We must be quite clear that this is self-condemnation—not damnation. To one critic, Kurtz's words, "The horror!" with their repetition, constitute both "summation" and "judgment" and he goes on: "There is the horror that has been perpetrated [the nature of this is not made clear in the article cited], the horror that descends as judgment either in this pitiless and empty death or in *whatever damnation there could be to come*"[7] (my italics). These vague personifications of the horror cast no light on the basis of Kurtz's self-condemnation—indeed the italicized words (which are especially vague) lead away from the crucial point: that Kurtz has eventually "pronounced a judgment upon the adventures of his soul on this earth." Damnation must involve some external agent or force, and nothing of the sort is shown in *Heart of Darkness*. Any specifically Christian reading of Kurtz's fate would be equally inappropriate, and Kurtz neither makes a pact with a "real" devil, nor is he diabolically possessed in a theological sense. The story is not recounted in those terms. The basis is humanistic and ethical. Kurtz retains, or rather regains, a capacity to judge himself, largely because of Marlow's determination to struggle with his "mad soul" and prevent Kurtz from surrendering his humanity once and for all to "the heavy, mute spell of the wilderness" which has called him back by "the awakening of forgotten and brutal instincts . . . the memory of gratified and monstrous passions." It is central to my argument that *Heart of Darkness* is set in a completely indifferent universe, and that Kurtz's debasement grows from within, and not through any "actively malign force",[8] represented by "the wilderness." True, the wilderness is frequently personified by Marlow, as a huge, brooding, even threatening presence, but this is clearly his subjective reaction—as when it "seemed [to Marlow] to draw [Kurtz] to its pitiless breast." Not only does Marlow find "no moral darkness in the black inhabitants of Africa",[9] but the "pure, uncomplicated savagery" of the wilderness is never shown to be in any way aggressive.[1]

Kurtz's "brutal instincts" bring about his surrender to "monstrous passions"; yet at the end Marlow tells us that he "struggled, he struggled." The struggle indicates the presence of some moral awareness as well. What counts in the end is that Kurtz can judge himself in the light of his own expressed ideals. When "his values at last connect with his life [they] reveal it to be a 'darkness' . . . and by recognizing that the values to which he had paid lip-service apply to himself, Kurtz has *made them real at last*".[2] This is a fine insight which clarifies enormously the whole question of positive value in this story. In particular, it refutes certain other views: "If Kurtz somewhere held to any glimmer of his original 'idea', he must have lost sight of it entirely amid the blackness of his end."[3] Not so, as has just been shown. Since (referring to the same critic) Kurtz not only "died at the hands of his own traitorous neglect of the ideal" but dies fully aware of his treachery (and loathing it), it follows that his "gifts of insight" must extend beyond insight *merely* "into darkness." His "cruel and lucid death" must be diminished if his lucidity is seen as expressive of nothing beyond "an abject and profound darkness." And why should Kurtz's "*so-called tragic recognition*" (I italicize the phrase because it is never explained) be seen as not only "nihilistic" (as this critic consistently argues) but "throttled"? Not, it is to be hoped, by Marlow's lie. A fatal weakness in this critic's argument is his failure even to mention the central issue of Kurtz's "victory."

When Marlow sees "together" Kurtz and the Intended, he sees not simply the "horror" of Kurtz's realization of his debasement but the deeper realization involved in his "moral victory." The tremendous power of *Heart of Darkness* consists in its revelation of the capacity of a human soul, without external religious sanctions of any sort, to struggle with itself, to find within itself values by which it can and must judge its actions—and condemn them. That is Kurtz's undoubted victory, a confirmation of the validity of his ideals, intentions, even his words. This is

8. Watt, p. 250.
9. Watt, p. 249.
1. See again McLauchlan, "The 'Something

Human' " for further discussion of this point.
2. Berthoud, p. 59, my italics.
3. Garrett Stewart, p. 327.

the great moral center of *Heart of Darkness*—and this is what robs the "darkness" of any "overwhelming" power.[4]

Marlow calls Kurtz's judgment: "an affirmation, a moral victory paid for by innumerable defeats, by abominable terrors, by abominable satisfactions. But it was a victory." This quotation leads directly to consideration of the nature of the inner conflict which culminates in Kurtz's victory, a conflict from which, it appears, he is never free. Marlow defines Kurtz's final "glimpsed truth" as "the strange commingling of desire and hate." Critics have too often dwelt upon analysis of the possible nature of Kurtz's desires and satisfactions (with fascinated horror, or even admiration). But what of the commingled "hate"? If Kurtz had given himself over to primitive instincts and passions without experiencing any conflict at all, he would simply have "gone native," and the story would have been banal and superficial. Some such simplistic notion seems to inhere in the assumption that Kurtz is "the heart and soul of darkness repressed beneath the accretions and delusions of civilization."[5] Why should any sense of "horror" arise when repressed passions have broken free from mere "accretions" and "delusions"? Kurtz's tragedy consists in an inner conflict (which this critic fails to see); the horror lies in the "strange commingling" of such opposites as "hate" and "desire." Even the Harlequin, whose insight into Kurtz is minimal, tells Marlow: "This man suffered too much. He hated all this and *somehow he couldn't get away*" (my italics). It now seems that Marlow's first "distinct glimpse" of Kurtz formed a precise image for that inability to escape from what he loathed.

Speaking of the Romans in Britain, Marlow has invited his auditors to imagine what it was like, and here every detail prefigures an aspect of Kurtz's conflict: "He has to live in the midst of the incomprehensible which is also detestable. And it is a fascination too, that goes to work upon him. The fascination of the abomination—you know. Imagine the growing regrets, the longing to escape, the powerless disgust, the surrender—the hate." As Marlow's narrative approaches the moment of Kurtz's final words, he asks: "Did he live his life again in every detail of desire, temptation, and surrender during that supreme moment of complete knowledge?" The partial parallel in these passages is obvious, and the implication of the rhetorical question is that Kurtz did so relive his experience. Kurtz's "mingled expression of wistfulness and hate," the "diabolic love and the unearthly hate" of "the mysteries" which his soul has "penetrated"; these are the elements in Kurtz which fight for the possession of his soul. The word "hate" is recurrent, and although Kurtz may have become a "shade," a "hollow sham," a mere "disinterred body," yet within Kurtz human values survive which account for his sense of revulsion, for his hatred of his own degradation.

Kurtz's moral judgment applies supremely to his own soul, but his final insight is all-encompassing; looking upon humanity in full awareness of his own degradation, he projects his debasement, failure, and

4. Watt, p. 251.   5. Garrett Stewart, pp. 322–23.

hatred universally. Realizing that any human soul *may* be fascinated, held irresistibly, by what it rightly hates, his stare is "wide enough to embrace the whole universe," "wide and immense . . . embracing, condemning, loathing all the universe." Having failed to prevent himself from penetrating that "lightless region of subtle horrors" where Marlow can never bear to follow him even in thought, Kurtz looks out from its depths with a gaze "piercing enough to penetrate all the hearts that beat in the darkness." Here he is seeing in terms of humanity's downward potential and can gaze straight into those hearts which, like his own, have been conquered by the darkness—and into all those which *might* be so conquered.

As is clearly shown in *Heart of Darkness*, there are hearts and souls which do not follow humanity's downward potential, and could never do so. Yet the wholly "light" hearts and souls are not endowed with full humanity. The Harlequin is too naïve, immature, dazzled by ideas, to see the evil which is plainly before his eyes. The Intended is too exalted, too remote from ordinary reality to see or hear anything but the "unearthly" and "heavenly." Marlow, the fully human, can comprehend the primitive; he can (because he must) look into the extremes in human nature, from the debased to the exalted. Significantly, at the beginning of the story, he calls for imaginative insight into past human experience which then parallels very closely the "present" experience of Kurtz. This imparts a strong sense of continuity between past and present, but timelessness and universality come only with Kurtz's all-embracing gaze. Among conflicting emotions at his death, Kurtz experiences "despair." It is, precisely, some slight *hope* which survives through Marlow's lie: the survival of ideals and aspirations will provide a standard by which humanity can at least continue to judge its degradation—as Kurtz has judged his.

But what, exactly, is the nature and extent of Kurtz's debasement? In particular, what is it that most appals Marlow, as "the moral man"? Why does he find many aspects of savagery readily comprehensible while other aspects (all connected with Kurtz) are "unspeakable" and "incomprehensible"—and must remain, I would argue, *literally* unspeakable and incomprehensible. (These and similar words called down F. R. Leavis's strictures upon Conrad's "adjectival insistence" and his "making a virtue out of not knowing what he means."[6]) I contend that Conrad knew and expressed exactly what he meant, and that Leavis's strictures are inappropriate, as are suggestions of "rhetorical overemphasis" or "attitudinizing."[7] To Marlow, the shrunken heads are simply "a savage sight," when contrasted to the proffered details of the "ceremonies used when approaching Mr. Kurtz." Marlow angrily prevents the Harlequin from giving him these details, which seem, significantly, to have transported him "into some lightless region of subtle horrors, where pure, uncomplicated savagery was a positive relief, being something that had a right to exist—obviously—in the sunshine." Rather similarly, Marlow

6. Leavis, pp. 179–80.   7. Watt. p. 233.

experiences later "a moral shock" when he discovers that Kurtz has left his cabin and gone ashore. He feels: "as if something altogether monstrous, *intolerable to thought* and odious to the soul, had been thrust upon me unexpectedly" (my italics). These italicized words point a contrast to Marlow's previously expressed conviction that the "mind of man" could contain and understand ("comprehend") all of humanity's past and future—for here he faces something which the human mind cannot bear to entertain or penetrate. The fact is that Kurtz has gone quite outside the human. He has descended below the savage in specific ways yet to be discussed—which must be discussed, since Marlow has recently been rebuked (not for the first time) for "opposing" Kurtz instead of "joining" him in his attempt to return to the wilderness.[8] It is a recurring critical view that Kurtz is not degraded at all.

He is. His debasement consists, in part, in the very heights to which he has permitted himself to be exalted while "getting himself adored" among the "simple people" of the wilderness; more important, it consists in the nature of the "rites" which Marlow denominates simply "unspeakable." Paradoxically, to the extent that Kurtz's "unlawful soul" has aspired to godhead and assumed it, to that same extent Kurtz as a human being becomes debased. But what, precisely, is the "lightless region of subtle horrors"—so horrible that Marlow cannot and will not admit it to his mind? What are the "unspeakable rites"? To go further, we must consider a question which seems naïve when posed (as it often is) by a newcomer to *Heart of Darkness: but what did Kurtz do?* It is not naïve at all, but absolutely basic. What *did* Kurtz do? Uncertainty has frequently led to vague hints that Kurtz sinks to "cannibalism"—but "cannibalism" as such does not lead very far. As one aspect of "pure, uncomplicated savagery" the potential cannibalism of Marlow's native companions has been quite comprehensible, prompted, as it was, by "all the gnawing devils of hunger." What amazes Marlow is "one of these human secrets," the restraint which prevents these "cannibals" from making a good meal of Marlow and the pilgrims. Restraint is a quality which Kurtz lacks—lacks, generally, but lacks specifically with regard to those rites over which he has presided. Conrad attaches precise and subtle significance to "cannibalism" in *Heart of Darkness*—a significance which has absolutely nothing to do with actual cannibalistic practice as it may, or may not, have been known in Africa or anywhere else. Conrad is not recording facts or judging actual practice.

Within the story, and in line with the painstaking development of its themes, "cannibalism" takes on great thematic importance. There are two circumstances in which those who are called "cannibals" in *Heart of Darkness* would be likely to eat human flesh. They would certainly eat the flesh of a vanquished enemy. "Eat 'im!" the headman says to Marlow, gazing pensively towards the attackers on the shore. They might (Marlow believes they would) eat one of their own number (the helms-

8. Peter J. Glassman, *Language and Being: Joseph Conrad and the Literature of Personality* (New York: Columbia University Press, 1976), p. 229.

man) once he has somehow met his death. Otherwise we see no evidence at all that the cannibals of the story eat "each other."[9] Although
the cannibals' restraint is given great human value, it does not follow
that "in the end it is cannibalism that is seen as the epitome of savage
abandon, the heart of darkness. . . ."[1] This view seems to spring from
some ill-defined assumption regarding Kurtz's own "cannibalism," since
"Kurtz's abandon . . . is in effect *the same* as that of the savages"[2] (my
italics). This is not defensible.

Let us consider the evidence of the text. On the *supposition* (only)
that Kurtz's people eat human flesh habitually, being perhaps short of
food, it would be an aspect of "pure, uncomplicated savagery." In the
context of *Heart of Darkness* we could not approve, but we could "comprehend" as Marlow comprehends his "cannibals." If Kurtz, a supposedly civilized human being, joins in, it is not "the same" but must
constitute some degree of degradation—a falling below human standards. But the supposition itself is false, because totally unsupported by
anything in the text. Kurtz's people are never classed as "cannibals" and
we know from the Harlequin that there is "game" to be shot. To understand the extent of Kurtz's degradation we must penetrate that "lightless
region of subtle horrors" where Kurtz presides over, not cannibal feasts,
but "unspeakable rites."

It seems most probable that, in the course of Kurtz's ivory raids, the
victors might seal and celebrate success by not only killing but eating
their defeated enemies. The full horror of Kurtz's participation would
consist in his allowing or encouraging human sacrifices to be offered up
to him: "to him—do you understand?—to Mr. Kurtz himself." Animal
sacrifices or ordinary libations, could not be denominated "unspeakable." Human sacrifices must be involved.[3] It is in this context, and not
in any vague sense of an atavistic turning to "cannibalism," that we must
see Kurtz's acceptance of human flesh.

How, precisely, does this show the extent to which Kurtz has fallen
below his expressed intentions? He has always seen man's civilizing role
in terms of god-like power. In his "moving appeal to every altruistic
sentiment" he has stated that white men "must necessarily appear to
them [savages] in the nature of supernatural beings—we approach them
with the might as of a deity." Although this may well seem overweening
or "unlawful," the stated aim is positive: "By the simple exercise of our
will *we can exert a power for good practically unbounded*" (my italics).

9. Daleski, p. 57.
1. Daleski, p. 57.
2. Daleski, p. 67.
3. See Stephen A. Reid, "The 'Unspeakable Rites'
in *Heart of Darkness,*" in *Conrad: A Collection of
Critical Essays,* ed. Marvin Mudrick (Englewood
Cliffs, New Jersey: Prentice-Hall, 1966). The whole
argument is most interesting, but relies too heavily
upon speculative material unsupported by textual
evidence. Reid starts from accounts in Fraser's *The*

Golden Bough of ceremonies "to circumvent the
inevitability of the man-god's aging and dying"
which involved "the sacrifice of a young and vigorous man, and the consuming of a portion of his
body" in order to revivify the ailing man-god. It
seems wrong to postulate a Kurtz who is not only
ill but aging and growing physically frail over a
considerably longer period than that covered by the
story.

Those are the stated intentions. The Harlequin tells Marlow that Kurtz has indeed come to them "with thunder and lightning . . . and very terrible." How then has he gone on to exercise his power? He has charmed or frightened his simple followers into "aggravated" forms of primitive ritual in his honor. In order to carry out his ivory raids he has incited his people to warfare, thus destroying the peace of the whole area. He has robbed of their human dignity his people and their chiefs by making them "crawl" into the presence of his assumed godhead. He has been responsible for the ruthless execution of so-called "rebels." Finally, instead of "humanizing, improving, instructing," he has encouraged and perhaps, again, "aggravated" the worst aspects of primitive worship: the ritual killing of human beings for sacrifice—not even for sacrifice to some (supposedly) supernatural being but to a man who has arrogated to himself a quite spurious godhead. Here we see the essence of Kurtz's debasement. We have penetrated "the lightless region of subtle horrors" so far below the natural savagery which has every right to live "in the sunshine." Kurtz's expressed intentions have embodied the most elevated concern for other human beings; from these intentions he has sunk to the "inconceivable ceremonies" of "initiation" into "rites" which involve the deliberate sacrificial killing and eating of other human beings.

What of Marlow's deep sense of moral shock and revulsion? It has been forcibly argued that: "the total reversal of moral attitudes in the intervening decades [since Conrad wrote *Heart of Darkness*] means that Marlow's moral outrage at Kurtz's participation in human sacrifices is bound to seem exaggerated or false to modern readers."[4] This seems quite unacceptable for, however relativist our moral views may have become, however unwilling we may be to call "manifestations of another culture 'ugly'," we must surely marvel with Marlow: "How can man, and especially civilized man, be and do what he [Marlow] has seen?" as this critic himself asks.[5]

Within this whole context, what is to be made of Marlow's "choice of nightmares"? Since Marlow declares himself to be incapable of comprehending, conceiving, penetrating, tolerating, thinking of, speaking of, the details of what Kurtz has done, how does he come to feel that some meaningful "choice" is "enforced" upon him? What can be worse than that "lightless region"? One critic would have us believe that there is an easy answer: "However intolerable to thought or odious to the soul, Marlow must at last understand that one's choice of nightmare is perfectly simple. One either wants forest or sepulchre, dance or death, being or nothingness."[6] Inclusion here in that generalizing "one" must entitle us to protest that one's choice cannot be reduced to these naïvely simplistic and ludicrously false antitheses. They take no account of the actual terms of Marlow's choice. At the moment of choice, Marlow comes to feel that he has "never breathed an atmosphere so vile." Why? Why "so vile

---

4. Watt, p. 233.
5. Watt, p. 240.

6. Glassman, p. 228.

[that] I turned mentally to Kurtz [from whom he has mentally recoiled] for relief—positively for relief"? He seeks relief from the atmosphere surrounding the manager—"vile" echoing precisely Conrad's own description of the ivory trade as "the vilest scramble for loot that ever disfigured the history of human conscience and geographical exploration."[7] The manager represents naked commercialism devoid of human concern of any sort. The turmoil in which Kurtz is leaving the natives is important to him only because "The district is closed to us for a time. Deplorable. [Because] upon the whole, the trade will suffer." He is worse than indifferent to the degradation and mortal illness of Kurtz, expressing concern only for the "harm" done by "unsound methods." Marlow has seen through the manager's cruel and devious scheme "to delay a man's relief, in conditions which virtually ensure that . . . the man will succumb to disease and death"; he has become aware that the manager's "murder plot" has succeeded.[8] The total inhumanity of the manager is evident here. The full significance of Marlow's choice becomes clear, however, only through retrospective consideration of a speech of the manager's which Marlow has overheard: "and the pestiferous absurdity of his talk . . . each station should be like a beacon on the road towards better things, a centre for trade, of course, but also humanizing, improving, instructing. Conceive you, that ass." During this outburst the manager finds himself "choked with excessive indignation," the only emotion which ever springs from his malevolent heart. The "road towards better things" is vague cliché; the "beacon" (cliché too) at least suggests a guiding point of light, and recalls the "torch" by which the "sacred fire" of civilization is traditionally supposed to be spread; "humanizing, improving, instructing," though imprecise, are key words expressive of Kurtz's declared aims. The manager's choking contempt for such aims places him morally: he is hostile to positive human values. By the time Marlow visits the Intended, Kurtz is a year dead; the manager has been seen for the last time in a state of triumphant survival, horrifyingly "serene," "quiet," "satisfied," in possession of a vast amount of ivory. All this is in shattering contrast to the struggle, torment, horror, and victory associated with Kurtz's death. But as the Intended says, she, too, has "survived." She represents total acceptance and devoted affirmation of Kurtz's expressed ideals. The manager represents contemptuous rejection (both in words and in practice) of all such ideals, and a total denial of their worth. I recur briefly here to a critical view cited earlier: to the idea that there is some "part of civilization worth saving" which involves "man's humanity." Such positive values are denied when "European idealism" is oversimplified to carry a totally negative connotation, when "the lie of idealism" is seen as implicit in Kurtz's death; when (again) it is "the lie of idealism" which "generates" Kurtz's tragedy. This is to say that "the lie" is implicit in the very fact of idealism—no idealism, it seems, can

7. Joseph Conrad, *Last Essays* (London: Dent,   8. Watts, p. 83.
1926), p. 25. [See p. 187, above—*Editor.*]

escape that taint.[9] Metaphysically or philosophically, even historically, this may be a tenable position—but it is far from what we have just been seeing in Conrad's *Heart of Darkness*.

What does *Heart of Darkness* show about the relationship of ideas and ideals to the language which serves to express them? Although the manager refers scornfully to Kurtz's "talk" he really hates and fears the ideas which the talk may disseminate. Coldly malevolent, motivated only by greed and ruthless ambition, he sees humane and idealistic intentions as no better than noxious nonsense: "pestiferous" and "absurdity" are exactly expressive of Conrad's meaning. To the manager, Kurtz's talk is dangerous because it may communicate high ideals which would ruin his business prospects if they were put into practice. Elsewhere (especially in *Nostromo*) Conrad shows many (quite different) ways in which eloquence must be suspect, even dangerous. There are, in fact, real dangers which spring from Kurtz's eloquence—not least the self-deception of Kurtz himself. Yet ideas must be formulated and communicated: words are essential preliminaries to putting them into practice. There is, therefore, no inherent falsity in words. The expressed aims to humanize, to improve, to instruct, would constitute, indeed, the only redeeming idea behind what Kurtz sets out to do in Africa among its primitive people. The aims must be affirmed. Falsity supervenes only when words are not realized in appropriate action.

Once ideals have been expressed in words, everything depends upon the way they are understood and accepted. In *Heart of Darkness* idealistic aims, together with the words which express them, remain constant, but responses to them convey crucial differences in tone.

9. See Garrett Stewart. Present-day readers can readily accept Stewart's detestation of nineteenth century (or any) "imperialism" with its "inevitable brutality," and can see this as "a mode of death." But they must reject his facile and total equation of imperialistic notions of "white supremacy" with "European [and all Western] idealism." All forms of idealism, it seems, are imperialistic masks and lies. Marlow is, of course, tainted, and indicted by Stewart for "deep-seated racism." Not surprisingly he adduces no proof of the charge, which he would doubtless extend to Conrad as well. Although Conrad and Marlow shared some of the assumptions and misconceptions of their time, they transcend such categories as "racist." Human and humane qualities are their deepest concern, whether these are found in black or white humanity; and the full savagery of Conrad's undoubted attack in *Heart of Darkness* is levelled at white cruelty and rapacity. A related point embodies Stewart's most incomprehensible and, certainly untenable, view: that Marlow's "lie of idealism [is] unconsciously resurrected from its own death in order to be traded in as the barter of return, the inevitably exacted price of repatriation to the European community." Where does Conrad (or Marlow) ever indicate that Marlow wants any such "repatriation"—or that he wants to "come back and go on"? In fact, having seen in Africa the unbelievable depths of European exploitation, greed, and hypocrisy, Marlow "come[s] back" to experience a lasting revulsion from the "European community"—and what sense of "community" is conveyed in the Europe of the sepulchral city, which is all we see? Having lied to save "the part of civilization worth saving," Marlow follows the sea and, so far as we are ever told, never feels the slightest inclination to "go on" serving Europe's imperialistic notions of white supremacy in any way.

In this context, Ian Watt's whole illuminating discussion of "the lie" (Watt, pp. 241–48 especially) should be studied. Pointing out that the lie to the Intended is the last in a series of enforced and, as it were, excusable lies (or evasions of the truth) by Marlow, he writes: "Speaking of Ibsen's view of the need for the saving lie, Thomas Mann makes an important distinction: 'clearly there is a vast difference whether one assents to a lie out of sheer hatred of truth and the spirit or for the sake of that spirit in bitter irony and anguished pessimism'. The latter [Watt concludes] is certainly the spirit of Marlow's lie to the Intended" (pp. 246–47).

Conrad presents these with the greatest subtlety. Marlow becomes aware
that his aunt has "represented" him as being an "exceptional and gifted
creature" and "something like an emissary of light." She makes him feel
"quite uncomfortable" with her talk of "weaning those ignorant millions
from their horrid ways." The aunt is parroting these words as part of that
mindless "rush" of reiteration which makes them "humbug" and "rot."
Basic civilizing aims are simply travestied by total unawareness of individual, different needs: the generalized "millions" are all necessarily
"ignorant"; all their "ways" are necessarily "horrid." Mere parroting occurs
again, but on a spiteful and cynical note, as the envious and ambitious
"brickmaker" calls Kurtz: " 'a prodigy . . . an emissary of pity, and science, and progress, and devil knows what else. We want,' he began to
declaim suddenly, 'for the guidance of the cause intrusted to us by Europe,
so to speak, higher intelligence, wide sympathies, a singleness of purpose.' " Not only Kurtz, but "lots of them" declaim thus, he tells Marlow. The cynical tone sharpens to sarcasm as he classes Marlow himself
with "the new gang—the gang of virtue." As noted above, the manager
at one and the same time parrots "civilizing" aims and angrily rejects
their worth.

He is at one extreme. At the opposite extreme is the Intended, to
whom Kurtz's words have been communicated directly as "the illuminating,—the most exalted . . . the pulsating stream of light." Doubtless
her lover has spoken the "noble, burning words" with passionate intensity and an air of deep conviction. She has quite simply accepted them.
She goes on believing in him (to return to an earlier point) because she
never receives any hint of his failure. She continues to the end to believe
in the worth of his ideals and to reaffirm them as faithfully and truly as
an echo—and with no more originality or real force than an echo. The
Harlequin speaks of Kurtz with "severe exaltation" as one who "has
enlarged my mind," "made me see things—things." Marlow does not
envy this "disciple" his blind devotion to Kurtz. In contrast to the Intended,
his is a wilful blindness: "transported" by the flow of Kurtz's words, he
remains faithful despite all he has actually seen.

What of Marlow? He can appreciate well enough the loftiness of Kurtz's
intentions and can even be moved by them: when Kurtz "soared" in his
"beautiful piece of writing" he carries Marlow with him—for a time.
Marlow's experience of Kurtz's practical failure enables him to see that
the same words may serve the light or the darkness, becoming, in the
latter case, "the bewildering . . . the most contemptible . . . the deceitful flow from the heart of an impenetrable darkness." First published in
1899, *Heart of Darkness* embodies an insight which has been brought
home to humanity time and time again during the Twentieth Century:
elevated words can serve the light or the dark depending upon the way
their embodied ideas and aims are, or are not, put into practice.

Finally, it is now possible to understand more clearly the insight which
enforced Marlow's fidelity to his choice of nightmares in the story's final
scene (which should not now be felt to have been "treated in a rather

strained, melodramatic, and repetitive way").[1] Of the two nightmares, the worse consists in the rejection and denial of expressed human values. The mentality which rejects and denies is a mentality obsessed by sheer rapacity, ruthless ambition, deep malevolence—"mentality" must be the word, since neither the manager himself nor any of his ilk, in *Heart of Darkness*, is granted a "soul." The lesser nightmare (though still unequivocally a nightmare) is Kurtz's degradation. Although he is "hollow" in that he has been false in practice to his ideals, ideas, and words, he can never reject human values or deny their worth. They make possible his "moral victory"; they "survive" in his Intended as an ideal, with all the limitations noted. There is no strong positive hope at the end of *Heart of Darkness*. Mere survival is assured. Yet the importance of the "saving illusion" is plain. Without Marlow's lie, all "light of visionary purpose," any "slender ray of light" would be extinguished and, with these, the whole concept of humanity's upward potential. Humanity, in future, could never know the struggle or the victory of a Kurtz, could never gain the insight of a Marlow into the "two extremes that can exist within the human mind." All hearts would have no choice but to "beat in the [triumphant] darkness."[2]

"It would have been too dark—too dark altogether."

MICHAEL LEVENSON

The Value of Facts in the *Heart of Darkness* †

Although the point has been strangely neglected, it is clear that Conrad markedly altered his conception of *Heart of Darkness* during the period of its composition. His act of writing was at the same time a discovery of his subject. This issue possesses independent interest, but it will be pursued here as a way of approaching a problem in the interpretation of the tale. *Heart of Darkness* does not simply record the unfolding of an action; it unfolds its own mode of understanding, and by the time it has reached its conclusion it has redrawn its own boundaries, redescribed its facts, and revaluated its values.

In a letter to William Blackwood dated 31 December 1898, Conrad refers to a new story that he is preparing for *Blackwood's Magazine*, "a narrative after the manner of *Youth*" that is already "far advanced." He discloses his working title, *The Heart of Darkness*, but quickly adds that "the narrative is not gloomy. The criminality of inefficiency and pure selfishness when tackling the civilizing work in Africa is a justifiable

1. Watt, p. 241.
2. A penetrating and illuminating discussion of aspects of *Heart of Darkness* which extend conceptually beyond the scope of my present essay should be warmly recommended: William F. Zak, "Conrad, F. R. Leavis, and Whitehead: *Heart of Darkness* and Organic Holism," *Conradiana*, 4:1 (1972), 6–24.
† From *Nineteeth-Century Fiction* 40 (1985): 261–80. © 1985 by The Regents of the University of California. Reprinted by permission.

idea." He remarks that "the subject is of our time distinctly" and compares it to "my *Outpost of Progress*," noting, however, that the new work is "a little wider—is less concentrated upon individuals."[1]

Two days later he tells David Meldrum, Blackwood's representative, that the story would have been finished the day before had his son not fallen ill and that he anticipates that the finished work will be under twenty thousand words. During the first week of January he completes the portion of the story that will ultimately become the first installment of the published work and that conforms well to the initial outline offered to Blackwood. The bitter evocation of imperialism merits the description "of our time," and the rapidly shifting attention among characters and incidents explains why Conrad thought of his story as somewhat diffuse. This early section, as carefully managed as it is, nevertheless remains within the relatively humble boundaries that Conrad had mentioned, a kind of *Youth*-cum- "An Outpost of Progress" in which the agency of Marlow is brought to bear upon the Social Question.

The early proposal contains no mention of Kurtz and no reference to the motif of atavism. If Conrad could write at the end of December that his tale was almost finished, that it would expose criminality, inefficiency, and selfishness, and that it would not focus upon particular characters, then he was doubtless envisioning a story in which the preponderant stress would continue to fall upon the abuses of imperialism. *Heart of Darkness*, in other words, was conceived in distinctly social and political terms, and well into its composition Conrad thought of it in this way. A work which has become perhaps the leading example of modern psychological fiction began with an expressed disregard for the fate of individuals.

Part One not only emphasizes the political question; it stays close to the historical facts. Conrad draws heavily on events he had witnessed; and given the initial statements to Blackwood, it is highly likely that he first projected the tale as a reasonably faithful rendering of the European entanglement in Africa, a series of sordid misadventures culminating in the pointless death of a European trader. Conrad's own experience with the trader Klein remains obscure; we know that Klein was brought aboard the *Roi des Belges* at Stanley Falls and that he died during the trip downriver; but we have no reason to suppose that Conrad's encounter with him bore any significant resemblance to Marlow's uncanny confrontation with Kurtz. Indeed the dissimilarity gives us a way to understand why Conrad thought that he would finish the story so quickly and why he assumed, even when it was well advanced, that it would not go much beyond the present end of Part One. For if he had continued to trace the pattern of his own unpleasant ordeal in the Congo, the meeting with Kurtz would doubtless have been rendered in far more modest terms and would have served more as a pendant to the angry social critique, a final senseless misfortune in a long sequence of unnecessary blunders. In fact,

1. Joseph Conrad, *Letters to William Blackwood and David S. Meldrum*, ed. William Blackburn (Durham, N.C.: Duke Univ. Press, 1958), pp. 36, 37. [See p. 201, above—*Editor*.]

it is difficult to see how Conrad could have achieved much else within the boundaries he had first planned. Certainly he could not have anticipated the force of Kurtz's provocation when on 2 January 1899, having not yet finished what would become Part One, he claimed that his account of European criminality in Africa was almost complete.

Because the manuscript remained almost entirely free of revision, *Heart of Darkness* stands not only as a narrative of Marlow's adventure in the Congo but as a record of Conrad's adventure in the English countryside, his own struggle to define his conception while hurrying to meet a deadline with *Blackwood's*.[2] Hence, its present form retains traces of the changing design. In the first mention of Kurtz, and almost certainly first in order of composition, Marlow identifies him as "the poor chap."[3] Surely it is not as a "poor chap" that we remember him, and by the end of the tale Marlow will describe his dark career in far more lurid terms. This at least raises the possibility that Kurtz was envisioned more as a victim than as a monster and thus closer to that unfortunate Klein, whose last days Conrad had witnessed; indeed, in the manuscript Conrad had written "Klein" on the first four occasions that he referred to Kurtz by name.

Halfway through Part One Marlow roundly denounces the European presence in Africa.

> I've seen the devil of violence, and the devil of greed, and the devil of hot desire; but by all the stars these were strong, lusty, red-eyed devils that swayed and drove men—men, I tell you. But as I stood on this hillside I foresaw that in the blinding sunshine of that land I would become acquainted with a flabby, pretending, weak-eyed devil of a rapacious and pitiless folly. How insidious he could be too I was only to find out several months later and a thousand miles farther.

The last comment furnishes a second reference to Kurtz's fall, but we should pay careful attention to the context. Speaking from his retrospective standpoint on the *Nellie*, Marlow invokes Kurtz as the most "insidious" manifestation of the "flabby, pretending, weak-eyed devil." And yet "flabby," "pretending" and "weak-eyed" are perhaps the last attri-

2. For a synopsis of the revisions see Jonah Raskin, "*Heart of Darkness*: The Manuscript Revisions," *Review of English Studies*, NS 18 (1976), 30–39.

3. Joseph Conrad, *Heart of Darkness*, ed. Robert Kimbrough, Norton Critical Edition, 3rd ed. (New York: Norton, 1987). At the beginning of his narrative Marlow recalls the Roman conquest of Britain, and in a brief vignette that is often taken to prefigure Kurtz's plight, he conjures the image of a young Roman soldier repelled by the English wilderness. Certainly the perception of a fundamental estrangement between nature and culture bears on the European experience in Africa, but it does not begin to capture the peculiarities of Kurtz's condition. Of the Roman, Marlow says that "there's no initiation . . . into such mysteries. He has to live in the midst of the incomprehensible which is also detestable." Kurtz, on the other hand, will experience a "devilish initiation" into the secrets of the jungle, and Marlow will speak of him as an "initiated wraith from the back of Nowhere." The idea of an "initiation" provides a useful way to think about the changing perspective in the tale; the only weakness more grave than the inability to comprehend turns out to be comprehension itself. When Marlow looks upon the wild mob of shouting natives, he asks Kurtz, "Do you understand this?" to which the latter chillingly replies, "Do I not?" At this point we have left the uncomprehending Roman far behind.

butes one would bestow on Kurtz, whose moral descent will far exceed the connotations of "folly." Furthermore, in this early passage Marlow *opposes* the corruption he will meet upriver to the "manly" devils of violence, greed, desire, and lust. But Kurtz, let us recall, will appear precisely as a man who "lacked restraint in the gratification of his various lust," who indulged "forgotten and brutal instincts," "gratified and monstrous passions."

In other words, this early reference suggests that Kurtz's afflictions will be thoroughly continuous with the criminality of imperialism, that there will be no "choice of nightmares," only one increasingly appalling phantasm. Within this conception Kurtz would pose no distinctly psychological problem; he would represent merely the most extreme, the most "insidious" example of the general corruption. At this point it even remains unclear whether Conrad had anticipated the celebrated motif of voluntary reversion to the primitive. No doubt he intended Kurtz to succumb to the "fascination of the abomination," but there is as yet no hint—in a tale which persistently offers hints—that this will go any further than the miserable plight of Kayerts and Carlier in "An Outpost of Progress," no further, that is, than "a flabby, pretending, weak-eyed" descent into criminal folly. The crucial transformation occurs when Conrad wrenches Kurtz free from the prevailing folly and recognizes in him an independent problem of monstrous proportions.

On 9 January 1899 Conrad sent off everything that he had written up to the day before, the body of material that would become Part One of the story. It is possible then to discern a second stage in the process of composition, whose beginning coincides with the beginning of Part Two. Apparently Conrad found himself at an impasse as he tried to continue beyond this point. On 13 January he wrote a frustrated letter to Garnett in which he referred to the "rotten stuff" he was preparing for *Blackwood's:* "Ah if I could only write! If I could write, write, write! But I cannot."[4] Three days later, however, his tone has changed. He tells Meldrum, "I don't' think [the tale] will be bad," remarking that "the thing has grown on me."[5]

What has grown evidently is Kurtz. Part Two begins with Marlow half asleep on the deck of his steamer, catching snatches of a conversation between the Manager and his uncle. The former bitterly describes how Kurtz had traveled hundreds of miles downriver with his ivory and then had abruptly decided to paddle a small dugout back into the wilderness. "As for me," says a waking Marlow, "I seemed to see Kurtz for the first time."[6] In the light of Conrad's own struggles with the story, it is tempt-

4. Joseph Conrad, *Letters from Joseph Conrad, 1895–1924,* ed. Edward Garnett (Indianapolis: Bobbs-Merrill, 1928), p. 150. [See p. 205, above—Editor.]

5. Joseph Conrad, *Letters to William Blackwood and David S. Meldrum,* p. 43. [See p. 206, above—Editor.]

6. Indeed, it is noteworthy that a break in the composition occurred just before this moment of

recognition. At the end of that portion of the manuscript that Conrad dispatched on 9 January 1899, Marlow remains in a state of drowsy confusion, unable to make anything of the conversation he is hearing. Only when Conrad resumes work on the story does Marlow come to waking consciousness and "see Kurtz for the first time." Consider, too, Edward Garnett's recollection: "Some time before [Conrad] wrote this story of his Congo ing to suppose that the "I" has a double reference, that the author, like his character, feels that he is seeing Kurtz for the first time, and that in the image of the "lone white man turning his back suddenly on the headquarters," Conrad experienced a turn in his conception of the tale.

This last supposition must of course remain speculative, but the general point should now be evident: that as the tale of "20,000 words" grew to almost twice that length, Conrad found himself far exceeding the boundaries of his initial design. By the time we arrive at the further reaches of Kurtz's degradation, "poor chap" and "flabby . . . devil" have long since ceased to apply; the tale is no longer "of our time distinctly"; and once Kurtz has uttered his final words and Marlow has lied to the Intended, no one would dream of saying that the subject of the work is "inefficiency." Indeed, Conrad himself came to acknowledge a transformation in his story. After Cunninghame Graham read Part One in *Blackwood's* he sent Conrad words of enthusiastic praise. Conrad was delighted, but he cautioned the socialist Graham that the next two installments might not please him so well. "So far," he wrote, "the note struck chimes in with your convictions—mais après? This is an après."[7] This remark establishes the problem that we must now pursue. How does a tale of imperialist exploitation generate an *après?* And why such an *après* as this?

I

Criticism of the novel has always, and naturally, focused upon the conclusion, that *après* which is the fiction's crux. The jungle, the horror, the return, the lie—these no doubt pose the most absorbing problems of the work. But part of our purpose is to see how the opening of the tale engenders its culmination, and if we rush too quickly to the conclusion we miss its motivation and diminish its force. We miss, for one thing, the extent to which *Heart of Darkness* is a drama of officialdom. Imperialism presents itself to Conrad as an affair of inefficient clerks, disaffected functionaries, envious subordinates, and defensive superiors—all arrayed within a strict hierarchy whose local peak is the General Manager and whose summit is the vague "Council in Europe." The Company gives identities, establishes purposes, assigns destinies, and with its bizarre configuration of Central and Inner Stations even constructs geography. The accumulation of ivory is the material goal,

experience, he narrated it at length one morning while we were walking up and down under a row of Scotch firs that leads down to the Cearne. I listened enthralled while he gave me in detail a very full synopsis of what he intended to write. To my surprise when I saw the printed version I found that about a third of the most striking incidents had been replaced by others of which he had said nothing at all" (Edward Garnett, introd., *Letters from Joseph Conrad, 1895–1924*, p. 14). [See p. 196, above—Editor.]

7. Conrad seems unduly apologetic in his response to Cunninghame Graham. He suggests that his

original "idea" has become increasingly "wrapped up in secondary notions"—a reversal of the metaphor in which the meaning of Marlow's tale is said to be "outside" like a haze rather than inside like a kernel—and insists that Graham will still be able to find the "right intention" if he examines the episodes carefully. It is almost as though Conrad, startled at how far he has strayed, were trying to reclaim the story for his original political design (*Joseph Conrad's Letters to R. B. Cunninghame Graham*, ed. C. T. Watts [Cambridge: Cambridge Univ. Press, 1969], p. 116). [See pp. 207–8, above—Editor.]

but it interests Conrad less than its social consequence, the scramble for position within the institution, which creates its own flabby passions and even its own flabby pentameter: "Am I the Manager—or am I not?"

The absurdist aspect of these early sections emerges in the empty assertion of an institutional formalism in the face of violently anti-institutional facts. The Company scrupulously pays brass wire to its nearly starving native employees; the accountant makes "perfectly correct transactions" while fifty feet away loom "the still tree-tops of the grove of death." The incongruity between the Company and the wilderness is a particular instance of that more general Conradian incongruity between value and fact, between the system of meanings that we devise and the world reluctant to accept them.

Here we may invoke Max Weber—not, of course, in order to provide a Weberian reading of *Heart of Darkness*, if such a thing is even conceivable, but to generate a distinction that may clarify Conrad's arrangement of values. Weber and Conrad were close contemporaries, and from the unlikely points of Germany, Protestantism, and sociology, Weber came to an intellectual bearing and a moral demeanor close to Conrad's own. In particular, his theory of social organization contains implications for a theory of modern character. He should help to illuminate Conrad, but no more than Conrad should help to illuminate him.

Certainly among Weber's most important contributions to sociological thought was his analysis of bureaucracy as one of three fundamental types of social authority, and the one under which he had the misfortune to live.[8] Within a general system of legal domination bureaucracy becomes the "means of transforming social action into rationally organized action." It presupposes a formal hierarchy, written regulation, and clearly defined relations of authority and subordination, all of which make the individual "a small cog in a ceaselessly moving mechanism which prescribes to him an essentially fixed route of march."[9] For Weber this social form extends well beyond governmental organization to inform every mode of modern authority. At the limit bureaucracy represents the triumph of reasoned method and "the exclusion of love, hatred, and every purely personal, especially irrational and incalculable, feeling from the execution of official tasks."[1]

Hence, from Weber's own historical standpoint the Bureaucrat ceases to be one type among others and becomes the representative figure of the modern age. Lacking both reverence for tradition and hope of revolutionary change, content to sustain the prevailing hierarchy, committed to discipline and routine, willing to follow directives from above but incapable of devising independent initiatives, the Bureaucrat has history on his side and can wait patiently while his dominion extends into every aspect of contemporary life. From the perspective of a "value-free" soci-

8. The other two types of social domination are patriarchal (or traditional) authority and charismatic authority. See Max Weber, *Economy and Society*, ed. Guenther Roth and Claus Wittich, trans. Ephraim Fischoff et al., 3 vols. (New York: Bedminster Press, 1968).

9. Weber, *Economy and Society*, III, 987, 988.

1. Max Weber, *Max Weber on Law in Economy and Society*, ed. Max Rheinstein (Cambridge, Mass.: Harvard Univ. Press, 1954), p. 351.

ology Weber dispassionately charts the rise of the bureaucratic sensibility, but a detectable bitterness enters his tone, and outside his formal
studies it erupts into derision and contempt.

> It is horrible to think that the world could one day be filled with
> nothing but those little cogs, little men clinging to little jobs and
> striving towards bigger ones. . . . This passion for bureaucracy . . .
> is enough to drive one to despair. . . . That the world should know
> no men but these: it is in such an evolution that we are already
> caught up, and the great question is therefore not how we can pro-
> mote and hasten it, but what can we oppose to this machinery in
> order to keep a portion of mankind free from this parcelling-out of
> the soul, from this supreme mastery of the bureaucratic way of life. [2]

Under the same historical pressures Conrad came to much the same
perception, and we need to recall a point too often neglected, namely,
that after Kafka, Conrad is our most searching critic of bureaucracy.
Like Weber he consistently sought a principle of opposition to social
machinery, and in the view offered here it is a Weberian rather than a
Freudian insight that lies at the origin of *Heart of Darkness*—at its origin, not at its end.

Within this set of concerns the Manager is the exemplary figure, and
we simply misread the work if we neglect the importance of this character who typifies the vulgar sensibility of petty officialdom and who
incarnates the criminality, inefficiency, and selfishness that Conrad first
set out to expose. A man with "no learning, and no intelligence," "neither civil nor uncivil," the Manager "was obeyed, yet he inspired neither
love nor fear, nor even respect." He jealously guards "trade secrets,"
deprecates "unsound method" and coldly submits human welfare to
institutional requirements. The epitome of the bureaucrat, he "originated nothing, he could keep the routine going—that's all." In important respects the Manager is the displaced center of *Heart of Darkness*
who would have held pride of place in the shorter work that Conrad had
first conceived. Conrad's own bitter experiences in Africa involved his
conflict with Camille Delcommune, upon whom the Manager is based,
and we need only set off Part One from the rest of the story in order to
recognize that Conrad's lingering antipathy toward Delcommune and
his contempt for European inefficiency would have provided sufficient
motive for the story that he originally forecast to Blackwood.

Not only the origins of the tale but its structure must be understood
in the context of Conrad's revulsion from the bureaucratic sensibility.
Kurtz enters the work, and perhaps entered Conrad's imagination as an
antithesis to the Manager, as though he were summoned into being
through the strength of Conrad's repugnance. Marlow first hears his
name from the chief accountant, who describes him as "a first-class

---

2. From a 1909 speech, quoted in Reinhard Bendix, *Max Weber: An Intellectual Portrait* (Garden City,
N.Y.: Doubleday, 1960), pp. 455–56.

agent," and then, noting Marlow's disappointment, adds that Mr. Kurtz "is a very remarkable person." The distinction between "agent" and "person" is fundamental; for in its initial movement the tale dramatizes the attempt to recover personality from a world of impersonal functionaries, an activity that begins within a strictly institutional context. Kurtz initially represents that distinctly modern figure, the organizational *wunderkind* who rapidly ascends the corporate ladder, destined to "be a somebody in the Administration before long." Furthermore, he has "moral ideas" and when he is still "just a word," Marlow posits him as the ethical alternative to economic privacy. *Heart of Darkness* begins, that is, by identifying a bureaucratic conflict, the struggle between the good and the bad official and, by implication, a struggle between moral and immoral forms of social organization.

These, of course, are not the struggles that we ultimately witness. But the transformation in the narrative must be understood against the background of this original problem—the need to find a perspective from which to oppose institutionalized depravity. Kurtz's turn to the wilderness, whatever else it becomes, is first of all a gesture of social rebellion. The Tribe is rejoinder to the Company. Under Kurtz's domination the Tribe possesses a seamless unity that avoids the endless articulations of bureaucracy; it knows no legal formalism, no reliance on a vague "They, above," whose lofty intentions dissipate in the long descent through hierarchy. For Conrad the inefficiency of imperialism is not one defect among many: it is a measure of the awful distance between intention and action so inimical to coherent social purpose. Within the Tribe authority exists not as a remote official dispatching instructions through the mail but as a visible body and a living voice—a "real presence." The distance between the will and its realization is overcome; inefficiency disappears as a problem; Kurtz makes the canoes run on time.

In Weberian sociology the antonym to the rule of bureaucracy is the rule of *charisma*, the "gift" that is invested in a leader whose authority depends on neither tradition nor law, who indeed overturns every traditional and legal norm in the name of a personal calling acknowledged by an entire society. Other forms of authority, argues Weber, accommodate themselves to history; they exist to satisfy quotidian needs and to permit stability in communal life. Charismatic leadership is "alien to all regulation and tradition"; it is "not a continuous institution, but in its pure type the very opposite."

> In radical contrast to bureaucratic organization, charisma knows no formal and regulated appointment or dismissal, no career, advancement or salary, no supervisory or appeals body, no local or purely technical jurisdiction, and no permanent institutions in the manner of bureaucratic agencies, which are independent of the incumbents and their personal charisma. Charisma is self-determined and sets its own limits. Its bearer seizes the task for which he is destined

and demands that others obey and follow him by virtue of his mission.[3]

Because it violates all custom and tradition and because it offers no justification but itself, charisma always appears supernatural and its edicts have divine warrant. All value emanates from the bearer of the "gift," and all social activity originates in the will of the leader. A community under charismatic domination necessarily breaks with its past, and for this reason Weber calls charisma "the specifically creative revolutionary force of history."[4]

It will have become obvious that this notion of "the gift" bears closely on Marlow's portrayal of "the gifted Kurtz": "The point was in his being a gifted creature. . . . I laid the ghost of his gifts at last with a lie." What Weber hypothesized, Conrad imagined: a social order dependent on one center, one value, one will.[5] The Russian reports that the natives "would not stir until Mr. Kurtz gave the word. His ascendancy was extraordinary. . . . [T]he chiefs came every day to see him. They would crawl." There is no need to accumulate examples; it is already clear that this is not like being "a somebody in the Administration." The point, which Weber lets us see clearly, is that a distinction between social orders generates a distinction between paradigms of character epitomized by the Manager and Kurtz. Indeed, all through our century the civil servant and the charismatic leader have served as representative types, competing extremes for the modern temperament. The one surrenders personality, the other accumulates too much. Following Weber, we may think of the difference in terms of contrasting modes of modern authority. Following Marlow, we may recognize it as a choice of nightmares, two besetting temptations for the contemporary world.

Within this configuration Kurtz himself retains a powerful ambiguity. On the one hand, he is the *reductio* of imperialism. He stands at the point where rational acquisition becomes irrational hoarding, where economic routine becomes primitive ritual, where a commodity becomes a fetish, and where indirect violence becomes overt barbarism. In this respect Conrad presents Kurtz as the suppressed truth of European immorality, a point well emphasized in the eagerness of the Company to exploit his sordid achievement. Moreover, from what we know of the

3. Weber, *Economy and Society*, III, 1115, 1113, 1112.

4. Weber, *Economy and Society*, III, 1117. Yet the pathos of charisma, and the pathos of Weber's sociology, is that quotidian needs make an inexorable return: "Every charisma is on the road from a turbulently emotional life that knows no economic rationality to a slow death by suffocation under the weight of material interests: every hour of its existence brings it nearer to this end" (III, 1120). Moments of ecstasy yield to enduring social structures. Institutions reform and traditions reestablish themselves. There occurs a "routinization of charisma," in which it "recedes as a creative

force" (III, 1146) and changes "from a unique, transitory gift of grace . . . into a permanent possession of everyday life" (III, 1121). No longer a supernatural endowment disclosed by revelation, it is appropriated by the king, the priest, or the bureaucrat who invokes its aura in virtue of his office, not in virtue of his mission.

5. V. J. Emmett, Jr., makes a passing reference to Weber's notion of charisma in the context of his discussion of Conradian heroism in relation to Carlyle. See "Carlyle, Conrad, and the Politics of Charisma: Another Perspective on *Heart of Darkness*," *Conradiana*, 7 (1975), 145–53.

composition of the story, this emphasis is thoroughly consistent with Conrad's original design. Insofar as Kurtz discloses the concealed logic of imperialism, then he indeed represents the most "insidious" example of a "rapacious and pitiless folly."

On the other hand, even as Kurtz takes the logic of accumulation to its unthinkable extreme, he discloses another logic altogether; folly reaches the point at which it becomes *folie*; and in presenting European abuses at their grotesque limit, he furnishes a principle of opposition to them. This is the complexity in Conrad's final conception. Kurtz represents both the *reductio* of imperialism and its antithesis. And it is when Conrad thought past the former possibility (the degradation of a virtuous man— "the poor chap"—which reveals the depravity of a social form) and when he recognized voluntary atavism as the nightmare from which it was possible to awake, that *Heart of Darkness* took its longest step and disclosed another region of experience.

II

There is a revealing lacuna in Weber's analysis of charisma. Having defined the concept and having named some historical instances, Weber proceeds quickly to the subject that dominates his analysis: the waning of charisma, its inevitable subordination to the forces of law and tradition, and its appropriation by those who seek to legitimize their power. In other words, as soon as charisma appears in Weber's own analysis it begins to recede. Social life under charismatic domination occupies just one paragraph of that immense tome, *Economy and Society*, and a phenomenon that Weber regarded as one of the three fundamental types of social authority almost completely escapes description.

It is not difficult to see why this is so. Charismatic leadership, *ex hypothesi*, breaks with rules and norms. In its pure form, holds Weber, it cannot be understood as a social organization in any customary sense. By definition it is "extra-ordinary," the product of the Gifted One who suspends all those conventions, institutions, and traditions that sociology takes as its proper subject. Charisma thus exists at the limit of Weber's sociological understanding. It is where the study of the group must become the study of the exceptional individual who molds the group according to his will. Sociology passes into psychology.

What is a puzzle for the system of academic disciplines—where does society stop and the mind begin?—is an opportunity for the literary imagination. Conrad, too, describes the limitations of bureaucracy; he, too, conceives a charismatic alternative; and to this point the analogy with Weber is extensive and heuristic. But because he is bound neither by theoretical presupposition nor by historical fact, Conrad willingly follows the movement from social to psychological experience. A tale that begins with bureaucratic folly imagines a ghastly alternative in tribal violence; and in carrying through that insight, it imagines the point at which social life passes into the life of the instincts. In *Heart of Darkness* and immediately afterward in *Lord Jim* Conrad built a theater for the psyche, not in an isolated individual, but in a social configuration that gave the mind an expanse on which to play itself out. When the Russian withholds ivory, Kurtz threatens to shoot him, "because he could do so, and had a fancy for it, and there was nothing on earth to prevent him killing whom he jolly well pleased." Conrad, in other words, envisions that form of community in which social organization becomes psychological expression.

After the Russian tells Marlow that the heads impaled on stakes are the heads of rebels, Marlow laughs skeptically: "Rebels! What would be the next definition I was to hear. There had been enemies, criminals, workers—and these were—rebels." But the next definition, the psychological definition, will indeed be telling. The story in effect offers a succession of concepts under which to sort human character, a series of definitions that unfold from one another and that lead Marlow to change his very categories of description. Through its own strenuous logic *Heart of Darkness* pursues the representation of bureaucracy until it becomes the representation of a monstrous passion; and fully to appreciate the tale as a psychological fiction is to appreciate the way it must excavate a place for the mind. Here is Conrad's promised *après*: the psyche is a sequel to society.

What is more, it is an alternative to society. As *Heart of Darkness* invents for itself a genre of psychological narrative, it discovers a standpoint from which to contest grotesque political abuse. Politics and the psyche are not two levels; they are two antagonists; *Heart of Darkness* challenges the structure of institutions with the structure of the mind. One must not be misled by the novel's most celebrated words. The unredeemable horror in the tale is the duplicity, cruelty, and venality of European officialdom. Kurtz himself, in *speaking* horror, immediately renders himself less horrible. He ensures his standing as "a remarkable man," a man who has "summed up" and so achieved "a moral victory paid for by innumerable defeats, by abominable terrors, by abominable satisfactions."

III

This last quotation already intimates another change in this continually changing design. Kurtz is not only modern Psychological Man; he becomes, improbably, unexpectedly, Moral Man. The end of his lust, his greed, his terror, his satisfaction is a "moral victory," and this curious begetting establishes the final problem that this essay will pursue. To this point I have considered how Conrad's social conception transformed to a psychological conception, how the institutional self metamorphosed to the instinctual self. But in this last phase of the argument I want to discuss a further and equally consequential tranformation, namely, from mental life to moral life, from psychology to ethics.

It is clear, first of all, that Kurtz's fall is not merely due to the surge of instinct that routs social values; it is due to a failure of the values themselves. The prelapsarian Kurtz had talked of pity, science, progress, love, justice, and the conduct of life—"burning noble words," Marlow calls them. They constitute an ideology of enlightenment, a collective moral inheritance that, plainly enough, arouses virtuous aspiration and then proves unequal to the passion it excites. Kurtz's words fall under the heading of "principles" that "fly off at the first good shake." But the failure of principle does not mark the demise of value in *Heart of Darkness*, only a change in its source. If value cannot descend from social ideals, it must ascend from the psychic abyss.

A perception of the distance between fact and value is fundamental to Conrad's assault on prevailing social conventions. The incongruity between the sound of moral words and the spectacle of sordid deeds excites his contempt and gives urgency to the representation of anarchic instinct. Certainly, a familiar approach to *Heart of Darkness* considers it a rejection of the values of progress and enlightenment in the name of such facts as passion, greed, and violence. But we need to acknowledge a third category of Conradian concepts that is distinct from both the class of groundless ideals and the class of amoral instincts.

During Kurtz's final crisis Marlow watches "the inconceivable mystery of a soul that knew no restraint, no faith, and no fear, yet struggling blindly with itself." Here is Conrad's improbable image for the foundation of morality, an image that locates the moral source not in social convention but in an inconceivably mysterious gesture of the individual mind. Kurtz, a man without restraint, struggles to restrain himself. It is a primitive psychological movement, the self confronting the self, an act of will originating *ex nihilo*. The importance of restraint in *Heart of Darkness* is thoroughly obvious but perhaps not thoroughly perspicuous. Restraint, after all, is a psychological concept that in itself implies no ethical norm; it presupposes no moral code and commits one to no opinions about love, progress, or the conduct of life. How, then, are we to understand its prominence?

When Marlow encounters the unlikely self-control of the hungry cannibals aboard his ship, he stands amazed: "Restraint! I would just as soon have expected restraint from a hyena prowling amongst the corpses of a battlefield." Then he immediately adds, "But there was the fact facing me—the fact, dazzling, to be seen, like the foam on the depths of the sea." "Restraint" thus possesses a strategic ambiguity. It belongs to the domain of objective description ("the fact facing me"), but it is already imbued with value ("dazzling to be seen"). It names a concrete perceptible datum and at the same time a basic virtue. Along with other subtle devices that we will consider in a moment, "restraint" gives Marlow a way to overcome the distance between description and evaluation. He need not struggle any longer to apply transcendent ethical concepts to refractory experience; now he can locate moral value *within* individual experience. A notion such as restraint suggests the possibility of natural basis for ethics, a nonmoral ground for morality, a reconciliation between fact and value.

As he watches the natives who howl and dance on the banks of the river, Marlow wonders what motives and impulses sway them. And what is most notable about the possibilities he considers—"joy, fear, sorrow, devotion, valour, rage"—is the casual compounding of emotions and virtues. States of mind (joy, rage) are not clearly distinguished from moral states (devotion, valor). Similarly, in his reflections on Kurtz's final words Marlow sees them as the expression of "belief," "candour," "revolt," "truth," "desire," and "hate," the sum of which, as we know, is a "moral victory." Perhaps as deep as any urge in Conrad is the desire to let evaluation emerge spontaneously out of description in accordance with his high aesthetic conviction that when he has described the world faithfully he will also have described his faith. Much like "restraint," terms such as "devotion," "belief," and "candour" suggest to Conrad both mental facts and moral values, and they suggest too that in the right circumstances the psychic life can lead naturally, almost imperceptibly, into ethical life.

In this way *Heart of Darkness* again transcends its own principles of structure. Having begun with a distinction between the good and the bad bureaucrat, and having rudely supplanted it with a nightmarish choice between social venality and passionate license, it ends by offering the individual moral psyche as a slim third term between these weighty alternatives. Marlow is the one who seeks to cultivate this vulnerable site; and to consider the fate of moral value in *Heart of Darkness* is finally to consider Marlow's fate. To conclude, then, we must ask how his fragile autonomy can be sustained. After the bureaucrat, after the atavist, how can he find a character of his own? How can Marlow by himself secure values for himself?

In an early expression of disgust at the feckless plotting of Company agents, Marlow observes that "there is something after all in the world allowing one man to steal a horse while another must not look at a halter." In its context the judgment seems unexceptionable, but it represents a precept difficult to sustain. What is this "something" that distinguishes the worthy horse thief from the wicked obeyer of laws? Marlow does not elaborate, but he persistently relies on this form of reasoning. He misleads the brickmaker merely in the hope that it might "somehow" help Kurtz. And in explaining his aversion to lies, he invokes no general canon but a personal response, even an eccentricity: Lying "makes me miserable and sick like biting something rotten would do. Temperament, I suppose." Marlow never shrinks from judgment, but he judges without abstract ideals, without general principles, indeed without consistency.

Kurtz had spoken to the Russian of love "in general," and later when he appears in the jungle surrounded by a thousand armed natives, Marlow comments bitterly, "Let us hope that the man who can talk so well of love in general will find some particular reason to spare us this time."

This is the foundation of Marlow's moral sense: a contempt for ethics "in general" and a demand for the "particular reason." He derides moral absolutes and willingly suspends universal in favor of concrete discriminations. We know that he abominates lies and that he recognizes justice as Kurtz's due, but when he meets the Intended, he complies with neither the maxim of honesty nor the claim of justice. Instead he acts as the Practical Moralist who overturns general ethical conceptions without overturning ethics.

When Marlow describes his "particular reason" for lying to Kurtz's Intended, he makes no appeal to those tainted ideas: progress, pity, conduct of life. He says simply that the truth "would have been too dark— too dark altogether." But what kind of moral concept is "darkness"? Clearly it is none at all; it is, if you will, a moral *sensation*—like the "flavour of mortality" Marlow finds in lies. In offering an image for the human predicament, Marlow describes the world as a place in which one must "breathe dead hippo so the speak and not be contaminated." When he discovers that Kurtz has left his cabin in the middle of the night, he experiences a "moral shock," and when he makes his choice of nightmares, he turns to Kurtz "for relief—positively for relief." Shock, relief, and the smell of dead hippo are further instances of moralized sensations that take the place of abstract principle. And the most decisive example is Kurtz's own valediction. "Horror" is the culminating instance of these almost punning Conradian concepts that engender an unmistakable moral assessment out of an intuitive psychic spasm. In each of these cases the act of judgment appears more as a reflex than a verdict—thus Kurtz's "summing up" is not a deliberation but a "cry." The moral sense becomes an immediate expression of the individual sensibility, existing not beyond but beneath good and evil.[6]

Conrad longs to overcome the separation between fact and value; he longs to see value lodged securely in fact—"the redeeming facts of life"— so that the individual need not rely on the rickety apparatus of social ethics. "Darkness" is the perfect moral term, a term that at once suggests a perception and a value and hence satisfies the impulse to merge description and appraisal.[7] The transitions from the literal gloom of the African jungle to Kurtz's gloomy horror, from the obscurtiy of the Intended's drawing room to Marlow's obscure dread, from the black bank of clouds above the Thames to the heart of darkness appear almost seam-

6. Peter Brooks, *Reading for the Plot: Design and Intention in Narrative* (New York: Knopf, 1984), p. 250, writes as follows: "More than a masterful, summary, victorious articulation, 'The horror!' appears as minimal language, language on the verge of reversion to savagery, on the verge of a fall from language." Brooks is certainly right to point to the liminal character of Kurtz's final words, but we can see them as ascent quite as readily as descent, language as it emerges from sensation, from word-less reflex to reflexive word.

7. Fredric Jameson, *The Political Unconscious:*

Narrative as a Socially Symbolic Act (Ithaca, N.Y.: Cornell Univ. Press, 1981), pp. 231, 230, has written of the "perceptual vocation of [Conrad's] style," which "offers the exercise of perception and the perceptual recombination of sense data as an end in itself." No doubt the activity of perception carries its own justification for Conrad, but that activity receives sufficient warrant only through its contribution to the moral vocation of the style. Marlow may not be an articulate moralist, but he has a moral style.

less. They do so, of course, only because this darkness is a metaphor which so reliably links facts and values.[8] It is indeed almost a dead metaphor. Its ethical associations are so highly conventional and Marlow repeats them so often that it scarcely seems a figure of speech at all. And yet it is just to Conrad's purpose that darkness be a dying metaphor. The more hackneyed the figure, the more secure is the association between literal and moral obscurity, and the more inevitable seems the link between perception and evaluation. By the end of the tale an event as natural as the darkening sky stands as a somber moral warning. Facts are inlaid with value until judgment has become a task for the senses.

Conradian Impressionism is habitually regarded as an epistemological event, an attempt to restore the priority of the sensory apparatus in the literary representation of knowledge. But we do not need to disregard Conrad's epistemology in order to recognize that his Impressionism is at least as significant a moral event. As *Heart of Darkness* moves from an institutional to an instinctual domain, it implicitly asks what lies between these warring regions, and it responds by offering the Impressionist temperament as itself a basis for individual moral autonomy. The ascent from Kurtzian horror is an ascent to a region of experience in which virtue and vice disclose themselves in sight and sound, taste and smell. Between fragile social conventions and blind passions morality finds a place in the educated impressions of the Practical Moralist. The world shimmers with value as it shimmers with color, and there is no need to rely on independent (and dubious) acts of the ethical mind once one has learned to trust intelligent sensations.

Thus the Practical Moralist makes a curious approach to the Working Artist—"too dark," after all, is something that a painter might observe of an unsatisfactory canvas. To say this is not to imply that there is anything frivolous in Marlow's convictions, only to suggest that a final consequence of the attempt to embed value in fact is that one comes to rely on intuitive perceptions of consonance and dissonance. "Somehow" and "something," "relief," "shock," "flavour" and "horror"—all reflect the desire to locate the moral sense so firmly within individual experience that no skein of ethical reflections need ever distract judgment. One simply inspects the world and arranges a balance in the shades of contrast. Darkness becomes the raw material of this aestheticized morality, an almost palpable substance that can be kneaded into form and then disposed according to intuitions of ethical fitness. Marlow takes it from Kurtz, flourishes it before the Manager, withholds it from the Intended, confers it upon his shipmates. Each of these acts has a reason, but they are all "particular reasons," so particular indeed, so securely lodged in individual circumstance, that they reveal Marlow as no moral metaphysician, only, perhaps, a sculptor in darkness.

8. For a useful discussion of Conradian metaphor, see William W. Bonney, "Joseph Conrad and the Betrayal of Language," *Nineteenth-Century Fiction*, 34 (1979), 128.

ROBERT KIMBROUGH

Conrad's *Youth* (1902): An Introduction †

In the year of his death (1924), Joseph Conrad said that the three stories in *Youth: A Narrative; and Two Other Stories* (1902)—*Youth, Heart of Darkness,* and *The End of the Tether*—represent the three ages of man—youth, maturity, and age. The comment is helpful, but only in a general, introductory way, even if supported by the relative length of each story: *Youth* is about thirteen thousand words; *Heart of Darkness,* about thirty-eight thousand; and *The End of the Tether,* about forty-seven thousand—Conrad's longest. (His shortest novel, *The Nigger of the "Narcissus"* [1897], is about fifty-four thousand words.) In fact, the very first sentence in Conrad's "Author's Note" written for an edition of *Youth* published in 1917 states that "the three stories in this volume lay no claim to unity of artistic purpose." Conrad did not set out to write about three separate periods of life; he wrote about life from three separate points of view, using three separate techniques—even though the first two are told by the same man, Marlow.

Not *The End of the Tether,* but *Lord Jim* in the form of a short story was to have been the third piece for a volume contracted in 1898 by the Edinburgh publisher, William Blackwood. *Youth* and *Heart of Darkness* had first appeared in *Blackwood's Magazine* ("*Maga*") in 1897 and 1899 as had *Lord Jim* in 1899–1900 (and as would *The End of the Tether*). Upon completion, however, *Lord Jim* had proved too long for inclusion as a short story and was published separately as a novel in 1900. Before the third story had been received, however, the first two stories had been set in print for the single volume. Thus, Conrad still had to provide about forty thousand words in order to fulfill his contract to complete the book.

Had *Lord Jim* remained short enough to be included, the resulting volume could have been entitled *Marlow,* because Marlow, that friend of the anonymous narrator of *Youth, Heart of Darkness,* and *Lord Jim,* is actually the principal narrator within all three. Thus, all three are *about* Marlow as well as *by* Marlow. But in writing *The End of the Tether* to complete *Youth: A Narrative; and Two Other Stories,* Conrad chose not to evoke Marlow, possibly because to do so would draw too much attention to the many ways that *The End of the Tether* is a kind of recasting of Lord Jim's story, which Marlow had already recounted.

Conrad's 1917 "Author's Note" to *Youth* remains the best introduction to Marlow and to the three stories in that volume—and to this present Norton Critical Edition of *Heart of Darkness.* Hence, any present reader might well wish to turn back at this point to Conrad's "Author's Note" on page 3, read it, and return. There, Conrad places the composition of the stories between the two critically acknowledged land-marks of his early career as a writer, *The Nigger of the "Narcissus"* (1897) and *Nostromo* (1904). He tells us that each of the three stories is based in part on his own experience:

> *Youth* is a feat of memory. It is a record of experience; but that experience, in its facts . . . begins and ends in myself. *Heart of Darkness* is experience too; but it is experience pushed a little (and only very little) beyond the actual facts of the case. . . . *The End of the Tether* is a story of sea-life. . . . [T]he pages of that story—a fair half of the book—are also the product of experience.

For the details of Conrad's experiences as the second mate on the barque *Palestine* in 1881–82 *(Youth)*, as the captain of a steamer on the Congo in 1890 *(Heart of Darkness)*, and as the first mate of the *Vidar* in 1888 *(The End of the Tether)*, the reader should consult Roger Tennant's 1981 biography and Norman Sherry's excellent volumes on Conrad's Eastern and Western worlds (see the Guide to Bibliography, which follows). When Conrad was forthright enough to say that "every novel contains an element of autobiography" (see above, p. 235), he did not mean that every novel is biographical. Indeed, he made it steamingly clear in a letter to his young friend Richard Curle in 1921 that scholarly, critical explicitness is fatal to art (see above, p. 232). In accordance with Conrad's wishes, the footnotes in my edition of *Heart of Darkness* do not link details of fiction to details of life. Indeed, the proper degree of scholarly, critical reserve that one should adopt before Conrad is exemplified by Conrad himself in his remarks on Marlow, that "most discreet, understanding man."

Conrad rightly laughs at those who debate whether Marlow is or is not Conrad. Clearly, Marlow is both, at the same time that he is neither. Marlow is, in the Elizabethan sense, an invention—something come across, something happened upon, something uncovered—something discovered in the very process of writing. Hence, we need not doubt that "Marlow and I came together in the casual manner of those health-resort acquaintances which sometimes ripen into friendships," that Marlow "haunts my hours of solitude," and that "as we part at the end of a tale I am never sure that it may not be for the last time" (this was written in 1917, four years after *Chance*, which turned out to be the fourth and last of the Marlow-stories). Because of the imaginative source of Marlow within Conrad, we can appreciate the warmth and humor in Conrad's "Yet I don't think that either of us would much care to survive the other."

I
Youth

The special appeal of *Youth* is that it simultaneously celebrates and laughs at young ideas and acts, that it is simultaneously sentimental and world-weary. This simultaneity, this mix, could not be achieved without Marlow. Had the story been told in the first-person during or immediately after the events, the egoism of youth—the self-congratulation, the self-centeredness, the self-glorification: in short, the romanticism of youth—would have been so central that the story would have sounded a single-noted effect: either of celebration or of derision. Or, had the story been told in a restricted third-person, either past or present tense, the effect, again, would be either/or: either of sentimentality or of embittered disillusionment. But with Marlow a character within someone else's narrative telling his own story from a recollective point of view, all of the either/or's disappear. Marlow can laugh at himself for having been foolhardy, stupid, and limited in vision; nevertheless, it was Marlow himself who was adventurous, brave, and guided by idealistic patterns superimposed on the world. As a result, Marlow's report has integrity—wholeness—truth.

Between Marlow and us is the anonymous narrator who, as had his four friends, "began life in the merchant service." To him, then, life at sea "is life itself." This statement prepares us for Marlow's "you fellows know there are those voyages that seem ordered from the illustration of life, that might stand for a symbol of existence." And at forty-two, Marlow looks back twenty years to recount his initiation into life, his movement from youth to manhood.

To the young Marlow, the *Judea* (with its simplistic motto of an arrested adolescence: "Do or Die" ["Death Before Dishonor," "Better Dead Than Red," "Love It or Leave It"]) was "the endeavor, the test, the trial of life," and his journey ends with "the thought that I had been tried in the ship and had come out pretty well. . . . I did not know how good a man I was till then." In present perspective, however, before he gets wine-soaked-sentimental at the end, Marlow can clear-sightedly say of his adventure, "It was like an absurd dream." The narrator, too, cynically concludes that the life of youth is "the romance of illusions." But because of the invention of Marlow, Conrad can rightly claim to have captured in *Youth* a double-layered "mood of wistful regret, of reminiscent tenderness" that is life in a larger perspective than that merely of past time or present.

II
Heart of Darkness

Once invented in *Youth*, Marlow allowed Conrad to turn to his deeply traumatic, cataclysmally catalytic venture into Africa in 1890 and to convert the experience into art. While a lot of autobiography is deeply hidden in *Heart of Darkness*, there is only surface biography because here, in addition to Marlow, we are given Kurtz. *Youth* is double-layered; *Heart of Darkness* is multilayered. Question: When Kurtz utters "The horror! The horror!" what do you think that Conrad thought that the narrator thought that Marlow thought that Kurtz thought? The answer to that question lies not in Conrad's biography, but is found at the heart of this dark story—or, it resides as well in the darkness surrounding the heart of the story, for all referents point inward and outward at the same time, which is the way symbols work on us.

In *Youth*, through Marlow, Conrad turned from his previous technique of straightforward, single-layered narrative to indirect and double. Still, the tensions, the potential ambiguities, were contained within the dimensions of Marlow's original experience. With the addition of Kurtz's experience, Conrad is able to add a symbolic dimension to his earlier narrative technique. In the surviving manuscript version of the story, Conrad included an episode that describes Marlow's arrival at the seat of colonial government within the estuary of the River Congo (see above, p. 18). Marlow says in part:

> I had heard enough in Europe about its advanced state of civilization; the papers, nay the very paper vendors in the sepulchral city were boasting about the steam tramway and the hotel—especially the hotel. I beheld that wonder. *It was like a symbol at the gate.* It stood alone, a grey high cube of iron with two tiers of galleries outside towering above one of those ruinous-looking foreshores you come upon at home in out-of-the-way places where refuse is thrown out. To make the resemblance complete it wanted only a drooping post bearing a board with the legend: rubbish shot here, and *the symbol* would have had the clearness of the naked truth. (emphasis added)

Conrad cancelled this passage in the typescript that was sent to *Blackwood's Magazine*; perhaps the symbolism of this mock sepulchral city linking Europe with Africa was too blatant, too naked. But the repetition of the word "symbol" indicates that Conrad realized that he was bringing a new kind of writing into *Heart of Darkness*. Where his earlier narratives were primarily objective, descriptive, and thematically clear, *Heart of Darkness* is also interior, suggestively analytic, and highly psychological. Indeed, Conrad realized that in comparison to *Youth*, *Heart of Darkness* is "written in another mood"; the "sombre theme had to be given a sinister resonance, a tonality of its own, a continued vibration" and the result is "like another art altogether."

While *Heart of Darkness* is the story of the story of Marlow's venture up the Congo River to Stanley Falls, Marlow's interest (to the regret of the reporting narrator) is centered in Kurtz:

> "I don't want to bother you much with what happened to me personally," he began, showing in this remark the weakness of many tellers of tales who seem so often unaware of what their audience would best like to hear; "yet to understand the effect of it on me you ought to know how I got out there, what I saw, how I went up that river to the place where I first met the poor chap."

Hence, it is Kurtz's story that Marlow is telling, even before he and we meet Kurtz. But Marlow's story is the mediating story between the inner one of Kurtz's invasion of the so-called Belgian Congo and the outer story that Conrad is telling of Europe's invasion of Africa. Without Kurtz's story, *Heart of Darkness* would, like *Youth*, be a simultaneous celebration of self and satire of society. But with Kurtz, the reverberations and implications multiply, for Kurtz is the central symbol—as Conrad clearly asserted in a letter of December 2, 1902, even though the assertion is carefully couched in the authorial language of uncertainty, indirection, and casualness—after all, Conrad was the present companion of James and Ford: "What I distinctly admit is the fault of having made Kurtz too symbolic or rather symbolic at all. But the story being mainly a vehicle for conveying a batch of personal impressions I gave rein to my mental laziness and took the line of least resistance." So, Kurtz is the central symbol, and what a symbol.

All of Europe, we are told, contributed to the making of Kurtz—Europe: safe, civilized, scheduled, masculine, literate, superficially Christian, and dead. Kurtz, a European "Knight," sets out on a crusade to win the hearts and minds of a "lesser" people, himself ignorant of the degree to which Africa is dangerous, wild, timeless, feminine, unfettered by letters, deeply religious, and vibrant. His love turns to rape when he discovers how unfitted he is to master the magnificent vitality of a natural world. The difference between Europe and Africa is the difference between two secondary symbols, the European woman who has helped to puff up Kurtz's pride and the African woman who has helped to deflate him.

The Intended (nameless, intended for someone else, not herself) is totally protected (helpless), rhetorically programmed (words without matter), nunlike in her adoration (sexually repressed), living in black, in a place of darkness, in a pre-Eliot City of the Dead, in the wasteland of modern Europe. She, like Europe, is primarily exterior, for her simple black garment hides nothing.

The Native Woman is Africa, all interior, in spite of her lavish mode of dress. While Kurtz is male, white, bald, oral, unrestrained, the native woman is female, black, stunningly coiffured, emotive, and restrained. Here, in part, is her introduction:

> She walked with measured steps, draped in striped and fringed cloths, treading the earth proudly with a slight jingle and flash of barbarous ornaments. . . . She was savage and superb, wild-eyed and magnificent; there was something ominous and stately in her deliberate progress. And in the hush that had fallen suddenly upon the whole sorrowful land, the immense wilderness, the colossal body of the fecund and mysterious life seemed to look at her, pensive, as though it had been looking at the image of its own tenebrous and passionate soul.

Africa, yes, but she is also Tellus Mater, Amazon, Dido, and a type of Venus. Kurtz is clearly a kind of Mars. While this does not mean that the arrows shot through the pilot-house door come from their son Cupid, these arrows are, however, a fine example of the phallic futility of a relationship which has none of the creativity and bonding of love, only love's hate and anger. Kurtz's lustful exploitation of the woman, then, is rape, just as were his raids in the lake region, just as was the fantastic invasion of Africa by Christian, capitalistic Western civilization—and its discontents.

Marlow's story links these inner and outer stories. In a sense, Marlow exploited the exploiters in order to carry out his boyhood dream of going to the center of Africa where there was "one river especially, a mighty big river that you could see on the map, resembling an immense snake uncoiled, with its head in the sea, its body at rest curving afar over a vast country and its tail lost in the depths of the land. And as I looked at the map of it in a shop-window it fascinated me as a snake would a bird—a silly little bird. . . . The snake had charmed me." The snake and the bird, age-old phallic symbols, set up the motif of sexual encounter. Recalling the map on the office wall in the sepulchral city, Marlow says, "I was going into the yellow. Dead in the centre. And the river was there—fascinating—deadly—like a snake." And as he departed in his French steamer he "felt as though instead of going to the centre of a continent I were about to set off for the centre of the earth."

Thus the river is a phallus within the vulva of Africa, the head of the penis touching the womb, the heart, the inner darkness. But the river itself is a vulva, open to the sea, inviting the sexually excited scavenger birds of Europe. The snake swallowing its own tail is the sign of fulfill-ment, of perfection, of androgynous wholeness because penis and vulva engaged can create a continuous circle. But in *Heart of Darkness* the phallus of Europe enters the oriface, moves inward to the heart of dark-ness, reaches climax, and is disgorged. Phallic futility, vaginal pain—no fulfillment, no contentment.

During Marlow's trip to Africa, the coast line was "smiling, frowning, inviting, grand, mean, insipid, or savage, and always mute with an air of whispering—Come and find out." This female image is counter-pointed by the masculine surf: "The voice of the surf heard now and then was a positive pleasure, like the speech of a brother. It was some-thing natural, that had its reason, that had a meaning," as did the native men who came out to the ship in canoes: "they had bone, muscle, a wild vitality, an intense energy of movement that was as natural and true as the surf along their coast"—a surf that is a "dangerous surf, as if Nature herself had tried to ward off intruders."

Within this self-contained, powerful, masculine-feminine context, we get a symbol of the intruders in the French man-of-war, "her ensign drooped limp like a rag," "shelling the bush" from "long six-inch guns" sticking out of its low hull:

In the empty immensity of earth, sky, and water, there she was, incomprehensible, firing into a continent. Pop, would go one of the six-inch guns; a small flame would dart and vanish, a little white smoke would disappear, a tiny projectile would give a feeble screech—and nothing happened. Nothing could happen. There was a touch of insanity in the proceeding, a sense of lugubrious drollery in the sight.

Interestingly, Conrad reduced these guns from "ten-inch" in the manuscript, to "eight-inch" in the typescript for *Blackwood's Magazine*, to "six-inch" for the 1902 *Youth* volume; "inch," of course, refers to muzzle/bore diameter, but the association of diminishing size with the self-conscious fears and fantasies of male penile pride is obvious.

Fittingly, when Marlow first hears the high-explosives used in clearing for the railroad that will connect the Lower and Central Stations, he is reminded of this French phallic futility: "A heavy and dull detonation shook the ground, a puff of smoke came out of the cliff, and that was all. No change appeared on the face of the rock. They were building a railway. The cliff was not in the way of anything, but this objectless blasting was all the work going on. . . . Another report from the cliff made me think suddenly of that ship of war I had seen firing into a continent."

After fifteen days and two hundred miles of tramping, Marlow gets from the Lower to the Central Station.[1] The cockiness of the Manager and the impotence of his underlings are caught at once: "They wandered here and there with their absurd long staves in their hands like a lot of faithless pilgrims bewitched inside a rotten fence. . . . And outside, the silent wilderness surrounding this cleared speck on the earth struck me as something great and invincible." This satirical allegory of masculine pretension and ineptitude, of phallic futility and failed interaction, is elaborated by the invasion, the infliction, the visitation of the Eldorado Exploring Expedition that follows, and Marlow overhears one night snatches of conversation between the manager and his uncle, the leader of the Expedition:

> I saw him extend his short flipper of an arm for a gesture that took in the forest, the creek, the mud, the river—seemed to beckon with a dishonouring flourish before the sunlit face of the land a treacherous appeal to the lurking death, to the hidden evil, to the profound darkness of its heart. . . . The high stillness confronted these two figures with its ominous patience, waiting for the passing away of a fantastic invasion.

At this point, Conrad's manuscript reads, "The thick voice was swallowed up, the confident gesture was lost in the high stillness . . . with

1. To keep the confrontation of Africa and Europe free of footnoted complications, Conrad does not have Marlow visit busy native market centers or rest in a missionary settlement, as had Conrad himself (see above, pp. 160–66).

its ominous air [of] patient waiting," and cancelled is a comparison of the voice and gesture to "bursting shells" and "blasted rocks." And the text continues: "In a few days the Eldorado Expedition went into the patient wilderness, that closed upon it as the sea closes over a diver. Long afterwards the news came that all the donkeys were dead. I know nothing as to the fate of the less valuable animals."

These episodes of droll stupidity, of stupid folly, serve as prelude to the central sexual experience of the book, the trip up the river by the men aboard that nineteenth-century symbol of Western civilization, the steamboat. Within the now clearly established contex of the story, the steamboat is simultaneously a phallus penetrating the river-vulva, and semen carrying sterile sperm within the river-phallus moving up to the mouth of the womb of Africa. This adventure to attempt to "rescue" Kurtz culminates in a sexual explosion of nature's fog and man's smoke, of natural noises and manmade ones, of arrows and bullets. What more appropriate than to find the Russian fool at the Inner Station, for the fool is another age-old phallic symbol. The Russian is many things— harlequin, court jester, existential man—but he is also the fool in the heart of darkness, which brings us full circle in the ironic world of Conrad. The traditional residence of folly is in the head of the penis. The folly of folly, folly within folly.

The whole experience is given an inner universality through a passage spoken by Marlow before he describes this ascent into the heart of darkness. Ostensibly for the benefit of his immediate audience, but actually for ours, he asks: "Do you see the story? Do you see anything? It seems to me I am trying to tell you a dream—making a vain attempt, because no relation of a dream can convey the dream-sensation, that commingling of absurdity, surprise, and bewilderment in a tremor of struggling revolt, that notion of being captured by the incredible which is the very essence of dreams." The description of the passage up-river "as we penetrated deeper and deeper into the heart of darkness" *is* a dream narrative, a prose-poem, that must be read aloud, slowly in order for the utter sensuality of the experience to be felt: from page 35—"Going up that river was like travelling back to the earliest beginnings of the world, when vegetation rioted on the earth and the big trees were kings"— through page 38—"They howled and leaped, and spun, and made horrid faces, but what thrilled you was just the thought of their humanity— like yours—the thought of your remote kinship with this wild and passionate uproar." The extent to which Conrad is here drawing from his creative imagination can be measured by comparing this Jungean exploration of the mind—"The mind of man is capable of anything—because everything is in it, all the past as well as all the future"—with Conrad's account of the actual up-river journey (see above, pp. 167–86). (Few of us will ever visit the river Congo, but may experience it through an excellent segment of the PBS/TV Series "River Journeys"—see Introduction.)

The manuscript of the story tells us that comprehension of the wil-

derness could not come to the travellers because they were merely passing by. Total comprehension could come only "by conquest—or by
surrender." Kurtz came to a full knowledge both ways, by conquest *and*
surrender: "The wilderness had patted him on the head, and behold, it
was like a ball—an ivory ball; it had caressed him and—lo!—he had
withered; it had taken him, loved him, embraced him, got into his veins,
consumed his flesh, and sealed his soul to its own by the inconceivable
ceremonies of some devilish initiation. He was its spoiled and pampered
favourite." In his sexually spent condition, Kurtz looks like Edmund
Spenser's Redcross Knight in Book I of *The Faerie Queene*, also the
victim of his own sexual pride in the House of Pride and Orgoglio's
castle. But the native woman is not Duessa, and the Intended is not
Una. Rather, the reverse, for when Kurtz conquered, and surrendered
to, the Native Woman he discovered Truth. It is not the Intended, but
the African, "wild and gorgeous," to whom Marlow refers when he says
that Kurtz "had conquered one soul in the world that was neither rudimentary nor tainted with self-seeking." It is she to whom Kurtz tries to
return at night, and Marlow is appalled: "I tried to break the spell, the
heavy mute spell of the wilderness that seemed to draw him to its pitiless
breast by the awakening of forgotten and brutal instincts, by the memory
of gratified and monstrous passions." These are Marlow's words, and
those who would have us believe that this is Conrad speaking do not
understand Kurtz, who in spite of what Marlow's and Conrad's reactions
to his sexual experiences might be, has learned all there is to learn about
Love and Will before Rollo May, with a debt to Schopenhauer, wrote
about the demonic within us. When the steamer is leaving, the woman
returns, puts out her hands, and screams something. Marlow asks Kurtz
if he understands: "He kept on looking out past me with fiery, longing
eyes, with a mingled expression of *wistfulness* and *hate*. . . . 'Do I not?'
he said slowly, gasping, as if the words had been torn out of him by a
supernatural power" (emphasis added).

When Kurtz says "The horror! The horror!" rhetoric and reality come
together, Europe and Africa collide, the Intended and the African. Kurtz
realizes that all he has been nurtured to believe in, to operate from, is a
sham; hence, a horror. And, the primal nature of nature is also, *to him*,
a horror, because he has been stripped of his own culture and stands
both literally and figuratively naked before another; he has been exposed
to desire but cannot comprehend it through some established, ready-at-
hand, frame of reference. That which we cannot understand we stand
over; that which we cannot embrace, we reject; that which we cannot
love, we hate. To Kurtz, both Europe and Africa have become nightmares—"The horror! The horror!"—and it is between these nightmares
that Marlow must make his choice.

Meditating on his own brush with death, Marlow wonders if he could
have reached the insight and self-discovery that Kurtz obtained through
his exposure to the timeless world of love and hate:

He had summed up—he had judged. "The horror!" He was a remarkable man. After all, this was the expression of some sort of belief; it had candour, it had conviction, it had a vibrating note of revolt in its whisper, it had the appalling face of a glimpsed truth— the strange commingling of *desire* and *hate*. . . . It was an affirmation, a moral victory paid for by innumerable defeats, by abominable terrors, by adominable satisfactions. But it was a victory. (emphasis added)

Because of his full experience of self and sexual knowledge, Kurtz could never go back to his Intended—the agony of this realization informs his doubled expression of "horror." Such as he had become would overwhelm the male-sheltered, carefully cultured, literally manufactured woman. That hers is a repressed sexuality is, further, part of Kurtz's "horror." On the one hand, he experienced lust unleashed—through carnal knowledge of Africa coming into self-knowledge of his European hollowness—but she, being European, has been rendered unable to share that knowledge. To force a sharing, to tell the truth, would be to inflict rape and slaughter merely of a different kind in a different place in the world. And for Marlow to have indicated to the Intended the way Kurtz lived and died would have been to carry out that rape and slaughter.

Conrad set up the ironic contrast between the European and the African women through the painting by Kurtz that he left behind at the Central Station. The picture represented "a woman draped and blind-folded carrying a lighted torch. The background was sombre—almost black. The movement of the woman was stately, and the effect of the torchlight on the face was sinister." Europe, symbolized by the Intended, in Africa, symbolized by darkness—but, the torch will be quenched, the blind woman swallowed whole. Marlow did not really lie: the last words Kurtz pronounced were, in part, in reference to his symbolic model within his symbolic picture.

Marlow knows that the Intended could not stand up to (understand) the raw truth as discovered by Kurtz, could never stand up to (understand) the Native Woman. Marlow neatly sums up the tragic relationship that was created among these three people:

She put out her arms, as if after a retreating figure, stretching them black and with clasped pale hands across the fading and narrow sheen of the window. Never see him! I saw him clearly enough then. I shall see this eloquent phantom as long as I live and I shall see her too, a tragic and familiar Shade resembling in this gesture another one, tragic also and bedecked with powerless charms, stretching bare brown arms over the glitter of the infernal stream, the stream of darkness.

Empty words, empty gestures. Europe and Africa. Each is a Heart of Darkness. A choice of nightmares.

III
The End of the Tether

After *Heart of Darkness*, Conrad began "Lord Jim: A Sketch," to be the third story in that volume of three to be published by Blackwood, but *Jim* went on to fill thirteen instalments in *Blackwood's Magazine* and became a separately published novel. In all that space, Marlow tells us no more of Africa or of any personal aftermath. Indirectly, however, *Lord Jim* is a minute examination of a "choice of nightmares" such as Marlow faced on a small scale and Kurtz on a large. Although five short stories came between *Lord Jim* and *The End of the Tether*, when Conrad sat down in 1902 to settle his account with Blackwood, the question of a "choice of nightmares" and the resultant psychological evaluation of its consequences returned to haunt Conrad, but now without his familiar, his attendant spirit, Marlow.

While no claim can be made that *The End of the Tether* achieves the artistic wholeness or creates the dramatic impact of either of the first two stories, to judge it solely in comparison with *Youth* and *Heart of Darkness* is a mistake—and is misleading. While *The End of the Tether* may seem to complete a pattern of youth-maturity-age among the three stories, it cannot be read as a "sequel" to the first two if only because it does not utilize the technique of a character-narrator. Yet, within the third-person narration of *The End of the Tether*, there is marvelous indirection at work, in both technique and tone. Critics complain that the story is too long, too vague, too sentimental—but these complaints arise only when Conrad's technique—his painter's style—and his tone—his creation of an urbane, ironic voice worthy of Henry James—are not comprehended. To understand *The End of the Tether*, one must be willing to take second takes, to view both broadly and up close. What one discovers is that the story is sketched broadly, but filled with minute dots and strokes—the technique is layered, and understanding must come from unlayering. The whole is accomplished through patient, ironic indirection—and the least discovery is the discovery of Captain Whalley's blindness, referred to as early as the first three paragraphs of the story, but indirectly.

The major discovery is that Captain Whalley is none of the persons any of the on-looking world thinks he is, including Whalley. A blind man blind to himself. Possibly his daughter Ivy, his romanticized "fair maid," measured him for the completely simple soul he is—but children have a built-in tendency to make such an assessment of parents anyway. But no one, not even the narrator, makes the assessment directly. That job is left to the reader.

In *Youth* and *Heart of Darkness*, we are forced by the narrator into the hands of Marlow and are compelled to listen to him for the clues and codes, signs and symbols of significance. If we come to *The End of the Tether* expecting to be charmed by the ancient magic of a story-teller, we will be disappointed. This is no oral discourse; it is literate—highly sophisticated and removed. The appeal is not based primarily in the story-line, but in the effects of interplay of character. Very little happens in the less than two days of the story. Even the melodramatic climax is undercut: Massy the owner is bailed out and Ivy receives her inheritance—unless lawyers are inept or corrupt. Whalley was incapable of figuring out either that he will save others when he commits suicide to escape the ignominy of a lost reputation, or that his reputation is so firmly established that his stupidity in trying to hide his blindness, had it been revealed at a board of inquiry, would have been interpreted as a noble, heroic endeavor.

Although there is no aural pun in Whalley/whale, there is a visual one, which is reinforced by Sterne's discovery by means of analogy of the captain's blindness: the Pilot/Serang is to Whalley as a pilot-fish is to a whale. And like a whale, Whalley is large and magnificent in appearance, at home only at sea, and has attributed to his simple mammalian brain all sorts of mysterious wisdom and dignity—Moby-Dick with a white beard.

Conrad's sea-fiction and his essays on his fellowship with the craft are filled with tributes to the simple souls of seamen. Possibly the archetypal one is Old Singleton of the *Narcissus*. But Whalley is not a simple Singleton; he is a simpleton—and Conrad seems to have been aware of the possibility of the accusation of betrayal in his drawing of the portrait of his captain. In his "Author's Note," Conrad tells us that *"The End of the Tether* is a story of sea-life *in a rather special way*; and the most intimate thing I can say of it is this: that having lived that life fully, amongst its men, its thoughts and sensations, I have found it possible, *without the slightest misgiving, in all sincerity of heart and peace of conscience*, to conceive the existence of Captain Whalley's personality and to relate the manner of his end" (emphasis added). Even if one does not agree that here Conrad protests too much, at least his assertions lead us to the basic irony of the story—the elevated Whalley is less the man whom the lesser persons look up to: the jolly, assured Ned Eliot; the paranoid, puny Massy; the self-contained, but racially intimidated Serang; the self-destructive opportunist Sterne; the byronic, romantic Van Wyk. Each of these is painted in small strokes, slowly, through indirect discourse, interior monologue, and deduced implications of reported dialogue. As a group they are unified by their reactions to Whalley: each reads Whalley from the point of view of his own defective character; each reads into him; each has a psychological need to see Whalley for what he is not. But not Ivy, who clings and kills.

Ivy may "kill" her father, but the fault is not hers: "He had named her Ivy because of the sound of the word, and *obscurely* fascinated by a *vague* association of ideas" (emphasis added). Here the narrator is at work; he, not Whalley, understands the ego that hears the "I" in the first syllable of Ivy and who knows that while Ivy clings and kills, it is also tough and hearty. Its roots are firmly planted. Through the narrator we can absorb the ironies and recognize the further one of the father tethering himself to the child.

There are two ends to a tether, one fixed and one free, as free as the length of the tether. One end of the tether is Ivy, the other is Whalley. Because Ivy is the fixed end, she is the tether holding the father, whose end ends the hold of the tether. In this sense, the end of the tether is the ending of his life and his ending is finally only the end or destiny of his life: dust to dust. But end as purpose takes us back to the other end, Ivy, the support of whom has been the sole end of Whalley's life. But in the final analysis, Ivy is not really the particular motivation force in Whalley's life: supporting her merely giving an overall end or purpose to Whalley's life. He gave up his "fair maid" three times: through marriage, through the sale of the *Fair Maid*, through suicide.

But these variations on the meaning of the title come only after reading the story. In its initial, primary sense, the title means Whalley's getting free from the bind of the contract with Massy; this is the primary relevance of Conrad's words: "the manner of his end" (just quoted): Whalley's suicide frees him from the tether of the contract.

The bold extent of Conrad's use of ironies is found in the fact that Conrad allows Whalley twice the use the titular phrase without any awareness of irony. In the midst of the apparent resolution of the two-day story, when Massy states that Whalley will get exposed, that the ship is lost, and that the insurance will not be paid, the narrator says:

> Captain Whalley did not move. True! Ivy's money. Gone in the wreck. Again he had a flash of insight. He was indeed at the end of his tether.

The great insight is that he must kill himself. The "indeed" is not loaded with multiple significance *for him*; it is a simple confirmation of the "insight" he had had before this voyage when he composed and left with the lawyer the letter delivered to Ivy upon his death in which he had, in effect, said, I really don't know what to do in my predicament: I am at my wit's end. Quite literally, that there might be any other solution lies *beyond* his comprehension. Whalley has always had a short hold on life—his comprehension does not reach beyond a fixed, measured, absolute length. The irony rings out in the narrator's report of the indirect, interior monologue, just quoted above: "True!"

The James-like irony of the subdued narrator is apparent on every page of *The End of the Tether* once the reader is alerted to its presence. Nowhere is this irony more withering than in the last paragraph of the story—which ends, "she felt she had loved him after all." Small wonder that of the three tales in *Youth* (1902), Henry James liked only *The End of the Tether*.

A Guide to Bibliography

I. BIBLIOGRAPHICAL AIDS

University libraries, most college libraries, and a great many public libraries can provide computer searching of bibliographical databases to create all kinds of general and special subject and topic bibliographies. Furthermore, most of these libraries have online computer catalogues to supplement and soon to replace the traditional author-title-subject card catalogues.

The most complete printed bibliographies on Conrad are Kenneth A. Lohf and Eugene P. Sheehy, *Joseph Conrad at Mid-Century: Editions and Studies, 1895–1955* (1957), and Theodore G. Ehrsam, *A Bibliography of Joseph Conrad* (1969). More helpful to the student, however, is Bruce E. Teets and Helmut E. Gerber, *Joseph Conrad: An Annotated Bibliography of Writings about Him* (1971), which covers the years 1895–1966. A sequel that will cover some fifteen more (massive) years is currently in press at Northern Illinois University Press. In the meantime, the best source of bibliographies on every aspect of Conrad can be found easily and handily in the bound volumes of *Conradiana*, founded in 1968 and now published at Texas Tech University. And, of course, there is the reliable annual *PMLA* bibliography, now available both in print and through the computer.

II. BIOGRAPHY

Much primary material on Conrad's life is readily available. Of autobiographical value are *The Mirror of the Sea* (1906), *A Personal Record* (1912), *Notes on Life and Letters* (1921), *Last Essays* (1926), and *Conrad's Prefaces*, ed. Edward Garnett (1937). *The Collected Letters of Joseph Conrad* under the general editorship of Frederick R. Karl will run to eight volumes, two of which have appeared (and are used in this book). In the meantime, the greatest body of letters by Conrad is in G. Jean-Aubrey, *Joseph Conrad: Life and Letters*, 2 vols. (1927), but other important edited collections are Richard Curle, *Conrad to a Friend* (1928); Edward Garnett, *Letters From Conrad, 1895–1924* (1928); G. Jean-Aubrey, *Lettres Françaises* (1929); John A. Gee and Paul J. Sturm, *Letters of Joseph Conrad to Marguerite Poradowska, 1890–1920* (1940); William Blackburn, *Joseph Conrad: Letters to William Blackwood and David S. Meldrum* (1958); and C. T. Watts, *Joseph Conrad's Letters to Cunninghame Graham* (1969). Of testimonial value are two books by Conrad's wife, Jessie, *Joseph Conrad as I Knew Him* (1926) and *Joseph Conrad and His Circle* (1935, 2nd ed. 1964), and two by his sons: Borys Conrad, *My Father: Joseph Conrad* (1970), and John Conrad, *Joseph Conrad: Times Remembered* (1981). Other books of reminiscence are various studies by Richard Curle, the most important of which is *The Last Twelve Years of Joseph Conrad* (1928), and those by literary friends, the fullest of which are by Ford Madox Ford, *Joseph Conrad: A Personal Remembrance* (1924) and *Portraits from Life* (1937). Engaging full biographies are G. Jean-Aubrey's 1947 recasting of the biographical part of his pioneer *Life and Letters*, which was translated by Helen Sebba as *The Sea Dreamer: A Definitive Biography of Joseph Conrad* (1957); Jerry Allen, *The Thunder and the Sunshine: A Biography of Joseph Conrad* (1958); Jocelyn Baines, *Joseph Conrad: A Critical Biography* (1960); Bernard C. Meyer, *Joseph Conrad: A Psychoanalytic Biography* (1967); Frederick R. Karl, *Joseph Conrad: The Three Lives* (1979); Zdzisław Najder, *Joseph Conrad: A Chronicle* and *Conrad Under Familiar Eyes* (both 1983); and Wit Tarawski, *Conrad the Man, the Writer, the Pole* (1982, 1984). For those who do not trust themselves to create their own biography of Conrad in the Congo out of the materials presented in Backgrounds and Sources, there are Norman Sherry, *Conrad's Western World* (1971), and Roger Tenant, *Joseph Conrad* (1981).

III. SELECTED STUDIES

All of the major books on Conrad and most of the major articles on *Heart of Darkness* are readily accessible through the texts and the footnotes of the preceding sections. Two other useful sources of titles are the first edition (1963) and the second edition (1971) of this present Norton Critical Edition. Other helpful collections of titles can be found in Adam Gillon, *Joseph Conrad*

(Twayne English Authors Series, 1982); Cedric Watts, *A Preface to Conrad* (1981); Norman Page, *A Conrad Companion* (1986); and Gary Adelman, *Heart of Darkness: Search for the Unconscious* (1987). Seven early reactions to the story can be found in *Conrad: The Critical Heritage*, ed. Norman Sherry (1973). Finally, *Conradiana* is an excellent source for essays of all kinds as well as for book reviews and for the bibliographies mentioned above.